W9-AHF-589

Tanzania

Mary Fitzpatrick

Contents

Lake Victoria
p213

Northern Tanzania
p163

Northeastern
Tanzania p137

Zanzibar
Archipelago
p91

Western Tanzania
p230

Dar es Salaam
p71

Southern Highlands
p246

Southeastern
Tanzania
p277

Lonely Planet books provide independent advice. Lonely Planet does not accept advertising in guidebooks, nor do we accept payment in exchange for listing or endorsing any place or business. Lonely Planet writers do not accept discounts or payments in exchange for positive coverage of any sort.

Vitabu vya Lonely Planet vinashauri wasafiri huru na wazi. Kampuni ya Lonely Planet haikubali matangazo kwenye vitabu vyake, wala haikubali malipo kwa ajili ya kutaja au kupendekeza biashara yoyote. Waandishi wa Lonely Planet wanakataa marupurupu au posho yoyote kwa ajili ya kuandika mambo mazuri ya mapendekezo.

Destination Tanzania

Few areas of the continent captivate the imagination as does Tanzania. From Mt Kiliman-jaro's snow-capped summit to the Serengeti's wildlife-filled expanses, the country embod-ies what is for many quintessential Africa. It's a melting pot of traditions, a crossroads of cultures and a supremely diverse and satisfying destination to explore. Moss-covered ruins of ancient Swahili city-states overlook fine white-sand beaches; cool, forested hillsides rise dramatically from the plains; and 100-plus ethnic groups amicably rub shoulders. Minarets are silhouetted against the skyline while nearby Christian churches resound with singing; wizened Makonde elders with facial etchings share seats with office workers in Western dress; Dar es Salaam's gleaming modern face gazes across the waters at the cobbled streets of Zanzibar's old Stone Town.

Despite its attractions, Tanzania is one of Africa's most unassuming and low-key destina-tions, and thus far has remained enviably untouched by the tribal rivalries and political upheavals that plague many of its neighbours. Thanks to these qualities, and to a booming tourism industry, it's an ideal choice for both first-time visitors and Africa old hands. The most popular areas – the northern safari circuit around Arusha, and the Zanzibar Archipelago – have sealed main roads and an array of hotels and restaurants, and can be easily (though not always cheaply) negotiated by everyone from backpackers to five-star connoisseurs. For more adventure, head south and west, where you'll soon find yourself well off the beaten path, surrounded by a Tanzania that's far removed from Western development.

Wherever you visit, the highlight inevitably winds up being Tanzanians themselves – with their characteristic warmth and politeness, and the dignity and beauty of their cultures. Chances are that you'll want to come back for more, to which most Tanzanians will say *'karibu tena'* (welcome again).

ARIADNE VAN ZANDBERGEN

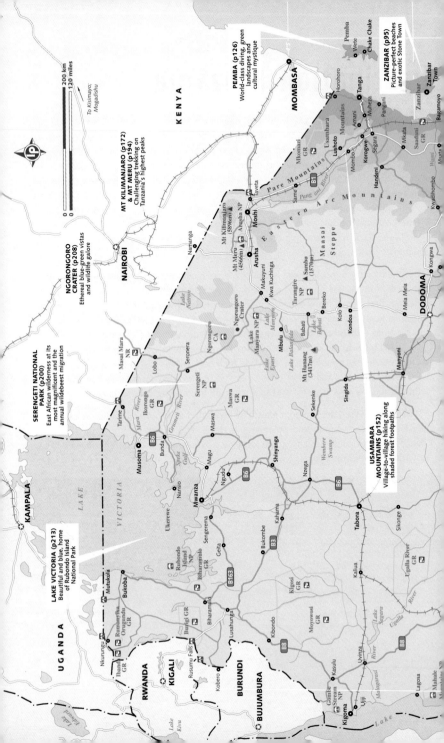

SERENGETI NATIONAL PARK (p200)
East African wilderness at its most magnificent and the annual wildebeest migration

NGORONGORO CRATER (p208)
Ethereal blue-green vistas and wildlife galore

MT KILIMANJARO (p172) & MT MERU (p194)
Challenging trekking on Tanzania's highest peaks

PEMBA (p126)
World-class diving, green landscapes and cultural mystique

ZANZIBAR (p95)
Picture-perfect beaches and exotic Stone Town

LAKE VICTORIA (p213)
Beautiful and blue, home of Rubondo Island National Park

USAMBARA MOUNTAINS (p152)
Village-to-village hiking along shaded forest footpaths

0   200 km
0   120 miles

UGANDA

KAMPALA

RWANDA

KIGALI

BURUNDI

BUJUMBURA

KENYA

NAIROBI

To Kisimayo;
Mogadishu

Nkurungu
Ibanda GR
Rumanyika
Orugundu GR
Mutukula
Bukoba
Burigi GR
Biharamulo
Biharamulo GR
Lusahunga
Rusumu Falls
Kobero
Kasulu
Gombe
Stream NP
Uvinza
Kigoma
Ujiji
Lagosa
Mahale
Lake Kivu
Lake
Lake Tanganyika

Rubondo Island NP
Biharamulo
Sengerema
Geita
Bukombe
Kahama
Kibondo
Moyowosi GR
Kigosi GR

LAKE VICTORIA

Ukerewe
Mwanza
Narsio
Magu
Ngudu
Nzega
Tabora
Kalua
Sikonge
Ugalla River GR
Lake Sagara
Ugalla River
Malagarasi River

Musoma
Bunda
Tarime
Ikorongo GR
Mara River
Grumeti River
Speke Gulf
Maswa
Maswa GR
Shinyanga
Wembere Swamp
Singida
Sekenke
Manyoni
Kolo
Kondoa
Mt Hanang (3417m)
Lake Balangida
Lake Eyasi

Masai Mara NR
Lobo
Seronera
Serengeti NP
Ngorongoro CA
Ngorongoro Crater
Lake Manyara
Lake Manyara NP
Mbulu
Babati
Lake Babati
Makuyuni
Kwa Kuchinga
Samu (1570m)
Tarangire NP
Bereko
Mbulu

Namanga

Lake Natron

Mt Kilimanjaro (5896m)
Arusha NP
Mt Meru (4566m)
Arusha
Moshi
Same
Pare Mountains
Mombo
Lushoto
Usambara Mountains
Amani
Muheza
Tanga
Pangani
Horohoro

Taveta

MOMBASA

Pemba
Wete
Chake Chake

Zanzibar
Zanzibar Town
Bagamoyo

Handeni
Korogwe
Segara
Mkata
Kwadikombo
Saadani GR
Wami River

Eastern Arc Mountains

Maasai Steppe

DODOMA
Kongwa
Mela Mela

B6
B3
B8
B163

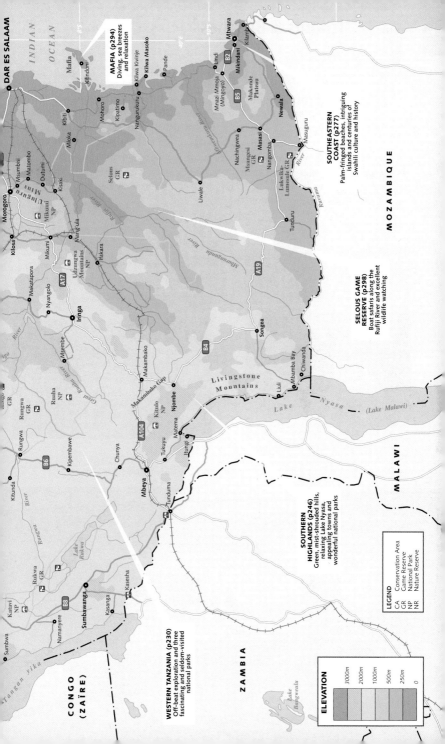

Turquoise tides, silver-white sands and intriguing island cultures bring Tanzania's coastline just one step away from paradise. Laze away by day on **Zanzibar's beaches** (p112), and explore exotic **Stone Town** (p97) by night; swim among shoals of colourful fish around tiny **Misali** (p131), offshore from Pemba; relax amidst the ruins at **Bagamoyo** (p138) or **Kilwa Masoko** (p289); or enjoy the ultimate tropical getaway at the beaches south of **Pangani** (p145), or on **Mafia** (p294). Treat yourself to a bit of surf and safari together at **Saadani Game Reserve** (p143), or head inland for off-beat explorations around the placid **Lake Nyasa** (p271) shoreline.

Play a game of soccer on the beach in Zanzibar (p95)

Explore the oldest of Kilwa Kisiwani's ruins, Husuni Kubwa (p292)

Visit the caves at one of Zanzibar's interesting beaches, Mangapwani (p113)

DAVID WALL

Camp out near Mt Meru, Arusha National Park (p191)

DAVID ELSE

Trek through the stunning Mt Kilimanjaro National Park (p172)

Enjoy watching the flamingos at Ngorongoro
Crater (p208)

GREG ELMS

HIGHLIGHTS **Parks & Wildlife**

Tanzania's unsurpassed array of parks and reserves is one of its biggest draw
cards. Crowning the collection is the magnificent **Serengeti** (p200), where million-
strong herds of wildebeest trammel the seemingly endless plains. Nearby, the
steeply sloping sides of **Ngorongoro Crater** (p208) serve as a backdrop for the ever-
changing drama of one of the highest concentrations of wildlife in Africa. **Ruaha**
(p262), with its sublime riverine setting, is worth as much time as you can give
it, as are the vast, baobab-studded expanses of the **Selous** (p298). **Katavi** (p243)
is as unspoiled as it gets, rivalled only by remote **Mahale Mountains National Park**
(p237), one of the best places on the continent for tracking chimps.

Colourful cultures abound in Tanzania, and exploring their diversity is one of the highlights of travel here. Let the monsoon winds carry you back through the centuries on **Zanzibar** (p95); walk with the Maasai amidst the rugged landscapes of the **Crater Highlands** (p206); watch skilled Makonde carvers at work at Dar es Salaam's **Mwenge market** (p84); or live like a Chagga for the day near **Marangu** (p170). Immerse yourself in fascinating Pare culture around **Same** (p159); learn about the hunting and gathering traditions of the ancient Hadzabe near **Lake Eyasi** (p211); step back into Haya history around **Bukoba** (p223); beat out pulsating Sukuma drumming rhythms near **Mwanza** (p220); and spend time with the Sambaa in the western **Usambaras** (p152).

WAYNE WALTON

Shop the Zanzibar (p95) market scene

Watch the Hadzabe people demonstrate hunting techniques at Lake Eyasi (p211)

ARIADNE VAN ZANDBERGEN

Visit Maasai women at a traditional Maasai boma (p187)

ARIADNE VAN ZANDE

Getting Started

Tanzania has a fast-growing selection of hotels and safari lodges, good air connections between major destinations and a wide array of tour operators. For mid-range and top-end budgets, travelling here is Africa made easy, with just enough adventure to keep things satisfying. However, to get under the country's skin, you'll need to put in time bumping over rough roads on crowded buses and staying in basic guesthouses.

See climate charts (p307) for more information.

Whatever your style, there's plenty to keep you busy – trekking, safaris, lazing on the beach or simply watching local life. Costs range from high for upmarket safari lodges and the popular northern circuit, to modest for living local style.

Spur of the moment visits are possible (and fun), but you'll get more out of your travels, plus better prices, with advance planning.

WHEN TO GO

Tanzania can be visited during all seasons. The weather is coolest and driest from late June to October, although hotels and park lodges are at their fullest and airfares most expensive. From late December until February, temperatures are higher, but not oppressive, and there are fewer tourists. Watch out for peak-season hotel prices around the Christmas–New Year holidays and during the July–August peak season.

During the rainy season from March to May, you can often save substantially on accommodation costs, and enjoy landscapes that are green and full of life. However, secondary roads may be impassable, and many coastal hotels close.

During peak season (July to August, December to January), many hotels levy a peak season surplus. In low season (March to early June), ask about discounted room and safari prices. Families: ask about children's discounts at parks and hotels.

COSTS & MONEY

Tanzania travel is relatively expensive, especially for organised tours and safaris, and low prices generally mean low quality. At the budget level, plan on US$25 per day for a basic room, local food and public transport, but excluding safaris (p38).

For tips on saving money see p313.

Mid-range travellers seeking some comforts and Western-style meals should plan on US$35 to US$150 per day, excluding safaris. Top-end luxury lodge travel costs from US$150 to US$400 or more per person per day,

---

DON'T LEAVE HOME WITHOUT...

You can buy almost anything you'll need in Dar es Salaam or Arusha, except specialist trekking and sporting equipment, and certain toiletries such as contact lens solution. However, choice is limited and prices high. Some things to bring from home:

- binoculars for wildlife watching
- torch (flashlight)
- mosquito repellent and net (p337)
- zoom lens for wildlife shots (p314)
- shoes appropriate for beach walking
- sleeping bag and waterproof gear for trekking
- sturdy water bottle
- travel insurance (p312)

TOP TENS

Great Cultural Experiences

There's nothing better than immersion for getting to know local life. For starters try:

- sharing a plate of *ugali* and sauce with Tanzanians (p65)
- celebrating Eid al-Fitr (p311) on Zanzibar
- hiking in the Usambara Mountains (p154)
- doing a Cultural Tourism Program (p331)
- spending the morning at a small-town market
- listening to church singing
- watching traditional dancing (p28)
- taking local transport
- sailing down Lake Tanganyika on the *Liemba* (p239)
- sampling Dar es Salaam's nightlife (p83)

Alluring Panoramas

Tanzania's topography ranges from lushly forested mountains to stunning tropical coastlines, and provides a magnificent backdrop for the country's diverse cultural palette. Some of the most impressive panoramas:

- elephants frolicking in the Rufiji River (p298) against a backdrop of borassus palms
- sunrise from atop Mt Meru (p194)
- sunset over the rooftops of Zanzibar's Stone Town (p97)
- waterbirds wading in the shallows of Lake Eyasi (p211)
- the patchwork quilt scenery of small farms and villages in the western Usambaras (p154)
- verdant mountains cascading down to the Lake Nyasa (p271) shoreline
- crashing waves and open ocean from the tip of Pemba's Kigomasha Peninsula (p135)
- Kilwa Kivinje dhow port at dawn (p293)
- the Rift Valley escarpment rising up from the plains near Lake Manyara (p196)
- moonrise over one the beaches on Zanzibar's east coast (p112)

Best Things to Do Away from the Crowds

Break away from the tourist trails and discover Tanzania's hidden corners:

- retrace history in Kilwa (p291), Pangani (p145) and Bagamoyo (p138)
- go on safari in Mahale Mountains (p237) or Katavi (p243) National Parks
- visit the rock paintings around Kolo (p190)
- explore Pemba (p126)
- discover Zanzibar (p95) in the rainy season
- bird-watch on Rubondo island (p222)
- spend a few days in Iringa (p259)
- travel overland between Mikindani and Songea, and on to Mbamba Bay (p274)
- explore the hills around Mbeya (p268)
- hike in Udzungwa Mountains National Park (p257)

with prices at the upper end of this spectrum usually for all-inclusive safari packages.

TRAVEL LITERATURE

The Tree Where Man Was Born by Peter Matthiessen offers a timeless portrayal of life on the East African plains. In the widely acclaimed *Sand Rivers*, the same author takes you on a hauntingly beautiful safari into the heart of Selous Game Reserve.

Zanzibari Abdulrazak Gurnah brings WWI-era East Africa to life in his evocative coming-of-age story, *Paradise*.

Kilimanjaro: To the Roof of Africa by Audrey Salkeld is a dramatic recounting of the climb up Africa's highest mountain – highly inspirational if you're planning a trek. To further whet your appetite, settle down with a copy of *Tanzania – African Eden* by Graham Mercer and Javed Jafferji, which takes you on the ultimate photographic journey through the country.

In *The Gunny Sack*, Tanzanian-bred MG Vassanji explores Tanzania's rich ethnic mix through several generations of an immigrant Indian family. *In Quest of Livingstone: A Journey to the Four Fountains,* by Colum Wilson and Aisling Irwin, retraces the East African journeys of the renowned explorer and missionary.

INTERNET RESOURCES

Government of Tanzania (www.tanzania.go.tz) The government site – dry, but with visa info.

Kamusi Project (www.yale.edu/swahili) A 'living' online dictionary for getting started with Swahili.

Lonely Planet (www.lonelyplanet.com) Travel tips, the Thorn Tree bulletin board and links at Subwwway.

Tanzania News (www.tanzanianews.com) News clippings.

Tanzania Page (www.sas.upenn.edu/African_Studies/Country_Specific/Tanzania.html) Good links.

Tanzania Tourist Board (www.tanzaniatouristboard.com) TTB's official site.

Zanzibar Tourism (www.zanzibartourism.net) The Zanzibar Commission for Tourism's official site.

HOW MUCH?

Mid-range safari US$200/person/day

Plate of *ugali* Tsh500

Serengeti NP entry US$30/person/entry

Papaya Tsh300

Short taxi ride Tsh1000

LONELY PLANET INDEX

Litre of petrol Tsh920

Litre of bottled water Tsh500

Safari Lager Tsh500

Souvenir T-shirt Tsh10,000

Street snack – *mishikaki* Tsh200

Itineraries

CLASSIC ROUTES

BEACH & BUSH
Two to Three Weeks / Arusha to Zanzibar

This well-trodden route combines wildlife watching *par excellence* with postcard-perfect beaches and the allure of the 'Spice Islands'. Two weeks gives a taste, but allow three or more to get off the main road.

From Arusha, you can explore the northern parks. Good combinations: **Serengeti** (p200) and **Ngorongoro Crater** (p208); Ngorongoro plus **Lake Manyara** (p196) or **Tarangire** (p199); **Arusha National Park** (p191), including a Mt Meru trek; or a trek to the top of Africa in **Mt Kilimanjaro National Park** (p172).

Head southeast via **Moshi** (p164) to leafy **Lushoto** (p154), the Usambaras and a network of hiking trails. If time is tight, continue straight to **Dar es Salaam** (p71) and the ferry or plane over to **Zanzibar** (p95). Alternatively, travel to **Tanga** (p147), with a detour to **Pangani** (p145), before flying or boating to **Pemba** (p126) and Zanzibar. On Zanzibar, base yourself at one of the beaches for relaxing, or in **Stone Town** (p97) for exploring.

Budget permitting, consider a less-travelled variant of this itinerary, combining Zanzibar's Stone Town with **Mafia** (p294) and **Selous Game Reserve** (p298), although this involves some flights.

This classic 1000km journey (more if you include detours and visit lots of parks) combines Tanzania's best – wildlife, beaches and culture – in one easy-to-manage package. Roads are generally good, and there are plenty of flights if you're on a tight schedule. Two weeks is just enough time to get everything in, but you'll need three or more to even start to get under the surface.

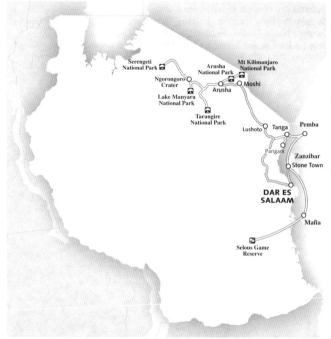

ROADS LESS TRAVELLED

THE GRAND TOUR   **Three Months**

Away from the Arusha-Zanzibar corridor, most of Tanzania is well off the beaten track. Do a grand circuit, or pick and choose as you please. One option: from Dar es Salaam, sojourn through the Southern Highlands, stopping at **Mikumi** (p255) and **Udzungwa Mountains** (p257) parks; **Iringa** (p259) and **Ruaha National Park** (p262); and **Mbeya** (p265) and **Lake Nyasa** (p271). Continue northwest towards **Katavi park** (p243), Mpanda, **Tabora** (p240) and the train back to Dar es Salaam, finishing on the **Zanzibar Archipelago** (p91).

Another route: travel from Dar es Salaam to **Tanga** (p147), via **Bagamoyo** (p138), **Saadani Game Reserve** (p143) and **Pangani** (p145), before continuing to the **Usambara Mountains** (p152), and on to **Moshi** (p164), **Arusha** (p178) and the northern parks. From Arusha, turn south to **Dodoma** (p247) and Iringa, visiting **Babati** (p189), **Mt Hanang** (p190) and the **Kolo rock paintings** (p190) en route. Once in Iringa, detour to Ruaha before heading southwest towards Mbeya or **Songea** (p274), or northeast to Dar es Salaam and Zanzibar.

Other options from Arusha: travel via the western Serengeti to Lake Victoria, and **Rubondo** (p222), **Ukerewe** (p221) or **Lukuba** (p227) islands; or charter a flight to **Mahale Mountains park** (p237). From Dar es Salaam: follow the southeastern coast, stopping in **Kilwa Kisiwani** (p291), **Lindi** (p287), **Mikindani** (p283) and **Mtwara** (p278), then continue south to Mozambique, or west along the rugged route to Songea.

To really get into the pulse of Tanzania, allow at least three months to make your 3000km-plus way around the country – longer if you plan on taking time out for hiking and exploring. The main stretches – Dar es Salaam to Mbeya, and Dar to Arusha – are tarmac. Elsewhere, expect lots of bumps and dust (or mud).

TAILORED TRIPS

SWAHILI SAMPLER

Tanzania's Swahili heritage fuses influences past and present, African and Arabian, Indian, Asian and European, and delving in brings you on a fascinating journey through the continents and the centuries. A good place to start is **Dar es Salaam** (p71), where modern-day urbanity is only a thin veneer over the area's deep Swahili roots. Nearby is sleepy **Bagamoyo** (p138), a historical treasure trove that is just beginning to come into its own on tourist

itineraries. Don't miss the handful of carved doorways, or the chance to watch the day come to life at the town's bustling harbour. **Pangani** (p145), once a major port on the Swahili coast, is best explored on a leisurely stroll. **Zanzibar** and **Pemba** (p126) are the jewels in the crown, and worth a long visit, although to immerse yourself in things Swahili, you'll need to get away from the resorts and into the villages. **Mafia** (p294) and the ruins on **Kilwa Kisiwani** (p291) carry you back to the days when this part of the coast was the centre of trading networks that stretched as far as Persia and the Orient. Further south are pretty, palm-fringed **Lindi** (p287) and tiny **Mikindani** (p283), the epitome of a traditional Swahili village. Time remaining? Follow old trade caravan routes inland to **Tabora** (p240), and then to **Ujiji** (p236), with its Swahili-style houses and flourishing tradition of dhow building.

HIKER'S PARADISE

Forested mountains, dramatic peaks and the Rift Valley escarpment combine with dozens of colourful tribal groups for some of the most enjoyable hiking in East Africa. Head first to **Lushoto** (p154) and the western Usambaras, where the cool climate, winding paths and picturesque villages will keep you walking for days. The nearby eastern Usambaras around **Amani Nature Reserve** (p152) are a botanist's dream, with a wealth of unique plants

and a network of trails. For something more vigorous, head to **Mt Hanang** (p190) – a straightforward climb offering views over the plains and the chance to get to know local Barabaig culture. To the south are the wild, forested slopes of the lush **Udzungwas** (p257), where you are guaranteed to be walking away from the crowds. For rugged beauty and Rift Valley vistas, it's hard to beat northern Tanzania's **Crater Highlands** (p206). Also in the north is **Mt Meru** (p194), with its stately silhouette, superb sunrise views and classic trek to the summit. Topping it all off is **Mt Kilimanjaro** (p172), where you can wander through moorlands and heather before ascending to the snowfields capping the continent's highest peak.

The Author

MARY FITZPATRICK

Originally from Washington, DC, Mary set off after graduate studies for several years in Europe. Her fascination with languages and cultures soon led her further south to sub-Saharan Africa, where she has spent much of the past decade living and working. She has authored numerous guidebooks on East Africa and elsewhere on the continent, speaks Swahili and is convinced she holds an unofficial record for kilometres travelled in buses along Tanzania's roads. Mary works as a full-time travel writer from her home base in Cairo, from where she continues to journey frequently to the land of Kilimanjaro.

My Favourite Trip

The sublime shoreline, vast baobab-studded expanses and intriguing cultures of the south have an irresistible allure. Heading south from Dar es Salaam, essential stops include **Mafia** (p294) for its tropical outpost ambience; **Selous Game Reserve** (p298) for its wilderness and wildlife; **Kilwa** (p291) with its ruins and time-warp feel; and the charming old Swahili trading settlement of **Mikindani** (p283). From **Mtwara** (p278), I'd cross the wild southern road to **Songea** (p274), next heading via **Iringa** (p259), **Ruaha National Park** (p262) and **Udzungwa Mountains National Park** (p257) to **Lushoto** (p154). I'd then spend days in the **Serengeti** (p200) before finishing up on the **Zanzibar Archipelago** (p91).

CONTRIBUTING AUTHOR

Dr Caroline Evans wrote the Health chapter. Caroline studied medicine at the University of London, and completed General Practice training in Cambridge. She is the medical adviser to Nomad Travel Clinic, a private travel health clinic in London, and also a GP specialising in travel medicine. She has been an expedition doctor for Raleigh International and Coral Cay expeditions.

Snapshot

Although it has been two decades since Julius Nyerere stepped down from the helm, his portrait still graces the walls of office buildings throughout the country. In many respects, the slight smile he wears is well-justified. Impelled by a remarkably egalitarian social vision, the fatherly Nyerere introduced Swahili as a unifying national language, managed to instil ideals of *ujamaa* (familyhood) among the majority of his people and initiated a long and respected tradition of regional political engagement. Thanks to this vision – Nyerere's greatest legacy – Tanzania today is one of Africa's most stable countries, and religious and ethnic conflicts are close to nonexistent.

On the economic front, there is less reason to be pleased – although Nyerere himself would have been one of the first to acknowledge this. When he left office, the country was close to bankruptcy, with a moribund socialist economy and a network of ailing parastatals. Even today Tanzania continues to be ranked near the bottom worldwide on the UNDP (United Nations Development Program) Human Development Index (160th out of 175 countries in a recent listing), and illiteracy and infant mortality rates are high. Yet, the outlook is not all grim: privatisation is proceeding apace, the economy is beginning to climb out of the depths – helped along in part by a booming tourism industry – and the country is routinely lauded for its progress by the international donor community.

Corruption – which the upstanding Nyerere managed to rise above completely – is another problem. In an effort to combat it, there are signs in banks, immigration offices and elsewhere advertising that you're in a corruption-free zone. And, in a recent politically correct move, the current president chose not to fly to a regional conference on poverty alleviation in his controversial new US$40 million jet.

Just as immediate in the lives of many Tanzanians is the HIV/AIDS infection rate, which is estimated at about 8% of the population. It is the focus of huge billboards in Dar es Salaam and elsewhere in the country, although national debate is still muted.

While an amicable path for coexistence has been found, keeping family ties happy between the mainland and proudly independent Zanzibar also requires ongoing attention. The task is made more challenging by the continued overwhelming dominance of Nyerere's Chama Cha Mapinduzi (CCM) party in the national government.

As Tanzania moves towards its 50th birthday and addresses these issues, it will need to hold another element of Nyerere's vision firmly in sight: education. Although Nyerere's goal of universal primary education still hasn't been realised, it is slowly coming closer to fulfilment. The key over the coming decades will be finding a way to ensure that more than 5% of youth (the current figure) can finish secondary school, and go on to university or find employment. If Tanzania manages to do this, it's something that would have been likely to cause 'Mwalimu' (or 'Teacher', as Nyerere is universally known) to positively beam.

FAST FACTS

Population: 34.4 million

Inflation: 4.5%

Highest point: Mt Kilimanjaro (5896m)

Lowest point: floor of Lake Tanganyika (358m below sea level)

Mainland population density: 39/sq km

Zanzibar Archipelago population density: 400/sq km

Black market price for a tonne of cloves: up to US$10 per kilo

Average life expectancy: 47.9 years

Literacy rate: 76%

Elephant population in Ruaha National Park: around 12,000

History

IN THE BEGINNING

Tanzania's history begins with the dawn of humankind. Hominid (human-like) footprints unearthed at Laetoli near Olduvai Gorge (p210), together with archaeological finds from Kenya and Ethiopia, show that our earliest ancestors may have been roaming the Tanzanian plains and surrounding areas over three million years ago. By about one million years ago, these creatures – by then known as *homo erectus* – had come to resemble modern humans, and had spread well beyond East Africa, including to Europe and Asia. Around 100,000 years ago, *homo sapiens,* or modern man, arrived on the scene. Although it's still a subject of debate, it's possible that early *homo sapiens* may have been going on safari in parts of present-day Tanzania as early as 50,000 years ago.

About 10,000 years ago, the picture starts to become clearer, with the arrival of scattered clans of nomadic hunter-gatherers in the area south of Olduvai Gorge. They spoke a language similar to that of southern Africa's Khoisan, and are considered to be cousins of Tanzania's modern-day Sandawe group. Impressive rock paintings from these peoples have been found scattered throughout central Tanzania around Kondoa.

See www.pbs.org/wgbh /evolution/humans /humankind/d.html for an overview of human evolution in East Africa.

THE FAMILY EXPANDS

Somewhere between 3000 and 5000 years ago, these Khoisan speakers were joined by Cushitic-speaking farmers and cattle herders who had made their way to the region from present-day Ethiopia. They moved mostly in small family groups, and brought with them traditions that are still practised by their descendents, including the Iraqw around Lake Manyara.

Most Tanzanians trace their ancestry to a series of more recent migrations that began around 1000 BC, when Bantu speakers from the distant Niger delta in west Africa started to move eastwards through Cameroon and Congo (Zaïre), reaching East Africa around the 1st century BC. Unlike their predecessors, the Bantu-speaking newcomers were skilled agriculturalists and iron workers who lived in settled villages. They soon displaced or absorbed many of their Cushitic- and Khoisan-speaking siblings and became by far the most numerous group in the area.

A final wave of migrations began somewhat later when small groups of Nilotic speakers arrived in Tanzania from the southern Sudan. This influx continued through to the 18th century, with the main migrations in the 15th and 16th centuries. Most of these Nilotic peoples – ancestors of the Maasai – were pastoralists, and many settled in the less fertile areas of north-central Tanzania where their large herds could have space for grazing.

DID YOU KNOW?

DNA lineages found in Tanzania are among the oldest anywhere on earth, making the country a strong contender for distinction as the 'cradle of humanity'.

MONSOON WINDS

As these migrations were taking place in the interior, coastal areas were being shaped by far different influences. Azania, as the East African coast was known to the ancient Greeks, was an important trading post as early as 400 BC. By the early part of the first millennium AD, thriving settlements

TIMELINE	c 8000 BC	c 750
	The Khoisan settle in around Olduvai Gorge	Islam arrives on the East African coast; Swahili civilisation begins to prosper

had been established as traders, first from the Mediterranean and later from Arabia and Persia, came ashore on the winds of the monsoon and began to intermix with the indigenous Bantu speakers, gradually giving rise to Swahili language and culture. The traders from Arabia also brought Islam, which by the 11th century had become entrenched.

Over the next few centuries, the Arabic traders established outposts all along the coast, including on the Zanzibar Archipelago and Kilwa Kisiwani. These settlements flourished – reaching their pinnacle between the 13th and 15th centuries – and trade in ivory, gold and other goods extended as far away as India and China.

EXPEDITIONING EUROPEANS

The first European to reach East Africa was the intrepid Portuguese explorer, Vasco da Gama, who arrived in 1498, en route to the Orient. Within three decades, the Portuguese had disrupted the old trading networks and subdued the entire coast, building forts at various places, including on Mafia island. Portuguese control lasted until the early 18th century, when they were displaced by Arabs from Oman. As the Omani Arabs solidified their foothold, they began to turn their sights westwards, developing powerful trade routes that stretched inland as far as Lake Tanganyika and Central Africa.

The slave trade also grew rapidly during this period, driven in part by demand from European plantation holders on the Indian Ocean islands of Réunion and Mauritius. Soon slave traders, including the notorious Tippu Tip, had established stations in Tabora, Ujiji and other inland towns.

THE FIRST MISSIONARIES

From about the mid-19th century, European missionaries, explorers and, later, imperialists began to penetrate the Tanzanian mainland. The first missionaries to reach the interior were Germans Johann Ludwig Krapf and Johannes Rebmann, who arrived at Mt Kilimanjaro in the 1840s. In the 1860s, Anglican and Catholic missionaries arrived on Zanzibar,

---

SWAHILI

The word 'Swahili' ('of the coast', from the Arabic word *sāhil*) refers to the Swahili language, as well as to the Islamic culture of the peoples inhabiting the East African coast from Mogadishu (Somalia) in the north down to Mozambique in the south. Both language and culture are a rich mixture of Bantu, Arabic, Persian and Asian influences.

Although Swahili culture began to develop in the early part of the first millennium AD, it was not until the 18th century, with the ascendancy of the Omani Arabs on Zanzibar, that it came into its own. Swahili's role as a *lingua franca* was solidified as it spread throughout East and Central Africa along the great trade caravan routes. European missionaries and explorers soon adopted the language as their main means of communicating with locals. In the second half of the 19th century, missionaries, notably Johann Ludwig Krapf, also began applying the Roman alphabet. Prior to this, Swahili had been written exclusively in Arabic script.

There are an increasing number of Tanzanians for whom Swahili is their mother tongue, although most speak it as a second language, or as a second mother tongue together with their tribal language.

---

c 1100	c 13th Century
Verses from the Quran are written in Swahili	Kilwa becomes the most powerful trade centre along the East African coast

and in 1868 the first mainland mission was established at Bagamoyo as a station for ransomed slaves. Over the next decades, missionaries from various denominations made their way inland, setting up mission stations as far west as Lake Tanganyika.

Around the same time, European explorers began to 'discover' and map large areas of the interior, principally by following established caravan routes. Among the earliest of these explorers were Richard Francis Burton and John Hanning Speke, who traversed the country in 1857 in search of the source of the Nile. Shortly thereafter came missionary-explorer David Livingstone and journalist Henry Morton Stanley.

The World of the Swahili by John Middleton is an excellent place to start for anyone wanting to learn more about Swahili life and culture.

COLONIAL CONTROL

As reports from the missionaries and explorers made their way back to Europe, East Africa became a known territory and Western interests were piqued. By the late 1880s, Britain had established a sphere of influence on the Zanzibar Archipelago and along the coast. In 1884 Carl Peters, a German acting independently of the German government, concluded various 'treaties' with unsuspecting local chiefs in order to secure a charter for his German East Africa Company (Deutsch-Ostafrikanische Gesellschaft or DOAG). The treaties were endorsed by the German government, which delegated the DOAG to administer the mainland. The challenge that this posed to Britain's coastal dominance was at least temporarily resolved in 1890, when Germany and Great Britain signed an agreement defining their spheres of influence and formally establishing a British protectorate over the Zanzibar Archipelago. In 1891 most of what is now mainland Tanzania came under direct German control as German East Africa.

COLONIALISM IN CRISIS

Colonialism brought Western education and health care to German East Africa, as well as road and rail networks. However, these developments benefited relatively few Africans, and the German administration was widely unpopular. Harsh labour policies, the imposition of a hut tax and numerous other measures contributed to the discontent. Local opposition began in earnest with the Abushiri Revolt in 1888 (see the boxed text, p145), and culminated in the Maji Maji rebellion (p275) of 1905 to 1907, which decimated much of southern Tanzania and is considered to contain the first seeds of Tanzanian nationalism.

The German era lasted until the end of WWI, when German East Africa came under British administration as a League of Nations mandate and was renamed Tanganyika. This arrangement lasted until WWII, after which the area became a UN trust territory, again under British administration.

During the interwar years, marketing cooperatives sprung up in several areas, notably among the Chagga around Kilimanjaro and the Haya around Bukoba, to promote cultivation of export crops. Many of these farmers' cooperatives soon took additional roles as channels for expressing nationalist aspirations and protests against the colonial system. In 1929 the African Association – a group similar to these cooperatives, but organised along political rather than economic lines – was founded in Dar es Salaam. The African Association assumed increasing importance

DID YOU KNOW?

Portuguese influence is still seen in architecture, customs (eg bull fighting on Pemba, p132) and language. The Swahili *gereza* (jail), from Portuguese *igreja* (church) dates to the days when Portuguese forts contained both edifices in the same compound.

1498	1840s
Vasco da Gama reaches East Africa	The Sultan of Oman sets up court on Zanzibar

as grass-roots resentment against colonial policies grew, and in 1948 was renamed the Tanganyika Africa Association (TAA).

A rallying point for the nationalist cause came in the early 1950s when several thousand Meru people were forcibly expelled from their lands in the western Kilimanjaro area to make room for a dozen European settlers to establish farms. When the Meru's protests were rebuffed via the normal channels, they sought redress of their grievances with local political groups. These groups in turn looked to the TAA for leadership and began to agitate for more radical action.

INDEPENDENCE AT LAST

In 1953 the TAA elected a teacher named Julius Nyerere as its president. Within a year, Nyerere had given up his teaching profession to devote himself full-time to the TAA, which by then was known Tanganyika African National Union (TANU), with the rallying cry of *uhuru na umoja* (freedom and unity).

One of the first items on TANU's agenda was independence. In 1958 and 1959, TANU-supported candidates decisively won general legislative elections, and in 1959 Britain agreed to the establishment of internal self-government, requesting Nyerere to be chief minister. On 9 December 1961 Tanganyika became independent and on 9 December 1962 it was established as a republic, with Nyerere as president.

'On 9 December 1961 Tanganyika became independent and on 9 December 1962 it was established as a republic, with Nyerere as president'

On the Zanzibar Archipelago, which had been a British protectorate since 1890, the main push for independence came from the radical Afro-Shirazi Party (ASP). Opposing the ASP were two minority parties, the Zanzibar & Pemba People's Party (ZPPP) and the sultanate-oriented Zanzibar Nationalist Party (ZNP), both of which were favoured by the British. As a result, at Zanzibari independence in December 1963, it was the two minority parties that formed the first government.

This government did not last long. Within a month, a Ugandan immigrant named John Okello initiated a violent revolution against the ruling ZPPP-ZNP coalition, leading to the toppling of the government and the sultan, and the massacre or expulsion of most of the islands' Arab population. The sultan was replaced by an entity known as the Zanzibar Revolutionary Council, which was comprised of ASP members and headed by Abeid Karume.

On 26 April 1964 Nyerere signed an act of union with Karume, creating the United Republic of Tanganyika (renamed the United Republic of Tanzania the following October). Formation of the union, which was resented by many Zanzibaris from the outset, was motivated in part by the then-prevailing spirit of pan-Africanism, and in part as a cold war response to the ASP's socialist programme.

Karume's government lasted until 1972, when he was assassinated and succeeded by Aboud Jumbe. Shortly thereafter, in an effort to subdue the ongoing unrest resulting from the merger of the islands with the mainland, Nyerere authorised formation of a one-party state and combined TANU and the ASP into a new party known as Chama Cha Mapinduzi (CCM, or Party of the Revolution). This merger, which was ratified in a new union constitution on 27 April 1977, marked the beginning of the CCM's dominance of Tanzanian politics which endures to this day.

1873	1889
The Zanzibar slave market is abolished	Kilimanjaro is scaled for the first time

TANZANIA JOINS THE SOCIALIST FOLD

Nyerere took the helm of a country that was economically foundering and politically fragile, its stability plagued in particular by the mainland's lack of control over the Zanzibar Archipelago. Education had also been neglected, so that at independence there were said to be only a handful of university graduates in the entire country.

This inauspicious beginning eventually led to the Arusha Declaration of 1967, which committed Tanzania to a policy of socialism and self-reliance. The policy's cornerstone was the *ujamaa* (familyhood) village – an agricultural collective run along traditional African lines, with an emphasis on self-reliance.

JULIUS NYERERE

Julius Kambarage Nyerere – Baba wa Taifa (Father of the Nation), but known by everyone simply as Mwalimu (Teacher) – rose from humble beginnings to become one of Africa's most renowned statesmen. He was born in 1922 in Butiama, near Lake Victoria, son of a chief of the small Zanaki tribe. After finishing his education, including graduate studies in Scotland, he embarked on a teaching career.

It wasn't long before Nyerere was drawn into politics. As president of the Tanganyika African National Union (TANU), Nyerere travelled widely advocating peaceful change, social equality and racial harmony. Soon his oratorical skills and political savvy earned him distinction as Tanganyika's pre-eminent nationalist spokesman, and by 1962, he was president of the independent United Republic of Tanganyika.

Nyerere is well known internationally for his philosophy of socialism and self-reliance, for which he drew inspiration from his studies of Karl Marx, his reading of the Bible and his obser-vations of the Chinese Communist system. Nyerere brought these various elements together in the African context, reasoning that there could be no justification for social or other inequities in Tanzania, given the value placed by traditional African culture on community and family. The African extended family cultivated its fields in common and shared its resources in times of need. Could not this communalism be applied at the national level, thereby avoiding large gaps between rich and poor? Nyerere chose the term *ujamaa* (familyhood) to describe his programme, to emphasise the blend of economic cooperation, racial and tribal harmony, and moralistic self-sacrifice that he sought to achieve.

Nyerere gained widespread respect for his idealism, for his success in shaping a society which was politically stable and free of divisive tribal rivalries, and for his contributions towards raising Tanzania's literacy rate, which during his tenure became one of the highest in Africa. He also earned international acclaim for his commitment to pan-Africanism and for his regional engage-ment – an area where he was active until his death in October 1999.

Despite criticisms of his authoritarian style and economic policies, Nyerere was indisputably one of Africa's most influential leaders, and the person almost single-handedly responsible for putting Tanzania on the world stage. He was widely acclaimed for his long-standing opposition to South Africa's apartheid system, and for his 1979 invasion of Uganda, which resulted in the deposition of the dictator Idi Amin Dada. In his later years, Nyerere continued to be active as an elder statesman, taking a leading role in seeking resolution of the Burundi crisis, and advocating African political and economic collaboration.

Nyerere wrote numerous books, and translated two Shakespeare plays and parts of Plato's *Republic* into Swahili. Many of his manuscripts, photos and other memorabilia are on display at the Nyerere Museum in Butiama (p227).

1905	1961
Maji Maji Rebellion begins, and nationalism takes root	Tanganyika gains independence

In the early days of the *ujamaa* system, progressive farmers were encouraged to expand in the hope that other peasants would follow their example. This approach proved unrealistic, and was abandoned in favour of direct state control. Between 1973 and 1978, 85% of Tanzania's rural population was resettled, often forcibly, into over 7000 planned villages in an effort to modernise the agricultural sector and improve access to social services. Yet, this approach was also unsuccessful, and resentment towards compulsory resettlement was widespread.

Tanzania's socialist experiment was widely acclaimed in the days following independence, and is credited with unifying the country and expanding education and health care. Economically, however, it was a failure. Per capita income plummeted, agricultural production stagnated and industry limped along at less than 50% of capacity. The decline was precipitated by a combination of factors, including steeply rising oil prices, the 1977 break-up of the East African Community (an economic and customs union between Tanzania, Kenya and Uganda) and sharp drops in the value of coffee and sisal exports.

DEMOCRACY DEBUTS

Nyerere was re-elected to a fifth term as president in 1980, amid continuing dissatisfaction with the socialist experiment. In 1985, he resigned, handing over power to Zanzibari Ali Hassan Mwinyi. Mwinyi tried to distance himself from Nyerere and his policies, and instituted an economic recovery programme. Yet the pace of change remained slow, and Mwinyi's presidency was unpopular. The fall of European Communism in the early 1990s, and pressure from Western donor nations, accelerated the move towards multiparty politics, and in 1992 the constitution was amended to legalise opposition parties.

'Nyerere was re-elected to a fifth term as president in 1980, amid continuing dissatisfaction with the socialist experiment'

The first elections were held in October 1995 in an atmosphere of chaos. On the mainland, the CCM, under Benjamin Mkapa, won 62% of the vote in relatively smooth balloting. On the Zanzibar Archipelago, however, the voting for the Zanzibari presidency was universally denounced for its dishonesty. The opposition Civic United Front (CUF) candidate, Seif Shariff Hamad, was widely believed to have won the presidential seat despite official results marginally favouring CCM incumbent Salmin Amour. In the ensuing uproar, foreign development assistance was suspended and most expatriates working on the islands left.

Elections in October 2000 proceeded without incident on the mainland, with a decisive victory for incumbent president Mkapa and the CCM. On Zanzibar, however, the balloting was highly controversial. In January 2001, the CUF called for demonstrations to protest the results. The government declared the demonstrations illegal, but they were held anyway. On Pemba, a CUF stronghold where demonstrators greatly outnumbered the police, government security units responded with force, resulting in at least several dozen deaths and causing many Pembans to temporarily flee the island.

In the wake of the violence, the CCM and CUF initiated renewed attempts to reach agreement through dialogue. An accord was signed aimed at ending the strife on the archipelago and negotiating a long-term solution to the crisis. However, progress on this front has been only modest at best, and tensions continue to simmer.

1964	1967
The United Republic of Tanganyika (later, Tanzania) is born	Arusha Declaration sets Tanzania on a course of 'socialism and self-reliance'

INTO THE FUTURE

One of the effects which the introduction of multiparty politics had on Tanzanian life was the unmasking of underlying political, economic and religious frictions, both on the mainland and between the mainland and the Zanzibar Archipelago. The tensions involving the archipelago are perhaps the most visible example. Yet – the Zanzibar situation notwithstanding – Tanzania as a whole remains reasonably well integrated, with comparatively high levels of religious and ethnic tolerance. Tanzanians have earned a name for themselves in the region for their moderation and balance, and most observers consider it highly unlikely that the country would disintegrate into the tribal conflicts that have plagued some of its neighbours.

For everything you ever wanted to know about the Tanzanian parliament, check out www.parliament.go.tz.

President Mkapa is constitutionally prevented from seeking another term in the 2005 presidential elections, and attention is now focused on choosing his successor. Perhaps more significant is the future of multiparty politics in Tanzania. If anything, these seem to have taken several steps backwards in recent years with entrenchment of the CCM and splintering of the opposition. Progressing beyond this situation may result in some growing pains in the short term. However chances are high that Tanzania will continue to move forward, maintaining the stable and moderate outlook that has characterised its development since independence.

1995	2005
First multiparty elections	Kilimanjaro's rapidly melting glaciers are estimated to disappear completely by 2020

The Culture

THE NATIONAL PSYCHE

It takes a lot to ruffle a Tanzanian, and the country's remarkably harmonious and understated demeanour is largely attributable to this fact. In contrast to Kenya and several other neighbours, tribal rivalries are almost nonexistent. It's rare for a Tanzanian to identify themselves at the outset according to tribe; primary identification is almost always as a Tanzanian, and the *ujamaa* (familyhood) ideals of Julius Nyerere permeate society. Religious frictions are also minimal, with Christians and Muslims living side by side in a relatively easy coexistence. Although political differences flare up – a glance at recent events on the Zanzibar Archipelago (p22) is enough proof of this – they rarely come to the forefront in interpersonal dealings.

The workings of society are oiled by a subtle but strong social code. Tanzanians place a premium on politeness and courtesy. Greetings in particular are essential, and you'll probably be given a gentle reminder should you forget this and launch straight into a question without first inquiring as to the wellbeing of your listener and their family. Tanzanian children are trained to greet their elders with a respectful *shikamoo* (I hold your feet), often accompanied in rural areas by a slight curtsey, and strangers are frequently addressed as *dada* (sister) or *mama*, in the case of an older woman; *kaka* (brother); or *ndugu* (relative or comrade).

Much of daily life is shaped by the struggle to make ends meet in an economy that is ranked as one of the world's poorest. Yet, behind these realities is the fact that Tanzania is home, and not a bad place at that. Combined with the inevitably warm reception that you'll receive as a visitor is a dignified reserve, often coupled with an appealing bemusement at the ways of Westerners.

LIFESTYLE

Rural rhythms set the beat, although you'll find lifestyle variants that span the spectrum. At one end, the main diet is *ugali* with sauce; women and children work small *shamba* (farm plots); and school fees (from about Tsh80,000 per year at the secondary level) are a constant worry. Home – often in varying stages of completion, waiting for the finances needed to finish construction – is of cinderblock or mud brick, with roofing of corrugated tin or thatch, a latrine outside and water drawn from a nearby pump or river. At the other end of the spectrum are a small number of wealthy people, often the families of government ministers, who drive fancy 4WDs and live in Western-style houses in posh residential areas of Dar es Salaam. The remainder of Tanzanians fall somewhere in-between these extremes, although far more are closer to the first scenario than to the latter. Women always work – whether outside the home, or tending to the family and *shamba*. Most students don't have the opportunity to finish secondary school, and many of those that do have unemployment to look forward to, especially in rural areas. Tourism provides opportunities, though good positions are for the lucky few.

Family life is central, with weddings, funerals and other events holding centre stage. Celebrations are grand affairs aimed at demonstrating status, and frequently go well beyond the means of the host family. It's expected that family members who have jobs will share what they have, and the extended family (which also encompasses the community) forms

Want to let someone know how you feel? Tanzanians say it with *kangas* – the writings around the edges of these wrap-around skirts range from amorous outpourings to pointed humour. For a sampling of what's being said around you, see www.glcom.com /hassan/kanga.html.

ETIQUETTE TANZANIAN STYLE

Tanzanians are conservative, and while they are likely to be too polite to tell you so directly, they'll be privately shaking their head about travellers doing things like not wearing enough clothing, sporting tatty clothes, or indulging in public displays of affection. Especially along the Muslim coast, you should cover up the shoulders and legs, and avoid plunging necklines, skin-tight fits and the like. A few other tips:

- Pleasantries count! Even if you're just asking for directions, take time to greet the other person. Handshake etiquette is also worth learning, and best picked up by observation. Tanzanians often continue to hold hands for several minutes after meeting, or even throughout an entire conversation, and especially in the south, a handshake may be accompanied by touching the left hand to the right elbow as a sign of respect.

- Don't eat or pass things with the left hand.

- Respect authority; losing your patience or undermining an official's authority will get you nowhere, while deference and a good-natured demeanour will see you through most situations.

- Want to visit a Tanzanian friend? Before entering their house, call out *hodi*, and then wait for the inevitable *karibu* (welcome).

- Avoid criticising the government.

- Receive gifts with both hands, or with the right hand while touching the left hand to your right elbow. Giving a gift? Don't be surprised if the appreciation isn't expressed verbally.

an essential support network in the absence of a government social security system. Given that the average per capita GDP is only about US$280 (compared with about US$24,000 in the UK), the system works remarkably well, with relatively few destitute on the streets.

Invisible social hierarchies lend life a sense of order. In the family, the man rules the roost, with the children at the bottom and women just above that. In the larger community, it's not much different. Child-raising is the expected occupation for women, and breadwinning for men. Village administrators (*shehe* on Zanzibar) oversee things, and make important decisions in consultation with other senior community members. Tribal structures, however, range from weak to nonexistent – a legacy of Nyerere's abolishment of local chieftaincies following independence.

In Tanzania, it's sometimes hard to know where the family ends and the community begins. Doors are always open, helping out others in the *jamaa* (clan, community) is expected, and celebrations involve everyone.

AIDS is not as widespread in Tanzania as in many southern African countries (an 8% adult HIV/AIDS infection rate compared, eg with about 20% in South Africa). However, its spectre looms on the horizon, and has prompted increased efforts at raising public awareness. You'll see AIDS-related billboards throughout major cities, although real public discussion is limited, and AIDS deaths are commonly explained away as 'tuberculosis', or with silence.

POPULATION

Tanzania's heart pulses with the blood of close to 120 tribal groups, plus Asians, Arabs, Europeans and more. Despite the diversity in the indigenous gene pool, most tribes are very small, with almost 100 of them combined accounting for only one-third of the total population. As a result, none have succeeded in dominating politically or culturally, although groups such as the Chagga and the Haya, who have a long tradition of education, are often disproportionately well-represented in government and business circles.

The vast majority of Tanzanians (about 95%) are of Bantu origin. These include the Sukuma (who live around Mwanza and southern Lake

---

BACK TO BASICS?

For a country that was founded by a teacher (even today, Julius Nyerere is still referred to as Mwalimu, Swahili for 'teacher'), Tanzania ranks near the bottom of the heap when it comes to education. It wasn't always like this. Nyerere was convinced that success for his philosophy of socialism and self-reliance depended on having an educated populace. He made primary education compulsory and offered government assistance to villagers to build their own schools. By the late 1980s, the country's literacy rate had become one of the highest in Africa.

Since then, much of the initial momentum has been lost. Although 85% of children enrol at the primary level (thanks in part to the elimination of primary school fees), about 20% of these drop out before finishing, and barely 5% complete secondary school. The reasons are many, with not enough trained teachers, not enough schools and not enough money topping the list. At the secondary level, school fees are a problem, as is language. Primary-school instruction is in Swahili, and many students lack sufficient knowledge of English to carry out their secondary level studies.

Although there is still a long way to go, help is on the way: the government is giving increased emphasis to education, especially at the primary level, where enrolment levels have been rising in recent years, and the private secondary school network is slowly expanding to fill the large gaps in the government system.

Victoria, and constitute about 13% of overall population), the Nyamwezi (around Tabora), the Makonde (southeastern Tanzania), the Haya (around Bukoba) and the Chagga (around Mt Kilimanjaro). The Maasai and several smaller groups including the Arusha and the Samburu (all in northern Tanzania) are of Nilo-Hamitic or Nilotic origin. The Iraqw, who live in the area around Karatu and northwest of Lake Manyara, are Cushitic, as are the tiny northern-central tribes of Gorowa and Burungi; the Sandawe and, more distantly, the Hadzabe (around Lake Eyasi), are considered to belong to the Khoisan ethno-linguistic family.

About 985,000 (or 3% of Tanzania's total population) live on the Zanzibar Archipelago, with about one-third of these on Pemba. Most African Zanzibaris belong to one of three groups, the Hadimu, the Tumbatu and the Pemba. Members of the non-African population are primarily Shirazi and consider themselves descendants of immigrants from Shiraz in Persia (Iran).

Filling out Tanzania's melting pot are small but economically significant Asian and Arabic populations, especially in Dar es Salaam, and a small European community.

Tanzania is one of the least urbanised countries in sub-Saharan Africa, with urban dwellers constituting only about one-third of the total population. However, the number of city dwellers is steadily growing, at about 4.9% per year in Dar es Salaam. Average population density is 39 people per sq km, although this varies radically from one area to the next. Among the most densely populated areas: Dar es Salaam and the surrounding coast; the Usambara and Pare mountains; the slopes of Mt Kilimanjaro; Mwanza region; and the Zanzibar Archipelago (with 400 people per sq km).

DID YOU KNOW?

Tanzania is the only African country boasting indigenous inhabitants from all of the continent's main ethnolinguistic families (Bantu, Nilo-Hamitic, Cushitic, Khoisan). They live in closest proximity around lakes Eyasi and Babati.

MEDIA

True to its rural roots, Tanzania still gets most of its news via the radio, with about 28 radios per 100 people (versus only about four televisions per 100 people).

A countrywide illiteracy rate of about 25%, and distribution difficulties in rural areas mean that the influence of newspapers is limited to urban centres. Despite this, the local press is quite lively, and relatively independent. However, because most of the main dailies are aligned in some degree with the governing CCM party, there is little outright political debate.

RELIGION

The vibrant spirituality that pervades much of the African continent fills Tanzania as well. All but the smallest villages have a mosque, a church, or both, religious festivals are generally celebrated with fervour – at least as far as singing, dancing and family gatherings are concerned – and almost every Tanzanian identifies with some religion.

Muslims, accounting for about 35% to 40% of the population, have traditionally been concentrated along the coast, as well as in the inland towns that lined the old caravan routes. There are several sects represented, notably the Sunni (Shafi school). The population of the Zanzibar Archipelago is almost exclusively Sunni Muslim.

About 45% to 50% of Tanzanians are Christians. Major denominations include Roman Catholic, Lutheran and Anglican, with a small percentage of Tanzanians adherents of other Christian denominations, including Baptist and Pentecostal. One of the areas of highest Christian concentration is in the northeast around Moshi, which has been a centre of missionary activity since the mid-19th century.

The remainder of the population follow traditional religions centring on ancestor worship, the land and various ritual objects. There are also small but active communities of Hindus, Sikhs and Ismailis.

Historically, the main area of friction has been between Tanzania's Muslim and Christian populations. Today, tensions – while still simmering – are at a relatively low level, and religion is not a major factor in contemporary Tanzanian politics.

WOMEN IN TANZANIA

Tanzania's stellar rankings for tourism and safaris fade when it comes to women in government and high profile positions. Although women arguably form the backbone of the economy – with most juggling child-rearing plus work on the family *shamba,* or in an office – they are near the bottom of the social hierarchy, and are frequently marginalised. This is especially so when it comes to education and politics. Only about 5% of girls complete secondary school, and of these, only a handful go on to complete university. While secondary school enrolment levels are low across the board, girls in particular are frequently kept home due to lack of finances, to help with chores, or because of pregnancy. With a few exceptions – one is the Minister of Natural Resources & Tourism – it's rare to find politically prominent women. Literacy rates (67% for women, versus 85% for men) are other indicators of women's status.

On the positive side, the situation is slowly improving. In 1996 the government guaranteed 20% of parliamentary seats for women, and there are now four female cabinet ministers (of 28 ministers, total). In education, the 'gender gap' has been essentially eliminated at the primary level.

About 56% of Tanzania's AIDS sufferers are women.

ARTS
Cinema

Tanzania's tiny and long languishing film industry received a major boost with the opening of the first annual Zanzibar International Film Festival (ZIFF) in 1998. Today, this festival is one of the best measures of the country's artistic pulse, and one of the region's premier cultural events.

DID YOU KNOW?

Tanzania has one of the lowest rates of secondary school enrolment in the world, with less than 7% of suitably aged youth enrolled.

DID YOU KNOW?

Especially in rural areas, it's common for a woman to drop her own name, and become known as *Mama* followed by the name of her oldest son (or daughter, if she has no sons).

The festival, which is held annually on Zanzibar, serves as a venue for artists from the Indian Ocean basin and beyond. Tanzanian prize winners have included *Maangamizi – The Ancient One,* shot in Tanzania and co-directed by Martin M'hando, who is also known for his film, *Mama Tumaini* (Women of Hope); and *Makaburi Yatasema* (Only the Stones are Talking), about AIDS and directed by Chande Omar Omar. For information on the festival, contact ZIFF (p311).

Literature

Tanzania's literary scene is dominated by renowned poet and writer, Shaaban Robert (1909–62). Robert, who was born near Tanga, is considered the country's national poet, and was almost single-handedly responsible for the development of a modern Swahili prose style. Among his best-known works are the autobiographical *Maisha yangu* (My Life), the poem *Utenzi wa Vita vya Uhuru* (An Epic in the War for Freedom) and several collections of folk tales.

Almost as well-known as Robert is Zanzibari Muhammed Said Abdulla, who gained fame with his *Mzimu wa watu wa kale* (Graveyard of the Ancestors) and other detective stories, and is considered the founder of Swahili popular literature. Other notable authors of Swahili-language works include Zanzibari novelist Shafi Adam Shafi, Joseph Mbele (known for his short stories) and Ebrahim Hussein (known primarily for his dramas and theatre pieces).

One of Tanzania's most widely acclaimed contemporary writers is Abdulrazak Gurnah, who was born on Zanzibar in 1948. His novel *Paradise,* which is set in East Africa during WWI, made the short list for the UK's Booker Prize in 1994.

Joining Gurnah among the ranks of English-language writers are Peter Palangyo, William Kamera and Tolowa Marti Mollel. Palangyo's novel *Dying in the Sun* tells the story of a young Tanzanian who, after questioning his existence, comes to terms with his family and his heritage in rural Tanzania. Kamera penned several collections of poetry, as well as *Tales of the Wairaqw of Tanzania.* The prolific Mollel has authored numerous short stories, and is particularly known for his folktales, including the collection *Waters of the Vultures and Other Stories.*

Complementing this formal literary tradition are proverbs, for which Tanzanians are famous. They're used for everything from instructing children to letting one's spouse know that you are annoyed with them. For a sampling see www.mwambao.com/methali.htm (featuring Swahili proverbs) or look for *Folk Tales from Buhaya* by R Mwombeki & G Kamanzi (Haya proverbs).

Swahili prose got a relatively late start, but Swahili oral poetry traditions have long roots. See www.humnet.ucla.edu/humnet/aflang/swahili/SwahiliPoetry/index.htm for an excellent overview and anthology.

Music & Dance
TRADITIONAL

Subtle, mesmerising rhythms and smooth dynamism in movement characterise Tanzanian traditional dance, or *ngoma,* as it's known locally. By creating a living picture and encompassing the entire community in its message, it serves as a channel for expressing sentiments such as thanks and praise, and of communicating with the ancestors. Institutions at the forefront of promoting and preserving Tanzanian dance include the renowned College of Arts (Chuo cha Sanaa; p140) in Bagamoyo, and Bujora Cultural Centre (p220) near Mwanza.

While *marimbas* (percussion instruments with metal strips of varying lengths that are plucked with the thumb) and other instruments are sometimes used to accompany dancing, the drum gets top billing and is the most essential element. The same word *(ngoma)* is used for both dance and drumming – testimony of the intimate relationship between the two – and many dances can only be performed to the beat of a particular type of drum. Some dances, notably those of the Sukuma, also make use of other accessories, including live snakes and other animals (p221). The Maasai leave everything behind, including drums, in their famous dancing, which is accompanied only by chants and often also by vigorous leaping.

Other traditional musical instruments include the *kayamba* (shakers made with grain kernels); rattles and bells made of wood or iron; xylophones (also sometimes referred to as *marimbas*); *siwa* (horns) and *tari* (tambourines).

The main place for masked dance is in the southeast, where it plays an important role in the initiation ceremonies of the Makonde (who are famous for their *mapiko* masks) and the Makua.

MODERN

The single greatest influence on Tanzania's modern music scene has been the Congolese bands that began playing in Dar es Salaam in the early 1960s, and which brought the styles of rumba and soukous *(lingala* music) into the East African context. Among the best known is Orchestre Super Matimila, which was propelled to fame by the renowned Dar es Salaam–based Remmy Ongala ('Dr Remmy'), who was born in the Congo (Zaïre). Many of his songs (most are in Swahili) are commentaries on contemporary themes such as AIDS, poverty and hunger, and Ongala has been a major force in popularising music from the region beyond Africa's borders. Other groups to watch for – Dar es Salaam (music capital of East Africa) is the place to be for this – include Mlimani Park Orchestra and Vijana Jazz.

Everyday life is full of art and elegance on the Indian Ocean's most exotic island – beautifully documented in the photo journey *Zanzibar Style* by Gemma Pitcher and Javed Jafferji.

In the shadow of the dance bands, but thriving nevertheless, are Swahili rap artists, including the classic rap group, Kwanza Unit, and a vibrant hip-hop scene (featuring X Plastaz, Sos B and many more). The easiest cassettes to find – you'll see them on small street carts in all major towns – are of church choir music *(kwaya),* which has an enthusiastic following.

During the colonial days, German and British military brass bands spurred the development of *beni ngoma* (brass *ngoma)* – dance and music societies combining Western-style brass instruments with African drums and other traditional instruments. Variants of these are still hugely popular at weddings. Stand at the junction of Moshi and Old Moshi Rds in Arusha on any weekend afternoon, and watch the wedding processions come by, all accompanied by a small band riding in the back of a pick-up truck.

Anyone serious about Tanzanian music should check out http://members.aol.com/dpaterson/index.htm.

On Zanzibar, the music scene has long been dominated by *taarab* (see p110), which has experienced a major resurgence in recent years. Rivalling *taarab* for attention, especially among younger generations is the similar *kidumbak,* distinguished by its defined rhythms and drumming, and its often hard-hitting lyrics. The best contact for music on the archipelago is the **Dhow Countries Music Academy** (☎ 0747-416529; www.zanzibarmusic.org; Old Customs House, Mzingani Rd), in Stone Town.

Visual Arts
PAINTING

In comparison with woodworking, painting has a fairly low profile in Tanzania. The most popular style by far is Tingatinga, which takes its name from painter Edward Saidi Tingatinga, who began it in the 1960s in response to demands from the European market. Tingatinga paintings are traditionally composed in a square, with brightly coloured animal motifs set against a monochrome background, and use diluted and often unmixed enamel paints for a characteristic glossy appearance.

The best place to buy Tingatinga paintings is at the Tingatinga Centre near Morogoro Stores in Dar es Salaam (p83). Other good spots include Msasani Slipway (p83), and the vendors along Hurumzi St in Zanzibar's Stone Town. Dar es Salaam's cultural centres (p75) and Nyumba ya Sanaa (p83) host occasional painting exhibitions by contemporary Tanzanian artists.

SCULPTURE & WOODCARVING

Tanzania's Makonde people, together with their Mozambican cousins, are renowned throughout East Africa for their original and highly fanciful carvings. Although originally from the southeast around the Makonde Plateau, commercial realities lured many Makonde north. Today, the country's main carving centre is at Mwenge in Dar es Salaam (p84), where blocks of hard African blackwood (*Dalbergia melanoxylon* or, in Swahili, *mpingo*) come to life under the hands of skilled artists.

Among the most common carvings are those with *ujamaa* motifs, and those known as *shetani,* which embody images from the spirit world. *Ujamaa* carvings are designed as a totem pole or 'tree of life' containing interlaced human and animal figures around a common ancestor. Each generation is connected to those that preceded it, and gives support to those that follow. Tree of life carvings often reach several metres in height, and are almost always made from a single piece of wood. Shetani carvings are much more abstract, and even grotesque, with the emphasis on challenging viewers to new interpretations while giving the carver's imagination free reign.

DID YOU KNOW?

Lurking inside many carvings are the spirits they represent, thus giving them supernatural powers.

Environment

THE LAND

Tanzania – East Africa's largest country – stretches over 943,000 sq km, almost four times the size of the UK. It's bordered to the east by the enticing turquoise- and emerald-coloured waters of the Indian Ocean, and to the west by the deep lakes of the Western Rift Valley. The narrow coastline consists of long, sandy stretches punctuated by dense stands of mangroves, especially around river mouths. Inland, the terrain rises abruptly into mountains, before levelling out onto an arid highland plateau averaging between 900m and 1800m in altitude. This central plateau area is nestled between the eastern and western branches of the Great Rift Valley, Africa's most distinctive relief feature. Due in large part to central Tanzania's relative aridity, the population is concentrated around the country's perimeter. Tanzania's mountain ranges are grouped into a sharply rising northeastern section (the Eastern Arc) and an open, rolling central and southern section (the Southern Highlands or Southern Arc). There is also a range of volcanoes, known as the Crater Highlands, that rises from the side of the Great Rift Valley in northern Tanzania.

The largest river is the massive Rufiji, which drains the Southern Highlands region as it winds its way to the coast. Other major waterways include the Ruvu, the Wami, the Pangani and the Ruvuma (which forms the border with Mozambique).

WILDLIFE
Animals

Tanzania's fauna is notable both for sheer numbers and for variety, with representatives of 430 species and subspecies among the country's more than four million wild animals. The more common ones include zebras,

DID YOU KNOW?

About 6% (59,000 sq km) of mainland Tanzania is covered by vast inland lakes.

DID YOU KNOW?

In addition to boasting Africa's highest mountain, Kilimanjaro (5896m), Tanzania also has the continent's lowest point – the floor of Lake Tanganyika, at 358m below sea level.

THE GREAT RIFT VALLEY

The Great Rift Valley is part of the East African rift system – a massive geological fault stretching 6500km across the African continent, from the Dead Sea in the north to Beira (Mozambique) in the south. The rift system was formed more than 30 million years ago when the tectonic plates that comprise the African and Eurasian landmasses collided and then diverged. As the plates moved apart, large chunks of the earth's crust dropped down between them. Over millennia, these movements resulted in the escarpments, ravines, flatlands and lakes that characterise East Africa's topography today.

The rift system is notable in particular for its calderas and volcanoes (including Mt Kilimanjaro, Mt Meru and the calderas of the Crater Highlands) and for its lakes. These lakes – including Lakes Tanganyika and Nyasa – are often very deep, with floors well below sea level, although their surfaces may be several hundred metres above sea level.

The Tanzanian Rift Valley consists of two branches formed where the main rift system divides north of Kenya's Lake Turkana. The western branch, or Western Rift Valley, extends past Lake Albert (Uganda) through Rwanda and Burundi to Lakes Tanganyika and Nyasa. The eastern branch (Eastern or Gregory Rift) runs south from Lake Turkana, past Lakes Natron and Manyara, before joining again with the Western Rift by Lake Nyasa. The lakes of the Eastern Rift are smaller than those in the western branch, with some of them only waterless salt beds. The largest are Natron and Manyara. Lake Eyasi is in a side branch off the main rift.

The escarpments of Tanzania's portion of the Rift Valley are most impressive in the north, in and around the Ngorongoro Conservation Area and Lake Manyara National Park.

elephants, wildebeests, buffaloes, hippos, giraffes, antelopes, dik-diks, gazelles, elands and kudus. There are also many predatory animals, including hyenas, wild dogs, lions and leopards, and bands of chimpanzees in Gombe Stream and Mahale Mountains parks. See the Wildlife Guide for descriptions of some of these animals, and the Safaris chapter (p37) for tips on the best times to watch them. In addition, Tanzania has over 60,000 insect species, about 25 types of reptiles or amphibians, 100 species of snakes and numerous fish species.

Complementing this natural wealth are over 1000 species of birds, including various types of kingfisher, hornbills (around Amani in the Eastern Usambaras), bee-eaters (along the Rufiji and Wami Rivers), fish eagles (Lake Victoria) and flamingos (Lake Magadi in the Ngorongoro Crater and Lake Natron, among other places). There are also numerous birds that are unique to Tanzania, including the Udzungwa forest partridge, the Pemba green pigeon, the Usambara weaver and the Usambara eagle owl.

The Kingdon Field Guide to African Mammals by Jonathan Kingdon makes a wonderful safari companion, with a wealth of information on Tanzania's wildlife. Field Guide to the Birds of East Africa by Terry Stevenson & John Fanshawe is similar for birding.

ENDANGERED SPECIES

The black rhino is the best known of Tanzania's endangered species; Ngorongoro Crater (p208) is one of the best places for trying to spot one. Other species fighting for survival include Uluguru bush shrikes; hawksbill, green, olive ridley and leatherback turtles; red colobus monkeys (best seen in Zanzibar's Jozani Forest, p124); wild dogs (most likely spotted in the Selous Game Reserve, p298); and Pemba flying foxes.

Plants

If you're interested in plants, few places on the continent surpass Tanzania's Eastern Arc range, where small patches of tropical rainforest provide home to an incredibly rich assortment of plants, many of which are found nowhere else in the world. One of the most famous is the Usambara or African violet (*Saintpaulia*), which is sold as a humble house plant in grocery stores throughout the West – a far cry from the splendid wildness of its natural habitat in the Eastern Arc forests. South and west of the Eastern Arc range, you'll see impressive stands of baobab, a tree whose root-like branches make it look as if it's standing on its head. Tarangire National Park (p199) has some particularly striking baobab-studded landscapes. One of the best places to start botanical exploration of Tanzania is Amani Nature Reserve (p152), where there is an information centre that also shows traditional medicinal uses of many of the plants. Once established, the planned Kitulo Plateau National Park, southeast of Mbeya, will be another highlight, and one of the few parks in Africa with flowers as its centre point.

Away from the mountain ranges, much of the country is covered by miombo, or 'moist' woodland, where the main vegetation is various types of *Brachystegia* tree. Much of the dry central plateau is covered with savanna, bushland and thickets, while grasslands cover the Serengeti plain and other areas that lack good drainage.

NATIONAL PARKS & RESERVES

Tanzania's unrivalled collection of parks and reserves includes 12 national parks (with two more – Saadani and Kitulo Plateau – on the way), 14 wildlife reserves, the Ngorongoro Conservation Area, two marine parks and several protected marine reserves. Each has its own character, all are highly worth visiting and several have been declared Unesco World Heritage Sites.

Until relatively recently, development and tourism have focused almost exclusively on the so-called 'northern circuit' – Serengeti National

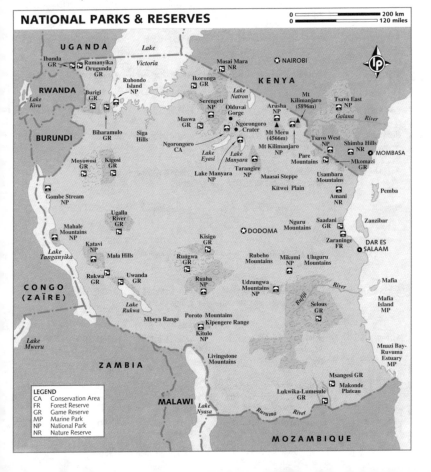

NATIONAL PARKS & RESERVES

0 — 200 km
0 — 120 miles

UGANDA — *Lake Victoria*

Ibanda GR — Rumanyika Orugundu GR — Rubondo Island NP — Ikoronga GR — Masai Mara NR — NAIROBI

RWANDA — Burigi GR — *Lake Natron* — Serengeti NP — Olduvai Gorge — Arusha NP — Mt Kilimanjaro (5896m) — Tsavo East NP

Lake Kivu — Biharamulo GR — Siga Hills — Maswa GR — Ngorongoro Crater — Mt Meru (4566m) — *Galana River*

BURUNDI — Ngorongoro CA — *Lake Eyasi* — *Lake Manyara* — Mt Kilimanjaro NP — Tsavo West NP — Shimba Hills NR — MOMBASA

Moyowosi GR — Kigosi GR — Tarangire — Pare Mountains — Mkomazi GR

Lake Manyara NP — Maasai Steppe — Usambara Mountains

Gombe Stream NP — Kitwei Plain — Amani NR — Pemba

Ugalla River GR — Nguru Mountains — Saadani GR — Zanzibar

Mahale Mountains NP — Katavi NP — Kisigo GR — DODOMA — Zaraninge FR — DAR ES SALAAM

Lake Tanganyika — Mala Hills — Rungwa GR — Rubeho Mountains — Mikumi NP — Uluguru Mountains — Mafia

Rukwa GR — Uwanda GR — Ruaha NP — Udzungwa Mountains NP — *Rufiji* — Mafia Island MP

CONGO (ZAÏRE) — *Lake Rukwa* — Mbeya Range — Poroto Mountains — Kipengere Range — Selous GR

Lake Mweru — Kitulo NP — Mnazi Bay-Ruvuma Estuary MP

ZAMBIA — Livingstone Mountains — Msangesi GR — Makonde Plateau

MALAWI — *Lake Nyasa* — Lukwika-Lumesule GR — *Ruvuma River*

MOZAMBIQUE

LEGEND
CA Conservation Area
FR Forest Reserve
GR Game Reserve
MP Marine Park
NP National Park
NR Nature Reserve

Park	Features	Activities	Best time to visit	Page
Arusha NP	Mt Meru, lakes & crater: zebras, giraffes, elephants	trekking, canoe & vehicle safaris, walking	year-round	p191
Gombe Stream NP	lake shore, forest: chimpanzees	chimp tracking	year-round	p236
Katavi NP	flood plains, lakes & woodland: buffaloes, hippos, antelopes	vehicle & walking safaris	Jun-Oct	p243
Kitulo NP	wildflowers & wilderness	hiking	Dec-Apr (for wildflowers), Sep-Nov (for hiking)	p271
Lake Manyara NP	Lake Manyara: hippos, water birds, elephants	canoe & vehicle safaris	Jun-Feb (Dec-Apr for birding)	p196
Mahale Mountains NP	remote lake shore & mountains: chimpanzees	chimp tracking	Jun-Oct, Dec-Feb	p237
Mikumi NP	Mkata flood plains: lions, buffaloes, giraffes, elephants	vehicle safaris	year-round	p255
Kilimanjaro NP	Mt Kilimanjaro	trekking	Jun-Oct, Dec-Feb	p172
Ngorongoro CA	Ngorongoro Crater: black rhinos, lions, elephants, zebras, flamingos	vehicle safaris	Jun-Feb	p208
Ruaha NP	Ruaha River, sand rivers: elephants, hippos, kudus, antelopes, birds	vehicle & walking safaris	May-Nov	p262
Rubondo Island NP	Lake Victoria: bird life, sitatungas, chimps	walks, chimp tracking, boating, fishing	Jun-Nov	p222
Saadani GR	Wami River, beach: birds, hippos, crocodiles	boat trips, wildlife drives & walks	Jun-Feb	p143
Selous GR	Rufiji River, lakes, woodland: elephants, hippos, wild dogs, black rhinos, birds	boat, walking & vehicle safaris	Jun-Oct, Jan-Feb	p298
Serengeti NP	plains & grasslands, Grumeti River: wildebeests, zebras, lions, cheetahs, giraffes	vehicle & balloon safaris	year-round	p200
Tarangire NP	Tarangire River, woodland, baobabs: elephants, zebras, wildebeests, birds	vehicle safaris	Jun-Oct	p199
Udzungwa Mountains NP	Udzungwa Mountains, forest: primates, birds	hiking	Jun-Oct	p257

TANZANIA'S UNESCO WORLD HERITAGE SITES

- Kilimanjaro National Park (p172)
- Kilwa Kisiwani (p291) & Songo Mnara ruins (p292)
- Ngorongoro Conservation Area (p205)
- Serengeti National Park (p200)
- Selous Game Reserve (p298)
- Zanzibar's Stone Town (p100)

Park and Ngorongoro Conservation Area, together with Lake Manyara, Tarangire and Arusha National Parks, as well as Kilimanjaro National Park for trekkers. As a result, all of these places are easily reached by road or air, well-equipped with facilities, and heavily visited. Apart from the evocative landscapes, the main attractions of the northern circuit are the high concentrations, diversity and accessibility of its wildlife.

The 'southern circuit' – primarily Ruaha National Park and the Selous Game Reserve, as well as Mikumi and Udzungwa Mountains National Parks – has been receiving increasing attention in recent years. However, it still doesn't see close to the number of visitors that the north does and most areas tend to have more of a wilderness feel. They also tend to be more time consuming to reach by road. The wildlife, however, is just as impressive although it's often spread out over larger areas.

In the far west of the country are Mahale Mountains and Gombe Stream National Parks, where the main draws are the chimpanzees and – for Mahale – the spectacularly remote setting. Katavi is also wonderfully remote, and probably the closest you can come to experiencing the pristine face of the wild. Rubondo Island National Park is set on its own in Lake Victoria, and is of particular interest to bird-watchers. Saadani Game Reserve, about to be gazetted as a national park, is easy to reach from Dar es Salaam and lets you mix beach and bush at the same time.

For a summary of Tanzania's national parks and reserves, see the table opposite.

See www.tourismconcern
.org.uk for more on 'fair
trade in tourism' and
travellers' guidelines.

National Parks

Tanzania's national parks are managed by the **Tanzania National Parks Authority** (Tanapa; ☎ 027-250 3471, 250 4082, 250 8216; www.tanzaniaparks.com). Entry fees must be paid in hard currency, preferably US dollars cash. For national park accommodation and guide fees see the table below; park entry fees can be found in the individual listings. Guide and vehicle fees for Ngorongoro Crater, and Selous and Saadani Game Reserves are given in those sections. For general information on park accommodation, see p303.

Accommodation	US$ (16 yrs +)	US$ (5-15 yrs)
Ordinary camp site	20	5
Special camp site	40	10
Hostel	10	-
Resthouse (Serengeti, Arusha, Ruaha, Katavi)	30 (Gombe Stream 20)	-
Banda or Hut	20 (Mt Kilimanjaro 50)	-

Other costs include guide fees of US$10 per day (US$15 overnight) and US$20 for walking safaris. Also, vehicle fees of US$30 per day for a foreign-registered car (Tsh5000 for a Tanzanian-registered car.)

KEEPING THINGS GREEN

Organisations in Tanzania working for environmental conservation include the following:

- **Wildlife Conservation Society of Tanzania** (WCST; Map p73; ☎ 022-211 2518; wcst@africaonline .co.tz; Garden Ave, Dar es Salaam) The best local contact for information on environmental issues; it also publishes the informative environmental newsletter *Miombo*.

- **Roots & Shoots** (☎ 022-270 0795; shoots@africaonline.co.tz) The local branch of the educational arm of Jane Goodall's institute.

- **African Wildlife Foundation** (☎ 027-250 9616/7; www.awf.org)

- **World Wildlife Fund** (☎ 022-277 5346, 270 0071; wwftpo@raha.com)

Wildlife Reserves

With the exception of Saadani, which is a national park in everything but name, and managed by Tanapa, wildlife reserves are administered by the **Wildlife Division of the Ministry of Natural Resources & Tourism** (☎ 022-286 6376, 022-286 6064; selousgamerserve@cats-net.com; cnr Nyerere & Changombe Rds, Dar es Salaam). Fees should be paid in US dollars cash. Saadani and Selous are the only reserves with tourist infrastructure. Large areas of many others have been leased as hunting concessions.

Marine Parks & Reserves

The Ministry of Natural Resources & Tourism's **Marine Parks & Reserves Unit** (Map p74; ☎ 022-215 0420, 022-215 0621; marineparks@raha.com; Olympio St, Upanga, Dar es Salaam) oversees marine parks and reserves. For information on Tanzania's marine parks, see p284 and the boxed text, p296.

ENVIRONMENTAL ISSUES

Although Tanzania has one of the highest proportions of protected land of any African country (about 39% is protected in some form), limited resources hamper conservation efforts, and erosion, soil degradation, desertification and deforestation continue to whittle away at the natural wealth. According to some estimates, Tanzania loses 3500 sq km of forest land annually as a result of agricultural and commercial clearing. In the national parks, poaching and inappropriate visitor use – especially in the northern circuit – threaten wildlife and ecosystems. Deforestation is also a problem on the offshore islands, with about 95% of the tropical high forest that once covered Zanzibar and Pemba now gone. Both on the archipelago and in mainland coastal areas, dynamite fishing has also been a serious threat, although significant progress has been made in halting this practice.

On the positive side, great progress has been made in recent years to involve communities directly in conservation, and local communities are now stakeholders in several lodges and other tourist developments.

Maximum speed limit in parks: 50km/h

Optimal speed for watching animals: 0km/h

Honking: not allowed

Safaris

The sight of hundreds of wildebeests moving across the plains, elephants silhouetted against a red-orange sunset, or a pink haze of flamingos wading in the shallows are likely to be among the most indelible images that you will take away from your time in Tanzania. Thanks to the number, variety and accessibility of its wildlife – all roaming around against a highly evocative natural backdrop – the country has become one of Africa's premier safari destinations, and its safari industry highly competitive. At the budget end there's often only a fine line between operators running no-frills but reliable safaris, and those that are either dishonest, or have cut things so close that problems are bound to arise. At the higher end of the price spectrum, ambience, safari style and the operator's overall focus are important considerations. This chapter provides an overview of factors to consider when planning a safari; many apply in equal measure to organised treks. See p63 for a few suggestions if you're arranging things on your own.

Check out Tanapa's website – www.tanzania parks.com – for help in deciding which parks to visit.

PLANNING A SAFARI
Booking

You can either wait until arriving in Tanzania to organise a safari, or book directly with the operator in advance. If you wait until arrival – Arusha is the best place to organise a safari, followed by Moshi (for Kilimanjaro treks) – you will be able to keep some flexibility in your schedule, plus you'll have the chance to meet up with other travellers to form a group (thereby lowering costs). At the budget level, you might benefit from cheaper walk-in rates, although the difference between walk-in rates and rates for advance bookings usually isn't more than about 5%.

The main disadvantage of booking in advance is decreased flexibility; however, if time is tight, if you are travelling in high season, or if you have specific ideas about which operator you want to use, it's much better to secure a booking before you leave home. Most mid-range and top-end safaris, are booked in advance and, outside the July–August peak season and the Christmas holidays, it can be difficult to find a group to join. During the high season, it's likely that you'll have to wait several days in Arusha or Moshi before an opening arises or a large enough group materialises (four is the minimum for many budget operators). Also, northern circuit lodges and camps (and increasingly those in the south as well) are generally booked out months in advance. If you're travelling on your own and hoping to find other travellers to join, you can still consider booking in advance, as many companies will permit you to adjust your booking on arrival. For example, if you've booked a safari for two people, but find another two companions to join you once you're in Tanzania, the per-person price should be adjusted downwards to reflect the lower four-person rate (although confirm this is an option in advance).

DID YOU KNOW?

The Serengeti is Tanzania's largest park (14,763 sq km), and home to the greatest concentration of large mammals in the world. About half of the park is pristine wilderness.

Booking in advance also allows you to minimise the amount of cash or travellers cheques that you'll need to carry. If you feel confident in your choice of operator, you can do an electronic funds transfer (EFT) for full payment. Most companies also accept an EFT deposit, with the balance to be paid in cash or travellers cheques upon arrival. Be sure to verify payment terms when booking. Another advantage of booking in advance is that you won't need to spend your time in Arusha shopping around at the various operators (which takes at least a day), leaving you free to do something more enjoyable instead. Finally, by booking in advance, you'll be able to minimise dealings with safari touts. While they're not all bad guys, many are quite aggressive, and the whole experience can be rather intimidating.

If you decide to book ahead, try to do so as much in advance as possible. For popular operators in the northern circuit, at least three to six months is recommended, and if your schedule is tight or you will be travelling during the high season, six months to a year in advance is not too soon. In order to maximise your chances of success with booking on arrival, build some flexibility into your itinerary, be prepared to wait and don't rush into any deals.

Costs

Quoted safari prices usually include park entrance fees, camping or lodge fees, fuel and (where applicable) tent rental. They normally exclude drinks (whether these are bottled water, soft drinks or alcoholic beverages), and budget camping safari prices usually exclude sleeping bag rental (which costs anywhere from US$5 per day to US$10 per trip). However, companies vary, so confirm what is included before booking. If you are dealing directly with lodges and tented camps (rather than going through a safari operator), you may be quoted 'all-inclusive' prices. In addition to accommodation, full board and sometimes park fees, these usually include two 'activities' (usually wildlife drives, or sometimes one wildlife drive and one walk, per day, each lasting about two to three hours). If accommodation-only prices are quoted, you'll need to pay extra to go out looking for wildlife – from about US$30 per person per day per 'activity'.

It's nearly always cheaper to deal directly with the operating company. If all or part of your itinerary is subcontracted, the commissions will be reflected in the prices you pay. Booking through an agency abroad (which will then subcontract to a Tanzania-based operator) is convenient, but will always be more expensive. Prices quoted by agencies or operators usually assume shared (double) room/tent occupancy. Most operators, lodges and tented camps charge a supplement for single occupancy ranging from 20% to 50% of the shared-occupancy rate.

In addition to the price quoted by the tour operator, you'll also be expected to tip your driver, guide, cook and porters, assuming that the service has been satisfactory. Many operators have tipping guidelines; in general expect to tip about US$10 per group per day to the driver and/or guide, and about US$8 per group per day to the cook – more for top-end safaris, groups with more people or if an especially good job has been done. For guidelines on tipping porters, and for tipping guidelines for treks on Mts Kilimanjaro and Meru, see p174 and p194.

BUDGET

Most safaris at the lower end of the price range are camping safaris. In order to keep costs to a minimum, groups often find themselves camping outside national park areas (thereby saving park admission and camping fees) or, alternatively, staying in budget guesthouses outside the park. Budget operators also save costs by working with larger groups to minimise per-person transport costs, and by keeping to a no-frills setup with basic meals and a minimum number of staff. For most safaris at the budget level, as well as for many mid-range safaris, daily kilometre limits are placed on the vehicles.

For any budget safaris, the bare minimum cost for a registered company is US$85 per person per day (camping), but most reliable companies

Bernhard Grzimek's 1959 film, *The Serengeti Shall Not Die*, was one of the most influential wildlife films ever made, drawing world attention to the Serengeti and conservation in Africa.

charge between US$90 and US$100. Be wary of anyone offering you prices much below US$90, as there are bound to be problems. To save money, bring drinks with you, especially mineral water, as it's expensive in and near the parks. For other ways to save, see p313. During the low season, it's often possible to find a lodge safari for roughly the price of a camping safari.

MID-RANGE

Most mid-range safaris use lodges, where you'll have a comfortable room and eat in a restaurant. One of the main variables here as far as price is concerned is which lodges or hotels are included. For the northern circuit, the main chains are the formerly government-owned 'Wildlife Lodges', Serena and Sopa. There are Wildlife Lodges at Lake Manyara National Park, at Seronera and Lobo in the Serengeti, and at Ngorongoro Crater. All have good (sometimes excellent) locations and no-frills but perfectly adequate accommodation. Hotels in both the Serena and Sopa chains are quite comfortable, but more expensive, although during the low season price differentials level out. Currently, neither Serena nor Sopa has hotels in the southern circuit parks, although several are planned in the near future. In addition to the three major chains, private mid-range hotels and lodges are sometimes used, which generally have less of an institutional feel, and can be very good deals.

In general, safaris in the mid-range category are comfortable, reliable and reasonably good value. A disadvantage is that they may have a packaged-tour atmosphere, although this can be minimised by selecting a safari company and accommodation carefully, and giving attention to who and how many other people you travel with. Expect to pay a minimum of about US$140 per person per day for a lodge safari, with most closer to US$160 and more.

TOP END

Private lodges or luxury tented camps and sometimes private fly camps are used in top-end safaris (p304). For the price you pay (from US$200 up to US$500 or more per person per day), expect a full range of amenities. Even in remote settings without running water you will be able to enjoy hot, bush-style showers, comfortable beds and fine dining. Also expect a high level of personalised attention, an often intimate atmosphere (many places at this level have fewer than 20 beds), excellent guiding and an emphasis on achieving as 'authentic' an experience of the bush as possible.

When to Go

Getting around is easier in the dry season (late June to October), and in many parks this is when animals are easier to find around water holes and rivers. Foliage is also less dense, making it easier to spot wildlife. However, as the dry season corresponds in part with the high-travel season, lodges and camps become crowded and accommodation prices are at a premium.

Apart from these general considerations, the ideal time to go on a safari depends on which parks and reserves you want to visit and what you want to see and do. Large sections of Katavi National Park, for example, are only accessible during the dry season, when vast herds of buffaloes, elephants and more jostle for space at scarce water sources. Tarangire National Park, although accessible year-round, is another park best visited during the dry season, when wildlife concentrations are far higher than at other times of the year. In the Serengeti, by contrast, wildlife concentrations are

SAFARI STYLE

While price can be a major determining factor in safari planning, there are other considerations that are just as important:

■ **Ambience** Will you be staying in or near the park? (If you stay well outside the park, you'll miss the good early morning and evening wildlife-viewing hours.) Are the surroundings atmospheric? Will you be in a large lodge or an intimate private camp?

■ **Equipment** Mediocre vehicles and equipment can significantly detract from the overall experience. On Kilimanjaro treks, inadequate equipment can mean the difference between reaching the summit or not, or worse.

■ **Access and activities** If you don't relish the idea of hours in a 4WD on bumpy roads, consider parks and lodges where you can fly in. Parks and reserves where walking and boat safaris are possible are the best bet for getting out of the vehicle and into the bush.

■ **Guides** A good driver or guide can make or break your safari. Staff at reputable companies are usually knowledgeable and competent. With borderline operators trying to cut corners, chances are that staff are unfairly paid, and are not likely to be particularly knowledgeable or motivated.

■ **Setting the agenda** Some drivers feel that they have to whisk you from one good 'sighting' to the next. If your preference is to stay in one strategic place for a while to simply experience the environment and see what comes by, don't hesitate to discuss this with your driver. Going off in wild pursuit of the 'Big Five' means you'll miss the more subtle aspects of your surroundings.

■ **Extracurriculars** On the northern circuit, it's common for drivers to stop at souvenir shops en route. While this gives the driver an often much-needed break from the wheel, most shops pay drivers commissions to bring clients, which means you may find yourself spending a lot more time souvenir shopping than you'd bargained for. If you're not interested in this, discuss it with your driver at the outset of your safari, ideally while you're still at the operator's offices.

■ **Less is more** If you'll be teaming up with others to make a group, find out how many people will be in your vehicle, and try to meet your travelling companions before setting off.

■ **Special interests** If bird-watching or other special interests are important, arrange a private safari with a specialised operator.

comparatively low during the dry season; it's during the wet season that you'll see the enormous herds of wildebeests in the park's southeastern section, although the dry season is best for lions and other predators. For birding, the wet season is the best time in many areas. If you are timing your safari around specific events such as the Serengeti wildebeest migration, remember that seasons vary from year to year and are difficult to accurately predict in advance.

What to Bring

Useful items to bring with you include binoculars; field guides; a good-quality sleeping bag (for treks or camping safaris); mosquito repellent; rain gear and waterproofs for wet-season travel – especially for camping safaris or treks; sunglasses; camera and film; and extra contact lens solution or your prescription glasses, as the dust can be irritating. Top-end lodges and tented camps usually have mosquito nets, but it doesn't hurt to bring one along, and you'll often need one for budget guesthouses. For walking safaris bring lightweight, long-sleeved/-legged clothing in subdued colours, a head covering and sturdy, comfortable shoes. For budget safaris, it's a good idea to bring extra food and snacks and a roll

(Continued on page 57)

Wildlife Guide

Tanzania teems with wildlife. With vast elephant herds around Ruaha and Tarangire parks, and the chimpanzee bands that frolic in the forests of Mahale Mountains and Gombe Stream parks, the country is one of Africa's premiere wildlife-watching destinations. Few other places on earth host such an impressive collection of large animals supported by such a range of environmental and climactic conditions within such a geographical area.

The best news is that much of this natural wealth is readily accessible to visitors, thanks to an enlightened conservation policy and an unparalleled collection of national parks and reserves. In the popular northern safari circuit around Arusha, the animals are often well habituated, and this, combined with some stunning topographical backdrops, makes for unforgettable safari memories. In the south and west, where visitor numbers are much lower, wildlife tends to be more skittish and difficult to spot, although the raw wilderness setting more than compensates.

Wherever you head, it's worth remembering that watching Tanzania's wildlife is about far more than just 'seeing' the animals, and ticking them off on checklists. It's about experiencing East African nature at its most untamed, getting a glimpse into nature's magnificent synchrony, and understanding how the rhythms of the wild can be best protected for future generations. Doing all this takes time – time to loiter for hours at a watering hole, to sit in one spot at dawn while the morning rises around you, or to learn about the animals' habits and migration patterns and the myriad factors affecting them. In Tanzania, it often takes money as well, although it's possible with some planning to keep costs at a reasonable level. And of course, the more understanding you have about the animals and their habitats, the more satisfied you'll be that your Tanzania safari has been money well spent.

Leopard (*Panthera pardus*) – Masai Mara National Reserve.
PHOTO BY ALEX DISSANAYAKE

Both bushbaby species are often found in family groups of up to six or seven individuals.

PHOTO BY MITCH REARDON

PRIMATES

BUSHBABIES
GREATER BUSHBABY
Otolemur crassicaudatus; East African lesser bushbaby Galago senegalensis

Named for the greater bushbaby's conspicuous, wailing nocturnal calls (the calls of lesser bushbabies are rarely noticed), bushbabies are nocturnal primates with small heads, large rounded ears, thick bushy tails and enormous eyes – look for their red eye reflection in torchlight. The greater bushbaby is dark brown; the tiny lesser bushbaby is light grey with yellow on its legs. Tree sap and fruit are the mainstay of their diet, supplemented by insects and, in the case of the greater bushbaby, lizards, nestlings and eggs. Fantastically agile, lesser bushbabies make spectacular treetop leaps. **Size:** Greater bushbaby length 80cm, including 45cm tail; weight up to 1.5kg. Lesser bushbaby length 40cm; weight 150g to 200g. **Distribution:** Both found in forests and woodlands throughout the country. **Status:** Common but strictly nocturnal.

The male vervet monkey has a distinctive bright-blue scrotum, an important signal of status in the troop.

PHOTO BY ARIADNE VAN ZANDBERGEN

VERVET MONKEY
Cercopithecus aethiops

A conspicuous inhabitant of the woodland-savanna, the vervet is easily recognised by its grizzled grey hair and black face fringed with white. Troops may number up to 30. The vervet has a sophisticated vocal repertoire, with, for example, different calls for different predators. It is diurnal and forages for fruits, seeds, leaves, flowers, invertebrates and the occasional lizard or nestling. It rapidly learns where easy pickings can be found around lodges and camp sites, but becomes a pest when it gets habituated to being fed. **Size**: Up to 130cm long, including 65cm tail; weight 3kg to 9kg; male larger than female. **Distribution**: Widespread throughout the country everywhere there are trees or bush, but especially in woodland-savanna and especially near water. **Status**: Very common and easy to see.

Blue monkeys are more arboreal than vervet monkeys and generally prefer dense forest and woodland rather than savanna.

PHOTO BY MITCH REARDON

BLUE (SAMANGO) MONKEY
Cercopithecus mitis

Similar to the vervet monkey, but slightly larger and much darker, blue monkeys have a grey to black face, black shoulders, limbs and tail, and a reddish-brown or olive-brown back. They feed largely on fruit, bark, gum and leaves. Social groups may be as large as 30 but generally number between four and 12. The groups usually consist of related females and their young, and a single adult male. A broad diet allows them to occupy relatively small home ranges. **Size**: 140cm long, including 80cm tail; weight normally up to 15kg, but as much as 23kg; male larger than female. **Distribution**: In most forests, which occur along the coast and in the north and far south. **Status**: Locally common; active by day; often difficult to see in foliage.

EASTERN BLACK-AND-WHITE COLOBUS
Colobus guereza

This colobus is glossy black with a white face, bushy white tail, and a white fur 'cape'. Newborns are initially white, gaining their adult coat at around six months. The colobus' low-energy diet means it is relatively inactive but it makes spectacular leaps when moving through the treetops. The ready availability of its food enables it to survive on quite small home ranges, usually maintained by troops of up to 12 animals, consisting of a dominant male, females and young.

Size: 140cm long, including 80cm tail; weight 3.5kg to 10kg; male larger than female. **Distribution:** Forests in the northwest and north-central regions. **Status:** Locally common; active during the day, but often difficult to see among foliage.

The black-and-white colobus spends most of its time in the forest canopy, where it feeds mostly on leaves.

PHOTO BY ARIADNE VAN ZANDBERGEN

BABOON
Papio cynocephalus

Baboons are unmistakable, but there are two subspecies in Tanzania: the yellow *(P. c. cynocephalus)* and the olive baboon *(P. c. anubis)*, named for their differing hair colour. Social interactions in the troop are complex with males accessing only certain females, males forming alliances to dominate other males, and males caring for unrelated juveniles. They forage by day, mostly in open woodland-savanna for grasses, tubers, fruits, invertebrates and occasionally small vertebrates. Ever the opportunist, baboons often visit camp sites and may become (dangerous) pests.

Baboons live in troops of between eight and 200; contrary to popular belief there is no single dominant male.

PHOTO BY JASON EDWARDS

Size: Shoulder height 75cm; length 160cm, including 70cm tail; weight up to 45kg; male larger than female, and twice as heavy. **Distribution:** Widespread, yellow baboon in the south and east, olive in the north and west. **Status:** Abundant.

CHIMPANZEE
Pan troglodytes

The chimpanzee is our closest living relative and behaves like it, engaging in cooperative hunting, tool manufacture and use, and war. They are highly sociable, living in communities numbering up to 120; however, all individuals in a social group rarely congregate and the typical group size is much smaller. Individuals may also spend considerable time alone. Primarily vegetarians consuming fruit, bark, stems and leaves, chimps also eat insects, nestling birds, eggs and larger prey, including monkeys.

Though requiring a rich year-round food supply and preferring productive, moist forests, the chimpanzee is adaptable and is found in a wide range of habitats.

PHOTO BY ARIADNE VAN ZANDBERGEN

Size: Up to 1.7m when standing; weight 25kg to 55kg, male larger than female. **Distribution:** Equatorial forest in western Tanzania; best seen in Gombe Stream and Mahale Mountains National Parks. **Status:** Threatened by habitat destruction and hunting (ie illegal chimp trafficking), chimpanzees are endangered and occur in small isolated populations.

Jackals scavenge from the kills of larger predators but are also efficient hunters themselves.

PHOTO BY CAROL POLICH

CARNIVORES

JACKALS
BLACK-BACKED JACKAL
C. mesomelas; side-striped jackal
C. adustus; golden jackal Canis aureus

The golden jackal is often the most numerous carnivore in open savanna and may be very active by day. The black-backed has a mantle of silver-grey hair and black-tipped tail; it is often the most common night scavenger. The side-striped is the least common and least studied, grey in colour with a light stripe along each side and a white-tipped tail. The three have similar social and feeding behaviour. Pairs are long lasting and defend small territories. Young of previous litters often help raise the new pups.

Size: Shoulder height 38cm to 50cm; length 95cm to 120cm, including 25cm to 40cm tail; weight up to 15kg. **Distribution**: The golden jackal occurs in the centre and northeast, the other two species are found throughout the country. **Status**: Abundant in parks; also in settled areas.

The huge ears of the bat-eared fox detect the faint sounds of invertebrates below ground, before it unearths them in a burst of frantic digging.

PHOTO BY ARIADNE VAN ZANDBERGEN

BAT-EARED FOX
Otocyon megalotis

The bat-eared fox eats mainly insects, especially termites, but also wild fruit and small vertebrates. It is monogamous and is often seen in groups comprising a mated pair and offspring. Natural enemies include large birds of prey, spotted hyenas, caracals and larger cats. It will bravely attempt to rescue a family member caught by a predator by using distraction techniques and harassment, which extends to nipping larger enemies on the ankles.

Size: Shoulder height 35cm; length 75cm to 90cm, including 30cm tail; weight 3kg to 5kg. **Distribution**: Throughout the country. **Status**: Common, especially in national parks; mainly nocturnal but often seen in the late afternoon and early morning.

The wild dog requires enormous areas of habitat and is one of the most endangered carnivores in Africa.

PHOTO BY DAVID WALL

WILD DOG
Lycaon pictus

The wild dog's blotched black, yellow and white coat, and its large, round ears, are unmistakable. It lives in packs of up to 40, though usually 12 to 20. Endurance hunters, the pack chases prey until exhaustion, then cooperates to pull it down. The wild dog is widely reviled by eating its prey alive, but this is probably as fast as 'cleaner' methods used by other carnivores. Mid-sized antelopes are preferred, but wild dogs take animals as large as buffaloes.

Size: Shoulder height 65cm to 80cm; length 100cm to 150cm, including 35cm tail; weight 20kg to 35kg. **Distribution**: Restricted to large reserves; Selous National Park probably has the largest population in East Africa. **Status**: Highly threatened; numbers reduced from naturally low density by persecution, disease and habitat loss.

CAPE CLAWLESS OTTER
Aonyx capensis

Similar to European otters but much larger, Cape clawless otters are a glossy chocolate brown with a white or cream-coloured lower face, throat and neck. Unlike most otters, only the hind feet of Cape clawless otters are webbed, and the front feet end in dexterous, human-like fingers with rudimentary nails.

Cape clawless otters are active during early morning and evening, though they become nocturnal in areas where they are hunted by humans.

PHOTO BY ROGER DE LA HARPE/ GALLO IMAGES

They are very entertaining to watch, being active and vocal – their repertoire includes whistles, mews and chirps. Their main foods include fish, freshwater crabs and frogs.

Size: Length 105cm to 160cm, including 50cm tail; weight up to 30kg. **Distribution**: Found in large freshwater bodies and coastal habitats throughout the country. **Status**: Locally common; active both day and night but usually seen in the early morning and late afternoon.

HONEY BADGER (RATEL)
Mellivora capensis

The ratel is pugnacious and astonishingly powerful for its size, and has a fascinating relationship with the honeyguide bird. The honeyguide leads them to bees' nests, which the ratel rips open for honey, and in doing so provides the honeyguide access to its most favoured food – beeswax. The ratel is highly

The ratel's thick, loose skin is an excellent defence against predators, bee stings and snake bites.

PHOTO BY LORNA STANTON/GALLO IMAGES

omnivorous, feeding on small animals, carrion, berries, roots, eggs, honey and especially on social insects (ants, termites and bees) and their larvae. In some parks, the ratel scavenges from bins, presenting the best opportunity for viewing this animal.

Size: Shoulder height 30cm; length 95cm, including 20cm tail; weight up to 15kg. **Distribution**: Found in most habitats throughout the country. **Status**: Generally occurs in low densities, but populations are sustainable; apparently active by day in parks but nocturnal in areas of human habitation.

SMALL-SPOTTED GENET
Genetta genetta; large-spotted genet G. tigrina

Relatives of mongooses, genets resemble long, slender domestic cats with pointed foxlike faces. The two species of genets can be differentiated by the tail tips – white in the small-spotted, black in the large-spotted. The small-spotted also has a crest along the spine, which it raises

Genets are solitary, sleeping by day in abandoned burrows, rock crevices or tree hollows.

PHOTO BY DENNIS JONES

when threatened. Genets hunt on land or in trees, feeding on rodents, birds, reptiles, eggs, insects and fruits. Genets deposit their droppings in latrines, usually in open or conspicuous sites.

Size: Shoulder height 18cm; length 85cm to 110cm, including 45cm tail; weight 1.5kg to 3kg. **Distribution**: The large-spotted occurs throughout the country, including human settlements; the small-spotted is absent from the west. **Status**: Very common but strictly nocturnal; often the most common small carnivore seen at night.

Collectively, mongooses can intimidate much larger enemies.

PHOTO BY ABI

MONGOOSES

Although common, most of the nine species (approximately) of mongooses in Tanzania are usually seen only fleetingly. A few species, such as the dwarf mongoose *(Helogale parvula)* and the banded mongoose *(Mungos mungo)* are intensely social, keeping contact with twittering calls while foraging. Others, such as the slender mongoose *(Galerella sanguinea)* – it has a distinctive black-tipped tail, which it holds aloft like a flag when running – and the white-tailed mongoose *(Ichneumia albicauda)* are usually solitary. Family groups are better than loners at spotting danger and raising kittens. Invertebrates are their most important prey.

Size: Ranging from the dwarf mongoose at 40cm in length and to 400g in weight, to the white-tailed mongoose at 120cm and up to 5.5kg. **Distribution**: In most of Tanzania there are at least two or three species. **Status**: Common; sociable species are diurnal, solitary species are generally nocturnal.

The male aardwolf assists the female in raising the cubs, mostly by babysitting at the den while the mother forages.

PHOTO BY ABI

AARDWOLF
Proteles cristatus

Smallest of the hyena family, the aardwolf subsists almost entirely on harvester termites (which are generally ignored by other termite eaters because they are so noxious), licking more than 200,000 from the ground each night. Unlike other hyaenids, it does not form clans; instead, it forages alone and mates form only loose associations with each other. The aardwolf is persecuted in the mistaken belief that it kills stock, and may suffer huge population crashes following spraying for locusts (the spraying also kills termites).

Size: Shoulder height 40cm to 50cm; length 80cm to 100cm, including 25cm tail; weight 8kg to 12kg. **Distribution**: Throughout the country, especially in open, dry, sandy areas in which the grass is grazed short. **Status**: Uncommon; nocturnal but occasionally seen at dawn and dusk.

The female spotted hyena is larger than, and dominant to, males and has male physical characteristics, including an erectile clitoris that renders the sexes virtually indistinguishable.

PHOTO BY LUKE HUNTER

SPOTTED HYENA
Crocuta crocuta

Widely reviled as a scavenger, the spotted hyena is actually a highly efficient predator with a fascinating social system. Clans, which can contain dozens of individuals, are led by females. The spotted hyena is massively built and appears distinctly canine, but is more closely related to cats than to dogs. It can run at a speed of 60km/h and a pack can easily dispatch adult wildebeests and zebras. Their 'ooo-oop' call is one of the most distinctive East African night sounds.

Size: Shoulder height 85cm; length 120cm to 180cm, including 30cm tail; weight 55kg to 80kg. **Distribution**: Throughout the country. **Status**: Common where there is suitable food and often the most common large predator in protected areas; mainly nocturnal but also seen during the day.

SERVAL
Felis serval

Tall, slender, long-legged cats, ser-vals, on first impression, may be mistaken for small cheetahs. The tawny to russet-yellow coat has large black spots, forming long bars and blotches on the neck and shoulders. All-black individuals occasionally occur. Other distin-guishing features include very large upright ears, a long neck and a relatively short tail. Servals are rodent specialists, feeding primarily on mice, rats and springhares. Birds, small reptiles and occasionally the young of small antelopes are also taken.

Servals are associated with vegetation near water and are most common in flood plain savanna, wetlands and woodlands near streams.

PHOTO BY DAVID WALL

Size: Shoulder height 60cm; length 95cm to 130cm, including 30cm tail; weight 7kg to 16kg.
Distribution: Throughout the region in areas of long grasses, especially along the edges of forests or marshes. **Status**: Relatively common but mainly nocturnal, sometimes seen in the early morn-ing and late afternoon.

CARACAL
Felis caracal

Sometimes called the African lynx due to its long tufted ears, the caracal is a robust, powerful cat that preys mostly on small antelopes, birds and rodents but also takes prey much larger than itself. The caracal is largely solitary, and although male-female pairs may associate more than most other cats, females raise their one to three kittens alone. The sandy body colour is excellent camou-flage, but the ears and face are strikingly patterned in black and white and are highly mobile and expressive – features used for visual signalling.

The caracal's long back legs power prodigious leaps – it even takes birds in flight.

PHOTO BY DAVE HAMMAN

Size: Shoulder height 40cm to 50cm; length 95cm to 120cm, including 30cm tail; weight 7kg to 18kg; male slightly larger than female. **Distribution**: Throughout the country but prefers semi-arid regions, dry savannas and hilly country; absent from dense forest. **Status**: Fairly common but largely nocturnal and difficult to see.

LEOPARD
Panthera pardus

Leopards are heard more often than seen; its rasping territorial call sounds very much like a saw cut-ting through wood. The supreme ambush hunter, leopards stalk close to its prey before attacking in an explosive rush. It eats everything from insects to zebras, but ante-lopes are their primary prey. It is solitary, except when a male and female remain in close association for the female's week-long oestrus.

The leopard is highly agile and climbs well, spending more time in trees than other big cats – it hoists its kills into trees to avoid losing them to lions and hyenas.

PHOTO BY DENNIS JONES

Size: Shoulder height 50cm to 75cm; length 160cm to 210cm, including 70cm to 110cm tail; weight up to 90kg; male larger than female. **Distribution**: Throughout the country in all habitats with dense cover. **Status**: Common but, being mainly nocturnal, they are very difficult to see.

The lion hunts – certainly as a group, perhaps cooperatively – virtually anything, but wildebeests, zebras and buffaloes are the main targets.

PHOTO BY ALEX DISSANAYAKE

LION
Panthera leo

The lion spends the night hunting, patrolling territories (of 50 to 400 sq km) and playing. It lives in prides of up to about 30, comprising four to 12 related females, which remain in the pride for life, and a coalition of unrelated males, which defend females from foreign males. Young males are ousted from the pride at the age of two or three, becoming nomadic until around five years old, when they are able to take over their own pride.

Size: Shoulder height 120cm; length 250cm to 300cm, including 100cm tail; weight up to 260kg (male), 180kg (female). **Distribution**: Largely confined to protected areas but present in all savanna and woodland parks. **Status**: Common where it occurs; mainly nocturnal but easy to see during the day.

Cheetahs' litters may be as large as nine, but in open savanna habitats most cubs are killed by other predators, particularly lions.

PHOTO BY JOHN HAY

CHEETAH
Acinonyx jubatus

The world's fastest land mammal, the cheetah can reach speeds of at least 105km/h but becomes exhausted after a few hundred metres and therefore usually stalks prey to within 60m before unleashing its tremendous acceleration – three out of every four hunts fail. The cheetah preys on antelopes weighing up to 60kg as well as hares and young wildebeests and zebras. Young cheetahs disperse from the mother when aged around 18 months. The males form coalitions; females remain solitary for life.

Size: Shoulder height 85cm; length 180cm to 220cm, including 70cm tail; weight 35kg to 65kg. **Distribution**: Largely restricted to protected areas or the regions surrounding them; absent from densely forested areas. **Status**: Uncommon, with individuals moving over large areas; active by day and frequently seen in national parks.

Elephant vocalisations include a deep rumble felt as a low vibration by humans; and a high-pitched trumpeting given in threat or when frightened.

PHOTO BY ANDERS BLOMQVIST

UNGULATES

AFRICAN ELEPHANT
Loxodonta africana

The African elephant usually lives in groups of 10 to 20 females and young and often congregate in larger herds at common resources. Bulls live alone or in bachelor groups, joining the herds when females are in season. A cow may mate with many bulls during oestrus. Consuming 250kg of vegetation daily, elephants can decimate woodlands, but such damage may be part of the savanna's natural cycle. An elephant lives for up to 100 years.

Size: Shoulder height up to 4m (male), 3.5m (female); weight five to 6.5 tonnes (male), three to 3.5 tonnes (female). **Distribution**: Widely distributed; large populations only occur in protected areas. **Status**: Very common in most of the larger national parks.

ROCK HYRAX
Procavia johnstoni; Yellow-Spotted Rock Hyrax Heterohyrax brucei

Despite their resemblance to large guinea pigs, hyraxes are actually related to the elephant.

PHOTO BY ARIADNE VAN ZANDBERGEN

Hyraxes (or dassies) occur nearly everywhere there are mountains or rocky outcrops. They are sociable, living in colonies of up to 60. The yellow-spotted is readily distinguished from the rock hyrax by the presence of a prominent white spot above the eye. Hyraxes spend much of the day basking on rocks or chasing other hyraxes. Where habituated to humans they are often approachable, but otherwise dash into rock crevices when alarmed, uttering shrill screams. Rocks streaked white by hyraxes' urine are often a conspicuous indicator of a colony's presence.
Size: Rock hyrax length 40cm to 60cm; weight 2kg to 5.5kg. Yellow-spotted length 30cm to 50cm; weight 1kg to 2.5kg. **Distribution**: Occur throughout the country, often inhabiting the same site; Serengeti National Park is excellent for observing both together. **Status**: Common and easily seen; regularly inhabit areas around tourist lodges.

BURCHELL'S ZEBRA
Equus burchelli

Yes, it's true – a zebra's stripes are as individual as a human's fingerprints.

PHOTO BY RICHARD I'ANSON

Thousands of Burchell's zebras (one of three zebra species in Africa) join blue wildebeests on their famous mass migration. The zebras' sociality centres on harems of five to six mares defended by a single stallion. Larger herds are usually temporary aggregations of smaller groups. Stallions may hold a harem for 15 years, but they often lose single mares to younger males, which gradually build up their own harems. When pursued by predators, zebras close ranks as they run off, making it hard for any individual to be singled out for attack.
Size: Shoulder height 140cm to 160cm; length 220cm to 260cm; weight up to 390kg; females are slightly smaller than males. **Distribution**: In savanna habitats from treeless grasslands to open woodlands in parks throughout the country. **Status**: Very common and easily seen.

BLACK (HOOK-LIPPED) RHINOCEROS
Diceros bicornis

The black rhino is solitary and aggressively territorial, usually only socialising during the mating season; however, in some areas they may form temporary associations.

PHOTO BY DAVID WALL

Poaching for their horns has made rhinos Africa's most endangered large mammal. In many countries they have been exterminated and the white rhino (*Ceratotherium simum*) is now extinct in East Africa (though still numerous in Southern Africa). The smaller of the two species, the black rhino is more unpredictable and prone to charging when alarmed or merely uncertain about a possible threat. They use their pointed, prehensile upper lip to feed selectively on branches and foliage.
Size: Shoulder height 160cm; length 3m to 4m; weight 800kg to 1400kg; front horn up to 130cm long. **Distribution**: Restricted to relict populations in a few reserves; best seen in Tanzania's Ngorongoro Crater. **Status**: Highly endangered in the region but seen in protected areas.

WARTHOG
Phacochoerus aethiopicus

The warthog grows two sets of tusks: the upper ones grow as long as 60cm, the lower ones are usually less than 15cm long. The distinctive facial warts can be used to determine the sex of warthogs – females have a pair of warts under the eyes; males have a second set further down the snout. Males form bachelor groups or are solitary, only associating with females during oestrus. The warthog feeds mainly on grass, but also fruit and bark. In hard times, it grubs for roots and bulbs. It dens in abandoned burrows or excavates its own.

Size: Shoulder height 70cm; weight up to more than 100kg, but averages 50kg to 60kg; male larger than female. **Distribution**: Throughout the country; abundant in savanna and woodland. **Status**: Common, diurnal and easy to see.

HIPPOPOTAMUS
Hippopotamus amphibius

The hippo is found close to fresh water, spending most of the day submerged and emerging at night to graze on land. It lives in large herds, tolerating close contact in the water but foraging alone when on land. Adult bulls aggressively defend territories against each other and most males bear the scars of conflicts (often a convenient method of sexing hippos). Cows with calves are aggressive towards other individuals. The hippo is extremely dangerous on land and kills many people each year, usually when someone inadvertently blocks the animal's retreat to the water.

Size: Shoulder height 150cm; weight 1000kg to 2000kg; male larger than female. **Distribution**: Widespread but restricted to large bodies of fresh water with nearby grasslands. **Status**: Common in major water courses and easy to see.

GIRAFFE
Giraffa camelopardalis

There are several distinctly patterned species of giraffes; of those found in Tanzania, the Masai giraffe, is the most common. The 'horns' (knobs of skin-covered bone) of males have bald tips, females' are hair covered. The giraffe forms loose, ever-changing groups of up to 50; females are rarely seen alone, while males are more solitary. A browser, it exploits foliage out of reach of most herbivores – males usually feed from a higher level than females. Juveniles are prone to predation and lions even take adults – it is most vulnerable when drinking.

Size: Height 3.5m to 4.5m (female), 4m to 5.5m (male); weight 700kg to 1000kg (female); 900kg to 1400kg (male). **Distribution**: Found in most parks and reserves in Tanzania, except the floor of Ngorongoro Crater. **Status**: Relatively common where it occurs and easy to see.

BUSHBUCK
Tragelaphus scriptus

Shy and solitary animals, bushbucks inhabit thick bush close to permanent water, where they browse on leaves at night. The bushbuck is chestnut to dark brown in colour and has a variable number of white vertical stripes on the body between the neck and rump, as well as a number of white spots on the

When startled, the bushbuck bolts and crashes loudly through the undergrowth.

PHOTO BY MITCH REARDON

upper thigh and a white splash on the neck. Normally only males grow horns, which are straight with gentle spirals and average about 30cm in length. It can be aggressive and dangerous when cornered.

Size: Height at shoulder 80cm; weight up to 80kg; horns up to 55cm long; male larger than female. **Distribution**: Throughout the country where there is dense vegetation (especially the inside margins of forests), usually near water. **Status**: Common, but shy and difficult to see.

GREATER KUDU
Tragelaphus strepsiceros; Lesser Kudu T. imberbis

The greater kudu is Africa's second-tallest antelope and the males carry massive spiralling horns. It is light grey in colour with six to 12 white stripes down the sides. The lesser kudu has 11 to 15 body stripes; males are blue-grey and females are bright rust coloured. In both species,

Strong jumpers, greater kudu flee with frequent leaping, clearing obstacles more than 2m high.

PHOTO BY ARIADNE VAN ZANDBERGEN

one to three females and their young form groups, and are joined by the normally solitary males during the breeding season. Kudus are browsers, finding their preferred diet in woodland-savanna with dense bush cover.

Size: Greater kudu shoulder height 120cm to 150cm (males); weight 190kg to 320kg; horns to 180cm. Lesser kudu shoulder height 95cm to 110cm; weight 90kg to 110kg; horns to 90cm. Females 10% shorter, 40% lighter. **Distribution**: Greater kudu widespread outside arid areas; lesser kudu found in northern arid region. **Status**: Greater kudu becoming scattered; lesser kudu still common.

ELAND
Taurotragus oryx

Africa's largest antelope, the eland is massive. The horns of both sexes average 65cm, spiralling at the base then sweeping straight back. The male has a distinctive hairy tuft on the head, and stouter horns. Herds consist of adults, adults and young, or sometimes just young – group membership and composition

The eland normally drinks daily, but can go for over a month without water.

PHOTO BY DAVID WALL

change often. The most common large groups consist of 10 to 60 females and young. Males are less gregarious, coming together more sporadically and in smaller numbers, but one or more often join female-young herds. Aggregations up to 1000 form where new grass is growing.

Size: Shoulder height 150cm to 180cm (male), 125cm to 150cm (female); weight 450kg to 950kg (male), 300kg to 500kg (female); horns up to 100cm long. **Distribution**: Widespread but patchy distribution in all habitats, except forest and desert. **Status**: Low density but relatively common.

Although generally docile, buffaloes can be very dangerous – most aggressive are lone bulls, and females protecting their young.

PHOTO BY DAVID WALL

AFRICAN BUFFALO
Syncerus caffer

Both sexes of the African buffalo have distinctive curving horns that broaden at the base to meet over the forehead in a massive 'boss' – the female's are usually smaller. Local populations of buffaloes inhabit large home ranges and at times herds of thousands form, but the population's social organisation is fluid: groups of related females and their young coalesce and separate into larger or smaller herds; males associate with the females during breeding, and at other times they form male herds or are solitary.

Size: Shoulder height 160cm; weight 400kg to 900kg; horns up to 125cm long; female somewhat smaller than male. **Distribution**: Widespread and in most habitats with abundant grass, water and cover. **Status**: Common and can be approachable where protected.

The duiker is predominantly a browser, often feeding on agricultural crops. This habit leads to it being persecuted outside conservation areas, though it is resilient to hunting.

PHOTO BY ROB DRUMMOND

COMMON (GREY) DUIKER
Sylvicapra grimmia

One of the most common small antelopes, the common duiker is usually solitary, but is sometimes seen in pairs. It is greyish light brown in colour, with a white belly and a dark brown stripe down its face. Only males have horns, which are straight and pointed, and rarely grow longer than 15cm. The common duiker is capable of going without water for long periods, but it will drink whenever water is available.

Size: Shoulder height 50cm; weight 10kg to 20kg; females slightly larger than males; horns up to 18cm long. **Distribution**: Found throughout the country in all habitats with cover, but especially in savanna and woodland with thick scrub. **Status**: Common; active day and night, but more nocturnal where disturbance is common.

The waterbuck always stays near water and is a good swimmer, readily entering water to escape predators.

PHOTO BY MITCH REARDON

WATERBUCK
Kobus ellipsiprymnus

The solid waterbuck has a shaggy, brown coat, and white rump, face and throat markings; only males have horns. Females have overlapping ranges, coming and going to form loose associations of normally no more than a dozen. Young, nonterritorial males behave similarly. Mature males hold territories, onto which females wander (nonterritorial males are also often allowed access). These essentially independent movements sometimes produce herds of 50 to 70. The waterbuck's oily hair has a strong, musky odour (especially that of mature males), potent enough for humans to smell.

Size: Shoulder height 130cm; weight 200kg to 300kg (males), 150kg to 200kg (females); horns to 100cm. **Distribution**: Widespread on grasslands near water. Two subspecies: defassa waterbuck in the east with all white rump; common waterbuck in the west with white bull's-eye ring around rump. **Status**: Common and easily seen.

COMMON REEDBUCK
Redunca arundinum; Bohor reedbuck R. redunca; mountain reedbuck R. fulvorufula

Reedbucks whistle repeatedly when advertising territories or when alarmed.

PHOTO BY ANDREW VAN SMEERDIJK

Reedbuck species look similar, except for size and always occur near water. The brown common reedbuck is most common in grassy woodland, the yellowish bohor reedbuck is prevalent on floodplains. The greyer mountain reedbuck inhabits grassy hill country. All have white underparts, and males have forward-curving horns. Common reedbucks form pairs, though mates associate only loosely; female mountain reedbucks form small groups that range over the territories of several males. Bohor males have ranges that overlap those of females, who generally remain separate.

Size: Common reedbuck – shoulder height 90cm; weight 70kg; horns to 45cm. Bohor reedbuck about 30% smaller; mountain reedbuck about 30% smaller again. Males 20% larger than females in common and bohor; sexes similar size in mountain. **Distribution**: Bohor found throughout Tanzania, mountain in central-north, common in south. **Status**: Common.

ROAN ANTELOPE
Hippotragus equinus

Roan antelopes prefer sites with tall grasses, shade and water.

PHOTO BY JASON EDWARDS

The roan antelope is one of Africa's rarest and largest antelopes. It is reddish fawn to dark rufous above, with white underparts and a mane of stiff, black-tipped hairs. Its face is patterned black and white, its long, pointed ears tipped with a brown tassel. Both sexes have long backward-curving horns. Herds of less than 20 females and young range over the territories of several adult males; other males form bachelor groups. Female herds up to 50 are regular and larger herds occur during the dry season when resources are more localised.

Size: Shoulder height 140cm; weight 200kg to 300kg; horns to 100cm. Females slightly smaller than males and have shorter horns. **Distribution**: Southwestern Tanzania; best seen in Ruaha National Park. **Status**: Despite a wide distribution, populations are declining and the species is threatened.

SABLE ANTELOPE
Hippotragus niger

Both the roan and the sable are fierce fighters, and are even known to kill attacking lions.

PHOTO BY JASON EDWARDS

Widely considered the most magnificent of Africa's antelopes, the sable antelope is slightly smaller than the roan antelope, but thicker set; and it has the longer horns, often more than 1m. Sables have a white belly and face markings; females are reddish brown, while mature males are a deep, glossy black. It favours habitat slightly more wooded than that of the roan antelope. Social organisation of the two species is also very similar, but sable female-young herds are slightly larger – usually 10 to 30, but up to 70 or so.

Size: Shoulder height 135cm; weight 180kg to 270kg; horns up to 130cm long – the male's are longer and more curved than the female. **Distribution**: Primarily seen in southern Tanzania. **Status**: Common and easily seen.

Adapted to aridity, the oryx can survive without drinking. To conserve water, it lets its body temperature rise to levels that would kill most mammals.

PHOTO BY DENNIS JONES

ORYX
Oryx gazella

The oryx is solid and powerful; both sexes carry long, straight horns. Principally a grazer, it also browses on thorny shrubs. In areas with better resources, populations are sometimes resident and adopt a social system like that of roan antelopes. More usually, nomadic herds number around a dozen, but can reach up to 50 or 60. Herds normally contain males and females, but there are strict dominance hierarchies within the sexes. Herds, especially if small, may also be single sex.

Size: Shoulder height 120cm; weight 170kg to 210kg (males), 120kg to 190kg (females); horns to 110cm. **Distribution**: The subspecies in Tanzania is known as the fringe-eared oryx; it is found in the dry scrublands of the northeast. **Status**: Relatively common and easy to see, but shy.

Hartebeests prefer grassy plains for grazing but are also found in sparsely forested savanna and hills.

PHOTO BY ARIADNE VAN ZANDBERGEN

HARTEBEEST
Alcelaphus buselaphus

Hartebeests are red to tan in colour, and are medium-sized and easily recognised by their long, narrow face and short horns. In both sexes, the distinctively angular and heavily ridged horns form a heart shape, hence their name, which comes from 'heart beast' in Afrikaans. Dominant males defend territories, through which pass herds of females and their young; other males wander in bachelor groups. Herds are typically of up to about a dozen (male herds generally smaller than female herds), but aggregations of hundreds and (in the past) thousands also occur.

Size: Shoulder height 120cm; weight 130kg to 170kg (males), 115kg to 150kg (females); horns to 85cm. **Distribution**: The subspecies in Tanzania is Coke's hartebeest, also known as the kongoni – it occurs throughout the east. Lichtenstein's hartebeest, found in Ruaha National Park and other areas of southern Tanzania, is usually considered a separate species. **Status**: Common.

Topis often stand on high vantage points (commonly termite mounds) as territorial advertisement and to observe their surroundings.

PHOTO BY MATT FLETCHER

TOPI
Damaliscus lunatus

The topi is reddish brown, with glossy violet patches on the legs and face. The horns, carried by both sexes, curve gently up, out and back. The social system is highly variable. In grassy woodlands, males hold territories with harems of up to 10 females. On floodplains with dense populations, nomadic herds of thousands may form, males establishing temporary territories whenever the herd halts. Elsewhere, males gather on breeding season display grounds; females visit these 'leks' to select their mates.

Size: Shoulder height 120cm; weight 110kg to 150kg (male), 75kg to 130kg (female); horns to 45cm. **Distribution**: Grassy plains, with or without other vegetation, in the west of the country. **Status**: Common; abundant in Serengeti National Park.

BLUE WILDEBEEST
Connochaetes taurinus

The wildebeest is a grazer, and moves constantly in search of good pasture and water, preferring to drink daily – this gives rise to the famous mass migration in the Serengeti-Masai Mara ecosystem. Elsewhere, especially where resources are more permanent, groups of up to 30 are more usual, with larger congregations being less frequent and more temporary. In both situations, males are territorial and will attempt to herd groups of females into their own territory.

The blue wildebeest is gregarious, and in some areas forms herds up to tens of thousands strong, often in association with zebras and other herbivores.

PHOTO BY RICHARD I'ANSON

Size: Shoulder height 140cm; weight 140kg to 230kg (females), 200kg to 300kg (males); horns to 85cm; male larger than female. **Distribution**: Open plains with short grass from the southeast to the north **Status**: Very common; 1.5 million occur in the Serengeti-Masai Mara ecosystem.

KLIPSPRINGER
Oreotragus oreotragus

A small, sturdy antelope, the klipspringer is easily recognised by its tip-toe stance – its hooves are adapted for balance and grip on rocky surfaces, enabling it to bound up impossibly rough and steep rock faces. The widely spaced short horns are prominent only on the male. The klipspringer normally inhabits rocky outcrops; it also sometimes ventures into adjacent grasslands, but always retreats to the rocks when alarmed. When disturbed, the pair often gives a duet of trumpet-like alarm calls.

The klipspringer forms long-lasting pair bonds and the pair occupies a territory, nearly always remaining within a couple of metres of each other.

PHOTO BY ARIADNE VAN ZANDBERGEN

Size: Shoulder height 55cm; weight 9kg to 15kg; horns to 15cm; female larger than male.
Distribution: Scattered distribution on rocky outcrops and mountainous areas throughout the country; absent from dense forests. **Status**: Common but wary; often seen standing on high vantage points.

STEENBOK
Raphicerus campestris

The steenbok is a very pretty and slender small antelope; its back and hindquarters range from light reddish-brown to dark brown with pale underparts markings. Its nose bears a black, wedge-shaped stripe useful for identification. Males have small, straight and widely separated horns. Although usually seen alone, it appears likely that steenboks share a small territory with a mate, but only occasionally does the pair come together. The steenbok is active in the morning and afternoon and by night; it may become more nocturnal where frequently disturbed.

If a predator approaches the steenbok lies flat with neck outstretched, zigzagging away only at the last moment.

PHOTO BY ARIADNE VAN ZANDBERGEN

Size: Shoulder height 50cm; weight 10kg to 16kg; horns to 19cm; female slightly larger than male.
Distribution: Widespread, except for the central- and northwest, wherever there is cover; often in habitats regenerating after destruction. **Status**: Relatively common, but easily overlooked; often seen in Serengeti National Park.

Dik-diks are identified by their miniature size, the pointed flexible snout and a tuft of hair on the forehead; only the males have horns.

PHOTO BY ARIADNE VAN ZANDBERGEN

KIRK'S DIK-DIK
Madoqua kirkii

Dik-diks are monogamous and pairs are territorial. If one is seen, its mate is usually nearby, as well as that year's young. Territories are marked by up to a dozen large piles of dung placed around the boundary. Both members of the pair, and their young, use the dung piles, placing their deposits as part of an elaborate ceremony. Dik-diks feed by browsing on foliage and, being well-adapted to their dry environments, don't need to drink water.

Size: Shoulder height 35cm to 45cm; weight 4kg to 7kg; horns to 12cm. **Distribution**: Throughout most of the country, except the west, inhabiting thick bushy cover with open ground underneath, often in dry, stony areas. **Status**: Common, but wary and easy to miss; active day and night.

The impala is known for its speed and ability to leap – it can spring as far as 10m in one bound, or 3m into the air.

PHOTO BY DENNIS JONES

IMPALA
Aepyceros melampus

Often dismissed by tourists because it is so abundant, the impala is a unique antelope with no close relatives. Males have long, lyre-shaped horns averaging 75cm in length. It is a gregarious animal, forming resident herds of up to 100 or so. The male impalas defend the female herds during the oestrus, but outside the breeding season they congregate in bachelor groups. The impala is common prey of lions, leopards, cheetahs, wild dogs and spotted hyenas.

Size: Shoulder height 85cm; weight 40kg to 80kg; horns to 90cm; male about 20% larger than female. **Distribution**: Patchily distributed throughout the country, preferring the edges of grassy woodlands near permanent water. **Status**: Very common and easy to see.

The social structure of gazelles is highly flexible, but herds often consist of females and young, with males defending territories centred on the feeding grounds of females.

PHOTO BY ARIADNE VAN ZANDBERGEN

THOMSON'S GAZELLE
Gazella thomsonii; Grant's gazelle G. granti

Counted among the most common medium-sized antelope in the region, gazelles are often the main prey of predators – consequently, they are particularly fleet of foot and wary of attack. Two species are common in Tanzania. Thomson's gazelle is the smallest and forms large aggregations (often of many thousands) on the open plains of the Serengeti. It often occurs with the impala-sized Grant's gazelle, which lacks the distinctive black side stripe of the 'tommy'.

Size: Thomson's gazelle – shoulder height 65cm; weight 15kg to 30kg; horns to 45cm. Grant's gazelle – shoulder height 85cm, weight 40kg to 80kg; horns to 80cm. Females of both around 20% smaller with greatly reduced horns. **Distribution:** Northern savanna and woodland. **Status:** Very common.

(Continued from page 40)

of toilet paper. In and near the parks, there's little available, except hotel meals and perhaps a few basics, so if you're on a tight budget, stock up on mineral water and supplies in Arusha or the nearest major centre.

TYPES OF SAFARIS

Traditionally, the main and often the only way to visit most of Tanzania's wildlife-viewing parks has been in a vehicle. Fortunately, this is changing, with walking and other activities gradually being introduced – a happy development which can't come too soon.

Vehicle Safaris

Vehicle safaris are by far the most common type of safari in Tanzania, and, in some parks, are still the only option. In the northern parks, these safaris must be done in a 'closed' vehicle, which means a vehicle with closed sides, although there is usually an opening in the roof which allows you to stand up and get a better view and take photographs. In wildlife reserves such as Selous, in some of the southern parks and in Katavi park, safaris in open vehicles are permitted. These are usually high vehicles with two or three seats at staggered levels and a covering over the roof, but open on the sides and back. If you have the choice, open vehicles are better as they are roomier, give you a full viewing range, and minimise barriers. The least-preferable vehicles are minivans, which are sometimes used, especially in the north. They accommodate too many people for a good experience, the rooftop opening is usually only large enough for a few people to use at a time and at least some passengers will get stuck in middle seats with poor views.

Whatever type of vehicle you are in, try to avoid overcrowding. Sitting uncomfortably scrunched together for several hours over bumpy roads puts a definite damper on the safari experience. Most safari quotes are based on groups of three to four passengers, which is about the maximum for comfort in most vehicles. Some companies put five or six passengers in a standard 4WD, but the minimal savings don't compensate for the extra discomfort.

Night drives are currently not permitted in any of Tanzania's parks and reserves except for Lake Manyara, although they're possible in adjacent wildlife areas.

Walking Safaris

Most walking safaris that you'll see advertised are for relatively short walks of two to three hours, usually done in the early morning or late afternoon. At the end of the walk, you'll then return to the main camp or lodge or alternatively to a fly camp, although sometimes it's possible to organise longer walks. Not much distance is covered in comparison to a straight walk for the same time period; the pace is measured and there will be stops en route for observation, or for your guide to pick up an animal's track. Some walking safaris are done within the park and reserve boundaries, while others are in adjacent areas that are part of the park or reserve ecosystem and which have similar habitats and wildlife.

Whatever the length and location, if you have the chance and inclination to do a walking safari, it's highly worthwhile. Although you may not see the numbers of animals that you would in a vehicle (since you won't cover as much ground), you'll experience the bush at a completely different level. There's nothing that quite conveys the vastness of the African plains, or the power and rawness of nature, as having your feet

Jane Goodall's pioneering chimpanzee research at Gombe Stream has grown into a world-wide organisation for promoting environmental conservation. See www .janegoodall.org and www.rootsandshoots.org.

on the ground with nothing between you and the sounds, the breeze, the smells and the grasses. Places where you can walk in 'big game' areas include Selous Game Reserve, Ruaha, Mikumi, Katavi and Arusha National Parks, and in wildlife areas bordering Tarangire National Park. There are also several parks – notably Kilimanjaro and Udzungwa Mountains – that can only be explored on foot. You'll be on foot in Gombe Stream and Mahale Mountains National Parks, and walks are easily arranged on Rubondo Island National Park.

Walks are always accompanied by a guide, who is usually armed, and with whom you will need to walk in close proximity.

Boat & Canoe Safaris

Like walking safaris, boat safaris are an excellent way to experience the East African wilderness, and a welcome break from dusty, bumpy roads. They are also the only way to fully explore riverine environments and they'll give you a new perspective on the terrestrial scene as you approach hippos or crocodiles at close range, float by a sandbank covered with birds, or observe animals on shore from a river vantage point.

The best place for boat safaris is along the Rufiji River in Selous Game Reserve (p298). They're also possible on the Wami River bordering Saadani Game Reserve (p143), although the scenery and wildlife here can't compare with that in the Selous. In Arusha National Park, you can take canoe safaris on the Momela Lakes (p192).

See www.friendsof ruaha.org for more on an organisation that is doing excellent work for the conservation of the magnificent but fragile Ruaha ecosystem.

Balloon Safaris

In a Jules Verne twist on the classic safari theme, it's possible to float over the Serengeti plains in a hot-air balloon at dawn (p202). While everything depends on wind and weather conditions, the captains try to stay between 500m and 1000m above ground, which means that if animals are there, you'll be able to see them.

Trekking

For information on trekking, see p172, p194, p207 and p190. Lonely Planet's *Trekking in East Africa* is well worth buying if you plan to make trekking a focal point of your holiday.

ITINERARIES

For safaris, the general rule is the longer, the better, particularly in large areas such as the Serengeti, Ruaha National Park and Selous Game Reserve. Much of the safari market focusing on the northern circuit has degenerated into quick in-and-out trips which – apart from the deleterious environmental effects – can make the whole experience seem like a bit of a zoo. While it is possible to 'see' plenty of wildlife on a day trip or an overnight excursion, you'll need time to experience the more subtle attractions of Tanzania's magnificent wilderness areas.

If you're serious about a safari, allow a minimum of five days from Arusha to get off the main roads and explore a bit. In the south, or anywhere if you fly in and out, three to four days, focused on one park or reserve, can work out quite well. Several itineraries are outlined following. For general itineraries combining the parks with other parts of the country, see p12.

Northern Circuit

Arusha National Park (p191) is the best bet for a day trip, while Tarangire (p199) and Lake Manyara (p196) parks are each easily accessed as overnight trips from Arusha, although all these parks deserve more time to do them justice. For a half-week itinerary, try any of the northern parks alone (although for the Serengeti, p200, it's worth flying at least one way, since it's a full day's drive from Arusha), or Ngorongoro Crater (p205) together with either Lake Manyara or Tarangire. With a week, you will have just enough time for the classic combination of Lake Manyara, Tarangire, Ngorongoro and the Serengeti, but it's better to focus on just two or three of these. Many operators offer a standard three-day tour of Lake Manyara, Tarangire and Ngorongoro (or a four- to five-day version including the Serengeti). However, distances to Ngorongoro and the Serengeti are long, and the trip is likely to leave you feeling that you've spent too much time rushing from park to park and not enough time settling in and experiencing the actual environments.

In addition to these more conventional itineraries, there are countless other possibilities combining wildlife viewing with visits to other areas. For example, you might begin with a vehicle safari in the Ngorongoro Crater followed by a climb of Oldoinyo Lengai (p205), trekking elsewhere in Ngorongoro Conservation Area (p205), or visiting Lake Eyasi (p211).

Southern Circuit

Mikumi National Park (p255) and Saadani Game Reserve (p143) are both good destinations if you only have one or (better) two nights. Three to four days would be ideal for Selous Game Reserve (p298) or Ruaha National Park (p262) if you fly. With a bit longer, you could combine the Selous and Ruaha, Ruaha and Katavi, in the west, or – for safari and hiking – Mikumi and Udzungwa Mountains (p257) parks.

Western Parks

Trips to Katavi (p243), Mahale Mountains (p237) or Gombe Stream (p236) parks will require a bit more planning and, unless you have lots of time, will involve some flights. For Katavi, a minimum of three days is ideal, given the effort it takes to reach the park. For Gombe Stream, budget at least two days and, for Mahale, a bit longer to revel in the remoteness.

OPERATORS

A good tour operator is the single most important variable for your safari or trek, and it's worth spending time thoroughly researching those you're considering. Following are lists of recommended companies, although the lists are by no means exclusive.

Arusha

If you organise a Kilimanjaro trek in Arusha, look for companies that have their own mountain-climbing licence (as opposed to the tour-operator licence required for safaris) and those that organise the treks themselves, rather than subcontracting to a Moshi- or Marangu-based operator. Recommended operators based in Arusha include the following:

Africa Travel Resource (ATR; ☎ UK 01306-880770; www.intotanzania.com; all budgets) A well-established web-based safari broker that matches your safari ideas with an operator, and helps you plan and book customised itineraries. The focus is on getting away from the crowds, and the website contains heaps of excellent background information on Tanzania, and the safari circuits and lodges.

East African Safari & Touring Company (Map pp180-1; ☎ 0744-741354; www.eastafrican safari.info; Goliondoi Rd; mid-range–top end) A specialist outfit focusing on customised itineraries for individuals and small groups. It has particular expertise in the ecosystems around Tarangire National Park, where it operates several luxury camps. Throughout, the emphasis is on personal attention.

DID YOU KNOW?

Lake Manyara has been declared a Unesco biosphere reserve in recognition of its impressive habitat and species diversity, including almost 400 types of birds.

Iain and Oria Douglas-Hamilton put Lake Manyara on the map with *Life Among the Elephants*. In *Battle for the Elephants*, the same authors describe the ongoing political battles over the ivory trade in Africa.

CHOOSING AN OPERATOR

Keep the following things in mind when choosing a safari or trekking operator, particularly if you're planning to book a budget safari on arrival in Tanzania.

- Get personal recommendations, and talk with as many people as you can who have recently returned from a safari or trek and who have used the company you're considering.

- Be sceptical of quotes that sound too good to be true, and don't rush into any deals, no matter how good they sound.

- Don't fall for it if a tout tries to convince you that a safari or trek is leaving 'tomorrow' and that you can be the final person in the group. Take the time to shop around at reliable outfits to get a feel for what's on offer and, if others have supposedly registered, ask to speak with them.

- Check the blacklist of the **Tanzania Tourist Board's Tourist Information Centre** (TTB; ☎ 027-250 3843; www.tanzania-web.com) in Arusha. Both TTB and the **Tanzanian Association of Tour Operators** (TATO; ☎ 027-250 4188; www.tatotz.org) maintain lists of licensed operators. While TATO isn't the most powerful of entities, going on safari with one of their members will at least give you some recourse to appeal in case of problems.

- Don't give money to anyone who doesn't work out of an office, and don't arrange any safari deals at the bus stand or with touts who follow you to your hotel room.

- Go with a company that has its own vehicles and equipment. If you have any doubts, don't pay a deposit until you've seen the vehicle that you'll be using, and be aware that it's not unknown for an operator to show you one vehicle, but then on the actual safari day, arrive in a far inferior one.

- Unless you speak Swahili, be sure your driver can speak English.

- Go through the itinerary in detail and confirm what is expected and planned for each stage of the trip. Check that the number of wildlife drives per day and all other specifics appear in the contract, as well as the starting and ending dates, and approximate times, and keep in mind that while two competing safari company itineraries may look the same, service can be very different. Normally, major problems such as vehicle breakdown are compensated for by adding additional time to your safari. If this isn't possible (eg, if you have an onward flight), reliable operators may compensate you for a portion of the time lost. However, don't expect a refund for 'minor' problems such as punctured tyres and so on. Also note that park fees are non-refundable.

- If you have any doubts about an operator, only organise local bookings with them. For example, don't book a Kilimanjaro trek from Dar es Salaam; if something goes wrong you'll be far away and without recourse.

George Mavroudis Safaris (☎ 027-254 8840; gmsafaris@gmsafaris.com; top end) An excellent operator, highly respected in industry circles, and headed by one of East Africa's best private safari guides. Its speciality is exclusive, customised mobile safaris in the northern circuit done in vintage style — the ultimate choice for well-heeled safari connoisseurs.

Green Footprint Adventures (☎ 027-250 2664; www.greenfootprint.co.tz; upper mid-range–top end) An experienced and enthusiastic operator, and *the* one to contact if you're interested in anything action-oriented in the northern circuit. Among its activities (most of which range from a few hours to a full day, rather than multiday) are canoe safaris in Arusha National Park, mountain biking and walking around Lake Manyara, and short hikes in the Crater Highlands. It also offers excellent bush guide courses for anyone who wants to learn more about wildlife and how to spot it.

Hoopoe Safaris (Map pp180-1; ☎ 027-250 7011; www.hoopoe.com; India St; upper mid-range–top end) A highly regarded company and one of the best in the industry, offering luxury camping and lodge safaris with an emphasis on individualised itineraries and service. Hoopoe has its own tented camps in the border areas of Tarangire, Lake Manyara and Serengeti National Parks and in other parts of the northern circuit, where they have formed partnerships with and made investments in the surrounding communities. Staff and guides are highly professional and prices, while not inexpensive, are good value.

IntoAfrica (☎ UK 44-114-255 5610; www.intoafrica.co.uk; mid-range) A small operator specialising in fair-traded cultural safaris and treks in northern Tanzania. It directly supports local communities in the areas where it works, and is the perfect choice if your interest is more in gaining insight into local life and culture, than in experiencing the luxury lodge atmosphere. Prices are reasonable and good value. Popular itineraries include treks on Mt Kilimanjaro (Machame route) and Mt Meru, plus a seven-day wildlife-cultural safari in Maasai and Chagga areas.

Kahembe's Trekking & Cultural Safaris (☎ 027-253 1088, 027-253 1377; www.authentic culture.org; budget) A small, solid and friendly operator offering good Mt Hanang treks and a range of no-frills cultural safaris around Babati. The tours are off the beaten track, prices are very reasonable, and the company is a fine choice if you want to experience Tanzania from a local perspective.

Nature Beauties (Map pp180-1; ☎ 027-254 8224; nature.beauties@habari.co.tz; Old Moshi Rd; budget) A low-key outfit offering Kilimanjaro treks and northern circuit safaris.

Nature Discovery (☎ 027-254 4063; info@naturediscovery.com; mid-range) Individualised, environmentally responsible northern-circuit safaris, and treks on Kilimanjaro, Meru and in the Crater Highlands.

Roy Safaris (Map pp180-1; ☎ 027-250 2115, 027-250 8010; www.roysafaris.com; Serengeti Rd; all budgets) A highly regarded, family-run company offering quality budget and semiluxury camping safaris in the northern circuit, as well as luxury lodge safaris at very competitive prices. It also organises treks on Mt Kilimanjaro, Mt Meru, and in the Crater Highlands. Its vehicle fleet is the cream of the crop, staff are knowledgeable and enthusiastic, and safaris and treks are consistently excellent value for money. Roy's has some good deals with the lodges, and can often arrange lodge-based safaris for close to the same price as camping safaris, as well as more upmarket offerings. It can also assist with Zanzibar hotel bookings and domestic flight reservations if you want to combine your safari or trek with other travels.

Safari Makers (Map pp180-1; ☎ 254 4446; www.safarimakers.com; India St; budget) A reliable outfit that runs no-frills northern circuit camping and lodge safaris and treks at surprisingly reasonable prices; some safaris and treks also incorporate Cultural Tourism Program tours.

Sunny Safaris (Map pp180-1; ☎ 027-250 8184, 027-250 7145; www.sunnysafaris.com; Colonel Middleton Rd; budget) A reliable and well-regarded budget operator with a wide selection of no-frills camping and lodge safaris at very reasonable prices, as well as Kilimanjaro and Meru treks and day walks in the area around Arusha.

Swala Safaris (☎ 027-250 8424; www.swalasafaris.com; budget–mid-range) A low-key, reasonably priced company that runs camps near the Serengeti, Lake Natron, Lake Manyara and Mkomazi Game Reserve, and can organise intriguing off-beat combination itineraries, usually involving hiking or walking. It's also one of the best contacts for anything involving Lake Natron.

Tropical Trails (☎ 027-250 0358, 027-254 8299; www.tropicaltrails.com; Masai Camp, Old Moshi Rd; upper mid-range) A long-standing and recommended company offering high-quality treks and walking safaris on Kilimanjaro, Meru, in the Crater Highlands and in the Monduli Mountains. Equipment is top notch, and staff have long experience on Kilimanjaro. Kosher treks, photographic camping safaris and other special interest tours can be arranged, and a portion of the company's profits goes towards supporting education projects in Maasai schools.

Tropical Trekking (Map pp180-1; ☎ 027-250 2417; www.tropicaltrekking.com; Joel Maeda St; mid-range–top end) A specialist operator affiliated with Hoopoe Safaris. In addition to Kilimanjaro and Meru treks, it is one of the best contacts for routes in the Crater Highlands, the Monduli Mountains and other speciality areas. An ideal choice if you want to combine trekking with your safari.

Moshi

Recommended Moshi-based companies focusing on Kilimanjaro treks include the following:

Akaro Tours Tanzania (Map p166; ☎ 027-275 2986; www.akarotours.com; Ground fl, NSFF House, Old Moshi Rd; budget) A small outfit offering good, no-frills Kilimanjaro treks, day hikes on Kilimanjaro's lower slopes and a range of very enjoyable cultural tours.

Hatari! (1962, John Wayne/Hardy Kruger) was filmed in Arusha National Park and Ngorongoro Crater. While it has little to do with safaris (the stars are capturing animals for zoos), it has great footage of local wildlife and scenery.

Key's Hotel (☎ 027-275 2250; www.keys-hotels.com; Uru Rd; mid-range) A long-established place offering reliable Kilimanjaro packages.

Moshi Expeditions & Mountaineering (Map p166; ☎ 027-275 4234; www.memtours.com; Kaunda St; budget–mid-range) An efficiently run place offering Kilimanjaro treks and northern circuit safaris at competitive prices.

Shah Tours (Map p166; ☎ 027-275 2370, 027-275 2998; www.kilimanjaro-shah.com; Mawenzi Rd; mid-range) A reliable and well-established operator offering quality Kilimanjaro and Meru treks at reasonable prices.

Zara Tanzania Adventures (Map p166; ☎ 027-275 0011; www.zaratravel.com; Rindi Lane; budget–mid-range) A professional and efficient outfit that does a brisk business with Kilimanjaro treks (its speciality) and northern circuit safaris.

DID YOU KNOW?

Tsetse flies can be unwelcome safari companions. To minimise the nuisance, wear thick, long-sleeved shirts and trousers in khaki or other drab shades, and avoid bright, contrasting and very dark clothing.

Marangu

Most hotels in Marangu organise Kilimanjaro treks. For listings, see p171. One to check out is the long-established **Marangu Hotel** (☎ 275 6591/4; www.maranguhotel.com), an upper mid-range operator with good Kilimanjaro treks. It also has a no-frills 'hard way' option that's one of the cheapest deals available for a reliable trek. For US$170 plus park fees for a five-day Marangu climb, the hotel will take care of hut reservations and provide a guide with porter; you must provide all food and equipment.

Dar es Salaam

The following agencies can help you book southern-circuit safaris, or combination itineraries involving Mikumi and Ruaha National Parks, Selous Game Reserve, and Zanzibar and Mafia islands.

Coastal Travels (Map p74; ☎ 022-211 7959, 022-211 7960; safari@coastal.cc; Upanga Rd; mid-range) A long-established and recommended outfit that has its own fleet of planes and runs

---

SAFARI SCAMS & SCHEMES

When it comes to booking safaris and treks, especially at the budget level, the need for caution can't be overemphasised. If you stick with reliable safari or trekking operators, including the ones recommended in this chapter, you shouldn't have major problems. Most difficulties arise when trying to book budget safaris on arrival. Remember that once your money is paid, it's as good as gone, and watch out for the following:

■ Touts who promise you a bargain safari or trek deal, but in order to seal it, payment must be made on the spot – of course with a receipt. The next day, the promised transport doesn't show up, the receipt turns out to be for a bogus company, and the tout is never seen again.

■ Sham operators trading under the same names as companies listed in this or other guidebooks. Don't let business cards fool you; they're easy to print up, and are no proof of legitimacy.

■ Questionable ethics on the part of disreputable operators, especially on Kilimanjaro treks. One of the most common problems is overloading porters. (The competition to be a porter on Kilimanjaro is so fierce that some porters may agree to heavy loads just to get employment.) Just as bad are companies that don't ensure that their porters and guides have suitable gear for cold-weather treks, or ones that underpay. A more innocuous example is smudging park fees (though it's not so innocuous if, for example, you planned on an extra day acclimatisation time on Kilimanjaro, but are forced up early because your operator played games with the park fees). For more on problems of porter overloading, etc, see p177.

If you do get taken for a ride, the main thing to do is to file a complaint with both the TTB and TATO (see p60). The police will be of little help, and it's unlikely that you will see your money again.

WILDLIFE WATCHING ON THE CHEAP

If your budget is tight, here are some ways to get at least fleeting glimpses of the wildlife:

- Take the train (either Tazara, or the private luxury train of Foxes African Safaris) from Dar es Salaam towards Kidatu, crossing the northern border of Selous Game Reserve.
- Take a bus along the Tanzam highway through the centre of Mikumi National Park.
- Take a bus through the Serengeti corridor, en route from Mwanza to Arusha, or camp near the start of the Serengeti's western corridor.

---

safari camps and lodges in Ruaha park, the Selous and on Mafia island. It has excellent-value 'last-minute' flight-and-accommodation deals, and is a good contact for putting together itineraries taking in different parts of the country, or combining safaris with non-safari touring. Offerings include competitively priced Ruaha packages, day trips to Zanzibar and Selous–Mafia combinations.

Foxes African Safaris (☎ UK 01452-862288, Tanzania 0744-237422; www.tanzaniasafaris.info; mid-range–top end) A highly regarded family-run company that owns lodges and camps in Mikumi, Ruaha and Katavi National Parks, on the coast near Bagamoyo and in the Southern Highlands. It is an excellent choice for personalised combination itineraries to these destinations using plane, road and its own private luxury train.

Hippotours & Safaris (Map p74; ☎ 022-212 8662/3; www.hippotours.com; Nyumba ya Sanaa, Ohio St; mid-range–top end) A well-respected specialist agency focusing on southern-circuit itineraries, especially in Selous Game Reserve and on Mafia island.

Tent with a View (☎ 022-211 0507, 0741-323318; www.saadani.com; upper mid-range) This helpful group runs lodges in Selous and Saadani Game Reserves and organises upmarket combination itineraries involving these and other areas.

DO-IT-YOURSELF SAFARIS

It is quite possible to visit the parks with your own vehicle, though less commonly done than in southern African safari destinations. Parks well-suited to exploring on your own include Mikumi (p255), with easy access from Dar es Salaam, and a reasonably good network of primary roads; Arusha (p191), with easy access from Arusha town, reasonable roads and a good variety of accommodation; and Ruaha (p262), which is straightforward to reach once you're in Iringa, and has the chance for walking safaris. Visits to Gombe Stream park (p236) are easy to sort out on your own, once you've managed to get to western Tanzania. The Selous (p298) is also well worth considering (especially since camping locations aren't as restricted as in most parks), but you'll need to be experienced at driving and surviving in the bush, and be completely self-sufficient.

For almost all parks and reserves, you'll need 4WD. In addition to park admission fees, there's a US$30 per day vehicle fee for foreign-registered vehicles (or Tsh5000 for locally registered vehicles). Guides are not required for most of the main parks, except as noted in the individual park entries. However, it's highly recommended to take one along to help you find your way through the bush, as well as for showing you the best areas to spot those elusive lions, or whatever else you may be looking for. Fees are given on p35.

You'll also need to carry extra petrol, as it's not available in any of the parks, except at Seronera in the Serengeti and at Ngorongoro Crater, where it's expensive; the lodges and hotels will not be able to provide you with petrol. It's also worth setting off well-prepared with spares and some mechanical knowledge.

You can rent safari vehicles in Dar es Salaam, Arusha and Mwanza, as well as at the Ngorongoro Crater (where you can hire a park vehicle

Serengeti: Natural Order on the African Plain by Mitsuaki Iwago is a superb photographic documentary of the majestic rhythms of nature on the East African plains.

with driver; advance notice required); Karatu (p209) and Mto wa Mbu (p198); and Katavi National Park (where you can arrange vehicle hire at park headquarters). Otherwise, there's no vehicle rental at any of the parks or reserves. Unless you are in a group, renting a car specifically for safari is usually at least as expensive as going through a tour operator, especially for the northern parks.

Camping will give you the most flexibility, as you can always find a spot. If you plan on staying in lodges, book well in advance, especially during the high season.

Food & Drink

Imagine dining under the stars, with your feet in the sand, and the scents and tastes of coriander and coconut transporting you to the days when the East African coast was a major port of call on the spice route from the Orient. Or sitting down in the shade of a palm tree to a plate of freshly grilled fish. Or relishing five-star cuisine at one of Tanzania's luxurious safari camps, with the sounds of the bush filling the night air around you. Of course, it's not all like this: it would be easy to come away from a Tanzania visit thinking that the entire country subsists on *ugali* – the main staple – and sauce, and that salads haven't yet been discovered. But, if you're happy to hunt around a bit, there are some surprising treats to be found. The Zanzibar Archipelago in particular is one of East Africa's culinary highlights and an essential stop for the gastronomically inclined. Elsewhere in the country, lively local atmosphere and unsurpassed Tanzanian hospitality more than compensate for what can otherwise be a rather bland diet.

STAPLES & SPECIALITIES

If there were a competition for the Tanzanian national dish, *ugali* – a staple made from maize or cassava flour, or both – would win hands down. This thick, filling, dough-like mass – beloved by most Tanzanians, and somewhat of an acquired taste for many foreigners – is found throughout the country. It varies slightly in flavour and consistency depending on the flours used and the cooking, and everyone has their favourite versions. In general, though, good *ugali* should be neither too dry nor too sticky. It's almost always served with a sauce containing meat, fish, beans or greens. Rice – best on the coast, where it is frequently flavoured with coconut milk – and *matoke* (cooked plantains) are other common staples, and chips are ubiquitous in larger towns.

Most visitors have more of an affinity for *mishikaki* (marinated meat kebabs), which are found almost everywhere – grilled over the coals at street stalls – or their upmarket cousin, *nyama choma* (seasoned roasted meat). Along the coast, this is complemented by an abundance of delectable seafood dishes, often grilled or cooked in coconut milk or curry-style. Excellent grilled fish is also a treat if you're travelling near any of Tanzania's lakes.

BEST BUDGET BITES

- **Forodhani Gardens** (p109) Street food at its best.
- **Salzburger Café** (p168) Great ambience.
- **Patwas Restaurant** (p150) Simple and homy.
- **Princess Lodge** (p254) More of the same.
- **Kuleana Pizzeria** (p218) Egalitarian and no-frills, and street children benefit.
- **Hasty Tasty Too** (p261) A great little place off the Dar-Mbeya highway.
- **Boma Guest House** (p184) Not quite budget, but authentic and delicious Tanzanian dining.
- **Sombrero Restaurant** (p267) Straightforward and unpretentious.
- **Radha Food House** (p109) Vegetarian heaven.

Many Tanzanians start their day with *uji*, a thin, sweet porridge made from bean, millet or other flour. Watch for ladies stirring bubbling pots of it on the street corners if you are out in the early morning. *Vitambua* – small rice cakes vaguely resembling tiny, thick pancakes – are another morning treat, especially in the southeast. On Zanzibar, look for *mkate wa kumimina*, a bread made from a batter similar to that used for making *vitambua*.

In the northeast around Tanga, and in the northwest near Lake Victoria you can find highly refreshing *mtindi* and *mgando*, cultured milk products similar to yogurt, and usually drunk with a straw out of plastic bags.

Three meals a day is the norm, although breakfast is frequently nothing more than *kahawa* (coffee) or *chai* (tea) and *mkate* (bread). The main meal – often *ugali* or another staple with a meat- or fish-based sauce – is eaten at midday. In out-of-the-way areas, many places are closed in the evening and the main option is street food.

> One of Zanzibar's great early-morning sights is the coffee vendors who carry around a stack of coffee cups and a piping hot kettle on a long handle with coals fastened underneath.

DRINKS

Tap water is best avoided unless your intestines have acclimated to local conditions. Bottled water is widely available, except in remote areas, where you should carry a filter or purification tablets.

Apart from the ubiquitous Fanta and Coca-Cola, the main soft drink is Tangawizi, a local version of ginger ale. Fresh juices, including pineapple, sugar cane and orange, are widely available and a treat, although you should check first to see whether they have been mixed with unsafe water. Western-style supermarkets sell imported fruit juices.

Tanzania's array of beers includes the local Safari and Kilimanjaro labels, plus Castle Lager and various Kenyan and German beers. Finding a beer is usually no problem, but finding a cold one can be a challenge.

Local brews fall under the catch-all term *konyagi*. In the Kilimanjaro area, watch for *mbege* (banana beer). *Gongo* (also called *nipa*) is an illegal distilled cashew drink, but the brewed version, *uraka*, is legal. Local brews made from papaw are also common.

Tanzania has a small wine industry based in Dodoma (p247), although the vintage is unlikely to give French wines much competition.

> **DID YOU KNOW?**
>
> Coconut rice is prepared with the help of a *mbuzi* (goat) – a small, wooden stool with a metal tongue for shredding the coconut.

WHERE TO EAT & DRINK

For dining local style, nothing beats taking a seat in a small *hoteli* – a small, informal restaurant – and watching life pass by. Many *hoteli* will have the day's menu written on a blackboard, and often a TV in the corner broadcasting the latest soccer match. Rivalling *hoteli* for local atmosphere are the bustling night markets that you'll find in many towns, where vendors set up grills along the road side and sell *nyama choma*, grilled *pweza* (octopus) and other street food. In rural areas, *hotelis* and street food are often your only choice.

For something more formal, or for Western-style meals, stick to cities or main towns, where you'll find a reasonable array of restaurants, most moderately priced compared with their European equivalents.

Throughout the country, lunch is served between noon and 2.30pm, and dinner from 7pm to 10pm. The smaller the town, the earlier its dining establishments are likely to close; after about 7pm in rural areas it can be difficult to find anything other than street food.

Self-caterers can stock up in main towns, most of which have at least one supermarket selling various imported products such as canned meat, fish and cheese, crackers and cereals (but not speciality items such as trail food or energy bars). In coastal areas, you can always find a fresh

> Always boil or purify water and be wary of ice and fruit juices diluted with unpurified water. With fruits and vegetables, it's best to follow the adage: 'Cook it, peel it, boil it or forget it'.

KARIBU CHAKULA

It would be hard to travel in Tanzania – a land renowned for its hospitality – without hearing the phrase *karibu chakula* (welcome – join us for some food) at least once. If you do hear it, try to accept, as an invitation to dine with Tanzanians at home is a treat not to be missed. The first step is hand washing. For this, your hostess will bring around a bowl and jug of water; you should hold your hands over the bowl while your hostess pours water over them. Sometimes soap is provided, as is a towel for drying off.

Next comes the meal itself, which will inevitably centre around *ugali*. To enjoy it Tanzanian-style, take some *ugali* with the right hand from the communal pot, roll it into a small ball with the fingers, making an indentation with your thumb, and dip it into whatever sauce is served. Eating with your hand is a bit of an art, but after a few tries it will start to feel natural. Some tips: don't soak the *ugali* too long (to avoid it breaking up in the sauce), and keep your hand lower than your elbow (except when actually putting the food in your mouth) so the sauce doesn't drip down your forearm.

Except for fruit, desserts are rarely served; meals conclude with a second round of hand washing. Saying *chakula kizuri* or *chakula kitamu* are ways to let your host know that the food was appreciated.

---

catch of fish and someone to prepare it for you; the best time to look is the early morning.

Quick Eats

The best fast food is at night markets – with the best in the country at Zanzibar's Forodhani Gardens (p109) – where you can wander around filling up on *mishikaki*, grilled *pweza* and other titbits for less than Tsh1000.

Otherwise, fast food Tanzanian-style is whatever the dish of the day is at the local *hoteli* – rice or *ugali* with chicken, fish or beans. If you go into these places at lunch time, you'll be served a plate of local fare within a few minutes, for about Tsh1000 or less. Outside of regular meal times, ask what is ready, as it can take hours if the cook needs to start from scratch.

VEGETARIANS & VEGANS

While there isn't much in Tanzania that is specifically billed as 'vegetarian', there are many veggie options and you can find *wali* (cooked rice) and *maharagwe* (beans) almost anywhere. The main challenges away from major towns will be keeping some variety and balance in your diet, and getting enough protein, especially if you don't eat eggs or seafood. In larger towns, Indian restaurants are the best places to try for vegetarian meals. Elsewhere, try asking Indian shop owners if they have any suggestions; many will also be able to help you find good yogurt. Peanuts (*karanga*) and cashews (*korosho*) are widely sold on the streets, and fresh fruits and vegetables are abundant. If you eat seafood, you'll have no problems along the coast or near the lakes, and even in inland areas good fish is often available from rivers and streams.

Most tour operators are willing to cater to special dietary requests, such as vegetarian, kosher or halal, as long as they have advance notice. Most food on safaris tends to be halal anyway, as many commercial sellers follow the halal ritual.

In restaurants catering to tourists, tip about 10%, assuming service warrants it. Tipping isn't expected in small, local establishments, though rounding up the bill is always appreciated.

CATERING FOR CHILDREN

Tanzanians are very family-friendly, and dining out with children is no problem. Hotel restaurants in tourist areas usually have high chairs, and

---

DOS & DON'TS

For Tanzanians, a shared meal is an expression of solidarity between hosts and guests, and the various customs, such as eating out of a communal dish, are simply expressions of this. As a result, there are several dos and don'ts to keep in mind:

- If you receive an invitation to eat and aren't hungry, it's OK to explain that you have just eaten, but you should still share a few bites of the meal in recognition of the bond with your hosts.

- Try to leave a small amount on your plate at the end of the meal to show hosts that you have been satisfied.

- For the same reason, don't take the last bit of food from the communal bowl or serving plate – your hosts may end the evening worrying that they haven't provided enough.

- Never handle or eat food with the left hand; in many areas, it's even considered impolite to give a person something with the left hand.

- If everyone else is eating with their hands, try to do the same, even if cutlery is also provided.

- It's usual to wash your hands before and after eating.

- Defer to your host for any customs that you are not sure about.

---

staff do their best to ensure everyone stays happy. While special children's meals aren't common, it's easy enough to find menu items that are suitable for young diners. The main things to avoid are curries and other spicy dishes, uncooked, unpeeled fruits and vegetables, meat from street vendors (as it's sometimes undercooked) and unpurified water. Child-size boxes of fresh juice are available at supermarkets in major towns and make good snacks, as do the many fresh fruits (tangerines, bananas and more) sold throughout most of the country. For more on travelling with children, see p306.

HABITS & CUSTOMS

Meals connected with any sort of social occasion are usually drawn-out affairs for which the women of the household will have spent several days preparing. Typical Tanzanian style is to eat with the (right) hand from communal dishes in the centre of the table. There will always be somewhere to wash your hands – either a basin and jug of water that are passed around, or a sink in the corner of the room. Although food is shared, it's not customary to share drinks. Sodas are the usual meal accompaniment, and there will also usually be a pitcher of water somewhere on the table, though this may be unpurified. Children generally eat separately. If there's a toast, the common salutation is *afya!* – (to your) health!

To get your mouth watering, look for *A Taste of Zanzibar – Chakula Kizuri* by Zarina Jafferji.

Street snacks and meals on the run are common. European-style restaurant dining – while readily available in major cities – is not really a part of local culture. Much more common are large gatherings at home, or perhaps at a rented hall, to celebrate special occasions, with the meal as the focal point.

EAT YOUR WORDS

Want to know *mkate* from *maandazi*? *Ndizi* from *nyama*? Get behind the cuisine scene by getting to know the language. For pronunciation guidelines, see p344.

Useful Phrases

I'm a vegetarian.	*Nakula mboga tu.*
I don't eat meat.	*Mimi sili nyama.*

Is there a restaurant near here?	*Je, kuna hoteli ya chakula hapo jirani?*
Do you serve food here?	*Mnauza chakula hapa?*
I'd like ...	*Ninaomba ...*
Without chilli pepper, please.	*Bila pilipili, tafadhali.*
Please bring me the bill.	*Lete bili tafadhali.*

Menu Decoder

biryani – casserole of spices and rice with meat or seafood
mchuzi – sauce, sometimes with bits of beef and very-well-cooked vegetables
mishikaki – kebab
nyama choma – roasted meat
pilau – spiced rice cooked in broth with seafood or meat and vegetables
supu – soup; usually somewhat greasy, and served with a piece of beef, pork or meat fat in it
ugali – thick, porridge-like maize- or cassava-based staple, available almost everywhere
wali na kuku/samaki/nyama/maharagwe – cooked white rice with chicken/fish/meat/beans

Food Glossary

BASICS

cold	baridi
cup	kikombe
fork	uma
hot	joto
knife	kisu
napkin	kitambaa cha mikono
plate	sahani
spoon	kijiko
sweet	tamu

STAPLES

beans	maharagwe
bread	mkate
chips	chipsi
plantains	ndizi ya kupika or (when cooked and mashed)
	matoke
potatoes	viazi
rice (cooked)	wali

OTHER DISHES & CONDIMENTS

eggs (boiled)	mayai (yaliyochemshwa)
salt	chumvi
sugar	sukari
yogurt	maziwa ganda

MEAT & SEAFOOD

beef	nyama ng'ombe
chicken	kuku
crab	kaa
fish	samaki
goat	nyama mbuzi
pork	nyama nguruwe
octopus	pweza (usually served grilled, at street markets)

FRUITS & VEGETABLES

banana	ndizi
coconut (green)	dafu

coconut (ripe)	nazi
fruit	tunda
mango	embe
onions	kitunguu
orange	chungwa
papaya	papai
pineapple	nanasi
potatoes	viazi
spinach (boiled)	sukuma wiki
tomatoes	nyanya
vegetables	mboga

DRINKS

beer (cold/warm)	bia (baridi/yamoto)
orange juice	maji ya machungwa
soda	soda
water (boiled/drinking/mineral)	maji (ya kuchemsha/ya kunywa/ya madini)

Dar es Salaam

CONTENTS

HIGHLIGHTS

- Shopping for crafts at **Msasani Slipway** or **Mwenge Carvers' Market** (p83)

- Strolling through the **city centre** (p77), getting a feel for the beat on the street

- Luxuriating at the exclusive seaside resorts on **Ras Kutani** (p90)

- Leaving the urban crush behind at one of the laid-back **beach haunts** (p88) north or south of the city

- Communing with nature at **Pugu Hills** (p86)

Beaches
Msasani Slipway
Mwenge Carvers' Market
City Centre
Beaches
Pugu Hills
Ras Kutani

■ TELEPHONE CODE: ☎ 022   ■ POPULATION: 2.5 MILLION

This was my first glimpse of Dar es Salaam...a vast rippling blue-black lagoon and all around the rim of the lagoon there were pale-yellow sandy beaches, almost white, and breakers were running up on to the sand, and coconut palms with their little green leafy hats were growing on the beaches, and there were casuarina trees, immensely tall and breathtakingly beautiful...And then behind the casuarinas was what seemed to me like a jungle, a great tangle of tremendous dark-green trees that were full of shadows and almost certainly teeming...with rhinos and lions and all manner of vicious beasts. Over to one side lay the tiny town of Dar es Salaam, the houses white and yellow and pink, and among the houses I could see a narrow church steeple and a domed mosque and along the waterfront there was a line of acacia trees splashed with scarlet flowers...

From *Going Solo* by Roald Dahl

Dar es Salaam has come a long way since the late 1930s when Roald Dahl first glimpsed it. With a population that is rapidly approaching three million and an area of more than 1350 sq km, it is Tanzania's major city, capital in everything but name, and one of the least likely places in the country for sighting rhinos and lions.

Despite its size, Dar es Salaam is a down-to-earth, manageable place with a picturesque seaport, an intriguing mixture of African, Arabic and Indian influences, and close ties to its Swahili roots. While there's not much to actually do, there are enough historical buildings, shops and good restaurants to keep most visitors busy for at least a few days.

For a break from the bustle, try the easily accessed beaches north and south of town, or head to Zanzibar – just a short ferry ride away. If none of this appeals, it's easy to bypass Dar es Salaam completely. With the increasing number of international flights to/from Kilimanjaro International Airport (between Arusha and Moshi), many travellers avoid the city, especially if they'll be focusing on northern Tanzania.

HISTORY

Until the mid-19th century, what is now Dar es Salaam was just one of many small fishing villages along the East African coast. In the 1860s, Sultan Seyyid Majid of Zanzibar decided to develop the area's inland harbour into a port and trading centre, and named the site Dar es Salaam ('Haven of Peace'). No sooner had development of the harbour begun, however, than the sultan died and the town again sank into anonymity, overshadowed by Bagamoyo, an important dhow port to the north. It wasn't until the 1880s that Dar es Salaam assumed new significance, first as a way-station for Christian missionaries making their way from Zanzibar to the interior, and then as a seat for the German colonial government, which viewed Dar es Salaam's protected harbour as a better alternative for steamships than the dhow port in Bagamoyo. In 1891 the colonial administration was moved from Bagamoyo to Dar es Salaam. Since then, the city has remained Tanzania's undisputed political and economic capital, even though the legislature and official seat of government were transferred to Dodoma in 1973.

ORIENTATION

The bustling, congested city centre runs along Samora Ave from the clock tower to the Askari monument, with banks, foreign-exchange bureaus, vendors and shops. Northwest of Samora Ave, around India and Jamhuri Sts, is the Asian quarter, where you'll find a warren of narrow streets lined with Indian merchants and traders.

GREATER DAR ES SALAAM

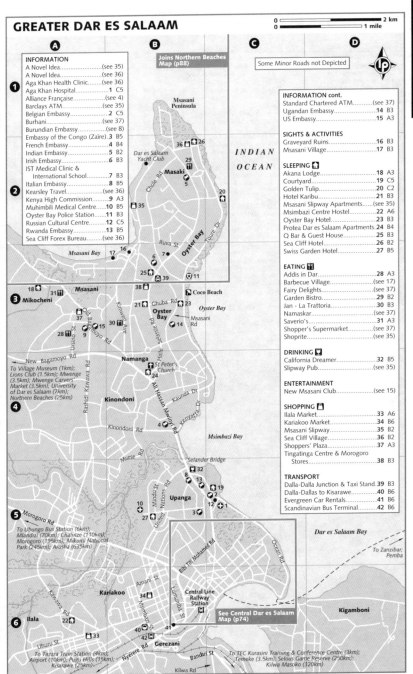

0 — 2 km
0 — 1 mile

Joins Northern Beaches Map (p88)

Some Minor Roads not Depicted

INDIAN OCEAN

INFORMATION
A Novel Idea.........................(see 35)
A Novel Idea.........................(see 36)
Aga Khan Health Clinic.......(see 36)
Aga Khan Hospital........................1 C5
Alliance Française................(see 4)
Barclays ATM........................(see 35)
Belgian Embassy.........................2 C5
Burhani...............................(see 37)
Burundian Embassy..............(see 8)
Embassy of the Congo (Zaïre)..3 B5
French Embassy............................4 B4
Indian Embassy............................5 B2
Irish Embassy..............................6 B3
IST Medical Clinic &
   International School...............7 B3
Italian Embassy...........................8 B5
Kearsley Travel....................(see 36)
Kenya High Commission...........9 A3
Muhimbili Medical Centre......10 B5
Oyster Bay Police Station......11 B3
Russian Cultural Centre...........12 C5
Rwanda Embassy.......................13 B5
Sea Cliff Forex Bureau.........(see 36)

INFORMATION cont.
Standard Chartered ATM..........(see 37)
Ugandan Embassy........................14 B3
US Embassy..................................15 A3

SIGHTS & ACTIVITIES
Graveyard Ruins..........................16 B3
Msasani Village............................17 B3

SLEEPING
Akana Lodge................................18 A3
Courtyard.....................................19 C5
Golden Tulip................................20 C2
Hotel Karibu................................21 B3
Msasani Slipway Apartments..(see 35)
Msimbazi Centre Hostel............22 A6
Oyster Bay Hotel.........................23 B3
Protea Dar es Salaam Apartments.24 B4
Q Bar & Guest House.................25 B3
Sea Cliff Hotel.............................26 B2
Swiss Garden Hotel....................27 B5

EATING
Addis in Dar.................................28 A3
Barbecue Village.........................(see 17)
Fairy Delights...............................(see 37)
Garden Bistro..............................29 B2
Jan - La Trattoria.........................30 B3
Namaskar.....................................(see 37)
Saverio's......................................31 A3
Shopper's Supermarket.............(see 37)
Shoprite.......................................(see 35)

DRINKING
California Dreamer......................32 B5
Slipway Pub.................................(see 35)

ENTERTAINMENT
New Msasani Club......................(see 15)

SHOPPING
Ilala Market.................................33 A6
Kariakoo Market.........................34 B6
Msasani Slipway.........................35 B2
Sea Cliff Village..........................36 B2
Shoppers' Plaza..........................37 A3
Tingatinga Centre & Morogoro
   Stores.....................................38 B3

TRANSPORT
Dalla-Dalla Junction & Taxi Stand..39 B3
Dalla-Dallas to Kisarawe...........40 B6
Evergreen Car Rentals...............41 B6
Scandinavian Bus Terminal.......42 B6

Msasani Peninsula

Dar es Salaam Yacht Club

Masaki

Chole Rd

Msasani Bay

Ruva St

Oyster Bay

Toure Dr

Coco Beach

Chuba Rd

Oyster Bay

Msasani Rd

Mikocheni

Msasani

Old Bagamoyo Rd

Msombo Rd

Ursino Rd

New Bagamoyo Rd

To Village Museum (1km);
Lions Club (1.5km); Mwenge
(3.5km); Mwenge Carvers'
Market (3.5km); University
of Dar es Salaam (7km);
Northern Beaches (25km)

Kimwei Ave

Hafie St

Namanga

St Peter's Church

Kinondoni

Ali Hassan Mwinyi Rd

Kaunda Dr

Kinondoni Rd

Msimbazi Bay

Msese Rd

Selander Bridge

Upanga

Mindu St

United Nations Rd

Morogoro Rd

To Ubungo Bus Station (6km);
Mlandizi (70km); Chalinze (110km);
Morogoro (195km); Mikumi National
Park (245km); Arusha (635km)

Dar es Salaam Bay

To Zanzibar;
Pemba

Bibi Titi Mohamed Rd

Ocean Rd

Central Line
Railway
Station

See Central Dar es Salaam
Map (p74)

Kigamboni

Amani St

Kariakoo

Lumumba St

Msimbazi St

Ilala

Uhuru St

Gerezani

Bandari St

Kilwa Rd

Nyerere Rd

To Tazara Train Station (4km);
Airport (10km); Pugu Hills (15km);
Kisarawe (25km)

To TEC Kurasini Training & Conference Centre (3km);
Temeke (3.5km); Selous Game Reserve (250km);
Kilwa Masoko (320km)

CENTRAL DAR ES SALAAM

INFORMATION
A Novel Idea.............................(see 50)
Alpha Internet Café........................**1** B5
American Express.......................(see 7)
Barclay's Bank & ATM...................**2** B4
British Airways..........................(see 40)
British Council...........................**3** C5
British High Commission................**4** C4
Canadian High Commission............**5** C5
Central Police Station...................**6** B6
Citibank..................................**7** B4
Coastal Travels..........................**8** B4
DSM Printers.............................**9** A5
Dutch Embassy..........................(see 4)
Extelecoms House......................**10** B5
Flying Doctors/AMREF..................**11** B4
German Embassy........................(see 4)
Kearsley Travel..........................(see 34)
Ket-Net Internet Café...................**12** A5
Kodak Express...........................(see 72)
Kool Surfing.............................**13** A5
Linhas Aéreas de Moçambique....(see 73)
Lions of Tanzania Safaris & Tours...(see 7)
Local Currency Outlet...................(see 8)
Main Post Office.........................**14** B5
Malawian High Commission.......(see 25)
Mealz Internet Café.....................**15** C5
Mozambican Embassy...................**16** C4
NBC Bank & ATM........................**17** B5
Regency Medical Centre................**18** A4
Rickshaw Travels.........................(see 7)
Rickshaw Travels Branch..............(see 40)
Royal Palm Forex Bureau...............(see 40)
Second-Hand Bookstalls................**19** B5
Skylink...................................(see 2)
Standard Chartered ATM..............**20** C5
Standard Chartered ATM............(see 73)
Standard Chartered Bank &
    ATM...................................(see 34)

Tanzania Tourist Board Information
    Centre................................**21** B6
Traffic Police Headquarters...........**22** A6
Wan Communications Café............**23** C5
Wizara ya mambo ya ndani...........**24** B4
Zambian High Commission............**25** C5

SIGHTS & ACTIVITIES
Askari Monument........................**26** B5
Botanical Gardens.......................**27** C4
Clock Tower..............................**28** A6
Marine Parks & Reserves Unit........**29** A4
National Museum........................**30** C5
State House..............................**31** D5
Surveys & Mapping Division Map Sales
    Office.................................**32** C5
Wildlife Conservation Society of
    Tanzania..............................**33** B5

SLEEPING
Harbour View Suites...................(see 73)
Holiday Inn..............................**34** C4
Jambo Inn...............................**35** A5
Kibodya Hotel...........................**36** A6
Luther House Centre Hostel...........**37** C5
New Africa Hotel........................**38** B5
Peacock Hotel...........................**39** A5
Royal Palm Hotel........................**40** B4
Safari Inn................................(see 35)
YMCA....................................**41** B4
YWCA...................................**42** B5

EATING
Al-Mahdi Tea Room.....................**43** A5
Alcove...................................**44** B5
Bandari Grill............................(see 38)
Baraza...................................(see 34)
Chef's Pride.............................**45** A5
City Garden..............................**46** B5

Cynics Café & Wine Bar................(see 2)
Dar Shanghai Restaurant..............(see 37)
Épi d'Or..................................**47** B5
Hong Kong Tai Yong Sun..............**48** A5
Kibo Bar.................................(see 40)
Salamander - The Patisserie...........**49** B5
Sawasdee................................(see 38)
Serengeti Restaurant...................(see 40)
Shoprite.................................(see 73)
Steers...................................**50** C5
Street Food..............................**51** B6
Tradewinds.............................(see 40)

DRINKING
Florida Pub.............................**52** B6
Mawazo Art Gallery & Café.......(see 41)

ENTERTAINMENT
Club Bilicanas...........................**53** B5

SHOPPING
Nyumba ya Sanaa.......................**54** B4

TRANSPORT
Air India.................................**55** B4
Air Tanzania............................**56** B5
Avis.....................................(see 2)
Business Rent-A-Car....................**57** B5
Coastal Aviation........................(see 8)
Dalla-Dallas to Temeke.................**58** A6
Dar Express.............................**59** A5
EgyptAir................................**60** B6
Emirates Airlines........................(see 72)
Ethiopian Airlines.......................(see 2)
Ferries to Zanzibar Archipelago......**61** B6
Ferry to Kigamboni & Southern
    Beaches..............................**62** D6
Hertz....................................(see 40)
Kenya Airways..........................(see 63)
KLM.....................................**63** B4
MV Safari Booking Office..............**64** B6
New Posta Transport Stand...........**65** B5
Old Posta Transport Stand............**66** B5
Precision Air............................**67** B5
Royal Coach............................(see 59)
South African Airways..................**68** B4
Stesheni Transport Stand..............**69** A6
Swiss International Airlines.............(see 37)
Tawfiq...................................(see 59)
Taxi Stand..............................**70** B5
Taxi Stand..............................**71** B4
Yemenia Yemen Airways..............(see 2)

OTHER
Haidery Plaza...........................**72** B5
Hippotours & Safaris..................(see 54)
JM Mall..................................**73** B6

On the other side of town, northeast of Askari monument, is a quiet area of tree-lined streets with the National Museum, Botanical Gardens and State House. Proceeding north from here along the coast, you first reach the upper–middle class area of Upanga and then, after crossing Selander Bridge, the fast-developing diplomatic and upmarket residential areas of Oyster Bay and Msasani. The city's only real stretch of sand is at Coco Beach, near Oyster Bay, but much nicer beaches to the north and south are only a short jaunt away (see p88).

Maps

The tourist information centre has free photocopied city maps. The best overview of the city's street layout is Dar es Salaam City Map & Guide (1:20,000; Tsh5000), although it's large and unwieldy to manage while walking around. It's available from the **Surveys & Mapping Division Map Sales Office** (cnr Kivukoni Front & Luthuli St; ⏱ 8am-2pm Mon-Fri), and bookshops.

INFORMATION
Bookshops

International newspapers and magazines are available from the Royal Palm Hotel (p80).

A Novel Idea (☎ 260 1088; www.anovelidea-africa .com) Msasani Slipway (Map p73; Msasani Slipway, Msasani Peninsula); Sea Cliff Village (Map p73; Sea Cliff Village, on Msasani Peninsula, next to Sea Cliff Hotel); Steers (Map opposite; cnr of Ohio St & Samora Ave) Dar es Salaam's best bookshop, with an excellent selection of classics, modern fiction, travel guides, Africa titles, maps and more.

DSM Printers (Map opposite; ☎ 213 1616; Jamhuri St) Swahili dictionaries and study guidebooks.

Second-hand Bookstalls (Map opposite; Sokoine Dr) Between Pamba Rd and Ohio St; a good bet for older books, especially on colonial-era history; bargaining is required.

Cultural Centres

Alliance Française (Map p73; ☎ 213 1406/2; fdar@africaonline.co.tz; Ali Hassan Mwinyi Rd)

British Council (Map opposite; ☎ 211 6574/5/6; info@britishcouncil.or.tz; cnr Ohio St & Samora Ave)

Nyumba ya Sanaa (Mwalimu Julius K Nyerere Cultural Centre; Map opposite; Ohio St)

Russian Cultural Centre (Map p73; ☎ 213 6578; cnr Ufukoni & Ocean Rds)

Emergency

Flying Doctors/Amref (Map opposite; Nairobi emergency ☎ 254-2-501280, 602492; Ali Hassan Mwinyi Rd) For emergency evacuations; see p312 for membership details.

Central police station (Map opposite; ☎ 211 5507; Sokoine Dr) Near the Central Line Railway Station.

Oyster Bay police station (Map p73; ☎ 266 7332; Toure Dr) North of Coco Beach; for Msasani Peninsula.

Traffic police headquarters (Map opposite; ☎ 211 1747; Sokoine Dr) Near the Central Line Railway Station.

Film & Photography

Burhani (Map p73; Shoppers' Plaza, Old Bagamoyo Rd) Film supplies and processing, including slide film.

Kodak Express (Map opposite; Haidery Plaza; cnr Kisutu & India Sts) Film supplies and processing.

Immigration Office

Wizara ya mambo ya ndani (Map opposite; ☎ 211 8640/3; uhamiaji@intafrica.com; cnr Ghana Ave & Ohio St; ⏱ 8am-1pm Mon-Fri for visa applications, until 3pm for visa collection)

Internet Access

Alpha Internet Café (Map opposite; Garden Ave; per hr Tsh500; ⏱ 8.30am-9pm Mon-Sat)

Ket-Net Internet Café (Map opposite; Jamhuri St; per hr Tsh500; ⏱ 8.30am-10.30pm)

Kool Surfing (Map opposite; off Jamhuri St; per hr Tsh500; ⏱ 8am-10pm Mon-Sat, 9am-10pm Sun)

Mealz Internet Café (Map opposite; cnr Pamba Rd & Sokoine Dr; per hr Tsh1000; ⏱ 8am-9pm Mon-Sat, 10am-6pm Sun)

Wan Communications Café (Map opposite; Ohio St; per hr Tsh1000; ⏱ 7am-10pm) Next to Steers.

Medical Services

All these hospitals provide 24-hour emergency service:

Aga Khan Health Clinic (Map p73; ☎ 260 1484, 24-hr line 0748-911111; Sea Cliff Village, Msasani Peninsula; ⏱ 8am-12.30pm & 2-4.30pm Mon-Fri, or by appointment) Western doctors on call.

Aga Khan Hospital (Map p73; ☎ 211 5151; cnr Ocean & Ufukoni Rds)

IST Medical Clinic (Map p73; ☎ 260 1307/8, 24-hr emergency line 0744-783393; daktari@raha.com; ⏱ 8am-6pm Mon-Fri, 9am-noon Sat) Western-run fully equipped clinic on the Masaki campus of the International School of Tanganyika; use Ruvu St entrance.

Muhimbili Medical Centre (Map p73; ☎ 215 1351; United Nations Rd) Tanzania's main teaching hospital, with well-qualified staff, but often lacking medicines and supplies.

Regency Medical Centre (Map opposite; ☎ 215 0500, 215 2966; Allykhan St) In Upanga, off Bibi Titi Mohamed Rd.

Money

Forex bureaus give the fastest service and best rates of exchange; there are many scattered around the centre of town on or near Samora Ave. Outside standard business hours, try some of the forex bureaus among following list:

American Express (Map p74; ☎ 211 0960, 211 4094; amex@intafrica.com; Upanga Rd) At Rickshaw Travels, next to Citibank; no cash advances and no replacement of stolen cheques, but does issue US-dollar travellers cheques up to US$1500 against an Amex card.

Coastal Travels' Local Currency Outlet (Map p74; Upanga Rd; ⏰ 9am-4pm Mon-Fri, 9am-noon Sat) With-draw Tanzanian shillings (or dollars, for an additional 6% commission) using Visa or MasterCard; withdrawal limit US$500 per transaction, amounts higher than this available with advance notice.

Galaxy Forex Bureau (International Arrivals Area, Airport; ⏰ for all flights) Cash and travellers cheques; to the right as you exit customs.

National Bank of Commerce (NBC; Map p74; cnr Azikiwe St & Sokoine Dr) Changes cash and travellers cheques, and has an ATM.

Royal Palm Forex Bureau (Map p74; Ohio St; ⏰ 8am-8pm Mon-Sat, 10am-1pm Sun & public holidays) At the Royal Palm Hotel; cash and travellers cheques.

Forex Bureau (International Arrivals Area, Airport; ⏰ for all flights) Straight ahead as you exit customs; cash and travellers cheques.

Sea Cliff Forex Bureau (Map p73; Sea Cliff Village; ⏰ 11am-9pm daily) Cash only.

ATMS

All ATMs give shillings on a Visa card, to a limit of Tsh400,000 per day at Barclays, Tsh1,000,000 per week at Standard Chartered, and Tsh300,000 per day at NBC. Locations following:

Barclays Opposite the Royal Palm Hotel (Map p74) and at the Msasani Slipway (Map p73).

NBC ATMs at all branches, including at headquarters (Map p74; cnr Azikiwe St & Sokoine Dr) and next to Ubungo Bus Terminal.

Standard Chartered At NIC Life House (Map p74; cnr Ohio St & Sokoine Dr); Shoppers' Plaza (Map p73); JM Mall (Map p74; Samora Ave); and next to Holiday Inn Hotel (Map p74).

Post

Main post office (Map p74; Maktaba St; ⏰ 8am-4.30pm Mon-Fri, 9am-noon Sat)

Telephone

Cardphones are everywhere, including in front of Extelecoms House and the main post office.

Extelecoms House (Bridge St & Samora Ave; ⏰ 7.30am to 6pm Mon-Fri, 9am-3pm Sat) Operator-placed calls from US$2 per minute to USA/Europe/Australia.

Tourist Information

What's Happening in Dar es Salaam (www.whats updar.com) Free monthly with tide tables, airline sched-ules, etc; available from hotels, travel agencies and the tourist information centre.

Dar es Salaam Guide More of the same.

Tanzania Tourist Board Information Centre (Map p74; ☎ 212 0373, 213 1555; www.tanzania-web.com; Samora Ave; ⏰ 8am-4pm Mon-Fri, 8.30am-noon Sat) Just west of Zanaki St, with free tourist maps and brochures and helpful city information.

Travel Agencies

For safari and trek operators, also see p59. For flight and hotel bookings, try the following places:

Coastal Travels (Map p74; ☎ 211 7959, 211 7960; safari@coastal.cc; Upanga Rd) A long-established place with its own airline, and flights around the country; espe-cially recommended for travel to Zanzibar, and to northern and southern safari circuit destinations.

Kearsley Travel (www.kearsleys.com) Holiday Inn (Map p74; Garden Ave); Sea Cliff Village (Map p73; ☎ 260 0538, 260 0467) A branch also in Arusha.

Lions of Tanzania Safaris & Tours (Map p74; ☎ 212 8161; www.lions.co.tz; Upanga Rd) Next to Citibank; does half- or full-day city tours from US$20 per person.

Rickshaw Travels Royal Palm Hotel (Map p74; Ohio St); Upanga Rd (Map p74; ☎ 211 0960, 211 4094; rickcliff@twiga.com) Amex agent.

Skylink (Map p74; ☎ 211 5381; www.skylinktanzania .com; Ohio St) Opposite Royal Palm Hotel.

DANGERS & ANNOYANCES

Dar es Salaam is safer than many other big cities in the region, notably Nairobi, though it has its share of muggings and thefts. During the day, watch out for pick-pocketing, particularly at crowded markets and bus and train stations, and for bag snatching through vehicle windows. Take the usual precautions, try to avoid carrying bags or cameras and, if possible, leave your valuables in a reliable hotel safe. At night take a taxi, rather than taking a *dalla-dalla* (minibus) or walking, and avoid walking alone along the path paralleling Ocean Rd, and on Coco Beach (which is only safe on weekend afternoons, when it's packed with locals).

SIGHTS & ACTIVITIES

Dar es Salaam's craft stands and markets are great for browsing (see p83), and its otherwise modest selection of attractions should be enough to keep you busy until you can escape to the beach or points further afield.

National Museum

The **National Museum** (☎ 212 2030, 211 7508; Shaaban Robert St; adult/child/student US$3/1/2; ⏰ 9.30am-6pm) is home to the famous fossil discoveries of *zinjanthropus* (nutcracker man) from Olduvai Gorge (see p210), plus some scattered but intriguing displays on a variety of other topics, including the Shirazi civilisation of Kilwa, the Zanzibar slave trade, and the German and British colonial periods. It's near the Botanical Gardens, between Samora Ave and Sokoine Dr.

Village Museum

The centrepiece of the open-air **Village Museum** (☎ 270 0437; village@nat.mus.or.tz; cnr New Bagamoyo Rd & Makaburi St; adult/child/student US$3/1/2, camera/video US$3/20; ⏰ 9.30am-6pm) is a collection of authentically constructed dwellings meant to show traditional life in various parts of Tanzania. The best time to come is in the afternoon, when there are often traditional music and dance performances (see p83).

The museum is situated 10km north of the city centre; via public transport take the Mwenge *dalla-dalla* from New Posta transport stand (Tsh150, 30 minutes) and get off at the museum.

Msasani Peninsula

On the western side of the Msasani Peninsula, on the site of one of the oldest Arabic settlements along the Swahili coast, is **Msasani fishing village** (Map p73). Nearby are **ruins** (Map p73) of what is said to be Dar es Salaam's oldest graveyard, dating back to the 17th century.

Bird Walks

Dar es Salaam boasts a surprisingly rich variety of bird life, especially once you get outside the centre. The best introduction is on one of the Wildlife Conservation Society of Tanzania's (see the boxed text, p36) free weekly **bird walks**, lasting around two to three hours, which depart from its office at about 7.30am on Friday.

WALKING TOUR

Central Dar es Salaam may be lacking in 'sights', but it is full of historical buildings, interesting architecture and atmosphere, and well worth exploring on foot. The following walk could easily be done in less than two hours, but set aside half a day to appreciate things en route.

The **Askari monument (1)**, at the intersection of Samora Ave and Azikiwe St, is a good place to begin. This bronze statue is dedicated to Africans killed in WWI. From the monument, head northeast on Samora Ave, crossing Pamba Rd, Ohio and Mirambo Sts. Directly after the next intersection (Shaaban Robert St) and to the left on Samora Ave are Dar es Salaam's languishing **Botanical Gardens** (**2**; admission free). To the south, down Shaaban Robert St, is the **National Museum** (**3**; see left).

THE MANY FACES OF DAR

Dar es Salaam is at its most exotic around Mosque St in the busy central area. Here, narrow, congested streets tumble into each other, Indian merchants rub shoulders with African traders, the sidewalks are lined with colourful *kangas*, and ramshackle colonial-era buildings with their shuttered windows and balconies jostle for space with faceless modern constructions. Stretching west and southwest of the city is a jumble of vibrant, earthy neighbourhoods, including Kariakoo, Temeke and Ilala. In these areas – seldom reached by travellers – sandy streets wind past small square houses with corrugated roofs, and bustling night markets do business to the light of dozens of small kerosene lanterns. For something more placid, head out to Msasani Peninsula, following Ocean Rd and Toure Dr along the coast, past the clipped lawns and stately residences of various foreign dignitaries to the peninsula's tip. Here – especially at Msasani Slipway and the nearby Sea Cliff Village – you can immerse yourself in all things Western. Southeast of town is Kigamboni Ferry, which takes you five minutes across the bay to laid-back villages and a string of relaxing beaches.

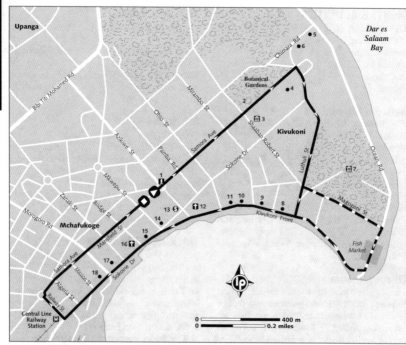

Continue east along Samora Ave past the botanical gardens for another half a block. On the right is **Karimjee Hall** (**4**; closed to the public) where Julius Nyerere was sworn in as president. This was the former house of parliament before the legislature was relocated to Dodoma. Now it's used for parliamentary committee meetings and political functions. Continue east along Samora Ave to Luthuli St. To the northeast is the striking **Ocean Road Hospital** (**5**), which is no longer operational but is nevertheless interesting architecturally with its appealing Moorish influences. It was built in 1897 and combines both Arabic and German influences. The small, white, **domed building** (**6**) just before the hospital is where Robert Koch carried out his pioneering research on malaria and tuberculosis around the turn of the 20th century.

From Ocean Road Hospital you can head south along Luthuli St. To your left, amid large grounds, is the imposing **State House** (**7**; closed to the public), which was originally built by the Germans and then rebuilt after WWI by the British. Just southeast of State House on the seafront is Dar es Sa-

laam's main **fish market** (p84), which makes an agreeable detour.

From the fish market, head west along Kivukoni Front (sometimes also called Azania Front), which meets up again with Luthuli St. Soon you'll see a row of government buildings on your right, including the **Bureau of Statistics** (**8**), the **Ministry of Foreign Affairs** and the **Ministry of Justice** (**9**), all dating from the German era. To your left is the colourful seafront, with an assortment of ageing boats and rows of vendors. Continue past the government buildings to the site of the old **Kilimanjaro Hotel** (**10**; Kivukoni Front), once a Dar es Salaam institution, and now being totally rebuilt. Just after the Kilimanjaro Hotel is the **Hotel Tourism & Training Institute** (**11**; Kivukoni Front), also known as Forodhani's, and currently closed. It enjoyed its heyday during the British era as the Dar es Salaam Club.

The next important building you will reach is the striking **Azania Front Lutheran Church** (**12**; cnr Sokoine Dr & Azikiwe St), with a red-roofed belfry that is one of Dar es Salaam's landmarks. The church was built at the turn of the 20th century by German missionaries and is still used for services. Diagonally opposite the church is the enormous headquarters of the **National Bank of Commerce (13)**. Shortly after passing the bank (and continuing southwest along the waterfront) you will reach first the **Old Post Office (14**; cnr Sokoine Dr & Mkwepu St) and then the **White Fathers' Mission House (15**; Sokoine Dr; closed to the public), which is one of the oldest buildings in the city. One block beyond this is the spired **St Joseph's Cathedral (16**; cnr Sokoine Dr & Bridge St), another famous landmark. The cathedral was built at the same time as the Lutheran church, also by German missionaries, and still contains many original German inscriptions and some artwork, including the carved relief above the main altar. From St Joseph's, if you still have energy left, continue a few blocks further west to the old German **boma (17**; Sokoine Dr, east of Morogoro Rd), which now houses various offices. In the next block is **City Hall (18**; Sokoine Dr, west of Morogoro Rd) dating from 1903, followed by the **Central Line Railway Station** (cnr Sokoine Dr & Railway St). To finish the walk, head one block north to Samora Ave, which you can then follow east, past rows of shops and foreign exchange bureaus back to the Askari monument.

For an mini overview of Tanzanian history, watch the street names as you walk. Luthuli St, for example, is named after Albert Luthuli, the former South African ANC (African National Congress) president. Shaaban Robert St honours one of Tanzania's most famous writers, while Sokoine Dr is named after Edward Moringe Sokoine, who served as prime minister and was considered to be Julius Nyerere's most likely successor until he was killed in a car crash in 1984.

DAR ES SALAAM FOR CHILDREN

With young ones in tow, good diversions include the beaches north of the city – especially their **water parks** (p89); the supervised **play area** at Sea Cliff Village, next to Sea Cliff Hotel (p81), where you can leave your child with a nanny while you go shopping; and **Msasani Slipway** (p83), with ice-cream cones, movies and a playground.

SLEEPING

If you're relying on public transport, it's cheaper and more convenient to stay in the city centre, which is also where most budget lodging is. If you don't mind paying for taxis, or travelling the distance from the airport (about 20km), the hotels on Msasani Peninsula are a break from the urban crush. To avoid the city entirely, head for the beaches north or south of Dar es Salaam (p88 and p89).

The closest places for camping are at Pugu Hills (p86), and at the beaches north and south of town.

All top-end hotels accept credit cards.

City Centre
BUDGET

Most budget lodging is clustered around the busy Kisutu area, or the equally busy area around the main post office.

YWCA (Map p74; ☎ 212 2439; Maktaba St; d Tsh12,000, s/d without bathroom Tsh7000/10,000) Just up from the post office, and a good budget deal. Rooms are clean, with net, fan and sink, and the convenient central location makes up for the street noise. Rooms around the inner courtyard are quieter. Men and women are accepted, and food is available.

YMCA (Map p74; ☎ 213 5457; Upanga Rd; s/d without bathroom US$10/13) Around the corner from the YWCA, and marginally quieter (though the step up in price from the YWCA isn't justified). Rooms have mosquito nets, and there's a canteen. Men and women are accepted.

Safari Inn (Map p74; ☎ 211 9104; safari-inn@lycos .com; off Libya St; s/d Tsh8400/15,000, d with air-con Tsh21,000; 🅿 🖵) A popular travellers haunt in Kisutu, on the western edge of the city centre. Rooms have fans, and are sprayed each evening.

Jambo Inn (Map p74; ☎ 211 4293, 211 0686; Libya St; s/d Tsh10,000/14,000, d with air-con Tsh20,000) Around the corner from Safari Inn, and also popular, with fans, flyscreens in the windows, erratic hot water supplies and a small restaurant with Indian dishes.

Luther House Centre Hostel (Map p74; ☎ 212 6247; luther@simbanet.net; Sokoine Dr; s/tw US$20/25; 🅿) Centrally located, about two blocks southeast of the post office, but not as good value as other places in this category. Rooms have fans and nets, and breakfast is available (at extra charge) at Dar Shanghai restaurant, downstairs.

Kibodya Hotel (Map p74; ☎ 211 7856; intersection of Samora Ave & Lindi St; d without bathroom Tsh8000) Large, clean, no-frills rooms with fans. It's in a busy area at the southwestern end of Samora Ave near the clock tower; there's no food.

Out of the city centre are two places run by the Archdiocese of Dar es Salaam:

TEC Kurasini Training & Conference Centre (☎ 285 1077; tec@cats-net.com; Nelson Mandela Rd; s/d/tr Tsh10,000/16,000/24,000, s in new wing Tsh12,000) Simple, quiet rooms with fans and nets, and a canteen for meals. Taxis from the centre charge Tsh2000.

Msimbazi Centre Hostel (Map p73; ☎ 286 3508, 286 3204; Kawawa Rd; s/d Tsh8500/12,000) Tiny, stuffy singles with fan and net, breezier doubles with two rooms sharing bathroom facilities, and a canteen. It's often noisy, especially on weekends, but otherwise is reasonable value. Take the Buguruni *dalla-dalla* from the Old Posta transport stand (Tsh2000 in a taxi) and ask to be dropped.

MID-RANGE

Harbour View Suites (Map p74; ☎ 212 4040; www .harbourview-suites.com; Samora Ave; s/d from US$85/95, breakfast extra; 🖂 🖵) New and very nice business travellers' studio apartments with views over either the city or the harbour, with broadband connections and a business centre. Rooms are spotless and good value, some have nets, and all have modern furnishings and a kitchenette. Long-term rates are available. Just underneath is JM Mall shopping centre, with an ATM, supermarket and forex bureau.

Peacock Hotel (Map p74; ☎ 211 4126; www.peacock -hotel.co.tz; Bibi Titi Mohamed Rd; s/d/tr US$75/85/110; 🖂 🖵) A busy, central location, rooms with TV, a restaurant and a bar. Caters primarily to a local business clientele.

TOP END

Royal Palm Hotel (Map p74; ☎ 211 2416; www.royal palmdar.com; Ohio St; s/d from US$185/210; 🖂 🖵 🖳) This five-star place is Dar es Salaam's classiest, with plush rooms and top-notch service. In addition to the large pool (Tsh10,000 for nonguests), there are fitness and business centres, several restaurants and a café-patisserie with chocolate éclairs and other delicacies. It's centrally located, in green, attractive grounds near the golf course.

Holiday Inn (Map p74; ☎ 213 7575; www.holiday -inn.com; Garden Ave; s/d US$139/155; 🖂 🖵) This is a pleasant and popular place, with modern

rooms and the standard amenities, including TV, telephone and a business centre that's open until 10pm. It's on a quiet side street near the National Museum and next to Standard Chartered Bank.

New Africa Hotel (Map p74; ☎ 211 7050; www.new africahotel.com; Azikiwe St; s/d US$131/147; 🖂 🖵) New Africa is very nice and worth a look, though the rooms are not quite what you'd expect for the price. There's a small business centre and two restaurants. It's in the busy and central area, close to the Askari monument.

Msasani Peninsula & Upanga
BUDGET

Q Bar & Guest House (Map p73; ☎ 260 2150; qbar@ cats-net.com; cnr Haile Selassie & Msasani Rds; dm US$15, d US$55-80; 🖂) Huge, spotless mid-range rooms, plus a four-bed budget dorm room. Food is served downstairs and there's also a popular bar with live music on Friday evenings.

MID-RANGE

Akana Lodge (Map p73; ☎ 270 0122, 277 5261; www .akanalodge.com; s/d US$50/70; 🖂) A good choice for escaping the hotel scene. Rooms are in a private house, with a few smaller ones next door in an annexe (the ones in the main house are more spacious), and local-style meals can be arranged. It's about 7km north of the city centre: go north on Old Bagamoyo Rd past Shoppers' Plaza. Watch for a tiny bridge, and then a sign on the left for the Tanzania Heart Institute. Turn left at the sign onto a small dirt road and then take the next left. Akana is in the first house to the right and signposted.

Courtyard (Map p73; ☎ 213 0130; info@thecourt yard-dar.com; Ocean Rd; s/d from US$109/129; 🖂 🖵 🖳) This place has comfortable, modern rooms around a small courtyard, with the better (brighter) ones on the upper level. There's a restaurant, business centre and efficient staff. It's 1km south of Selander Bridge. If you don't like air-con, note that the windows don't have flyscreens.

Swiss Garden Hotel (Map p73; ☎ 215 3219; swissgarden@bluewin.ch; Mindu St; s/d from US$50/70; 🖵) A cosy B&B in a quiet, leafy neighbourhood, with small, spotless rooms and helpful hosts. Breakfast is included; other meals can be arranged. It's in Upanga, just off United Nations Rd.

Hotel Karibu (Map p73; ☎ 260 2946; www.hotel karibu.com; Haile Selassie Rd; s/d US$80/90; 🔀 💺) A quirky place in Oyster Bay with reasonable rooms (ask for one that has been refurbished) and a large free-form pool that's usually a hit with children.

Msasani Slipway Apartments (Map p73; ☎ 260 0893; r US$60; apt US$80) Slick, modern apartments in a good location at the Msasani Slipway (look for the multistorey yellow building). All have a hotplate, sink and refrigerator, and some have superb views over the bay. Discounted weekly and monthly rates are available, and it also has day rooms. For meals, you have all the Slipway restaurants at your doorstep.

Protea Dar es Salaam Apartments (Map p73; ☎ 266 6665; proteadar@africaonline.co.tz; cnr Haile Selassie & Ali Hassan Mwinyi Rds; fully-serviced apt from US$120; 🔀 🖥 💺) Modern apartments in a secure compound just north of Selander Bridge. All come with kitchenette, TV and access to the fitness and business centres; both short- and long-term rentals are possible.

TOP END

Sea Cliff Hotel (Map p73; ☎ 260 0380/7; www .hotelseacliff.com; Toure Dr; s/d without/with sea view US$160/180; 🔀 🖥 💺) Sea Cliff has an excellent, breezy setting overlooking the ocean at the northern tip of Msasani Peninsula. On the grounds are a small fitness centre, aromatherapy, a resident masseuse and a good restaurant. Avoid the less appealing, view-less rooms in the annex next door in Sea Cliff Village.

Golden Tulip (Map p73; ☎ 260 0288; www.golden tulip.com; Toure Dr; s/d US$180/200, s/d ste US$275/295; 🔀 🖥 💺) Overlooking the ocean, this place is just south of Sea Cliff Hotel. It has a good pool and a business centre, and caters primarily to conference groups. All rooms have small balconies, and the suites have lovely sea views.

Oyster Bay Hotel (Map p73; ☎ 260 0352/4; obhotel@ acexnet.com; Toure Dr; s/d US$100/120; 🔀 🖥) The location of this place – across the road from the seafront – is pleasant, and the grounds are a little like walking through grandmother's attic, with an eclectic collection of sculptures and artwork. It's often overlooked for the slicker and more modern places in this price range, though some of the rooms are surprisingly OK (take a look at a few, as they vary considerably).

EATING

Dar es Salaam has a good selection of moderately priced restaurants scattered around the city centre, and at Msasani Slipway. Most restaurants in the centre are closed on Sunday.

City Centre
BUDGET

For street food, try the stalls near the corner of Garden Ave and Pamba St, and along Kivukoni Front by the harbour, all of which are busiest around midday, dishing up plates of rice or *ugali* with sauce. For inexpensive Indian food and takeaways, head to the area around Zanaki and Jamhuri Sts. The best place to start here is **Al-Mahdi Tea House** (Map p74; Zanaki St; snacks from Tsh200; 🕑 8am-8pm Mon-Fri, 8am-2pm Sat) a tiny place oozing local flavour.

Nyumba ya Sanaa (Map p74; Ohio St; meals from Tsh2000; 🕑 lunch & dinner) A small, informal eatery in the Nyumba ya Sanaa crafts and cultural centre, serving up plates of chicken and chips, and other local fare.

Épi d'Or (Map p74; ☎ 213 6006; Samora Ave; light meals from Tsh1500; 🕑 7am-7pm Mon-Sat) A cosy French-run bakery-café with a mouthwatering selection of delicious breads, pastries and light lunches, as well as hummus and other Middle Eastern dishes. It's near the corner of Bridge St.

Salamander – the Patisserie (Map p74; cnr Samora Ave & Mkwepu St; light meals from Tsh700; 🕑 7am-5.30pm Mon-Fri, 7am-3pm Sat) Friendly and welcoming, and a good stop for snacks, light meals or breakfast before hopping on the early ferry to Zanzibar (the terminal is just a two-minute walk away). Mac, the owner, is helpful with information on Dar es Salaam.

Chef's Pride (Map p74; Chagga St; meals from Tsh1500; 🕑 lunch & dinner, closed during Ramadan) A longstanding and popular local eatery within easy walking distance of the Kisutu budget hotels. The large menu features standard fare, plus pizzas, Indian and veg dishes, and even some Chinese cuisine.

City Garden (Map p74; cnr Pamba & Garden Sts; meals from Tsh2000; 🕑 lunch & dinner) This place offers a lunch buffet and á la carte, featuring standard favourites such as grilled fish/chicken and rice. The main attraction is the nice, shady outdoor seating area. It's also one of the few places in the centre open on Sunday.

Other recommendations:

Shoprite (Map p74; JM Mall, Samora Ave & Mission St) For self-catering.

Steers (Map p74; cnr Samora Ave & Ohio St; meals from Tsh2000; 🕑 8am-11pm) Burgers and fast food.

MID-RANGE & TOP END

Cynics Café & Wine Bar (Map p74; ☎ 213 8422; cynicscafé@satconet.net; sandwiches & salads Tsh2000-5000; 🕑 10am-6pm Mon-Thu, 10am-9pm Fri) A great little place tucked in next to Barclay's bank, between Ohio St and Upanga Rd, with sandwiches and salads – it also does takeaways – plus good juices and coffees, yogurt and cakes.

Dar Shanghai Restaurant (Map p74; ☎ 213 4397; Luther House Centre Hostel, Sokoine Dr; meals from Tsh3000; 🕑 breakfast, lunch & dinner, closed Sun lunch) The best bet for tasty Chinese food, with a wide menu selection, reasonable prices and friendly staff. It's behind Swiss Airlines in the Luther House Centre Hostel building.

Hong Kong Tai Yong Sun (Map p74; ☎ 213 6622; Bibi Titi Mohamed Rd; meals from Tsh4000; 🕑 lunch & dinner) Delicious but pricey Chinese food.

Kibo Bar (Map p74; ☎ 211 2416; Royal Palm Hotel, Ohio St; 🕑 lunch-11.30pm) Features a great-value lunch special on weekdays for around Tsh4000 to Tsh8000, with design-your-own pasta, sandwich, omelette and salad stations. Portions are large, service is fast and it's usually packed. Next door are **Serengeti Restaurant** (Map p74; ☎ 211 2416; buffet Tsh15,000-20,000; 🕑 breakfast, lunch & dinner), with a full-course buffet and á la carte dining, and the more upmarket **Tradewinds** (Map p74; meals from Tsh20,000; 🕑 from 7pm Mon-Sat), with impeccably prepared seafood and steaks, and an excellent wine selection.

Baraza (Map p74; ☎ 213 7575; Holiday Inn Hotel; meals from Tsh6000; 🕑 breakfast, lunch & dinner) A popular, top-end place with a small luncheon buffet, and good á la carte dining featuring seafood grills and Swahili cuisine.

Alcove (Map p74; ☎ 213 7444; Samora Ave; meals from Tsh4500; 🕑 lunch & dinner, closed lunch Sun) Dark, heavy décor and delicious Indian and Chinese cuisine, including a decent selection of vegetarian dishes.

Bandari Grill (Map p74; ☎ 211 7050; New Africa Hotel, Azikiwe St; buffet Tsh12,000; 🕑 lunch & dinner Mon-Fri) A weekday lunch buffet, complemented by views over Kivukoni Front and the harbour. Upstairs, on the rooftop, is **Sawasdee** (Map p74; meals from Tsh12,000; 🕑 dinner), a Thai restaurant, with buffets on Tuesday and Friday evenings.

Msasani Peninsula
BUDGET

Namaskar (Map p73; 1st fl, Shoppers' Plaza; 🕑 11am-8pm Mon-Sat) Small and informal, with good vegetarian dishes – mostly southern Indian, Mughlal and Punjabi.

Fairy Delights (Map p73; Ground fl, Shoppers' Plaza; meals from Tsh2000; 🕑 breakfast, lunch & dinner) Indian and local meals, including some vegetarian dishes, plus ice cream.

For self-catering:

Shopper's Supermarket (Map p73; Shoppers' Plaza; Old Bagamoyo Rd)

Shoprite (Map p73; Msasani Slipway)

MID-RANGE & TOP END

Addis in Dar (Map p73; ☎ 0741-266299; 35 Ursino St; meals from Tsh4500; 🕑 lunch & dinner Mon-Sat) One of Dar es Salaam's best insider tips if you like Ethiopian food, with *doro wat* and other delicacies, and a good range of vegetarian dishes. It's signposted off Mgombani St.

Jan – La Trattoria (Map p73; ☎ 255 7640, 0742-766922; Kimweri Ave; meals from Tsh4000; 🕑 lunch & dinner) A homy, long-standing place that attracts a loyal group of regulars with its good pizzas and Italian dishes.

Saverio's (Map p73; Old Bagamoyo Rd; meals from Tsh3500; 🕑 lunch & dinner Tue-Sun) Another good bet for pizzas, grills and seafood.

Msasani Slipway (Map p73; Msasani Slipway; 🕑 all day) Everything from burgers to sushi. There's also an ice-cream shop, and a Melela Bustani outlet for bakery and gourmet products.

Sea Cliff Village (Map p73; Toure Dr; 🕑 all day) Another good collection of eateries, including **Turquoise** (☎ 260 0979; meals from Tsh4000; 🕑 lunch & dinner Tue-Sat, lunch Sun) with Turkish cuisine and delectable pastries; and **Manchu Wok** (☎ 260 0963), for Chinese takeaways.

Other recommendations:

Garden Bistro (Map p73; ☎ 260 0800; Haile Selassie Rd) Indian dishes and grills served in nice garden *bandas*.

Barbecue Village (Map p73; ☎ 266 7929; Nkomo St; 🕑 dinner Tue-Sun) In Msasani village, with Indian and Chinese dishes and grills.

DRINKING

Neither the café nor the pub scene have made their way into local Dar es Salaam life, but there are a few good spots to quench your thirst.

Cynics Café & Wine Bar (see opposite) Live music on some Friday evenings.

Mawazo Art Gallery & Café (Map p74; ☎ 0748-782770; mawazogallery@hotmail.com; Upanga Rd; ⊙ 10am-6pm Mon-Fri, 10am-2pm Sat) A small, bright art gallery–café in the YMCA grounds.

Slipway Pub (Map p73; ☎ 260 0893; Msasani Slipway; ⊙ noon-11pm) British pub near the water, with drinks and meals.

Épi d'Or (see p81) Good coffee and juices, and a great place for a midday break.

Kibo Bar (see opposite) Upmarket sports bar at the Royal Palm Hotel.

Garden Bistro (see opposite) The latest 'in' spot for a drink, with live music on weekends.

Q-Bar (see p80) Happy hours (⊙ 5-7pm Mon-Fri) and live music on Fridays.

Coco Beach Packed with locals on weekends, and the best seaside setting for an inexpensive beer; however, it's recommended for the weekends only (see p76).

Florida Pub (Map p74; Mansfield St) An earthy place catering to the downtown office crowd; also has meals.

ENTERTAINMENT

For the latest on what's going on around town, check the listings magazines (p76), the bulletin board at Nyumba ya Sanaa (see p83) and www.naomba.com.

Nightclubs

Dar es Salaam is the music hub of East Africa, though it takes time to discover all it has to offer. Most nightspots only get going after 11pm. Admission averages Tsh3000 to Tsh5000 on weekends.

California Dreamers (Map p73; Ali Hassan Mwinyi Rd) Upmarket Western-style disco.

Club Bilicanas (Map p74; Mkwepu St) More of the same.

Lions Club (Sheikilango Rd) Lots of local flavour, best on Friday and Saturday; in Sinza, just off New Bagamoyo Rd.

New Msasani Club (Map p73; Old Bagamoyo Rd) Near the US embassy, and with a moderately upmarket clientele; Friday, Saturday and Sunday.

Cinemas

Showing occasional free cultural films is the British Council (p75). Movies are also shown at the Msasani Slipway (right) on Friday, Saturday and Sunday evenings.

Traditional Music & Dance

Mwalimu Julius K Nyerere Cultural Centre (Map p74; Nyumba ya Sanaa, Ohio St) The centre has traditional dance performances at 7pm on Fridays, and it's the best place to find out about other traditional dance events around town.

Village Museum (☎ 270 0437; village@natmus.or.tz; cnr New Bagamoyo Rd & Makaburi St) The museum hosts *Ngoma* (drumming) performances for Tsh2500 from 4pm to 6pm on Saturday and Sunday; it also has occasional special programmes highlighting the dances of individual tribes.

SHOPPING

Dar es Salaam is one of the best places in Tanzania for craft shopping.

Handicrafts

Nyumba ya Sanaa (Map p74; Ohio St, next to Royal Palm Hotel; ⊙ daily) This local artists cooperative sells textiles and crafts from various parts of the country; you can also watch some of the artists at work.

Msasani Slipway Weekend Craft Market (Msasani Slipway, Msasani Peninsula; ⊙ Sat & Sun) Prices are slightly higher here than elsewhere in town, but quality is good and the atmosphere calm. Once you've stocked up on crafts, there are lots of other shops for browsing. The market is on the western side of Msasani Peninsula, just off Chole Rd.

Also worth checking is Mawazo Art Gallery & Café (see left), with a small collection of high-quality paintings and woodcarvings.

If you save your craft shopping until the last minute, **Out of Africa** (Dar es Salaam International Airport) and several other shops in the departures lounge at the airport have good selections.

There are curio shops scattered throughout the city centre around Samora Ave near the Askari monument, where you can buy batiks, woodcarvings and other crafts. Most of the top-end hotels have expensive boutiques with high-quality crafts.

Tingatinga Paintings

Tingatinga Centre (Map p73; Morogoro Stores, Haile Selassie Rd, Oyster Bay; ⊙ 8.30am-5pm) This centre is at the spot where Edward Saidi Tingatinga (p29) originally marketed his designs, and is still the best place to buy Tingatinga paintings. You can watch the artists at work and stroll among their wares.

There are also Tingatinga artists at Msasani Slipway's weekend craft market.

DAR'S MARKETS

For a gentle initiation into Dar es Salaam's markets, head to the **fish market** (Ocean Rd), near Kivukoni Front. It's fairly calm as urban markets go, and you can watch fish auctions taking place and browse through stalls selling an assortment of Indian Ocean delicacies. For more excitement, get a reliable taxi driver or Tanzanian friend to take you to **Ilala Market** (Map p73; Uhuru St, near Shaurimoyo Rd), or to the huge, sprawling **Kariakoo Market** (Map p73; Msimbazi & Mkunguni Sts), Tanzania's largest market; don't bring any valuables, and watch out for pickpockets! For Western-style shopping, try **Msasani Slipway** (Map p73) or **Sea Cliff Village** (Map p73), both at the northern end of Msasani Peninsula, and the less glitzy **Shoppers' Plaza** (Map p73; Old Bagamoyo Rd), all with a good assortment of shops.

Woodcarvings

Mwenge Carvers' Market (Sam Nujoma Rd; 🕒 8am-6pm) The Mwenge market, opposite the Village Museum, and just off New Bagamoyo Rd, is packed with vendors, and you can watch carvers at work. Via public transport, take the Mwenge *dalla-dalla* from New Posta transport stand to the end, from where it's five minutes on foot down the small street to the left.

GETTING THERE & AWAY
Air

Dar es Salaam International Airport is the major international arrival point for overseas flights and the main hub for domestic services. For more information, including international flight connections, see p318. For flights to Zanzibar, the best contacts are Coastal Aviation and ZanAir. Airline offices in Dar es Salaam include the following:

Air India (Map p74; ☎ 215 2642; cnr Ali Hassan Mwinyi & Bibi Titi Mohamed Rds)

British Airways (Map p74; ☎ 211 3820, 284 4082; Royal Palm Hotel, Ohio St)

Coastal Aviation (Map p74; ☎ 211 7959/60, 284 3293; aviation@coastal.cc; Upanga Rd) Also at Terminal One, Airport.

EgyptAir (Map p74; ☎ 022-211 0333; Samora Ave)

Emirates Airlines (Map p74; ☎ 022-211 6100; Haidery Plaza, cnr Kisutu & India Sts)

Ethiopian Airlines (Map p74; ☎ 022-211 7063; Ohio St) Opposite Royal Palm Hotel.

Kenya Airways (Map p74; ☎ 022-211 9376/7; Upanga Rd, cnr Ali Hassan Mwinyi & Bibi Titi Mohamed Rds)

KLM (Map p74; ☎ 022-213 9790/1; Upanga Rd) Together with Kenya Airways.

Linhas Aéreas de Moçambique (Map p74; ☎ 022-213 4600; 1st fl, JM Mall, Samora Ave) At Fast-Track Travel.

Oman Air (Map p74; ☎ 213 5660; omanair@cats-net .com; Samora Ave)

Precision Air (Map p74; ☎ 022-212 1718, 284 3547; cnr Samora Ave & Pamba Rd)

South African Airways (SAA; Map p74; ☎ 022-211 7044; Raha Towers, cnr Bibi Titi Mohamed & Ali Hassan Mwinyi Rds)

Swiss International Airlines (Map p74; ☎ 022-211 8870; Luther House, Sokoine Dr)

Yemenia Yemen Airways (Map p74; ☎ 022-212 6036; Ohio St) Opposite Royal Palm Hotel.

ZanAir (☎ 284 3297; Terminal 1, Airport)

The airport has two terminals. Most regularly scheduled domestic flights and all international flights depart from Terminal Two (the 'new' terminal, and the first one you reach coming from town), while many flights on small planes and most air charters depart from Terminal One (the 'old' terminal), about 700m further down the road. Verify the departure terminal when purchasing your ticket.

Boat

The main passenger routes are between Dar es Salaam, Zanzibar and (sporadically) Pemba; and Dar es Salaam and Mtwara.

TO/FROM ZANZIBAR & PEMBA

Three 'fast' ferries trips (*Sea Star* or *Sea Bus*) run daily from Dar es Salaam to Zanzibar, departing at 7am, 10.30am, noon and 4.15pm. All take 1½ hours and cost US$35/40 regular/ VIP (VIP gets you a seat in the air-con hold, but isn't worth the extra money). There's also one slow ferry called the *Flying Horse*, which doesn't fly at all, but takes almost four hours. It departs daily at 12.30pm and costs US$20 one way. The ticket window for non-resident tickets for all ferries is opposite St Joseph's Cathedral near the *Flying Horse* sign.

Travelling in the other direction, departures from Zanzibar are daily at 7am (8am on Sunday), 10.30am (Monday to Saturday), 1pm, 4.15pm and 10pm (*Flying Horse*, which arrives before dawn the next day).

Only buy your tickets at the ticket window, and don't fall for touts at the harbour trying to collect extra fees for 'doctors' certificates', departure taxes and the like. The only fee is the ticket price (which includes the US$5 port tax). Also, avoid touts who want to take you into town to buy 'cheaper' ferry tickets, or who offer to purchase ferry tickets for you at less expensive resident rates; although it's easy enough to get resident-rate tickets and get on the boat with them, you're likely to have problems later when the tout or his buddies come around to collect payment for the favour.

For information on ferry connections to Pemba, see p133.

TO/FROM MTWARA
The only connection is on the ailing MV *Safari*, which sails approximately weekly in each direction to no set schedule. The trip takes 25 to 30 hours, sometimes less, and costs US$25, including port tax. Sailing times are posted at the **MV Safari office** (Map p74; ☎ 2124504/6; Sokoine Dr) at the port, just down from the Zanzibar ferry terminal. Most passengers describe the trip as uncomfortable; the VIP lounge on the lower level of the boat has no windows.

Bus
All buses except Scandinavian Express depart from and arrive at the main bus station at Ubungo, about 8km west of town on Morogoro Rd. It's a sprawling place with the usual assortment of bus station hustle and touts trying to drum up business for their lines. Keep an eye on your luggage and your wallet and try to avoid arriving at night. Just outside (east) of the compound is an NBC bank branch with an ATM. *Dalla-dallas* to Ubungo (Tsh150) leave from New Posta and Old Posta local transport stands, as well as from various other spots in town. Taxis from the city centre cost about Tsh8000. If you're coming into Dar es Salaam, you can sometimes stay on the bus past Ubungo until the bus line's town office – which is worth doing as it will be less chaotic and you'll have a cheaper taxi fare to your hotel. It doesn't work out as well leaving the city, since departures from the booking offices are usually about two hours before Ubungo departures. To book tickets, head to the bus line offices (listed following), which are in Kisutu, near

the Libya St post office. As usual, only buy tickets inside the bus office itself.

Dar Express (Map p74; Libya St) runs daily buses to Arusha: 'ordinary' bus (Tsh8000, once daily); semi-luxury (Tsh10,000, one daily); and luxury (Tsh12,000, three daily). **Royal Coach** (Map p74; ☎ 212 4073; Libya St) also has daily departures to Arusha in the morning (Tsh17,000). **Tawfiq** (Map p74; Libya St) runs buses daily to Arusha, Mombasa, Mwanza, Nairobi and Tanga, all departing Ubungo between about 6am and 8am.

Scandinavian Express (Map p74; ☎ 218 4833/4; www.scandinaviagroup.com; cnr Msimbazi St & Nyerere Rd) has its own slick terminal for arrivals and departures (which is also where you book tickets). It's much calmer than Ubungo, and closer to the city centre and for some routes, you can even book online. All Scandinavian buses also pass by Ubungo. Below is a table giving price and frequency for the various locations:

Destination	Price (Tsh)	Frequency
Arusha	13,000-22,000	2 per day
Dodoma	6500-9000	2 per day
Iringa	8000-9000	3 per day
Kampala	40,000	1 per day
Kyela	15,000-17,000	2 per day
Mbeya	13,500-20,000	3 per day
Mombasa	17,000	1 per day
Mwanza	38,000	1 per day
Nairobi	35,000	1 per day
Tanga	7000	1 per day
Songea	15,000-17,000	2 per day
Tunduma	15,000	1 per day

Minibuses to Kilwa Masoko depart from Temeke bus stand, located about 5km southwest of the city centre, just off Nelson Mandela Rd.

For information about buses between Dar es Salaam and Kenya, Uganda, Zambia and Malawi, see p321.

Car & Motorcycle
See p330 for rental agencies.

Train
For information about the Tazara line between Dar es Salaam, Mbeya and Kapiri Mposhi (Zambia), see p332. For more on Central Line trains between Dar es Salaam and Kigoma and Mwanza, see p332.

The **Tazara station** (☎ 286 5187; www.tazara.co
.tz; cnr Nyerere & Nelson Mandela Rds) is about 6km
southwest from the centre of town (Tsh4000
in a taxi). *Dalla-dallas* to the station leave
from either New or Old Posta transport
stands, and are marked Vigunguti, U/
Ndege or Buguruni.

Tanzanian Railways Corporation (Central Line)
station (☎ 211 7833; www.trctz.com; cnr Railway St &
Sokoine Dr) is in the centre of town just southwest of the ferry terminal.

GETTING AROUND
To/From the Airport
Dar es Salaam International Airport is about
12km from the city centre. *Dalla-dallas*
(marked U/Ndege) go to the airport from
New Posta transport stand. In heavy traffic
the trip can take over an hour, and there's
generally no room for luggage.

Taxis cost Tsh6000 to Tsh10,000, depending on your bargaining abilities.

Car & Motorcycle
Most of the rental agencies listed on p330
offer special business packages within Dar
es Salaam.

Public Transport
The main form of public transport is the
dalla-dalla (minibus). These go almost
everywhere in the city for Tsh100 to Tsh200,
are invariably packed to overflowing, and
are difficult to board with luggage. First and
last stops are shown in the front window,
but routes vary, so confirm that the driver
is really going to your destination. Main
terminals include the following:

New Posta (Map p74; Maktaba St) In front of the main
post office.

Old Posta (Map p74; Sokoine Dr) Just down from the
Azania Front Lutheran Church.

Stesheni (Map p74; Algeria St) Just off Samora Ave near
the Central Line Railway Station; *dalla-dallas* to Temeke
bus stand also leave from here; ask for 'Temeke *mwisho*'.

Taxi
Taxis don't have meters. Short rides within
the city centre cost Tsh1000 to Tsh2000.
Fares from the city centre to Msasani Pe-
ninsula start at Tsh2500 (Tsh4000 to Sea
Cliff Village).

There are taxi ranks throughout the city,
including opposite the Royal Palm Hotel,
on the corner of Azikiwe St and Sokoine

Dr (located opposite the Azania Front Lutheran Church) and on the Msasani Peninsula on the corner of Msasani and Haile
Selassie Rds.

AROUND DAR ES SALAAM

PUGU HILLS
Make your way through the outskirts of Dar
es Salaam, and you'll step straight into the
rhythm of rural Tanzanian life. Pugu Hills,
which begins about 15km southwest of
Dar es Salaam and extends past Kisarawe,
is lightly wooded, with several small forest
reserves, and offers a complete change of
pace from the urban scene. It makes a good
destination if you have a day or two in Dar
es Salaam and want to avoid the city, or for
a short day or weekend getaway. Despite its
proximity to Dar es Salaam, the Pugu area
is not urbanised at all, and many communities have remained quite traditional and
conservative. Pugu Hills is also interesting

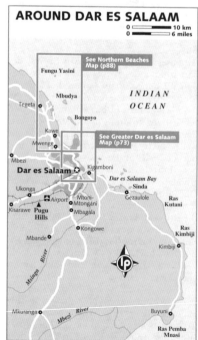

AROUND DAR ES SALAAM

THE ZARAMO WORLD VIEW

The original inhabitants of the area around Dar es Salaam are the Zaramo, who are known for their skilled woodworking, and for their intriguing beliefs about creation. In the beginning, according to the Zaramo, was Nyalutanga, the common mother from whom springs forth all life and knowledge. Nyalutanga herself had no creator and no husband, but rather emerged from the female earth, later bringing forth a line of daughters, from whom all Zaramo are descended. Men fit into the picture as nourishers of the female creative power, and as the source of the cultural qualities that complement women's biological contribution. Thus, while family lines are continued through the mother, Zaramo children take the name of their father's mother's clan and are considered to inherit the cultural qualities of their father.

Also interesting are Zaramo beliefs relating to life and death. The Zaramo believe that all life arises from death. Death is seen as part of the natural continuum of life, as a transition rather than a transformation. The rituals that mark this transition extend into many areas. For example, Zaramo traditional healers often place newly procured medicinal plants on compost heaps for a few days to gain potency. As the plants wither, they take on new powers, and a place connected with death and decay (the compost heap) assumes the symbolism of a place of regeneration.

For more on the Zaramo, look for a copy of *Blood, Milk and Death: Body Symbols and the Power of Regeneration Among the Zaramo of Tanzania* by Marja-Liisa Swantz with Salome Mjema and Zenya Wild, on which this text is based.

---

from a historical perspective: several mission stations were established here, and it is the site of Pugu Secondary School, where Julius Nyerere worked as a teacher before entering into politics full time.

Pugu's roads (most of which are unsealed) are only lightly travelled, and good for biking. There are also two short WCST hiking trails. If you want to try them, you will need to go first to the *Mali Asili* (Natural Resources) office in Kisarawe, which is just south of the main roundabout, to get a permit (Tsh4000). The trailheads are about 15 minutes from the office on foot; each trail takes approximately 30 minutes. Note that there's a military base in Pugu, which means that you must not take pictures anywhere unless you're sure that you're nowhere in the vicinity.

Pugu Hills (☎ 0744-489230, 565498; www.puguhills .com; entry Tsh2000, camping per person Tsh6000, 4-6 person bandas US$50; meals Tsh6000) is a good, breezy place set on a hillside backing onto a forest reserve. There's an area to pitch your tent, shower facilities and a restaurant with vegetarian dishes and other meals. There are also four spacious and very relaxing *bandas* (thatched-roof huts with wooden or earthen walls). Large groups and overland trucks cannot be accommodated. Nearby are some hiking paths, including a short walk that takes you to a lookout with views over Dar es Salaam. Pugu Hills is also a good base for biking. The compound is open on Saturday and Sunday only; during the week, you'll need to call in advance to make arrangements.

Getting There & Away

Dalla-dallas to Kisarawe leave from Msimbazi St in Kariakoo. You can also get them on Nyerere Rd at the airport turn-off. For Pugu Hills camping ground and restaurant, ask the driver to drop you at the old Agip station (about 7km before Kisarawe, and about 7km past the airport). From here, continue straight along the unsealed Kisarawe road for about 200m, to the end of a tiny group of shops on your left, where there is a dirt path leading up to Pugu Hills (about 15 minutes further on foot); ask for Bwana Kiki's place. By vehicle, from the old Agip station follow the sealed road to the left, continue about 1.2km, then turn right at an unmarked dirt path running past a chicken warehouse (the turn-off is about 50m before the railroad tracks). Continue about 2km uphill, along a rough road, to Pugu Hills.

OFFSHORE ISLANDS

The islands of Bongoyo, Mbudya, Pangavini and Fungu Yasini, shimmering on the horizon just off the coast of Dar es Salaam, were gazetted in 1975 as part of the Dar es Salaam Marine Reserve system. They boast some pristine patches of sand, a decent array of fish and enjoyable diving and snorkelling, particularly around Bongoyo and Mbudya. There's a Tsh1000 per person entry fee to enter the reserve area (including the islands), which is usually included in the price of excursions.

Bongoyo Island Marine Reserve

Bongoyo Island Marine Reserve, about 7km north of Dar es Salaam, is the most popular of the islands, with a quiet (except on holiday weekends) stretch of beach and some short walking trails. You can arrange a seafood meal with locals on the beach, but you'll need to bring your own drinks. Swimming here is not tide dependent as it is on the mainland beaches. There's no accommodation.

There is a boat that travels to the island from the Msasani Slipway, that departs at 9.30am, 11.30am and at 1.30pm, and then returns at 10.30am, 12.30pm and either 2.30pm or 4.30pm (US$10 return, minimum four people, this includes the marine reserve entry fees and lunch).

Mbudya

Mbudya, about 4km north of Bongoyo, has snorkelling, swimming and nothing else (no food, no accommodation). It's best reached from the beaches north of Dar es Salaam (below), and most of the northern beaches hotels can arrange excursions. Expect to pay from about US$10 per person in a group of four.

NORTHERN BEACHES

The beaches about 25km north of Dar es Salaam and east of New Bagamoyo Rd are lined with resorts and are popular weekend getaways. While they lack the exotic tropical island ambience of Zanzibar's beaches, they make a relaxing break from the city and – with a good selection of swimming pools and water parks – are an ideal destination for families. They are close enough to Dar es Salaam that you can visit for the day, or base yourself here if you want to avoid the city completely.

Diving & Snorkelling

Diving around Bongoyo and Mbudya islands, and diving certification courses (PADI and NAUI), can be arranged at **Sea**

NORTHERN BEACHES

0 — 3 km
0 — 2 miles

SIGHTS & ACTIVITIES
Kunduchi Ruins.............................1 A3
Kunduchi Wet 'n' Wild................2 A3
Sea Breeze Dive Centre...........(see 8)
Village Museum...........................3 A4
Water World...................................4 A3

SLEEPING
Beachcomber..................................5 A3
Jangwani Sea Breeze Lodge.......6 A3
Silver Sands Beach Hotel...........7 A2
White Sands Hotel.......................8 A3

SHOPPING
Mwenge Carvers' Market...........9 A4

TRANSPORT
Mwenge Dalla-Dalla Stand......10 A4

Breeze Dive Centre (seabreeze@afsat.com) at White Sands Hotel (opposite). There's also a small dive centre at Silver Sands Beach Hotel (opposite).

Ruins

Just north of Kunduchi Wet 'n' Wild are the atmospheric **Kunduchi ruins**, which include the remnants of a late 15th-century mosque as well as Arabic graves from the 18th or 19th centuries, with some well-preserved pillar tombs. Fragments of Chinese pottery found here testify to ancient trading links between this part of Africa and the Orient. The best way to visit is by arranging a guide with your hotel; it's not safe to walk to the ruins, as there have been muggings.

ARIADNE VAN ZANDBERGEN

St Joseph's Cathedral (p79), Dar es Salaam

DENNIS JOHNSON

An ebony wood sculpture (p84), Dar es Salaam

Local fisherman on a beach at Ras Kutani (p90)

DAVE LEWIS

JOHN BORTHWICK

Art on the street in Stone Town (p97),
Zanzibar

EDWARD SNIJDERS

Strolling along the beach at Stone
Town (p97), Zanzibar

ARIADNE VAN ZAND

Swahili girl in decorative doorway,
Zanzibar (p95)

Children enjoying the late afternoon sun, Zanzibar (p95)

LEANNE

Water Parks

In Kunduchi, just east of New Bagamoyo Rd, are several water parks that might be worth considering if you're travelling with children, or if you can't leave Western, Disney-style entertainment behind.

Kunduchi Wet 'n' Wild (☎ 265 0326, 265 0332; wetnwild@raha.com; adult/child Tsh3950/3750; ♈ 9am-6pm, Tue women only) This is a huge place, with several pools, water slides, bumper cars, video arcades and more. It's usually packed. To get here, take a *dalla-dalla* to Mwenge and then a taxi.

Water World (☎ 264 7621; www.hotelwhitesands .com; admission Tsh4000; ♈ 10am-6pm Wed, Fri, Sat & Sun, Wed women only) A pool and water slides, just up from White Sands Hotel.

Sleeping & Eating

Silver Sands Beach Hotel (☎ 265 0567/8; www.silver sands.co.tz; camping per person/vehicle US$3/2, dm US$7, s/d from US$20/30) The best budget choice, with camping facilities plus hot water, and dorm beds with mosquito nets. There are also rooms set around a grassy lawn near the beach with hot water and nets, and some with air-con. Meals are available from about Tsh3000, and staff can help you organise snorkelling trips to Mbudya island.

Jangwani Sea Breeze Lodge (☎ 264 7215, 0741-320875; www.jangwani.com; s/d from US$90/115; ✖ ⬛ ⬛) A tidy German-run establishment with comfortable if somewhat over-furnished rooms (all across the road from the beach), a bougainvillea-draped beach-side courtyard, and a restaurant with weekend barbecues and buffets (from Tsh8000). Airport pickups can be arranged.

Beachcomber (☎ 264 7772/3; www.beachcomber .co.tz; s/d US$104/122; ✖ ⬛ ⬛) The place to stay if you want to keep fit during your holiday, with modern rooms, a large pool, gym, sauna and more. It's about 500m north of White Sands Hotel.

White Sands Hotel (☎ 264 7621, 211 3678; www .hotelwhitesands.com; s/d US$100/115, on weekends US$85/95; ✖ ⬛ ⬛) A sprawling hotel right on the beach just north of Jangwani. Rooms have TV, mini-fridge and small sea-view balconies; diving, windsurfing, deep-sea fishing and excursions to Bongoyo and Mbudya can be arranged. The hotel also owns Water World (above), which guests can use for half price. There's a nightclub and disco on Friday and Saturday evenings.

Getting There & Away

Jangwani Sea Breeze Lodge, White Sands Hotel and the Beachcomber are all reached via the same signposted turn-off from the Bagamoyo road. About 3km further north along the Bagamoyo road is the signposted turn-off for Silver Sands.

Via public transport, take a *dalla-dalla* from New Posta in Dar es Salaam to Mwenge. For Jangwani, White Sands and The Beachcomber, get a *dalla-dalla* from Mwenge towards Tegeta and get out at the Africana Junction, from where you can find a taxi to the hotels (from Tsh1500). For Silver Sands Beach Hotel, stay on until the Kunduchi Junction, where you'll need to look for a taxi for the remaining 2km or so (about Tsh1500). Don't walk, as there have been several muggings along this stretch of road.

Taxis direct from Dar es Salaam cost from Tsh10,000 to Tsh15,000 one way, depending on your bargaining abilities; from the airport, expect to pay about Tsh20,000.

SOUTHERN BEACHES

The coastline south of Dar es Salaam gets more attractive, tropical and rural the further south you go, and makes a great and easily accessible getaway. The budget places are spread out, beginning just south of Kigamboni, which is opposite Kivukoni Front and reached in just a few minutes by ferry. About 25km further south are a few exclusive resorts.

Kigamboni

The beach south of Kigamboni, around Mjimwema village, is the closest spot to Dar es Salaam for camping. It's also an easy day trip if you're staying in town and want some sand and surf.

SLEEPING & EATING

Kipepeo Village (☎ 282 0877, 0744-276178; www .kipepeovillage.com; s/d/tr banda US$40/50/70) consists of raised cottages lined up about 200m in from the beach, all with balconies and mosquito nets, and overlooking the water in the distance. Breakfast is not included. On the beach itself is **Kipepeo Campsite** (☎ 282 0877; www.kipepeocamp.com; camping per person US$3, dm US$5, s/d banda US$11/16), with a restaurant and bar, a grill and simple beachside *bandas* (thatched-roof hut with wooden or earthen walls) and dorm beds. On Saturday and Sunday, there's a Tsh3000 fee for day use of the beach and facilities. Kipepeo is 8km south of the ferry dock.

Gendayeka Beach Village (☎ 0748-612212; camping per person Tsh5000, r per person without bathroom Tsh10,000) A simple, locally-run place on a good stretch of beach about 700m south of Kipepeo Campsite, near the site of the last British governor's weekend retreat. In addition to camping, there are no-frills bungalows with nets and shared facilities, and staff can help you sort out trips to Sinda island offshore (from Tsh5000 return), and to Gezaulole. You can also make bookings and arrange transport through Chef's Pride restaurant (p81).

GETTING THERE & AWAY
Making a good excursion in itself, the Kigamboni (Magogoni) ferry (Tsh100/800 per person/vehicle, five minutes) runs throughout the day between the eastern end of Kivukoni Front and Kigamboni village. Once on the other side, catch a *dalla-dalla* heading south, and ask the driver to drop you. Taxis from Kigamboni charge about Tsh2000 to Kipepeo and Gendayeka.

If you have a car, an alternative route back to the city is to turn right along the tarmac road just south of Kipepeo, and follow it past extensive stands of coconut palms and scattered villages to Dar es Salaam via Kongowe (at the junction with Kilwa Rd), Mbagala and Mtoni-Mtongani.

Gezaulole
About 13km south of Kigamboni on the beach, Gezaulole village has a good Cultural Tourism Program where you can get introduced to Zaramo life (see the boxed text, p87), learn about local history and sail out to nearby Sinda island. The starting point is at the green and welcoming **Akida's Garden** (☎ 0744-505725, or through WCST, see the boxed text, p36, ☎ 211 2518; wcst@africaonline .co.tz; camping Tsh2500, bandas per person without bathroom Tsh4000), signposted about 1km off the main road. There's also **camping** (per person Tsh2000) under the palms on the sublime Kim Beach, nearby. If you start early enough, it's possible to visit Gezaulole as a day trip from Dar es Salaam on public transport. Cultural Tourism Program fees are about Tsh7000 per person per half day, and Sinda island trips cost Tsh5000.

Via public transport, take a *dalla-dalla* from the Kigamboni ferry dock heading towards Kimbiji or Gezaulole, and ask the driver to drop you at the turn-off for Akida's Garden (Tsh300). Taxis from Kigamboni charge about Tsh5000.

Ras Kutani
This cape juts into the sea about 30km south of Dar es Salaam, isolated from the rest of the world by extensive tracts of bush and palm trees. It's a haven for those seeking secluded tropical surroundings, water sports and good fishing. There are two places to stay, both accessed via the same signposted turn-off, and both require advance bookings. Nearby is an airstrip for charter flights.

Ras Kutani (www.ccafrica.com; per person all-inclusive US$265) This intimate retreat is set between the sea and a small lagoon, and comes about as close as you can get to a tropical island getaway without actually leaving the mainland. Accommodation is in rustic, barefoot luxury style bungalows with views over the water. When you're not reclining in your bungalow, you have your choice of bird-watching, forest walks, horse riding, canoeing in the lagoon and water sports. Deep-sea fishing can also be arranged.

Amani Beach Club (☎ 0744-410033; www.protea hotels.com; s/d full board US$140/240; 🅿 🖵 🏊) If you're looking for more of a resort atmosphere, head just south and around the bend from the Ras Kutani bungalows to Amani Beach Club. It's an exclusive establishment spread across large, manicured lawns overlooking the sea. The spacious, luxurious cottages have all the amenities, and there's a full array of excursions and water sports to keep you busy.

Zanzibar Archipelago

CONTENTS

HIGHLIGHTS

- Wandering through the **Stone Town's** (p100) labyrinth of narrow, cobbled streets

- Relaxing under the palms on picture-perfect **beaches** (p112)

- Discovering **Pemba's** (p126) unknown corners and culture

- Diving and snorkelling amidst shoals of colourful fish around **Mnemba Atoll** (p126) or **Misali island** (p131)

- Browsing for **souvenirs** (p110) in tiny shops fragrant with spices or filled to the rafters with carved wooden chests

Pemba ★
Misali Island ★
★ Mnemba Atoll
★ Beaches
Stone Town ★

■ TELEPHONE CODE: ☎ 024 | ■ POPULATION: 990,000

Step off the boat (or plane) onto Zanzibar, and you'll be transported through the miles and the centuries – to the ancient kingdom of Persia, to the Oman of bygone days with its caliphs and sultans, to the west coast of India with its sensual rhythms and heavily laden scents. In Stone Town – the heart of the archipelago – narrow, cobbled alleyways take you past Arabic-style houses with brass-studded wooden doors. Elderly men in their *kanzu* (white robes) and *kofia* (caps) sit on small *baraza* (stone benches), chatting animatedly over cups of strong *kahawa* (coffee) while playing a seemingly never-ending game of *bao* (a board game). Nearby, veiled women in their flowing, black *bui-bui* (cover-alls) pause to share the latest gossip, while children chase balls through the streets.

Along the coast, life seems to go on as it has for centuries, its slow pace set by the rhythm of the tides and the winds of the monsoon. Fishermen repair nets in the shade, while seaweed harvesters spread their crop on large wooden racks to dry. Chickens and the occasional cow wander along sandy village lanes, coconut palms rustle in the breeze and ethereally turquoise waters lap the sun-baked white sands.

Just across the deep, dark waters of the Pemba channel lies hilly, verdant Pemba – the archipelago's 'other' island, seldom-visited and steeped in mystique. Dense mangrove swamps line its coast, opening occasionally onto stunning white-sand coves; a patchwork of neat farm plots covers the hillsides; and the scent of cloves from the island's plantations hangs in the air.

There is, of course, another side to life on the archipelago: hassles from Zanzibar's ever-present street touts will probably be your first introduction, development threatens to overwhelm some areas of the coast, costs seem to creep constantly skywards and noisy *piki-piki* (motorbikes) careen recklessly through Stone Town's streets. However, there are still plenty of quiet, unspoiled spots left and good deals to be found. And, while your reverie on caliphs and sultans may not last, the archipelago's allure will continue to captivate long after you've finished your visit.

History

The archipelago's history stretches back at least to the start of the first millennium, when Bantu-speaking peoples from the mainland ventured across the Zanzibar and Pemba channels – perhaps in search of bigger fish and better beaches. The islands had probably been visited at an even earlier date by traders and sailors from Arabia. The *Periplus of the Erythraean Sea* (p18) documents small Arabic trading settlements along the coast that were already well established by the 1st century, and makes reference to the island of Menouthias, which many historians believe to be Zanzibar. From around the 8th century, Shirazi traders from Persia also began to make their way to East Africa, where they established settlements on Pemba, and probably also at Zanzibar's Unguja Ukuu.

Between the 12th and 15th centuries, the archipelago came into its own, as trade links with Arabia and the Persian Gulf blossomed. Zanzibar became a powerful city-state, supplying slaves, gold, ivory and wood to places as distant as India and Asia, while importing spices, glassware and textiles. With the trade from the east also came Islam and the Arabic architecture that still characterises the archipelago today. One of the most important archaeological remnants from this era is the mosque at Kizimkazi (p123), whose mihrab (prayer niche showing the direction to Mecca) dates from the early 12th century.

The arrival of the Portuguese in the early 16th century temporarily interrupted this golden age, as Zanzibar and then Pemba fell under Portuguese control. Yet Portuguese dominance did not last long. It was challenged first by the British, who found Zanzibar an amenable rest stop on the long journey to India, and then by Omani Arabs, who, in the mid-16th century, gave the Portuguese the routing that they no doubt deserved. By the early 19th century, Oman had gained the upper hand on Zanzibar, and trade on the island again flourished, centred around slaves, ivory and cloves. Caravans set out for the interior of the mainland, and trade reached such a high point that in the 1840s the Sultan of Oman relocated his court here from the Persian Gulf.

From the mid-19th century, with increasing European interest in East Africa and the end of the slave trade, Omani rule over Zanzibar began to weaken, and in 1862 the sultanate was formally partitioned. Zanzibar became independent of Oman, with Omani sultans ruling under a British protectorate. This arrangement lasted until 10 December 1963 when Zanzibar gained its independence. Just one month later, in January 1964, the sultans were overthrown in a bloody revolution instigated by the Afro-Shirazi Party (ASP), which then assumed power. On 12 April 1964 Abeid Karume, president of the ASP, signed a declaration of unity with Tanganyika (mainland Tanzania) and the union, fragile from the outset, became known as the United Republic of Tanzania.

Karume was assassinated in 1972 and Aboud Jumbe assumed the presidency of Zanzibar until he resigned in 1984. A succession of leaders followed, culminating in 2000 with the highly controversial election of Aman Abeid Karume, son of the first president.

Today, the two major parties in the archipelago are the Chama Cha Mapinduzi (CCM) and the opposition Civic United Front (CUF), which has its stronghold on Pemba. Tensions between the two peaked in the disputed 1995 national elections (p22) and have been simmering ever since.

In 1999 negotiations moderated by the Commonwealth secretary general concluded with a brokered agreement between the CCM and CUF. However, the temporary hiatus this created was shattered by the 2000 elections and the resulting violent incidents on Pemba in January 2001 (p22). Since then, renewed efforts at dialogue be-

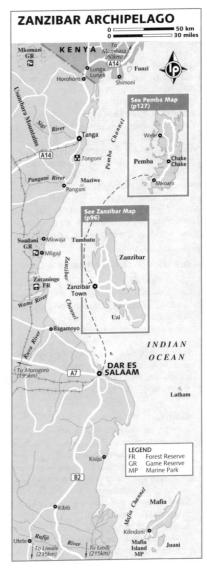

tween the CCM and CUF have restored a fragile calm, although little progress has been made at resolving the underlying issues.

Climate

Zanzibar's climate is shaped by the monsoon, with tropical, sultry conditions all year, and just enough sea breezes to keep things comfortable. The main rains fall from March until May, when many hotels and eateries close. There's also a short rainy season from November into early December, and showers can come at any time, especially on Pemba.

Dangers & Annoyances

While Zanzibar remains a relatively safe place, robberies, muggings and the like occur with some frequency, especially in Zanzibar Town and along the beaches.

Follow the normal precautions: avoid isolated areas, especially isolated stretches of beach, and keep your valuables out of view. If you go out at night in Zanzibar Town, take a taxi or walk in a group. Also avoid walking alone in Stone Town during the predawn and dawn hours. As a rule, it's best to leave valuables in your hotel safe, preferably sealed or locked. Should your passport be stolen, get a written report from the police. Upon presentation of this report, Immigration will issue you a travel document that will get you back to the mainland.

If you've rented a bicycle or motorcycle, avoid isolated stretches of road, including the section between Jambiani and Makunduchi on the southeast coast, and don't stop if you're flagged down in isolated areas.

Given the ongoing history of political tensions on Zanzibar and Pemba, and the overall world political situation, it's a good idea to check for updates on your government's travel advisory site (see the boxed

---

DIVING THE ZANZIBAR ARCHIPELAGO

The archipelago's turquoise waters are just as amazing below the surface as they are from above, with a magnificent array of hard and soft corals and a diverse collection of sea creatures, including shadowy manta rays, hawksbill and green turtles, barracudas and sharks. Other draws include the possibility for wall dives, especially off Pemba; the fascinating cultural backdrop; and the opportunity to combine wildlife safaris with underwater exploration. On the down side, visibility isn't as reliable as in some other areas of the world, although sometimes you'll be treated to ranges of 25m to 30m. Another thing to consider, if you're a serious diver and coming to the archipelago exclusively for diving, is that unless you do a live-aboard arrangement, you'll need to travel – often for up to an hour – to many of the dive sites. Also, prices are considerably higher than in places like the Red Sea or Thailand.

Seasons

Diving is possible year-round, although conditions vary dramatically. Late March until mid-June is generally the least favourable time because of erratic weather patterns and frequent storms. However, even during this period you can have some good days, particularly in March when water temperatures are also warmer. July or August to February or March tends to be the best time overall, although again, conditions vary and wind is an important factor. On Pemba, for example, the southeastern seas can be rough around June and July when the wind is blowing from the south, but calm and clear as glass from around November to late February when the monsoon winds blow from the north. On both islands, the calmest time is generally from around September to November during the lull between the annual monsoons.

Water temperatures range from lows of about 22°C in July and August to highs of about 29°C in February and March, with the average about 26°C. Throughout, 3mm wetsuits are standard; 4mm suits are recommended for some areas during the July to September winter months, and 2mm are fine from around December to March or April.

Costs, Courses & Planning

Costs are fairly uniform throughout the archipelago, though somewhat cheaper on Zanzibar than on Pemba. Expect to pay from US$350 for a four-day PADI open water course, about US$45/75 for a single-/double-dive package, and from about US$50 for a night dive. Most places discount about 10% if you have your own equipment, and for groups. In addition to open water certifica-

text, p308), especially if you plan on travelling to the archipelago in late 2005, when elections are scheduled.

ZANZIBAR

☎ 024 / pop 990,000

Zanzibar gets the lion's (sultan's?) share of attention on the archipelago, and with good reason. Its old Stone Town, where everyone arrives, is one of Africa's most evocative locations, with a mesmerising mix of influences from the Indian subcontinent, the Arabian peninsula, the African mainland and Europe. Just an easy drive away are the island's beaches, which are among the finest stretches of sand to be found anywhere. Zanzibar is small enough that you can base yourself either in Stone Town or at one of the beaches to do all your exploring, and tourist infrastructure is highly developed, with hotels and restaurants for every taste and budget.

Getting There & Around

Getting to Zanzibar is easy, with lots of daily flights plus several daily ferries between Dar es Salaam and Zanzibar Town. There are also daily flights between Zanzibar Town, Pemba and Tanga, and a boat several times weekly between Zanzibar and Pemba. Once on Zanzibar, taxi and motorbike hire is quite affordable, and there is a good network of cheap, slow and crowded *dalla-dallas* (minibuses) and faster private minivans that will take you wherever you want to go.

ZANZIBAR ARCHIPELAGO

---

tion, many operators also offer other courses, including Advanced Open Water, Medic First Aid, Rescue Diver, and speciality courses including underwater photography and navigation.

As for deciding where to dive: very generally speaking, Zanzibar is known for the corals and shipwrecks offshore from Stone Town, and for fairly reliable visibility, high fish diversity and the chance to see pelagics to the north and northeast. While some sites are challenging, there are many easily accessed sites for beginning and mid-range divers.

Unlike Zanzibar, which is a continental island, Pemba is an oceanic island located in a deep channel with a steeply dropping shelf. Because of this, diving tends to be more challenging, with an emphasis on wall and drift dives, though there are some sheltered areas for beginners, especially around Misali island. Most dives are to the west around Misali, and to the north around the Njao Gap.

Wherever you dive, allow a sufficient surface interval between the conclusion of your final dive and any onward/homeward flights. According to PADI recommendations, this should be at least 12 hours, or more than 12 hours if you have been doing daily multiple dives for several days. Another consideration is insurance, which you should arrange before coming to Tanzania. Many policies exclude diving, so you'll probably need to pay a bit extra, but it's well worth it in comparison to the bills you will need to foot should something go wrong. The closest recompression centres are in Kenya and South Africa.

Most of the archipelago's dive operators also offer snorkelling. Equipment rental costs from US$5 to US$15; when you're selecting it pay particular attention to getting a good mask. Most snorkelling sites are only accessible by boat. Trips average US$20 to US$50 per half day, often including a snack or lunch.

Dive Operators

When choosing a dive operator, quality rather than cost should be the priority. Consider: the operator's experience and qualifications; knowledgeability and competence of staff; and the condition of equipment and frequency of maintenance. Assess whether the overall attitude is serious and professional, and ask about safety precautions – radios, oxygen, emergency evacuation procedures, boat reliability and back-up engines, first aid kits, safety flares and life jackets. On longer dives, do you get an energising meal, or just tea and biscuits? An advantage of operators offering PADI courses is that you'll have the flexibility to go elsewhere in the world and have what you've already done recognised at other PADI dive centres.

Dive operators are listed by location elsewhere in this chapter.

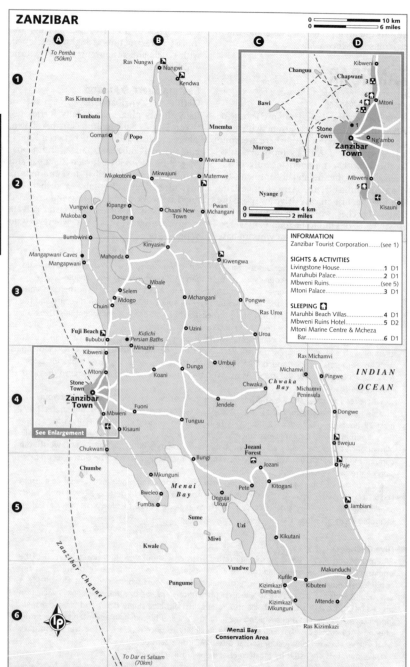

ZANZIBAR

0 — 10 km
0 — 6 miles

A
To Pemba
(50km)

1

Ras Nungwi
Nungwi
Kendwa

Ras Kinunduni

Tumbatu

Gomani
Popo

Mnemba

2

Mwanahaza

Mkokotoni
Mkwajuni
Matemwe

Pwani
Mchangani

Vungwi
Kipange
Chaani New Town
Makoba
Donge

Bumbwini

Kinyasini

Mangapwani Caves
Mahonda
Kiwengwa

Mangapwani

3

Mbale
Selem
Mchangani
Mdogo
Pongwe
Chuini
Ras Uroa

Fuji Beach
Uzini
Uroa
Bububu
Kidichi
Kibweni
Persian Baths
Minazini

Mtoni
Dunga
Umbuji
Ras Michamvi

Stone Town
Koani
Michamvi
Pingwe

4

Zanzibar Town
Chwaka
Chwaka Bay
Michamvi Peninsula

Mbweni
Fuoni
Dongwe

See Enlargement
Kisauni
Tunguu
Jendele

Bwejuu

Chukwani
Bungi
Paje

Chumbe
Jozani Forest
Jozani

Mkunguni
Pete
Kitogani

Bweleo
Menai Bay
Unguja Ukuu
Jambiani

Fumba
Sume
Uzi

5

Miwi
Kikutani

Kwale

Vundwe
Makunduchi

Pungume
Kufile
Kizimkazi
Dimbani
Kibuteni

Kizimkazi
Mkunguni
Mtende

6

Ras Kizimkazi

Menai Bay
Conservation Area

To Dar es Salaam
(70km)

Zanzibar Channel

INDIAN OCEAN

Menai Bay

Enlargement (Stone Town area)

0 — 4 km
0 — 2 miles

Changuu
Kibweni
Chapwani 3
Bawi
6
4
Mtoni
2
Murogo
Stone Town
Pange
Zanzibar Town
Ng'ambo
Nyange
Mbweni 5
Kisauni

INFORMATION
Zanzibar Tourist Corporation.......(see 1)

SIGHTS & ACTIVITIES
Livingstone House.......................**1** D1
Maruhubi Palace.........................**2** D1
Mbweni Ruins............................(see 5)
Mtoni Palace.............................**3** D1

SLEEPING
Maruhbi Beach Villas..................**4** D1
Mbweni Ruins Hotel....................**5** D2
Mtoni Marine Centre & Mcheza
  Bar.....................................**6** D1

ZANZIBAR ARCHIPELAGO

ZANZIBAR TOWN
Orientation
Zanzibar Town, on the western side of the island, is the heart of the archipelago, and the first stop for most travellers. The best-known section by far is the old Stone Town, surrounded on three sides by the sea and bordered to the east by Creek Rd. Directly east of Stone Town is the bustling but much less atmospheric section of Ng'ambo, which you'll pass through en route to some of the beaches. Almost all the listings mentioned in this information section are in Stone Town.

MAPS
Commission for Lands & Environment (Map pp98-9) Also known as the 'Planning Office'; the place to go for dated topographical maps of Zanzibar Town and of the archipelago; it's tucked in behind the Shangani St tunnel.

MaCo Map The best, with a detailed map of Stone Town on one side and Zanzibar on the other; it's widely available in Stone Town.

Information
BOOKSHOPS
Zanzibar Gallery (Map pp98-9; ☎ 223 2721; cnr Kenyatta Rd & Gizenga St; ☿ 9am-7pm Mon-Sat, 9am-1pm Sun) Has an exotic ambience conducive to browsing and an excellent selection of books and maps, including travel guides, Africa titles and historical reprint editions.

CONSULATES
Mozambique (Map pp98-9; ☎ 223 0049; Mapinduzi Rd)
Oman (Map pp98-9; ☎ 223 0066; Vuga Rd)

INTERNET ACCESS
There are dozens of Internet cafés in Stone Town, including the following:

UNGUJA VERSUS ZANZIBAR

Unguja is the Swahili name for Zanzibar. It's often used locally to distinguish the island from the Zanzibar Archipelago (which also includes Pemba), as well as from Zanzibar Town. In this book, for ease of recognition, we've used Zanzibar.

The word 'Zanzibar' comes from the Arabic *Zinj el-Barr* or 'Land of the Blacks'. It was used by Arab traders from at least the 8th or 9th century until the arrival of the Portuguese to refer to both the archipelago and the adjacent coast (*Zanguebar*). Now, the name refers just to the archipelago. Azania – the name given by the early Greeks to the East African coast – is perhaps a Hellenised version of the Arabic *zinj*.

Azzurri Internet Café (Map pp98-9; New Mkunazini Rd; per hr Tsh500; ☿ 8.30am-10.30pm) A cheap place, around the corner from the Anglican cathedral.

Macrosoft Internet Café (Map pp98-9; Hurumzi St; per hr Tsh500; ☿ 9am-11pm) One of the cheapest connections in town.

Shangani Internet Café (Map pp98-9; Kenyatta Rd; per hr Tsh1000; ☿ 8.30am-10pm)

Too Short Internet Café (Map pp98-9; Shangani St; per hr Tsh1000; ☿ 8.30am-11pm) Near the tunnel at the end of Forodhani Gardens.

Zanzibar Cyber Café (Map pp98-9; Kiponda St; per hr Tsh1000; ☿ 8.30am-11pm)

MEDICAL SERVICES
Afya Medical Centre (Map pp98-9; ☎ 223 1228; ☿ 8am-10pm Mon-Fri, 8am-9pm Sat & Sun) Off Kenyatta Rd, between Baghani St and Vuga Rd.
Shamshuddin Pharmacy (Map pp98-9; ☎ 223 1262, 223 3814; Market St; ☿ 9am-8.30pm Mon-Thu & Sat, 9am-noon & 3pm-8.30pm Fri, 9am-1.30pm Sun) Just behind (west of) the Darajani market.

MONEY
There are many forex bureaus – most open until about 8pm Monday to Saturday, and often also on Sunday – where you can change cash and travellers cheques with a minimum of hassle. Rates vary, so it pays to shop around; rates in Stone Town are better than elsewhere on the island, but slightly lower than those on the mainland, and rates for dollars are generally better than those for British pounds, euros and other hard currencies. Officially, accommodation on

---

ZANZIBAR ETIQUETTE

Zanzibar is a conservative, Muslim society, and many locals take offence at scantily clad Westerners. Women should avoid sleeveless tops and plunging necklines, and stick with slacks, skirts or at least knee-length shorts. For men, keep your shirt on when wandering around town, preferably also with slacks or knee-length shorts. During Ramadan, take particular care with dress, and show respect by not eating or drinking in the street or other public places.

ZANZIBAR ARCHIPELAGO

ZANZIBAR TOWN

A **B** **C** **D**

❶

INFORMATION
Afya Medical Centre...........................1 F5
Azzurri Internet Café.........................2 G5
Commission for Lands & Environment..3 D4
Easy Travel & Tours...........................4 H3
Eco + Culture Tours...........................5 G4
Fernandes Tours & Safaris..................6 F5
Fisherman Tours & Travel....................7 F5
Institute of Swahili & Foreign
  Languages...................................8 G5
Local Currency Outlet.........................9 C5
Macrosoft Internet Café....................10 G4
Madeira Tours & Safaris....................11 D6
Mozambique Consulate.....................12 G6
NBC Bank & ATM.............................13 D4
Omani Consulate..............................14 F5
Queen Bureau de Change.............(see 19)
Robin's Collection............................15 D5
Sama Tours......................................16 F4
Shamsuddin Pharmacy......................17 G4
Shangani Forex Bureau.....................18 D5
Shangani Internet Café.....................19 D5
Shangani Post Office.........................20 D5
Suna Tours......................................21 F4
Tima Tours......................................22 G3
Too Short Internet Café.....................23 D4
Tropical Tours..................................24 D6
Zan Tours..25 H3
Zanzibar Cyber Café........................26 G4

❸

SIGHTS & ACTIVITIES
Aga Khan Mosque............................27 G3
Anglican Cathedral...........................28 G4
Bahari Divers...................................29 D4
Beit el-Ajaib (House of Wonders) &
  Zanzibar National Museum of
  History & Culture..........................30 F4
Beit el-Amani (Peace Memorial Museum)
  Natural History Collection..............31 G6
Beit el-Amani (Peace Memorial
  Museum)......................................32 G6
Beit el-Sahel (Palace Museum) &
  Makusurani Graveyard...................33 G3
Darajani Market................................34 H4
Forodhani Gardens...........................35 F3
Hamamni Persian Baths.....................36 G4
Ijumaa Mosque................................37 G3
Mr Mitu's Office (Spice Tours)...........38 H2
Msikiti wa Balnara............................39 H3
Old Dispensary................................40 H3
Old Fort & Zanzibar Cultural Centre..41 F4
Old Slave Chambers.....................(see 69)
Old Slave Market.........................(see 28)
One Ocean/The Zanzibar Dive
  Centre...42 D4
St Joseph's Cathedral........................43 F4
State House.....................................44 F6
Victoria Hall & Gardens....................45 F6

❺

SLEEPING
Africa House Hotel............................46 C6
Annex of Malindi Lodge..............(see 65)
Baghani House Hotel........................47 D6
Bandari Lodge.................................48 H2
Beit al-Aman...................................49 F5
Chavda Hotel..................................50 D6
Clove Hotel.....................................51 G4
Coco de Mer Hotel...........................52 D5
Dhow Palace...................................53 D6
Emerson & Green.............................54 G4
Flamingo Guest House.......................55 G5
Florida Guest House..........................56 F5
Garden Lodge..................................57 F5
Haven Guest House...........................58 F5
Hotel International............................59 G4
Hotel Kiponda.................................60 G3
Hotel Marine...................................61 H2

❻

Jambo Guest House...........................62 G5
Karibu Inn......................................63 D5
Malindi Guest House.........................64 H2
Malindi Lodge.................................65 H3
Manch Lodge.............................(see 58)
Mazsons Hotel.................................66 D5
Mtoni Marine Centre Town
  Booking Office............................(see 9)
Narrow St Hotel...............................67 H3
Riverman Hotel................................68 G4
St Monica's Hostel............................69 G5
Shangani Apartment.........................70 C5
Shangani Hotel................................71 D5
Tembo House Hotel...........................72 C4
Victoria House.................................73 F5
Vuga Hotel......................................74 F5
Warere Town House...........................75 H2
Zanzibar Serena Inn.........................76 C5

EATING
Amore Mio......................................77 C6
Archipelago Café-Restaurant.............78 D4
Baracuda..................................(see 81)
China Plate Restaurant.....................79 D4
Dolly's Patisserie.............................80 D5
Dolphin Restaurant..........................81 D5
Emerson's & Green Tower Top
  Restaurant...............................(see 54)
Fany's Green Restaurant...............(see 81)
Green Garden............................(see 62)
Kidude.....................................(see 54)
La Fenice.......................................82 C5
Le Spice Rendez-Vous.......................83 E5
Mercury's.......................................84 G3
Monsoon Restaurant.........................85 F4
Neem Tree Café..........................(see 41)
Pagoda Chinese Restaurant...............86 C6
Radha Food House............................87 D4
St Monica's Restaurant.................(see 69)

Sambusa Two Tables
  Restaurant..................................88 F5
Shamsuddin's Cash & Carry...............89 G4
Sweet Eazy......................................90 D4

DRINKING
Dharma Lounge..........................(see 91)
Garage Club....................................91 D5
Starehe Club....................................92 C5

ENTERTAINMENT
Culture Musical Club....................(see 56)

SHOPPING
Craft Vendors.............................(see 35)
Memories of Zanzibar..................(see 19)
Moto..93 F4
Zanzibar Curio Shop........................94 F4
Zanzibar Gallery..............................95 D5

TRANSPORT
Air Tanzania....................................96 G5
Asko Tours & Travel.....................(see 20)
Coastal Aviation...........................(see 9)
Ferry Tickets....................................97 H2
Kenya Airways.................................98 F5
Oman Air..99 G3
Precision Air..............................(see 66)
Traffic Police.................................100 H3
Transport Stand..............................101 H4
ZanAir......................................(see 25)

OTHER
Big Tree...102 G3
Ciné Afrique...................................103 H3
Customs & Immigration....................104 H2
High Court......................................105 F5
Mnazi Mmoja Hospital 106 F6
Old Customs House..........................107 G3

Zanzibar Channel

0 —————— 100 m

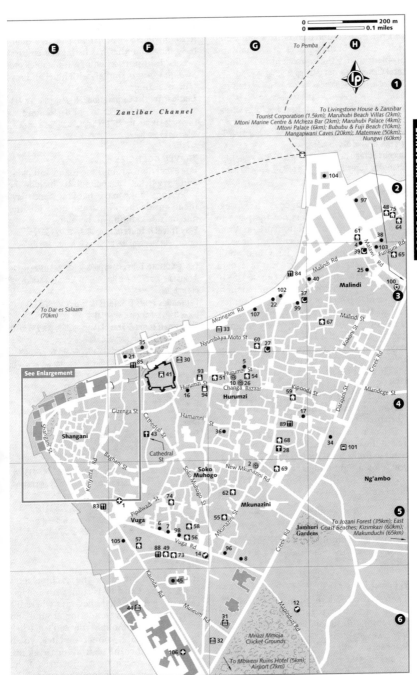

0 — 200 m
0 — 0.1 miles

E   F   G   H

1

Zanzibar Channel

To Pemba

2

To Livingstone House & Zanzibar
Tourist Corporation (1.5km); Maruhubi Beach Villas (2km);
Mtoni Marine Centre & Mcheza Bar (2km); Maruhubi Palace (4km);
Mtoni Palace (6km); Bububu & Fuji Beach (10km);
Mangapwani Caves (20km); Matemwe (50km);
Nungwi (60km)

● 104

● 97

48 75
64

61
4   38
39   103
25   65
100

84
40   Malindi
Malindi Rd

To Dar es Salaam
(70km)

102   37
22   99

107   Malindi St

33

Mizingani Rd

Nyumbaya Moto St   60   27

35

21
85   30

See Enlargement

41
16   93   5
Hurumzi St   54
51   10 @ 26
94   Changa Bazaar
Hurumzi

Gizenga St
Hamamni St   59
Kiponda St

Shangani
36 ●   17

43   89
68
Cathedral   28
St
Soko   2 @
Muhogo   New Mkunazini Rd   69

Ng'ambo

83   1
74   62
Vuga   Mkunazini

6   7   55
98   58   To Jozani Forest (35km); East
105   57   Coast Beaches; Kizimkazi (60km);
88   49   96   Jamhuri   Makunduchi (65km)
14   8   Gardens

● 45

44   12

31

32
Mnazi Mmoja
Cricket Grounds

106   To Mbweni Ruins Hotel (5km);
Airport (7km)

3

4

5

6

Zanzibar must be paid for in US dollars, and prices are quoted in dollars, but especially at the budget places, it's usually no problem to pay the equivalent in shillings.

Local Currency Outlet (Map pp98-9; Shangani St) Situated next to Zanzibar Serena Inn and run by Coastal Travels, this place offers dollars or shillings on Visa or MasterCard at rates similar to those in their Dar es Salaam office (p76).

NBC (Map pp98-9; Shangani St) Changes cash and travellers cheques and has an ATM.

Queens Bureau de Change (Map pp98-9; Kenyatta Rd)

Shangani Forex Bureau (Map pp98-9; Kenyatta Rd)

Costs

Despite its initial appearance as a backpacker's paradise, Zanzibar is not the place to come looking for rock-bottom prices. While it doesn't need to be expensive, prices are higher than on the mainland, and you'll need to make an effort to keep to a tight budget. Plan on spending at least US$10 to US$15 per night for accommodation, and from Tsh7000 per day for food (unless you stick to street food only), plus extra for transport, excursions and diving or snorkelling. During the low season, for longer stays, or if you're in a group, you'll often be able to negotiate discounts, although even at the cheapest places it won't go much below US$8/16 per night per single/double. Many mid-range and top-end hotels charge peak-season supplements during August and the Christmas/New Year holiday period.

Prices are higher away from Stone Town, and at the budget beach hotels it can be difficult to find a meal for less than Tsh4000. If you're on a tight budget, consider stocking up on food and drink in Stone Town. Many hotels and restaurants close from March to May.

POST

Shangani post office (Map pp98-9; Kenyatta Rd; ☽ 8am-4.30pm Mon-Fri, 8am-12.30pm Sat) Has poste restante.

TELEPHONE & FAX

There are several shops around town offering international calls for about US$2 per minute, including **Robin's Collection** (Map pp98-9; Kenyatta Rd; ☽ 9am-8pm Mon-Sat).

Shangani post office (Map pp98-9; Kenyatta Rd; ☽ 8am-10pm Mon-Fri, 8.30am-9pm Sat & Sun) Operator-assisted calls for Tsh1800 per minute, and card phones.

TOURIST INFORMATION

Recommended in Zanzibar is a free quarterly magazine that has listings of cultural events, transport schedules, tide tables etc. *Swahili Coast* is similar, with hotel and restaurant listings.

Zanzibar Tourist Corporation (ZTC; Map p96; ☎ 223 8630; ztc@zanzinet.com; Bububu road) Headquartered in Livingstone House, the ZTC has helpful staff and a small selection of brochures.

TRAVEL AGENCIES

For excursions around the island and plane and ferry tickets, agencies to try include the following. Only make bookings and payments inside the offices, and not with anyone outside claiming to be staff.

Easy Travel & Tours (Map pp98-9; ☎ 223 5372; easytravel@zitec.org) Has branches in Arusha and Dar es Salaam.

Eco + Culture Tours (Map pp98-9; ☎ 223 0366; www .ecoculture-zanzibar.org; Hurumzi St) Also has a branch in Jambiani.

Fernandes Tours & Safaris (Map pp98-9; ☎ 223 0666; fts@zanlink.com; Vuga St)

Fisherman Tours & Travel (Map pp98-9; ☎ 223 8790; www.fishermantours.net; Vuga Rd)

Madeira Tours & Safaris (Map pp98-9; ☎ 223 0406; madeira@zanzinet.com) An efficient operator working with all price ranges.

Sama Tours (Map pp98-9; ☎ 223 3543; samatours@zitec.org; Hurumzi St) A reliable choice for everything from spice tours to excursions to the outlying islands.

Suna Tours (Map pp98-9; ☎ 223 7344)

Tima Tours (Map pp98-9; ☎ 223 1298; tima@zitec .org; Mizingani Rd)

Tropical Tours (Map p98-9; ☎ 223 0868, 0747-413454; tropicalts@hotmail.com; Kenyatta Rd) Friendly and helpful, this place is targeted at the budget market.

Zan Tours (Map pp98-9; ☎ 223 3042, 223 3116; www.zantours.com; Malawi Rd) Offers a wide range of quality upmarket tours on Zanzibar and Pemba and beyond.

Sights

If Zanzibar Town is the archipelago's heart, Stone Town is its soul, with a magical jumble of cobbled alleyways where it's easy to spend days wandering around and getting lost – although you can't get lost for long because, sooner or later, you'll end up on either the seafront or Creek Rd. Nevertheless, each twist and turn of the narrow streets brings something new – be it a school full of children chanting verses from the Quran, a beautiful old mansion with overhanging verandas, a coffee vendor with his long-spouted pot fastened over coals, clacking cups to attract custom, or a group of women in *bui-bui* sharing a joke and some local gossip. Along the way, watch the island's rich cultural melange come to life: Arabic-style houses with their recessed inner courtyards rub shoulders with Indian-influenced buildings boasting ornate balconies and latticework, and bustling oriental bazaars alternate with street-side vending stalls as lively as any on the Tanzanian mainland.

While the best part of Stone Town is simply letting it unfold before you, it's worth putting in an effort to see some of its major features.

BEIT EL-AJAIB (HOUSE OF WONDERS)

One of the most prominent buildings in the old Stone Town is the elegant **Beit el-Ajaib**, now home to the **Zanzibar National Museum of History & Culture** (Map pp98-9; Mizingani Rd; adult/child US$2/1; ⏰ 9am-6pm Mon-Fri, 9am-3pm Sat & Sun). It's also one of the largest structures in Zanzibar. It was built in 1883 by Sultan Barghash (1870–88) as a ceremonial palace. In 1896 it was the target of a British naval bombardment, the object of which was to force Khalid bin Barghash, who had tried to seize the throne after the death of Sultan Hamad (1893–96), to abdicate in favour of a British nominee. After it was rebuilt, Sultan Hamoud (1902–11) used the upper floor as a residential palace until his death. Later it was used as the local political headquarters of the CCM. Its enormous doors are said to be the largest carved doors in East Africa. Inside it houses exhibits on the dhow culture of the Indian Ocean (on the ground floor, and not yet completed) and on Swahili civilisation and 19th-century Zanzibar (1st floor). Everything is informatively labelled in English and Swahili, and well

---

PAPASI

In Zanzibar Town, you will undoubtedly come into contact with street touts. In Swahili, they're known as *papasi* (ticks). They are not registered as guides with the ZTC, although they may carry (false) identification cards, and while a few can be helpful, others can be aggressive and irritating. The main places that you'll encounter them are at the ferry dock in Zanzibar Town – where they can be quite overwhelming, especially if it's your first visit to the region – and in the Shangani area around Tembo House Hotel and the post office. Many of the more annoying ones are involved with Zanzibar's drug trade and are desperate for money for their next fix, which means you are just asking for trouble if you arrange anything with them.

If you do decide to use the services of a tout (and they're hard to avoid if you're arriving at the ferry dock for the first time and don't know your way around), tell them where you want to go or what you are looking for, and your price range. You shouldn't have to pay anything additional, as many hotels pay commission. If they tell you your hotel of choice no longer exists or is full, take it with a grain of salt, as it could well be that they just want to take you somewhere where they know they'll get a better commission.

Another strategy is to make your way out of the port arrivals area and head straight for a taxi. This will cost you more, and taxi drivers look for hotel commissions as well, but most are legitimate and once you are 'spoken for', hassles from touts usually diminish.

Most *papasi* are hoping that your stay on the island will mean ongoing work for them as your guide, so if you do use one to help you find a hotel, he'll invariably be outside waiting for you later. If you're not interested in this, explain this (politely) once you've arrived at your hotel. If you want a guide to show you around Stone Town, it's better to arrange one with your hotel or a travel agency. For any dealings with the *papasi*, if you're being hassled, a polite but firm approach usually works best – yelling or showing irritation, although quite tempting at times, just makes things worse. Another thing to remember is that you have a better chance of getting a discount on your hotel room if you arrive alone, since the hotel can then give you the discount that would have been paid to the touts as commission.

When arranging tours and excursions, never make payments on the street – be sure you're paying at a legitimate office, and get a receipt.

worth visiting. Greeting you at the entrance is a life-size *mtepe* – a traditional Swahili sailing vessel made without nails, the planks held together with only coconut fibres and wooden pegs.

BEIT EL-SAHEL (PALACE MUSEUM)

Just north of the Beit el-Ajaib is this palace, **Beit el-Sahel** (Map pp98-9; Mizingani Rd; admission US$3; 9am-6pm Mon-Fri, 9am-3pm Sat & Sun), which served as the sultan's residence until 1964, when the dynasty was overthrown. Now it is a museum devoted to the era of the Zanzibar sultanate.

The ground floor displays details of the formative period of the sultanate from 1828 to 1870, during which commercial treaties were signed between Zanzibar and the USA (1833), Britain (1839), France (1844) and the Hanseatic Republics (1859). There is also memorabilia of Princess Salme, a Zanzibari princess who eloped with a German to Europe and later wrote an autobiography. The exhibits on the 2nd floor focus on the period of affluence from 1870 to 1896, during which modern amenities such as piped water and electricity were introduced to Zanzibar under Sultan Barghash. The 3rd floor consists of the modest living quarters of the last sultan, Khalifa bin Haroub (1911–60), and his two wives, each of whom clearly had very different tastes in furniture. Outside is the Makusurani graveyard, where some of the sultans are buried.

OLD FORT

Just south of the Beit el-Ajaib is the **Old Fort** (Map pp98-9), a massive, bastioned structure originally built around 1700 on the site of a Portuguese chapel by Omani Arabs as a defence against the Portuguese. In recent years, it has been partially renovated to house the **Zanzibar Cultural Centre**, as well as the offices of the Zanzibar International Film Festival (ZIFF). Inside is an open-air theatre that hosts music and dance performances. There's also a small information centre that has schedules for performances, and the Neem Tree Café (p109). The tree growing inside the fort, in the area in front of the café, is known in Swahili as *mwarobaini* (forty) because its leaves, bark and other parts are used to cure up to 40 different ailments.

ANGLICAN CATHEDRAL & OLD SLAVE MARKET

Constructed in the 1870s by the Universities' Mission to Central Africa (UMCA), the **Anglican cathedral** (Map pp98-9; admission Tsh1000; 8am-6pm Mon-Sat) was the first Anglican cathedral in East Africa. It was built on the site of the old slave market alongside Creek Rd, although nothing remains of the slave market today other than some holding cells under St Monica's Hostel next door. Services are still held at the cathedral on Sundays; the entrance is next to St Monica's Hostel.

ST JOSEPH'S CATHEDRAL

One of the first sights travellers see when arriving at Zanzibar by ferry is the spires of **St Joseph's Roman Catholic cathedral** (Map pp98–9). Yet the church is deceptively difficult to find in the narrow confines of the adjacent streets. (The easiest route is to follow Kenyatta Rd to Gizenga St, then take the first right to the back gate of the church, which is usually open, even when the front entrance is closed.) The cathedral, which was designed by French architect Beranger and built by French missionaries, celebrated its centenary in 1998. There's a brief summary of the mission's history just inside the entrance. The church is still in use.

MOSQUES

The oldest of Stone Town's many mosques is the **Msikiti wa Balnara** (Malindi Minaret Mosque; Map p96), originally built in 1831, enlarged in 1841 and extended again by Seyyid Ali bin Said in 1890. Others include the **Aga Khan Mosque** and the impressive **Ijumaa Mosque**. It's not permitted to enter many of the mosques, as they're all in use, although exceptions may be made if you are appropriately dressed.

HAMAMNI PERSIAN BATHS

Built by Sultan Barghash in the late 19th century, these were the first public **baths** (Map pp98-9; admission Tsh500; Hamamni St) on Zanzibar. Although they're no longer functioning and there's no water inside, they're still worth a visit, and it doesn't take much imagination to envision them in bygone days. To get in, you'll need to ask the caretaker across the alley to unlock the gate.

BEIT EL-AMANI (PEACE MEMORIAL MUSEUM)

The larger of the two buildings that make up this **museum** (Map pp98-9; cnr Kaunda & Creek Rds) previously contained a poorly presented history of the island from its early days until independence, while the smaller building across the road housed a decaying natural history collection. Both are in the process of being rehabilitated and merged with the Zanzibar National Museum of History & Culture at the Beit el-Ajaib (p101), and are currently closed.

LIVINGSTONE HOUSE

Located about 2km north of town along the Bububu road, **Livingstone House** (Map p96) was built around 1860 and used as a base by many of the European missionaries and explorers before they started their journeys to the mainland. Today it's mostly remembered as the place where David Livingstone stayed before setting off on his last expedition. Now it houses the office of the Zanzibar Tourist Corporation. You can walk from town, or take a 'B' *dalla-dalla*.

OLD DISPENSARY

Near the port you'll find the **Old Dispensary** (Map pp98-9; Mizingani Rd), built at the turn of the 20th century by a wealthy Indian merchant. It has been impressively renovated by the Aga Khan Charitable Trust, and now houses boutiques and shops, and small displays of local artists' work.

FORODHANI GARDENS

One of the best ways to ease into life on the island is to stop by **Forodhani Gardens** (Jamituri Gardens; Map pp98-9) in the evening, when the grassy plaza comes alive with dozens of vendors serving up such delicacies as grilled *pweza* (octopus), plates of goat meat, Zanzibari pizza (rolled-up, omelette-filled chapati), a thick, delicious local version of naan, plus piles of chips, samosas and much more. The gardens are also a major social meeting point, with women sitting on the grass chatting about the events of the day, children playing and men strolling along the waterfront. It's all lit up, first by the setting sun, and then by small lanterns, and the ambience is superb. The gardens are along the sea opposite the Old Fort.

DARAJANI MARKET

The dark, narrow passageways of the chaotic **Darajani market** (Map pp98-9) assault the senses, with occasional whiffs of spices mixing with the stench of fish, the clamour

ZANZIBAR ARCHIPELAGO

STONE TOWN'S ARCHITECTURE

Stone Town's architecture is an evocative and practical fusion of Arabic, Indian, European and African influences. Arabic buildings are often square, with two or three storeys. Rooms line the outer walls, allowing space for an inner courtyard and verandas, and cooling air circulation. Indian buildings, also several storeys high, generally include a shop on the ground floor and living quarters above, with ornate façades and balconies. A common feature is the *baraza*, a stone bench facing into the street which serves as a focal point around which townspeople meet and chat.

The most famous feature of Zanzibari architecture is the carved wooden door. There are more than 500 remaining today in Stone Town, many of which are older than the houses in which they are set. The door, which was often the first part of a house to be built, served as a symbol of the wealth and status of a household. While older (Arabic) doors have a square frame with a geometrical shape, 'newer' doors – many of which were built towards the end of the 19th century and incorporate Indian influences – often have semicircular tops and intricate floral decorations.

Many doors are decorated with carvings of passages from the Quran. Other commonly seen motifs include images representing things desired in the household, such as a fish (expressing the hope for many children), chains (displaying the owner's wish for security), or the date tree (a symbol of prosperity). The lotus motif signifies regeneration and reproductive power, while the stylised backwards 'S' represents the smoke of frankincense and signifies wealth. Some doors have large brass spikes, which are a tradition from India, where spikes protected doors from being battered down by elephants. For more, look for a copy of the beautifully photographed and highly informative *Doors of Zanzibar* by Uwe Rau & Mwalim A Mwalim.

of vendors hawking their wares, neat, brightly coloured piles of fruits and vegetables, and dozens of small shops selling everything from plastic tubs to auto spares. It's just off Creek Rd, and at its best in the morning, before the heat and the crowds, and when everything is still fresh.

VICTORIA HALL & GARDENS

Diagonally opposite Mnazi Mmoja hospital on Kaunda Rd is the imposing **Victoria Hall** (Map pp98–9), housed the legislative council during the British era. The hall is not open to the public, but you can walk in the small surrounding gardens. Opposite is the **State House**, also closed to the public.

RUINS

There are a number of historical sites around Zanzibar Town. All can be easily reached as short excursions from town, and many are included in spice tours (p104).

Mbweni

Mbweni (Map p96), located around 5km south of Zanzibar Town, was the site of a 19th-century UMCA mission station that was used as a settlement for freed slaves. In addition to the small and still functioning St John's Anglican church, dating to the 1880s, you can see the atmospheric ruins of the UMCA's St Mary's School for Girls, set amidst lush gardens on the grounds of the Mbweni Ruins Hotel (p108).

Maruhubi Palace

The once-imposing Maruhubi Palace (Map p96), around 4km north of Zanzibar Town, was built by Sultan Barghash in 1882 to house his large harem. In 1899 it was almost totally destroyed by fire, although the remaining ruins – primarily columns that once supported an upper terrace, an overhead aqueduct, and small reservoirs covered with water lilies – hint at its previous scale. The ruins are just west of the Bububu road and signposted.

Mtoni Palace

The ruins of Mtoni Palace (Map p96), built by Sultan Seyyid Said as his residence in the early 19th century, are located just northeast of Maruhubi. In its heyday, the palace was a beautiful building with a balconied exterior, a large garden courtyard complete with pea-

cocks and gazelles, an observation turret and a mosque. By the mid-1880s the palace had been abandoned, and during WWI, parts of the compound were used as a supplies storehouse. Today, nothing remains of Mtoni's grandeur other than a few walls, although you can get an idea of how it must have looked once by reading Emily Said-Reute's *Memoirs of an Arabian Princess*. To get here, continue north on the main road past the Maruhubi Palace turn-off for about 2km, from where the ruins are signposted to the west.

Kidichi Persian Baths

The Kidichi Persian Baths, northeast of Zanzibar Town, are another construction of Sultan Seyyid, built in 1850 for his Persian wife at the island's highest point. Like the other nearby ruins, they're rather unremarkable now, but with a bit of imagination, you can see the Sultan's lavishly garbed coterie disrobing to test the waters. The décor, with its stylised birds and flowers, is typically Persian, though it's now in poor condition. To get here, take a No 502 *dalla-dalla* to the main Bububu junction, from where it's about a 3km walk east down an unsealed road. Look for the bathhouse to your right.

Activities

DIVING

For more on diving around the archipelago, see the boxed text on p94. Recommended dive operators:

Bahari Divers (Map pp98-9; ☎ 0748-245786, 0747-415011; www.zanzibar-diving.com) A small, friendly and professional outfit that primarily organises dives around the islands offshore from Stone Town. They offer a range of PADI certification courses, and cater to families (including rental of children's masks and fins).

One Ocean/The Zanzibar Dive Centre (Map pp98-9; ☎ 223 8374, 0748-750161; www.zanzibaroneocean .com) A PADI five-star centre, and one of the best dive operators on the islands, with more than a decade of experience on Zanzibar. They have branches at Matemwe Beach Village (Matemwe) and Bluebay Beach Resort (north of Kiwengwa) and can organise dives along the east coast, as well as around Stone Town, for divers of all levels. Their main office – just down from the tunnel and NBC bank – rents underwater cameras, prescription masks and Suunto computers.

SPICE TOURS

While spices no longer dominate Zanzibar's economy as they once did, plantations still dot the centre of the island. It's possible to visit them on 'spice tours', learning about what cloves, vanilla and other spices look like in the wild. These half-day excursions from Zanzibar Town take in some plantations, as well as some of the ruins described earlier and other sights of historical interest. Along the way you'll be invited to taste many of the spices, herbs and fruits that the island produces, including cloves, black pepper, cardamom, cinnamon, nutmeg, breadfruit, jackfruit, vanilla and lemongrass.

One of the best places to organise tours is through **Mr Mitu's office** (☎ 223 4636), which is signposted off Malawi Rd near Ciné Afrique. Tours cost US$10 per person in a group of about 15, and include a lunch of local food seasoned with some of the spices you've just seen. They depart about 9.30am and return by about 2.30pm (later, if a stop at Mangapwani beach is included). It's best to book a day in advance (they will then come to get you at your hotel), though it's usually no trouble to just show up in the morning.

To arrange other excursions around the island, see Travel Agencies (p100).

Festivals & Events

Muslim holidays are celebrated in a big way on Zanzibar. **Eid al-Fitr** (p311) especially is a fascinating time to be in Stone Town, with countless lanterns lighting the narrow passageways, families dressed in their best, and a generally festive atmosphere. Note that many restaurants close down completely during Ramadan.

Some festivals unique to Zanzibar (see p310 for more details):

Sauti za Busara (Voices of Wisdom) A celebration of all things Swahili, which got its start at Forodhani Gardens; well worth timing your visit to catch it in February.

Festival of the Dhow Countries and Zanzibar International Film Festival Film screenings, performing arts groups from around the region, village events and a wonderful, festive atmosphere; check www.ziff.or.tz or with the Zanzibar Cultural Centre at the Old Fort for details. Yearly in July.

Mwaka Kogwa The Shirazi New Year, also in July, is at its best in Makunduchi.

Sleeping
BUDGET

Stone Town has a large selection of budget guesthouses, most costing about the same, and with similar facilities – nets and fans, and usually shared bathrooms and cold-water showers. The standard price is US$10 per person (from US$15 with bathroom), though it's usually easy to negotiate this down to about US$8 in the off-season.

Mkunazini

The following options are in the Mkunazini area, on the eastern edge of town near the Anglican cathedral.

Riverman Hotel (Map pp98-9; ☎ 223 3188; river manhotel@yahoo.com; r per person without bathroom US$10) Basic rooms with net and fan, made more appealing by the friendly and ever-welcoming staff and a pleasant breakfast room on an adjoining porch. Just behind the Anglican cathedral.

St Monica's Hostel (Map pp98-9; ☎ 223 0773; monicaszanzibar@hotmail.com; s/d US$28/32, s/d/tr without bathroom US$12/24/36) An old, rambling place next to the Anglican cathedral, with spacious rooms, including some with a small veranda. Next door is the inexpensive St Monica's Restaurant (p109).

Flamingo Guest House (Map pp98-9; ☎ 223 2850; flamingoguesthouse@hotmail.com; Mkunazini St; s/d US$10/20, without bathroom US$8/16) No-frills but fine, with straightforward rooms and a TV.

Jambo Guest House (Map pp98-9; ☎ 223 3779; jamboguest@hotmail.com; r per person without bathroom US$10; ☒) Just around the corner from Flamingo Guest House, Jambo has free tea and coffee, clean rooms, decent breakfasts and an Internet café opposite. Green Garden Restaurant (p109) is just out front.

Soko Muhogo

Just south of Mkunazini, off Soko Muhogo St are a few more good places:

Haven Guest House (Map pp98-9; ☎ 223 5677/8; d US$25, r per person US$10) This place has clean rooms, a travellers' bulletin board, free coffee and tea and a small kitchenette.

Manch Lodge (Map pp98-9; ☎ 223 1918; moddy best@yahoo.com; r per person US$10) Around the corner from Haven Guest House and similar, though without the kitchenette; some rooms have a bathroom.

Vuga

The following places are near the southern edge of Stone Town, around Vuga Rd:

Florida Guest House (Map pp98-9; ☎ 0747-421421, 0747-411335; floridaznz@yahoo.com; Vuga Rd; r per person

US$15) This guesthouse has small, clean rooms (check out a few as they're all different) – many with bathroom – and solicitous proprietors. It's next to Culture Musical Club, and there are discounts for stays of more than two days.

Vuga Hotel (Map pp98-9; ☎ 223 3613; vuga hotel2001@yahoo.com; s/d US$25/38, without bathroom US$18/28) The Vuga Hotel has clean, no-frills rooms set around an uninspiring grey-toned interior courtyard; breakfast is not included. It's just off Vuga Rd in a small alley.

Garden Lodge (Map pp98-9; ☎ 223 3298; garden lodge@zanlink.com; Kaunda Rd; s/d/tr downstairs US$15/25/35, upstairs US$25/40/50) Friendly, family-run and somewhat pricier than others in this category, but the location – diagonally opposite the High Court – is convenient and rooms are good value, especially the upstairs ones, which are clean, bright and spacious. All have hot water, and there's a rooftop breakfast terrace.

Victoria House (Map pp98-9; ☎ 223 2861; r per person without bathroom US$10) This place has large, airy rooms, including a quad with its own shower, and an agreeably green location just off Kaunda Rd.

Malindi

On the northern side of town, and about a five-minute walk from the port, is a clutch of good places:

Bandari Lodge (Map pp98-9; ☎ 0747-423638; r per person US$12) Clean, bright rooms, plus a common kitchen and fridge. Turn right as you exit the port – it's just two minutes ahead.

Warere Town House (Map pp98-9; ☎ 223 3835; www.wareretownhouse.com; r per person US$10-15) Offers good-value rooms – some with small balconies and all with hot water – plus a rooftop terrace. It's just minutes from the port (they'll come meet you), and around the corner from Bandari Lodge.

Malindi Guest House (Map pp98-9; ☎ 223 0165; malindi@zanzinet.com; r per person with air-con US$20, without bathroom US$15; ✿) This guesthouse has whitewashed walls and attractive, atmospheric and well-maintained rooms.

Malindi Lodge (Map pp98-9; ☎ 223 2350; sunset bungalows@hotmail.com; s/d US$15/25; ✿) Clean and nicely decorated, and with hot water; it's just around the corner from Malindi Guest House.

Annex of Malindi Lodge (Map pp98-9; s/d without bathroom US$10/20) This is under the same management as the nearby Malindi Lodge, and just a small step down in standards.

Hotel Kiponda (Map pp98-9; ☎ 223 3052; hotel kiponda@email.com; Nyumbaya Moto St; d/tr US$45/55, s/d/tr without bathroom US$18/35/45) This hotel is pricier than others in this category, but rooms are spotless, the building is atmospheric, and the location – tucked away in a small lane near the waterfront – is convenient. There's also a restaurant.

Narrow St Hotel (Map pp98-9; ☎ 223 2620; narrow 22@yahoo.com; s/d US$25/40; ✿) This place has clean, straightforward rooms. Just off Malindi St, and roughly due south of the port.

Shangani

Karibu Inn (☎ 223 3058; karibuinn@zanzinet.com; dm US$10, s/d/tr without bathroom US$20/30/40) Karibu Inn has a convenient location in Shangani, at the western edge of Stone Town, but drab and pricey rooms; look at a few as they vary. Dorm rooms have either four, six or seven beds, and the hotel is often used by overland groups.

MID-RANGE
Shangani

Most mid-range places are in or near Shangani. All have fans, nets and bathroom with hot water, and some have air-con.

Baghani House Hotel (Map pp98-9; ☎ 223 5654; baghani@zanzinet.com; s/d US$30/55) This small, atmospheric hotel is one of the best value choices in this category, with rooms that are full of character – most on the upper level, reached via a steep staircase – dark wood and Zanzibari furnishings. Advance bookings and reconfirmations are recommended. It's just off Kenyatta Rd.

Chavda Hotel (Map pp98-9; ☎ 223 2115; chavda hotel@zanlink.com; Baghani St; s/d US$70/90) Chavda is a quiet, reliable hotel with some period décor and a range of bland, carpeted rooms with TV, telephone and minibar. The rooftop bar and restaurant are open during the high season only. It's just around the corner from Baghani House Hotel.

Mazsons Hotel (Map pp98-9; ☎ 223 3694; mazsons@zanlink.com; Kenyatta Rd; s/d US$60/80; ✿) The long-standing Mazsons has impressively restored lobby woodwork and a convenient location, which go some way to compensating for its rooms – modern and quite comfortable, though rather pallid. There's also a restaurant.

Africa House Hotel (Map pp98-9; ☎ 0747-432340; theafricahouse@zanlink.com; d from US$125; 🛇) This long-standing place is still brushing the dust away after a lengthy restoration, but if you don't mind a few paint chips on the carpets, it's worth a look. Some of the rooms have a sea view, and all are OK, although they don't quite live up to their potential. The best part of the hotel is its sunset terrace. There's also a mediocre restaurant, and a nightclub downstairs. It's near Mazsons Hotel, and just off Kenyatta Rd.

Other recommendations:

Shangani Hotel (Map p96; ☎ 223 3688, 223 6363; shanganihotel@hotmail.com; Kenyatta Rd; s/d US$65/80) An unpretentious place opposite Shangani post office, with cluttered but comfortable rooms, most with TV, fridge and fan, plus a restaurant.

Coco de Mer Hotel (Map p96; ☎ 223 0852; cocode mer_znz@yahoo.com; s/d/tr US$35/50/60) Conveniently located just off Kenyatta Rd, near the tunnel, and vaguely reminiscent of the Algarve, with white walls and tile work. Avoid the closet-sized room on the first floor, and the downstairs rooms – many of which have only interior windows.

Elsewhere in Stone Town

Outside the Shangani area are several more choices.

Clove Hotel (Map pp98-9; ☎ 0747-484567; www .zanzibarhotel.nl; Hurumzi St; s/d/f US$30/45/55) Newly renovated in pleasing shades of lavender and peach, Clove has good-value rooms with nets and fans. The family rooms also have small balconies with views down onto the small square below. On the rooftop is a terrace for breakfast, drinks and views.

Hotel International (Map pp98-9; ☎ 223 3182; hotelinter@zanlink.com; s/d US$45/60; 🛇) The International, a cavernous multistorey place, is just off Kiponda St, with a forex bureau, a restaurant and rather soulless rooms, though some aren't bad. It's worth checking a few (avoid those on the lower floor). Most have TV, fridge and small balcony, and there's a rooftop terrace.

Beit al-Aman (Map pp98-9; ☎ 0747-414364; beit2000@hotmail.com; s/d US$30/60, house US$250; 🛇) This attractively furnished private house has six rooms and a small kitchen, and can be rented out by the room, or in its entirety. It's ideal if you know Zanzibar and want a place to relax away from the hotel scene;

breakfast is included in the price. It's on a small side street between Kaunda and Vuga Rds, near Victoria Gardens.

TOP END
Shangani

Tembo House Hotel (Map pp98-9; ☎ 223 3005; www. tembohotel.com; s/d from US$85/95; 🛇 🛋) This attractively restored building has a prime waterfront location, and comfortable rooms – some with sea views – in new and old wings. Most have a TV and fridge, and there's a small pool, a restaurant and a good buffet breakfast on the seaside terrace, though no alcohol is served. The hotel is a favourite with tour groups.

Dhow Palace (Map pp98-9; ☎ 223 3012; dhow palace@zanlink.com; s/d US$60/80; 🛇 Jun-Mar; 🛋) This is another classic place with old Zanzibari décor, a fountain in the tastefully restored lobby and comfortable, well-appointed rooms. It's just off Kenyatta Rd, and under the same management as Tembo House Hotel.

Zanzibar Serena Inn (Map pp98-9; ☎ 223 2306, 223 3587; zserena@zanzinet.com; s/d from US$190/240; 🛇 🛋) The Zanzibar Serena, in the refurbished Extelecoms House, is Zanzibar Town's most upmarket accommodation, with a beautiful setting on the water, plush rooms with all the amenities, and a business centre.

Shangani Apartment (Map pp98-9; www.allabout zanzibar.com; apt US$150) This atmospheric two-bedroom is in a restored building with views. It's off Kenyatta Rd in Shangani; discounted long-term rates are available.

Hurumzi

Emerson & Green (Map pp98-9; ☎ 223 0171, 0747-423266; www.emerson-green.com; Hurumzi St; r US$165-200) Emerson & Green – in two adjacent historic buildings that have been completely restored – is full of character and has become a Zanzibar institution. Each room is unique – one even has its own private rooftop teahouse – and all are decadently decorated to give you an idea of what Zanzibar must have been like in its heyday. There's also a famous rooftop restaurant with wide views over town (p108). It's several winding blocks east of the Old Fort.

Outside Stone Town

Just outside Stone Town are a few more options that make agreeable bases if you want proximity to the town as well as greenery and relaxing surroundings.

Mtoni Marine Centre (Map p96; ☎ 225 0140; mtoni@zanzibar.cc; budget s/d US$25/30, 2/3-bed bungalows US$100/150, sea view s/d US$70/100; ⚙ ⚘) This family-friendly establishment has a range of accommodation options, including small budget rooms, larger family-style cottages set around pleasant gardens, and spacious sea-view rooms with private balconies. There's a small beach, a popular waterside bar and good dining in the main restaurant. It's in large grounds overlooking the water about 3km north of town along the Bububu road. The hotel is run by Coastal Travels (p62), and they have various package deals from Dar es Salaam. Their town booking office is next to Zanzibar Serena Inn.

Mbweni Ruins Hotel (Map p96; ☎ 223 5478; www.mbweni.com; s/d US$95/175; ⚙ ⚘) Mbweni is a quiet, genteel establishment set in large, lushly vegetated gardens about 5km from town, and several kilometres off the airport road. In addition to well-appointed rooms and a relaxing ambience, it has stands of mangroves for bird-watching and a restaurant. The property was formerly the site of the UMCA mission school for the children of freed slaves.

Maruhubi Beach Villas (Map p96; ☎ 0747-451188; maruhubi@zanlink.com; 6-person self-catering villa US$200, s/d in serviced villa US$80/120, air-con per villa per day US$20; ☽ Jun–mid-Apr; ⚙) A promising place (once the gardens grow in), with five chalets lined up facing the water just south of Mtoni Marine Centre, and nearing completion when this book was researched. Each of the chalets has two en suite bedrooms, a fully equipped kitchen and a porch, and there's a restaurant and a barbecue area. The chalets are rented on either a self-catered or serviced basis, with breakfast included in the serviced price.

Eating

Stone Town has a wide selection of eateries, enough to keep even the most avid gastronomes happily occupied for days. Note that during the low season and Ramadan, many restaurants close or operate reduced hours.

RESTAURANTS

Monsoon Restaurant (Map pp98-9; ☎ 0747-411362, 0747-410410; meals Tsh4000-10,000; ☽ noon-midnight)

The impeccably decorated Monsoon is one of the most atmospheric options, with traditional-style dining on floor cushions, and excellent Swahili cuisine served to a backdrop of *taarab* (see the boxed text, p110) or other traditional music. It's at the southwestern edge of Forodhani Gardens.

Archipelago Café-Restaurant (Map pp98-9; ☎ 223 5668; mains from Tsh3500-6000; ☽ lunch & dinner) This new place has an excellent, breezy location on a 1st-floor terrace overlooking the water just opposite NBC bank in Shangani, and a menu featuring such delicacies as vegetable coconut curry, orange and ginger snapper and chicken pilau, topped off by an array of home-made cakes and sweets. There's no bar, but you can bring your own alcohol.

La Fenice (Map pp98-9; ☎ 0747-411868; Shangani St; meals Tsh8000; ☽ lunch & dinner) A breezy little patch of Italy on the waterfront, La Fenice has the best Italian cuisine in Stone Town and outdoor tables where you can enjoy your pasta while gazing out at the turquoise sea in front of you. For dessert, try a scoop of the smooth and delicious home-made Italian ice cream.

Amore Mio (Map pp98-9; Shangani St; ☽ high season only) Across the road from La Fenice, Amore Mio also has delectable ice cream, as well as light meals and good coffees and cappuccinos.

Sweet Eazy (Map pp98-9; ☎ 0747-416736; sweet eazy@retom.com; meals Tsh4000-8000; ☽ noon-midnight) With its relaxing ambience, good Thai and African cuisine, and varied entertainment offerings, this place is one of Stone Town's more popular evening destinations. It's also one of the few spots in town where you can get food late at night. In addition to the main menu, there are luxuries such as fresh fruit shakes, salads and light meals. It's on the waterfront near NBC bank, and just down from One Ocean/The Zanzibar Dive Centre.

Emerson & Green Tower Top Restaurant (Map pp98-9; ☎ 223 0171, 0747-423266; www.emerson -green.com; Hurumzi St; meals US$25-30; ☽ dinner) Dinner at this rooftop restaurant has become a Zanzibar institution, and while its popularity means that it is no longer the intimate dining experience it once was, it still makes an enjoyable evening out. The menu is fixed, and reservations are essential. On Friday, Saturday and Sunday, meals are served to a backdrop of traditional music and dance.

Kidude (Map pp98-9; ☎ 0747-423266; Hurumzi St; meals Tsh4000-8000; lunch & dinner) If the Tower Top Restaurant is booked out, you can console yourself with a meal at Emerson & Green's very nice and air-con ground-level restaurant. The lunch menu features sandwiches, salads and cakes; in the evening, there's a set menu, a happy hour and a well-stocked bar.

Mtoni Marine Centre (Map p96; ☎ 225 0140; mtoni@zanzibar.cc; meals Tsh8000-Tsh20,000; dinner) The main restaurant here has what many connoisseurs consider to be the finest cuisine in Stone Town, with a range of seafood and meat grills, and waterside barbecues (Tsh17,500) on Tuesday and Saturday, with a backdrop of *taarab* or other traditional music.

Mcheza Bar (Map p96; meals about Tsh5000; lunch & dinner) This beachside spot with burgers and pub food is next door to the Mtoni Marine Centre.

Mercury's (Map pp98-9; ☎ 223 3076; meals Tsh5000; 10am-midnight) Named in honour of Queen vocalist Freddie Mercury (who was born just a few blocks away), this is Stone Town's main waterside hang-out. On offer are good seafood grills and pizzas, a well-stocked bar and a terrace that's a prime location for sipping sundowners.

Sambusa Two Tables Restaurant (Map pp98-9; ☎ 223 1979; meals Tsh8000; dinner) For sampling authentic Zanzibari dishes, it's hard to beat this small, family-run restaurant just off Kaunda Rd, where the proprietors bring out course after course of delicious local delicacies. Advance reservations are required.

Radha Food House (Map pp98-9; ☎ 223 4808; thalis Tsh4500) This great little place is tucked away on the small side street just before the Shangani tunnel. The menu – strictly vegetarian – features *thalis*, refreshingly cool lassis, home-made yogurt and other dishes from the subcontinent.

Other recommendations:

China Plate Restaurant (Map pp98-9; ☎ 0744-846569; lunch & dinner) Tasty Chinese food served on a breezy 1st-floor terrace overlooking the water.

Pagoda Chinese Restaurant (Map pp98-9; ☎ 223 1758; meals Tsh5000; lunch & dinner) More of the same, but without the breezes or sea views and with a good-value lunch menu.

Le Spice Rendez-Vous (Kenyatta Rd; meals Tsh6000; 11.30am-3pm & 6.30pm-late Tue-Sun) Pricey Indian and French cuisine in a Western ambience.

Neem Tree Café (Map pp98-9; Old Fort; meals Tsh3000-5000; 8am-10pm) Reasonable local grub, and traditional dance and drum performances (see p110).

Zanzibar Serena Inn (Map pp98-9; ☎ 223 2306, 223 3587; meals from Tsh9000; lunch & dinner) Fine dining overlooking the sea. Wednesday evening features a sumptuous Swahili buffet (US$25) served on the outside terrace.

QUICK EATS

Forodhani Gardens (Map pp98-9; meals from Tsh500; dinner) These fantastic waterside gardens (see p103) have the best-value street food in Zanzibar, if not in all Tanzania, with piles of grilled fish and meat, chips, snacks and more, all served up on a paper plate or rolled into a piece of newspaper, and eaten while sitting on benches or on the lawn, soaking up the atmosphere and enjoying the passing scene. The ambience is superb, and once you've given it a try, it's likely you'll come back night after night for more. Locals advise against eating fish and meat during the height of the low season (when food turnover is slower), but countless travellers come here, and we've never heard of any problems.

For something more mundane, there are plenty of places where you can eat well for under Tsh5000. All serve up a mix of local dishes and grills; most are around Kenyatta Rd and the Shangani area.

Fany's Green Restaurant (Map pp98-9; ☎ 223 3918; Kenyatta Rd; 7.30am-10pm)

Dolphin Restaurant (Map pp98-9; Kenyatta Rd; lunch & dinner) Next to Fany's Green Restaurant.

Baracuda (Kenyatta Rd; lunch & dinner) Also next to Fany's Green Restaurant.

Green Garden (Map pp98-9; meals Tsh2500; lunch & dinner) Nice outdoor tables in front of Jambo Guest House, off Mkunazini St.

St Monica's Restaurant (Map pp98-9; ☎ 223 0773; monicaszanzibar@hotmail.com; meals from Tsh1500; 8am-3pm Mon-Sat) Cheap and reliable; next to the Anglican cathedral in Mkunazini.

Dolly's Patisserie (Map pp98-9; cnr Shangani St & Kenyatta Rd; snacks from Tsh500; 7am-8pm) Breads, cakes, yogurt and other snacks.

SELF-CATERING

Shamshuddin's Cash & Carry (Map pp98-9; Soko St) Just behind the Darajani market.

ZANZIBAR ARCHIPELAGO

Drinking & Entertainment

Stone town isn't known for its nightlife, but there are a few popular spots.

BARS & NIGHTCLUBS

Sweet Eazy (Map pp98-9; ☎ 0747-416736; sweet eazy@retom.com) Live music Friday and Saturday evenings, daily happy hour and sundowners overlooking the water, big-screen sports and movie viewings, and more.

Garage Club (Map pp98-9; Shangani St; ☯ from 10pm Wed-Mon) Diagonally opposite Tembo House Hotel, this is Stone Town's main disco. Taxis wait outside, and it's a good idea to take one back to your hotel rather than walking.

Dharma Lounge (Map pp98-9; Shangani St; ☯ 5pm-late Wed-Mon) Zanzibar's first and only cocktail lounge, with big cushions for relaxing, a well-stocked bar, air-con, a good selection of music and even a karaoke night (Thursday). It's next to the Garage Club.

Other recommendations:

Mercury's (Map pp98-9; ☎ 223 3076; meals Tsh5000) Waterside sundowners, and live music many nights.
Starehe Club (Map pp98-9; Shangani St) Very laid back (in fact sometimes it doesn't happen at all), with occasional reggae nights.
Mcheza Bar (Map p96; ☎ 225 0140; mtoni@zanzibar .cc) A happening sports bar that draws mainly an expat crowd.

TRADITIONAL MUSIC & DANCE

Zanzibar's most famous contribution to the world music scene is *taarab*; for more information and details on where to hear it, see the boxed text, p110.

On Tuesday, Thursday and Saturday evening from 7pm to 10pm, there are traditional *ngoma* (dance and drumming) performances at the Old Fort (Tsh4000, with dinner Tsh10,000), although be prepared for rather flat tourist displays.

Shopping

Stone Town has wonderfully atmospheric craft shopping, and – if you can sort your

---

TAARAB MUSIC

No visit to Zanzibar would be complete without spending an evening listening to the evocative strains of *taarab*, the archipelago's most famous musical export. *Taarab*, from the Arabic *tariba* (roughly, 'to be moved'), fuses African, Arabic and Indian influences, and is considered by many Zanzibaris to be a unifying force among the island's many cultures. A traditional *taarab* orchestra consists of several dozen musicians using both Western and traditional instruments, including the violin, the *kanun* (similar to a zither), the accordion, the *nay* (an Arabic flute) and drums, plus a singer. There's generally no written music, and songs – often with themes centring around love – are full of puns and double-meanings.

Taarab-style music was played in Zanzibar as early as the 1820s at the sultan's palace, where it had been introduced from Arabia. However, it wasn't until the 1900s, when Sultan Seyyid Hamoud bin Muhammed encouraged formation of the first *taarab* clubs, that it became more formalised.

One of the first clubs founded was Akhwan Safaa, established in 1905 in Zanzibar Town. Since then, numerous other clubs have sprung up, including the well-known Culture Musical Club and the smaller, more traditional Twinkling Stars, which is an offshoot of Akhwan Safaa. Many of the newer clubs have abandoned the traditional acoustic style in favour of electronic equipment, although older musicians tend to look down on this as an adulterated form of *taarab*. The performances themselves are quite an event. In the more traditional clubs, men and women sit separately, with the women decked out in their finest garb and elaborate hairstyles. Audience participation is key, and listeners frequently go up to the stage to give money to the singer.

For an introduction to *taarab* music, stop by the Zanzibar Serena Inn, where the Twinkling Stars play on Tuesday and Friday evening on the veranda from about 6pm to 7.30pm. For something much livelier, head to the **Culture Musical Club** (Vuga Rd), with a classic old-style club atmosphere and rehearsals from about 7.30pm to 9.30pm Monday to Friday. Akhwan Safaa has rehearsals several times weekly from about 9.30pm in the area off Creek Rd near the traffic police; locals can point you in the right direction. An excellent time to see *taarab* performances is during the Festival of the Dhow Countries (p311) in July.

way through some of the kitsch – there are some excellent buys to be found. Items to watch for include finely crafted Zanzibari chests, *kanga* (cotton wraps worn by women all over Tanzania), *kikoi* (the thicker striped or plaid equivalent worn by men on Zanzibar and in other coastal areas), spices and handcrafted silver jewellery.

A good place to start is Gizenga St, which is lined with small shops and craft dealers. **Zanzibar Gallery** (Map pp98-9; ☎ 223 2721; cnr Kenyatta Rd & Gizenga St; ☒ 9am-7pm Mon-Sat, 9am-1pm Sun) is also excellent, with a large collection of souvenirs, textiles, woodcarvings, antiques and more, in addition to its books. **Memories of Zanzibar** (Kenyatta Rd) has a large selection of jewellery, textiles and curios, while the **Zanzibar Curio Shop** (Hurumzi St) is a grandmother's attic-type place filled with many antique look-alikes, plus a few of the real thing. At the western end of Forodhani Gardens are vendors selling woodcarvings, Maasai beaded jewellery and other crafts. **Moto** (Hurumzi St), a small crafts outlet opposite the Zanzibar Curio Shop, sells baskets, mats and other woven products, plus batiks and textiles – all made by a local women's cooperative. The cooperative itself is based in Pete, shortly before Jozani Forest (p124), and welcomes visitors to see how the crafts are made using environmentally sustainable technologies.

Getting There & Away
AIR
There are daily flights connecting Zanzibar with Dar es Salaam (US$55), Arusha (US$140 to US$175), Pemba (US$70), Selous Game Reserve and the northern parks on Coastal Aviation and ZanAir. Coastal Aviation also goes daily to/from Tanga via Pemba (US$80), and has a special value day excursion package from Dar es Salaam to Stone Town for US$80 including return flights, lunch and airport transfers – excellent value for anyone who is short on time. Air Tanzania and Precision Air also fly daily between Zanzibar and Dar es Salaam, with connections to Nairobi. Precision Air, in partnership with Kenya Airways, has a direct flight between Zanzibar and Nairobi. Note that the Nairobi–Zanzibar flight is routinely overbooked, and passengers are frequently bumped (especially if they've booked through Precision Air). Reconfirm

your seat many times, and arrive early at the airport.

There are direct international connections from Zanzibar on Oman Air via Muscat and on Kenya Airways via Nairobi.

Airline offices in Zanzibar Town include the following:

Air Tanzania (Map pp98-9; ☎ 223 0213; Vuga Rd)
Coastal Aviation (Map pp98-9; ☎ 223 3112, 0747-334582) Next to Zanzibar Serena Inn, and at the airport.
Kenya Airways (Map pp98-9; ☎ 223 2041/3; Vuga Rd) At ZAT Travel.
Oman Air (Map pp98-9; ☎ 223 8308; Mizingani Rd) Just southeast of the Big Tree.
Precision Air (Map pp98-9; ☎ 223 4520; www .precisionairtz.com; Kenyatta Rd)
ZanAir (Map pp98-9; ☎ 223 3670; www.zanair.com) Just off Malawi Rd, opposite Ciné Afrique.

BOAT
For information on ferry connections between Zanzibar and Dar es Salaam see p84. For ferry connections between Zanzibar and Pemba, see p133. You can get tickets at the port, or through a travel agent. If you leave Zanzibar on the *Flying Horse* night ferry, take care with your valuables, especially when the boat docks in Dar es Salaam in the early morning hours.

Dhows link Zanzibar with Dar es Salaam, Tanga, Bagamoyo and Mombasa (Kenya). Foreigners are not permitted on dhows between Dar es Salaam and Zanzibar. For other routes, the best place to ask is at the beach behind Tembo House Hotel. Allow anywhere from 10 to 48 hours or more to/from the mainland; also see the boxed text, p328.

TRAIN
Riverman Hotel (p105) can help you make bookings for the Tazara line for a Tsh1000 fee; you pay for the ticket at the Tazara train station in Dar es Salaam.

Getting Around
TO/FROM THE AIRPORT
The airport is about 7km southeast of Zanzibar Town and Tsh6000 in a taxi, though you'll need to bargain hard to get this rate. The No 505 bus line also does this route, departing from the corner opposite Mnazi Mmoja hospital. Many Stone Town hotels offer free airport pick-ups for confirmed bookings, though some charge. For hotels elsewhere on the island, transfers usually

cost about US$25 to US$30, depending on location.

CAR & MOTORCYCLE

It's easy to arrange car, moped or motorcycle rental and prices are reasonable, although breakdowns are fairly common, as are moped accidents. Considering how small the island is, it's often more straightforward and not that much more expensive just to work out a good deal with a taxi driver.

You'll need either an international driving licence, a licence from Kenya, Uganda or South Africa, or a Zanzibar permit – there are lots of police checkpoints along the roads where you'll be asked to show one or the other. Zanzibar permits can be obtained on the spot at the **traffic police office** (cnr Malawi & Creek Rds) for Tsh6000. If you rent through a tour company they'll sort out the paperwork.

Daily rental rates average about US$25 for a moped, US$30 for a motorcycle, and from US$50 to US$70 for a Suzuki 4WD, with better deals available for longer-term rentals. You can rent through any of the tour companies, through **Asko Tours & Travel** (☎ 223 0712; askotour@hotmail.com; Kenyatta Rd) next to Shangani post office, or by asking around in front of the market, near the bus station. If you're not mechanically minded, bring someone along with you who can check that the motorbike or vehicle you're renting is in reasonable condition, and take a test drive. Full payment is usually required at the time of delivery, but don't pay any advance deposits.

PRIVATE MINIVAN

Private minivans run daily to Nungwi and to Paje, Bwejuu and Jambiani on the east coast, although stiff competition and lots of hassles with touts mean that a splurge on a taxi isn't a bad idea. Book through any travel agency the day before you want to travel, and the vans will pick you up at your hotel in Stone Town between 8am and 9am. Travel takes 1½ to two hours to any of the destinations, and costs a negotiable Tsh3000 per person. Don't pay for the return trip in advance as you'll probably see neither the driver nor your money again. Most drivers only go to hotels where they'll get a commission, and will go to every length to talk you out of other places, including telling you that the hotel is closed/full/burned down etc.

DALLA-DALLAS

Dalla-dallas packed with people and produce link all major towns on the island, leaving from Creek Rd opposite Darajani market. For most destinations, including all the main beaches, there are several vehicles daily, with the last ones back to Stone Town departing by about 3pm or 4pm. None of the routes cost more than Tsh1000, and all take plenty of time (eg about three hours from Zanzibar Town to Jambiani). All have destination signboards and numbers. Commonly used routes include the following:

Route No	Destination
101	Mkokotoni
116	Nungwi
117	Kiwengwa
118	Matemwe
121	Donge
206	Chwaka
214	Uroa
308	Unguja Ukuu
309	Jambiani
310	Makunduchi
324	Bwejuu
326	Kizimkazi
501	Amani
502	Bububu
504	Fuoni
509	Chukwani
505	Airport (marked 'U/Ndege')
501	Mtoni/Kidatu

TAXI

Taxis don't have meters, so you'll need to agree on a price with the driver before getting into the car. Town trips cost Tsh1000 to Tsh1500, and Tsh2000 at night.

AROUND ZANZIBAR

BEACHES

Zanzibar has superb beaches, with the best along the island's east coast and to the north. Although some have become overcrowded and built-up, all offer a wonderful respite from bumping along dusty roads on the mainland, or from dreary London winters. The east-coast beaches are protected by coral reefs offshore and have fine, white coral sand. Depending on the season, they may also have a lot of seaweed (most abun-

BEST BEACHES

Almost all of Zanzibar's beaches would be considered superlative if they were located anywhere else, but a few stand out, even here:

- Matemwe – for its powdery, white sands and intriguing village life
- Pongwe – for its crystal waters and lack of crowds
- Jambiani – for the otherworldly turquoise shades of its waters
- Bwejuu – 'palm fringed coastline' takes on a new dimension here
- Kendwa – wide, white and swimmable around the clock

dant from December to February). Locals harvest the seaweed for export, and you'll see it drying in the sun in many villages.

Everyone has their favourites, and which beach you choose is a matter of preference. For meeting other travellers, enjoying some nightlife, and staying at relatively inexpensive accommodation, the best choices are Nungwi in the far north, followed by Paje on the east coast. Bwejuu and Jambiani on the east coast are also popular – and have some of the finest stretches of palm-fringed sand you'll find anywhere – but everything is more spread out and quieter here than in the north. For a much quieter atmosphere, try Matemwe, Pongwe or the southern end of Kiwengwa. If you're seeking the large resort scene, the main area is the beach north of Kiwengwa towards Pwani Mchangani. The attractive section of coast north of Bwejuu near the tip of Ras Michamvi is ideal if you're looking for top-end standards away from the large resorts. Except for Nungwi (and nearby Kendwa beach), where you can take a dip at any time, swimming at all of the beaches is tide dependent.

Bububu (Fuji Beach)

This modest stretch of sand, 10km north of town in Bububu, is the closest place to Zanzibar Town for swimming, though if you're after a beach holiday, it's better to head further north or east. It's accessed via the dirt track heading west from just north of the Bububu police station.

SLEEPING

Salome's Garden (www.salomes-garden.com; house per day US$425) The decadently luxurious Salome's Garden, set in large gardens a few hundred metres from the beach, is a rehabilitated plantation house which once belonged to the Omani royal family. It's now sumptuously decorated in traditional Zanzibari style, and can be rented in its entirety (up to 10 people). Rates double during peak season.

Bububu Beach Guest House (☎ 225 0110; www.bububu-zanzibar.com; s/d US$15/25) This good budget haunt has clean, airy no-frills rooms near the beach, and meals can be arranged. Next door, and under the same management, is an eight-person self-catering house that can be rented in its entirety. The guesthouse is at the end of the dirt track heading west from the Bububu police station; the staff will come and collect you free from the airport or Stone Town, and can organise excursions around the island.

Imani Beach Villa (☎ 225 0050; www.imani.it; d from US$60; 🏊) This small villa, set in lush gardens just back from the beach and south of Bububu Beach Guest House, has good-value rooms and a very good restaurant. Dining is at low tables with floor cushions, and features intriguing cuisine mixing Swahili, Mediterranean and other influences.

Mangapwani

The small and unremarkable beach at Mangapwani is notable mainly for its nearby caves, and is frequently included as a stop on spice tours.

The caves are located about 20km north of Zanzibar Town along the coast, and are an easy walk from Mangapwani beach. There are actually two locations. The first is a large **natural cave** with a freshwater pool that is rumoured to have been used in connection with the slave trade. North of here is the sobering **slave cave**, a dank, dark cell that was used as a holding pen to hide slaves after the legal trade was abolished in the late 19th century.

There are no facilities at Mangapwani other than the **Mangapwani Seafood Grill** (☎ 223 2306, 223 3587; meals Tsh6000-8000; 🍴 lunch), with a bar, sandwiches and seafood grills. It's run by Zanzibar Serena Inn (p107).

To get to the beach, follow the main road north from Zanzibar Town past Bububu to

ZANZIBAR ARCHIPELAGO

Chuini, from where you head left down a dirt road for about 8km towards Mangapwani village and the beach. Zanzibar Serena Inn provides a shuttle twice daily in the high season, departing from the hotel at 10am and 3.30pm, and returning at 2.30pm and 6.30pm. *Dalla-dallas* also run between Stone Town and Mangapwani village, from where it's a short walk to the beach. Just before reaching the restaurant area, there's a small sign for the caves, or ask locals to point the way.

Nungwi

This large village, nestled among the palm groves at Zanzibar's northernmost tip, is a dhow-building centre, and one of the island's major tourist destinations. It's also where traditional and modern knock against each other with full force. On the beautiful white-sand beach, fishermen sit in the shade repairing their nets while the morning's catch dries on neat wooden racks nearby, and rough-hewn planks slowly take on new life as skilled boat builders ply their centuries-old trade. Yet you only need to take a few steps back from the sand to enter into another world, with blaring music, a slick Internet café, a rather motley collection of guesthouses packed in against each other, and a definite party atmosphere. For some travellers it's the only place to be on the island (and it's one of the few places on Zanzibar where you can swim round the clock, without needing to wait for the tides to come in); others will probably want to give it a wide miss. Most hotels, the better beaches, and the centre of all the action are just north and west of Nungwi village, where it can get quite crowded. If partying isn't your scene, there are some lovely, quiet patches of sand on Nungwi's eastern side, and quiet Kendwa (p116) is only a short boat-ride away.

INFORMATION

There's Internet access at Amaan Bungalows and at Nungwi Inn Hotel, and a forex bureau at Amaan Bungalows that changes cash and travellers cheques at a high commission.

THE SLAVE TRADE

Slavery has been practised in Africa throughout recorded history, but its greatest expansion in East Africa came with the rise of Islam, which prohibits the enslavement of Muslims. Demands of European plantation holders on the islands of Réunion and Mauritius were another major catalyst, particularly during the second half of the 18th century.

At the outset, slaves were taken from coastal regions and shipped to Arabia, Persia and the Indian Ocean islands. Kilwa Kisiwani was one of the major export gateways. As demand increased, traders made their way further inland, so that during the 18th and 19th centuries, slaves were being brought from as far away as Malawi and the Congo. By the 19th century, with the rise of the Omani Arabs, Zanzibar had eclipsed Kilwa Kisiwani as East Africa's major slave-trading depot. According to some estimates, by the 1860s from 10,000 to as many as 50,000 slaves were passing through Zanzibar's market each year. Overall, close to 600,000 slaves were sold through Zanzibar between 1830 and 1873, when a treaty with Britain finally ended the regional trade.

As well as the human horrors, the slave trade caused major social upheavals on the mainland. In the sparsely populated and politically decentralised south, it fanned up inter-clan warfare as ruthless entrepreneurs raided neighbouring tribes for slaves. In other areas the slave trade promoted increased social stratification and altered settlement patterns. Some tribes, for example, began to build fortified settlements encircled by trenches, while others – notably the Nyamwezi and other central-Tanzanian peoples – concentrated their populations in towns as self-defence. Another fundamental societal change was the gradual shift in the nature of chieftaincy from religiously based position to one resting on military power or wealth – both among the 'gains' of trade in slaves and commodities.

The slave trade also served as an impetus for European missionary activity in East Africa – prompting establishment of the first mission stations, as well as missionary penetration of the interior. After the abolishment of slavery on Zanzibar, the Universities' Mission to Central Africa (UMCA) took over the slave market, and built the Anglican cathedral that still stands on the site today.

Because of the large number of tourists in Nungwi, it's easy to overlook the fact that you're in a traditional, conservative environment. Be respectful, especially in your dress and in your interactions with locals, and ask permission before snapping photos. Also, watch your valuables, and don't walk along the beach alone or with valuables, especially at night.

SIGHTS & ACTIVITIES

Other than diving, snorkelling and relaxing on the beach, you can watch the dhow builders, or visit the **Mnarani Aquarium** (admission Tsh1000; 9am-6pm), home to a small family of hawksbill turtles. It's near the lighthouse at the northernmost tip of Ras Nungwi. The lighthouse, which dates to 1886, is still in use and not open to the public.

The area's main attraction is diving. The best diving in the north is around Mnemba, which can be readily arranged from Nungwi, though it's a bit of a ride to get there. Leven Bank is closer and can be quite rewarding, but you'll need previous experience. Otherwise, there are a collection of sites closer in that are good for beginners. For more on diving around Zanzibar, see the boxed text, p94. Locally based operators include the following:

East Africa Diving & Water Sport Centres (0747-420588; www.diving-zanzibar.com) Next to Amaan Bungalows.

Ras Nungwi Beach Hotel (223 3767; www.rasnungwi.com) A PADI five-star centre based at Ras Nungwi Beach Hotel.

Sazani Beach Dive Centre (024-224 0014; www.sazanibeach.com) At Sazani Beach hotel; caters primarily to couples and small groups.

Spanish Dancer Dive Centre (224 0091, 0747-417717; www.spanishdancerdivers.com) At Nungwi Inn Hotel.

SLEEPING & EATING

The main cluster of guesthouses is on the western side of Nungwi, where there's not much ambience (and little to distinguish between the various places), but plenty of activity. Just northeast of here are Nungwi's only camping area and a few other decent shoestring options. Further east, around the tip of the cape and past the lighthouse, everything gets much quieter, with a handful of hotels spread along a low cliff overlooking the water, surrounded by empty tracts of scrub vegetation. Many of Nungwi's hotels have restaurants, and in the village there's a tiny shop with a few basics. For anything more than that, you'll need to shop in Zanzibar Town.

Budget

In the village centre there are several basic guesthouses, the best of which is the no-frills **Morning Star Guest House** (224 0045; r per person without bathroom US$10). However, almost everyone stays in one of the places on the beach, all of which are within a few minutes' walk of each other.

Cholo's (camping per person US$5, bandas per person without bathroom US$10) Very chilled out, and the only spot to pitch a tent; they also have some basic *bandas* (thatched-roof huts with wooden or earthen walls), plus Nungwi's best bar.

Jambo Brothers (s/d without bathroom US$15/25) Low key, with clean, no-frills rooms on the sand, just next to Cholo's, and meals (order early).

Union Beach Bungalows (s/d without bathroom US$15/25) Next to Jambo Brothers, this is another agreeable shoestring option.

Amaan Bungalows (224 0026; www.amaanbungalows.com; s US$25-40, d US$30-60, s/d with sea views US$50/75; meals Tsh4000;) At the centre of activity, and the biggest place, with various levels of accommodation, including nicer sea view rooms, plus several restaurants.

Baraka Beach Bungalows (0747-415569; barakabungalow@hotmail.com; s/d US$20/40) Small and friendly, just around the bend from Amaan Bungalows.

Paradise Beach Bungalows (0747-418860, 0747-416308; s/d US$20/35) These bungalows are next to Baraka and on the beach, with hot water and mirrors in the rooms.

Safina Bungalows (s/d US$15/30, with hot water US$20/35) Spiffy bungalows around a small garden, just in from the beach in the centre of Nungwi.

Nungwi Inn Hotel (224 0091; thenungwi_inn@hotmail.com; s/d US$30/50) Located at the southwestern end of the main hotel strip, the Nungwi Inn Hotel has reasonable rooms and a restaurant.

Baobab Beach Bungalows (0747-429391; www.baobabbeachbungalows.com; s/d from US$50/60) The last of the bunch, and a bit quieter, with standard bungalows plus some nice 'deluxe' rooms that are closer to the beach, and worth the splurge.

ZANZIBAR ARCHIPELAGO

Mid-Range & Top End

The better places in this category are on Nungwi's eastern side.

Mnarani Beach Cottages (☎ 224 0494; www.light housezanzibar.com; s/d US$60/84, d/q cottage US$104/177) This small lodge is the first place you come to on the placid eastern side of Nungwi, and a fine choice. It's set on a small outcrop overlooking the sea, with a dozen unassuming cottages, some with sea views, plus a few larger sea-facing family cottages with minifridge, and a honeymoon chalet.

Smiles Beach Hotel (☎ 224 0472; smilesbeach hotel@zanzinet.com; s/d US$65/85; 🏊) Smiles – on the eastern edge of Nungwi centre – has impeccably maintained two-storey cottages overlooking a manicured lawn and the beach. While a tad pretentious, they're spotless and good value, all with small sea-facing balconies, and with more space and quiet than at the other central hotels.

Sazani Beach (☎ 224 0014; www.sazanibeach.com; s/d US$60/80) Sazani is a small, quiet place with 10 rustic but agreeable thatched cottages on a hill overlooking the sea and a dive centre. It's on the eastern side of Nungwi, past Mnarani Beach Cottages.

Ras Nungwi Beach Hotel (☎ 223 3767; www .rasnungwi.com; s/d full board US$195/270, with sea view from US$235/350; 🌙 Jun-Mar) This is the most upmarket hotel at Nungwi, with a low-key ambience, airy sea-view chalets nestled on a hillside overlooking the sea, and less expensive 'garden-view' rooms in the main lodge. The hotel can organise fishing and water sports, and there's a dive centre. It's just past Sazani Beach on Nungwi's eastern side.

Other recommendations:

Langi-Langi Beach Bungalows (☎ 224 0470; langi _langi@hotmail.com; s/d US$45/60) An appealingly named place in the centre of Nungwi next to Amaan Bungalows, and just in from the water (no sea views). Rooms are clean and undistinguished, and there's a restaurant.

Nungwi Village Beach Resort (☎ 224 0476, 022-215 2187; www.nungwivillage.com; s/d r US$60/80, s/d bungalow US$95/140) A large beachside establishment that's a reasonable choice if you want to be close to Nungwi's facilities, but away from the main cluster of hotels. Accommodation is in either spacious two-storey thatched bungalows or less appealing and overpriced 'standard' rooms, clustered around a small courtyard. It's next to Smiles Beach Hotel.

GETTING THERE & AWAY

The No 116 bus runs daily between Nungwi and Zanzibar Town (Tsh700), but almost everyone uses one of the private minivans (p112). If you're driving on your own, it's faster to take the sealed route from Mahonda via Kinyasini (to the east), rather than the deteriorated road via Donge and Mkokotoni.

Kendwa

About 3km southwest of Nungwi along the coast is Kendwa, a long, wide and wonderful stretch of sand known among other things for its laid-back atmosphere and its full-moon parties. Apart from the full-moon parties, when it's loud until the wee hours, the beach is much quieter than at Nungwi, and more spread out, without Nungwi's crush of activity and accommodation. Offshore are some reefs for snorkelling, and at high tide you still have some beach – unlike at Nungwi, where it essentially disappears.

SLEEPING

All the hotels are within about a 700m stretch, so you can easily go from one place to the next on foot. Just about everywhere has sea views. Under construction is a five-star place, Gemma dell'Est, at the far northern end of Kendwa.

White Sands (☎ 0747-480987; www.zanzibar-white -sands-hotel.com; d US$35-55) One of Kendwa's best, with cheery, good-value en suite cottages on a small cliff above the beach (prices vary according to size), and a great beachside bar and restaurant.

La Rosa dei Venti (☎ 0747-411314; www.rosa zanzibar.com; 2-3 person bungalow US$75, s/d from US$30/45; 🏊) Friendly and family-run; this small guesthouse is set just behind a grove of palm trees leading down to the beach, with a choice of a few simple but spacious bungalows, or smaller rooms in the main family house. The bungalows come with minifridge and air-con, the rooms have ceiling fan, and the cuisine is very good.

Kendwa Rocks (☎ 0747-415474; www.kendwa rocks.com; bandas per person US$12, s/d from US$30/45) A Kendwa classic, with beach *bandas*, simple wooden bungalows on the sand, some cooler stone and thatch versions nearby and the biggest full-moon parties. Scuba Shack diving is on the beach out front.

Sunset Bungalows (☎ 223 2350; sunsetbungalows@ hotmail.com; d cottages US$35-45, d beachfront with air-con US$55) Straightforward cottages on a small cliff overlooking the beach, plus some pricier ones closer to the water, as well as a dive operator and a beachside restaurant-bar. You can also book through Malindi Lodge (p106) in Stone Town.

Amaan Kendwa Beach Resort (☎ 0747-492552; amaankendwa@hotmail.com; s/d US$35/50, with sea view US$50/70) Huge and sprawling, with three rows of rooms on a hillside sloping down to the beach. Most face the garden (or the back of the row in front), but a few have sea views. There's a restaurant that's right on the water, and **Sensation Divers** (☎ 0747-422975; www.sensationdivers.com) is based here.

GETTING THERE & AWAY

You can walk to Kendwa from Nungwi at low tide in about 25 to 30 minutes, but take care as there have been some muggings. Alternatively, inexpensive boats go from near Amaan Bungalows (p115) a few times daily depending on demand. Via public transport from Stone Town, have the No 116 *dalla-dalla* drop you at the sign for Kendwa Rocks (a few kilometres south of Nungwi), from where it's about a 2km walk to the beach. (If you're driving, this access road is supposed to be rehabilitated soon, but even now it's passable in 2WD, with some care needed over the rocky patches.)

Matemwe

The long, idyllic beach at Matemwe has some of the finest sand on Zanzibar. It's also the best base for diving and snorkelling around Mnemba, which lies just offshore. In the nearby village, life moves at its own pace, with women making their way across the shallows at low tide to harvest seaweed, strings of fish drying in the sun, and cows and chickens wandering across the road – all thousands of miles removed from the world of ringing mobile phones, traffic jams and high-rise office buildings that most of Matemwe's visitors have left behind.

SLEEPING

Matemwe Beach Village (☎ 0747-417250, 024-223 8374; www.matemwebeach.com; s/d US$60/100, with air-con US$70/110, ste half board US$180-300; ⚡) This recommended beachfront place has a won-derful setting on a beautiful stretch of coast, a low-key ambience and spacious, airy bun-galows with small verandas. Most are on the beach, separated only by a low wall of vegetation, with a few more set back about 100m on a low rise. There's also a plush and very private beachfront honeymoon suite complete with its own plunge pool, out-door bathroom, chef and separate stretch of sand, plus several appealingly designed two-storey 'shamba suites' and a convivial open lounge area where you can relax on large throw pillows while looking out to sea. One Ocean/The Zanzibar Dive Centre (see p104) has a branch here, which means if you start with them in Stone Town, you can get in some good east-coast diving as well. Half-board arrangements are available, as are discounts for children. In Stone Town, book through One Ocean, which can also help with transport arrangements.

Matemwe Bungalows (☎ 0747-425788; www .matemwe.com; bungalows/ste per person full-board US$130/165, d/tr/q villas US$550/660/730; ⚡ mid-Jun–Easter) Matemwe Bungalows, about 1km north of Matemwe Beach Village, is a relax-ing, upmarket place with a row of spacious and impeccably decorated bungalows lined up along the sea. It has a genteel, pampered atmosphere and receives consistently rave reviews. All the bungalows have their own veranda and hammock, and there are also more luxurious suites, including one for honeymooners with its own beach. A swim-ming pool is planned, as are a few exclu-sive villas set off on their own, where you'll be able to take your dinner and drinks in tropical seaside seclusion. The owners have made great efforts to reduce the impact of their establishment on the local commu-nity, and have set up various small-scale conservation and development projects.

Zi Villa (☎ South Africa 011-807 2682; www.zivilla .co.za; villa per 2/8 persons ZAR2500/5400; ⚡) This new place is about 700m north of Matemwe Bungalows on the beach. It's a large and exclusive private villa that can sleep up to eight persons in four enormous bedrooms (one with its own spa bath). There's also a kitchen reminiscent of something you'd find in a country estate in Tuscany, plus a large wooden terrace overlooking the sea, and dining and entertainment rooms.

Matemwe Baharini Villas Beach Resort (☎ 0747-417768; kibwenibeachvilla@zitec.org; s/d r with-out bathroom US$25/40, s/d bungalow US$35/60) Quiet and unassuming, Baharini Villas is on the beach between Matemwe Beach Village and Matemwe Bungalows. There's a somewhat dilapidated but well-located main house

HONEYMOON HEAVEN

Tanzania has become a hugely popular destination for honeymooners, and many upmarket hotels, both on Zanzibar and on the mainland (especially along the coast and on the northern safari circuit) offer special honeymoon suites, private candlelit dinners and other luxuries to help you ease into betrothed bliss. We've mentioned a few of the suites in the listings in this book, but it's always worth asking. Web-based tour operators who specialise in arranging up-market honeymoon safari/beach packages in Tanzania include **Africa Travel Resource** (www.allaboutzanzibar.com), which also has heaps of good background information on the archipelago (and elsewhere in the country), and **Encounter Zanzibar** (www.encounterzanzibar.com). Most of the mid-range and top-end safari operators listed on p59 can also help you arrange special honeymoon packages.

with a few no-frills rooms and an airy sitting area upstairs, plus some simple beach-facing rooms on the sand, and a small restaurant (order well in advance). It's possible to rent out the whole house, and there's a kitchenette.

Mohammed's Place (☎ 0747-431881; r per person without bathroom US$10) Last but not least, this is the only truly shoestring option, with three very simple rooms in a local house set back from the beach in Matemwe village. (Look for the hand-painted signs, or ask staff at Matemwe Beach Village to point out the way.) Grilled fish and other local meals can be arranged.

GETTING THERE & AWAY
Matemwe village is located about 25km southeast of Nungwi, and is reached via an unsealed road branching east off the main road by Mkwajuni. *Dalla-dallas* travel here daily from Stone Town, passing the Matemwe Beach Village hotel on the way, and stopping within about 2km of Matemwe Bungalows; all the upmarket hotels can organise transfers.

Pwani Mchangani
As you head south along the coast, the sands of Matemwe slide almost impercep-

tibly into those of Pwani Mchangani, a large fishing village that acts as a buffer before the string of Italian resorts further south at Kiwengwa.

There are a few inexpensive local guest-houses that seem to change name with some frequency, so just ask around. Otherwise, try **Uzioni Beach Bungalows** (☎ 0747-417701; uzionipm@hotmail.com; d US$40), which has basic rooms around a sandy courtyard set back about 100m from the sea, hot water for bathing and a nice, long beach.

Kiwengwa
Kiwengwa village is spread out along a fine, wide beach, much of which is occupied by large, Italian-run resort hotels, although there are some quieter stretches to the north and south.

SLEEPING
Shooting Star Inn (☎ 0747-414166; www.zanzibar .org/star; bandas per person without bathroom US$15, s/d US$75/110, sea-view cottages US$85/130) Cosy and intimate, Shooting Star is the best of the bunch, with comfortable stone-and-thatch cottages on a small cliff overlooking the sea, and good cuisine. There are also rooms set around a small garden, and some budget *bandas* with sand floors. The overall ambience is tranquil, and the inn is an ideal place to relax. On the beach below (reached via a small staircase) are some thatched *bandas* for shade. Renovations are planned, and prices and facilities are likely to change.

Reef View (☎ 0747-413294, 0747-414030; bandas per person without bathroom US$15, d US$50) This is the only budget choice, and a good place to sit back for a while. It's on the beach in the Kumba Urembo section of Kiwengwa, with simple *makuti bandas* sharing facilities, plus a newer en suite double. There's a restaurant and bar and a book exchange, and snorkelling trips and town transfers can be arranged. It's about 20-minutes' walk from Kiwengwa centre (along the beach at low tide), or you can pay the No 117 bus driver about Tsh1000 extra for a drop.

Bluebay Beach Resort (☎ 224 0240/1; www .bluebayzanzibar.com; d half board from US$130-320; 🍴 💻 🏊) Of the various large resorts along the Kiwengwa coastline, this is one of the nicest, with a quieter, more subdued atmosphere than those of its neighbours. Rooms have two large beds and all the amenities, and the grounds are expansive, green and serene. One Ocean/The Zanzibar Dive Centre (p104) has a base here, and the pool can be used for introductory lessons.

Other recommendations:

Ocean Paradise Resort (☎ 0747-439990; www .oceanparadisezanzibar.com; s/d half board US$140/240; ⓧ 🖳 🖳) Another agreeable choice if you're seeking a resort, with accommodation in spacious, round bungalows, a raised restaurant with commanding views over the water, and large, green gardens dotted with palms and sloping down to the beach.

GETTING THERE & AWAY
The No 117 *dalla-dalla* runs daily between Kiwengwa and Stone Town. The village itself is divided into three parts: Cairo to the north; Kiwengwa proper in the centre and just east of the main junction; and Kumba Urembo to the south. Public transport will drop you in Kiwengwa proper unless you pay the driver extra to take you further.

The road south of Kiwengwa turns into a rough dirt lane winding through the tropical vegetation and coconut palms to Pongwe, where it then becomes tarmac. Apart from a few rocky patches between Kiwengwa and Pongwe that need to be negotiated with care, 2WD is fine during most times of year.

Pongwe
This quiet arc of beach, about 5km south of Kiwengwa, is dotted with palm trees and backed by dense vegetation, and is about as close to the quintessential tropical paradise as you can get. Thanks to its position in a semisheltered cove, it also has the advantage of having less seaweed than nearby Chwaka and other parts of the east coast.

The attractive, intimate and unassuming **Pongwe Beach Hotel** (☎ 0747-413973; www.pongwe .com; s/d US$70/110) has just 10 bungalows (including one honeymoon bungalow with a large, Zanzibari bed), nestled amongst the palms on the best section of beach. All are sea-facing, spacious and breezy, the cuisine is good, and when you tire of the turquoise panoramas at your doorstep, you can amuse yourself with such pursuits as game and deep-sea fishing ($200 per boat per day) or excursions to Stone Town ($30 per transfer).

Set on a beautiful stretch of sand just to the south of the Pongwe Beach Hotel and Pongwe village, **Santa Maria Coral Park** (☎ 0747-432655; s US$25-35, d US$35-50) ranks among the most laid-back budget beach haunts on the island. For sleeping, there are a handful of simple *makuti bandas* with different colour themes. The restaurant serves up fresh prawns and other delicacies, and you can arrange snorkelling or excursions in the local fishing boats. The beachside bar has music in the evenings, and sometimes a bonfire.

Uroa
This rather centreless and nondescript village lies on an attractive and seldom-visited stretch of beach that's of similar appeal to that at nearby Chwaka (p120), just to the south. It's a reasonable choice if you want to enjoy the sea breezes and sand away from the resort crowds.

SLEEPING & EATING
For something upmarket, the best choice is the Zanzibar Safari Resort, south of Tamarind Beach Hotel, which was in the process of changing hands when we passed through.

Tamarind Beach Hotel (☎ 223 7154, 0747-411191; www.tamarind.nu; s/d US$35/50) One of the oldest hotels on the east coast, Tamarind has recently been renovated and is an ideal choice for families. Accommodation is in good-value bungalows within just a few metres of a placid pine-fringed beach, all with sea views and small porch. The stonework and arches of the main building give the place a pleasing, homy ambience. There's a good restaurant, and staff are helpful with organising excursions to Michamvi or Stone Town.

Uroa White Villa (☎ 0741-326874; www.uroa whitevilla.net; d from US$50, bungalow s/d US$50/70) This small, quiet place consists of a four-room house and a nearby two-room bungalow annexe, both with a few pleasant, spotless rooms – most with bathroom – and a restaurant. It's on the beach 1km north of Tamarind Beach Hotel, and is another good choice for families. There's a 20% discount on room prices if you book direct.

Jambo Beach Restaurant (meals Tsh2000) Situated on the opposite side of the road from the Uroa White Villa, this place has in-expensive local food.

GETTING THERE & AWAY
The No 214 *dalla-dalla* runs between Zan-zibar Town and Uroa several times daily. Sometimes you can get this at Darajani market, but usually you need to take bus 501 (Amani Stadium) to a junction known as Mwembe Radu (just ask the *dalla-dalla* driver), where you can pick up the No 214. Alternatively, bus 206 (Chwaka) sometimes continues northwards as far as Uroa. The last departure from Uroa back to Stone Town is at about 4pm.

Chwaka
Chwaka, a small fishing village on Chwaka Bay, due east of Zanzibar Town, doesn't receive too many visitors these days, and as a consequence has an appealing, sleepy charm. The modest beach, which would be considered fine if it were anywhere else, is below average compared with others on Zanzibar's east coast, though it's still at-tractive. There are also other diversions, including excursions to Michamvi penin-sula across the bay, strolls around the vil-lage, or just taking in the tranquillity of the coastline.

The only place to stay is the attractive and completely renovated **Chwaka Bay Re-sort** (☎ 224 0289; chwaka@zanlink.com; s/d with fan US$38/55, with air-con US$50/65; ☒) – it's quite an agreeable spot to spend a few days. Accom-modation is in simple, clean bungalows set on a small hillside a bit in from the beach, and in nicer rooms in two-storey cottages with sea views and balconies, some with air-con. Staff are attentive, and there's a good restaurant with a mix of local and conti-nental cuisine and a Sunday evening buffet. Boat trips over to Michamvi are included in the room price.

Bus 206 runs several times daily between Zanzibar Town and Chwaka.

Paje
Paje is a very wide, white beach at the end of the tarmac where the coastal road north to Bwejuu and south to Jambiani joins with the road from Zanzibar Town. There's a cluster of places here, and somewhat of a party atmosphere, though it's much quieter and more low key than in Nungwi. Many

hotels in Paje organise dolphin trips to Kiz-imkazi for about Tsh15,000 per person in a group. For diving, there's **Paje East Coast Dive** (☎ 224 0191; pajediving@zanzinet.com), on the beach next to Kitete Guest House.

SLEEPING
Kinazi Upepo (☎ 0748-655038; www.kinaziupepo.com; bandas without bathroom US$20-25, bungalows US$35-40) Good vibes and good value are the main attractions at this place nestled amidst the palms and coastal pines on a very nice section of beach. You can sleep in simple *makuti bandas* on low stilts, or in large bun-galows with Zanzibari beds – most bunga-lows have a private bathroom. The food is the among the tastiest to be found along this part of the coast, and there's a well-stocked bar with fruit smoothies, among other drinks. Evenings there's often music, and Saturday evenings currently feature an all-night East Coast Beach Party with the hugely popular DJ Yusuf (the force behind Sauti za Busara, p105).

Paradise Beach Bungalows (☎ 223 1387; saori@cats-net.com; s/d US$25/35; meals Tsh4000) This very nice Japanese-run place is hidden among the palms on the beach at the northern edge of Paje. Each room has two large beds, and there's excellent food, including sushi and other Japanese cuisine if you order in advance.

Kitete Guest House (☎ 224 0226; www.kitete beach.com; s/d US$25/40) This place is a small family-run guesthouse situated right on the beach with spotless rooms and tasty meals, although we have received mixed reviews from readers.

Paje by Night (☎ 0747-460710; www.pajebynight .net; s US$20, d US$30-50) This fairly raucous place known mainly for its bar has straight-forward rooms around a courtyard a few hundred metres in from the beach. Staff can help you organise dolphin excursions and boating forays with local fishermen. The pricier doubles are spacious and have hot water, and there's a restaurant with a pizza oven.

Other options:
Paje Ndame Village (☎ 223 6577; s/d US$20/40) Friendly but a bit tatty and overpriced; it's on the northern edge of Paje, en route to Bwejuu.
Paje Beach Bungalows (☎ 0747-438149; pajebeach@hotmail.com; d/tr US$40/60) A new place that's still brushing away the paint chips. You'll find a row

Anglican Cathedral (p102), Zanzibar Town

Old Arab Fort (p102), Zanzibar Town

Old Dispensary (p103) historic building, Zanzibar Town

Forodhani Gardens (p103) and Old Stone Town harbour

DAVID ELSE

Machame Route (p175), Shira Cave trekkers' camp, Mt Kilimanjaro National Park

Lion on the prowl, Serengeti National Park (p200)

ARIADNE VAN ZANDBERGEN

Fisherman pulling fishing net, Saadani Game Reserve (p143)

ARIADNE VAN ZAN

Irente viewpoint (p154) at the edge of the Usambara Mountains

ARIADNE VAN ZAN

of no-frills thatch-and-cement bungalows set back from the water. It's just south of Kitete Guest House.

GETTING THERE & AWAY

Bus 324 runs several times daily between Paje and Stone Town en route to/from Bwejuu, with the last departure from Paje at about 3pm.

Bwejuu

The large village of Bwejuu lies about 3km north of Paje on a long, wonderful and palm-shaded beach. It's very spread out, quieter than Paje, and much less crowded than Nungwi, with a mellow atmosphere and nothing much more to do other than wander along the sand and listen to the breezes rustling the palm trees.

SLEEPING & EATING

Mustapha's Nest (☎ 224 0069; www.fatflatfish.co.uk /mustaphas/; r per person US$20-25, without bathroom US$10-15) This chilled-out, welcoming place has a laid-back Rasta atmosphere and a variety of simple, cheery and very creatively decorated rooms, some with their own bathroom and all with their own theme. Meals are taken family style, and Mustapha and family are very helpful in sorting out things like bike hire, drumming lessons and other diversions. It's south of Bwejuu village, and just across the road from the beach.

Robinson's Place (☎ 0747-413479; www.robinsons place.net; s/d from US$20/40) This recommended Robinson Crusoe–style getaway has a small collection of appealingly designed rooms nestled amidst the palms directly on the beach. The two-storey Robinson House has an upstairs tree-house double that's one of the most natural and charming rooms on the island, open to the sea and the palms. Downstairs is a tidy single, and there are a few more rooms in a separate house – all spotless and appealingly decorated. Some have their own bathroom, and the shared bathroom is about the cleanest and most attractive imaginable. Eddy, the Zanzibari owner, cooks up great breakfasts and dinners (for guests only) served in a seaside *banda*. It's at the northern end of Bwejuu – just keep heading up the sandy track until you see the sign.

Palm Beach Inn (☎ 224 0221; mahfudh28@hotmail .com; s/d US$50/70; ⊠) The friendly, beachside

Palm Beach Inn has small, well-maintained rooms, all with hot water and minifridge. There's also a larger family room, a tree-house lounge-library area overlooking the beach, a good restaurant and helpful staff.

Sunrise Hotel & Restaurant (☎ 224 0170; www .sunrise-zanzibar.com; s/d US$65/75, s/d bungalow with sea view US$80/90; ⊠) The Belgian-run Sunrise has rooms and bungalows set around a small garden area and a highly regarded restaurant. The beach-facing bungalows are worth the extra money, as they are much nicer than the dark rooms. It's on the beach about 3km north of Bwejuu village.

The following (all of which are located along the beach north of Bwejuu village) are also recommended:

Bahari Beach Village (hisdory@hotmail.com; r per person without bathroom US$10) On the beach north of Robinson's place, with a few rooms in a small house, some nice simple bungalows, and good local meals.

Shells (☎ 0748-310980; s/d US$15/25) Spiffy white thatched cottages on the beach.

Evergreen Bwejuu (☎ 224 0273; www.evergreen -bungalows.com; r without/with bathroom from US$30/35) Pricey but nice two-storey bungalows. The upper-level rooms have their own balcony.

Twisted Palm (☎ 0747-438121; s/d from US$15/25) OK bungalows (the ones closest to the water are better), plus a beachside bar and a raised restaurant overlooking the water.

Jamal's Restaurant (meals Tsh1500) Inexpensive local meals; it's on the land side of the road near Palm Beach Inn.

GETTING THERE & AWAY

Bus 324 goes daily between Stone Town and Bwejuu village, and private minivans come here as well.

Michamvi Peninsula

Beginning about 4km north of Bwejuu, the land begins to taper off into the narrow and seldom-visited Michamvi Peninsula, where budget accommodation disappears, and a few upmarket retreats are the only options. In Michamvi, there are a few simple *bandas* where you can arrange grilled fish or other local fare.

Breezes Beach Club (☎ 0741-326595; www.breezes -zanzibar.com; s/d half board from US$133/220; ⊠ ▭ ⊠) is one of the best choices around and is pleasantly free of the hectic, homogenised resort atmosphere that you get at some of the other east-coast places. There are various levels of accommodation here, all with a full range of amenities, plus diving, a gym and plenty of other activities to balance out time on the beach. Next door and under the same management is the lovely and very exclusive **Palms** (www.palms-zanzibar.com; s/d all-inclusive US$545/730), with six luxurious villas, each with their own private outdoor spa bath.

Further north towards the end of the Michamvi peninsula are **Karafuu Hotel Beach Resort** (www.karafuuhotel.com; s/d half board from US$140/220) and the quieter and luxurious **Sultan Palace** (www.sultanzanzibar.com; s/d full board US$390/580).

Once past Bwejuu, there's no public transport. Local boats cross between Michamvi village (on the northwestern side of the peninsula opposite Karafuu Hotel) to Chwaka, usually departing Michamvi in the early morning (Tsh1000), or you can arrange to hire one at any time of day (about Tsh15,000 return).

Jambiani

Jambiani is a long village on a stunning stretch of coastline. The village itself – a sunbaked and somnolent collection of thatch and coral-rag houses – is stretched out over more than a kilometre. The sea is an ethereal shade of turquoise and is usually dotted with *ngalawa* (outrigger canoes) moored just offshore. It's quieter than Paje and Nungwi, and has a good selection of accommodation – mostly budget, but a few mid-range places as well. In the village, there's a post office (with bicycle rental nearby), and a shop selling a few basics.

SLEEPING

Oasis Beach Inn (☎ 224 0259; d US$25, s/d without bathroom US$8/16) One of the cheapest places, the beachside Oasis has simple but quite decent rooms with shared bathroom, and friendly staff who will help you sort out grilled fish or other meals.

Blue Oyster Hotel (☎ 224 0163; www.zanzibar.de; s/d US$45/50, without bathroom US$20/30) German run, this place has pleasant, spotless, good-value rooms, a breezy terrace restaurant, and a convenient setting at the northern end of the beach.

Auberge Coco Beach (☎ 0747-413125; cocobeach@ zitec.org; s/d US$20/40, with air-con US$25/50; 🖭) Clean, simple rooms, a good restaurant and vaguely French overtones are the main

attractions at this beachfront place just north of Jambiani village.

Kimte Beach Inn (☎ 224 0212; www.kimte.com; dm US$10, d without/with bathroom US$25/30) At the southern end of Jambiani, this friendly and laid-back Rasta-run place has spotless rooms on the land side of the road (about half a minute's walk from the beach), a good vibe, delicious meals and a beachside bar with music and evening bonfires.

Gomani Bungalows (☎ 224 0154; gomanibunga lows@yahoo.com; s/d US$15/30) This pleasant and spiffy beachside place is at the southern end of Jambiani just after Kimte Beach Inn. Rooms are set around a garden on a tiny cliff overlooking the sea, and there's a restaurant.

Red Monkey Bungalows (☎ 224 0207; standard@ zitec.org; s/d US$15/25) Located at Jambiani's far southern end, this place has clean, agreeable sea-facing bungalows set along a nice garden on the beach.

Other recommendations:

Mt Zion Long Beach (☎ 0747-439001, 0747-439034; www.mountzion-zanzibar.com; s/d/tr US$30/50/65) Another Rasta-run place with nicely decorated, spotless stone-and-thatch bungalows set around large, lush gardens just up from the beach. They also have a couple of less expensive no-frills *makuti bandas* directly on the sand, plus a bar built around polished driftwood and tasty food. It's about 1.5km north of Jambiani village.

Hakuna Majiwe (☎ 0747-454505; hakunamajiwe@ hotmail.com; d US$110, 4-bed US$130; 🖭) A new and promising mid-range place that was having the finishing touches put on it when we passed through. Accommodation is in nicely decorated cottages with shady porches and Zanzibari beds, and the décor is a pleasing fusion of mostly Zanzibar with a touch of Italy. A small private marine sanctuary is planned on the beach near the lodge, as is a clothing boutique where Italian fashion design meets Zanzibari flair. It's at the far northern end of Jambiani, near Mt Zion Long Beach.

Shehe Bungalows (☎ 224 0149; shehebungalows@ hotmail.com; r per person US$15) Straightforward rooms at the southern end of Jambiani. Most have bathroom, some have a minifridge, and there's a seaside restaurant.

Villa de Coco (☎ 0747-430750, 0747-464038; www .villadecoco.com; s/d US$35/45) Nice, airy chalets – all with ceiling fans and hot water – in gardens bordering the beach. It's just north of Mt Zion Long Beach.

Sau Inn Hotel (☎ 224 0169; www.sauinn.net; s/d US$60/70; 🖭 🖭) One of the few mid-range places, though overpriced for what you get, with modern rooms scattered around manicured green grounds.

EATING

Molly's Restaurant (meals Tsh2000) For inexpensive local meals, try this place under a thatched *banda* on the beach just north of Blue Oyster Hotel; you'll need to order a few hours in advance.

Kikundi cha Akina Mama (meals Tsh500) At this eatery in the village centre the Jambiani women's group serves up inexpensive local fare at midday.

GETTING THERE & AWAY

To get to Jambiani, there are private minivans, or take bus 309 from the market in Stone Town. Public transport from Jambiani back to Stone Town usually departs by 6am. South of Jambiani the road deteriorates to become a sandy track with very rocky patches, and there's no public transport.

Makunduchi

The main reason to come to Makunduchi is for the Mwaka Kogwa festival (p311), when this small and otherwise workaday town is bursting at its seams with revellers. There's nowhere to stay, but you can easily visit as a day trip from Stone Town or Kizimkazi, and it shouldn't be too hard to arrange something with locals as it's considered an unfavourable omen if you don't have at least one guest during the festival days. Bus 310 runs to Makunduchi on no set schedule, and during Mwaka Kogwa you shouldn't have trouble finding transport from either Stone Town or Kizimkazi.

Kizimkazi

This small village – at its best when the breezes come in and the late afternoon sunlight illuminates the sand – actually consists of two adjoining settlements: Kizimkazi Dimbani to the north and Kizimkazi Mkunguni to the south. It has a beach, but the main reason people visit is to see the dolphins that favour the nearby waters. Trips can be organised through tour operators in Stone Town from about US$20 per person, depending on group size. Some of the hotels at Paje and Jambiani also organise tours from Tsh15,000 per person, and both places listed under Sleeping & Eating, following, organise trips for Tsh40,000 per boat (up to eight people) plus an extra Tsh2500 per person for rental of poor-quality snorkelling equipment. While the dolphins are beautiful, the tours are often quite unpleasant, due to the hunt-and-chase tactics used by many of the tour boats, and they can't be recommended. If you do go out, the best time is early morning when the water is calmer and the sun not as hot. Late afternoon is also good, although winds may be stronger (and if it's too windy, it's difficult to get in and out of the boats to snorkel).

Kizimkazi is also the site of a Shirazi **mosque** dating from the early 12th century and thought to be one of the oldest Islamic buildings on the East African coast, although much of what is left today are later restorations. The building isn't impressive from

---

WATCHING THE DOLPHINS

Unfortunately for Kizimkazi's dolphins, things have gotten out of hand these days, and it's not uncommon to see a group of beleaguered dolphins being chased by several boats of tourists. If you want to watch the dolphins, heed the advice posted on the wall of the Worldwide Fund for Nature (WWF) office in Zanzibar Town, which boils down to:

- As with other animals, viewing dolphins in their natural environs requires time and patience.
- Shouting and waving your arms around will not encourage dolphins to approach your boat.
- Be satisfied with simply seeing the dolphins; don't force the boat operator to chase thè dolphins, cross their path or get too close, especially when they are resting.
- If you decide to get in the water with the dolphins, do so quietly and calmly and avoid splashing.
- No one can guarantee that you will see dolphins on an outing, and swimming with them is a rare and precious occurrence.
- Remember – dolphins are wild and their whereabouts cannot be predicted. It is they who choose to interact with people, not the other way around…

the outside, apart from a few old tombs in front. Inside, however, in the mihrab are inscribed verses from the Quran dating to 1107 and considered to be among the oldest known examples of Swahili writing. If you want to take a look, ask for someone to help you with the key. You'll need to take off your shoes, and you should cover up bare shoulders or legs. The mosque is in Kizimkazi Dimbani, just north of the main beach area.

SLEEPING & EATING

Kizidi Restaurant & Bungalows (☎ 223 0081; www .kizidibungalows.com; s/d/tr US$30/40/50) A large place on the northern end of the beach in Kizimkazi Dimbani – you'll see it as soon as you come into town – with the best rooms in the area, although there isn't much competition. All are in nice no-frills cottages overlooking the water, with nets, hot water and twin or double beds, plus there's a large restaurant.

Dolphin View Village (☎ 0747-434959; d/tr from US$25/50) Offers basic rooms in a grove of palm trees, and dolphin tours. It's about 1km south of Kizidi (and not necessarily worth the extra walk) in Kizimkazi Mkunguni and reached via a sandy track running parallel to the beach.

GETTING THERE & AWAY

To reach Kizimkazi take bus 326 (Kizimkazi) direct, or take No 310 (Makunduchi) as far as Kufile junction, where you'll need to get out and wait for another vehicle heading towards Kizimkazi, or walk (about 5km). The last vehicle back to Stone Town usually leaves Kizimkazi about 4pm. The mosque is about 2km north of the main section of town in the Dimbani area. As you approach from Stone Town go right at Kufile junction (ie towards Kizimkazi), and then right again at the next fork to Kizimkazi Dimbani. Kizimkazi Mkunguni is to the left at this last fork.

JOZANI FOREST

This cool and shady patch of green is the largest area of mature forest left on Zanzibar. Living among Jozani's tangle of vines and branches are populations of the rare red colobus monkey, as well as Sykes monkeys, bushbabies, Ader's duikers (although you won't see many of these), hyraxes,

more than 50 species of butterflies, about 40 species of birds and several other animals. There's a nature trail in the forest, which takes about 45 minutes to walk, the tiny Colobus Café with sodas, and the small Jozani Restaurant nearby with a modest selection of meals.

Jozani Forest (adult/child incl guide US$8/4; ⏲ 7.30am-5.30pm) is about 35km southeast of Zanzibar Town off the road to Paje, and best reached via bus 309 or 310, by chartered taxi, or with an organised tour from Zanzibar Town (often in combination with dolphin tours to Kizimkazi). The best times to see red colobus monkeys are in the early morning and late evening.

When observing the monkeys, take care not to get too close – park staff recommend no closer than 3m – both for your safety and the safety of the animals. In addition to the risk of being bitten by the monkeys, there's considerable concern that if the monkeys were to catch a human illness it could spread and rapidly wipe out the already threatened population.

Along the main road near Pete village, shortly before the Jozani Forest entrance, is the impressive Moto workshop and showroom (see p111), where you can buy crafts and watch the artisans at work.

MENAI BAY & UNGUJA UKUU

Tranquil Menai Bay, fringed by the sleepy villages of Fumba to the west and Unguja Ukuu to the east, is home to an impressive assortment of corals, fish and mangrove forests, some idyllic sandbanks and deserted islets, and a sea-turtle breeding area. Since 1997 it's been protected as part of the **Menai Bay Conservation Area** (admission US$3). The main reasons to visit are to enjoy the placid ambience, to take advantage of some good sailing around the islets and sandbanks offshore, and the chance to see dolphins. Unguja Ukuu is notable as the site of what is believed to be the earliest settlement on Zanzibar, dating to at least the 8th century, although there is little remaining today from this era.

The best place to stay is **Menai Bay Beach Bungalows** (☎ 0747-413915; www.menaibaybungalows .com; s/d US$30/50), on the bay at the southern edge of Unguja Ukuu village. It has pleasant cottages scattered around leafy grounds just in from the beach, a nice stretch of sand and a restaurant. A small museum is planned near the neighbouring (and still under construction) Southern Kaebona Beach Hotel with displays on the history of Unguja Ukuu.

You can organise excursions on the bay or to sandbanks through Menai Bay Beach Bungalows. Eco + Culture (p100) in Stone Town also organises trips to Unguja Ukuu and the offshore islands.

OFFSHORE ISLANDS

Once you've had your fill of the main island, there are various smaller islands and islets nearby that make enjoyable excursions and offer some good snorkelling.

Changuu

Also known as Prison island, **Changuu** (admission US$5, payable in US$ only), lies about 5km and an easy boat ride northwest of Zanzibar Town. It was originally used to detain 're-calcitrant' slaves and later as a quarantine station. Today the island is usually pushed as a day excursion, although it's a bit over-rated. The main attraction is a large family of giant tortoises, who are believed to have been brought here from Aldabra in the Sey-chelles around the turn of the 20th century. There's also a small beach and a nearby reef offering some novice snorkelling, for which you'll need your own gear. In the former house of the British governor, General Lloyd Matthews, there's an undistinguished **restaurant** (meals Tsh5000).

Any of the Zanzibar Town tour operators can arrange an excursion. Alternatively, fishing boats can be hired from the beach near Tembo House Hotel (p107) for about Tsh15,000 for a day return trip. Upper-end hotel development is planned, so ask around in Stone Town for an update.

Bawi

Tiny Bawi, about 7km west of Zanzibar Town and several kilometres southwest of Changuu, offers a beautiful beach and snor-kelling. There's nothing else, however, so you'll need to bring food, water and other drinks, and snorkelling equipment with you from Zanzibar Town. Fishing boats can be hired from Zanzibar Town near Tembo House Hotel (p107) from about Tsh15,000; the trip takes about 40 minutes. Various tour operators run day trips to Bawi with a stop en route at Changuu from about Tsh15,000, usually including lunch. There are rumours of forthcoming development here, so get an update before heading out.

Chapwani

This tiny, privately owned island (also known as Grave Island, thanks to its small cemetery and the tombs of colonial-era British seamen) is about 4km north of Zanzibar Town. It's surrounded by crystal waters, with a postcard-perfect white-sand beach backed by lush vegetation running down one side, and it makes an agreeable getaway from Stone Town. The only de-velopment on the island is the comfortable **Chapwani Island Lodge** (www.chapwaniisland.com; s/d full board US$170/240; ☺ Jun-Mar) with cosy bun-galows along the sand. The lodge provides transfers from Stone Town from US$10 per person.

Tumbatu

The large and seldom-visited island of Tum-batu, just off Zanzibar's northwest coast, is populated by the Tumbatu people, one of the three original ethnic groups on the ar-chipelago. Although Tumbatu's early his-tory is somewhat murky, ruins of a mosque have been found at the island's southern tip that possibly date to the early 11th century, and it's likely the island was settled even earlier. As recently as the last century, there were no water sources on Tumbatu and vil-lagers had to come over to the mainland for supplies. In between Tumbatu and Zan-zibar lies the tiny and uninhabited island of Popo.

There's no accommodation, but Tum-batu can be easily visited as a day trip from Kendwa or Nungwi, where the hotels can help you organise a boat (from US$35 to US$50 per boat). Alternatively, local boats sail throughout the day between Tum-batu and **Mkokotoni** village, which lies just across the channel on Zanzibar, and which is known for its bustling fish market. The trip takes anywhere from 30 minutes to three hours, depending on the winds (or much less with a motor), and costs about Tsh100. Residents of Tumbatu aren't used to tourists – they are actually notorious for their lack of hospitality – so if you're head-ing over on your own or if you want to try to arrange an overnight stay with locals, it's best to get permission first from the police station in Mkokotoni, or from the *shehe* (village chief) in Nungwi, who will probably request a modest fee. There's at least one bus daily between Mkokotoni and Stone Town. Once on Tumbatu, the main means of transport are bicycle (ask around by the dock) and walking.

Mnemba

Tiny, idyllic Mnemba, just northeast of Matemwe, is the ultimate tropical paradise for those who have the money to enjoy it, complete with white sands, palm trees, turquoise waters and total isolation. While the island itself is privately owned with access restricted to guests of Mnemba Island Lodge, the surrounding – and stunning – coral reef can be visited by anyone. It's one of Zanzibar's best diving and snorkelling sites, with a huge array of fish, including tuna, barracuda, moray eels and reef sharks and lots of colourful smaller species.

The very exclusive 'barefoot luxury'–style **Mnemba Island Lodge** (www.ccafrica.com; per person all-inclusive US$650) is a playground for the rich and famous, and is often rented out in its entirety.

Chumbe

The uninhabited island of Chumbe, about 12km south of Zanzibar Town, has an exceptional shallow-water coral reef along its western shore that is in close to pristine condition and abounding with fish life. Since 1994, when the reef was gazetted as Zanzibar's first marine sanctuary, the island has gained widespread acclaim, including from the UN, as the site of a highly impressive ecotourism initiative centred around an ecolodge and local environmental education programmes. It's now run as Chumbe Island Coral Park, a private, nonprofit nature reserve.

The excellent state of Chumbe's reef is due largely to the fact that from the 1960s it was part of a military zone and off limits to locals and visitors. In addition to nearly 200 species of coral, the island's surrounding waters host about 370 species of fish, and groups of dolphins who pass by to feed on the abundant fish life. The island also provides a haven for hawksbill turtles, and more than 50 species of birds have been recorded to date, including the endangered roseate tern. There are three historical

buildings on Chumbe: a lighthouse and a small mosque dating from the early 1900s, and the former warden's house.

Chumbe island can be visited as a day trip, although if you have the money and an interest in conservation, staying overnight in one of the seven wonderfully rustic **eco-bungalows** (223 1040; www.chumbeilsand.com; s/d all-inclusive US$230/400) is highly recommended. Each of these intimate structures has its own rainwater collection system and solar power, and a cosy loft sleeping area that opens to the stars. Advance bookings are essential. Day visits (also by advance arrangement only) cost US$70 per person.

Other Islets

Just offshore from Zanzibar Town are several tiny islets, many of which are ringed by coral reefs. These include Nyange, Pange and Murogo, which are sandbanks that partially disappear at high tide, and which offer snorkelling and diving (arranged through Stone Town dive operators, see p104).

PEMBA

024 / pop 362,200

For much of its history, Pemba has been overshadowed by Zanzibar, its larger, more visible and more politically powerful neighbour to the south. Although the islands are separated by only about 50km of water, relatively few tourists make their way across the channel for a visit. Those who do, however, are seldom disappointed.

Unlike flat, sandy Zanzibar, Pemba's terrain is hilly, fertile and heavily vegetated. In the days of the Arab traders it was even referred to as 'al Khuthera' or 'the Green Island'. Throughout much of the period when the sultans of Zanzibar held sway over the East African coast, it was Pemba, with its extensive clove plantations and agricultural base, that provided the economic foundation for the archipelago's dominance.

Pemba has also been long renowned for its voodoo and traditional healers, and people come from throughout East Africa seeking cures or to learn the skills of the trade.

Much of the island's coast is lined with mangroves, and Pemba is not a beach destination. However, there are a few good stretches of sand and some idyllic offshore

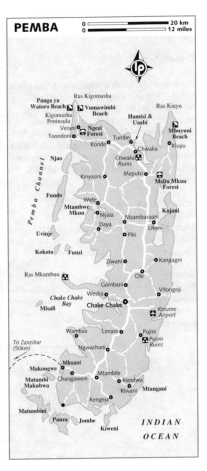

PEMBA

0 _____ 20 km
0 _____ 12 miles

Panga ya Watoro Beach
Ras Kigomasha
Vumawimbi Beach
Kigomasha Peninsula
Verani
Toondoni
Ngezi Forest
Tumbe
Konde
Hamisi & Usubi
Ras Kiuyu
Mbuyuni Beach
Kiuyu
Chwaka
Chwaka Ruins
Njao
Kinyasini
Maputo
Mtambwe Mkuu
Wete
Nyala
Mzambarauni
Kojani
Mitu Mkuu Forest
Fundo
Daya
Piki
Likoni
Uvinje
Kokota
Funzi
Ziwani
Kangagni
Ras Mkumbuu
Ole
Gombani
Vitongoji
Wesha
Misali
Chake Chake Bay
Chake Chake
Karume Airport
Wambaa
Limani
Pujini
Pujini Ruins
To Zanzibar (50km)
Ngwachani
Mkoani
Makongwe
Matumbi Makubwa
Changaweni
Mtambile
Kendwa
Kiwani
Mtangani
Kengeja
Matumbini
Panza
Jombe
Kiweni
INDIAN OCEAN

History

Pemba is geologically much older than Zanzibar and is believed to have been settled at an earlier date, although little is known about its original inhabitants. According to legend, the island was once peopled by giants known as the Magenge. More certain is that Pemba's first inhabitants migrated from the mainland, perhaps as early as several thousand years ago. The Shirazi presence on Pemba is believed to date from at least the 9th or 10th century, with Shirazi ruins at Ras Mkumbuu, northwest of Chake Chake, indicating that settlements were well established on Pemba by that point.

The Portuguese attacked Pemba in the early 16th century and sought to subjugate its inhabitants by ravaging towns and demanding tributes. As a result, many Pembans fled to Mombasa. By the late 17th century, the Busaidi family of Omani Arabs had taken over the island and driven away the last remaining Portuguese. Before long, however, the Mazrui, a rival group of Omanis based in Mombasa, gained the upper hand and governed the island until 1822. In 1890 Pemba, together with Zanzibar, became a British protectorate.

Following the Zanzibar revolution in 1964, the archipelago's president, Karume, closed Pemba to foreigners in an effort to contain strong antigovernment sentiment. The island remained closed until the 1980s, although the situation continued to be strained. Tensions peaked during the 1995 elections and relations deteriorated thereafter, with Pembans feeling increasingly marginalised and frustrated. This was hardly surprising, considering that illiteracy rates are as high as 95% in some areas, and roads and other infrastructure are badly neglected. In January 2001 in the wake of the October 2000 elections, tensions again peaked, resulting in at least several dozen deaths and causing many people to flee the island (p22). Since then, most have returned, and daily life is back to normal.

Getting There & Around

Pemba is small, and getting around isn't difficult with a bit of time and patience. A plodding local bus network connects the three main towns and several smaller ones. To reach destinations off these routes, take one of the buses to the nearest intersection,

islets. In the surrounding waters, coral reefs, the steeply dropping walls of the Pemba channel and an abundance of fish offer some rewarding diving.

The tourism industry on Pemba is still in its infancy, and infrastructure is for the most part fairly basic, although this is slowly changing and the island even has its first five-star resort. It will be a while, however, before tourism here reaches the proportions it's taken on Zanzibar. Much of Pemba is relatively 'undiscovered' and you'll still have things more or less to yourself, which is a big part of the island's charm. The main requirement for travelling around independently is time, as there's little regular transport off the main routes.

from where you'll either have to walk, rely on sporadic pick-ups, or negotiate an additional fee with the bus driver. There are no regular taxis as there are on Zanzibar or the mainland, but there are plenty of pick-up trucks that you can charter – best arranged in Chake Chake. The main roads between Mkoani and Wete are tarmac in various stages of repair; no secondary routes are paved.

Cycling is an excellent way to get around Pemba, although you'll need to bring your own (mountain) bike and spares, unless you're content with one of the single-speed bicycles available locally. Distances are relatively short and roads are only lightly travelled.

CHAKE CHAKE

Lively Chake Chake, set on a ridge overlooking Chake Chake Bay, is Pemba's main town and the best base for diving and for excursions to Misali. Although it has been occupied for centuries, there is little architectural evidence of its past other than the ruins of an 18th-century fort near the hospital, and some ruins at nearby Ras Mkumbuu (p132).

Orientation

MAPS

Commission for Lands & Environment Map Maps of Chake Chake are a rarity, but the Bureau of Lands & Environment, just outside Chake Chake in Machomane, sells a Pemba map. Head north from the town centre for about 1km, take the first right onto the road leading to the Essential Oil Distillery and continue about 700m to the two-storey white building on the right. The Commission for Lands & Environment in Zanzibar Town (p97) sells topographical maps of Pemba.

Information

INTERNET ACCESS

Adult Computer Centre (connection fee Tsh1000 plus per min Tsh300; ☼ 8am-8pm) On the main Mkoani–Wete road, opposite the telecom building.

MONEY

People's Bank of Zanzibar (PBZ) Changes cash and travellers cheques to a daily limit of US$200, and requires lots of time and patience. It's at the main junction in the town centre.

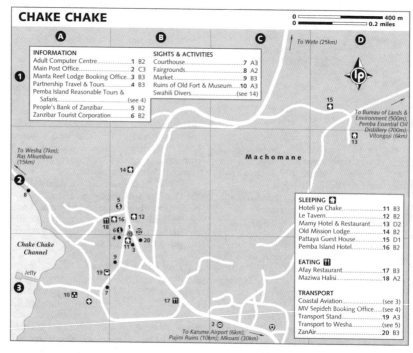

CHAKE CHAKE

0 — 400 m
0 — 0.2 miles

INFORMATION
Adult Computer Centre....................1 B2
Main Post Office...............................2 C3
Manta Reef Lodge Booking Office...3 B3
Partnership Travel & Tours..............4 B3
Pemba Island Reasonable Tours &
   Safaris.......................................(see 4)
People's Bank of Zanzibar...............5 B2
Zanzibar Tourist Corporation..........6 B2

SIGHTS & ACTIVITIES
Courthouse......................................7 A3
Fairgrounds.....................................8 A2
Market...9 B3
Ruins of Old Fort & Museum.....10 A3
Swahili Divers............................(see 14)

To Wete (25km)

To Bureau of Lands &
Environment (500m);
Pemba Essential Oil
Distillery (700m);
Vitongoji (6km)

To Wesha (7km);
Ras Mkumbuu
(15km)

Machomane

Chake Chake
Channel

Jetty

SLEEPING
Hoteli ya Chake.............................11 B3
Le Tavern.......................................12 B2
Mamy Hotel & Restaurant............13 D2
Old Mission Lodge........................14 B2
Pattaya Guest House.....................15 D1
Pemba Island Hotel.......................16 B2

EATING
Afay Restaurant............................17 B3
Maziwa Halisi................................18 A2

TRANSPORT
Coastal Aviation........................(see 3)
MV Sepideh Booking Office.....(see 4)
Transport Stand............................19 A3
Transport to Wesha...................(see 5)
ZanAir...20 B3

To Karume Airport (6km);
Pujini Ruins (10km); Mkoani (30km)

POST
Main post office (🕙 8am-4pm Mon-Fri, 9am-noon Sat) On the main Mkoani–Wete road.

TELEPHONE
There are several card telephones around town, including opposite the old fort.
Adult Computer Centre (🕙 8am-8pm) On the main Mkoani–Wete road. Calls can be placed/received for Tsh3000/500 per minute.

TOURIST INFORMATION
Zanzibar Tourist Corporation On the main road, just south of the bank. This office is on the 2nd floor of the building with the flag.

TRAVEL AGENCIES
Partnership Travel & Tours (☎ 245 2278) This place at the main junction arranges ferry tickets and island excursions.
Pemba Island Reasonable Tours & Safaris (☎ 0747-435266) A clued-up agency that organises spice tours (Tsh10,000 per person), trips to Vumawimbi and Ngezi Forest (Tsh20,000 per person, minimum four), to Misali island (Tsh35,000 per person) and other excursions, plus ferry tickets. It's next to Partnership Travel & Tours.

Sights & Activities
Chake Chake's appealingly scruffy main street is lined with small shops and makes for an interesting walk. Apart from the small but bustling **market**, buildings of note include the **courthouse**, with its clock tower, and the old Omani-era **fort**, which dates to the 18th century, and was probably built on the remains of an earlier structure. Inside is a tiny and dusty **museum** (admission Tsh1000; 🕙 8.30am-4.30pm Mon-Fri, 9am-4pm Sat & Sun), with a few rather forlorn displays of pottery shards and old photos. About 2km west of town along the Wesha road are **fairgrounds** dating from Pemba's Socialist days and now opened only on holidays.

Just out of town to the northeast is the sleepy **Pemba Essential Oil Distillery** (admission Tsh1500; 🕙 7.30am-3.30pm Mon-Fri), where you can smell lemon grass and cloves and see how spices are made into oil. It's best visited in combination with a **spice tour**, which can be arranged through any of the hotels or through Pemba Island Reasonable Tours & Safaris. About 6km further on, reached via an easy bike ride past the oil distillery, are some tiny, baobab-dotted **beaches** near Vitongoji.

Most diving from Chake Chake focuses on Misali island (p131). **Swahili Divers** (☎ 245 2786; www.swahilidivers.com) are a professional, well-managed outfit, and one of Pemba's main dive operators. In addition to diving, they offer overnight camping safaris on a small, outlying island (US$540 for three nights, including rustic accommodation in tents, full board and two dives per day), plus PADI certification courses, and – with the help of two Tornado rigid inflatable boats – can access dive sites all around Pemba. They're based at the Old Mission Lodge (below).

Sleeping & Eating
Pemba Island Hotel (☎ 245 2215, 0747-435266; s/d Tsh15,000/30,000; 🍴) New and spotless, this hotel is good budget value, with small rooms with nets, TV, minifridge and hot water, a rooftop terrace restaurant, and a 10% discount for longer stays. It's on the Wesha road, about 100m downhill from the bank.

Old Mission Lodge (☎ 245 2786; www.swahili divers.com; dm with full board US$20, d US$77, r without bathroom US$44-66, lunch/dinner about US$5/10) This clued-up lodge is in a restored Quaker mission house in the centre of Chake Chake and has spacious, rustic rooms complete with creaky wooden floors and high ceilings. There's also a veranda with sunset views and a small garden. It's the home of Swahili Divers (p129) and primarily a dive base, but plenty of non-divers stay here too. Rooms aren't cheap, but rates become more reasonable if you book one of their special dive-accommodation deals (cash and advance bookings only), some of which can be quite decent value. Apart from the diving, the main draws are the atmospheric surroundings and the convivial ambience; check out their website for an idea of what to expect. It's on the main road in the town centre, about 200m north of the bank. No travellers cheques accepted, and there's a 10% surcharge on credit cards.

Le Tavern (☎ 245 2660; 0747-429057; s/d with aircon US$25/30; meals Tsh4000; ✶) This reliable but slightly tatty establishment – on the main road diagonally opposite the Old Mission Lodge – has clean, no-frills rooms with nets and is a reasonable budget choice. Included in the price is an early morning wake-up call from the mosque next door. Meals can be arranged.

Hoteli ya Chake (☎ 245 2069; r US$15) This cavernous, usually empty government hotel is fairly bleak. However, the rooms are large and, overall, it's not as bad as its reputation would suggest, especially if you don't mind the lack of amenities such as water and electricity. If you stay, you'll probably be the only one here.

Pattaya Guest House (☎ 245 2827; r US$20) Pattaya is inconveniently located, but worth a look if the others are full. It has small, clean rooms in a brightly painted building. It's 2km north of town, and about 200m along the road leading to the Essential Oil Distillery.

Mamy Hotel & Restaurant (☎ 0747-432789; s/d without bathroom Tsh6000/12,000) A small family house, this is one of the cheapest places on the island, with a handful of no-frills rooms and meals available on request. It's about a 15-minute walk from the centre of Chake Chake, down the dirt road that branches southeast near Pattaya Guest House.

Afay Restaurant (meals Tsh2000; ✶ lunch & dinner) is a homy local haunt with good rice and fish and other standard fare. There's also a lively night market in the town centre, where you can get grilled *pweza* (octopus), *maandazi* (doughnuts) and other local delicacies at rock-bottom prices, and experience a slice of Pemban life. Most shops sell only basic supplies, but there are a few which have more exotic items, such as tinned cheese and peanut butter.

The small Maziwa Halisi shop, downhill from the bank and just after Pemba Island Hotel, has highly refreshing yogurt, plus simple but delicious Pemba-style milkshakes made with cold milk, cardamom and grenadine syrup.

Getting There & Away

AIR

Both **ZanAir** (☎ 245 2990), on the main road near the post office, and **Coastal Aviation** (☎ 245 2162, 0747-418343), opposite ZanAir, fly daily between Chake Chake and Zanzibar Town (US$70), with direct connections on to Dar es Salaam (US$85). Coastal also goes daily between Pemba and Tanga (US$55).

BOAT

See p133 for ferry schedules between Zanzibar and Mkoani (from where you'll need to take a bus up to Chake Chake). The MS *Sepideh* has a booking office in Chake Chake opposite the post office, or you can arrange tickets through hotels or travel agencies.

BUS

Main routes include the following (with prices on all averaging about Tsh700, and departures from the transport stand in the town centre):

Route No	Destination
303	Mkoani
306	Wete via the 'old' road
334	Wete via the 'new' (eastern) road
335	Konde

There's a shuttle bus from Chake Chake (Tsh1000) to Mkoani connecting with *Sepideh* departures and arrivals, departing from in front of Partnership Travel & Tours about two hours before the *Sepideh's* scheduled departure time. Book a place when buying your boat ticket, as the bus gets crowded.

Getting Around

TO/FROM THE AIRPORT

Karume airport, about 6km east of town, is Pemba's only airfield. There's no regular bus service to/from the airport, but at

EQUALITY IN PARADISE

When you see Misali, you may wonder why such a paradisal island hasn't been snatched up by developers. The answer in part is that it has been gazetted as a conservation area in order to protect it from this very scenario. However, this conservation status is fragile, and given the right (or wrong) set of factors, it could be reversed.

The idea of Misali as the site of a luxury lodge might be appealing to some. However, there is another side to the picture – namely, the equity issue involved when traditional resource users (ie the indigenous population) are excluded from an area in the name of conservation. The Misali Island Conservation Project seeks to empower locals to manage their own natural resources, thereby ensuring promotion of both environmental conservation and also the well being of the at least 8000 people who depend on the island and its waters for their sustenance. An additional benefit of this approach is that the conservation area remains accessible to tourists from various socioeconomic and national backgrounds. Contrast this with a scenario that would exclude not only local fishers, but also any tourist unable to pay several hundred dollars a night to experience their own private and (now) deserted tropical isle.

By visiting Misali you are making an important contribution to a model of ecological conservation that supports community development and 'egalitarian' ecotourism. The more successful the Misali Island Conservation Area is financially, the stronger the argument for resisting developers' attempts to wrest control from the fishermen, and the greater the likelihood that it will remain available both to traditional local users and the average tourist, rather than becoming the fenced-off domain of a wealthy few.

least one vehicle meets incoming flights (Tsh5000 to Chake Chake centre).

CAR & MOTORCYCLE

Cars and motorbikes can be hired in Chake Chake through the Old Mission Lodge or either of the travel agencies. Prices are fairly standard – US$15 between Mkoani and Chake Chake; US$10 one way between Chake Chake and Wete and US$25 to US$30 return between Chake Chake and Ras Kigomasha, including stops at Vumawimbi beach and Ngezi.

AROUND CHAKE CHAKE
Misali

This little patch of paradise lies offshore from Chake Chake, surrounded by crystal waters and stunning coral reefs. Nesting turtles and breeding sea birds favour the beaches on its western side, which have been set aside just for them. Also on the western side are some of the best reefs. On the northeast of the island is **Mbuyuni beach**, with fine, white sands and a small visitors centre, and to the southeast are some mangroves. About a 10-minute walk south of the visitors centre is **Bendera cave**, which is believed to be inhabited by the spirits of ancestors, and is used by Pembans from the main island for rituals. To the west are the larger **Mpapaini**

caves. Thanks to Misali's lack of fresh water, development of permanent settlements has been limited, but the island is in active use by local fishermen, and there are several fishing camps.

In 1998 the island and surrounding coral reef were gazetted as the **Misali Island Marine Conservation Area** (adult/student US$5/3), with the goal of maintaining the island's ecosystems in harmony with usage by local fishermen. There are underwater and terrestrial nature trails, and you can arrange guides at the visitors centre. Camping is not permitted.

To get to the island on your own, head first to Wesha, northwest of Chake Chake, via bus 305, which departs Chake Chake from in front of the People's Bank of Zanzibar to no set schedule, though it usually leaves fairly early. Alternatively, hiring a car costs about Tsh6000. Once in Wesha, you can negotiate with local boat owners to take you over to Misali. Expect to pay about Tsh35,000 per person return. There's no food or drink on the island, so bring whatever you'll need with you. It's easier, and only slightly more expensive (from about Tsh40,000 per person) to arrange Misali excursions through the Old Mission Lodge or travel agencies in Chake Chake, through Sharouk Guest House in Wete, or through Jondeni Guest House in Mkoani.

PEMBA PECULIARITIES

Unlike Zanzibar, where tourist infrastructure is well developed, Pemba is very much a backwater once away from its three main towns. (And, if you're coming from somewhere like London or Melbourne, these will probably seem like backwaters as well.)

■ Away from the pricier hotels, allow plenty of time for getting around and for meals. At budget places, you'll usually need to put in an order for a meal a few hours in advance. Apart from guesthouses, the main places to eat are at the island's lively night markets. These are found in all the major towns, but are best in Chake Chake. They sell *mishikaki* (skewered meat), *maandazi* (doughnuts), grilled *pweza* (octopus) and other delicacies. Wete has the best selection of vegetables from the mainland.

■ Other than local brews (the most common of which is *nazi*, a fermented coconut wine), there's little alcohol available on the island once away from the hotels. If you try the *nazi*, be sure it's fresh (made within the past 24 hours), otherwise it goes bad.

■ Chake Chake is the only town with banking facilities, so come prepared with enough cash (a mix of US dollars and Tanzanian shillings is best).

■ Most businesses operate from 8am to 4pm, and almost everywhere shuts down for about half an hour for prayers from about 4pm or 4.30pm, and at midday on Friday.

Ras Mkumbuu

Ras Mkumbuu is the long, thin strip of land jutting into the sea northwest of Chake Chake. At its tip are the ruins of a settlement known in ancient times as Qanbalu, which is thought to have risen to prominence in the early 10th century, when it may have been one of the major settlements along the East African coast. The main ruins, consisting of a mosque and some tombs and houses, are estimated to date from around the 14th century, and are now quite overgrown.

The best way to visit the area (which is also referred to by locals as Ndagoni, the name of the nearest village, or Makutani) is by boat from Chake Chake, although this can be expensive. If you go via road, you'll have at least an hour's walk at the end; one section of the path often becomes submerged at high tide, so plan accordingly.

AROUND PEMBA

Pemba offers opportunities for some enjoyable and very laid-back exploring. The following places are covered roughly south to north.

KIWENI

Tranquil Kiweni, marked as Shamiani or Shamiani island on some maps, is just off Pemba's southeastern coast. It's a remote backwater area, neglected by the government and overlooked by most visitors, where little seems to have changed for decades. With its undisturbed stretches of sand and quiet waterways, it's also one of the island's more scenic and alluring corners, as well as home to five of Pemba's six endemic bird species and a nesting ground for some sea-turtle colonies. Offshore is some good snorkelling.

Near Kiweni, in the area around Kengeja (as well as other spots on Pemba), you'll occasionally come across light-hearted '**bull fights**', said to date back to the days of Portuguese influence on the island.

At the moment, there's nowhere around Kiweni to stay. However, there's a hotel complex which is currently closed but that may one day start operating again, so ask around for an update.

To get here, catch any bus running along the Mkoani–Chake Chake road to Mtambile junction. From Mtambile, you can find pick-ups or other transport to Kengeja, from where you'll have to walk a few kilometres to the water and then take a boat over to Kiweni (about Tsh2000).

MKOANI

Although it's Pemba's major port, Mkoani has managed to fight off all attempts at development and remains a very small and boring town. However, its good budget guesthouse goes a long way to redeeming it, and it makes a convenient and reasonable base for exploring the southern and central parts of the island.

Information

An advantage of basing yourself in Mkoani is that the Chinese-run government hospital here has Pemba's best medical care, although the standards leave much to be desired.

The immigration officer usually meets all boat arrivals. Otherwise, if you're coming from anywhere other than Zanzibar, you'll need to go to the immigration office and get stamped in. It's 500m up the main road from the port in a small brown building with a flag.

Sleeping & Eating

Jondeni Guest House (☎ 245 6042; jondeniguest@ hotmail.com; dm/s/d US$8/20/30, s/d without bathroom US$15/20; meals Tsh6000) The only choice at the moment is this good backpackers' guesthouse, with clean, no-frills rooms and good meals. Staff have lots of information on Pemba, and can help you arrange excursions elsewhere on the island. To get here, head left when exiting the port, and walk about 800m up to the top of the hill.

Apart from Jondeni Guest House, which has Mkoani's best cuisine, it can be difficult to find meals, although there is decent street food in the evenings by the port.

Getting There & Away

BOAT

The unreliable **MS Sepideh** (☎ 0748-791433, 0747-418343) in theory sails Monday and Friday in both directions between Dar es Salaam and Pemba via Zanzibar, departing Dar es Salaam at 7.30am and Zanzibar around 9.30am, reaching Pemba about 11.30am. In the other direction, the boat departs Pemba at 12.30pm, reaching Zanzibar at 3pm, and then on to Dar es Salaam at 4pm. The *Sepideh* is good when it runs, but service is very sporadic. The fare is US$40/50 in economy class between Pemba and Zanzibar/Dar es Salaam, including port tax (which means that between Dar es Salaam and Pemba it's US$35 more and about three hours faster to take the plane).

The much less comfortable and marginally more reliable *Serengeti* sails three times weekly between Zanzibar and Pemba, de-

parting Pemba at 10am Tuesday, Thursday and Saturday, reaching Zanzibar between 4pm and 5pm (US$25, six to seven hours). Departures from Zanzibar are at 10pm, reaching Pemba the next morning at about 6am. If you take the night run, try to get to the port early to get one of their '1st class' couches; there's no extra charge, but it's more comfortable than the other seating, although 'comfortable' is an overstatement. Both boats have their main booking offices at the port in Mkoani. You can also arrange tickets through travel agencies in Chake Chake, and with Sharouk Guest House in Wete.

The *Sepideh* also occasionally sails between Mkoani and Tanga (US$35 one way); it's scheduled to do this twice weekly in each direction, but more often than not sailings are cancelled.

BUS

Bus 303 runs throughout the day to/from Chake Chake (Tsh700, two hours). The bus station is about 200m east of the port, up the hill and just off the main road. For Wete, you'll need to change vehicles in Chake Chake.

WAMBAA

The main reason to come to Wambaa is to luxuriate in Pemba's only five-star resort.

The exclusive **Fundu Lagoon Resort** (☎ 223 2926; www.fundulagoon.com; s/d full-board US$425/600; ✷ mid-Jun–mid-Apr) is set on a low hillside overlooking the sea, with luxurious bungalows tucked away amidst the vegetation and an excess of amenities. Particularly notable are its bar, set over the water on a long jetty, and its cuisine. In addition to the usual excursions, there's a good dive operator here, primarily operating around Misali and off Pemba's southern tip. It's also possible to arrange private yacht charter and deep-sea sport fishing.

PUJINI RUINS

About 10km southeast of Chake Chake at Pujini are the overgrown and atmospheric ruins of a town dating from about the 14th century, and perhaps earlier. It was here that the infamous Mohammed bin Abdul Rahman, who ruled Pemba around the 15th century, prior to the arrival of the Portuguese, had his seat. Locally, Rahman is known as Mkame

Ndume (Milker of Men), and for Pembans, his name is synonymous with cruelty due to the harsh punishments he meted out to his people. The main area of interest is framed by what were once the ramparts surrounding Rahman's palace, although several other ruins, including those of a mosque, have been found nearby. While the ramparts are in many places little more than a mound of earth, they show the scale of the residence, and, with some imagination, give an indication of Pujini's power in its heyday.

There's no regular public transport to Pujini. The best way to get here is by bicycle, following the road from Chake Chake southeast past farm plots, small villages and mangroves. Car hire from Chake Chake costs Tsh10,000 return.

WETE

The lively port- and market-town of Wete makes an agreeable base from which to explore northern Pemba. The port here is Pemba's second largest after Mkoani, and serves as the export channel for much of the island's clove crop. The centre of Wete's social life is the market, which is just off the main road at the eastern end of town.

Information

The best place for arranging excursions is Sharouk Guest House, which can also help with booking ferry tickets. **Raha Tours & Travel** (☎ 245 4228), just off the main road near the post office, also does *Sepideh* bookings.

Sleeping

Wete has a small collection of good budget guesthouses.

Sharouk Guest House (☎ 245 4386; s/d US$15/30, without bathroom US$10/20, lunch/dinner Tsh4000) This welcoming and recommended guesthouse, just off the main road at the western end of town, has simple, clean rooms, all with mosquito net and fan. The owner is very knowledgeable about Wete and the surrounding area and is the best contact for organising excursions to Vumawimbi beach, Ngezi Forest and elsewhere, making ferry bookings, bicycle (Tsh5000 per day) or motorbike (Tsh20,000 per day) rentals and the like. If all this doesn't persuade you to stay here, you get a free breakfast if you arrive at the guesthouse in the morning. Transfers from the Mkoani port (Tsh40,000) or the airport (Tsh25,000) can be arranged.

Bomani Guest House (☎ 245 4384; d US$20, s/d without bathroom US$10/15) Just opposite Sharouk Guest House, this place has straightforward rooms and no food.

North Lodge (☎ 0747-427459; s/d Tsh6000/12,000) A small, friendly establishment, formerly known as Super Guest House. There are several no-frills, adequate rooms, and meals can be arranged with advance notice. It's on the dirt lane that's parallel to and just south of the main road as you come into town.

Eating

Sharouk Guest House is the main place to eat in town (order meals ahead). Otherwise,

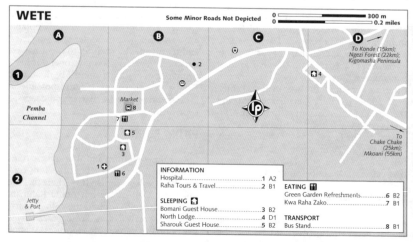

WETE

Some Minor Roads Not Depicted

0 — 300 m
0 — 0.2 miles

Pemba Channel

Market

To Konde (15km);
Ngezi Forest (22km);
Kigomasha Peninsula

To Chake Chake (25km); Mkoani (55km)

Jetty & Port

INFORMATION	
Hospital	1 A2
Raha Tours & Travel	2 B1

SLEEPING	
Bomani Guest House	3 B2
North Lodge	4 D1
Sharouk Guest House	5 B2

EATING	
Green Garden Refreshments	6 B2
Kwa Raha Zako	7 B1

TRANSPORT	
Bus Stand	8 B1

try the tiny local haunt, **Kwa Raha Zako** (meals Tsh500), near the market, or Green Garden Refreshments, at the western edge of town, for plates of *ugali* or rice and a few outdoor tables on a tiny patio.

Getting There & Away
BOAT
The small and sometimes wind- and wave-buffeted *Takrima* sails roughly weekly on a constantly changing schedule between Wete and Tanga, but usually departs Wete at 10am (US$25, five hours). The ageing and scruffy *Aziza* sails weekly between Zanzibar and Wete, departing in each direction at around 10pm (US$25, eight hours). Both boats change schedules frequently (and frequently don't run at all). Sharouk Guest House is the best place for updated information.

Wete is also the best place on Pemba to look for a dhow to the mainland, although captains are often unwilling to take foreigners. Inquire at the Wete port; passage costs about Tsh5000 between Wete and Tanga. There are also sporadic dhows between Wete and Mombasa. See also p328.

BUS
A tarmac road (the 'old' road) connects Wete with Chake Chake via Ziwani, winding its way past hills, villages and lots of banana trees en route. East of here, the 'new' road, also tarmac, connects Wete with Chake Chake via Ole. The main bus routes are No 306 (Wete to Chake Chake via the 'old' road), No 334 (Wete to Chake Chake via the 'new' road) and No 324 (Wete to Konde).

There's also a shuttle bus from Wete (Tsh 1000) to Mkoani connecting with *Sepideh* departures and arrivals, departing Wete about three hours before the *Sepideh's* scheduled departure time. Get an update at Sharouk Guest House, but currently the main pick-up point is at Raha Tours & Travel.

TUMBE
The large village of Tumbe lies on a sandy cove fringed at each end by dense stands of mangroves. It's the site of Pemba's largest fish market, and if you're in the area, it's well worth a stop, especially in the mornings when the catch of the day is brought in and the beach bustles with activity. Just

offshore are the two small islands of Hamisi and Usubi.

About 2km southeast from Tumbe at Chwaka are some overgrown **ruins**, including those of a mosque, an 18th-century fort, and some tombs. There are several sites, the best of which is known as the Haruni site, marked by a tiny signpost to the east of the main road. It's named after Harun, who was the son of Mkame Ndume (p133) and, according to local tradition, just as cruel as his father.

There's no accommodation in Tumbe. To get here, take the No 335 bus and ask the driver to drop you at the junction, from where it's an easy walk.

NGEZI
The small, dense and in parts wonderfully damp and lush forest at Ngezi is part of the much larger natural forest that once covered wide swathes of Pemba. It is notable in that it resembles the highland rainforests of East Africa more than the lowland forests found on Zanzibar. Ngezi is also known among botanical types as the home of *Pteropus voeltzkowi*, or the Pemba flying fox, a bat unique to the island and Pemba's only fully endemic mammalian species. The forest is now a protected **reserve** (admission Tsh4000; ☑ 8am-4pm) with a short nature trail that winds its way beneath the shady forest canopy. If you want to see Scops owls and other nocturnal birds, it's possible to arrange evening tours in advance with the caretaker.

Ngezi is along the main road between Konde and Tondooni. To get here via public transport, take the bus to Konde, from where it's a 3km to 4km walk. Bus drivers are sometimes willing to drop you at the information centre for an additional Tsh1000 to Tsh2000. The best idea is to combine Ngezi with a visit to Vumawimbi beach (see below). Despite what the Ngezi caretaker may tell you, you don't need to pay the forest entry fee if you're just passing through en route to the beach.

KIGOMASHA PENINSULA
The main reason to come to the Kigomasha peninsula in Pemba's northwestern corner is to relax on the beautiful, palm- and forest-fringed **Vumawimbi beach** on the peninsula's eastern side. There's nothing here other

than a small fishing village, so it's likely you'll have it completely to yourself (although don't wait too long, as development will inevitably come). Bring whatever food and drink you will need with you.

The best way to get to Vumawimbi is on bicycle from Konde. The road is sealed until the Ngezi Forest, then dirt, and thereafter loose sand. You can also hire a car in Chake Chake, or alternatively, try to negotiate a lift with one of the Konde bus drivers, although you'll then need to make arrangements for your return. Hitching is usually slow going, as there's little vehicle traffic.

On the northwestern end of the Kigomasha peninsula are **Panga ya Watoro Beach**, and the relaxing and superbly situated **Manta Reef Lodge** (☎ 0747-424637, 423930; www.mantareeflodge.com; s/d full board US$150/220; ◷ mid-Jun–mid-Apr), on a windy cliff top with spectacular views over the open ocean. Accommodation is in comfortably rustic sea-facing cabins, and they can help you organise diving, including live-aboard arrangements, as well as sea kayaking and fishing charters. To get here, stop by Manta Reef's booking office on the main street in Chake Chake, opposite ZanAir. Otherwise, there's usually at least one pick-up daily in the morning from Konde to Makangale village, about 4km or 5km south of Manta Reef, from where you'll need to walk or pay the driver extra to bring you all the way up.

OFFSHORE ISLANDS

There are dozens of tiny islets dotted along Pemba's coastline. Most have nothing on them, but they make enjoyable excursions. If you have any ideas of camping, keep in mind that many of the islands off Pemba's western coast are badly rat-infested. Some good destinations include **Hamisi** and **Usubi** (tiny fishing islands offshore from Tumbe village), **Mtambwe Mkuu** (actually a peninsula southwest of Wete) and the large **Kojani** in the northeast, with areas of protected forest. **Ras Kiuyu**, Pemba's far northeastern corner, is also well worth exploring, with forest, villages and beaches, including **Mbuyuni beach**, with some interesting water-sculpted rocks. Swahili Divers (p129) organises island camping getaways.

Northeastern Tanzania

CONTENTS

NORTHEASTERN TANZANIA

HIGHLIGHTS

- Meandering along winding foot-paths in the cool and scenic **Usambara Mountains** (p152)

- Lazing in a hammock on the wonderful beaches around **Pangani** (p145)

- Savouring sun and safari at **Saadani** (p143), Tanzania's only coastal game reserve

- Stepping back into history in the former colonial capital of **Bagamoyo** (p138)

- Discovering **Pare culture** (p158) in the secluded hills and valleys around Usangi and Mbaga

★ Pare Mountains

Usambara Mountains ★

★ Pangani & Beaches

Saadani Game Reserve ★

Bagamoyo ★

Northeastern Tanzania has been attracting visitors for at least 2000 years. In the first century AD, the author of the mariners' chronicle, *Periplus of the Erythraean Sea,* mentioned the existence of the mystery-shrouded trading outpost of Rhapta, which is thought by some to have been somewhere around present-day Pangani. Several centuries later – during the days when vast Swahili trading networks held sway on the high seas – a string of settlements sprung up along the coast with links to far-flung ports in Arabia and the Orient. Today, this long history, combined with easy access and a lack of crowds, make the northeast's long, tropical, ruin-studded coastline and its lush, mountainous inland areas among the most appealing parts of the country for exploring in depth.

Culturally and historically, there's a wealth of attractions. Inland, hike along shaded forest footpaths while following the lively cycle of bustling, colourful market days of the Sambaa, or learning about the intriguing burial rituals of the Pare. Along the coast, explore the medieval ruins at Kaole and Tongoni, step back to the days of Livingstone in Bagamoyo, relax on superb stretches of palm-fringed sand around Pangani, or have your beach and bush at the same time at Saadani, Tanzania's only seaside game reserve.

Whether you fly into Dar es Salaam or Arusha, most of the region is within an easy half-day's drive or bus ride away. Main roads are in good-to-reasonable condition, there's enough choice in accommodation to satisfy most tastes and the local transport network reaches many areas of interest. It's easily possible to combine coastal destinations, such as Saadani and the beaches north or south of Pangani, with inland areas such as Amani Nature Reserve and the western Usambaras – all within a reasonable time frame and budget.

National Parks & Reserves

The northeast is home to Saadani (p143), about to become Tanzania's newest national park, and the only one on the coast. Northwest of here, on the Kenyan border, is the rarely visited Mkomazi Game Reserve (p161), known for its black rhinos.

Getting There & Around

There are commercial flights to Tanga and Saadani, and several airstrips for charter flights around Pangani. Otherwise, you'll need to rely on the road network. The major routes are the tarmac roads connecting Dar es Salaam with Tanga and Arusha.

DID YOU KNOW?

Tanzania was once the world's largest producer and exporter of sisal, most of which was grown in the northeast, and handled in Tanga's port – one of East Africa's largest. Today, northeastern Tanzania continues to be one of the country's breadbasket areas, producing tea, coffee, cardamom and fruit, among other crops.

Secondary routes are mostly unsealed but in reasonable condition, except for along the coast, where things are still rough in spots (4WD needed). There's no ferry over the Wami River (though the old one may be rehabilitated soon), so it's not yet possible to drive from Dar es Salaam up the coast to Tanga.

Large buses connect towns along the main highways; elsewhere public transport is limited to *dalla-dallas* (minibuses).

BAGAMOYO

☎ 023

Strolling through Bagamoyo's narrow, unsealed streets, or sitting at the port watching dhows load up, takes you back in time to the early and mid-19th century when the town was one of the most important settlements along the East African coast and terminus of the trade caravan route linking Lake Tanganyika with the sea. Slaves, ivory, salt and copra (the dried, oil-yielding kernel of coconuts) were unloaded here before being shipped to Zanzibar and beyond, and many European explorers, including Burton, Stanley and Livingstone, began and

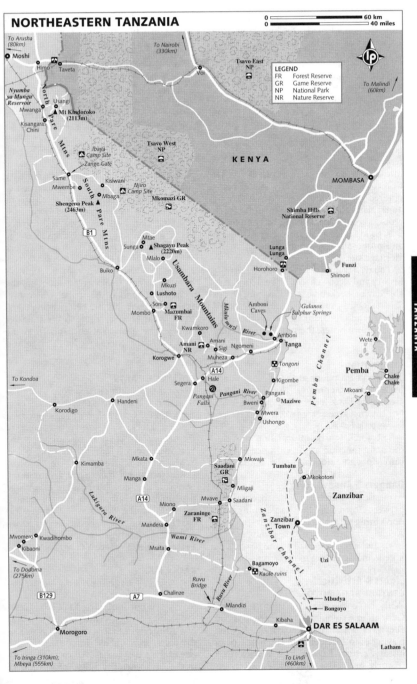

NORTHEASTERN TANZANIA

0 |————————————| 60 km
0 |————————————| 40 miles

LEGEND
FR Forest Reserve
GR Game Reserve
NP National Park
NR Nature Reserve

To Arusha
(80km)
Moshi
Himo
Taveta
To Nairobi
(330km)
Voi
Tsavo East
NP

To Malindi
(60km)

Nyumba
ya Mungu
Reservoir
Mwanga
Usangi
Mt Kindoroko
(2113m)
Kisangara
Chini

North Pare Mtns

Ibaya
Camp Site
Zange Gate
Tsavo West
NP

KENYA

MOMBASA

Same
Mwembe
Kisiwani
Njiro
Camp Site
Mbaga
South Pare Mtns
Mkomazi GR

Shimba Hills
National Reserve

Shengena Peak
(2463m)

B1

Mtae
Sunga
Shagayu Peak
(2220m)
Mlalo

Lunga
Lunga

Horohoro

Funzi
Shimoni

Buiko

Usambara Mountains

Mkuzi
Lushoto
Soni
Mombo
Mazumbai
FR
Kwamkoro
Amani
NR
Amani
Sigi
Ngomeni

Mkulumuzi River

Amboni
Caves
Galanos
Sulphur Springs
Amboni
Tanga

Wete

Pemba

Chake
Chake

Korogwe
Muheza

Tongoni

Kigombe

Pemba Channel

A14
Hale

Segera
Pangani
Falls
Pangani River
Pangani
Bweni
Maziwe
Mwera
Ushongo

Mkoani

To Kondoa

Handeni

Korodigo

Kimamba

Mkata

Manga

Saadani
GR
Mkwaja

Tumbatu

Mkokotoni

Zanzibar

A14
Miono
Mvave
Mligaji
Saadani

Lukigura River

Mandera
Zaraninge
FR

Mvomero
Kwadihombo
Kibaoni

Msata

Wami River

Zanzibar Channel

Zanzibar
Town

Uzi

To Dodoma
(275km)

Bagamoyo
Kaole ruins

B129
A7
Chalinze
Ruvu
Bridge

Ruvu River

Mlandizi

Mbudya
Bongoyo

Kibaha

Morogoro

DAR ES SALAAM

Latham

To Iringa (310km);
Mbeya (555km)

To Lindi
(460km)

NORTHEASTERN TANZANIA

ended their trips here. In 1868 French missionaries established Freedom Village at Bagamoyo as a shelter for ransomed slaves, and for the remainder of the century the town served as an important way station for missionaries travelling from Zanzibar to the country's interior.

From 1887 to 1891 Bagamoyo was the capital of German East Africa, and in 1888 it was at the centre of the Abushiri revolt, the first major uprising against the colonial government. In 1891 the capital was transferred to Dar es Salaam, sending Bagamoyo into a slow decline from which it has yet to recover. It is only recently – after being ignored for decades by most tourists and Tanzanians alike – that the town has been rediscovered, spurred along by completion of a good sealed road from Dar es Salaam and proposals to make it a Unesco World Heritage site.

Today, Bagamoyo's unhurried pace, long history and sleepy charm make it an agreeable day or weekend excursion from Dar es Salaam. Once you've had enough of historical explorations, head to the southeastern edge of town, where there are some relaxing beaches.

Information

There's a card phone at the telecom building at the town entrance. The National Microfinance Bank, next door, changes cash. For Internet access, try **4MSK** (Holy Ghost Catholic Mission; per hr Tsh2000; ⊙ 9am-6pm).

The small tourist information office at the main junction at the entrance to town can help with guides and excursions.

Dangers & Annoyances

Avoid isolated stretches of beach, especially between town and the Kaole ruins, and don't bring valuables to the beach with you. At night, it's best to walk in a group, both in town and along the road to the beach-side hotels, and again not to carry valuables.

Sights & Activities
CENTRAL BAGAMOYO

With its cobwebbed portals, crumbling German-era colonial buildings and small alleyways where the sounds of children playing echo together with the footsteps of history, central Bagamoyo is well worth a leisurely stroll. The most interesting area is

along Ocean Rd. Here, among other buildings, you'll find the imposing remains of the old **German boma** (fortified living compound), built in 1897; a **school**, which dates to the late 19th century and was the first multiracial school in what is now Tanzania; and **Liku House**, which served as the German administrative headquarters until the capital was moved to Dar es Salaam. Directly on the beach are the **German Customs House** (1895) and Bagamoyo's colourful **port**, where you can while away the time watching boat builders at work. The port is also the site of a busy **fish market** (on the site of the old slave market) with lively auctions most afternoons. Northwest of here are several small streets lined with Zanzibari-style **carved doors**.

About 2km north of town and reached via a long mango-shaded avenue is the **Holy Ghost Catholic Mission**, with its excellent **museum** (☎ 244 0010; admission free, donations appreciated; ⊙ 10am-5pm) – one of Bagamoyo's highlights, and an essential stop. In the same compound is the chapel where Livingstone's body was laid before being taken to Zanzibar Town en route to Westminster Abbey. The mission itself dates from the 1868 establishment of Freedom Village, and is the oldest in Tanzania.

COLLEGE OF ARTS

About 500m south of Bagamoyo along the road to Dar es Salaam is **Chuo cha Sanaa** (College of Arts; ☎ 244 0149, 244 0032; www.college-of-arts.org), a renowned theatre and arts college, home of the national dance company and one of the best measures of Tanzania's artistic pulse. When school is in session there are occasional traditional dancing and drumming performances, and it's possible to arrange drumming or dancing lessons. The annual highlight is the Bagamoyo Arts Festival (p311). For more on the Chuo cha Sanaa and arts in Bagamoyo, see the website of the **Bagamoyo Friendship Society** (www.bagamoyo.com).

KAOLE RUINS

Just south of Bagamoyo, time slides several centuries further into the past at the overgrown but intriguing **Kaole ruins** (admission Tsh1500). At their centre are the remains of a 13th-century mosque, which is one of the oldest in mainland Tanzania, and also one of the oldest in East Africa. It was built in the days when the Sultan of Kilwa held

THIS OPEN SORE OF THE WORLD

David Livingstone – one of Africa's most famous explorers and missionaries – was born in 1813 in Blantyre, Scotland, the second of seven children in a poor family. After a childhood spent working at a local cotton gin, followed by medical studies and ordination, he set off for Africa, arriving in Cape Town (South Africa) in 1841. Over the next two decades, Livingstone penetrated into some of the most inaccessible corners of the continent on a series of expeditions – making his way north into the Kalahari, west to present-day Angola and the Atlantic coast, and east along the Zambezi River and to Victoria Falls. In 1866 he set off from the area around Mikindani for what was to be his final expedition, seeking to conclusively solve the riddle of the Nile's source. He made his way as far as Ujiji, where he was famously 'found' by the American journalist Henry Morton Stanley.

After exploring parts of Lake Tanganyika with Stanley and spending time near Tabora, Livingstone set off again on his quest. He died in 1873 in Chitambo, in present-day Zambia. After cutting out and burying his heart, his porters carried his embalmed body in an epic 1500km journey to Bagamoyo and the sea, where it was then taken to England.

During his travels, Livingstone was tormented by the ravages of the slave trade that surrounded him. On his trips back to Europe, he spoke and wrote ceaselessly against it, in an effort to expose its horrors and injustices to the rest of the world. These efforts, combined with the attention attracted by his well-publicised funeral, the establishment of Freedom Village in Bagamoyo and reports from other missionaries, marked a point of no return for the slave trade. British attempts to halt the trade were mobilised, and it finally ground to a halt in the early 20th century.

In 1874 Livingstone was buried with full honours in London's Westminster Abbey. Today, a plaque memorialises his efforts to end the horrors of the slave trade with what were purportedly his last written words: 'All I can add in my solitude, is, may heaven's rich blessing come down on every one, American, English or Turk, who will help to heal this open sore of the world'.

sway over coastal trade, and long before Bagamoyo had assumed any significance. Nearby is a second mosque dating to the 15th century, as well as about 22 graves, many of which also date back to the same period. Among the graves are several Shirazi pillar-style tombs reminiscent of those at Tongoni (p151), but in somewhat better condition.

The most direct way to reach the ruins on foot is by following the beach south for about 5km past Kaole village into the mangrove swamps. Where the beach apparently ends, go a few hundred metres inland and look for the stone pillars. There's an easier, slightly longer route along the road running past Chuo cha Sanaa. Both routes, and especially the beach route, have a reputation for muggings, so it's best to walk in a group and with a guide, and not carry valuables.

EXCURSIONS

The coast around Bagamoyo is full of interesting water birds, mangrove ecosystems and some uncrowded stretches of sand. The tourist information office and most of the hotels can arrange excursions to **Mbegani lagoon**, the **Ruvu River delta** and **Mwambakuni sand bar**, all nearby. Expect to pay from US$20 to US$25 per person with four people.

Sleeping & Eating

BUDGET

Mary Nice Place (☎ 0744-024015; maryniceplace@yahoo .co.uk; r Tsh10,000-15,000) Simple and homy, this is the best budget bet – a converted house with a small garden, clean, no-frills rooms with fan, and the possibility of meals. It's just in from the road to the left, a few minutes on foot after passing Chuo cha Sanaa, and unsignposted. Anyone should be able to point you in the right direction, or look for the thatched entry gate covered with bougainvillea blossoms.

Double M Guesthouse (☎ 244 0227; r Tsh4000) This is a reasonable alternative if Mary Nice Place is full, and the cheapest recommendable option. The rooms all have fans, nets and a small double bed. Follow Majengo Rd from the bus stand past some small houses for about 400m until the signposted turn-off to the left.

For cheap local meals, try New Top Life Inn, two blocks northwest of the market.

MID-RANGE

Travellers Lodge (☎ 244 0077; www.travellers-lodge
.com; camping per person with shower Tsh3500, s/d without bathroom Tsh14,000/18,000, s/d garden cottage from
Tsh25,000/30,000, s/d beach cottage Tsh40,000/45,000;
meals from Tsh3500) With its relaxed atmosphere and reasonable prices, this is the best
value of the beach places. Accommodation
is in cottages scattered around expansive
grounds, with some on the beach. The least-
expensive ones are a hike from the bathroom, but otherwise are decent value, and
there's a restaurant. It's on the road running parallel to the beach, just south of the
entrance to the Catholic mission.

Bagamoyo Beach Resort (☎ 244 0083; bbr@baga
net.com; bandas per person without bathroom Tsh9000, s/d
with fan Tsh26,000/32,000, with air-con Tsh34,000/42,000;
meals about Tsh4000; 🗷) Fine and friendly with
adequate but undistinguished rooms in two
blocks (ask for the one closer to the water),
a few no-frills *bandas* (thatched-roof hut
with wooden or earthen walls) on the beach
that have just a bed and net and are good
budget value; and a seaside location just
north of Travellers Lodge. The cuisine is
vaguely French, and tasty.

Badeco Beach Hotel (☎ 244 0018; www.badeco
beachhotel.com; camping per person with showers Tsh3000,
d without bathroom Tsh12,000, d/tr Tsh24,000/30,000; meals
from Tsh3000) This long-standing German-run
place has a large, thatched restaurant and
en suite rooms – all with Zanzibar-style
beds – that have been renovated and are
good value. There are also cheaper rooms
sharing facilities. It's on the beach at the
southern end of town. Near the entrance is
a monument marking the spot where the
'rebellious Africans' who fought against
the German colonial government were
hanged.

Gemini Lodge (☎ 022-286 5395, 022-286 1191) If
this place (formerly the Old Market Guesthouse) reopens, it will be an excellent
choice in an atmospheric restored house
just opposite the old market in the most
historic part of town.

In addition to these places, Bagamoyo
has a string of bland mid-range hotels, most
of which cater to conferences and groups,
and none of which are particularly notable.
Among the better ones:

Livingstone Club (☎ 244 0080/59; www.livingstone
-club.com; s/d US$65/85; 🗷 🗷) The best of the bunch,
with an opulent reception area and luxurious rooms.

Paradise Holiday Resort (☎ 244 0136/40; www
.paradiseresort.net; s/d from US$45/66; 🗷 🗷) Modern
rooms, some with sea views, in a large, sterile, apartment-
style complex. Add 6% to these prices if you're paying by
credit card. It's along the beach road north of Bagamoyo
Beach Resort.

Millennium Sea Breeze Resort (☎ 244 0201;
reservation@millennium.co.tz; s/d from US$60/80; 🗷)
A large and architecturally ponderous establishment with
reasonable rooms in round double-storey *bandas*, all with
TV and minifridge; avoid the smaller rooms at the back
of the property. It's on the beach between Kaole and
the port.

TOP END

Lazy Lagoon (☎ 0748-237422, 0744-237422; www
.tanzaniasafaris.info; s/d full board & boat transfers
US$160/240; 🗷) For curling up with a book,
lazing by the pool, snorkelling or digging
your toes into the soft, wet sand, it's hard
to beat this relaxing, upmarket place about
10km south of Bagamoyo on the secluded
Lazy Lagoon peninsula. Accommodation
is in cosy thatched *bandas,* where you'll be
lulled to sleep by the sound of lapping waters
mixing with the night-time symphony from
the surrounding brush. To get here by road,
follow signs from the main highway to the
Mbegani Fisheries compound, from where
it's just a short boat ride over to the lodge.
You can leave your vehicle in the fisheries
compound. Transfers from Dar es Salaam
can be arranged and there's an airstrip for
charter flights.

Getting There & Away

Bagamoyo is about 70km north of Dar es
Salaam and an easy drive along good tar-
mac. With a 4WD it's also possible to reach
Bagamoyo from Msata (65km west on the
Dar es Salaam–Arusha highway, north of
Chalinze).

On public transport, there are buses and
minibuses between Bagamoyo and Dar es
Salaam (Tsh1000, three hours) throughout
the day.

Dhows to Zanzibar cost about Tsh5000,
but before jumping aboard, read the boxed
text on p328. You'll need to register first
with the immigration officer in the old
customs building. Departures are usually
around 1am, arriving in Zanzibar sometime
the next morning if all goes well. There is
no regular dhow traffic direct to Saadani
or Pangani.

SAADANI GAME RESERVE

About 70km up the coast from Bagamoyo and directly opposite Zanzibar is tiny Saadani Game Reserve, a 1000-sq-km patch of coastal wilderness that is only centimetres away from being declared Tanzania's newest national park (only awaiting final approval by parliament). Laid-back and relaxing, it's one of the few spots in Tanzania where you can enjoy the beach and bush at the same time. It's also easily accessed from Dar es Salaam as an overnight excursion and is a good choice if you don't have time to explore further afield.

To the south of the reserve is the languidly flowing Wami River, where you'll probably see hippos, crocodiles and many birds, including lesser flamingos (in the delta), fish eagles, hammerkops, kingfishers, bee-eaters and more. It's interesting to watch the vegetation along the river banks change with the decreasing salinity of the water as you move upstream. In some sections, there are also marked variations between the two banks, with areas of date palms and lush foliage on one side, and whistling thorn acacias reminiscent of drier areas of the country on the other. While terrestrial wildlife viewing isn't close to what it is in the national parks, animal numbers are slowly but surely increasing now that poaching is being brought under control. In addition to hippos and crocs, it's quite likely that you'll see giraffes. With more effort, you may also see elephants, Lichtenstein's hartebeests and even lions, although these are more difficult to spot.

The beach stretches as far as you can see in each direction, and because it faces due east you'll be treated to some beautiful sunrises. Just south of the main reserve area is tiny Saadani village, which – although it doesn't look like much today – was once one of the major ports in the area. Among other things, you can still see the crumbling walls of an Arab-built fort that was used as a holding cell for slaves before they were shipped to Zanzibar. During German colonial times it served as the customs house.

Information

Entry to the reserve costs US$20/5 per day per adult/child aged five to 15 years, and guides cost US$10 per day. Camping costs US$20/5 per adult/child aged five to 15 years. Although the reserve stays open year-round, access during the rainy season is difficult. If you do make it in during this time, you're likely to be limited to the area around the beach and the camps. Saadani is administered by Tanapa (p35), and the **park office** (saadani@bushlink.co.tz; Mkwaja) is at the park's northern end.

For information on Saadani's history and wildlife, browse through the excellent *Saadani: An Introduction to Tanzania's Future 13th National Park* by Dr Rolf Baldus, Doreen Broska and Kirsten Röttcher, available free at http://wildlife-programme.gtz .de/wildlife/tourism_saadani.html.

Sights & Activities

In addition to relaxing on the beach and observing bird life, the main activities are **boat trips** along the Wami and **wildlife drives** and **walks**. There's also a **cultural tourism programme** (per person per tour Tsh10,000, plus a Tsh1000 per-person village development fee), with tours of Saadani village focused on learning about local life and a bit of the area's long history. It's based at Warthog Camp (p144), and can be organised there, through the Saadani lodges, or through the WCST office in Dar es Salaam (p36).

Sleeping

Saadani Safari Lodge (☎ 022-277 3294, 0741-555678; www.saadanisafarilodge.com; s/d with full board & park fees US$193/310) This delectable beach-side retreat is the only lodging within the park, and a fine base from which to explore the area. Each of the nine cosy cottages is set directly on the beach with nothing in front of you except the sea and the sunrise, or the night sky full of stars. There's an open, thatched restaurant, also directly on the sand, with a raised sundowner deck, and a tree house overlooking a small waterhole. The atmosphere is unpretentious and comfortable, staff unfailingly friendly and helpful, and the cuisine is excellent. Safaris – including boat safaris on the Wami River, vehicle safaris, walks and snorkelling excursions to a nearby sandbank – cost US$35 per person per excursion, with a minimum of three people.

Tent With a View Safari Lodge (☎ 022-211 0507, 0741-323318; www.saadani.com; s/d full board US$220/350) For a secluded, tropical hideaway with a touch of the wild, this wonderful lodge is the place to come, with luxurious raised *bandas* hidden away among the coconut groves on the beach just outside the park boundaries. It makes an ideal base for exploring Saadani, or for simply immersing yourself in the sounds of the bush and the surf. The *bandas* all have large verandas where you can curl up in a hammock and gaze out to sea, and everything is very plush, but in a low-key, comfortable way. In addition to safaris in the park (US$70 per person for a full-day safari, including a boat safari along the Wami River; US$35 for a half-day vehicle safari; US$15 for a walking safari – all prices per person, minimum two people), there's the chance for various excursions around the camp, including guided walks to a nearby green turtle nesting site. Park entry fees need only be paid for days you go into the park on safari. No children under six years old.

Camping is possible at the basic **Warthog Camp** (camping per person US$8, tent rental US$10), outside the park in Saadani village, with pit latrines and bucket showers, and occasionally a tent for rent. WCST (see the boxed text, p36) can help you make a booking. Also check with Saadani Safari Lodge, which is planning to open a camping ground near the village.

Getting There & Away

AIR
ZanAir has daily flights connecting Dar es Salaam, Zanzibar and Saadani (US$50 one way Zanzibar–Saadani, US$75 one way Dar es Salaam–Saadani via Zanzibar). Coastal Aviation flies between Saadani and Selous Game Reserve (US$130 one way, minimum two passengers).

Air charters cost about US$170/290 one way from Zanzibar/Dar es Salaam for a three-passenger plane.

BOAT
Local fishing boats sail regularly between Saadani and Zanzibar (from behind Tembo House Hotel in Zanzibar Town), but the journey is known for being rough and few travellers do it. Better are boat transfers with Saadani Safari Lodge from the Wami River to their camp.

CAR & MOTORCYCLE
Both lodges provide road transport to/from Dar es Salaam for between US$155

and US$200 per vehicle. Allow about four hours for the journey.

From Dar es Salaam, the route is via Chalinze on the Morogoro road, and then north to Mandera village (situated about 50km north of Chalinze on the Arusha highway). At Mandera you should bear east along quite a reasonable dirt road (you will need a 4WD) and continue about 60km to Saadani. It's easy to get to Mandera by bus, but from there to Saadani there is no public transport.

To reach Saadani from Pangani, you need to first cross the Pangani River by ferry, then continue south along a rough road past stands of cashew, sisal and teak via Mkwaja to the reserve's northern gate at Mligaji. Although much improved in recent years, this route is only possible with 4WD. Tent With a View Safari Lodge and Tides (p146) provide transfers for US$100 per vehicle each way (about one hour).

BUS
There's a daily and very slow bus between Tanga and Mkwaja (Tsh4500, five hours), from where you could arrange to be collected by the lodges. However, the bus is prone to frequent breakdowns and the whims of the Pangani River ferry.

Until the ferry over the Wami River is repaired, there's no direct road access to Saadani from Bagamoyo, although Saadani Safari Lodge will come and pick you up at the Wami in its boat and sail you into the camp.

TRAIN
It's possible to get within about 8km of Saadani Game Reserve by train on a spur line. From Dar es Salaam, take any bus heading towards Chalinze and ask to be dropped at 'Ruvu Bridge,' which is nothing more than a railway overpass on the highway about 5km west of Mlandizi. Climb up the embankment to the bridge, get on the train and take it to Mvave, 8km west of Saadani. Departures heading north are at around 9am on Wednesday and Saturday. In the other direction, the train passes Mvave around noon on Tuesday and Friday. Ask the lodges to help you out with arrangements, as the schedule changes frequently; they may also be able to meet you in Mvave.

PANGANI

About 55km south of Tanga is the small and charmingly dilapidated Swahili outpost of Pangani. It rose from obscure beginnings as just one of many coastal dhow ports to become a terminus of the caravan route from Lake Tanganyika, a major export point for slaves and ivory, and one of the largest ports between Bagamoyo and Mombasa. Sisal and copra plantations were established in the area, and several European missions and exploratory journeys to the interior began from here. By the end of the 19th century the focus had shifted to Tanga and Dar es Salaam and Pangani again faded into anonymity.

Today, the town makes a fascinating step back into the centuries, especially in the area within about three blocks of the river, where you'll see some carved doorways, buildings from the German colonial era and old houses of Indian traders. The best place to base yourself is on one of the beaches running north and south of town.

History

Despite Pangani's ages-old feel, the town is relatively modern compared with Tongoni, Kaole and other settlements along the coast. It rose to prominence during the mid-19th century, when it was a linchpin between the Zanzibar sultanate and the inland caravan routes, and it was during this era that the river-front **slave depot** was built. Pangani's oldest building is the old **boma**, which dates to 1810, and was originally the private residence of a wealthy Omani trader. More recent is the **Customs House**, built a decade later. Probably several centuries older is the settlement at Bweni, diagonally opposite Pangani on the southern bank of the river, where a 15th-century grave has been found.

In September 1888 Pangani was the first town to rebel against the German colonial administration in the Abushiri revolt (p145).

Orientation

The centre of Pangani, with the market and bus stand, is on the corner of land where the Pangani River meets the sea. About 2km north of here is the main junction where the road from Muheza joins the coastal road, and where you should get out of the bus if you're arriving from Muheza and staying at the beaches north of town.

Information

The closest banks are in Tanga. The sporadically functioning **Pangani Cultural Tourism Program office** (8am-5pm Mon-Fri, 8am-noon Sat) on the river front can help organise town tours, river cruises and excursions to Maziwe island, as can any of the hotels.

It's not safe to walk along the beaches close to town.

Sights & Activities

Meandering along the southern edge of town is the **Pangani River**, which attracts many water birds, as well as populations of crocodiles and sometimes other animals as well. It's best explored on a river cruise via

THE ABUSHIRI REVOLT

Although usually associated with Bagamoyo, Pangani was the birthplace of the Abushiri revolt, one of East Africa's major colonial rebellions. The catalyst came in 1884, when a young German, Carl Peters, founded the German East Africa Company (Deutsch-Ostafrikanische Gesellschaft or DOAG). Over the next few years, in an effort to tap into the lucrative inland caravan trade, Peters managed to extract agreement from the Sultan of Zanzibar that the DOAG could take over the administration of customs duties in the sultan's mainland domains. However, neither the sultan's representative in Pangani nor the majority of locals were amenable to the idea. When the DOAG raised its flag next to that of the sultan, simmering tensions exploded. Under the leadership of an Afro-Arab trader named Abushiri bin Salim al-Harth, a loosely organised army, including many of the sultan's own guards, ousted the Germans, thus igniting a series of fierce power struggles that continued in other port towns along the coast. The Germans only managed to subdue the revolt over a year later after the arrival of reinforcements, the imposition of a naval blockade and the hanging of Abushiri. In the wake of the revolt, the DOAG went bankrupt, and the colonial capital was moved from Bagamoyo to Dar es Salaam.

local dhow, which can be arranged by any of the hotels. For impressive views over the river, climb up the bluff on the southern bank to the currently closed Protea Pangani River Hotel.

Shimmering in the sun about 10km offshore is tiny **Maziwe Marine Reserve** (admission Tsh1000), an idyllic sand island with some excellent snorkelling in the surrounding crystal-clear waters. Dolphins favour the waters as well, and are frequently spotted. Maziwe can only be visited at low tide; there's no food or drink available on the island.

Sleeping & Eating
TOWN CENTRE
New River View Inn Restaurant & Lodge (Jamhuri St; s/d without bathroom Tsh2500/4000) This is the cheapest recommendable place, with no-frills rooms sharing facilities. It's on the waterfront road, just east of the Customs House.

Safari Lodge (r Tsh7500-10,000) This scruffy establishment is the only other choice in the town centre, with a mixture of large no-frills rooms with net and fan, and a few small, dark cubicles, all with the advantage of a usually functioning bathroom. There's also a restaurant, though Pangani's lively night-time street markets are a better bet. It's on the road running parallel to the waterfront Jamhuri St, and one block in from the water.

NORTH OF PANGANI
There are several good options north of Pangani, just off the coastal road to Tanga.

Peponi Holiday Resort (☎ 0748-202962, 0741-540139; www.peponiresort.com; camping per person US$4, d banda US$40) This recommended and relaxing place is set in expansive grounds on a long, good beach about 19km north of Pangani. In addition to simple, breezy double *bandas,* there are several larger five-person chalets, a camp site and ablution blocks. It's popular with backpackers and families, and there are discounted rates for both. Tasty cuisine (about Tsh4000) and a nearby reef for snorkelling complete the picture. The proprietors are very helpful with information about excursions and onward connections, and the camp has its own *mashua* (motorised dhow) for sailing. If you're camping, bring supplies with you, and if you'll be staying in the *bandas,* book in

advance if possible. Take any bus running along the Pangani–Tanga coastal route and ask the driver to drop you near Kigombe village at the Peponi turn-off (Tsh500 from Pangani, Tsh800 from Tanga), from where it's just a short walk. Taxis from Tanga cost Tsh15,000 to Tsh25,000, depending on road conditions and your bargaining abilities.

Argovia Tented Lodge (☎ 0741-511600; argovia@kaributanga.com; camping per person US$5, s/d bandas US$27/38, s luxury tents US$56-60, d luxury tents US$66-82) Architecturally eclectic and appealingly subdued in ambience, this good-value establishment is the only upmarket accommodation along the northern coast. Most accommodation is in raised luxury tents of the sort you find in classy safari camps. There are also some small stone *bandas,* a good restaurant and a range of excursions. It's on a low cliff overlooking the sea, and signposted about 3km north of the main junction.

Tinga Tinga Resort (☎ 027-263 0022, 027-264 3419; tingatingapga@yahoo.com; camping per person Tsh4000, s/d/tr US$25/35/45; meals about Tsh4000) The very low-key Tinga Tinga is laid-back, friendly and a reasonable mid-range choice, though the other beach places are better value. Accommodation is in large, faded twin-bedded bungalows set inland, and just north of the main junction. Five minutes' walk away is a restaurant-bar gazebo overlooking the water, with swimming possible just below.

SOUTH OF PANGANI
Though rarely featuring on tourist itineraries, the long, excellent, palm-fringed beach about 15km south of Pangani around Ushongo makes a wonderful coastal getaway. Swimming isn't tide-dependent, and apart from the area in the immediate vicinity of Ushongo village, you'll have most spots to yourself.

Tides (☎ 027-264 0844, 0748-225812; www.thetideslodge.com; s/d half board US$95/150) This unpretentious place is one of the finest lodges along the Tanzanian coast, mixing an intimate seaside location with spacious, breezy bungalows and excellent cuisine. The bungalows – there are seven, lined up amid the coconut palms along the beach – are wonderful, with huge beds surrounded by billowing mosquito nets, large bathrooms and stylish, subdued décor. At night, you can step out directly onto the sand to gaze at the star-studded skies, or be lulled to sleep by the crashing of the waves on the shore. There's a beach-side bar, and staff can sort out whatever excursions you'd like, including Maziwe island, inshore and offshore fishing, dhow cruises on the Pangani River and bicycle rental. For a honeymoon location or beach-side retreat, it's hard to beat the value here, especially in comparison with similar-quality places elsewhere on the coast. Pick-ups from Pangani (US$16) can be arranged, as can transfers to/from Saadani Game Reserve (US$100 per vehicle) and to/from Segera (US$70 per vehicle), where there are connections to the Scandinavian Express bus between Dar es Salaam and Arusha.

Emayani Beach Lodge (☎ 027-250 1741; www .emayanilodge.com; s/d/tr US$63/79/100) Emayani, on the beach about 2km north of Tides, has a row of agreeably rustic bungalows strung out along the sand and a restaurant, and is about as laid-back as it gets. Everything is very open and natural – the bungalows are made entirely of *makuti* (plaited palm fronds) – and very conducive to chilling out. Small kayaks and windsurfing equipment are available to rent, and staff can arrange sails on a *ngalawa* (outrigger canoe) and excursions to Maziwe island, Pangani and elsewhere in the area. Pick-ups from Pangani cost US$20 return.

Other recommendations:

Coco Beach Resort (☎ 0741-333449; camping per person US$6; s/d without bathroom US$18/36, s/d/tr US$21/42/60) Small, serviceable cottages set among the palm trees just in from the beach south of Emayani Beach Lodge, and a restaurant. A good place if you're on a budget.

Beach Crab Resort This new place was under construction on the beach south of Tides, with rooms and various water sports planned.

Getting There & Away

AIR
There's an airstrip within about 1km of Ushongo for charter flights. ZanAir and Coastal Aviation are the best lines to check with, as both have scheduled flights to nearby destinations (ZanAir to Saadani and Coastal to Saadani and Tanga).

BOAT
Dhows sail regularly between Pangani and Mkokotoni, on the northwestern coast of Zanzibar.

The vehicle ferry over the Pangani River runs in theory between 6.30am and 6.30pm daily (Tsh100/4000 per person/vehicle), and there are small passenger boats (large enough to take a motorcycle) throughout the day (Tsh200).

BUS
The best connections between Pangani and Tanga are via the rehabilitated coastal road, with about five buses daily (Tsh1500, 1½ hours), except during the height of the rainy season. The first departs Pangani at about 6.30am so you can connect with a Tanga–Arusha bus. It's also possible to reach Pangani from Muheza (Tsh1000), from where there are connections to Tanga or Korogwe, but the road is worse and connections infrequent.

Getting Around
To get to Ushongo and the beaches south of Pangani, all the hotels do pick-ups. Alternatively, there's a bus that runs between Tanga and Mkwaja (at the edge of Saadani Game Reserve) that passes Mwera village (6km from Ushongo) daily about 7am going north, and about 3.30pm going south.

Another possibility is to rent a bike in Pangani and cycle down to Ushongo.

TANGA
☎ 027

Tanga, a major industrial centre until the collapse of the sisal market, is Tanzania's second-largest seaport and its third-largest town behind Dar es Salaam and Mwanza. Despite its size, it's a pleasant-enough place with a sleepy, semicolonial atmosphere and faded charm. While there's little reason to make a special detour to visit, it makes an agreeable stop if you're en route to or from Mombasa, and a convenient springboard to the good beaches around Pangani.

History
Although there has probably been a reasonably sized settlement at Tanga since at least the Shirazi era, the town first came into its own in the early to mid-19th century as a starting point for trade caravans to the interior. Ivory was the main commodity traded, with a turnover of about 70,000 lbs annually in the late 1850s, according to explorer Richard Burton, who visited here.

The real boom, however, came with the arrival of the Germans in the late 19th century, who built up the town and harbour as part of the construction of a railway line linking Moshi and the Kilimanjaro region with the sea. The Germans also introduced sisal to the area, and Tanzania soon became the world's leading producer and exporter of the crop, with sisal the centre of local economic life. In WWI, Tanga was the site of the ill-fated Battle of Tanga (later memorialised in William Boyd's novel, *An Ice-Cream War*), in which poorly prepared British troops were soundly trounced by the Germans.

As the world sisal market began to collapse in the 1970s, Tanga's economy spiralled downward. Today, much of the town's infrastructure has been abandoned and the economy is just a shadow of its former self, although you'll still see vast plantations stretching westwards along the plains edging the Usambara Mountains.

Orientation

The town centre is set along the waterfront and is easily covered on foot. About 1.5km south of here, and south of the railway tracks in the Ngamiani section, is the bus station. It costs Tsh1000 from here into town in a taxi. About 2km east of town, and reached by following Hospital Rd (which runs parallel to the water) is the suburban Ras Kazone section, with a few hotels.

Information

INTERNET ACCESS

Impala Internet Café (Sokoine St; per hr Tsh500; 9am-10pm)

Kaributanga.com (Sokoine St; per hr Tsh500; 9am-9pm)

MEDICAL SERVICES

MD Pharmacy (☎ 264 4067; cnr Sokoine St & Mkwakwani Rd; 8am-12.45pm & 2-6pm Mon-Fri, 8am-12.45pm Sat & Sun) Opposite the market.

MONEY

NBC (cnr Bank & Sokoine Sts) Just west of the market. This bank changes cash and travellers cheques. No ATM yet, but one is planned.

POST

Main post office (Independence Ave) Near the southeastern corner of Jamhuri Park, just off Independence Ave.

TOURIST INFORMATION

A new tourist information centre is planned for the corner of Usambara St and Independence Ave.

Tourcare Tanzania (☎ 264 4111; Mkwakwani Rd; 8am-5pm) Helpful with information on nearby attractions and arranging guides for excursions (Tsh10,000 per group per day).

Dangers & Annoyances

The harbour area is seedy and best avoided. In the evenings, take care around Port Rd and Independence Ave near Jamhuri Park.

Sights & Activities

Despite its size, Tanga has remarkably few 'sights', apart from its atmospheric colonial-era architecture. The most interesting areas for a stroll are around Jamhuri Park overlooking the harbour, near which you'll find the old German-built **clock tower**, and the park and cemetery surrounding the **Askari monument** at the end of Sokoine St.

Directly offshore is the small, mangrove-ringed **Toten Island** (Island of the Dead) with the overgrown ruins of a mosque (dating to the 17th century) and some 18th- and 19th-century gravestones. Fifteenth-century pottery fragments have also been found on the island, indicating that it may have been settled during the Shirazi era. The island's long history ended in the late 19th century, when its inhabitants moved to the mainland. Its ruins are much less accessible and atmospheric than those at Tongoni, and it's only worth a look if you have extra time.

There are fishing boats on the western side of the harbour that can take you over, although we've only heard unhappy tales from the few travellers we know who have tried this. A better approach is to organise an excursion through the tourist information office.

SWIMMING

Tanga Yacht Club (admission Tsh2500; Ras Kazone) has a tiny beach and is popular with resident expats on weekend afternoons. For more of a local ambience, try **Raskazone Swimming Club** (admission Tsh500), about 400m southwest of the yacht club, with a small beach, showers, changing rooms and meals. Given the dubious cleanliness of Tanga's water, both places are more appealing for sitting around than for swimming.

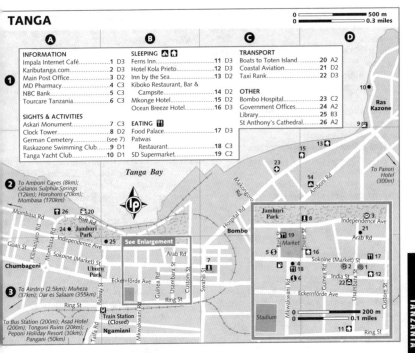

TANGA

INFORMATION	
Impala Internet Café	1 D3
Kaributanga.com	2 D3
Main Post Office	3 D2
MD Pharmacy	4 C3
NBC Bank	5 C3
Tourcare Tanzania	6 C3

SIGHTS & ACTIVITIES	
Askari Monument	7 C3
Clock Tower	8 D2
German Cemetery	(see 7)
Raskazone Swimming Club	9 D1
Tanga Yacht Club	10 D1

SLEEPING	
Ferns Inn	11 D3
Hotel Kola Prieto	12 D3
Inn by the Sea	13 D2
Kiboko Restaurant, Bar & Campsite	14 D2
Mkonge Hotel	15 D2
Ocean Breeze Hotel	16 D2

EATING	
Food Palace	17 D3
Patwas Restaurant	18 C3
SD Supermarket	19 C2

TRANSPORT	
Boats to Toten Island	20 A2
Coastal Aviation	21 D2
Taxi Rank	22 D3

OTHER	
Bombo Hospital	23 C2
Government Offices	24 A2
Library	25 B3
St Anthony's Cathedral	26 A2

Sleeping

Tanga doesn't distinguish itself when it comes to hotels. If you have a choice, head to the beaches south of town near Pangani (p146).

BUDGET

Kiboko Restaurant, Bar & Campsite (☎ 264 4929; jda-kiboko@bluemail.ch; Amboni Rd; camping per person US$4) A great addition to Tanga's struggling accommodation scene, with good, secure camping in a large yard, spotless ablutions, power points, a well-stocked bar and a nice garden restaurant. Management is very helpful with excursions and information on Tanga. It's about 300m in from Hospital Rd; the turn-off is signposted about 500m before Inn by the Sea.

Inn by the Sea (☎ 264 4614; Hospital Rd; r with fan/air-con Tsh8000/10,000; ❄) Inn by the Sea has a delightful water-side setting on the south-western edge of Ras Kazone and very run-down rooms, although they're fair enough value for the price. Meals can be arranged; allow about two hours.

Other recommendations:

Ocean Breeze Hotel (☎ 264 4445; cnr Tower & Sokoine Sts; r with fan/air-con Tsh7000/12,000; ❄) Rooms here are on the scruffy side, but OK, and many have nets. It's just east of the market, and one of the better budget choices in the town centre.

Ferns Inn (☎ 0748-481609; Usambara St; s/d Tsh5000/6000) Small and friendly with undistinguished, noisy rooms, meals and lots of local flavour. It's at the southern end of Usambara St, just before the railway tracks.

Asad Hotel (☎ 264 4711, 264 6801; d Tsh12,500; ❄) Functional rooms with views over the bus stand, and worth considering if you have an early-morning departure; it's in a multistorey building just off Taifa Rd in the Ngamiani area.

MID-RANGE

Panori Hotel (☎ 264 6044; panori@africaonline.co.tz; Ras Kazone; s/d in new wing Tsh25,000/30,000, in old renovated wing Tsh18,000/22,000, in old wing Tsh15,000/18,000; ❄) If you don't mind the location, in a residential area about 3km from the centre (no public transport), this is one of the better mid-range choices. There are clean, modern rooms in the new wing, all with nets and fan, and a nice outdoor restaurant with slow service and tasty meals. Take Hospital Rd east to Ras Kazone, and follow the signposts.

Hotel Kola Prieto (☎ 264 4206; kolaprieto@hotmail.com; India St; r Tsh22,700; ✕) This centrally located high-rise hotel has good modern rooms (no nets or screens), efficient service and, despite the bland ambience, does a good job of fulfilling the promise of its business card to provide you with the 'finest hospitality sensation'.

Mkonge Hotel (☎ 264 3440; Hospital Rd; d US$55; ✕) Sits imposingly on a grassy lawn overlooking the sea with a grand façade that masks a very ordinary, soulless interior. The rooms are OK, and some overlook the water, but they aren't particularly good value.

Eating

Tanga compensates for its dearth of good accommodation with a few culinary gems (all geared to budget travellers).

Patwas Restaurant (Mkwakwani Rd; meals from Tsh1500; ✕ 8am-8pm Mon-Sat) An unassuming place and the best restaurant in Tanga, with lassis, fresh juices, tasty, good-value meals and helpful owners. It's just south of the market.

Food Palace (☎ 264 6816; Sokoine St; ✕ lunch Mon, breakfast, lunch & dinner Tue-Sun) Another good choice, with an array of tasty Indian snacks and meals, including some good vegetarian selections.

Kiboko Restaurant & Bar (☎ 264 4929; jda-kiboko@bluemail.ch; Amboni Rd; meals from Tsh3000) Nice garden seating, a well-stocked bar and a huge menu featuring *kiboko*- (hippo-) sized portions of such delicacies as prawns *kiboko* with green pepper-sauce, king fish curry, sandwiches and *mishikaki* (skewered meat). For dessert, there's ice cream, plus chocolate truffle and other indulgences on order.

Good, cheap Indian meals are available in the evenings at Raskazone Swimming Club (p148). For self-catering try **SD Supermarket** (Bank St), behind the market.

Getting There & Away
AIR

There are daily flights on **Coastal Aviation** (☎ 264 6548; cnr Independence Ave & Usambara St) between Tanga, Dar es Salaam, Zanzibar and Pemba (one way between Tanga and Pemba/Dar es Salaam US$55/100). The airstrip is about 3km west of town along the Korogwe road (Tsh2000 in a taxi).

BOAT

The *Takrima* sails roughly weekly between Tanga and Wete on Pemba, departing in each direction at 10am (US$25, five hours).

BUS

To Dar es Salaam, the fastest connection is on Scandinavian, departing Tanga (en route from Mombasa) about 12.30pm (Tsh7000 Tanga to Dar es Salaam, four hours; book in advance). Otherwise, Raha Leo and several other lines depart Tanga every few hours between about 8am and 3pm (Tsh5500, five hours).

To Arusha, there are at least three departures between 6am and 11am (Tsh8000, seven hours). To Lushoto (Tsh3500, three to four hours), there are a couple of direct buses that depart by 7am, otherwise you can take any Arusha bus and transfer at Mombo.

To Pangani (Tsh1500, 1½ hours), there are small buses throughout the day along the coastal road.

For Mombasa, see p322; the Scandinavian bus from Dar es Salaam to Mombasa passes Tanga about noon.

Getting Around

There are taxi ranks at various places around town, including at the bus stand, and at the junction of Usambara and India Sts. Tourcare Tanzania (p148) can help with bicycle rental.

AROUND TANGA
Amboni Caves

Long the subject of local legend, these **limestone caves** (admission Tsh2000) are one of the most extensive subterranean systems in East Africa, and an intriguing offbeat excursion for anyone with an interest in spelunking. Now home to thousands of bats, they were traditionally believed to house various spirits, and continue to be a place of worship and ritual. The caves were originally thought to extend up to 200km or more, and are said to have been used by the Kenyan Mau Mau during the 1950s as a hide-out from the British. Although a

1994 survey concluded that their extent was much smaller – with the largest of the caves studied only 900m long – rumours of them reaching all the way to Mombasa persist.

It's possible to visit a small portion of the cave network, which is quite interesting once you get past the litter at the entrance. Bring along a torch, and wear closed shoes to avoid needing to pick bat droppings off your feet afterwards.

The caves are located about 8km northwest of Tanga off the Horohoro–Mombasa road, and an easy bicycle ride from town. Otherwise charter a taxi, or take a *dalla-dalla* towards Amboni village and get off at the turn-off for the caves, which is near the forestry office. From here, it's about 2.5km on foot to Kiomoni village; the caves stretch west of Kiomoni along the Mkulumuzi River. Guides can be arranged locally or at the tourist office in Tanga.

Galanos Sulphur Springs

If bending and crawling around the caves has left you feeling stiff in the joints, consider finishing the day with a visit to these green, odoriferous sulphur springs nearby. They take their name from a Greek sisal planter who was the first to recognise their potential for relaxation after the rigours of a long day in the fields. Now, although still in use, they are quite unappealing despite their supposedly therapeutic properties.

The unsignposted turn-off for the springs is along the Tanga–Mombasa road, about 2km north of the turn-off for the caves, and just after crossing the Sigi River. From here, it's around 2km further on. *Dalla-dallas* from Tanga run as far as Amboni village, from where you will need to continue on foot.

Tongoni Ruins

Basking in the coastal sun about 20km south of Tanga are the time-ravaged but historically intriguing **Tongoni ruins** (admission Tsh2000). They include the crumbling remains of a mosque and about 20 overgrown Shirazi pillar-style tombs – the largest collection of such tombs on the East African coast. Both the mosque and the tombs are estimated to date from the 14th or 15th century, when Tongoni was a major coastal trading port. Although most of the pillars have long since toppled to the ground, you can still see the recessed areas on some where decorative porcelain vases and offering bowls were placed. There are also about two dozen more recent, and largely unremarkable, tombs, dating from the 18th or 19th century.

To get here, take any vehicle heading towards Pangani along the coastal road and get out at the turn-off (look for a rusty signboard). From here, the ruins are about 1km east on foot. It's worth getting an early start, as finding a lift back in the afternoon can be difficult.

MUHEZA

Muheza is a scrappy junction town where the roads to Amani Nature Reserve and Pangani branch off the main Tanga highway. If you need to stay here, there are a few guesthouses, the most tolerable of which are the grubby **Hotel Ambassador** (s/d without bathroom Tsh2500/3500), on the main road towards Tanga, with no-frills rooms and meals, and the **Elephant Guest House** (d without bathroom Tsh3500), west of the Ambassador and just in from the main road. Muheza's central area, dominated by rows of rickety wooden market stalls, is about 1km in, and uphill from the main highway.

PLACE OF RUINS

Together with Mafia, Kilwa and other now-sleepy settlements along the coast, Tongoni (Place of Ruins) was once a major port in the network of Swahili trading towns that linked the gold, slave and ivory markets of Africa with the Orient. Its heyday was in the 15th century, when it had its own sultan, and was an inadvertent port of call for Vasco da Gama, whose ship ran aground here. By the early 18th century Tongoni had declined to the point of nonexistence, with the Portuguese disruption of local trade networks and the fall of Mombasa. In the late 18th century, it was resettled by Shirazis fleeing Kilwa (who named it Sitahabu, or 'Better Here than There') and experienced a brief revival, before declining completely shortly thereafter. For more on this period, and on the Tongoni ruins, see the excellent article *Antiquities of Tanga* by AA Mturi, available on the web at http://208.184.18.238/tangatz/Pages/Orientation/Greater/Text/Antiquities.html.

There's a Scandinavian Express bus booking office next to Hotel Ambassador (for buses between Dar es Salaam and Mombasa via Muheza and Tanga). Buses to Amani Nature Reserve leave from the main junction along the road leading towards the market.

KOROGWE

Korogwe is primarily of interest as a transport junction. In the western part of town, known as 'new' Korogwe, are the bus stand and several accommodation options. To the east is 'old' Korogwe with the train station (no passenger service).

The large road-side rest stop **Motel White Parrot** (☎ 264 1068; r Tsh15,000-25,000; meals Tsh4000; ✗) was just about to open as we passed through, with spiffy rooms and an efficient restaurant serving much better than the usual highway fare. It also has chilled fruit juices to go. It's on the main highway and unmissable.

For something cheaper, try **Travellers Inn** (d Tsh7500), opposite the bus stand, with clean rooms with enormous bathtubs, and a restaurant, or **White House Inn** (☎ 264 0554; r Tsh5000), just up the road on the opposite side.

USAMBARA MOUNTAINS

With their wide vistas, cool climate, winding paths and picturesque villages, the Usambaras are one of northeastern Tanzania's highlights. Rural life here revolves around a cycle of bustling, colourful market days that rotate from one village to the next, and is largely untouched by the booming safari scene and influx of fancy 4WDs in nearby Arusha. It's easily possible to spend at least a week hiking from village to village, or relaxing in one spot and doing your exploring as a series of day walks.

The Usambaras, which are part of the ancient Eastern Arc chain, are divided into two ranges separated by a 4km-wide valley. The western Usambaras, around Lushoto, are the most accessible and have the better road network, while the eastern Usambaras, around Amani, are less developed. Both ranges are densely populated, with an average of more than 300 people per sq km. The main tribes are the Sambaa, the Kilindi, the Zigua and the Mbugu.

Although the climate is comfortable year round, paths get too muddy for hiking during the rainy season. The best time to visit is from July to October, after the rains and when the air is at its clearest.

AMANI NATURE RESERVE

This often overlooked reserve is west of Tanga in the heart of the eastern Usambara mountains. It's a peaceful, beautiful place with some pleasant walks along shady forest paths, and is a highly worthwhile detour if you are ornithologically or botanically inclined.

History

Although Amani was only gazetted as a nature reserve in 1997, research in the area began about a century earlier when the Germans established a research station and extensive botanical gardens here. Large areas of forest were cleared and numerous new species introduced. Within a few years the gardens were the largest in Africa, totalling 304 hectares and containing between 600 and 1000 different species of plants, including numerous unique species. Soon after though, exploitation of the surrounding forest began and the garden began to decline. A sawmill was established and a railway link was created connecting Sigi, situated about 12km below Amani, with the main Tanga–Moshi line in order to facilitate the transport of timber to the coast.

During the British era, research was shifted to Nairobi, and the railway was replaced by a road linking Amani with Muheza. Many of the facilities at Amani were taken over by the nearby government-run malaria research centre and the gardens fell into neglect.

In more recent years, the real work at Amani has been done within the framework of the East Usambara Conservation Area Management Programme, with funding from the Tanzanian and Finnish governments and the EU. In addition to promoting sustainable resource use by local communities, one of the main focuses of the project has been to facilitate visitor access to the forests of the eastern Usambaras. There is now a good network of trails, several comfortable guesthouses and an association of local guides.

Information

At Sigi, there is a good **information centre** (8am-6pm) at the old station master's house full of information about the area's plants and animals, history, the traditional uses of medicinal plants and more.

The main **reserve office** (☎ 027-264 0313; entry fee per person US$5, per small/large vehicle US$2/4) is at Amani. Entry and guide fees (US$10 per person per day) can be paid here, or at the Sigi information centre.

Most trails take between one and three hours. They are detailed in the booklet *A Guide to Trails and Drive Routes in Amani Nature Reserve*, on sale at the information centre at Sigi and at the reserve office in Amani. In addition to the large variety of plants, you may see several unique bird species, including Amani and banded green sunbirds, and the green-headed oriole.

Sleeping & Eating

Amani Resthouse (☎ 027-264 0303; r per person full board without bathroom US$30) This rambling, old house, owned by the Amani Medical Research Centre, has several reasonable rooms and a large bathroom, though it's not as well maintained as the other resthouses and there is no breakfast-only option. To get here, branch right at the 'resthouse' signpost.

The **Amani Conservation Centre** (☎ 027-264 0313) runs two guesthouses, the **Amani Conservation Centre Rest House** (r without bathroom Tsh5000; Amani) and the **Sigi Rest House** (r Tsh5000; Sigi). Both are good, with hot water for bathing and filtered water for drinking. The rooms at Sigi have bathrooms and are marginally more comfortable, while the setting and rustic atmosphere are better at Amani. Meals (breakfast for Tsh1500, lunch and dinner for Tsh4000) are also available at both, though it's a good idea to bring fruit and snacks as a supplement. The Sigi Rest House is directly opposite the Sigi information centre. To reach the Amani Conservation Centre Rest House, once in Amani, continue straight past the main fork, ignoring the 'resthouse' signpost, to the reserve office. The Rest House is next to the office.

Camping (US$5 per person) is possible at both Sigi and Amani with your own tent and supplies.

Getting There & Away

Amani is 32km northwest of Muheza along a dirt road that is in fair condition the entire way, except for the last 7km, which are rocky and in bad shape (4WD only). There is usually at least one truck daily between Muheza and Sigi, sometimes continuing onto Amani (Tsh1500) and Kwamkoro, which is about 9km beyond Amani. The best time to catch this in Muheza is between about noon and 2pm. Going in the other direction, transport usually passes Amani at about 6.30am.

In the dry season, you can make it in a 2WD as far as Sigi, after which you'll need a 4WD. Allow 1½ to two hours travel time between Muheza and Amani. You can also walk from Sigi up to Amani along one of the trails, which takes about 2½ to three hours.

If you're driving from Muheza, the route is straightforward and signposted until the final junction, where you'll see Bulwa signposted to the right; Amani is about 2km further to the left.

LUSHOTO

☎ 027

Lushoto is a leafy highland town nestled in a fertile valley at about 1200m and surrounded by pines and eucalypts mixed with banana plants and other tropical foliage. It's the centre of the western Usambaras and makes an excellent base for hikes into the surrounding hills.

History

Lushoto's charms were first discovered by outsiders during the German era when the town (then known as Wilhelmstal) was a favoured holiday spot for colonial administrators, a local administrative centre and an important mission station. It was even slated at one point to become the colonial capital. Today, thanks to a temperate climate, it's best known for its bustling market (at its liveliest on Sunday), its abundant pears and plums and its superb walking.

Due in part to the high population density of the surrounding area and the resulting deforestation, erosion has long been a serious concern. Erosion control efforts were first initiated during the British era and today there are various projects under way, which you're likely to see as you hike in the area.

Information

INTERNET ACCESS

ELCT Office (per hr Tsh2000; ◷ 8am-8pm Mon-Sat) On the main road, next to Tumaini Hostel.

MONEY

National Microfinance Bank (◷ 8am-3pm Mon-Fri) On the main road. Changes cash and travellers cheques (minimum US$40 commission for travellers cheques).

TOURIST INFORMATION

If would-be guides approach you on the street, stop by the tourist office to verify that they are official before starting out.
Tourist information centre (☎ 264 0132) Just down the small road running next to the bank. This is the main spot in town for arranging hikes and guides.

Hiking

The western Usambaras around Lushoto offer some wonderful walking. Routes follow well-worn footpaths that weave among villages, cornfields and banana plantations, and range from a few hours to several days. An easy one to get started is to **Irente viewpoint** (about 1½ hours return), which be-

LUSHOTO

0	300 m
0	0.2 miles

INFORMATION	
ELCT Office.....................................**1** B4
National Microfinance Bank....................**2** A4
Tourist Information Centre......................**3** B4

SLEEPING ⌂	
Lawn's Hotel.......................................**4** B5
Lushoto Sun..**5** A3
New Teacher Safarini Club.....................**6** A4
Tumaini Hostel....................................**7** B4
Usambara Lodge..................................**8** B3
View Point Guest House.........................**9** A4
White House Annex............................**10** A4

EATING	
Tumaini Restaurant.........................(see 7)

TRANSPORT	
Bus Stand..**11** A4

CHIEF KIMWERI

Kimweri, chief of the powerful Kilindi (Shambaa) kingdom during the first half of the 19th century, is one of the Usambara region's most legendary figures. From his capital at Vuga (on the main road between Mombo and Lushoto), he ruled over an area stretching from Kilimanjaro in the north to the Indian Ocean in the east, levying tributes on towns as distant as Pangani. The extent of his dominion in the coastal regions soon brought him into conflict with Sultan Seyyid Said of Zanzibar, who also claimed sovereignty over the same areas. Ultimately, the two leaders reached an agreement for joint governance of the northeastern coast. This arrangement lasted until Kimweri's death in 1869, after which the sultan assumed full authority.

Tradition holds that Kimweri had magical powers, including control of the rain and the ability to call down famines upon his enemies. His kingdom was highly organised, divided into subchiefdoms ruled by his sons and districts ruled by governors, prime ministers and local army commanders. It was Kimweri to whom the missionary Johann Ludwig Krapf went to request land to build his first church for the Anglican Church Missionary Society.

Following the death of Kimweri, interclan rivalries caused the kingdom to break up, and fighting over who was to succeed him continued until the Germans arrived in the region.

gins on the road running southwest from the Anglican church. En route is **Irente Farm** (☺ 8am-4pm Mon-Fri, 10am-4pm Sat & Sun), where you can buy fresh cheese, yogurt, homemade wheat bread and granola. There's also a good three- to four-day hike from Lushoto to Mtae, and a two- to three-day walk to the Mazumbai Forest. The tourist office has a wall map detailing some of the routes and can offer suggestions for other hikes. Several are also described in detail in Lonely Planet's *Trekking in East Africa*. Lushoto can get chilly and wet at any time of year, so bring a jacket and warm, waterproof clothes.

You can hike on your own, or organise things through the tourist information centre. The Irente viewpoint hike is easily done independently. However, for longer hikes, especially if you don't speak Swahili, it's highly recommended to take a guide along to show you the way and provide introductions in remote areas. Rates vary depending on the hike, but expect to pay from Tsh8000 per person for a half-day hike to Irente viewpoint to about Tsh25,000 per person per day (less in a group) on multiday hikes, including camping or accommodation in basic guesthouses, guide and village development fees, but excluding food. For any hikes that enter forest reserves (which includes most hikes from Lushoto), you'll also need to pay an additional reserve fee of Tsh4000 per person per day. Note that if you're fit and keen on covering some distance, most of the set stages for the popular hikes are quite short, and it's easy to do two in a day. However, most guides will then want to charge you for two days, so you'll need to negotiate an amicable solution.

Sleeping & Eating
BUDGET

Karibuni Lodge (☎ 0748-403825; www.karibunilodge .com; camping US$3, dm US$4, d US$12-15) This small backpackers' house, surrounded by a small patch of forest, has a cosy, woodsy feel, large rooms (some with bathroom), a book swap and a crackling fire for curling up in front of. There's also a restaurant (breakfast extra) with delectable meals, tents can be hired and staff are helpful with information on the area. It's about 1.5km south of the town centre, near the district hospital, and is signposted; ask the bus to drop you at the hospital.

Tumaini Hostel (☎ 264 0094; tumaini@elct-ned.org; s/d Tsh10,000/17,000) Functionality is the theme here, with a couple of long hallways of clean, reasonable-value rooms housed in a two-storey compound along the main road near the Telecom building. For good, cheap meals try **Tumaini Restaurant** (☎ 264 0027; meals from Tsh1500; ☺ breakfast, lunch & dinner), next door.

White House Annex (☎ 264 0177; d without bathroom Tsh6000, s/d Tsh7000/8000) Once the main budget haunt, this place is cramped, faded and noisy compared with the other options, though still decent value. Rooms are no-frills and there's hot water and meals on order. It's on the southwestern edge of town and five minutes' walk from the bus stand: head over the small bridge, turn left and go up the hill.

NORTHEASTERN
TANZANIA

Usambara Lodge (s/d without bathroom Tsh3500/6000) The main attractions at this unassuming guesthouse are airy, no-frills rooms, and a good location near the park, away from the clutch of budget hotels near the bus stand.

Lawn's Hotel (☎ 264 0005/66; lawnstony@yahoo .com; camping per person with hot shower Tsh4500, s/d without bathroom Tsh14,000/18,000, s/d Tsh30,000/35,000) This Lushoto institution has rooms that are very faded and tatty these days, but still with a few vestiges of rustic charm. They come complete with dark wood floors, small fireplaces that don't work and ancient plumbing. However, the proliferation of better-value places means it doesn't see much custom these days. There's camping on the surrounding lawn, with hot showers. It's at the entrance to town.

Lushoto Sun (☎ 264 0082; d Tsh10,000) Rooms here are clean and have hot water, though they lack completely in ambience and aren't particularly good value. Out front is a restaurant serving *ugali* and sauce, and other inexpensive dishes. It's on the main road, just south of the Catholic church.

At Irente viewpoint, there's camping at **Irente Viewpoint Campsite** (camping per person Tsh2500), on the edge of the escarpment, and at the nearby **Irente Farm** (☎ 264 000; camping per person Tsh2000, r without bathroom Tsh6000), which also has a few very tiny rooms (cold water only). Irente Farm does picnic lunches for Tsh2000 per person (minimum Tsh5000, order in advance).

There are lots of no-frills guesthouses near the market, all with serviceable, grubby rooms:

View Point Guest House (☎ 264 0031; r without bathroom Tsh5000) The best of this bunch, though it can't compare with the similarly priced Usambara Lodge; ask for rooms in the annex. Hot-water buckets are available on request. It's diagonally opposite, and just before, White House Annex.

New Teacher Safarini Club (r without bathroom Tsh3500) Cheap and noisy; opposite White House Annex.

MID-RANGE

St Eugene's Hostel (☎ 264 0055; steugenes_hostel@ yahoo.com; s/tw/d Tsh18,000/28,000/40,000) This quiet place has spotless, comfortable rooms, all with good, hot showers and balconies with views over the hills, and is the best accommodation in this range close to the town centre. It's run by an order of sisters, and

---

BACK TO THE BASICS

Tucked away in the Usambara Mountains near Lushoto, in the tiny village of Mazinde Juu, is St Mary's Secondary School, one of Tanzania's most notable education success stories. The school was founded in 1989 by a Benedictine missionary, based on the idea that Tanzania's long-term development can only be achieved through the education and empowerment of the country's women. The area around Mazinde Juu – long neglected and lagging behind much of the rest of the region economically – was an ideal place to put this belief into practice. Most local families made (and continue to make) their living from small-scale farming, and education for girls, especially secondary education, was traditionally perceived as an unattainable or unnecessary luxury.

Initially, the school had only basic resources and just 42 girls. Today, it has around 300 students and is ranked near the top among the approximately 60 girls' schools in Tanzania, and in the top 20 of about 600 secondary schools in the country. Its reputation has also spread well beyond the Usambara Mountains; close to 700 girls from all over Tanzania competed in the most recent entrance exam for places, although, true to its original mission, the school reserves 50% of its seats for applicants from the Lushoto–Mazinde Juu area.

While St Mary's is still dependent on outside contributions to make ends meet (write to PO Box 90, Lushoto, if you'd like to help), strong emphasis is placed on achieving sustainability. The headmistress and all of the teachers are Tanzanians, and most are women. Students are taught ecologically sound farming methods and help out on the school farm, which supplies about 80% of the food needs in the compound. The school grows timber used in the construction of new buildings, raises livestock and maintains fruit trees as cash crops.

Although St Mary's is less than three decades old, there is already tangible proof of its success. Several former students are now teaching at the school and at other schools in the area. Others are pursuing further professional training, including nursing and accountancy, and a few are studying at university level.

profits go to support their work with local children. Meals are available (Tsh4000), and home-made cheese and jam are sold on the premises. St Eugene's is along the main road, about 3km before Lushoto, on the left coming from Soni. Ask the bus to drop you at the Montessori Centre.

About 15km outside of Lushoto, in the scenic, lush countryside around Migambo village, are several more places. All are well situated for walking, though because of the distance from town, they're better bets if you have your own transport.

Mullers Mountain Lodge (☎ 264 0204; mullers mountainlodge@yahoo.com; camping Tsh3500, s/d Tsh20,000/36,000, 4-bed r Tsh60,000) A sprawling family homestead set in extensive, green grounds, with cosy rooms in the main house or in nearby cottages. There are also a few less-appealing cement huts with shared bathroom, and a large grassy camping area with a covered cooking area. Meals (from Tsh5000) are made with produce from the surrounding gardens, and are very tasty. Transport from Lushoto can be arranged. The same owners also have a self-catering cottage closer to town.

Swiss Farm Cottage (☎ 264 0161; camping per person Tsh3000, r per person Tsh15,000) Friendly and homy, with only two rooms (one double and one triple). It's much smaller and simpler than Mullers, but good value if you have enough people to rent the entire house. The cuisine (lunch or dinner Tsh5000) is delicious, and the price includes free coffee, tea and biscuits.

Getting There & Around

Daily buses travel between Lushoto and Tanga (Tsh3500, three to four hours), Dar es Salaam (Tsh7000, seven to nine hours) and Arusha (Tsh6000, six hours), all departing in the morning, and *dalla-dallas* go throughout the day between Lushoto and Mombo (Tsh1000, one hour). If you're going from Lushoto to either Dar es Salaam, Moshi or Arusha, instead of taking a direct bus from Lushoto, it's faster to take a bus to Mombo, the junction town on the main highway, and then get one of the larger express buses to Dar es Salaam. The place to wait is at New Liverpool Hotel, on the main road about 1km west of the Mombo junction, where all the Dar es Salaam–Arusha buses stop for a rest break. Buses from Dar es Salaam arrive at the New Liverpool from about 10am, with another bunch coming through at around 1pm.

From Lushoto, to get to the lodges near Migambo (Mullers and Swiss Farm), take the road heading uphill and northeast of town to Magamba, turn right at the sign-posted junction and continue for about 7km to Migambo, where the two lodges are signposted. Swiss Farm Cottage is the first one you'll reach, about 1km off the main road to the left. Mullers is about 1km further down the Migambo road. Via public transport, there's a daily bus between Tanga and Kwamakame that goes to within around 2km of the lodges, departing Tanga at about 9am or 10am and reaching the Migambo area at around 2pm.

AROUND LUSHOTO
Mtae

Tiny Mtae is perched on a cliff about 55km northwest of Lushoto, with fantastic views over the Tsavo Plains and down to Mkomazi Game Reserve. It makes a good destination if you only have time to visit one village from Lushoto. Just to the southeast of Mtae is **Shagayu** (2220m), one of the highest peaks in the Usambaras Mountains. In addition to its many hiking paths, the area is also known for its traditional healers.

Staff at the Lutheran church will usually allow you to camp on their grounds, or there's the no-frills **Muivano II Guest House** (s/d without bathroom Tsh1500/2000) near the bus stand. Meals are available up the road at Muivano I.

Near Sunga village, 7km southwest of Mtae, there's accommodation at the simple but pleasant **Limbe Travellers Camp** (camping per person Tsh1500, r without bathroom Tsh3500) in green grounds about 1km south of the village along the main road.

The road between Lushoto and Mtae is full of turns and hills, and particularly beautiful as it winds its way up the final 7km to Mtae. If travelling by public transport you'll need to spend at least one night in Mtae as buses from Lushoto (about Tsh1500) travel only in the afternoons, departing Lushoto by about 1pm. The return buses from Mtae to Lushoto depart between 4am and 5.30am, en route to Dar es Salaam.

Mlalo

Set in a valley cut through by the Umba River, Mlalo is an incongruous place with a Wild West feel, a modest selection of basics and a guesthouse. Nearby is Kitala Hill, home of one of the Usambara subchiefs.

The walk between Mlalo and Mtae (five to six hours, 21km) is beautiful, passing by terraced hillsides, picturesque villages and patches of forest.

Afilfx Guest House (r without bathroom Tsh3000) in the town centre has no-frills rooms with shared bucket showers and meals.

Buses run daily between Dar es Salaam and Mlalo via Lushoto, departing Lushoto by about 2pm and Mlalo by about 5am.

Soni

Tiny Soni lacks Lushoto's infrastructure, but makes a good change of pace if you'll be staying for a while in the Usambaras. It's known for nearby **Kwa Mungu hill**, about 30 minutes away on foot, and for the small **Soni Falls** (admission Tsh300), which you can see to the left on the road up from Mombo. There are several good walks that start from Soni, including a three-day hike to the Mazumbai Forest and a short stroll (three to five hours return) to **Sakharani**, a Benedictine mission that sells locally produced wine. Guides can be arranged at Maweni Farm.

Maweni Farm (☎ 027-264 0426; maweni@maneno .net; camping per tent US$10, s/d without bathroom US$20/35, d US$50) This atmospheric old farmhouse is set in lush, rambling grounds about 3km from the main junction, against a backdrop of twittering birds, flowering gardens and a pond covered with water lilies. Rooms are very no-frills but spacious. There are also some tented *bandas*, plus good meals (lunch for Tsh5000, dinner for Tsh10,000) prepared with produce from the organic garden, and experienced guides for organising walks (the lodge director is the head of the Lushoto guides association). Coming from Lushoto, take the dirt road branching left at the main Soni junction, and continue straight for about 2km.

Soni is about halfway along the road between Mombo and Lushoto, and easy to reach via *dalla-dalla* from either destination; Maweni Farm provides free pick-ups if you're staying in its rooms.

Mombo

Mombo is the junction town at the foot of the Usambaras Mountains where the road to Lushoto branches off the main Dar es Salaam–Arusha highway. If you get stuck here overnight, the best accommodation option near the junction is **Midway Express** (r from Tsh2000).

Tembo Lodge & Campsite (☎ 027-264 1530/9, 0748-663205; tembo.lodges@iwayafrica.com; camping per site US$4, s/d US$14/18; 🐘) Much better than staying in Mombo is to head out to this place, at the foot of the mountains about 15km west of town. In addition to camping, it has rooms, food and a bar, and will come and collect you from Mombo free. There are also numerous hikes in the area to keep you busy. It's about 1km off the main highway and signposted.

Further up, about 45km northwest of Mombo, is the attractive **Pangani River Camp** (camping per person with shower US$3). It's set amid the palms on the Pangani River and makes a good spot to stop for the night. It's just off the main road, and signposted.

PARE MOUNTAINS

The fascinating and seldom-visited Pare Mountains – divided into northern and southern ranges – lie southeast of Kilimanjaro and northwest of the Usambara range. Like the Usambaras, they form part of the ancient Eastern Arc chain, and their steep cliffs and forested slopes host an impressive number of unique birds and plants. Also like the Usambaras, the Pares are densely populated, with many small villages linked by a network of paths and tracks. The main ethnic group here is the Pare, also called the Asu. While there are some historical and linguistic differences among various Pare groups, socially they are considered to be a single ethnic entity.

The Pare Mountains are not as accessible or developed for tourism as the Usambaras, which is a large part of their appeal. Thanks to their relative isolation, the rich traditions and folklore of the Pare have remained largely untouched. Also, unlike the Usambaras, there is no major base with developed infrastructure from which a series of hikes can be undertaken. The best way to begin exploration is to spend a night at Mwanga (for the north Pares) or Same (for the south Pares) getting organised, and then head up to either Usangi or Mbaga. From each of these places there are several good hikes, ranging from half a day to three days or more.

PARE FACTS & FABLES

Northeastern Tanzania's Pare people hail originally from the Taita Hills area of southern Kenya, where they were herdsmen, hunters and farmers. It was the Maasai, according to Pare oral traditions, who pursued them into the mountains, capturing and stealing their cattle.

Today many Pare are farmers, cultivating well-organised plots of vegetables, maize, bananas, cassava and cardamom. Thanks to significant missionary activity, the Pare also distinguish themselves as being among Tanzania's most-educated groups. During the 1940s, leading Pares formed the Wapare Union, which played an important role in the drive for independence. Although many Pare are now Christian or Muslim, Pare culture abounds with traditional beliefs and legends.

Traditional Pare society is patrilineal. Fathers are considered to have great authority during their lifetime as well as after death, and all those descended from a single man through male links share a sense of common fate. Once a man dies, his ghost influences all male descendants for as long as the ghost's name is remembered. After this, the dead man's spirit joins a collectively influential body of ancestors. Daughters are also dependent on the goodwill of their father. Yet, since property and status are transmitted through the male line, a father's ghost only has influence over his daughter's descendants until her death.

The Pare believe that deceased persons possess great powers, and because of this, they have developed elaborate rituals centring on the dead. Near most villages are sacred areas in which the skulls of tribal chiefs are kept, although you're unlikely to see these unless you spend an extended period in the mountains. When people die, they are believed to inhabit a netherworld between the land of the living and the spirit world. If they are allowed to remain in this state, ill fate will befall their descendants. The prescribed rituals allowing the deceased to pass into the world of the ancestors are thus of great importance.

To learn more about Pare culture, look for copies of *The Shambaa Kingdom* by S Feierman (1974), on which some of this section was based, and the intriguing *Lute – The Curse and the Blessing* by Jakob Janssen Dannholz (revised translated edition 1989), who established the first mission station at Mbaga.

Information

Lodging and food in the Pares are, for the most part, very basic. With the exception of Hill-Top Tona Lodge (p160), most accommodation is with villagers or camping (for which you'll need your own equipment). Prices for both average about Tsh2000 per person per night. For all destinations except Mbaga and Usangi, it's a good idea to bring a portable stove.

Most organised hiking is done within the framework of the Cultural Tourism Program (CTP), which charges around Tsh17,500/25,000 for one/two people per day, including a guide, camping fees and meals. Note that individual stages of the hikes are often quite short, and two (or three) can usually easily be combined, though you'll probably still need to pay for the same number of days. For the South Pares, the CTP is based in Same (p159), 105km south of Moshi on the Arusha–Dar es Salaam highway. For the North Pares, the CTP is based in Usangi (p161), reached via Mwanga along the same highway. There is a Tsh4000 per-visit forest fee for any walks that go into forest reserves, including walks to Shengena Peak. The fees are payable at the Catchment Office in Same, or through the CTP.

The Pares can be visited comfortably at any time of year, except during the March to May long rains, when paths become too muddy.

SAME

Same (*sah*-may) is a lively market town, and the largest settlement in the southern Pares. You'll need to pass through here to get to Mbaga, the centre for hikes in this area. Unlike Lushoto in the Usambaras, Same has little tourist infrastructure and the town is more suitable as a starting point for excursions into the Pares rather than as a base. If you do want to stay a few days before heading into the villages, there are several walks into the hills behind town, although for most of the better destinations you will need to take local transport at least part of the way. Sunday is the main market day, when traders from towns all over the Pares come to trade their wares.

The **Cultural Tourism Program information office** (dioceseofsame@kilionline.com; Padeco Bldg) is diagonally opposite the bus stand. If it's closed, check at Safari Grill, opposite the bus stand, where Hill-Top Tona Lodge in Mbaga has a representative, or at Elephant Hotel (which is also run by the CTP) for information. Otherwise, head directly to Hill-Top Tona Lodge, where there's a knowledgeable, resident, English-speaking guide for arranging treks. The Catchment Office (for paying forest reserve fees) is at the end of town, on the main road past the market.

Sleeping & Eating

Amani Lutheran Centre (☎ 027-275 8107; s/d without bathroom Tsh3500/4000) Simple rooms around a quiet compound and a restaurant.

Elephant Motel (☎ 027-275 8193; www.elephant motel.com; s/d Tsh10,000/15,000) Same's most 'up-market' accommodation, with faded but reasonable rooms, a cavernous restaurant serving up good meals, and a TV. It's on the main highway about 1km southeast of town.

Safari Grill (meals Tsh1000) Serves up cheap meals, and is opposite the bus stand.

Getting There & Away

Most buses on the Dar es Salaam–Arusha highway stop at Same on request. Otherwise, minibuses travel daily between Same, Dar es Salaam and Moshi, leaving Same in the morning. There is a direct bus between Arusha and Same, departing Arusha at around 8am (Tsh3500, 2½ hours). To Mbaga, transport leaves Same most days between about 11am and 2pm.

MBAGA

Mbaga, perched in the hills southeast of Same at about 1350m, is a good base for hikes deeper into the surrounding southern Pare mountains. You can also trek from here in two or three days to the top of **Shengena peak** (2463m), the highest peak in the Pares. Mbaga, an old Lutheran mission station, has long been an influential town due to its location near the centre of the Pare Mountains, and even today it is in many respects a more important local centre than Same.

A good three-day circular route is from Mbaga to **Chome** village, where you can spend a night, before ascending Shengena Peak on the second day, and then returning to Mbaga.

Sleeping & Eating

Hill-Top Tona Lodge (☎ 0744-852010; tona_lodge@ hotmail.com; camping US$5, r per person without bathroom US$10; meals Tsh2500) This rustic place is the former mission house of Jakob Dannholz (see the boxed text, p159), and one of the best bases in the Pares, with good views, helpful staff, simple cottages and reasonable hiking prices (guides US$6 per group of up to three people; village development fee US$2 per person per day).

Kisaka Villa Inn (☎ 027-275 6722; kisakas@yahoo .co.uk; camping per person US$10, r per person US$25; meals US$5) A quite nice although rather overpriced mountain lodge in a good setting in Chome village. For help in getting to Chome or making bookings, stop by Tukutane Guest House in Same, along the road past the Catholic church.

Getting There & Away

There are one or two vehicles daily around midday between Same and Mbaga, with the last one departing Same by about 2pm (Tsh2000, two to three hours, 40km). If you're coming from Moshi, this means that you'll need to get a bus by 8am in order to get to Mbaga the same day. Travelling from Dar es Salaam, you'll probably need to overnight in Same. Hiring a vehicle up to Mbaga costs about Tsh35,000 to Tsh40,000 one way; ask around at Safari Grill. From Mbaga back to Same, transport departs by 7am or earlier.

If you're driving, there is an alternative route via Mwembe, which can be reached by following the Dar es Salaam–Arusha highway 5km south to the dirt road leading off to the left.

MWANGA

The scruffy, windy town of Mwanga sprawls across the plains at the foot of the Pares about 50km north of Same on the Dar es Salaam–Arusha highway. The main reason to come here is to change vehicles to get to Usangi, the starting point for excursions in the northern Pares. To stay overnight, try the clean but noisy **Angela Guesthouse** (d Tsh6500), about 1km in from the main highway near the new market.

If you have time to linger, **Kisangara Chini**, about 10km south of Mwanga, is the site of a Cultural Tourism Program of sorts that offers the chance to do some walking and to visit a herbal hospital. At the nearby Nyumba ya Mungu (House of God) reservoir, there are Luo fishing communities that originally migrated here from the Lake Victoria area. Take any bus heading south from Mwanga and ask the driver to drop you at Kisangara Chini, from where the tourism programme base is about a 30-minute walk eastwards; ask for the Hasha Project, which also has a camp site. Costs, including guide fees and lunch, total about Tsh15,000 per day, more for overnight and meals.

USANGI
Pretty Usangi, lying in a verdant valley ringed by mountains about 25km east of Mwanga, is the centre of the northern Pares and the best base for hiking in this area.

The main point of interest in town, as far as hiking is concerned, is **Lomwe Secondary School** (☎ Usangi 7), which is the Cultural Tourism Program base, where you'll find guides and accommodation. There's a camping ground here with water, and the school serves as a **hostel** (camping & dm per person Tsh2000) when classes are not in session. If you can't find anyone at the school, ask for Mr Kangero. Other than Lomwe, accommodation options include home stays in the village (generally in houses near the school), or the **guesthouse** (r without bathroom Tsh3500) in town near the main mosque, with basic rooms and food.

In addition to various short jaunts, it's possible to hike in a long day through Kindoroko Forest Reserve (which begins about 7km south of Usangi village) to the top of **Mt Kindoroko**, at 2113m, the highest peak in the North Pares. From the upper slopes of Mt Kindoroko, it's possible to see over the Maasai Steppe to the west, and to Lake Jipe and into Kenya to the northeast.

Getting There & Away
Several pick-ups run daily along the unsealed but decent road between Mwanga and Usangi (one to two hours). From Arusha and Moshi there is also a direct bus to Usangi, departing in the morning (Tsh4000, four hours from Arusha). Ask the driver to drop you at Lomwe Secondary School. To give yourself time to get here and organise things, budget at least two days for an excursion to Usangi.

MKOMAZI GAME RESERVE
The wild and completely undeveloped Mkomazi Game Reserve spreads along the Kenyan border in the shadow of the Pare Mountains, its dry savannah lands contrasting sharply with the moist forests of the Pares. The reserve, which is contiguous with Kenya's Tsavo West National Park, is known for its black rhinos, which were introduced into the area from South Africa for breeding, and which are part of a little-publicised conservation success story (for more, see www .mkomazi.com/programs.htm and www.ifaw .org/ifaw/general/default.aspx?oid=82095). In addition to the rhinos, there are wild dogs (also reintroduced), elephants, giraffes, zebras and antelopes, although it takes luck and effort to spot these, as well as the rarely seen gerenuk, numerous snakes and reasonably good bird-watching.

Less happily, Mkomazi is also known as a classic example of 'conservation' measures clashing with human welfare, following the 1988 eviction of several thousand Maasai from their grazing areas within the reserve's boundaries. For background, see George Monbiot's No Man's Land (see the boxed text, p189), or check out the websites www .maninnature.com/Management/Conser vation/WConservation1d.html and www .ucl.ac.uk/herg/east_africa_mkomazi.htm for two different perspectives.

Conservation issues aside, if you happen to be in the area and want to get off the beaten track, Mkomazi makes an interesting albeit very offbeat safari destination. It's appealing primarily for the chance it offers for wilderness walking, rather than for its wildlife watching, which can't compare with the northern parks.

Information
Reserve entry costs US$20 per day and camping costs US$20 per person. Visits to the black rhino breeding area can be arranged with park staff at Zange Gate (the main entrance to the reserve, about 5km east of Same) or through Mkomazi Camp (p162). Walking tours are the reserve's main

attraction. You'll need to be accompanied by an armed ranger, who can be arranged at reserve headquarters at Zange Gate.

Roads in and around Mkomazi may be impassable during the rainy season.

Sleeping

There is a basic camp site (bring everything with you) at Ibaya, about 15km from Zange Gate, and several other cleared areas elsewhere in the reserve without any facilities where camping is permitted.

Mkomazi Camp (www.mkomazi.net; s/d half board US$110/170) This new mid-range camp was just getting started as this book was being researched. Once in full swing, it should make Mkomazi a first-rate wilderness activity destination. It's run by a couple of zoologists, who plan to offer walking safaris, animal tracking, canoeing, birding and more, all with a conservation-oriented focus. They can also help you arrange overnight stays in a hide in the rhino sanctuary, plus night wildlife drives and two- to three-day biking safaris.

Getting There & Away

Dalla-dallas between Same and Mbaga can drop you at Zange Gate, from where you can begin a walking safari.

Northern Tanzania

HIGHLIGHTS

- Waking up to the sounds of the **Serengeti** (p200), and savouring the rhythms of life in the wild

- Descending into the ethereal blue-green vistas of **Ngorongoro Crater** (p208), surrounded by more animals than you ever imagined

- Trekking on **Mt Kilimanjaro** (p172), Africa's highest peak, or catching the first rays of the rising sun from Mt Meru's **Rhino Point** (p194)

- Watching elephants wander among gnarled baobabs in **Tarangire National Park** (p199)

- Heading off the beaten track to experience the otherworldliness of **Lake Eyasi** (p211), the vibrancy of a **Maasai market** (p185), or the views from **Mt Hanang** (p190)

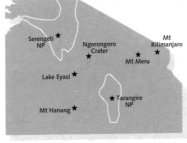

NORTHERN TANZANIA

There are few areas of the continent that attract as much tourist attention as northern Tanzania. Mt Kilimanjaro's stately snow-capped summit hovers majestically over the horizon, hundreds of flamingos stand sentinel in the salt pans on the floor of Ngorongoro Crater, and the hoof beats of thousands of wildebeest echo over the Serengeti plains. This is the Africa of legend, the quintessential snapshot of the continent, where hot, dusty afternoons end abruptly in glorious blazes of sunset, and velvet-black star-filled skies enfold the plains. It's a place where world-class safari lodges jostle for space with mud-thatch houses, where red-cloaked Maasai warriors follow centuries-old traditions, and where lively rural markets draw traders from miles around to haggle over everything from a head of cattle to a kilo of maize.

The main attractions are Mt Kilimanjaro and the northern safari circuit, which offers among the finest wildlife watching on the continent. Yet, there's much more. Haunting calls of waterbirds fill the air at serene Lake Eyasi; beautiful Mt Meru beckons with unforgettable sunrise panoramas from its summit; and the barren landscapes of the Crater Highlands offer rugged but satisfying hiking.

Exploring northern Tanzania is relatively easy. Tourist infrastructure is good, with plenty of accommodation and dining options in major towns. There's also direct air access from Europe and elsewhere in East Africa via Kilimanjaro International Airport (KIA), which is becoming an increasingly important hub. The main caveat is price – the north is Tanzania's most costly region, and for safaris, you'll need to plan on at least a mid-range budget. If you don't mind roughing things a bit, there are some inexpensive alternatives, including Cultural Tourism Programs (p331), the seldom-visited Mt Hanang, and intriguing rock-paintings around Kolo.

National Parks & Reserves

It's northern Tanzania's parks that have put this region on the tourist map, with the famed 'northern circuit' taking in the most popular parks and protected areas in the country: Serengeti (p200), Tarangire (p199), Lake Manyara (p196) and Arusha (p191) National Parks; Ngorongoro Conservation Area (p205); and Mt Kilimanjaro National Park (p172) for trekking. Other protected areas include the extended ecosystems of the Serengeti and Tarangire National Parks.

Getting There & Around

There are good air connections into KIA and Arusha airport, and to airstrips in Serengeti, Lake Manyara and Tarangire parks.

The main road is the tarmac highway running from Dar es Salaam via Moshi through to the Ngorongoro Crater. Heading southwest, the route is tarmac as far as Kwa Kuchinja, near Tarangire National Park. The bus network is good, with connections in all directions.

MOSHI

☎ 027

Moshi, which sits at about 800m at the foot of Mt Kilimanjaro, makes an unassuming introduction to the splendours of the north. It's a low-key place with a self-sufficient, moderately prosperous feel, due in large part to its status as the centre of one of Tanzania's major coffee-growing regions. It's also the capital of the densely populated Kilimanjaro region and a major educational centre, with one of the highest per-capita concentrations of secondary schools in the country.

Most visitors use Moshi as a starting point for climbing Mt Kilimanjaro, although it's a pleasant enough place in its own right to relax for a couple of days. It also tends to be less expensive than nearby Arusha.

Information

IMMIGRATION OFFICE

Immigration office (Boma Rd; ⏲ 7.30am-3.30pm Mon-Fri) Visa extensions are usually handled while you wait.

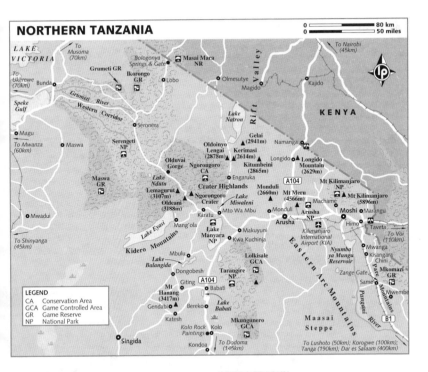

NORTHERN TANZANIA

INTERNET ACCESS

Fahari Cyber Café (Hill St; per hr Tsh800; 8.30am-8pm Mon-Sat, 10.30am-8pm Sun) One of the cheapest places in town.

Kicheko.com (Mawenzi Rd; per hr Tsh1000; 8.30am-8pm)

Twiga Communications Cybercafé (Old Moshi Rd; per hr Tsh1000; 9.30am-10pm) One block northeast of the clock tower roundabout, down from the KNCU Coffee Tree Hotel.

MEDICAL SERVICES & EMERGENCIES

Kilimani Pharmacy (☎ 275 1100; Hill St; 8am-8pm Mon-Sat, 9am-1pm Sun)

Kilimanjaro Christian Medical Centre (☎ 275 4377/8; Sokoine Rd) The best place in town, 3km northwest of town.

MONEY

There are ATMs at **Standard Chartered bank** (Rindi Lane) and at **NBC** (clock tower roundabout), which also changes cash and travellers cheques.

Chase Bureau de Change (Rindi Lane) Changes cash and travellers cheques.

Executive Bureau de Change (Boma Rd) Changes cash and travellers cheques.

PHOTOGRAPHY

Burhani Colour Lab (cnr Hill & Selous Sts; 8.30am-8pm Mon-Sat, 10.30am-8pm Sun) Sells Kodak print film and sometimes slide film.

Fahari Cyber Café (Hill St) Does CD burning for digital pictures.

TELEPHONE

Telephone Service (7am-6pm) Opposite TTCL.

TTCL (cnr Boma & Mawenzi Rds) Near the clock tower.

TOURIST INFORMATION

Coffee Shop (☎ 275 2709; Hill St) Has a handy travellers' bulletin board, and it's a good place to meet some fellow travellers. It also sells the small *Moshi Guide* (Tsh2500), which is good for information if you're staying for a while.

Kindoroko Hotel (☎ 275 4054; Mawenzi Rd) The rooftop bar here is also a good place to meet fellow travellers.

TRAVEL AGENCIES

For trekking operators, see the boxed text, p60.

Emslies (☎ 275 2701; emslies@eoltz.com; Old Moshi Rd) For airline bookings etc.

MOSHI

0 ————— 400 m
0 ————— 0.2 miles

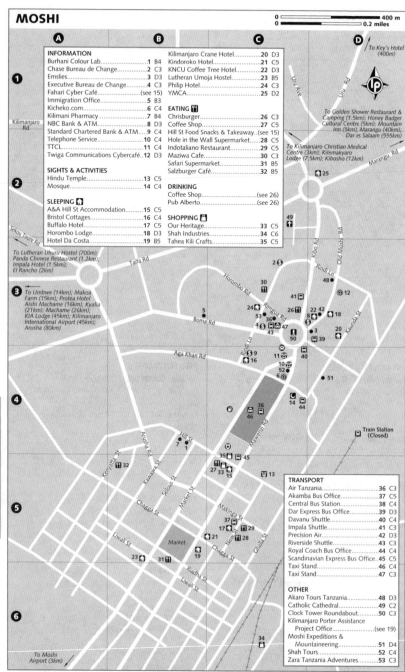

INFORMATION
Burhani Colour Lab..........................1 B4
Chase Bureau de Change.................2 C3
Emslies..3 D3
Executive Bureau de Change..........4 C3
Fahari Cyber Café....................(see 15)
Immigration Office..........................5 B3
Kicheko.com..................................6 C4
Kilimani Pharmacy..........................7 B4
NBC Bank & ATM............................8 D3
Standard Chartered Bank & ATM......9 C4
Telephone Service........................10 C4
TTCL...11 C4
Twiga Communications Cybercafé..12 D3

SIGHTS & ACTIVITIES
Hindu Temple...............................13 C5
Mosque.......................................14 C4

SLEEPING
A&A Hill St Accommodation...........15 C5
Bristol Cottages............................16 C4
Buffalo Hotel...............................17 C5
Horombo Lodge............................18 D3
Hotel Da Costa.............................19 B5

Kilimanjaro Crane Hotel.................20 D3
Kindoroko Hotel...........................21 C5
KNCU Coffee Tree Hotel................22 D3
Lutheran Umoja Hostel..................23 B5
Philip Hotel.................................24 C3
YMCA...25 D2

EATING
Chrisburger.................................26 C3
Coffee Shop.................................27 C5
Hill St Food Snacks & Takeaway..(see 15)
Hole in the Wall Supermarket.........28 C4
Indotaliano Restaurant...................29 C5
Maziwa Cafe................................30 C3
Safari Supermarket.......................31 B5
Salzburger Café...........................32 B5

DRINKING
Coffee Shop............................(see 26)
Pub Alberto.............................(see 26)

SHOPPING
Our Heritage...............................33 C5
Shah Industries...........................34 C6
Tahea Kili Crafts..........................35 C5

To Key's Hotel
(400m)

To Golden Shower Restaurant &
Camping (1.5km); Honey Badger
Cultural Centre (5km); Mountain
Inn (5km); Marangu (40km);
Dar es Salaam (555km)

To Kilimanjaro Christian Medical
Centre (3km); Kilemakyaro
Lodge (7.5km); Kibosho (12km)

Kilimanjaro Rd

Sekou Toure Rd

To Lutheran Uhuru Hostel (700m);
Panda Chinese Restaurant (1.2km);
Impala Hotel (1.5km);
El Rancho (2km)

To Umbwe (14km); Makoa
Farm (15km); Protea Hotel
Aishi Machame (16km); Kyalia
(21km); Machame (26km);
KIA Lodge (45km); Kilimanjaro
International Airport (45km);
Arusha (80km)

Uru Ave
Uru Rd
Kibo Rd
Rindi Ln
Old Moshi Rd
Marangu Rd
Kaunda St

Taifa Rd
Horombo Rd
Rengua Rd
Boma Rd
Rindi Ln
Aga Khan Rd
Arusha Rd
Kenyatta St
Kawawa St
Selous St
Market St
Chagga St
Mawenzi Rd
Makinga St
New St
Chagga St
Chhila St
Liwali St
Liwali St
Riadha St

Hill St

Market

Train Station
(Closed)

To Moshi
Airport (3km)

TRANSPORT
Air Tanzania................................36 C3
Akamba Bus Office.......................37 C5
Central Bus Station.......................38 C4
Dar Express Bus Office..................39 D3
Davanu Shuttle............................40 C4
Impala Shuttle.............................41 C3
Precision Air................................42 D3
Riverside Shuttle..........................43 C3
Royal Coach Bus Office.................44 C4
Scandinavian Express Bus Office....45 C5
Taxi Stand..................................46 C4
Taxi Stand..................................47 C3

OTHER
Akaro Tours Tanzania....................48 D3
Catholic Cathedral........................49 C2
Clock Tower Roundabout...............50 C3
Kilimanjaro Porter Assistance
    Project Office.......................(see 19)
Moshi Expeditions &
    Mountaineering.......................51 D4
Shah Tours.................................52 C4
Zara Tanzania Adventures..............53 C3

NORTHERN TANZANIA

Sights & Activities

Central Moshi is full of activity and atmosphere and makes an interesting walk, especially the area around the market and Mawenzi Rd, with its vaguely Asian flavour, Hindu temple, several mosques and many Indian traders. More impressive perhaps is catching a glimpse of Kilimanjaro's snow-covered peak, which hovers regally over the horizon to the north, and is best seen in the evening when the clouds part.

A dip in the 25m **swimming pool** (adult/child Tsh3000/1500; ☺ 9am-6pm Mon-Sat, 9am-4.30pm Sun) at the YMCA (p167) is a good way to beat the heat.

The area outside Moshi is beautiful, and Machame, Umbwe and other towns above Moshi on Kilimanjaro's lower slopes are all linked by easy-to-follow footpaths. Staff at the Coffee Shop (p169) can help you find a guide.

Another option is the **Machame Cultural Tourism Program** (☎ 027-275 7033), based in Kyalia village, about 14km north of Arusha–Moshi road near Kilimanjaro's Machame trail head. Their small office is in the centre of Kyalia near the *dalla-dalla* (minibus) stop, but it's usually closed so call in advance to be sure someone will be around. Everything is very basic, and you'll need to be self-sufficient with food and water. Another easy way to get a glimpse of the area is to take a *dalla-dalla* from the central bus station to Kibosho (Tsh500, 12km), where there's an old German church. Alternatively, and more comfortably, base yourself out of town at Kilemakyaro Lodge or Protea Hotel Aishi Machame (p168), both of which organise hikes for their guests.

Makoa Safaris (☎ 0744-312896; www.makoa-farm .com) has wonderful horse-riding safaris based out of their farm, which is set amid coffee plantations 16km west of Moshi off the Machame road. Rides (which require a minimum of two people) range from half a day (US$60) to eight days (US$1800 all-inclusive), with days spent in the bush and nights in a rustic, comfortable farmhouse setting or camping. Depending on the route, it's common to see monkeys, baboons, Grant's and Thomson's gazelles, zebras, warthogs and many birds, as well as the occasional elephant or giraffe. Previous riding experience is required.

Sleeping

BUDGET

Honey Badger Cultural Centre (☎ 275 4608/3365; honeybadger@africamail.com; camping per person Tsh3000; r per person Tsh10,000; meals Tsh2000-4000) The appealingly named and welcoming Honey Badger has enclosed grassy grounds for camping; rooms – either in a large family house, or in a separate block nearby; and meals on order. They can arrange traditional drumming performances or lessons, plus other cultural activities, such as Chagga cooking lessons. Overlanders and groups are welcome. It's about 5km from town off the Marangu road, and signposted.

Golden Shower Restaurant (☎ 275 1990; Taifa Rd; camping US$3) This place is conveniently located, with`a small area to pitch your tent, grubby showers and an atmospheric restaurant-bar. It's about 1.5km northeast of the centre along the Marangu road.

Buffalo Hotel (☎ 275 0270, 275 2775; buffalocom pany2000@yahoo.com; New St; s/d Tsh10,000/15,000, r without bathroom Tsh8000) The long-standing and popular Buffalo Hotel has straightforward rooms with fan and net, and a restaurant. The entrance is on a small street off Mawenzi Rd, directly behind Hotel New Castle.

Kindoroko Hotel (☎ 275 4054; kindoroko@kilionline .com; Mawenzi Rd; s/d from US$15/30; ▣) Kindoroko's spotless, good-value rooms, rooftop bar and central location make it a justifiably popular choice. Other services include a forex bureau and a restaurant.

Other recommendations:

A&A Hill St Accommodation (☎ 275 3455; Hill St; s/d Tsh6500/9000) Six clean rooms with fan in a convenient location near the bus stand, with an Internet café and inexpensive restaurant just below. There's no breakfast.

Hotel Da Costa (☎ 275 5159; hoteldacosta@yahoo.com; Mawenzi Rd; s/d without bathroom Tsh5500/8800) Small, clean rooms, plus a bar, restaurant and a convenient central location. Under the same management as Kindoroko Hotel.

Lutheran Umoja Hostel (☎ 275 0902; uhuru@elct .org; cnr Market & Liwali Sts; s/d Tsh10,000/12,000, without bathroom Tsh5000/8000) Clean, no-frills rooms around a small courtyard.

KNCU Coffee Tree Hotel (☎ 0744-485791; Old Moshi Rd; d Tsh8000-10,000; s without bathroom Tsh5000) Reasonable rooms in a drab, cavernous high-rise building, with unappealing shared bathrooms, a restaurant and views over Moshi from the rooftop.

YMCA (☎ 275 1754; Taifa Rd; s/d without bathroom US$10/13; ▣) Spartan, noisy rooms, some with views over Kilimanjaro. It's north of the clock tower on the roundabout between Kibo and Taifa Rds.

MID-RANGE

Lutheran Uhuru Hostel (☎ 275 4084; www.uhuru hostel.org; Sekou Toure Rd; s/d US$15/20, in newer wing US$35/45, in annexe without bathroom US$14/19; ▢) This place has spotless good-value rooms – those in the new wing have balconies – in leafy, expansive grounds and a good restaurant with meals from Tsh4000. Across the street are some budget rooms in a pleasantly rustic annexe with shared facilities and a kitchen. Staff are helpful, and the hostel can organise safaris. It's about 3km northwest of the town centre on the Arusha road (Tsh2000 in a taxi) and an ideal choice for families.

Bristol Cottages (☎ 275 5083/2833; briscot@kilion line.com; Rindi Lane; s/d cottage about US$53/66, r US$40/53; ▨) Bristol has a reserved demeanour, and spotless, modern attached cottages – some with air-con and others with fans – in quiet grounds just next to the Standard Chartered bank. There are also newer rooms in a two-storey block, and a small restaurant serving snacks, and dinner with advance notice.

Key's Hotel (☎ 275 2250; www.keys-hotels.com; Uru Rd; r US$50, air-con plus US$10; ▨ ▣) Key's, about 1.5km northeast of the clock tower on a quiet side street, has been popular with travellers for years. Rooms in the main building are spacious and high-ceilinged, and there are discounts for guests who book a Kilimanjaro trek with the hotel. There are also smaller rondavels (a circular building with a conical roof) out back for the same price, plus a small pool, a restaurant and a bar.

Kilimanjaro Crane Hotel (☎ 275 1114; www.kili manjarocranehotels.com; Kaunda St; s/d US$30/40, d with air-con US$60; ▨) Good-value rooms, with fans, nets, TV and large beds, are the main selling points in this solid mid-range establishment. Downstairs is a restaurant and souvenir shop. It's on a small side street running parallel to and just east of Old Moshi Rd.

Mountain Inn (☎ 275 5622; kilimanjaro@kilinet.co; Marangu road; s/d half board from US$45/65; ▣) About 5km northeast of town, Mountain Inn has clean rooms, all with private bathroom, plenty of hot water and a restaurant. It's run by Shah Tours (p62) and you get a discount if you organise your trek with them.

Other recommendations:

Horombo Lodge (☎ 275 0134; horombolodge@ kilionline.com; Old Moshi Rd; s/d US$20/30) Diagonally opposite the Precision Air office, with sterile rooms with fans, and a restaurant.

Philip Hotel (☎ 275 4746/8; philipht@africaonline .co.tz; cnr Rindi Lane & Horombo Rd; s/d US$30/40) A central location, and soulless twin-bed rooms with TV, fan and net.

KIA Lodge (☎ 255 4194; www.kialodge.com, d US$140; ▣) Not in Moshi at all, but directly at Kilimanjaro airport. The thatched, upmarket bungalows make an agreeable spot to relax if you have a night flight or early arrival; day rooms are available.

TOP END

Impala Hotel (☎ 275 3443/4; impala@kilinet.co.tz; Lema Rd; s/d US$72/83; ▣) Moshi's only upmarket option offers well-appointed rooms in prim and tranquil grounds, plus a good restaurant. It's about 4km northwest of the clock tower roundabout in Shantytown, and under the same management as Impala Hotel in Arusha.

Kilemakyaro Lodge (☎ 275 4925; www.kilimanjaro safari.com; s/d/tr US$65/110/165) Rooms here – in en suite stone rondavels with TV – are fine, though undistinguished, but the beautiful hilltop setting in a good walking area more than compensates. It's about 7km from the town centre off the Kibosho road. There's a restaurant and outdoor tables for sipping sundowners while gazing at Kilimanjaro in the distance. Taxis from town charge Tsh6000.

Protea Hotel Aishi Machame (☎ 275 6948; 275 6941; proteaaishi@africaonline.co.tz; s/d US$115/145; ▣) The Aishi Machame is the classiest hotel in the area, with beautiful, lush surroundings just below Kilimanjaro's Machame trailhead, well-appointed rooms, walking in the surrounding area and horse riding nearby.

Makoa Farm (☎ 0744-312896; www.makoa-farm .com; d US$80-100) This scenic place is just down the road from Protea Hotel Aishi Machame and in equally beautiful surroundings. It's primarily a base for doing horse-riding safaris (p167), but also has a few lovely, rustic guest cottages and rooms where you can arrange a farm stay.

Eating & Drinking

Salzburger Café (☎ 275 0681; Kenyatta St; meals Tsh2500-4000; ☷ 7am-midnight) The Alps meet

TANZANIA & COFFEE

Together with Bukoba, Moshi is one of Tanzania's major coffee-growing centres, and it's this aromatic bean that has (together with trekking, in more recent years) kept the town's economy alive for much of the past century.

Coffee, which is said to have originated in southwestern Ethiopia, came to Tanzania around the turn of the 19th century, after being introduced by Jesuit missionaries from Réunion island. During the British colonial era, the industry began to flourish, with the formation of successful coffee-marketing cooperatives among the Chagga people in and around Moshi. During the 1960s it surpassed sisal as Tanzania's main export crop, and today – despite taking a beating from adverse weather conditions and volatile world prices – is still a linchpin of the national economy.

There are two types of coffee. *Coffea arabica*, which accounts for just under 75% of Tanzanian coffee exports, is used to make higher-quality speciality coffees, and is what you'll see growing around Mt Kilimanjaro, Mt Meru and in the Southern Highlands. *Coffea robusta*, more neutral in taste and used to make less expensive blends and soluble coffees, is grown around western Lake Victoria. More than 90% of Tanzanian coffee is grown on tiny smallholder farms, with the rest coming from cooperatives and private estates.

Good places to buy bags of fresh coffee to bring home as gifts include the Coffee Shop (below) in Moshi, and Msumbi Coffee Shop (p185) in Arusha.

Africa at this classic place, which comes complete with waitresses sporting faux-leopard skin vests, Austrian bar décor on the walls and a selection of good, cheap dishes (try Chicken Mambo Yote), all with amusing menu descriptions.

Coffee Shop (☎ 275 2707; Hill St; snacks & meals from Tsh1000; ☺ 8am-8pm Mon-Fri, 8am-4.30pm Sat) Good coffee, plus a delectable assortment of home-made breads, cakes, yogurt, breakfast and light meals. Proceeds go to a church project.

Indotaliano Restaurant (☎ 275 2195; New St; meals about Tsh3000; ☺ 10am-11pm) This homey restaurant, with chequered tablecloths and good food, had the Indo portion of its menu going when we passed by, with Italian dishes planned to start soon. It's opposite the Buffalo Hotel.

Hill Street Food Snacks & Take Away (Hill St) Cheap plates of local fast food.

Maziwa Café (Rindi Lane; meals Tsh300; ☺ 7am-5.30pm) This small, local favourite dishes up *maziwa mtindi* (yogurt) and plates of *ugali* (maize and/or cassava meal pap) and sauce.

Chrisburger (☎ 275 0419; Kibo Rd; ☺ 8am-5pm Mon-Fri, 8am-2pm Sat) Good burgers and snacks. Next door is **Pub Alberto** (☺ 6pm-dawn Tue-Sun), Moshi's most popular bar, and outside is a small **coffee shop** (☺ from 7am).

Panda Chinese (☎ 0744-838193; ☺ lunch & dinner Wed-Mon) Come here for tasty Chinese meals and your choice of indoor or garden seat-

ing. It's a hike (about 3km) from the centre, just off Lema Rd near the Impala Hotel.

El Rancho (☎ 275 5115; meals from Tsh3500; ☺ closed Monday) Good Indian food, including some vegetarian dishes, in a green, suburban setting. It's about 3km northwest of the town centre off Lema Rd (no public transport).

For self-catering:

Hole in the Wall Supermarket (Solanki's; New St)

Safari Supermarket (Riadha St)

Shopping

Some places to try for crafts:

Our Heritage (Hill St)

Shah Industries Just south of town over the railway tracks; they also offer tours of their leather workshop.

Tahea Kili Crafts (Hill St) Opposite the Coffee Shop, with a good array of batiks, basketry, woodcarvings and more, and some of the profits going to a local women's group.

Getting There & Away

AIR

Almost all flights to Moshi use Kilimanjaro International Airport (KIA), about 50km west of town off the main highway. There's also the small Moshi airport about 3km southwest of town along the extension of Market St, which handles occasional charters. There are daily flights connecting KIA with Dar es Salaam (US$95), Zanzibar (US$95) and Entebbe on **Air Tanzania** (☎ 275 5205; Rengua Rd), near the clock tower. **Precision Air** (☎ 275 3495; Old Moshi Rd) has daily flights connecting KIA with Dar es Salaam, Mwanza (via

NORTHERN TANZANIA

Shinyanga, US$145 to Mwanza) and Nairobi (US$112).

BUS
Buses and minibuses run throughout the day to Arusha (Tsh1000, one to 1½ hours) and Marangu (Tsh700, one hour).

The best way to get to Nairobi is with one of the shuttle buses, though you'll need to wait an hour in Arusha in transit, see p322. **Davanu** (clock tower roundabout) is in Kahawa House on the clock tower roundabout; **Riverside** (Boma Rd) is opposite, in the THB building, and **Impala** (☎ 275 3444; Kibo Rd) is just north of the clock tower. Departures from Moshi are at about 6.30am and noon.

To Dar es Salaam, the best lines are Royal Coach (Tsh17,000) departing Moshi at 10.15am, and Scandinavian Express, departing at 8.30am (Tsh15,000) and 9.45am (Tsh13,000 for ordinary and Tsh22,000 for luxury). All start in Arusha, except the 8.30am Scandinavian bus, which comes from Kampala and is often fully booked. If you're trying to get to Dar es Salaam in time for the afternoon ferry to Zanzibar, Dar Express has a bus departing Moshi at 6.30am (Tsh8000) that usually arrives in time, as well as later departures at 7.30am (Tsh12,000) and 9am.

To get to Mwanza (Tsh25,000) and Nairobi, the best lines are Scandinavian and Akamba, both of which should be booked in advance.

Except for the following lines, all transport leaves from the central bus station in the town centre between Market St and Mawenzi Rd. The station is chaotic and full of touts and disreputable types wanting to take advantage of new arrivals, and it can be quite intimidating getting off the bus (which is a good reason to take Scandinavian or one of the other lines that let you disembark at their offices). To minimise hassles, look for the area of the station where the taxis are gathered before disembarking and head straight over and hire a driver there, rather than getting caught in the fray by the bus door. Unless you know Moshi, it's worth paying the Tsh1000 for a taxi to your hotel, even if it's close enough to walk, just to get away from the station. When leaving Moshi, the best thing is to go to the station the day before without your luggage and book your ticket then, so that the next morning you can just arrive and board.

Bus offices include the following:
Akamba (☎ 275 3908; cnr New & Makinga Sts) Just around the corner from the Buffalo Hotel.
Dar Express (Old Moshi Rd) Opposite KCNU Coffee Tree Hotel, off the clock tower roundabout.
Royal Coach (Aga Khan Rd) Opposite the bus stand, and just down from the mosque.
Scandinavian Express (☎ 275 1387; Mawenzi Rd) One block south of the bus stand, opposite the Hindu temple.

Getting Around
TO/FROM THE AIRPORT
Both Air Tanzania and Precision Air have free transport to/from KIA for most of their flights, departing from their offices two hours before flight time. Riverside and Impala (left) have a shuttle to/from KIA (US$10), departing from their Moshi offices at 6pm daily and coordinated with KLM flight departures. They also wait to meet arriving passengers on KLM.

TAXI & DALLA-DALLA
There are taxi stands near the clock tower and at the bus station. *Dalla-dallas* depart from the bus station.

MARANGU
☎ 027
Nestled modestly on the lower slopes of Mt Kilimanjaro 40km northeast of Moshi is the lively, leafy market town of Marangu. It has an agreeable highland ambience, a cool climate and a good selection of mid-range hotels, all of which organise treks. While you'll get better budget deals in Moshi, it makes a convenient and atmospheric base for Kili climbs using the Marangu or Rongai routes. It's also the heartland of the Chagga people, and you can do cultural walks in the surrounding area.

Thanks to the large influx of foreign trekkers, the contrasts between the tourist scene (or the 'developed' world in general) and local life are just as stark in Marangu as in Arusha, although they stand out more in Marangu as it's so much smaller. Well-heeled trekkers come into town outfitted with the latest gear and climbing accessories, and drop from several hundred to several thousand dollars into the coffers of trekking companies, while, nearby, local vendors hawk their wares and struggle to find US$200 per year to pay secondary-school tuition fees for their children.

Information

Marangu Internet Café (per hr Tsh2000; 8am-6pm) At the main junction, behind the post office.

Sights & Activities

There is a Cultural Tourism Program of sorts in Marangu, and you can arrange tours to see traditional blacksmiths at work, visit nearby caves and waterfalls, and experience local Chagga life. Guides are best arranged through the hotels; expect to pay about US$15 per person, including lunch and entry fees to the various attractions.

You can do a day hike in Mt Kilimanjaro National Park from Marangu Gate as far as Mandara Hut (about two hours up, one hour down; US$30 per person for park fees, plus US$10 per guide, arranged at the park gate).

Sleeping & Eating

Coffee Tree Campsite (275 6513/6604; kilimanjaro@iwayafrica.com; camping US$8, per person per day fireplace-use fee Tsh500, rondavel per person US$10, chalet per person US$12) Prices are high for camping, but the grounds are green and well maintained, and there are hot-water showers, tents for hire (Tsh10,000 per day), and a few four- to six-person rondavels and chalets. The camp site is about 700m east of the main road down a steep hill and signposted near Capricorn Hotel.

Marangu Hotel (275 6591/4; www.maranguhotel.com; camping per person with hot showers US$3, s/d half board US$70/100;) This long-standing place is the first hotel you reach coming from Moshi, with expansive grounds, inviting rooms and a good camp site (for people doing treks with the hotel, or independent travellers). Room discounts are available if you join one of the hotel's fully equipped climbs.

Kibo Hotel (275 1308; www.kibohotel.com; camping per person US$5, s/d US$30/50) The rustic but genteel Kibo has wooden flooring, large old-fashioned windows and spacious rooms that are quite decent value despite being well past their prime. There's a restaurant and, at the entryway, a huge sign announcing that Jimmy Carter stayed here several years ago. It's in nice gardens about 1.5km west of the main junction.

Babylon Lodge (275 1315; babylon@africaonline.co.tz; camping US$5, s/d US$25/40) The Babylon – a budget hotel at heart, masquerading behind mid-range prices – has a row of small, no-frills rooms clustered around a small enclosed green area, and is often somewhat more flexible than the other places on negotiating packages for Kili treks. It's about 700m east of the main junction. Next door is the small **Mt Kilimanjaro Guest Wing** (r Tsh15,000), with basic, cramped rooms.

Bismarck Hut Lodge (0744-318338; r per person without bathroom US$10) This is one of the few budget places in Marangu, but rooms are quite run-down these days. It's along the road to the park gate, shortly before the turn-off to the Capricorn Hotel.

Capricorn Hotel (275 1309; www.africaonline.co.tz/capricornhotel; s/d US$85/120) The Capricorn is probably the most upmarket of the Marangu hotels, at least on the surface, with a slightly pretentious feel, spacious rooms that are fine but don't quite seem worth the price, a restaurant and a good in-house trekking operator. It's about 3km north of the main junction.

Nakara Hotel (275 6571; www.nakara-hotels.com; r per person US$50; meals US$10-15) This reliable mid-range establishment has reasonable rooms

YOHANI KINYALA LAUWO

The first Tanzanian to scale Kilimanjaro was Yohani Kinyala Lauwo. Lauwo, whose memory is revered in his home town of Marangu, was only 18 in 1889 when he was appointed by Chief Marealle I to be the guide for Hans Meyer (the first Westerner to reach Uhuru Peak). In those days, climbing the mountain was quite different: the route was not defined, climbing equipment was rudimentary at best and wages were much lower. During his trek, Lauwo earned just one Tanzanian shilling a day.

Following this successful ascent, Lauwo remained in Marangu, where he spent much of the remainder of his life leading foreign trekkers up the mountain and training new guides. In 1989 at the 100th anniversary celebration of the first ascent of Kilimanjaro, Lauwo was the only person present who had been around at the time of the first ascent. Lauwo died in 1996 at the age of 125. His family still lives in Marangu.

and a restaurant. You'll find it just off the main road and it's signposted near the Capricorn Hotel.

Banana Jungle Lodge (☎ 027-275 6565, 0744-270 947; www.yellowpages.co.tz/jungle/index.htm; camping per person US$10, s/d US$35/60; meals US$4-6) Banana Jungle is a new place in a private home, where you can sleep in modernised and rather pricey 'Chagga huts', eat Chagga food and arrange cultural walks in the area. It's set amid pleasant gardens about 4km east of Marangu, more or less en route to the Rongai Route trailhead. Head right at the main junction, go about 2km to the Mamba Lutheran church, stay left at the fork, and continue another 2.5km.

Getting There & Away

Minibuses run throughout the day between Marangu and Moshi (Tsh700). In Marangu they drop you off at the main junction. From here, there are sporadic pick-ups to the park gate (Tsh300). Otherwise, you'll need to walk (5km).

TREKKING MT KILIMANJARO

Since its official opening in 1977, Kilimanjaro National Park has become one of Tanzania's most visited parks. Unlike the other northern parks, this isn't for the wildlife – although wildlife is there. Rather, it's to gaze in awe at a mountain on the equator capped with snow, and to take advantage of the chance to climb to the top of Africa.

At the heart of the park is the 5896m Mt Kilimanjaro, Africa's highest peak and one of the continent's magnificent sights. It's also one of the highest volcanoes and among the highest freestanding mountains in the world, rising from cultivated farmlands on the lower levels, through lush rainforest to alpine meadows, and finally across a barren lunar landscape to the twin summits of Kibo and Mawenzi. The lower rainforest is home to many animals, including buffaloes, leopards and monkeys, and elands are occasionally seen in the saddle area between Kibo and Mawenzi peaks.

A trek up Kili lures hundreds of trekkers each year, in part because it's possible to walk all the way to the summit without ropes or technical climbing experience. Yet, the climb is a serious (as well as expensive) undertaking, and only worth doing with the right preparation.

The Kilimanjaro massif has an oval base about 40m to 60km across, and rises almost 5000m above the surrounding plains. The two main peak areas are Kibo, the dome at the centre of the massif, which dips inwards to form a crater that can't be seen from below, and Mawenzi, a group of jagged pinnacles on the eastern side. A third peak, Shira, on the western end of the massif, is lower and less distinct than Kibo and Mawenzi. The highest point on Kibo is Uhuru Peak, the goal for most trekkers. The highest point on Mawenzi, Hans Meyer Point (5149m), cannot be reached by trekkers, and is only rarely visited by mountaineers.

Kilimanjaro is considered an extinct volcano, although it still releases steam and sulphur from vents in the crater centre.

Information

Mt Kilimanjaro can be climbed at any time of year, though weather patterns are notoriously erratic and difficult to predict. During November and March/April, it's more likely that paths through the forest will be slippery, and that routes up to the summit, especially the Western Breach, will be covered by snow. That said, you can also have a streak of beautiful, sunny days during these times, and should come prepared for rain and bitter cold at any time of year. Overall, the best time for climbing the mountain is in the dry season, from late June to October, and from late December to February or early March, just after the short rains and before the long rains.

Don't underestimate the weather on Kilimanjaro. Conditions on the mountain are frequently very cold and wet, and you'll need a full range of waterproof cold-weather clothing and gear, including a good-quality sleeping bag. It's also worth carrying some additional sturdy water bottles. No matter what time of year you trek, waterproof everything, especially your sleeping bag, as things rarely dry on the mountain. It's often possible to rent sleeping bags and gear from trekking operators, or – for the Marangu Route – from the Kilimanjaro Guides Cooperative Society stand just inside Marangu Gate. However, quality and availability can't be counted on, and it's best to bring your own.

Apart from a small shop at Marangu Gate selling a limited range of chocolate bars and tinned items, there are no shops inside the

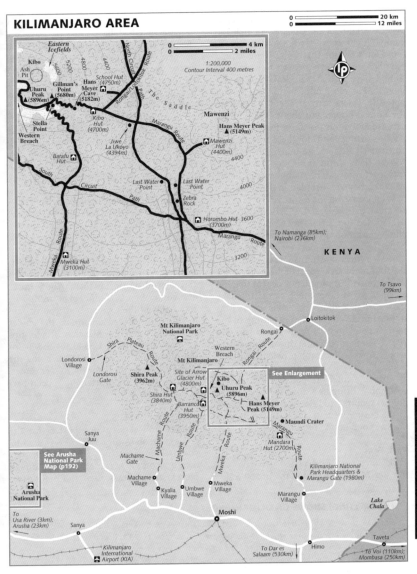

KILIMANJARO AREA

0 _____ 20 km
0 _____ 12 miles

NORTHERN TANZANIA

park. You can buy beer and sodas at high prices at huts on the Marangu Route.

COSTS

All treks on Kilimanjaro must be organised through a tour company. For listings and some tips see p59. No-frills five-day/four-night treks up the Marangu Route start at about US$600, including park fees, and no-frills budget treks of six to seven days on the Machame Route start at around US$700 to US$800, although it's *highly recommended* to budget at least one additional night for the ascent. Better-quality six-day trips on the Marangu and Machame routes start at about US$850. The Umbwe Route is often sold by budget operators for about the same price as Marangu, and billed as a quick and comparatively inexpensive way to reach the top. Don't fall for this – the route should only be done by experienced trekkers, and should have an extra acclimatisation day built in. For more information, see Routes opposite. Prices start at about US$650 on the Rongai Route, and about US$850 for a seven-day trek on the Shira Plateau Route. As the starting points for these latter routes, particularly Rongai, are much further from Moshi than those for the other routes, transport costs can be significant, so clarify whether they are included in the price.

Whatever you pay for your trek, remember that at least US$370 of this goes to park fees for a five-day Marangu Route climb, and more for longer treks. The rest of the money covers food, tents (if required), guides, porters and transport to and from the start of the trek. Most of the better companies provide dining tents, decent to good cuisine and various other extras to make the experience more enjoyable (as well as to maximise your chances of getting to the top). If you choose a really cheap trip you risk having inadequate meals, mediocre guides, few comforts and problems with hut bookings and park fees. Also remember that an environmentally responsible trek usually costs more. Bringing a stove and fuel, for example, requires additional porters because of the greater weight. (It's not permitted to use firewood on the mountain.)

Park Fees

Park entry fees – calculated per day, and not per 24-hour period – are US$30/5 per adult/child aged five to 15 years, and must be paid in US dollars, cash or travellers cheques. Huts (Marangu Route) cost US$50 per person per night, and there is a US$20 rescue fee per person per trip for treks on the mountain. Camping costs US$50 per person per night on the Marangu Route, and US$40 per person per night for all other camping. Park fees are generally included in price quotes, and paid on your behalf by the trekking operator, but you'll need to confirm this before making any bookings. Guide and porter fees (but not tips) are handled directly by the trekking companies.

Kilimanjaro National Park Headquarters (☎ 275 6605, 275 6602) are at the **park gate** (⏱ 8am-6pm) in Marangu.

Tipping

Most guides and porters receive only minimal wages from the trekking companies and depend on tips as their major source of income. As a guideline, plan on tipping about 10% of the total amount you've paid for the trek, divided up among the guides and porters. For the Marangu Route, tips are commonly from US$40 to US$60 for the guide, and from US$15 each for the porters. Plan on more for the longer routes, or if the guide and porters have been particularly good.

GUIDES & PORTERS

Guides, and at least one porter (for the guide), are obligatory and are provided by your trekking company. You can carry your own gear on the Marangu Route, although porters are generally used, but one or two

---

THE (MELTING) SNOWS OF KILIMANJARO

Since 1912, when they were first measured, Kilimanjaro's glaciers have lost over 80% of their ice, which means that they will have disappeared completely by 2020 if things continue at the present rate. Many factors are blamed, one of which is loss of forest cover on the mountain's lower slopes. (Fewer trees means there is less moisture in the air, which in turn means less precipitation, more solar rays getting through to the ice and faster evaporation.)

Various schemes have been dreamed up to halt further disappearance of the glaciers, including spreading huge white sheets over the remaining ice fields, à la the artist Christo, although no one has yet come up with a sure remedy. Meanwhile, speculation is rife about what the disappearance of one of Tanzania's national symbols will mean for the country's tourist industry. For now, perhaps the only certain thing is that if you want to see the top of Kilimanjaro as Ernest Hemingway described it in his classic *The Snows of Kilimanjaro* – 'wide as all the world, great, high, and unbelievably white in the sun' you shouldn't wait too long to book your trek.

SERIOUS BUSINESS

Whatever route you choose, remember that climbing Kilimanjaro is a serious undertaking. While many hundreds of trekkers reach Uhuru Peak without major difficulty, many more don't make it because they ascend too quickly and suffer from altitude sickness. And, every year a few trekkers die on the mountain. Come prepared with appropriate footwear and clothing, and most importantly, allow yourself enough time. If you're interested in reaching the top, seriously consider adding at least one extra day onto the 'standard' climb itinerary, no matter which route you do. Although paying an additional US$100 or so per extra day may seem a lot when you're planning your trip, it will appear as relatively insignificant savings later on if you've gone to the expense and effort to start a trek and then need to come down without having reached the top. And, don't feel badly about insisting on an extra day with the trekking companies: standard medical advice is to increase sleeping altitude by only 300m per day once above 3000m – which is about one-third of the daily altitude gains above 3000m on the standard Kili climb routes offered by most operators. Another perspective on it all: Uhuru Peak is several hundred metres higher than Everest Base Camp in the Nepal Himalaya, which trekkers often take at least two weeks to reach from Kathmandu.

It's also worth remembering that it is not essential to reach Uhuru Peak, and you haven't 'failed' if you don't. If time (or money) is limited, you'd be far better off choosing other treks – you could experience several different mountain areas for the price of a single Kili climb. If you really want to sample Kili, instead of just pushing on for the summit, consider trekking up to an area such as the Saddle, the top of the Barranco Wall or the Shira Plateau to appreciate the splendour and magnificence of the mountain from there before descending.

porters per trekker are essential on all other routes.

All guides must be registered with the national park authorities. If in doubt, check that your guide's permit is up to date. On Kili, the guide's job is to show you the way and that's it. Only the best guides, working for reputable companies, will be able to tell you about wildlife, flowers or other features on the mountain.

Porters will carry bags weighing up to 15kg (not including their own food and clothing, which they strap to the outside of your bag), and your bags will be weighed before you set off.

The guides and porters provided by some of the cheaper trekking outfits leave a lot to be desired. If you're a hardy traveller you might not worry about basic meals and substandard tents, but you might be more concerned about incompetent guides or dishonest porters. We've heard stories about guides who leave the last hut deliberately late on the summit day, to avoid going all the way to the top. The best way to avoid scenarios like this is by going with a reputable company, familiarising yourself with all aspects of the route, and – should problems arise – being polite but firm with your guide.

MAPS

Topographical maps include *Map & Guide to Kilimanjaro* by Andrew Wielochowski and *Kilimanjaro Map & Guide* by Mark Savage. MaCo's *New Map of the Kilimanjaro National Park* has useful gradient profiles, though you'll need to complement it with a topographical map for serious trekking.

Trekking Routes

There are at least 10 trekking routes that begin on the lower slopes but only three continue to the summit. Of these, the **Marangu Route** is the easiest and the most popular. A trek on this route is typically sold as a five-day, four-night return package, although at least one extra night is highly recommended to help acclimatisation, especially if you've just flown in to Tanzania or just arrived from the lowlands. The standard stages are described on p176.

Other routes on Kili usually take six days (which costs more, but helps acclimatisation) and pass through a wider range of scenic areas than the Marangu Route, although trekkers must use tents. The increasingly popular **Machame Route** has a gradual ascent, including a spectacular day contouring the southern slopes before approaching the summit via the top section of the Mweka

NORTHERN TANZANIA

Route. The **Umbwe Route** is much steeper, with a more direct way to the summit – very enjoyable if you can resist the temptation to gain altitude too quickly. Unfortunately, some trekking companies now push attractively priced five-day four-night options on the Umbwe Route in an effort to attract business. Although the route is direct, the top, very steep section up the Western Breach is often covered in ice or snow, which makes it impassable or extremely dangerous. Many trekkers who attempt it without proper acclimatisation are forced to turn back. An indication of its seriousness is that until fairly recently, the Western Breach was considered a technical mountaineering route. It has only gained in popularity recently because of intense competition for business and crowding on other routes. The bottom line is that you should only consider this route if you are experienced and properly equipped, and travelling with a reputable operator. Reliable operators will suggest an extra night for acclimatisation.

Another thing to watch out for is operators who try to sell a 'short' version of the Machame Route, which ascends the Machame Route for the first few stages, but then switches near the top to the final section of the Umbwe Route and summits via the Western Breach. This version is a day shorter (and thus less expensive) than the standard Machame Route, but the same considerations outlined in the preceding paragraph apply here, and you should only consider this combination if you are experienced, acclimatised and properly equipped.

The **Rongai Route**, which has also become increasingly popular in recent years, starts near the Kenyan border and goes up the northern side of the mountain. It's possible to do this in five days, but it's better done in six. The attractive **Shira Plateau Route** (also called the Londorosi Route) is somewhat longer than the others, but good for acclimatisation if you start trekking from Londorosi Gate (rather than driving all the way to the Shira Track road head), or if you take an extra day at Shira Hut.

Trekkers on the Machame and Umbwe routes descend via the Marangu Route or the **Mweka Route**, which is for descent only. Some Marangu treks also descend on the Mweka Route.

Officially a limit of 60 climbers per route per day is in effect on Kilimanjaro. It is currently not being enforced, except on the Marangu Route, which is self-limiting because of maximum hut capacities. If and when this limit is enforced, expect the advance time necessary for booking a climb to increase, with less flexibility for last-minute arrangements.

MARANGU ROUTE

This route starts at Marangu Gate near Marangu village, on the southeastern side of Mount Kilimanjaro and about 40km by road northeast of Moshi. Most trekking companies will provide transport to the gate. For information on public transport, see p172.

For details of hotels at the 'base' towns of Moshi and Marangu, see p167 and p171 respectively. Accommodation on the route itself consists of three 'huts' (actually groups of bunkhouses) spaced a day's walk apart. They are administered by the national park and you pay overnight fees with your entrance fees.

Stage 1: Marangu Gate to Mandara Hut
(7km, 4-5hr, 720m ascent)

From Marangu Gate (1980m) the path is wide and clear, passing through a section of forest. A short distance from the gate the path divides: the right fork is the main route; the left fork is a slightly longer alternative designed to give you more opportunity to enjoy the forest and observe the birds and monkeys. The paths rejoin after about two hours, and again after 2½ hours. From this final junction it's another one to 1½ hours to Mandara Hut (2700m), with beds for about 80 people.

From Mandara Hut you can visit nearby Maundi Crater, a small mound to the north. It's a two-hour return walk and the path is clearly signposted. Views from the top of the crater, over the forest up to the main peaks of Kibo and Mawenzi, provide plenty of inspiration for the trek to come.

Stage 2: Mandara Hut to Horombo Hut
(11km, 5-7hr, 1000m ascent)

From Mandara Hut two paths run roughly parallel through the forest and then through a zone of giant heather, meeting near the start of the moorland. The eastern path is slightly longer, but more pleasant. As you leave the forest you'll get your first clear view of the top of the Kibo dome. To the right are the jagged peaks of Mawenzi, looking higher than Kibo from this angle. The path, although undulating and steep in places, is easy to follow all the way up to Horombo Hut (3700m) – a large group of bunkhouses sleeping about 120 people.

While most standard Kilimanjaro packages allocate only one night at Horombo, it's highly recommended (we consider it essential) to spend two nights to help acclimatisation. A good rest-day walk is to go up to the Saddle and the lower slopes of Mawenzi.

Stage 3: Horombo Hut to Kibo Hut
(10km, 5-7hr, 1000m ascent)

After Horombo Hut the path divides. The western path is more popular; it gradually gains height, passing the landmark Last Water point, and crossing the Saddle.

The eastern path (reached by forking right after Horombo) is steep and rough, passing the aptly named Zebra Rock and another Last Water point. It isn't often used but is worth considering if you want to escape the crowds plodding along the western path. The two paths meet at Jiwe La Ukoyo (Pointed Rocks), at 4394m. From here to Kibo Hut takes one to 1½ hours.

Kibo Hut (4700m) is more basic than Horombo and Mandara, with space for about 60 people. There is no reliable water supply, so all water must be carried from Horombo or one of the Last Water points. From the perspective of combating altitude sickness, it would be ideal to spend two nights at Kibo as well. However, this is rarely done, in part because of overcrowding at Kibo, and in part because of the general unpleasantness of conditions in Kibo Hut – all of which are reasons to consider one of the other, longer routes up the mountain that spend more time above

---

KILIMANJARO'S PORTERS

Kilimanjaro guides and porters have a reputation for being aggressive and demanding when it comes to tips, and higher tips are expected here than elsewhere in the region. Yet, there's another side, too, with porter abuse and exploitation a serious concern.

Most of the porters who work on Kilimanjaro are local residents who work freelance, usually with no guarantees of a salary beyond the present job. The work is hard, rates are low, and it's safe to say that even the best-paid porters earn only a pittance in comparison with the salaries of many of the trekkers whose bags they are carrying. Due to stiff job competition, it's common for porters to agree to back-to-back treks without sufficient rest in between. It's also common for porters to work without proper shoes or equipment, and without adequate protection at night from the mountain's often cold and wet conditions. Equally concerning are cases where unscrupulous guides – perhaps interested in keeping an extra porter's salary for themselves – bribe the rangers who weigh porters' loads. This leaves the porter with the choice of carrying an overly heavy load or not getting the job at all.

Porters depend on tourism on the mountain for their livelihood, but as a trekker you can help ensure that they aren't exploited and that working conditions are fair. When selecting a trekking operator, tell them this is a concern. Be aware of what goes on around you during your trek. If you see exploitative treatment, tell the tour operator when you get back. Also get in touch with the UK-based **Tourism Concern** (www.tourismconcern.org.uk), which has mounted a worldwide campaign to improve the conditions of porters. Another very clued-up group is the **International Mountain Explorers Connection** (IMEC; www.mountainexplorers.org), which runs the **Kilimanjaro Porter Assistance Project** (info@mountainexplorers.org), a not-for-profit group that's doing great work in channelling trekking-clothing donations to porters (trekkers coming from the USA are invited to ferry bags of surplus clothes – contact IMEC directly about this); arranging informal English language training opportunities; and lobbying local tour operators to establish a code of conduct on porter pay and conditions. They have a good set of guidelines at www .hec.org/club/properporter.htm#guidelines, and a very helpful **office** (Mawenzi Rd) next to Hotel Da Costa in Moshi. Both they, as well as Tourism Concern, keep lists of trek operators who promote fair treatment of their staff.

3000m before attempting the final assault on the summit.

Stage 4: Kibo Hut to Uhuru Peak & Descent to Horombo Hut

(4km, 7-8½hr, 1200m ascent, plus 14km, 4½-7hr, 2200m descent)

This stage of the trek can often involve up to 16 hours of strenuous walking, although it's easy to bail out at any point and return the way you've come. It's usual to start very early in the morning, to see the sunrise from the crater rim, and to give you a chance of avoiding the mist. Also, the scree slope up to Gillman's Point and the snow on the path to Uhuru Peak will still be frozen, which will make walking safer and less tiring. Sunrise is around 6am; allow five to six hours to get from Kibo Hut to Gillman's Point plus another two hours to reach Uhuru Peak. This normally means leaving Kibo Hut between midnight and 1am.

If you're only going to Gillman's Point, it is important not to arrive too early, as this will mean waiting for sunrise, sometimes in extremely cold conditions. Experienced guides will assess your abilities and pace the walk to arrive on the rim at the right time.

From Kibo Hut, the path is easy to follow as it zig-zags up the scree. After Hans Meyer Cave (5182m) the gradient gets steeper and the walk becomes, without doubt, a slog. It seems endless but when you finally get to the rim at Gillman's Point (5680m), it's all worthwhile. You can see down into Kibo's snow-filled crater, across to the spectacular cliffs of the Eastern Icefields, back down to the Saddle with the dark bulk of Mawenzi behind, and along the edge of the rim to Uhuru Peak.

Most people are happy reaching Gillman's Point, especially when they see how much further it is to Uhuru, but if you're feeling good and there's still time, it's well worth carrying on to the summit. The walk around the crater rim, with the steep drop into the crater on one side and the smooth snow-covered outer slopes of the dome on the other, is one of the most spectacular in Africa. From Gillman's to Uhuru takes another two to 2½ hours.

At Uhuru Peak (5896m) there's a flag-pole, a plaque inscribed with a quote by President Nyerere, and a sign to say you've reached the highest point in Africa. If the weather's good you might want to revel in your success and take in the views. If the weather is bad you'll probably take a quick photo and hightail it down again.

The return from Uhuru to Gillman's takes about one to 1½ hours. You should aim to be back at Gillman's about three hours after sunrise, as after this time the top layer of snow becomes wet and much harder for walking.

From Gillman's back down to Kibo Hut the scree is blissfully easy-going compared with the slog up. An easy walk takes about two hours. If you've got strong knees and nerves of steel you can run down the scree and be back at Kibo Hut in less than an hour. From here, retrace the path to Horombo Hut – another two to three hours.

Stage 5: Horombo Hut to Marangu Gate

(18km, 5-7hr, 1900m descent)

On the last day, retrace the route, following the clearly marked path down to Marangu Gate. Mandara Hut is about halfway down – a good place for a break.

ARUSHA

☎ 027

Cool, lush and green, Arusha is one of Tanzania's most developed and fastest-growing towns. It sprawls near the foot of Mt Meru at about 1300m altitude, and enjoys a temperate climate throughout the year. Arusha is also the gateway to the Serengeti and the other northern parks. As such, it is the safari capital of Tanzania and a major tourism centre. Although it's further from Kilimanjaro than Moshi and the trailhead towns, it's also the main base for organising Kilimanjaro treks.

Arusha is fringed by coffee, wheat and maize estates tended by the Arusha and Meru people, whom you may see in the market area of town, and who have occupied this area since about the 18th century. The present-day town traces its roots to the waning days of the 19th century, when the German boma (colonial-era administrative office) was constructed. In 1967 Arusha became headquarters of the now defunct original East African Community. Today it is the seat of the new East African Community – a revived attempt at regional collaboration; the seat of the Tanzanian-moderated negotiations on Burundi; and the site of the Rwanda genocide tribunal.

Orientation

Arusha is divided into two sections by the small Naura River valley. To the west are the bus station, the market and the central area with many budget hotels. To the east are most of the upmarket hotels, the post office, immigration, government buildings, safari companies, airline offices, craft shops and the Arusha International Conference Centre (AICC). In the centre is the clock tower roundabout, which is a good landmark. It's also where the two main roads – Sokoine Rd to the west and Old Moshi Rd to the east – meet.

MAPS

MaCo puts out a good map of Arusha, widely available around town, and there are small, free photocopied town maps at the tourist information centre.

Information

BOOKSHOPS

Bookmark (☎ 250 4053; bookmark@bol.co.tz; Jacaranda St) The best bookstore in town, plus a café with cakes, juices and shakes.

IMMIGRATION OFFICE

Immigration office (Simeon Rd; ☒ 7.30am-3.30pm Mon-Fri) Near the junction with Makongoro Rd; visa extensions are usually processed while you wait.

INTERNET ACCESS

Cybernet Café (India St; per hr Tsh1000; ☒ 9am-5pm Mon-Fri, 9am-1pm Sat) Only a few computers, but a fast connection.
Impala Hotel (☎ 250 2398, 250 8448/51; www.impala hotel.com; cnr Moshi & Old Moshi Rds; per hr Tsh6000; ☒ 8am-11pm)
KamNet (per hr Tsh1000; ☒ 8am-8.30pm) Just off Boma Rd, opposite Coastal Aviation.
New Safari Hotel (☎ 250 3261; Boma Rd; per hr Tsh2000; ☒ 24hr)
Patisserie (Sokoine Rd; per hr Tsh1000; ☒ 7.30am-7.30pm Mon-Sat, 8.30am-2pm Sun)

MEDICAL SERVICES & EMERGENCIES

Accident Air Rescue (AAR; ☎ 250 8020; Haile Selassie Rd, Plot 54) Just off Old Moshi Rd; lab tests and a doctor on call 24 hours.
Hakima Pharmacy (☎ 250 3583; Wapare St; ☒ 9am-6pm Mon-Fri, 9am-1pm Sat, 10am-12.30pm Sun)
Moona's Pharmacy (☎ 0741-510590; Sokoine Rd; ☒ 8.45am-5.30pm Mon-Fri, 8.30am-2pm Sat) Just west of NBC bank.

Selian Lutheran Hospital (☎ 250 9974/75, 0744-095450) About 12km north of town in Ngaramtoni and signposted about 3km off the main road.

MONEY

There are several forex bureaus clustered around the northern end of Boma Rd. You can also try:
Colobus Bureau de Change (TFA Centre, Sokoine Rd; 8am-6pm Mon-Sat, 9am-2pm Sun) Next to Shoprite (2km west of the town centre), and one of the few forex bureaus open on Sunday.
Impala Hotel (☎ 250 2398, 250 8448/51; www.impala hotel.com; cnr Moshi & Old Moshi Rds; ☒ 8am-midnight) Their business centre has a forex bureau, and gives cash shillings and US dollars on credit cards at poor rates.
Rickshaw Travels (☎ 250 6655; ricktours@twiga.com; Sokoine Rd) The Amex representative, but doesn't issue travellers cheques.

There are several ATMs:
Barclays (Sopa Lodges Bldg, Serengeti Rd) Visa and MasterCard.
NBC (Sokoine Rd) Visa card; also the best place to change travellers cheques.
Standard Chartered (Goliondoi Rd) Takes Visa card.

POST

Main post office (Boma Rd)
Meru post office (Sokoine Rd)

TELEPHONE

TTCL (Boma Rd; ☒ 8am-8pm Mon-Sat, 9am-8pm Sun & public holidays) Domestic and international calls, and card phones.

TOURIST INFORMATION

There are travellers' bulletin boards at the Patisserie (p184) and the Tourist Information Centre, which is also a good spot to find safari companions.
Ngorongoro Conservation Area Authority (NCAA) Information Office (☎ 254 4625; www.ngorongoro -crater-africa.org; Boma Rd; ☒ 8am-1pm & 2-5pm Mon-Fri, 8am-1pm Sat) Just down from the TTB tourist office, with booklets on Ngorongoro and a relief map of the Ngorongoro Conservation Area.
Tanzania National Parks Headquarters (Tanapa; ☎ 250 3471/4082/8216; www.tanzaniaparks.com) About 5km west of town along the Dodoma road.
Tanzania Tourist Board (TTB) Tourist Information Centre (☎ 250 3843; ttb-info@habari.co.tz; Boma Rd; ☒ 8am-4pm Mon-Fri, 8.30am-1pm Sat) Just up from the post office; staff are helpful and have information on Arusha, the nearby parks and other attractions, and brochures

ARUSHA

Some Minor Roads Not Depicted

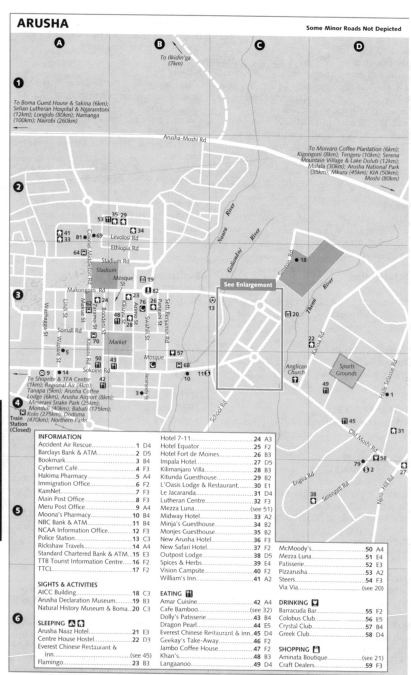

To Ilkidin'ga
(7km)

To Boma Guest House & Sakina (6km);
Selian Lutheran Hospital & Ngaramtoni
(12km); Longido (80km); Namanga
(100km); Nairobi (260km)

Arusha-Moshi Rd

To Moivaro Coffee Plantation (6km);
Kigongoni (8km); Tengeru (10km); Serena
Mountain Village & Lake Duluti (12km);
Mufala (30km); Arusha National Park
(35km); Mkuru (45km); KIA (50km);
Moshi (80km)

Levolosi Rd
Ethiopia Rd
Stadium Rd
Stadium
Mosque
St
Makongoro Rd
Market
Mosque
Sokoine Rd

To Shoprite & TFA Centre
(1km); Regional Air (4km);
Tanapa (5km); Arusha Coffee
Lodge (6km); Arusha Airport (8km);
Meserani Snake Park (25km);
Monduli (40km); Babati (175km);
Kolo (275km); Dodoma
(470km); Northern Parks
Train
Station
(Closed)

Wachaga St
Lindi St
Wajale St
Somali Rd
Colonel Middleton Rd
Makua St
Zaramo Rd
Boriden St
Kuoni Rd
Kikuvu St
Azimio St
Pangani St
Seth Benjamin Rd
Swahili St
Jacaranda St
School Rd

Naura River
Goliondoi River
Simeon Rd
Themi River
Kalus Rd
Old Moshi Rd
Haile Selassie Rd
Engira Rd
Serengeti Rd
Njiro Hill Rd

See Enlargement

Anglican
Church

Sports
Grounds

INFORMATION

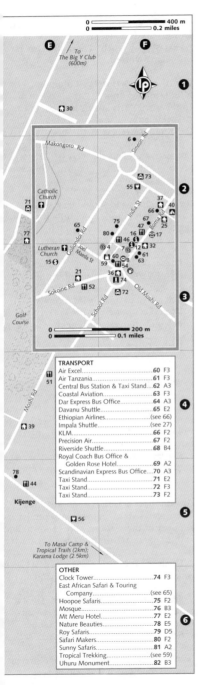

for the Cultural Tourism Program, which has a representative here. There are also copies of a 'blacklist' of tour operators as well as a list of registered tour companies.

TRAVEL AGENCIES

For listings of Arusha-based safari and trekking operators, see p59.

Coastal Aviation (☎ 250 0087; arusha@coastal.cc; Boma Rd) For northern and southern circuit itineraries, Zanzibar and flight charters.

Rickshaw Travels (☎ 250 6655; ricktours@twiga.com; Sokoine Rd) For domestic and international flight bookings.

Dangers & Annoyances

Arusha is the worst place in Tanzania for street touts and slick tour operators who prey on the gullibility of newly arrived travellers by offering them safaris and treks at ridiculously low prices. Their main haunts include Boma Rd and Goliondoi Rd, at the bus station and near the budget hotels at the northern and western ends of town. If you are booking on arrival, make sure that any tour company you choose to sign up with is properly registered; get recommendations from other travellers and check the current 'blacklist' at the Tourist Information Centre on Boma Rd. Also see p60 and p62.

At night, take a taxi if you go out. It's not safe to walk, especially over the bridge on Old Moshi Rd near the clock tower, and in the area between Mt Meru Hotel and the AICC building (p181).

Sights & Activities

The small **Arusha Declaration Museum** (☎ 250 7800; Makongoro Rd; adult/student US$2/1; ☼ 9am-6pm) near the Uhuru monument has an interesting display on postcolonial Tanzanian history, while the even smaller **Natural History Museum** (☎ 250 7540; nnhm@habari.co.tz; Boma Rd; adult/student US$2/1; ☼ 9.30am-5.30pm), in the old German boma, has a few fossils, and is worth a quick stop if you are in the area. Other diversions include the **market**, and the **swimming pool** (cnr Moshi Rd & the Arusha-Moshi road; admission Tsh4000) at Mt Meru Hotel.

It's possible to observe the proceedings of the UN International Criminal Tribunal for Rwanda at the AICC building on Simeon Rd, which take place Monday to Thursday; admission is free but you'll need your passport.

Sleeping

BUDGET

Guesthouses & Hotels – Clock Tower Roundabout

All the following places are in the green and pleasant eastern part of town, within easy access of the post office and many safari operator offices.

Centre House Hostel (☎ 250 2313, 250 3027; angelo.arusha@habari.co.tz; Kanisa Rd; r per person without bathroom Tsh6000; meals Tsh3000) Run by the Catholic diocese, this no-frills place has clean, spacious rooms with shared facilities, and is mercifully free of flycatchers. Most rooms are doubles, but there is also a quad and a triple. Meals can also be arranged. The compound gates shut at 10pm unless you've made previous arrangements. It's in a large green yard about 300m in from Old Moshi Rd.

Lutheran Centre (☎ 250 8855/7; elcthq@elct.or.tz; Boma Rd; r per person without bathroom Tsh5000) If the drab, institutional atmosphere doesn't put you off, rooms here – all with shared facilities – are good value. There's no food, and unless you've made prior arrangements, check-in and check-out are during regular business hours Monday to Friday only. It's diagonally opposite the post office in a grey multistorey building.

Everest Chinese Restaurant & Inn (☎ 250 8419; everesttzus@yahoo.com; Old Moshi Rd; s/d/tw/tr US$25/40/40/55) This recommended establishment has clean, homy, good-value rooms at the edge of a quiet garden behind the Everest Chinese Restaurant. There's a triple in the main house, and twins and doubles in a small block building in the garden behind. All come with nets and bathroom, and a good breakfast – your choice of Western or Chinese. It's about 500m southeast of the clock tower roundabout, and signposted along Old Moshi Rd.

Outpost Lodge (☎ 254 8405; www.outposttanzania.com; Serengeti Rd; dm US$18, s/d US$35/45; 💻) The Outpost, in a leafy residential area about 500m off Old Moshi Rd and about 1km southeast of the clock tower roundabout, has a few dorm rooms in an old two-storey house, small en suite garden bungalows and a restaurant.

Arusha Naaz Hotel (☎ 257 2087; Sokoine Rd; s/d US$25/40; 💻) Naaz's atmosphere is uninspiring, but the location is convenient and the rooms – all recently renovated – are decent and clean, all with TV, fan and hot water. Downstairs is a self-service snack bar for breakfast and lunch. The hotel also hires out safari vehicles.

Guesthouses & Hotels – Colonel Middleton Rd Area

In the small dusty streets just east of Colonel Middleton Rd and north of the stadium (a 10-minute walk from the bus station) is a clutch of cheap places. The area isn't great, but many travellers stay here because prices are among the lowest in town. While some of the accommodations are fine and quite decent value, others let flycatchers onto their premises and should be avoided at all costs. Watch out for smooth talkers wanting to sell you safaris or trying to steer you to a hotel other than the one you've picked out. There are several reliable places:

Kitunda Guesthouse (r Tsh10,000, s/d without bathroom Tsh5000/8000) This place offers hot water and clean rooms, most of which have received a coat of fresh paint recently.

Monjes Guesthouse (d Tsh3500-5000) A friendly and family run establishment, with basic rooms and hot water.

Minja's Guesthouse (r without bathroom Tsh3500) Similar to Monjes, but with shared facilities.

William's Inn (☎ 250 3578; s/d Tsh6000/8000) Short on ambience, but the rooms (the doubles have one large bed) are clean and reasonable value. It's on the other side of Colonel Middleton Rd from the previous three listings, and it's a bit quieter.

Midway Hotel (☎ 250 2790; r without/with bathroom US$10/16) Next door to William's Inn and similar.

Guesthouses & Hotels – Market Area

These places are all in the busy central market area in the western part of town, and within about a 10-minute walk from the bus stand.

Flamingo (☎ 254 8812; Kikuyu St; r US$15) Clean rooms that come with hot water and morning tea, and are good value for doubles.

Kilimanjaro Villa (☎ 250 8109; Azimo St; s/d without bathroom Tsh5000/7000) Tatty but reasonable rooms, and hot water; there's no food.

Hotel Fort de Moines (☎ 250 7406; s/d US$20/25) A few steps up from the others in this listing, in both price and standard, with bland straightforward rooms with fans but no nets.

Hotel 7-11 (☎ 250 1261; s/d/tw US$20/20/25) At the bus station itself (look for the white multistorey building directly opposite), with clean, noisy rooms that are decent value for the doubles.

Camping
Masai Camp (☎ 250 0358; masaicamp@africamail.com; camping per person US$3; banda per person without bathroom US$5, r per person without bathroom US$7; meals Tsh3000; ❑) Masai Camp is a longtime favourite and popular with overlanders. It has hot showers, pool tables, satellite TV, and a good restaurant with pizzas, burgers, Mexican dishes and other meals, plus an on-site telephone, a happening bar and even a children's play area. Tents and sleeping bags can be hired, and if you've had enough of your tent, there's a dorm-style accommodation and a few no-frills rooms. It's in large, green grounds about 3km southeast of town off Old Moshi Rd (Tsh2000 in a taxi), and also the base for Tropical Trails (p61).

Vision Campsite (camping per person US$3) Small, shaded and very basic, this is the only place to pitch a tent in the town centre. It's just off Boma Rd.

Meserani Snake Park (☎ 253 8282; www.feinc.net /SnakePark; camping per person incl admission to snake park 1st night Tsh3000, per night thereafter Tsh2000; meals Tsh4000) This overlander-oriented place has good facilities, including hot showers and a couple of emergency rooms if you're ill. Walks in the area can be organised. It's about 25km west of Arusha, just off the Dodoma road.

MID-RANGE
Le Jacaranda (☎ 254 4624; jacaranda@cybernet.co.tz; s/d US$40/45; meals Tsh5000) Spacious, pleasantly faded and good-value rooms in a large house set in pretty gardens make Le Jacaranda an appealing choice. There's a good restaurant featuring Swahili and Indian dishes, plus *raclette* (similar to a fondue) and a few other European favourites. (Advance notice is required for the *raclette*.) Other attractions include an outdoor pizza oven, a bar and a minigolf course. It's on a quiet side street about 100m north of Old Moshi Rd at the eastern end of town.

L'Oasis Lodge & Restaurant (☎ 250 7089; www .loasislodge.com; backpackers r per person without bathroom US$15, s/d/tr US$60/75/89; meals Tsh5000; ❑ ❒) This place has small African-style rondavels

and some nicer, airy stilt houses set around a garden, plus a few 'corporate rooms' with their own telephone/Internet connection and power-surge protection. There are also 'backpacker' doubles with shared facilities, including hot water, in a separate building nearby. The well-regarded restaurant does a mix of grills, salads and even some vegetarian dishes; there's a sports bar, and a tree-house dining/drinking area. All accommodation prices include a full breakfast, and discounts for Peace Corps volunteers, VSOs and other volunteers are available for the non-backpacker rooms. It's about 2km northwest of the clock tower, and about 1km off the main Moshi–Nairobi road; the signposted turn-off is diagonally opposite Mt Meru Hotel.

Mezza Luna (☎ 254 4381; Moshi Rd; s/d/tr US$35/45/75; ❄) In addition to tasty Italian cuisine, this restaurant also has several spotless, modern rooms. The ones at the back are quieter. It's signposted at the eastern end of town, just off Moshi Rd.

Other recommendations:
New Safari Hotel (☎ 250 3261; Boma Rd; s/d US$55/75; ❄ ❑) Completely renovated and recently reopened, this hotel has good-value rooms in a very central location, plus a restaurant, secure parking and 24-hour Internet access.

Hotel Equator (☎ 250 8409/3727; reservations@ newarusha.com; Boma Rd; s/d US$60/70; ❄) Also recently renovated, though not to quite the same standards as the New Safari Hotel. The garden-view rooms are much nicer.

TOP END
Impala Hotel (☎ 250 2398, 250 8448/51; www.impala hotel.com; cnr Moshi & Old Moshi Rds; s/d US$72/83; ❄ ❑ ❒) Large, reliable and centrally located, this establishment is good value, with efficient staff, a forex bureau, several restaurants, a small garden area and good, hot showers in rooms in the new wing.

Karama Lodge (☎ 250 0359, 0744-475188; www .karama-lodge.com; s/d US$79/107; day r US$40) Karama is nestled under the trees on a forested hillside in the Suye Hill area just south of town, and is an ideal choice if you want to be close to both nature and the town centre. Accommodation is in 12 rustic bungalows, each raised on stilts, and each with a large veranda where you can look out to both Kilimanjaro and Meru on clear days. There are short walking trails nearby, and a good restaurant. Follow Old Moshi Rd south about 2km from the edge of town to the signpost; turn left and continue 1.5km further.

Moivaro Coffee Plantation (☎ 255 3242/3; www .moivaro.com; d US$136; 🖳 🖾) Set amid the coffee plantations about 6km east of Arusha, this is another fine spot to spend a few days recovering from jet lag or relaxing after a Kilimanjaro climb. Accommodation is in cosy cottages, each with its own fireplace, and there are extensive gardens plus the chance for walks. It's about 2km south of Arusha–Moshi road and signposted. Day rooms are also available.

Kigongoni (☎ 255 3189, 255 3099; www.kigongoni .net; s/d/tr US$140/172/205; 🖾) Kigongoni has a tranquil hilltop perch about 8km outside Arusha, a cosy common area with fireplaces and reading nooks, a restaurant and spacious cottages, all with porches, wonderful large bathtubs and wide views. Birding and village walks are possible in the surrounding area, and a portion of the lodge's profits go to support a nearby clinic for mentally disabled children. Follow the Moshi road east for about 8km to the signposted turn-off, from where it's another 1km.

New Arusha Hotel (☎ 250 7777/8870; reserva tions@newarusha.com; s/d from US$130/150; buffet lunch US$12; 🖳) Directly on the clock tower roundabout, the New Arusha has been completely renovated and is now the most upmarket option in the town centre. Rooms are of a high standard, and there's a good restaurant and expansive gardens out back.

Arusha Coffee Lodge (☎ 250 0630/39; info@ sopalodges.com; s/d US$175/260) This lodge is about 6km west of town on the Dodoma road, with luxury chalets in the midst of a coffee plantation. It was in the process of changing management when we passed through, and should reopen soon.

Eating

There are dozens of places for burgers, pizza and other Western-style fast food for between Tsh1000 and Tsh3000. Popular ones include the ever-popular **Patisserie** (Sokoine Rd; snacks & meals from Tsh1000; ⏲ 7am-5pm), which also has soup, good light meals, baked goods and an Internet café; the similar **Dolly's Pa tisserie** (Sokoine Rd; ⏲ 8am-8pm Mon-Sat, 9am-4pm Sun); **McMoody's** (Sokoine Rd; ⏲ 11am-10pm Tue-Sun),

with mostly burgers; and a branch of the South African chain, **Steers** (Joel Maeda St).

For more local flavour, try **Geekay's Take-Away** (India St; meals from Tsh1000; ⏲ 7.30am-6pm Mon-Sat), which serves plates of rice, *ugali* and sauce; or try **Khan's** (Mosque St; mixed grill Tsh4000; ⏲ from 5.30pm), an auto-spares store by day and a popular barbecue by night, with a huge spread of grilled, skewered meat and salads.

Jambo Coffee House (Boma Rd; meals Tsh3500-5000; ⏲ to 10pm) European café chic in a Tanzanian setting. There's an à la carte menu and a good-value plate of the day for about Tsh4500.

Via Via (meals from Tsh3000; ⏲ 10am-10pm Mon-Sat) Via Via is set in the gardens behind the Natural History Museum. The cuisine and atmosphere – a mixture of local and European – are highly agreeable, and it's the best spot in town for drinks.

Café Bamboo (☎ 250 6451; Boma Rd; meals Tsh2000; ⏲ 8am-5.30pm Mon-Sat) Sandwiches, cakes and light meals, diagonally opposite the post office.

Amar Cuisine (☎ 250 6911; meals about Tsh4000; ⏲ 11am-3pm, 6pm-midnight) Amar's is just off Sokoine Rd at the end of Bondeni St, and has tandoori and other wonderfully spiced Indian dishes, including some vegetarian selections. Allow 30 to 45 minutes' preparation time for meals.

Boma Guest House (☎ 0745-880078; s/d with half board US$30/50; meals from Tsh6000; ⏲ lunch & dinner) A small, family-run place, and one of the best spots to sample authentic Tanzanian (Chagga) cuisine. It's under the same management as IntoAfrica (p61), and also has some rooms. It's in Sakina, about 6km north of town and difficult to find, but they'll come pick you up and bring you back to town again after your meal.

Everest Chinese Restaurant & Inn (☎ 250 8419; everesttzus@yahoo.com; Old Moshi Rd; meals Tsh4000-Tsh7000; ⏲ breakfast, lunch & dinner) Everest serves up tasty Chinese food in a pleasant outdoor garden, or indoors in an old, atmospheric house. The restaurant also runs a small guesthouse (p182).

Dragon Pearl (☎ 254 4107; Old Moshi Rd; meals Tsh4000-Tsh8000; ⏲ lunch & dinner) This is another good bet for delicious Chinese food, with an equally appealing garden setting, fast service and an attentive host. It's just around the corner from the Impala Hotel.

Mezza Luna (☎ 254 4381; Moshi Rd; meals from Tsh3500-Tsh8000; ☽ lunch & dinner) This is the place to go for wonderful thin-crust pizzas, pasta and other Italian dishes, garden seating and music in the evenings.

Pizzarusha (pizzas from Tsh3000; ☽ dinner) This unassuming place is trying to get on its feet again after the death of its owner, and is just a shadow of its former self, but still worth a look. When the ingredients are around, the pizza is good, and the homy décor is soothing. It's just off Colonel Middleton Rd near the budget guesthouses.

If you've had your fill of Tanzanian fare, **Spices & Herbs** (☎ 250 2279, Moshi Rd; meals from Tsh3500; ☽ lunch & dinner) is a great spot for some Ethiopian cuisine. For more flavours from Ethiopia, head up the road to the newer **Langaanoo** (Old Moshi Rd; meals from Tsh4000; ☽ lunch & dinner).

Just out of town next to Shoprite is the TFA Centre, a small shopping mall with everything to satisfy cravings for things Western, including Ciao Gelati (fantastic ice cream); Stigbucks Coffee (good coffee and pastries); and Msumbi Coffee Shop (more good coffee; closed Sunday). Most shops at the mall are open from about 9am to 6pm Monday to Saturday, and between around 10am and 2pm on Sunday.

For self-caterers:

Shoprite (Dodoma Rd; ☽ 9am-7pm Mon-Fri, 8am-5pm Sat, 9am-1pm Sun) About 2km west of the town centre; a huge selection.

Drinking & Entertainment

Via Via (Boma Rd) This is the best place in town for a drink and to find out about upcoming music and traditional dance events; it's in the grounds of the Natural History Museum.

Greek Club (cnr Old Moshi & Serengeti Rds; ☽ closed Mon & Thu) A popular expat hang-out, especially on weekend evenings; they have free movies on Sunday afternoon, pizza, and a lively sports bar.

Colobus Club (Old Moshi Rd; admission Tsh3000; ☽ 10pm-dawn Fri & Sat) This is Arusha's loudest and brashest nightclub. If you get bored with the dancing, there's also a small Internet café.

The Big Y Club Totally local flavour, with a breezy upstairs terrace and live music and dancing on weekends. It's about 1km off the Moshi–Nairobi road, with the un-

marked turn-off diagonally opposite Mt Meru Hotel.

Other recommendations:

Barracuda Bar (Makongoro Rd) A local haunt and a reasonable spot for a cold drink during the day.

Crystal Club (Seth Benjamin Rd; ☽ from 11pm Fri & Sat) Dancing until late.

Shopping

The small alley just off Joel Maeda St opposite the Northern Bureau de Change is full of vendors selling woodcarvings, batiks and other crafts. Hard bargaining is required. There are also several large craft stores west of town well signposted along the Dodoma road. **Aminata Boutique** (Sokoine Rd) in the entryway to the Arusha Naaz Hotel has good textiles.

Colourful local-produce markets include the Ngaramtoni market, on Thursday and Sunday, about 12km north of town on the Nairobi road, which draws Maasai from miles around; and the Tengeru market, on Saturday, about 10km east of town along the Moshi road.

Getting There & Away
AIR

There are daily flights to Dar es Salaam and Zanzibar (with ZanAir, Coastal Aviation, Precision Air and Air Tanzania), Nairobi (Precision Air), Seronera and other airstrips in Serengeti National Park (Coastal Aviation, Air Excel, Regional Air); Mwanza (Precision Air, via Shinyanga), and Lake Manyara and Tarangire National Parks (Coastal Aviation, Air Excel, Regional Air). Some flights use Kilimanjaro International Airport (KIA), about halfway between Moshi and Arusha off the main highway, while others use Arusha airport, 8km west of town along the Dodoma road; verify the departure point when buying your ticket. International airlines flying into KIA include KLM and Ethiopian Air. Some sample prices: Arusha–Dar (US$100 to $140), Arusha–Mwanza (US$130) and Arusha–Seronera (US$145).

Airline offices include the following:

Air Excel (☎ 254 8429, 250 1597; reservations@airexcel online.com; Joel Maeda St)

Air Tanzania (☎ 250 3201, 250 3203; www.airtanzania .com; Boma Rd)

Coastal Aviation (☎ 250 0087; arusha@coastal.cc; Boma Rd)

Ethiopian Airlines (☎ 250 6167, 250 7512; tsm-a@ethair.co.tz; Boma Rd)

KLM (☎ 250 8062/3; reservations.arusha@klm.com; Boma Rd)

Precision Air (☎ 250 2818/2836; www.precisionairtz.com; Boma Rd)

Regional Air (☎ 250 4477, 250 2541; www.airkenya.com; Nairobi Rd)

BUS

The central bus station is chaotic and a popular haunt for flycatchers and touts. Watch your luggage and don't negotiate any safari deals at the station. If you're arriving for the first time, head straight for a taxi, or duck into the lobby of Hotel 7-11 across the street to get your bearings. Staff there can point you in the right direction. Unless you're staying in the budget-hotel area downtown, in which case it makes sense to stay on the bus until it reaches the station, you can avoid the bus station altogether by asking the driver to drop you off in front of Mt Meru Hotel. All buses coming from Dar es Salaam and Moshi pass by here. There are taxis at the hotel and across the street, and the scene is less hectic than at the central station. Fares from here to central hotels shouldn't be more than Tsh1500. When leaving Arusha, the best thing to do is book your ticket the day before, so that in the morning when you arrive with your luggage you can get straight on your bus.

Except as noted, buses to Dar es Salaam and Nairobi leave from the southern end of the bus station, near Somali Rd. Buses to most other destinations depart from about half a block north of here opposite Hotel 7-11. For pre-dawn buses, take a taxi to the station and ask the driver to drop you directly at your bus. Despite what you may hear, there are no luggage fees (unless you have an extraordinarily large pack). The main connections to Dar es Salaam include the following:

Dar Express (Colonel Middleton Rd) Tsh9000/12,000 ordinary/luxury; buses depart Arusha at 6am sharp and, with luck, arrive in Dar es Salaam in time to catch the 4.15pm ferry to Zanzibar. If you're trying to do this, don't get off at Ubungo bus station in Dar es Salaam, but stay on the bus until it terminates at its offices in the city centre near Kisutu, from where it's Tsh1000 and about 10 minutes in a taxi to the ferry docks. If the bus is running behind schedule from Arusha, it's occasionally faster to get off at Ubungo and get a taxi from there straight to the ferry

dock, but only marginally so, and the taxi from Ubungo will cost you several times as much. There are also buses at 7.15am and 8.15am. The booking office is just south of Sunny Safaris.

Royal Coach (☎ 250 7959; royalty2000@hotmail.com; Colonel Middleton Rd) Tsh17,000; departures at 9am from the central bus station, before stopping by the booking office at the Golden Rose Hotel.

Scandinavian Express (☎ 250 0153; cnr Somali & Kituoni Rds) Tsh13,000/22,000 ordinary/luxury; departures at 7am (coming from Kampala or Mwanza) and 8.30am (both ordinary and luxury buses).

Moshi

Buses and minibuses run throughout the day between Arusha and Moshi (about Tsh1200, one hour). It's pricier but safer and more comfortable to take one of the Arusha–Nairobi shuttles (p322, Tsh4000 between Moshi and Arusha).

Nairobi (Kenya)

For information on this route see p322.

Babati, Kolo, Kondoa & Dodoma

Mtei line buses run three to four times daily between Arusha and Babati (Tsh3500, four to six hours), departing between 6.30am and 1pm. There are occasional direct buses from Arusha to Kolo, Kondoa and on to Dodoma (about 10 hours), but usually you'll need to change vehicles at Babati (Tsh3000 between Babati and Kondoa), as most transport to Dodoma uses the longer, but tarmac, route via Chalinze. The section of road between Kondoa and Dodoma is in rough shape and transport south of Babati becomes sporadic during the rains.

Musoma & Mwanza

Scandinavian Express buses go to Mwanza via Nairobi and Musoma (Tsh24,000 plus US$20 for a Kenyan transit visa, 20 hours), departing Arusha at about 3.30pm.

The other option is to go via Singida and Shinyanga in a large and very rugged southwestern loop, but the road is in bad shape, and the trip can take three days or more.

Kampala (Uganda)

Scandinavian Express goes daily between Arusha and Kampala (Tsh30,000, 17 hours), departing in each direction about 3pm. For more information on connections to Kampala see p324.

Lushoto

Fasaha buses depart daily at 6.30am (Tsh7500, eight hours). It's faster but more expensive to take an express bus heading for Dar as far as Mombo, and then get local transport from there to Lushoto.

Tanga

Tashriff departs Arusha daily for Tanga at 8.30am and 11.30am (Tsh8000, seven hours). Otherwise, take any Dar es Salaam bus and transfer at Segera junction.

Mbeya

Hood line runs a daily bus to Mbeya, departing Arusha at 5.30am (Tsh25,000, 16 hours).

Getting Around

TO/FROM KILIMANJARO INTERNATIONAL AIRPORT

Both Air Tanzania and Precision Air have shuttles to both airports for their passengers, departing from their offices about two hours before the scheduled flight departure. In the other direction, look for the airlines' buses in the airport arrivals area.

Riverside Shuttle has a daily bus to Kilimanjaro International Airport (KIA) coordinated with KLM departures and arrivals. It costs US$10 and departs at 6pm sharp from Mt Meru Hotel. It also waits for arriving passengers; look out for the bus in the airport arrivals area.

Taxis from town to KIA charge about Tsh25,000, more at night.

TO/FROM ARUSHA AIRPORT

Any *dalla-dalla* heading out along the Dodoma road can drop you at the junction, from where you'll have to walk about 1.5km to the airstrip. Taxis from town charge about Tsh8000.

Precision Air sometimes runs a shuttle from its office at the AICC to Arusha airport, leaving the AICC about 1½ hours before scheduled flight departures (Tsh1500).

CAR & MOTORCYCLE

Arusha Naaz Rent-a-Car (☎ 250 2087; www.arushanaaz.com) This efficient, reliable outfit based at Arusha Naaz Hotel (p182) has a selection of 2WD and 4WD vehicles, with or without driver. Rates (from US$80 to $100 per day for 4WD) include 120 free kilometres per day.

TAXI

There are taxi stands around the central bus station, opposite Mt Meru Hotel, on the southern side of the clock tower roundabout near New Arusha Hotel, and at the eastern end of Makongoro Rd. Town rides cost Tsh1000 to Tsh2000.

AROUND ARUSHA
Cultural Tourism Program

Several villages outside Arusha have organised Cultural Tourism Programs that offer an alternative to the safari scene in town and a good opportunity to experience local culture. All can be booked through the TTB Tourist Information Office (p179), which can also tell you the best transport connections. Book a day in advance for the more distant ones; for Ng'iresi and other programmes close to town, guides usually wait at the TTB office on stand-by each morning. (Check with the TTB to ensure the one you go with is authorised). There are various tours, starting from Tsh15,000/25,000 per person for a half-/full-day programme with lunch (less for two or more people):

Ng'iresi A popular tour to Ng'iresi village, about 7km northeast of Arusha on the slopes of Mt Meru; visit local irrigation projects, see Maasai houses, enjoy some walking and visit a local farm. There's also a longer overnight option with a hike up a small volcano.

Longido Hike to the top of Longido Mountain (2629m; eight to 10 hours return from the main road), visit Maasai bomas or get a taste of a Maasai cattle market at Longido, about 80km north of Arusha.

Ilkidin'ga Walking (from half-day strolls to a three-day 'cultural hike') and the chance to experience the traditional culture of the Arusha people, are the main attractions in this well-organised programme around Ilkidin'ga, 7km north of Arusha.

Mulala About 30km northeast of Arusha; this is the only tour completely implemented by women, and a good choice if you want to learn more about the life of your Tanzanian sisters. It involves visits to a local women's cooperative and some short walks; an overnight stay is also possible if you have camping gear. With an early start, it's no problem to do this tour as a day trip from Arusha.

Mkuru A camel camp near Arusha National Park's Momela Gate, where you can take camel safaris ranging from a half-day to several days, or climb nearby Ol Doinyo Landaree mountain (about two hours to the summit). This tour is more time-consuming to organise than the others, but you'll have the chance to experience life in a small and relatively isolated Maasai community and you're unlikely to see many other tourists. Bring everything with

AROUND ARUSHA

Village (☎ 027-250 4158, 250 4153; www.serenahotels
.com; s/d US$150/190), part of the Serena chain,
with small stone-and-thatch cottages covered with ivy. For diversion, there is the
green and peaceful Lake Duluti on your
doorstep. To get here from Arusha, head
east along the main road for about 10km to
Tengeru, take the second right (signposted),
and go about 2km to the hotel.

GETTING THERE & AWAY

Via public transport, have any bus or *dalla-
dalla* along the Arusha–Moshi road drop
you at the Tengeru junction, from where it's
about 1.5km walk in to the lake. Pick-ups
from Arusha can be organised with Green
Footprint Adventures (p60) if you'll be
doing canoeing with them.

Usa River

This tiny, nondescript town on the Arusha–
Moshi road about 20km east of Arusha, is of
interest for its proximity to Arusha National
Park, and for its handful of atmospheric, upmarket lodges.

Rivertrees Country Inn (027-255 3894; www.river
trees.com; s/d US$125/150, river cottage US$240; ☐) is
the nicest accommodation by far, with a genteel old-world ambience, impeccable service,
excellent cuisine served family-style around
a large wooden dining table and luxuriously
rustic rooms. There's a choice of rooms,
either in the main building – a beautifully
renovated colonial-era farmhouse – or in
the gardens, plus two private 'river cottages', each with their own fireplaces and one
with wheelchair access. It's in lush, shaded
grounds running along the Usa River, and
signposted off the main highway.

There is also **Ngare Sero Mountain Lodge**
(☎ 255 3638; www.ngare-sero-lodge.com; per person full
board US$90), a colonial-era throwback with
accommodation either in small, attached
cottages set around the gardens or in a few
nicer, luxurious suites in the main house,
reminiscent of an old hunting-lodge estate.
To get here turn north off the Arusha–Moshi
road at the sign for Hotel Dik-Dik, then follow signs for Ngare Sero. From the end of
the road, there's a small footbridge and path
through the gardens up to the lodge.

Monduli Mountains

The seldom-visited Monduli range, northwest of Arusha and west of Mt Meru, offers

you, including all food and drinking water, especially for
overnight tours. Riding camels entails at least one night
in Mkuru or at the nearby Momella Wildlife Lodge (p193)
to organise things; there's also a 5km walk from Ngare
Nanyuki village (p193) to reach the camel camp. If you
have several days, it's possible to combine the Mkuru
programme with the Longido programme on a three-day/
two-night camel safari from Mkuru to Longido Mountain,
with the final night spent in Longido, and then easy
transport back to Arusha at the end of the trip.

Lake Duluti

This small and tranquil crater lake lies about
11km east of Arusha, just off the main road
near the village of Tengeru (known for its
colourful Saturday market). It's part of a
forest reserve, and there's a fledgling ecotourism programme of sorts here, where
you can arrange to go canoeing (per person
US$20) or take guided nature walks around
the lake. The best contact for this is Green
Footprint Adventures (p60), which has its
base at Serena Mountain Village.

Accommodation includes a basic **camp
site** (camping per person US$7) on the banks of
the river and the upmarket **Serena Mountain**

some offbeat walking, particularly on its northern side, from where you'll be treated to wide views over the Rift Valley plains and to the distant cone of Ol Doinyo Lengai on the horizon. There are no set routes. All walks follow old cattle trails that become overgrown during the rains, and a local guide is essential. The base for trekking is the area of Monduli Juu, near Emairete village (9km from Monduli town), where you can arrange a guide and pay the fees. All walks (Tsh15,000 per day including guide and lunch, plus Tsh4000 for any walks that enter the forest) need to be arranged either through the cultural tourism representative, who lives along the main road in Emairete, or through the village chief. They can also help you find a spot to camp (Tsh2000, bring everything with you from Arusha) or arrange an overnight stay in a Maasai boma (Tsh3000), and sort out meals. The best contact in Arusha on this area is Tropical Trails (p61). Bring plenty of water, sunscreen, shade and long pants, as many of the trails are overgrown with thick, thorny brush.

Babati

The lively, agreeable market town of Babati is set in fertile countryside along the edge of the Rift Valley escarpment, about 175km southwest of Arusha. It's the main jumping-off point for Mt Hanang climbs, and for travel to Singida and beyond along the wild southern loop via Ngeza and Shinyanga to Mwanza and Lake Victoria. Flanking Babati to the southwest is the tranquil **Lake Babati**, fringed by tall reeds and home to hippos and lots of waterbirds.

INFORMATION

There's an Internet café on the main road near the bank and not far from the market, and another connection at the Cultural Tourism Program (CTP) office adjoining Kahembe's Guest House (across the large field in front of the bus stand). The National Microfinance bank on the main road changes major currencies, cash only.

In addition to Hanang climbs, the CTP office can organise trips with local fishermen on the lake.

MAASAI LAND ISSUES   *David Else*

Although the Maasai have grazed cattle for many centuries in the Serengeti, the Crater Highlands and in surrounding parts of the Great Rift Valley, over the last three decades they have been forcibly excluded from much of their traditional homeland. This is due to wildlife conservation – it has long been believed by some conservationists that the Maasai cattle compete with wild animals for grazing and water, and that their large herds contribute to soil erosion.

Conservationists who take a broader view hold that the needs of indigenous people must be included in any plan to conserve wildlife or natural resources, not simply for humanitarian reasons but because without the full support of local people any conservation project is ultimately doomed to failure. This subject is discussed in the book *No Man's Land* by George Monbiot, in which the author – a highly respected investigative journalist – points out that in the name of conservation the Maasai have been completely excluded from Serengeti National Park and Mkomazi Game Reserve simply because 'tourists did not like to see them there'. The Maasai were forced onto private farmland on the edge of these areas and became 'trespassers', unable to return to their traditional grazing lands. Of those Maasai who dared enter the protected areas, many were fined and imprisoned. Those who stayed outside, and managed to avoid trespassing on farmland, were safe, but, cut off from essential migration routes and grazing lands, their cattle died of starvation. Meanwhile, the Maasai have seen new roads and hotels built for tourists. This has led many to feel that they are seen as less important than wildlife or tourists, and has fostered resentment. Many have turned to poaching – some simply for meat because their cattle have died, others for ivory and rhino horn. The Maasai and wildlife have coexisted for hundreds of years, but Monbiot says conservation has forced the Maasai to become enemies of nature: 'Conservation has done as much as anything to destroy the East African environment'.

Of course, there are those who argue against George Monbiot's assertions, but most of the Maasai would probably agree with him. Reading *No Man's Land* before you visit Tanzania will increase your awareness of these issues and add another dimension to your travels.

SLEEPING & EATING

All accommodation in Babati is no-frills:

Kahembe's Guest House (s/d without bathroom Tsh2500/3000) Just across the large field in front of the bus stand. Renovations are underway and soon there will be some nice en suite singles (Tsh6000), plus doubles (Tsh4000) with a large bed and shared facilities – all with hot-water showers.

Motel Paa Paa (☎ 253 1111; r with/without bathroom Tsh3000/2500) Slightly more upmarket; near the old bus stand in the town centre.

Dodoma Transport Hotel (☎ 253 1089; r Tsh6500) On the Dodoma road opposite the petrol station and vying with Motel Paa Paa for the honour of Babati's best lodging, though once Kahembe's is renovated that should be the place to go; secure parking.

For meals, you should try **Abida Snacks** (meals Tsh1000) near Kahembe's Guest House, with curries, chips, *ugali* and even a few vegetarian offerings.

GETTING THERE & AWAY

Mtei line buses run between Arusha and Babati, departing between 6.30am and 1pm (Tsh3500, four to six hours, three to four daily).

Mt Hanang

The volcanic Mt Hanang (3417m) rises steeply above the surrounding plains about 180km southwest of Arusha. It's Tanzania's fourth-highest mountain, with a satisfying trek to the summit, but few visitors know of its existence. The surrounding area is home to a colourful array of ethnic groups, including the Barabaig, who still follow a traditional seminomadic lifestyle and are recognisable by their goatskin garments. Over the past few decades, they have been displaced from some of their lands by large-scale wheat-farming projects in the area surrounding Mt Hanang.

The most popular route to the top, and the easiest to organise, is the Jorodom Route, which begins in the town of **Katesh** on the mountain's southern side, and can be done in one long day. While a guide isn't strictly essential, it's recommended to go with one. This is best arranged through Kahembe's Trekking & Cultural Safaris (p61), which is the best contact for doing anything around Hanang or Babati (US$30 to US$40 per person per day for a three-day Hanang climb from Arusha). If you're

trekking independently, you can arrange a guide through the local municipality office (Idara ya Mkuu wa Ilaya) in Katesh for about Tsh5000 per day. Don't go with any of the freelancers who hang around Katesh and Babati saying they're with Kahembe's or the municipality.

For all trekking on the mountain you'll need to pay a US$5 forest reserve fee per person per trip, plus a Tsh2500 village fee per person per trip for climbs on the Jorodom Route. If you're organising things on your own, both fees should be paid prior to the trek at the local municipality office. If you've organised your trek through Kahembe's, staff there will take care of paying the fees for you (though they're in addition to Kahembe's daily climbing rate). The climbing route is described in Lonely Planet's *Trekking in East Africa* guidebook. Allow 10 to 12 hours for the return trek, and get an early start so as to have most of the ascent behind you before the sun gets too high. Water supplies up high are unreliable; carry at least 4L with you, and even with this you'll probably wish you had more. It's possible to camp at a small, flat area below the summit, although it's somewhat exposed and has no water; you'll need permission from the forestry office.

There are numerous basic guesthouses in Katesh, the best of which is **Colt** (☎ 253 0030; s/d Tsh2500/3500), just past the market. For something cheaper, try **Hanang View Guesthouse** (s/d Tsh1500/2500), with nondescript rooms around a cement courtyard and shared bucket baths. For meals, try **Kabwogi's**, near the Lutheran church.

Several of the Mtei buses from Arusha to Babati pass through Katesh on their way to Singida; the last bus to do this leaves Arusha at 9am. Otherwise, you'll need to spend a night in Babati and catch one of these buses to Katesh the next morning, or take your chances hitching a lift.

Kolo Rock Paintings

The tiny village of Kolo lies at the centre of one of the most impressive – and most overlooked – collections of ancient rock paintings on the African continent. For anyone with a bent for the offbeat and tolerance for a bit of rugged travel, the rock paintings make a very intriguing and worthwhile detour.

The history of most of the paintings remains shrouded in mystery, with little known about either their artists or their age. While some of the paintings date back more than 3000 years, others are much more recent, probably not more than a few hundred years old. One theory maintains they were made by the Sandawe, who are distantly related linguistically to South Africa's San, a group also renowned for its rock art. Others say the paintings, particularly some of the more recent ones, were done by various Bantu-speaking peoples, who moved into the area at a later date.

The paintings, which range in colour from white to shades of red, orange and brown, were probably made at least in part using the hands and fingers, as well as brushes made of reeds or sticks. Some of the colours were probably made by mixing various pigments with animal fat to form crayons. They contain stylised depictions of humans – often hunting, playing musical instruments or pursuing other activities – as well as various animals, notably giraffes and antelopes. Still others are unintelligible forms, perhaps early attempts at abstract art.

To visit, you'll first need to arrange a guide and a permit (Tsh4000) with the Department of Antiquities in Kolo. You'll then need to walk about two to 2½ hours from Kolo to reach the paintings. With your own vehicle (4WD), you can drive to within a few kilometres of the first sites.

You can also organise trips to Kolo through Arusha-based tour operators. A good budget option is Kahembe's Trekking & Cultural Safaris (p61; US$60 per day plus transport costs).

There's a basic **camp site** (camping per person Tsh2000) near Kolo, for which you'll need to be fully equipped. Otherwise, the closest overnight base is Kondoa, 20km south, where there are numerous guesthouses, the best of which is **New Planet** (r Tsh6000), near the bus stand.

Kolo is about 100km south of Babati and 275km southwest of Arusha. The best bus connections are from Babati, from where several small buses run daily to Kolo and on to Kondoa (20km further on). Alternatively, there's at least one direct bus daily between Arusha and Kondoa via Kolo, leaving Arusha about 6am or 7am and reaching Kolo about six hours later. Going in the other direction, there are several daily buses from Kondoa to Arusha, departing between about 6am and 10am. Kolo can also be reached from Dodoma, 180km to the south, see p251.

ARUSHA NATIONAL PARK
☎ 027

Arusha National Park, although one of Tanzania's smallest parks, is one of its most beautiful and most topographically varied. Its main features include Ngurdoto Crater (often dubbed Little Ngorongoro) and the Momela Lakes to the east. To the west is beautiful Mt Meru. The two areas are joined by a narrow strip, with Momela Gate at its centre. The park's altitude, which varies from 1500m to more than 4500m, has a variety of vegetation zones supporting numerous animal species.

Ngurdoto Crater is surrounded by forest, while the crater floor is a swamp. West of the crater is Serengeti Ndogo (Little Serengeti), an extensive area of open grassland and the only place in the park where herds of Burchell's zebras can be found.

The **Momela Lakes**, like many in the Rift Valley, are shallow and alkaline and attract a wide variety of wader birds, particularly flamingos. The lakes are fed by underground streams; due to their varying mineral content, each lake supports a different type of algal growth, which gives them different colours. Bird life also varies quite distinctly from one lake to another, even where they are only separated by a narrow strip of land.

Mt Meru is a mixture of lush forest and bare rock with a spectacular crater. For further information on the mountain, see Trekking Mt Meru, p194.

Animal life in the park is abundant. You can be fairly certain of sighting zebras, giraffes, waterbucks, reedbucks, klipspringers, hippos, buffaloes, elephants, hyenas, mongooses, dik-diks, warthogs, baboons, vervet and colobus monkeys, although there is dense vegetation in some areas. You may even catch sight of the occasional leopard. There are no lions and no rhinos due to poaching.

While tour companies often relegate the park to a day trip, it's better to allow at least a night or two to appreciate the wildlife and do a walking or canoe safari.

NORTHERN TANZANIA

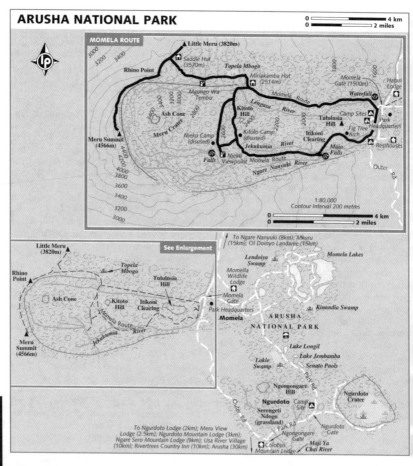

ARUSHA NATIONAL PARK

Information

Entry fees are US$25/5 per day per adult/
child aged five to 15 years. For camping
fees see p35. There is a US$20 rescue fee
per person per trip for treks on Mt Meru.
Armed rangers (required for all walks) cost
US$15 per day, and the huts on Mt Meru
cost US$20.

The main park entrance is at Ngongongare Gate, about 10km from the main
road. The **Park headquarters** (☎ 027-255 3995;
🕙 6.30am-6.30pm) – the main contact for making camp site or resthouse reservations and
for arranging guides and porters to climb
Mt Meru – are about 14km further in near
Momela Gate. There is another entrance at
Ngurdoto Gate, on the southeastern edge

of the park. All gates are open from 6am
to 6pm. Walking is permitted on the Mt
Meru side of the park, and there is now
also a beautiful walking trail along part of
the Ngurdoto Crater rim (though it's not
permitted to descend either on foot or in
a vehicle to the crater floor). Green Footprint Adventures (p60) does **canoe safaris**
(per person US$40, plus transfer from Tengeru US$10, park
& canoeing fees US$20, cash only) on the Momela
Lakes. These are highly recommended and
a great way to get a different safari perspective. Transport from Arusha or from
Serena Mountain Village hotel (p188) can
be arranged.

The best map of the park is the MaCo
Arusha National Park map.

Sleeping & Eating

The park has four ordinary camp sites, three near Momela Gate (including one with a shower), and one near Ngurdoto Gate. There are also two resthouses with kitchen facilities near the park headquarters.

Hatari Lodge (☎ 255 3456/7; www.hatarilodge .com; r per person full board plus safaris US$250) Hatari is the most atmospheric of all the park lodges, with an upmarket ambience, creative 'modern retro' room décor, a wonderful location on large lawns frequented by giraffes, and great views that take in both Meru and Kilimanjaro on clear days. Rooms are spacious, with large windows, and there's a cosy fireplace and good food. It's on the edge of the park, about 2km north of Momela Gate. The property was originally owned by Hardy Kruger, of *Hatari!* film fame.

Momela Wildlife Lodge (☎ 250 6423/6; www .lions-safari-intl.com/momela.html; s/d/tr half board US$68/98/128) This long-standing establishment is just northeast of Hatari Lodge and about 1.5km off the road from Momela Gate. Small, serviceable cottages are set around modest gardens, and the lodge can provide a vehicle and driver for visiting the park for a very reasonable US$30/60 per half/full day.

Ngurdoto Mountain Lodge (☎ 255 5217; www .thengurdotomountainlodge.com; s/d/tr US$130/160/210; 🖳 🛋 🖲) A vast, new compound that can accommodate over 1000 guests, with a mix of rooms, chalets and presidential suites. The chalets have their own sitting room and fireplace, and many of the rooms have spa baths. While there's no shortage of amenities (there's even a golf course), the lodge lacks intimacy, though the chalets are cosy enough. All in all, it's a good place to come if you crave a resort backdrop for your safari. It's just off the road leading from the Arusha–Moshi road to Ngongongare Gate, and under the same management as the Impala Hotel in Arusha. Some rooms have wheelchair access.

Other recommendations:

Colobus Mountain Lodge (☎ 255 3632; www.colobus mountainlodge.com; camping per person US$5; s/d US$35/50) Just a two-minute walk from Ngongongare Gate, with large bougainvillea-dotted grounds, a camping area, reasonable budget-style rooms and a restaurant.

Ngurdoto Lodge (☎ 255 3701; ngurdoto-lodge@ habari.co.tz; r per person full board US$150) An upmarket lodge with warm and attentive hosts, and five spacious double bungalows set on a large, peaceful lawn with views of Kilimanjaro and Meru. It's about 7km north of the main highway along the road to Ngongongare Gate.

Meru View Lodge (☎ 255 3876; meru.view.lodge@ habari.co.tz; s/d US$35/50) An unassuming place with a mix of large and small cottages (all priced the same) set in pleasant grounds just before Ngurdoto Lodge on the main park road.

Getting There & Away

Arusha National Park gate is about 35km from Arusha. Take the main road between Arusha and Moshi until you reach the national park signboard, where you turn left. From here, it's about 10km to Ngongongare Gate, where you pay your fees. This is also where the road divides, with both forks joining up again at Momela Gate.

Via public transport, there's a daily bus between Arusha and Ngare Nanyuki (10km north of Momela Gate) that departs Arusha at 1pm (Tsh1500, 1½ hours to Ngongongare Gate) and Ngare Nanyuki at 7am, and can drop you at the park gate. Otherwise, take any bus between Arusha and Moshi, and get off at Usa River village, 1km east of the park junction. From Usa River there are sporadic pick-ups that run most days through the park en route to Ngare Nanyuki village (Tsh400 between Usa River and Momela Gate).

Transport from Arusha can also be arranged with all of the lodges (about US$100 per vehicle for a drop at the gate, and up to double this for an all-inclusive one-day safari). If you arrive at the park without your own vehicle, most of the lodges can arrange wildlife-viewing drives for guests from about US$50 per day, transport only. The park does not rent vehicles. If you arrive with your own vehicle and are planning to trek on Mt Meru, you can leave it at Momela Gate (where you will have to pay standard park fees) or, less expensively, at Momella Wildlife Lodge.

Once in the park, there's a good series of gravel roads and tracks that will take you to all the main features and viewing points. Most are suitable for all vehicles, though some of the tracks get slippery in the rainy season, and a few areas are accessible only with a 4WD. From the road near Hatari Lodge, it's possible to continue via a rough track that joins the main Nairobi highway near Longido.

NORTHERN TANZANIA

TREKKING MT MERU

At 4566m, Mt Meru is the second-highest mountain found in Tanzania. Although completely overshadowed by Kilimanjaro and frequently overlooked by trekkers, it is a spectacular volcanic cone with one of East Africa's most scenic and rewarding climbs. A trek to the summit takes you through grassland and lush forest on the mountain's lower slopes, followed by a dramatic and exhilarating walk along the knife edge of the crater rim.

Mt Meru has a circular base some 20km across at 2000m, where it rises steeply above the plains as an almost perfect cone with an internal crater surrounded by a steep wall of cliffs. At about 2500m the wall has broken away so the top half of the mountain is shaped like a giant horseshoe. The cliffs of the inner wall below the summit are more than 1500m high – among the tallest in Africa. Inside the crater, more recent volcanic eruptions have created a subsidiary peak called the Ash Cone.

Information

COSTS

Most of the companies listed in the Safaris chapter for Mt Kilimanjaro also organise treks on Mt Meru, and the same considerations outlined in that chapter apply here. Rates for a four-day trip range from about US$400 to US$600.

That said, organised treks are not obligatory, and you can do things quite easily on your own. Costs for an independent trek are mostly park entrance, hut and guide fees. Porters are optional. You'll also need to add in the costs of food (which you should get in Arusha, as there's nowhere to stock up near the park), and of transport to the park (minimal, if you take a *dalla-dalla*). After paying your entry fees, continue to Momela Gate, where everything can be arranged. As this can all take a couple of hours, it's worth getting an early start or making arrangements the night before.

Park Fees

See p192 for park entry fees, all of which are payable at Ngongongare Gate. If you enter the park at Ngurdoto Gate, you can pay your entry fees there. Mountain-climbing fees are paid at Momela Gate.

Tipping

Generally the guides and porters on Mt Meru are hard-working and reliable, and do not expect the huge tips sometimes demanded by their counterparts on Kilimanjaro. However, the guides receive a fixed monthly salary for their work as rangers, and get no additional payment from the park for guiding, which means that tips are much appreciated, particularly for going to the summit. In fact, without tips a guide has little extra incentive to take you to the top, so you should calculate this in as part of your fixed costs. Make it clear to the guide that you will tip, but that payment is conditional on him guiding you at an appropriate pace over the full route. We've heard all-too-frequent reports of poorly motivated guides doing everything possible to avoid going to the summit. One of the most common ploys is to rush clients on the early stages of the climb, with the result that the trekkers themselves are forced to bail out early. As a guideline, for a good guide who has completed the full trek with you, plan on a tip of about Tsh10,000 per day per group. Tips for porters average about Tsh5000 per porter per group per trip.

GUIDES & PORTERS

A guide is mandatory and can be arranged at Momela Gate. The fee of US$15 per day is paid to the national park rather than to the guide himself. Unlike on Kilimanjaro, guides on Meru are armed rangers whose purpose is to assist you in case you meet some of the park's buffaloes or elephants, rather than to show you the way (although they do know the route). It's unlikely that an animal will have to be shot, but you should not underestimate the danger and walk too far away from your guide.

Most trekkers go up Mt Meru with only a guide, but if you want porters they are also available at Momela Gate. They come from one of the nearby villages and are not park employees. The charge is Tsh4000 or US$5 per porter per day. This is paid at Momela Gate and given to the porters by park staff after the trip. You will also need to pay park entrance and hut fees for porters (Tsh1500 per day park fee plus Tsh800 per night hut fee). Porters will carry rucksacks weighing up to 15kg (not including their own food and clothing). Heavier bags will be carried for a negotiable extra fee.

MAPS

The only map is on the reverse of MaCo's *Arusha National Park* map.

Momela Route

The **Momela Route** is the only route up Meru. It starts at Momela Gate on the eastern side of the mountain and goes to the summit along the northern arm of the horseshoe crater. The route is steep but can be done comfortably in four days (three nights), although trekkers often do it in three days by combining Stages 3 and 4 of the trek. Although Meru appears small compared with Kilimanjaro, don't underestimate it. It's still high enough to make the effects of altitude felt, so don't try to rush up if you are not properly acclimatised.

If you have the time and money for two treks, a visit to Meru is a good way to prepare for Kilimanjaro. It helps you acclimatise, and the views across the plains to Kili's dome rising above the clouds provide plenty of inspiration for the trek to come.

For information on getting to the trailhead at Momela Gate, see p193.

SLEEPING

On Mt Meru, the Momela Route has two blocks of bunkhouses ('huts'), conveniently spaced for a three- or four-day trek. Especially during the July–August and December–January high seasons, they are often full, so it's a good idea to carry a tent (though if you camp, you'll still need to pay hut fees). It's currently not possible for independent trekkers to make bookings for the bunkhouses, which operate on a first-come, first-served basis. Each bunkhouse has a cooking and eating area; you'll need to bring your own stove and fuel. There's also a separate dorm for guides and porters.

STAGE 1: MOMELA GATE TO MIRIAKAMBA HUT

(10km, 4-5hr, 1000m ascent)

Two routes are available from Momela Gate. The first is a track that goes through the forest towards the crater floor, and then steeply up to Miriakamba Hut (2514m). The second is a path that climbs gradually through the grassland direct to Miriakamba. The first option is more interesting and is described here. The second option is shorter and makes a suitable descent route. Some

guides prefer to go up and down the short route, and it may require some persuading to take the forest route.

From Momela Gate, cross the Ngare Nanyuki River and follow the track into the forest. The track winds uphill, to reach Fig Tree Arch about one hour from the gate. This parasitic wild fig originally grew around two other trees, eventually strangling them. Now only the fig tree remains, with its distinctive arch big enough to drive a car through.

The track continues to climb, reaching Itikoni clearing on the left side of the track after another 15 minutes. From a small hill on the right, you can often see buffaloes grazing. Half an hour further, the track crosses a large stream, just above Maio Falls. Continue for another hour to reach Kitoto Camp, with excellent views over the Momela Lakes and out to Kilimanjaro in the distance.

Continue following the track and you will reach a junction after 30 minutes. Take the right track – the left track leads to the floor of Meru Crater – over flat ground, to cross a rocky stream bed (usually dry) and descend slightly through trees, ignoring the path that comes in from the left, to reach Miriakamba Hut, one hour from Kitoto Camp.

From Miriakamba you can walk to Meru Crater floor (a two- to three-hour return trip) either in the afternoon of Stage 1 or before Stage 2. The path across the floor leads to Njeku Camp (an old forest station) and Njeku Viewpoint, on a high cliff overlooking a waterfall, with excellent views of the Ash Cone and the entire extent of the crater.

STAGE 2: MIRIAKAMBA HUT TO SADDLE HUT

(4km, 2-3hr, 1050m ascent)

From Miriakamba the path climbs steeply up through pleasant glades between the trees to reach Topela Mbogo (Buffalo Swamp) after 45 minutes and Mgongo Wa Tembo (Elephant Ridge) after another 30 minutes. From the top of Mgongo Wa Tembo there are great views down into the crater and up to the main cliffs below the summit. Continue through some open grassy clearings and over several stream beds (usually dry) to Saddle Hut (3570m).

From Saddle Hut you can walk up to the summit of **Little Meru** (3820m) in about an hour on a clear path. From the top you'll get impressive views of Meru's summit, the horseshoe crater, the top of the Ash Cone, and the sheer cliffs of the crater's inner wall. In the other direction, across the top of the clouds, you can see the great dome of Kilimanjaro. As the sun sets behind Meru, casting huge jagged shadows across the clouds, the snows on Kili turn orange and then pink, as the light fades. Allow 45 minutes to get back to Saddle Hut.

Alternatively, you can go to **Rhino Point** (about two hours return from Saddle Hut), from where the views of Kili are similarly stunning and you can also see down to the base of the Ash Cone and across the crater floor. You'll pass this point on your way both to and from the summit, but the views are so impressive it's worth going at least twice.

STAGE 3: SADDLE HUT TO MERU SUMMIT & RETURN

(5km, 4-5hr, 1000m ascent, plus 5km, 2-3hr, 1000m descent)

This stage, along a very narrow ridge between the outer slopes of the mountain and the sheer cliffs of the inner crater, is one of the most dramatic and exhilarating sections of trekking anywhere in East Africa. Some trekkers leave Saddle Hut early in the morning (2am to 3am) to reach the summit in time to see the sun rising from behind Kilimanjaro, and to stand a chance of avoiding the late morning mist, although others find this section too exposed for comfort, especially when done in the dark, or find the altitude makes the going beyond Saddle Hut a bit tough. If the sunrise is your main point of interest, there's no need to go to the top. It's just as impressive from Rhino Point (about an hour from Saddle Hut), and perhaps even more so because you also see the main cliffs of the inner wall of the crater being illuminated by the rising sun. The ideal combination is sunrise at Rhino Point, then up to the summit for the views (depending on the mist). If you spend two nights at Saddle Hut you can still see the sunrise at Rhino Point, then trek up to the summit and back in daylight. Many trekkers combine Stages 3 and 4, but this doesn't leave a margin for delays.

If you decide to go for the summit, take plenty of water. Even though it can be below freezing just before dawn, as soon as the sun rises the going becomes hot and hard. During the rainy season, ice and snow can occur on this section of the route, so take care.

For the ascent take the path from behind Saddle Hut, across a flat area, then steeply up through bushes. After an hour the vegetation gives way to bare rock and ash. Rhino Point is marked by a cairn and a pile of bones (presumably a rhino, but what was it doing up here?).

From Rhino Point the path drops slightly then rises again to climb steeply around the edge of the rim over ash scree and bare rock patches. Continue for three to four hours to reach Meru summit (4566m). The views are spectacular. To the west, if it's clear, you can see towards the Rift Valley and the volcanoes of Kitumbeini and Lengai, while down below you can see the town of Arusha, and the plains of the Maasai Steppe beyond.

To descend from the summit, simply retrace the route around the rim back to Saddle Hut (two to three hours).

STAGE 4: SADDLE HUT TO MOMELA GATE

(9km, 3-5½hr, 2000m descent)

From Saddle Hut, retrace the Stage 2 route to Miriakamba (1½ to 2½ hours). From Miriakamba, you can either return through the forest (2½ to three hours), or take a shorter route down the ridge that leads directly to Momela Gate (1½ to 2½ hours). This direct route goes through forest for some of the way, then through open grassland, where giraffes and zebras are often seen.

LAKE MANYARA NATIONAL PARK

Lake Manyara National Park is one of Tanzania's more underrated parks, and is often allocated only a quick stop on a larger northern circuit loop including Tarangire National Park and Ngorongoro Crater. Yet, while Manyara doesn't have the raw drama and variety of animals that you will find elsewhere on the northern circuit, it has much to offer and many visitors are surprised by how nice it really is. In addition to a striking setting and peaceful surroundings, Manyara's main attractions are

LAKE MANYARA'S FLAMINGOS

Flamingos are one of Lake Manyara's hallmarks, with their vast numbers – estimated at close to three million – often giving the lake a hazy, pink tint when viewed from a distance. In one of nature's still unsolved mysteries, thousands of the flamingos (about 10,000, according to park estimates, almost all lesser flamingos), died on the shoreline between June and July 2004. As this book went to print, the cause of the deaths was still being investigated. Based on similar mass flamingo deaths in some of Kenya's lakes in past decades, it's suspected that the culprits may be toxins in the algae that is the flamingos' preferred food. If you're planning a safari in Lake Manyara National Park, there are still plenty of flamingos to be seen and, at least in the short term, hyenas, fish eagles and various vultures on the shoreline scavenging the remains.

its superb birdlife, its tree-climbing lions (though these aren't often seen) and its hippos, which you can observe at closer range here than at most other places. There are also elephants, although the population has been declining in recent years. The park, which is between 900m and 1800m above sea level, is bordered to the west by the dramatic western escarpment of the Rift Valley. To the east is the alkaline Lake Manyara, which at certain times of year hosts tens of thousands of flamingos, as well as a diversity of other birdlife. Depending on the season, about two-thirds of the park's total 330 sq km area is covered by the lake. Despite the park's small size, its vegetation is diverse, ranging from savanna to marshes and acacia woodland, enabling it to support a remarkable variety of habitats.

Information

Entry fees are US$25/5 per adult/child aged five to 15 years, valid for multiple entries within 24 hours. For camping fees see p35. For booking camp sites contact the **senior park warden** (☎ 027-253 9112/45). The park gate and park headquarters are at the northern tip of the park near Mto Wa Mbu village. Both MaCo and Harms-ic put out good park maps, available at the park gate. A bird checklist is also available at the gate.

Green Footprint Adventures (p60) organises village walks, mountain biking and forest hikes (all US$25) around Lake Manyara, as well as full-day 'Manyara active excursions' (US$60) where you can get some culture, nature and exercise all at the same time. They also do night drives in the park (Manyara is the only northern park where you can do this) for US$45 per person plus park fees. Their Manyara base is at Lake Manyara Serena Lodge (p197). Budget

cultural walks outside the park can be organised through the Mto Wa Mbu Cultural Tourism Program (p198).

Up-close wildlife viewing opportunities are scarce at Manyara in comparison with the other northern parks, and it's a good idea to bring binoculars.

Sleeping

There are several camp sites, luxury lodges and tented camps near the park gate. If you're trying to save money, it's cheaper to stay in Mto Wa Mbu village, about 3km east of the park gate on the Arusha road.

LODGES & TENTED CAMPS

Kirurumu Luxury Tented Camp (☎ 250 7011, 250 7541; www.kirurumu.com; s/d full board US$165/250) A genteel, low-key ambience, closeness to the natural surroundings and memorable cuisine are the hallmarks of this highly regarded camp. It's set on the escarpment about 12km from the park gate and 6km from the main road, with views of Lake Manyara in the distance. The 20 double tents are hidden away in the vegetation and well spaced for privacy, and there are several larger 'family suite' tents. Low-season discounts are available.

Lake Manyara Serena Lodge (☎ 250 4158, 250 4153; www.serenahotels.com; s/d full board US$270/400; 🐾) Serena is a large complex and not the least bit intimate, but the views are great, and accommodation – in appealing two-storey conical thatched bungalows – is very comfortable, with all the amenities. It's southwest of Kirurumu on the escarpment overlooking the Rift Valley, and about 2km from the main road.

E Unoto Retreat (☎ 0744-360908; www.maasai village.com; s/d full board US$204/370) This classy, new lodge with Maasai overtones and spacious luxury bungalows nestles at the base of the Rift Valley escarpment near Lake Miwaleni. There's rewarding birding in the area, as well as the chance for cycling and cultural walks, including one focusing on traditional medicinal plants. E Unoto is about 10km north of Mto Wa Mbu, just off the road to Lake Natron.

Other recommendations:

Lake Manyara Wildlife Lodge (☎ 254 4595/4795; www.hotelsandlodges-tanzania.com; r per person full board US$175; 🏊) The best-located lodge – with a striking perch on the edge of the escarpment – and undistinguished but perfectly adequate rooms.

Lake Manyara Tree Lodge (www.ccafrica.com; per person all-inclusive US$560; ⊙ Jun-Mar; 🏊) Lake Manyara's most exclusive lodge, and the only one within the park boundaries, with 10 intimate 'tree-house suites' set in the forest at the southern end of the park.

CAMPING

Near the main gate, the park has two ordinary camp sites, about 10 double **bandas** (per person US$20) with bathrooms, and a student hostel. The *bandas* (thatched-roof hut with wooden or earthen walls) have bedding, a cooking area and (if you're lucky) hot water, but otherwise, and for all the camp sites, you'll need to be self-sufficient. There is a good selection of basic foodstuffs available in Mto Wa Mbu. At Endala on the lakeshore, and at Msasa on the escarpment, are picnic sites, where you can stretch your legs.

Mto Wa Mbu
☎ 027

Mto Wa Mbu (River of Mosquitoes) is a small village redeemed from scruffiness by its lively market and its beautiful vegetation – a profusion of palms, baobabs and acacia trees framed by the backdrop of the Rift Valley escarpment. It's just north of Lake Manyara, which is fed by the town's eponymous river, and makes a good base for visiting the park. There are also good cultural walks in the surrounding area, best organised through the very clued-up and enthusiastic **Cultural Tourism Program office** (☎ 253 9393; mtoculturalprogramme@hotmail.com) at the Red Banana Café on the main road, opposite the post office. Rates for one/two/three people are Tsh23,500/27,000/30,500 per day, and there's bike rental for Tsh4000 per person per day.

SLEEPING & EATING

There are several inexpensive guesthouses in town, all with basic rooms from about Tsh2500 (shared facilities) to Tsh6000 (with bathroom). Among the better ones are Sayari Lodge, behind the market, and Sunlight Lodge and Manyara Guest House, both along the main road in the town centre.

Migunga Forest Camp (☎ 257 8428, 250 8424; www.swalasafaris.com; camping per person US$8; per person full board US$50) Migunga's main attraction is its setting, in a grove of fever trees that echoes with bird calls. The tents are rustic but quite adequate, and there are good package deals for safaris to Lake Manyara National Park and Ngorongoro Crater. It's about 2km south of the main road and signposted.

Twiga Campsite & Lodge (☎ 253 9101; twigacampsite@hotmail.com; camping US$10, groups per person US$5, tent rental per person US$5, d/tr without bathroom US$25/35; 🏊) This large compound has cooking facilities, a restaurant, and ablution blocks with hot and cold water, and is often full. Car hire to visit Lake Manyara and Ngorongoro Conservation Area costs US$140 per day, including petrol and driver. It's often possible to negotiate cheaper camping and room rates, especially in the low season. The camp is along the main road and signposted.

Jambo Campsite & Lodge (☎ 253 9170; m_stock@yahoo.com; camping per person Tsh4000, s/d without bathroom Tsh5000/10,000) Cheap, scruffy and shadeless. This camp site is signposted along the main road, about 200m east of Twiga. Vehicle rental costs US$120/140 per half-/full day.

Getting There & Away
AIR

Coastal Aviation, Air Excel and Regional Air offer scheduled daily, or near-daily, services between Arusha and Lake Manyara for about US$55 one way. The airstrip is at the northwestern edge of the park.

BUS

By public transport, the best connections are on the Ngorongoro Crater bus (p210), which passes Mto Wa Mbu about 12.30pm coming from Arusha, and about 10.30am in the other direction. The fare between Arusha and Mto Wa Mbu is Tsh2000. Otherwise, the only option is sporadic *dalla-dallas*.

CAR & MOTORCYCLE

The only road access into the park is from Arusha via Makuyuni and Mto Wa Mbu. It's not possible to rent vehicles at the park, and most visitors come as part of an organised safari or with their own vehicles. Petrol is available in Mto Wa Mbu.

Getting Around

While it's easy to reach Mto Wa Mbu with public transport, once there you'll need to hire a vehicle to explore the park, which can be arranged through some of the places listed on p197, and will cost from US$140 per day. You may be able to negotiate something better if you will only be visiting Lake Manyara (rather than combining it with Ngorongoro Crater, which involves much more driving).

TARANGIRE NATIONAL PARK

Beautiful, baobab-studded Tarangire park stretches southeast of Lake Manyara around the Tarangire River. Like nearby Lake Manyara National Park, it's often assigned no more than a day visit as part of a larger northern circuit safari, although it is well worth longer exploration. Tarangire is a classic dry-season destination, particularly between August and October, when it has one of the highest concentrations of wildlife of any of the country's parks. Large herds of zebras, wildebeests, hartebeests and – in particular – elephants can be found here until October when the short wet season allows them to move on to new grasslands. Elands, lesser kudus, gazelles, giraffes, waterbucks, impalas and the occasional leopard or rhino can be seen at Tarangire year-round. The park is also good for bird-watching, especially between October and May, with more than 300 different species recorded.

Tarangire is part of an extended ecosystem where animals roam freely. It includes the large Mkungunero Game Controlled Area to the south, and the Lolkisale Game Controlled Area to the northeast. It's possible to do walks and night drives in the Lolkisale area, with local villagers benefiting from tourist revenues.

Information

Entry fees are US$25/5 per adult/child aged five to 15 years, valid for multiple entries within 24 hours. For bookings, contact the **senior park warden** (☎ 027-253 1280/1, 027-250 8642). The entry gate and park headquarters are at the northwestern tip of the park. Walking safaris within certain areas of the park have been approved in principle, but this has not yet been implemented, so for now the only walks are outside the park boundaries.

MaCo puts out the best Tarangire map, available in Arusha and at the park gate.

Sleeping

LODGES & TENTED CAMPS

All of the private lodges and tented camps are in, or near, the northern half of the park.

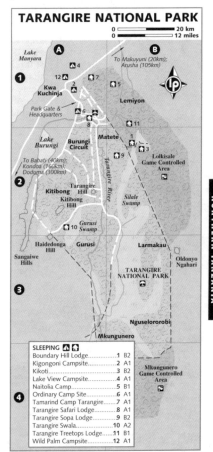

TARANGIRE NATIONAL PARK

SLEEPING	
Boundary Hill Lodge	1 B2
Kigongoni Campsite	2 A1
Kikoti	3 B2
Lake View Campsite	4 A1
Naitolia Camp	5 B1
Ordinary Camp Site	6 A1
Tamarind Camp Tarangire	7 A1
Tarangire Safari Lodge	8 A1
Tarangire Sopa Lodge	9 B2
Tarangire Swala	10 A2
Tarangire Treetops Lodge	11 B1
Wild Palm Campsite	12 A1

NORTHERN TANZANIA

Tarangire Safari Lodge (☎ 254 4752; www .tarangiresafarilodge.com; s/d tents full board US$114/170; 🖭) This large lodge is very good value, with a prime location on a bluff overlooking the Tarangire River, about 10km inside the park gate, and accommodation in tents or thatched bungalows. Apart from the fact that the tents are rather too close together if you're after space, it's a good choice, and probably the best overall deal in the park.

Tamarind Camp Tarangire (☎ 250 7011, 250 7541; www.kirurumu.com; s/d/tr full board US$165/250/330; ☙ Apr & May) Intimate and rustic, this comfortable camp is a fine base if you're interested in doing nature or wildlife walks together with your safari. It's outside the park boundaries, which means night drives are also possible. The camp is about 20 minutes' drive from the park gate and signposted off the Makuyuni road.

Naitolia Camp (☎ 0744-470447, 0744-275451; info@ tarangireconservation.com; per person all-inclusive US$175) This intimate, low-key lodge has just three very rustic tented cabins, all with attached bathroom and open-air showers. There's also a highly atmospheric tree house set off on its own, built around a baobab tree and open on three sides. It's just outside the park's northern border (about 45 minutes by vehicle to the gate) with the chance for walks and night drives. The same management also runs the soon-to-open **Boundary Hill Lodge** (www.eastafricansafari.info; per person all-inclusive US$245), set on an escarpment just northeast of the park.

Kikoti (☎ 250 8790; www.tzphotosafaris.com; s/d full board plus bush walk US$295/400) On a rise just east of the park boundaries, this camp offers spacious, well-appointed luxury tents and the chance for nature walks and night drives.

Other recommendations:
Tarangire Treetops Lodge (☎ 250 0630/39; info@sopalodges.com; s/d full board US$265/410, incl wildlife drives US$470/720) Pampered and upmarket, with spacious bungalows set on low stilts or built treehouse—style around the baobabs. Since it's outside the park, there's also the chance for walking safaris and night drives. It's set outside Tarangire's northeastern border amid baobabs and forest.
Tarangire Sopa Lodge (☎ 250 0630/39; info@ sopalodges.com; s/d full board US$160/250) Luxurious accommodation with all the amenities compensates in part for the architectural excesses of this lodge. It's in the northeastern section of the park, about 30km from the gate.

Tarangire Swala (☎ 250 9816; www.sanctuarylodges .com; per person all-inclusive US$385) Tarangire's most exclusive option, nestled in a grove of acacia trees and overlooking the Gurusi wetlands in the southwestern part of the park.

CAMPING
There is an ordinary camp site near park headquarters with basic toilet and shower facilities, and about 12 special camp sites, all in the upper-eastern and upper-western areas, near Matete, Burungi and Kitibong. As with all special camp sites, you'll need to book them in advance, and be completely self-sufficient.

Other options:
Kigongoni Campsite (camping per person US$5) A rather bleak camp site about 6km from the park gate along the road towards Makuyuni. The area for tents is rocky and dusty and there's no food, but it's the cheapest place in immediate proximity to the park.
Wild Palm Campsite (camping per person US$7) Further from the park gate (about 10km), but within walking distance of Lake Manyara. It's signposted just before the park gate turn-off.
Lake View Campsite (☎ 027-254 4057; www.bobby camping.com; camping per person US$5) Marginally nicer than Wild Palm, and overlooking Lake Manyara in the distance. It's several kilometres northeast of Kwa Kuchinja and west of the Makuyuni road.

Getting There & Around
AIR
Coastal Aviation, Air Excel and Regional Air all stop at Tarangire on request on their flights between Arusha and Lake Manyara (approximately US$60 per seat). The airstrip is in the northern section of the park near Tarangire Safari Lodge.

CAR & MOTORCYCLE
To visit Tarangire you will need to join an organised tour or use your own vehicle, as the park doesn't rent vehicles. The closest petrol is in Makuyuni, 32km from the park gate.

The park is reached via the Makuyuni road from Arusha. At Kwa Kuchinja village, there's a signposted turn-off to the park gate, which is 7km further down a good dirt access road.

SERENGETI NATIONAL PARK
The Serengeti is where legend meets reality, where Africa's mystery, rawness and power

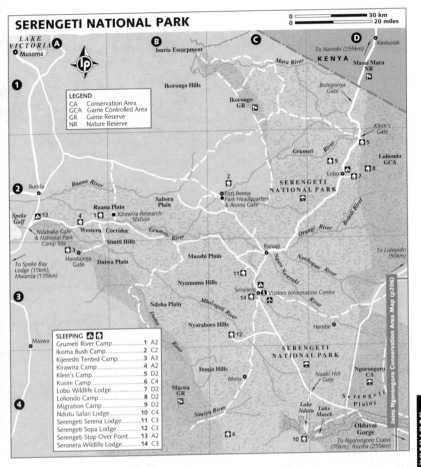

SERENGETI NATIONAL PARK

LEGEND

CA	Conservation Area
GCA	Game Controlled Area
GR	Game Reserve
NR	Nature Reserve

0   30 km
0   20 miles

SLEEPING

Grumeti River Camp	1 A2
Ikoma Bush Camp	2 C2
Kijereshi Tented Camp	3 A3
Kirawira Camp	4 A2
Klein's Camp	5 D2
Kusini Camp	6 C4
Lobo Wildlife Lodge	7 D2
Loliondo Camp	8 D2
Migration Camp	9 D2
Ndutu Safari Lodge	10 C4
Serengeti Serena Lodge	11 C3
Serengeti Sopa Lodge	12 C3
Serengeti Stop Over Point	13 A2
Seronera Wildlife Lodge	14 C3

Joins Ngorongoro Conservation Area Map (p206)

surround you, and where the beauty and synchrony of nature can be experienced as in few other places. On its vast, treeless plains, one of earth's most impressive natural cycles plays itself out again and again, as tens of thousands of hoofed animals, driven by primeval rhythms of survival, move constantly in search of fresh grasslands. The most famous, and the most numerous, are the wildebeests – of which there are more than one million – and their annual migration is the Serengeti's biggest drawcard. During the rainy season (between December and May), the wildebeests are widely scattered over the southern section of the Serengeti and the Ngorongoro Conservation Area. As these areas have few large

rivers and streams, they dry out quickly when the rains cease, nudging the wildebeests to concentrate on the few remaining green areas, and to form thousands-strong herds that migrate north and west in search of food. They then spend the dry season, from July to October, outside the Serengeti and in the Masai Mara (just over the Kenyan border), before again moving south in anticipation of the rains. Around February, the calving season, more than 8000 wildebeest calves are born per day, although about 40% of these die before they are four months old.

The 14,763 sq km Serengeti is also renowned for its predators, especially its lions, many of which have collars fitted with transmitters so their movements can be studied and their locations tracked. Keeping the lions company are cheetahs, leopards, hyenas, jackals and more. You'll also see zebras (of which there are about 200,000), large herds of giraffes, Thomson's and Grant's gazelles, elands, impalas, klipspringers and warthogs, and fascinating birdlife, including vultures brooding in the trees, haughty secretary birds surveying you from the road side and brightly coloured Fisher's lovebirds.

Wildlife concentrations in the park are greatest between about December and June, and comparatively low during the dry season (between about July and October). However, the Serengeti can be rewarding to visit at any time of year. If you are primarily interested in wildebeests, the best base from about December to April is at one of the camps near Seronera or in the southeastern part of the park. The famous crossing of the Grumeti River, which runs through the park's Western Corridor, usually takes place somewhere between May and July, although the viewing window can be quite short. In particularly dry years, the herds tend to move northwards sooner, avoiding or only skirting the Western Corridor. There are several camps in or near the Western Corridor, and it's also easily accessed from Seronera. The northern Serengeti, around Lobo and Klein's Gate, is a good base during the dry season, particularly between about August and October. As well as the migrating wildebeests, there are also small resident populations of wildebeests in the park, which you'll see at any time of year.

Almost all of the shorter safaris, and those done as part of a quick northern circuit loop, use Seronera as a base, although other sections of the park are just as rewarding, if not more so. In the low season, you will see few other vehicles outside of Seronera, although even in the high season the park is large enough that it doesn't feel overrun. With the move of the park headquarters to Ikoma several years ago, as well as various other steps, park administration is making an effort to decrease vehicle and tourist congestion in the Seronera area, and to promote use of the, until now, underutilised northern and western sectors.

Overall, the opportunities for wildlife viewing are unparalleled and, if you are able to visit, it's a chance not to be missed. Try to schedule as much time here as possible in order to explore the park's varied zones and to appreciate its vastness.

Information

Entry fees are US$30/5 per adult/child aged five to 15 years per 24-hour period, and valid for only one entry. Bookings for camp sites, resthouses and the hostel should be made through the Chief Park Warden or the **Tourism Warden** (☎ 028-262 0091, 028-262 1515, 028-262 1504; www.serengeti.org). The park headquarters are at Fort Ikoma, just outside the park, while the tourism division is at Seronera. If you're on a do-it-yourself safari, it's not mandatory to take a guide with you in the Serengeti, although having one along is likely to greatly enhance both your wildlife watching and your navigation through the park – especially if you've never been to the Serengeti. Vehicle rentals from both Arusha and Mwanza (the main Serengeti gateways) almost always include a driver-guide.

There is an excellent **Visitors Information Centre** at Seronera – the only one of its kind that we've seen anywhere in the region. Among other things, it has a self-guided walk through the Serengeti's history and ecosystems. Explanations are in English and Swahili and very well done, and it's well worth spending a few hours here before beginning your exploration of the park.

The small gift shop at the Seronera Visitors Information Centre sells various booklets and maps, including the informative MaCo *Serengeti* map.

For information on entry-gate locations see p205.

Activities

An expensive but highly enjoyable way to experience the Serengeti is by balloon. This costs US$399 per person for about an hour floating over the plains at dawn, followed by a champagne breakfast in the bush under the acacia trees, complete with linen tablecloths. The flight route varies depending on the winds, but often follows a stretch of the Grumeti River. Bookings can be made in Arusha through **Serengeti Balloon Safaris** (☎ 027-250 8578, 027-254 8967; www.balloonsafaris .com) or through any of the central Serengeti lodges listed on p203.

Walking safaris in the park have been preliminarily approved but not yet implemented, although this may change within the lifetime of this book. For an update, check with the park, or alternatively with Green Footprint Adventures (p60). Most of the lodges and camps outside the park boundaries also organise walks.

Sleeping
LODGES & TENTED CAMPS
Central Serengeti
The main lodge area is at Seronera, in the centre of the park.

Seronera Wildlife Lodge (☎ 027-254 4595/4795; www.hotelsandlodges-tanzania.com; r per person full board US$175) This is the best overall value, with a good location convenient to prime wildlife-viewing areas, modest but pleasant rooms and a lively end-of-the-day safari atmosphere at the evening buffet.

Serengeti Serena Lodge (☎ 027-250 4153/8; www.serenahotels.com; s/d full board US$270/400; ☒) About 20km northwest of Seronera airstrip, this place is not as favourably located as Seronera Wildlife Lodge but is otherwise a good choice and very comfortable. Accommodation is in intriguing two-storey Maasai bungalows with all the amenities.

Serengeti Sopa Lodge (☎ 027-250 0630/39; info@sopalodges.com; s/d full board US$160/250; ☒) Though ponderous and architecturally unappealing, the rooms here – all spacious, with small sitting rooms and two double beds – have all the comforts, and facilities are on a par with those at the other Sopa lodges.

Northern Serengeti
The wild and rugged northern Serengeti receives relatively few visitors, but makes a good base between August and October, when you may catch a glimpse of the wildebeest migration.

For connoisseurs, the main choices – both highly regarded – are the luxurious **Migration Camp** (☎ 250 0630/39; info@sopalodges.com; s/d full board incl wildlife drives US$470/720; ☒), which has an intimate bush atmosphere, and views over the Grumeti River in a good wildlife-viewing area; and the exclusive, strikingly situated **Klein's Camp** (www.ccafrica.com; per person all-inclusive US$560; ☒), just outside the northeasternmost park boundary, with eight luxurious cottages, and the chance to do night wildlife drives.

Loliondo Camp (☎ 027-250 7011, 027-250 7541; www.kirurumu.com; s/d full board US$500/700; ☽ Apr & May) This intimate five-tent camp is east of Lobo Wildlife Lodge, and just outside the park boundary in the Loliondo Game Controlled Area – a scenically stunning area of grasslands and wooded hills dotted with huge granite boulders. It's a good choice if you want to combine your safari with some cultural interaction with the local Maasai. It's also ideally situated for night drives and walking safaris, including longer walks with donkeys to carry your packs and nights spent in a fly camp; special family safaris can also be arranged.

Other recommendations:

Lobo Wildlife Lodge (☎ 027-254 4595/4795; www.hotelsandlodges-tanzania.com; r per person full board US$175) Well located and similar in standard to the Seronera Wildlife Lodge. If your budget is limited, it's the best value in this part of the park.

Serengeti Safari Camp (www.nomad-tanzania.com; per person all-inclusive US$590/930) A highly exclusive mobile camp that follows the wildebeest migration, with some of the best guides in the Serengeti. The camp can only be booked through upmarket travel agents.

Western Serengeti
Apart from the park camp sites, the western Serengeti is the only area that has options for budget travellers (all outside the park). It also has several very upmarket lodges.

Ikoma Bush Camp (☎ 250 8424; swala@swalasafaris.com; camping per person US$12; per person full board US$80, per person all-inclusive except park fees US$120) This small camp is just outside the park boundary and 3km from Ikoma Gate and is ideal for those on a tighter budget. It has 12 simple tents with bathrooms and hot water, plus the chance for night drives and guided walks in the surrounding area, and is good overall value.

Grumeti River Camp (www.ccafrica.com; per person all-inclusive US$560; ☒) One of the most exclusive camps in the Serengeti. It's in a wild bush location near the Grumeti River that's especially prime around June and July when the wildebeests are often around. Accommodation is in 10 wonderfully appointed, spacious luxury tents with all the amenities.

Kirawira Camp (☎ 027-250 4153/8, 028-262 1518; www.serenahotels.com; s/d all-inclusive US$850/1300; ☒) Kirawira, set on a small rise about 90km west of Seronera, is more open and somewhat tamer in feel than Grumeti, with luxurious tents in what its advertising describes as an ambience of 'colonial opulence'.

Serengeti Stop Over Point (☎ 028-262 1531, 027-253 7095; www.serengetistopover.com; camping per person US$5, tent rental per person US$10, s/d US$20/30) This friendly, clued-up camp site is directly on the Mwanza–Musoma road about 1km from Ndabaka Gate. There's space to pitch a tent and a few simple, clean rooms, plus food and a small bar, and staff can help you organise local boat trips on Lake Victoria and Sukuma cultural excursions. Any bus along the Mwanza–Musoma road will drop you nearby, and the camp rents out a safari vehicle (with advance notice) for about US$150 per day.

Other recommendations:

Kijereshi Tented Camp (☎ 028-250 0127, 028-262 1231; www.hoteltilapia.com; s/d US$35/55, with full board US$50/75; 🏊) A budget place just outside the park boundaries, 18km east of the Mwanza–Musoma road and signposted, and about 2km from the Serengeti's Handajega Gate. It's a popular base for overlanders, with functional tented accommodation (you can also pitch your own for US$5) plus a few rooms, a restaurant and cooking facilities for self-caterers.

Speke Bay Lodge (☎ 028-262 1236; spekebay@ africaonline.co.tz; s/d tents without bathroom US$31/44, s/d bungalows US$80/100) On Lake Victoria about 15km southwest of Ndabaka Gate and 125km north of Mwanza, this is a good choice if you want to combine the Serengeti with Lake Victoria, though you'll need your own car as there are none for rent. Accommodation is in simple tents with shared facilities, or in spotless, if rather soulless, en suite four-person bungalows. The hotel can help you organise boat, fishing or birding excursions on the lake.

Southeastern Serengeti

The Serengeti's southeastern corner makes a good base for wildlife viewing, especially during the wet season (December to April), when it's full of wildebeests.

Ndutu Safari Lodge (☎ 027-250 6702/8930; www.ndutu.com; s US$68-144 d US$90-185) This relaxed, good-value place is just outside the Serengeti in the far western part of Ngorongoro Conservation Area (NCA). It's well placed for wildlife viewing, especially for observing the enormous herds of wildebeests during the wet season, and makes a good stop if you're en route between Ngorongoro Crater and central or western Serengeti. It also has the advantage that walking safaris are possible in the surrounding NCA. In addition to NCA fees, you'll need to pay Serengeti fees any time that you cross into the park. Accommodation is in unpretentious but comfortable en suite cottages, and the atmosphere is relaxed and rustic.

Other recommendations:
Olduvai Tented Camp (see p211).

Southwestern Serengeti

Kusini Camp (☎ 250 9816; www.sanctuarylodges.com; per person all-inclusive US$385) Laid-back luxury in a good wet-season setting amid rocky outcrops in the remote southwestern Serengeti.

CAMPING

There are about nine ordinary camp sites in the Serengeti, including six around Seronera, one at Lobo, one at Kirawira in the Western Corridor, and one near Ndabaka Gate in the far west along the Mwanza–Musoma road. Several have pit toilets and at least one has a shower, though for most you'll need to be self-sufficient, including with water. There are also several resthouses at Seronera with running water, blankets and cooking facilities, as well as an 80-person hostel for student groups. The hostel has no showers, and for both resthouses and hostel, you'll need to bring your own food, although there's a small shop at Seronera selling soft drinks, water and a few basics.

There are at least two dozen special camp sites including in the areas around Lake Ndutu, Kirawira Research Station, Seronera, Lobo, Naabi Hill Gate and elsewhere. These should be booked well in advance, especially for groups; a 30% nonrefundable deposit is required one month before your arrival date.

Getting There & Around
AIR

Coastal Aviation, Air Excel and Regional Air all have daily flights from Arusha to several of the Serengeti airstrips, including Seronera (US$145 per person one way) and Grumeti (US$170). There are also airstrips at Serengeti South, Lobo and most other ranger posts. Some of Coastal's flights continue on to Mwanza and Rubondo Island National Park on demand.

CAR & MOTORCYCLE

The majority of travellers visit the Serengeti with an organised safari or in their own vehicle. For shoestring travellers the only other option to try to get a glimpse of the animals is to take a bus travelling between Arusha and Mwanza or Musoma via the Western Corridor route, although you won't be able to stop to observe the wildlife. You will need to pay park fees and, if you get out at Seronera, you'll have the problem of getting onward transport, as hitching is not permitted in the park.

Access from Arusha is via the heavily used **Naabi Hill Gate** (6am-6pm) at the southeastern edge of the park. From here, it's 75km further to Seronera. The **Ndabaka Gate** (6am-4pm) is about 140km northeast of Mwanza along the Mwanza–Musoma road, and gives you direct access to the Western Corridor. The road from Ndabaka to Seronera is in decent to good condition; allow two to three hours. Ikoma Gate is also accessed from the Mwanza–Musoma road, from a rough track running east from Bunda. Bologonya Gate, 5km from the Kenyan border, is the route to/from Kenya's Masai Mara National Reserve, but the border is open only to East African residents or citizens. There are other entry points at Handajega (Western Corridor) and in the north near Klein's Camp. Driving is not permitted in the park after 7pm.

Petrol points en route from Arusha include Makuyuni, Mto Wa Mbu and Karatu. Petrol is also usually available at Ngorongoro Crater (Park Village) and at the Seronera Wildlife Lodge, although it's expensive. It is not available anywhere else in the park, so if you have your own vehicle come prepared with sufficient supplies. Coming from the west, the most reliable petrol points are Mwanza and Musoma. You may also be able to find petrol in Bunda.

NGORONGORO CONSERVATION AREA

The world-renowned Ngorongoro Crater is just one part of a much larger area of interrelated ecosystems consisting of the Crater Highlands (to which the Ngorongoro Crater belongs) together with vast stretches of plains, grasslands, bush and woodland. The entire Ngorongoro Conservation Area (NCA) – a Unesco World Heritage Site – covers about 8300 sq km. Near its centre is Olduvai Gorge, where many famous fossils have been unearthed. To the west are the alkaline Lakes Ndutu and Masek, although Ndutu is just over the border in the Serengeti. Both lakes are particularly good areas for wildlife viewing between December and April, when they are practically overrun with wildebeests. In the east of the conservation area is a string of volcanoes and craters (collapsed volcanoes, often referred to as calderas); most, but not all, are inactive. Further east, just outside the NCA's boundaries, is the mysterious archaeological site of Engaruka. Nestled in the barren landscape along the NCA's southern border is Lake Eyasi, while to the northeast of the NCA in the arid expanses near the Kenyan border is the alkaline Lake Natron.

Information

The NCA is under the jurisdiction of the Ngorongoro Conservation Area Authority (NCAA), which has its **headquarters** (253 9108, 253 7019, 253 7060; ncaa_hq@habari.co.tz) at Park Village at Ngorongoro Crater. The NCAA has a tourist information office in Arusha (p179).

Entry fees – which you'll need to pay not only to visit Ngorongoro Crater, but for all activities within the NCA – are US$30 per person per 24-hour period (US$5 for children five to 16 years old, and free for children under five). Guides are mandatory and cost US$15 per day per group (US$20 for walking safaris). There is a vehicle fee of US$30 per entry and an additional 'crater-service' fee of US$15 per vehicle per entry to drive down into Ngorongoro Crater. Camping fees are US$20/40 per person in an ordinary/special camp site.

The two official entry points to the NCA are **Lodoare Gate** (253 7031; 6.30am-6pm), just south of Ngorongoro Crater, and **Naabi Hill Gate** (253 7030; 6am-6pm), on the border with Serengeti National Park.

Both MaCo and Harms-ic put out maps of the NCA, and they can be purchased at the NCA tourist information office in Arusha and at Lodoare Gate.

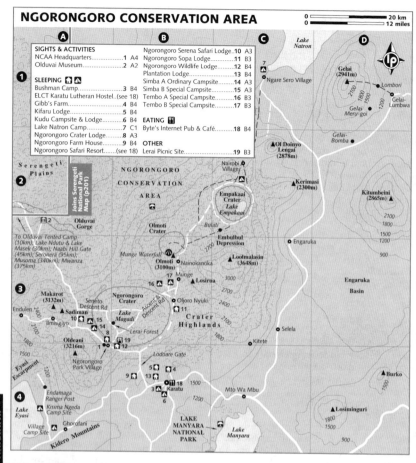

NGORONGORO CONSERVATION AREA

| 0 | 20 km |
| 0 | 12 miles |

SIGHTS & ACTIVITIES
NCAA Headquarters.................1 A4
Olduvai Museum.....................2 A2

SLEEPING
Bushman Camp.......................3 B4
ELCT Karatu Lutheran Hostel..(see 18)
Gibb's Farm...........................4 B4
Kifaru Lodge...........................5 B4
Kudu Campsite & Lodge.........6 B4
Lake Natron Camp.................7 C1
Ngorongoro Crater Lodge.......8 A3
Ngorongoro Farm House.........9 B4
Ngorongoro Safari Resort......(see 18)

Ngorongoro Serena Safari Lodge..10 A3
Ngorongoro Sopa Lodge...........11 B3
Ngorongoro Wildlife Lodge........12 B4
Plantation Lodge......................13 B4
Simba A Ordinary Campsite......14 A3
Simba B Special Campsite.........15 A3
Tembo A Special Campsite.........16 B3
Tembo B Special Campsite.........17 B3

EATING
Byte's Internet Pub & Café..........18 B4

OTHER
Lerai Picnic Site.........................19 B3

THE CRATER HIGHLANDS

The ruggedly beautiful Crater Highlands consist of an elevated range of volcanoes and collapsed volcanoes that rises up from the side of the Great Rift Valley and runs in a chain along the eastern edge of the NCA. The peaks include Oldeani (3216m), Makarot (Lemagurut; 3107m), Olmoti (3100m), Loolmalasin (3648m), Empakaai (also spelled Embagai; 3262m), the still-active Ol Doinyo Lengai ('Mountain of God' in Maasai; 2878m) and of course, Ngorongoro (2200m). The different peaks were created over many millions of years by a series of eruptions connected with the birth of the Great Rift Valley, and the older volcanoes have since collapsed to form the craters that

give the range its name. The main residents of the area are the Maasai, who have grazed cattle here for hundreds of years.

Apart from Ngorongoro Crater, much of the Crater Highlands area is remote and seldom visited, although it offers some of Tanzania's most unusual scenery, as well as good trekking. It can also be visited on a vehicle safari arranged through one of the Arusha-based tour operators, although you'll miss much of the area's essence by not exploring on foot. If you want to use your own vehicle, keep in mind that roads are isolated, and you'll need to be self-sufficient with petrol and water. You will also need to get permission and a guide from the NCAA.

Trekking the Crater Highlands

The best way to explore the Crater Highlands is on foot, although because of the logistics involved, trekking here is expensive. Treks range from short day jaunts to excursions of up to two weeks or more. For all routes, you'll need to be accompanied by a guide, and for anything except day hikes, you will need donkeys or vehicle support to carry water and supplies.

Nearly all visitors arrange treks through a tour company. A number of Arusha-based companies do treks to Empakaai and to Ol Doinyo Lengai (just outside the NCA boundaries), but for most trekking in this region you'll need to contact a specialist operator. For some recommendations, see p59, and Lonely Planet's *Trekking in East Africa*. Costs vary widely, but expect to pay a minimum of US$150 per person per day in a group of four, including NCA entry fees.

The only other option is to contact the NCAA directly and arrange your trek through them. This requires at least one month's notice, and usually winds up costing about the same as going through a tour company. You'll need to provide all camping equipment and supplies yourself, including water; you'll also need to hire a vehicle (essential for accessing all treks) and arrange for someone to drive the car

to the end of the trek to collect you, as most routes are not circuits. The NCAA will then take care of arranging the camp sites, guides and donkeys. The hikes are usually based at designated Maasai 'cultural bomas', each of which has a Tsh5000 entry fee.

There are no set routes, and the possibilities are numerous. A popular multiday trek starts just north of Ngorongoro Crater and crosses the highlands to finish at Ngare Sero village near Lake Natron. This normally takes four days, but can be cut to three by starting at Nainokanoka or extended by one day to climb Ol Doinyo Lengai.

If you want to experience the area but still stay within a reasonable budget, there are several good short hikes, including up Makarot or Oldeani, or at Empakaai or Olmoti Craters. All of these can easily be done in a day or less from a base at Ngorongoro Crater, and apart from transport costs, involve only the US$30 NCA entry fee and US$20 guide fee. If you're trying to do things on your own through the NCA, rather than through a tour operator, the least complicated option would probably be Oldeani, which is accessed from Park Village, where you can also arrange a ranger/guide. From Oldeani, it's then possible to continue on down to Lake Eyasi, though for this you'll need an overnight stay or two.

THE MAASAI

Travelling in northern Tanzania, you are almost certain to meet some Maasai, one of the region's most colourful tribes. The Maasai are pastoral nomads who have actively resisted change, and still follow the same lifestyle that they have for centuries. Their culture centres around their cattle, which provide many of their needs – milk, blood and meat for their diet, and hides and skins for clothing – although sheep and goats also play an important dietary role, especially during the dry season. The land, cattle and all elements related to cattle are considered sacred.

Maasai society is patriarchal and highly decentralised. Elders meet to decide on general issues but ultimately it is the well-being of the cattle that dominates proceedings. One of the most important features of Maasai society is its system of social stratification based on age. Maasai boys pass through a number of transitions throughout life, the first of which is marked by the circumcision rite. Successive stages include junior warriors, senior warriors, junior elders and senior elders; each level is distinguished by its own unique rights, responsibilities and dress. Junior elders, for example, are expected to marry and settle down – somewhere between the ages of 30 and 40. Senior elders assume the responsibility of making wise and moderate decisions for the community. The most important group is that of the newly initiated warriors, *moran*, who are charged with defending the cattle herds.

Maasai women play a markedly subservient role and have no inheritance rights. Polygyny is widespread and marriages are arranged by the elders, without consulting the bride or her mother. Since most women are significantly younger than men at the time of marriage, they often become widows; remarriage is rare.

There are no camps or lodges apart from the facilities at Ngorongoro Crater.

NGORONGORO CRATER

With its ethereal blue-green vistas, close-range viewing opportunities and unparalleled concentrations of wildlife, Ngorongoro is one of Tanzania's most visited destinations, and one of Africa's best-known wildlife-viewing areas. At about 20km wide it is also one of the largest calderas in the world. Its steep, unbroken walls provide the setting for an incredible natural drama, as lions, elephants, buffaloes, and plains herbivores such as wildebeests, Thomson's gazelles, zebras and reedbucks graze, stalk and otherwise make their way around the grasslands, swamps and forests on the crater floor. Chances are good that you'll also see a black rhino or two, and for many people this is one of the crater's main draws. The birding is also excellent, including around Lake Magadi, the soda lake at the crater's base, which attracts hundreds of flamingos to its shallows.

Despite the crater's steepness, there is considerable movement of animals in and out, thanks to the permanent water and grassland on the crater floor. Animals and birds share the crater with the local Maasai people, who have grazing rights, and you may come across them tending their cattle. During the German colonial era there were two settlers' farms in the crater; you can still see one of the huts.

Because of the crater's popularity, it's easy to get distracted from the natural magnificence, especially when there are several dozen vehicles crowded around one or two animals, all to a backdrop of clicking cameras and radio static. One of the best ways to minimise these distractions is by getting into the crater early (there are relatively few vehicles before about 9am). It also helps to pick one or several strategic spots and then to stay put for a while, letting the nuances and subtleties of the crater's environment gradually come to you rather than joining the mad dashes across the crater floor when drivers radio each other about particularly good sightings.

Information

For fee information, see p205. Ngorongoro can be visited at any time of the year, but during April and May it can be wet and difficult to negotiate. If there's particularly heavy rain, access to the crater floor may be restricted.

The gates down to the crater floor open at 7am and close (for descent) at 4pm; all vehicles must be out of the crater area before 6pm.

It can get quite chilly and raw on the crater rim, so bring a jacket and come prepared, especially if you're camping.

Sleeping

LODGES

There are four lodges on, or near, the rim of the crater.

Ngorongoro Wildlife Lodge (☎ 254 4595/4795, or direct ☎ 253 7058, 253 7073; www.hotelsandlodges -tanzania.com; r per person full board US$175) Ngorongoro Wildlife Lodge has a beautiful setting on the southern crater rim, and straightforward rooms.

Ngorongoro Crater Lodge (www.ccafrica.com; per person all-inclusive US$595) This lodge – actually three separate camps – is the most interesting in terms of design, with an eclectic collection of styles and décor. Service and amenities are ultra-top-end, and prices include your own butler. It's on the southwestern crater rim.

Ngorongoro Serena Safari Lodge (☎ 250 4153/8; www.serenahotels.com; s/d full board US$270/400) The perennially popular Serena lodge is in a good location on the southwestern crater rim, past Ngorongoro Crater Lodge and near the main crater descent route. It's a comfortable, attractive place with standards and facilities at least as good as those at the other Serena hotels, if not better. Green Footprint Adventures (p60) has a base here and organises short hikes from the lodge, including nature walks and day hikes to Olmoti.

Ngorongoro Sopa Lodge (☎ 027-250 0630/39; info@sopalodges.com; s/d full board US$160/250) This place is also well located, but off on its own on the eastern crater rim, just before the track leading up to Olmoti Crater, and near a crater descent/ascent road. Accommodation is in spacious rooms, each with two double beds, and standards and service are commendable.

CAMPING

The only ordinary camp site is Simba A, which has basic facilities (latrines and cold showers) and isn't very clean, but it has great views over the crater if you're lucky enough to be there when there is no cloud cover. It's along the road from Lodoare Gate, and not far from NCAA headquarters.

There are numerous special camp sites (none of which have any facilities), including Simba B, just up the road from Simba A, Tembo A and B north of the Ngorongoro Sopa Lodge; a cluster of sites near Lakes Ndutu and Masek; and one on the southern rim of Lake Empakaai.

Karatu
☎ 027

This small, scruffy town 20km southeast of Lodoare Gate is surrounded by some beautiful countryside, and makes a convenient base for visiting Ngorongoro. Many camping safaris out of Arusha use Karatu as an overnight stop to economise on entry fees for Ngorongoro, but it's also worth basing your trip here if you want to get in some walking in the nearby rolling hills.

There is a post office, an NBC branch that exchanges cash and travellers cheques and has an ATM, and **Bytes Internet Pub & Café** (per hr Tsh2000; ☉ 8am-11pm), which also has some great food (see right).

SLEEPING & EATING
Budget
In addition to the following listings, there are several basic guesthouses in the centre of town, all of about the same standard and all with no-frills rooms for about Tsh3000. A modest selection of supplies is available in Karatu, but if you're on a tight budget, it's cheaper to stock up in Arusha.

Ngorongoro Safari Resort (☎ 253 4059/4287; safariresort@yahoo.com; camping US$5, s/d US$65/80) This place has good, though crowded, camping facilities, hot showers, a covered dining area and meals from Tsh2000. There are also rooms, which are fine, but overpriced for what you get. It's on the main road in the town centre. Car hire can be arranged to Ngorongoro or Lake Manyara for US$110/120 per half-/full day.

ELCT Karatu Lutheran Hostel (☎ 253 4230; s/d/tr Tsh16,000/22,000/32,000; meals Tsh5000) The Lutheran Hostel has simple, clean rooms with hot water, and good meals. It's on the main road at the western end of town.

Kudu Campsite & Lodge (☎ 253 4055; kuducamp@habari.co.tz; camping per person US$7, s/d/tr bungalows US$55/75/90; meals US$5-8) Kudu, at the western end of town and signposted to the south of the main road, has good facilities, including quiet gardens; a large lawn to pitch your tent; hot-water showers; clean, comfortable bungalows; and a bar. Meals are available with notice.

Bushman Camp (☎ 0744-578045; faidabushman camp@yahoo.com; camping per person with hot shower US$5; d without bathroom US$16; meals US$5) An agreeable spot to pitch your tent, with large grounds dotted with bougainvillea bushes, and some basic rooms planned. It's about 1km off the main road and signposted.

Bytes Internet Pub & Café (☎ 253 4488; bytes@afsat.com; meals from Tsh4000; ☉ 8am-11pm) If you're craving an injection of Western comforts, this is an essential stop, with excellent freshly squeezed juices, cappuccino, freshly baked cakes and gourmet-style meals. They also do takeaway picnic lunches (with three days' advance notice) with quiche and other delicacies. Next door is a stand selling fresh vegetables and other produce, and there's a sports bar with satellite TV. It's along the main road behind the Crater Highlands petrol station.

For self-catering, in addition to the food stall at Bytes, there are several small supermarkets along the main road, including Olduvai Supermarket and Karatu Mini-Market.

Mid-Range & Top End
Karatu and surrounding area offer some excellent choices in this category.

Gibb's Farm (☎ 253 4040; www.gibbsfarm.net; s/d half board US$154/207; ☉ mid-May–mid-Apr) The long-established Gibb's Farm has a rustic atmosphere, a wonderful setting with wide views over the nearby coffee plantations, good walking and cosy garden bungalows. It gets consistently good reviews, as does the cuisine, which is made with home-grown produce and is excellent. The farm is about 5km north of the main road and signposted.

Plantation Lodge (☎ 253 4364/5, 254 4360; plantation-lodge@habari.co.tz; s/d half board US$135/187; ☒) This is a genteel place, with spacious, well-appointed cottages set in green and expansive grounds, and has large verandas with views over the hills, a crackling fireplace and a cosy, highland ambience. It's about

2km north of the main road, with good walking in the surrounding area.

Other recommendations:

Ngorongoro Farm House (☎ 250 4093; www.africa wilderness.com; s/d half board US$125/190) An atmospheric farmhouse set in a coffee plantation just a few kilometres from Lodoare Gate.

Kifaru Lodge (☎ 253 4402; www.kifarulodge.com; s/d US$120/170; 🖭) Another old farmhouse with simple, homy rooms. It's about 6km north of the main road and slightly west of Gibb's Farm.

Getting There & Away

The large, white Ngorongoro Crater bus goes daily between Arusha's central bus station and the NCAA headquarters (Tsh4000, seven hours), departing Arusha at 10am and Park Village (where vehicles can be rented) at 7am. It's also possible to get the bus in Karatu (Tsh3000 from Arusha, passing Karatu going west about 2pm, and going east about 9am) or Mto Wa Mbu. From Arusha, the bus often fills up, so it's worth getting to the station early or booking a seat the day before at the NCAA Tourist Information Office (p179). In Karatu, the bus stand is at the western end of town, behind the Total petrol station.

Getting Around

You can arrange guides and vehicle hire at NCAA headquarters for Ngorongoro Crater as well as other areas of the NCA. Car hire costs US$100/140 for a half/full day and should be booked in advance. You can also rent vehicles in Karatu for about the same price. The only petrol between Karatu and Seronera in the Serengeti is at the NCAA headquarters.

If you are coming with your own vehicle, only 4WDs are allowed down into the crater, except at certain times during the dry season when the authorities may allow 2WD vehicles to enter. All roads into the crater, except the road from Ngorongoro Sopa Lodge on the eastern side, are very steep, so if you are driving your own vehicle, make sure it can handle the conditions. The main route into the crater is via the Seneto descent road, which enters the crater on its western side, putting you at a point just west of Lake Magadi. To come out, use the Lerai ascent road, which starts near the Lerai picnic site to the south of Lake Magadi and puts you on the rim near

Ngorongoro Crater Lodge. There is a third access route on the northeastern edge of the crater near the Ngorongoro Sopa Lodge, which can also be used for ascents and descents. These routes are occasionally reversed if heavy rains render one or another impassable.

OLDUVAI GORGE

Slicing its way close to 100m down into the plains northwest of Ngorongoro Crater, and through millennia of history is Olduvai Gorge – a dusty, 50km long ravine that has become one of the continent's best-known archaeological sites. Thanks to its unique geological history, in which layer upon layer of volcanic deposits were laid down in an orderly sequence over a period of almost two million years, it provides remarkable documentation of ancient life, allowing us to begin turning the pages of history back to the days of our earliest ancestors.

The most famous of the fossils yielded by Olduvai has been the 1.8 million-year-old ape-like skull known as *Australopithecus boisei*, which was discovered by Mary Leakey in 1959 and gave rise to a heated debate about human evolution. The skull is also often referred to as 'zinjanthropus', which means 'nutcracker man', referring to its large molars. In 1972, 3.75-million-year-old hominid (human-like) footprints – the oldest known – were discovered at Laetoli, about 45km south of the Olduvai Gorge. Based on these findings as well as other ancient fossils excavated in Kenya and Ethiopia, it has been posited that there were at least three hominid species in the region about two million years ago, including *Australopithecus boisei*, *Homo habilis* and *Homo erectus*. While *Australopithecus boisei* and *Homo habilis* appear to have died out (or in the case of *Homo habilis*, been absorbed by or evolved into *Homo erectus*), it is theorised that *Homo erectus* continued and evolved into *Homo sapiens*, or modern man. Other lesser-known but significant fossils excavated from the upper layers of Olduvai provide some of the oldest evidence of *Homo sapiens* in the area.

There is a small and very interesting **museum** (☉ 8am-3pm) here, just off the road to Serengeti, and an adjoining picnic area. It's also possible to go down into the gorge, accompanied by a guide, who can be arranged at the museum. As well as the standard fees applying to the Ngorongoro Conservation Area, there's an additional US$2 per person per day fee for visiting Olduvai Gorge, including the museum.

Olduvai Tented Camp (olduvai@intotanzania.com; per person all-inclusive about US$300) This rustic camp is nestled among some *kopjes* (small, isolated hills) with wide views over the surrounding area. Standards are quite rudimentary in comparison with other places in this price range, but the setting is good, and if you're into the offbeat, it makes an ideal spot to watch wildebeests during the wet season and for getting a feel for this part of the country. Advance bookings are essential.

ENGARUKA

Dusty Engaruka, on the eastern edge of the Ngorongoro Conservation Area near the foot of Empakaai, is a small village known for its extensive ruins of a complex irrigation system with terraced stone housing sites estimated to be at least 500 years old. Scientists are not sure of the origin of the ruins; some speculate they were built by ancestors of the Iraqw (Mbulu) people, who live in the area today, while others suggest that the site was built by the Sonjo, a Bantu-speaking people. Those interested in Engaruka can read more about the site in the first chapter of Henry Forsbroke's *The Eighth Wonder*. The ruins are best viewed from the air, although archaeology buffs will probably find a ground visit more interesting.

There's a **Cultural Tourism Program** of sorts here, which in addition to tours of the ruins and Maasai cultural tours, offers a two-day hike to Ol Doinyo Lengai mountain or a day climb of Kerimasi mountain (2614m). You can arrange things through the tourist information office in Arusha, or at Jerusalem Campsite (below) in Engaruka.

There are several camp sites, including one in Engaruka village, and the nicer Jerusalem Campsite just after the river, on the left near the Engaruka Juu primary school.

Engaruka is about 60km north of Mto Wa Mbu along an unsealed road, which is in reasonable shape for the first 10km or so, and rough thereafter. Pick-ups traverse the stretch sporadically, usually departing Mto Wa Mbu in the late afternoon and Engaruka around dawn. It's also possible to

hike in from the Empakaai Crater, but you will need a guide from the NCAA.

LAKE NATRON

Shimmering amid the parched, sun-scorched landscapes along the Kenyan border northeast of the NCA is Lake Natron, a 60km-long alkaline lake known for the huge flocks of flamingos that gather here at the end of the rainy season. The surrounding country is remote, with a desolate, otherworldly beauty and an incomparable feeling of space, and can be a rewarding – albeit very hot – off the beaten track excursion. The lake also makes a good base for climbing Ol Doinyo Lengai, 25km to the south. Because the lake has no outlet, its size varies dramatically depending on the time of year. Whenever you visit, the swampy marshes around the banks make access difficult, and you'll need a 4WD.

The Lake Natron area has been plagued by banditry in the past. While the situation seems to have long since calmed down, the lake and its access route are remote, so if you're heading up here independently, check with Lake Natron Camp (below) and other Arusha-based safari operators familiar with the area for an update.

Lake Natron Camp (☎ 250 8424; www.swalasafaris .com; camping per person US$8; s/d tented camp full board US$70/110; ⌘) This is the only established accommodation, with nine straightforward en suite tents and an adjoining camp site. It's about 4km southwest of the lake, and isolated from the stark and barren surroundings by a clump of vegetation and a small stream. The camp is the best contact for organising treks up Ol Doinyo Lengai, and can also help with arranging hikes in the Crater Highlands. Full-board arrangements need to be booked in advance.

Lake Natron Camp can also organise transfers to the lake from Mto Wa Mbu (US$35 per person, minimum of two people). Otherwise, there's no public transport. In your own vehicle, you'll need to be completely self-sufficient, with extra supplies of petrol and water, as there is nothing to be found along the way. There's a US$20 per person district council fee to enter the area.

LAKE EYASI

Starkly beautiful Lake Eyasi lies at about 1000m between the Eyasi Escarpment in the north and the Kidero Mountains in the south. It's a hot, dry area, around which live the Hadzabe (also known as Hadzapi or Tindiga) people who are believed to have lived here for nearly 10,000 years and continue to follow hunting and gathering traditions. Their language is characterised by clicks and may be distantly related to that of the San of southern Africa, although it shows only a few connections to Sandawe, the other click language spoken in Tanzania. Also in the area are the Iraqw (Mbulu), a people of Cushitic origin who arrived about 2000 years ago, as well as Maasai and various Bantu groups. The area is Tanzania's main onion-growing centre, and there are impressive irrigation systems along the Chemchem River near the camp sites. The main village is Ghorofani, at the lake's northeastern end.

Although visitor numbers are relatively small, Eyasi makes a rewarding detour on a Ngorongoro trip. Guides can be easily arranged if you're interested in visiting nearby Hadzabe communities; plan on paying about Tsh15,000 per small group.

Near the Chemchem River and about 2km from Ghorofani is a **village camp site** (Tsh3000). It has a small spring for water and is popular with overland groups.

About 5km further on, in a sublime setting on the lakeshore with doum palms in the background, is **Kisima Ngeda** (☎ 027-253 4128, 027-254 8840; kisima@habari.co.tz; camping per person US$5, s/d luxury tented bungalow full board US$150/250). It has six beautiful luxury tented bungalows, each with lake views and plenty of peace and quiet. Further along the lake shore and well away from the luxury camp area are three good camp sites where you can pitch a tent. All have toilet and shower, and for a modest tip the guard can arrange hot water. Nearby is a large hill with excellent sunset views.

Full board is included at the luxury camp if you're staying there. If you're camping, you can get basics in Ghorofani, but it's worth stocking up in Karatu before heading to the lake.

There's public transport several times daily – usually in old 4WDs – between Karatu and Ghorofani (Tsh2000, two hours), from where you'll need to walk to the camp sites or pay a bit extra to have the driver drop you off. Alternatively, you can hitch a lift with one of the onion trucks.

Lake Victoria

HIGHLIGHTS

- Dancing and drumming with the Sukuma at the **Bujora Cultural Centre** (p220) near Mwanza

- Relaxing amid the serenity of **Rubondo Island National Park** (p222), and enjoying its excellent birding

- Treating yourself to a night or two at **Lukuba Island Lodge** (p227), a rustic but luxurious angler's hideaway off-shore from Musoma

- Delving into history at the **Nyerere museum** (p227), near Musoma

- Exploring **Mwanza** (p215) and other lake shore towns before heading off on safari in the Serengeti's Western Corridor

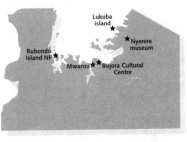

LAKE VICTORIA

Were it not Africa's largest lake, and the second-largest freshwater lake in the world, it would be easy to overlook Lake Victoria. The Tanzanian part of this enormous patch of blue sees only a trickle of tourists; lake shore towns, apart from a sleepy waterside charm, have little to hold passing visitors, and the infrastructure lags behind that in many other parts of the country. Yet, if you have a bent for the offbeat, the surrounding region holds a number of attractions. There's the Bujora Cultural Centre near Mwanza, where you can learn Sukuma dancing and immerse yourself in the culture of Tanzania's largest tribal group. Further north near Musoma is the Nyerere museum, an essential stop for anyone interested in the great statesman. On the opposite side of the lake is Bukoba, heartland of the Haya people, who were thought to have had one of the most highly developed early societies on the continent. Mwanza, on the lake's southeastern edge, is Tanzania's second largest town after Dar es Salaam, and a useful stocking-up point before heading into the Serengeti's Western Corridor. Serene Rubondo Island National Park, completely surrounded by the lake, is an ideal destination for bird-watching and relaxing.

The best way to explore the Lake Victoria region is as part of a larger East African loop combining Uganda and/or Kenya with Tanzania's northern circuit via the western Serengeti, although you'll need plenty of time, and a tolerance for rough roads. There are a few idyllic getaways – notably on Rubondo and Lukuba islands, and near Mwanza – but otherwise most accommodation is without frills. Most locals you'll meet en route rely on fishing and small-scale farming for their living, although industry and commercial agriculture – especially coffee and cotton – are playing increasingly important roles. To the south of Lake Victoria near Shinyanga and Geita are gold and mineral mining areas.

National Parks & Reserves

Rubondo Island National Park (p222), found in the southwestern corner of Lake Victoria, is the region's only national park. The Serengeti's Western Corridor is covered in the Northern Tanzania chapter (p200). To the west of Lake Victoria are several game reserves, including Rumanyika Orugundu, Ibanda, Burigi and Biharamulo. None of these are fully developed for tourism.

Getting There & Around

Mwanza, Musoma, Bukoba, Shinyanga and Geita all have airports, and there's an airstrip on Rubondo island.

Together with western Tanzania, the Lake Victoria region has long had the distinction of having among the worst roads in the country. Apart from the tarmac roads connecting Mwanza with Musoma and the Kenyan border; and Mwanza with Shinyanga; the road from Mutukula (on the Ugandan border) via Bukoba to Biharamulo; and the unsealed but well-maintained road from Bunda through the Serengeti's Western Corridor to Seronera, almost the entire road network is unsealed and rough. This will probably change soon, with roadworks underway at a remarkable pace. For now, however, travelling by boat (there are several ferries on Lake Victoria, see p328) or air is the best bet.

Direct buses run along the main routes; otherwise, you'll need to do most journeys in stages.

LAKE VICTORIA FACTS

Lake Victoria is

- 68,800 sq km in area, about half of which is in Tanzania
- 100m above sea level
- the world's second largest freshwater lake after Lake Superior in North America
- infested with bilharzia in many shoreline areas (swimming in the lake is not recommended, see p338)
- inhabited by some of the largest Nile perch in the world

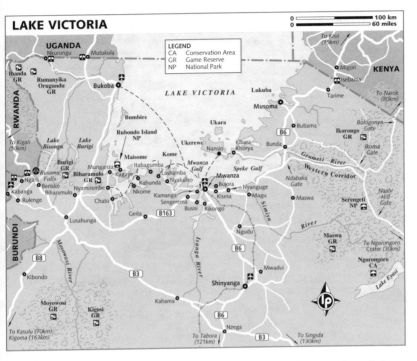

MWANZA

☎ 028

Booming Mwanza is Tanzania's second largest town, and the economic heart of the lake region. It has a profusion of industries and a busy port that handles much of the cotton, tea and coffee grown in the fertile western part of the country. The surrounding area is home to the Sukuma, Tanzania's largest tribe.

Although dusty in the dry season and muddy during the rains, Mwanza is an attractive place set among hills strewn with enormous boulders. The atmosphere is liveable and low-key, and most travellers who spend time here come to like it. Mwanza is the best base for visiting Rubondo Island National Park. It's also a convenient starting or finishing point for a safari through the western Serengeti, but don't expect many budget deals.

Orientation

The central part of town can easily be covered on foot. To the west, and just a short walk from the clock tower, are the passenger ferry docks and several banks and shops. East of the town centre are more shops, guesthouses, and mosques. Still further east, and about 10 minutes on foot from the clock tower, are the market and bus stand. In the southwestern corner of town, about five minutes on foot from the clock tower, is the train station. Just beyond is Capri Point, a small peninsula with breezes, lake views and the upmarket Hotel Tilapia (p218).

Information

EMERGENCY & MEDICAL SERVICES

Aga Khan Medical Centre (☎ 250 2474, 42407; Mitimrefu St; ☼ 24hr) Southeast of the bus station, behind the Ismaili mosque and before Bugando Hospital.

FDS Pharmacy (☎ 250 3284; Post St; ☼ 8am-11pm Mon-Sat, 9am-11pm Sun) At New Mwanza Hotel; the best pharmacy in town.

Mission Aviation Fellowship (MAF) office (☎ 250 3190) About 5km out of town on the airport road; may be able to assist with emergency medical evacuations.

INTERNET ACCESS

Barmedas.com (Nkrumah St; per hr Tsh1000; ☼ 8am-8.30pm) One block north of Nyerere Rd.

MWANZA

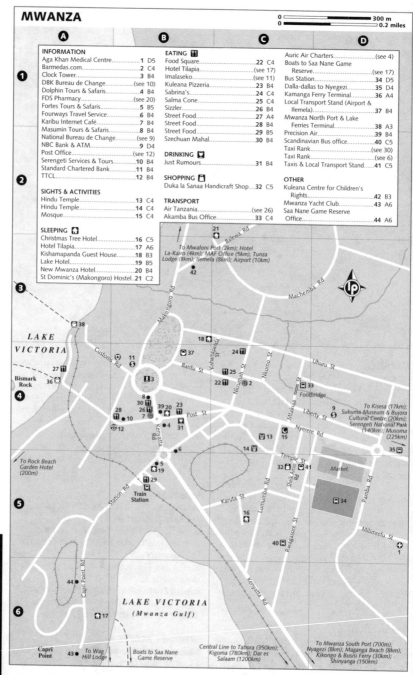

0 ——————— 300 m
0 ——————— 0.2 miles

INFORMATION
Aga Khan Medical Centre.................1 D5
Barmedas.com....................................2 C4
Clock Tower.......................................3 B4
DBK Bureau de Change...............(see 10)
Dolphin Tours & Safaris....................4 B4
FDS Pharmacy...............................(see 20)
Fortes Tours & Safaris.......................5 B5
Fourways Travel Service.....................6 B4
Karibu Internet Café..........................7 B4
Masumin Tours & Safaris...................8 B4
National Bureau de Change...........(see 9)
NBC Bank & ATM..............................9 D4
Post Office.....................................(see 12)
Serengeti Services & Tours..............10 B4
Standard Chartered Bank................11 B4
TTCL..12 B4

SIGHTS & ACTIVITIES
Hindu Temple.................................13 C4
Hindu Temple.................................14 C4
Mosque..15 C4

SLEEPING
Christmas Tree Hotel.......................16 C5
Hotel Tilapia...................................17 A6
Kishamapanda Guest House............18 B3
Lake Hotel......................................19 B5
New Mwanza Hotel.........................20 B4
St Dominic's (Makongoro) Hostel...21 C2

EATING
Food Square....................................22 C4
Hotel Tilapia...............................(see 17)
Imalaseko....................................(see 11)
Kuleana Pizzeria.............................23 B4
Sabrina's..24 C4
Salma Cone....................................25 C4
Sizzler..26 B4
Street Food.....................................27 A4
Street Food.....................................28 B4
Street Food.....................................29 B5
Szechuan Mahal.............................30 B4

DRINKING
Just Rumours..................................31 B4

SHOPPING
Duka la Sanaa Handicraft Shop....32 C5

TRANSPORT
Air Tanzania...............................(see 26)
Akamba Bus Office.........................33 C4

Auric Air Charters........................(see 4)
Boats to Saa Nane Game
  Reserve.....................................(see 17)
Bus Station.....................................34 D5
Dalla-dallas to Nyegezi...................35 D4
Kamanga Ferry Terminal.................36 A4
Local Transport Stand (Airport &
  Ilemela)......................................37 B4
Mwanza North Port & Lake
  Ferries Terminal..........................38 A3
Precision Air...................................39 B4
Scandinavian Bus office..................40 C5
Taxi Rank...................................(see 30)
Taxi Rank.....................................(see 6)
Taxis & Local Transport Stand........41 C5

OTHER
Kuleana Centre for Children's
  Rights...42 B3
Mwanza Yacht Club........................43 A6
Saa Nane Game Reserve
  Office...44 A6

Karibu Internet Café (cnr Post St & Kenyatta Rd; per hr Tsh1000; ☺ 8am-8.30pm Mon-Fri, 8am-6pm Sat, 9am-5pm Sun)

MONEY

There are ATMs at **Standard Chartered bank** (Makongoro Rd) near the clock tower, and at **NBC** (Liberty St). NBC also changes travellers cheques.

DBK Bureau de Change (Post St) At Serengeti Services & Tours, and the easiest place to change cash or travellers cheques.

National Bureau de Change (Liberty St) Next to NBC; often willing to change travellers cheques without the purchase receipt.

POST

Main post office (Post St; ☺ 8am-5pm Mon-Fri, 9am-noon Sat)

TELEPHONE

TTCL (Post St; ☺ 7am-8pm) Operator-assisted calls.

TRAVEL AGENCIES

All of the following can help with flight bookings, organising trips to Rubondo Island and Serengeti National Parks, and car hire. Prices for 4WD rental start at about US$90 per day plus petrol. For a two-day, one-night return trip to Seronera in Serengeti National Park, transport only, expect to pay from US$350 per vehicle (four to six persons) including petrol. It's not that easy to meet other travellers in Mwanza, so organising a Serengeti safari from the town works best if you're already in a group.

Dolphin Tours & Safaris (☎ 250 0096, 250 0128; www.auricair.com; cnr Post St & Kenyatta Rd) Vehicle and flying safaris in partnership with Auric Air Charters, including packages to Rubondo Island park and the Serengeti.

Fortes Tours & Safaris (☎ 250 0561, 0748-520550; fortes@thenet.co.tz; Station Rd) Serengeti safaris.

Fourways Travel Service (☎ 250 2620, 250 2273; www.fourwaystravel.net; Station Rd) Long-established agency offering Rubondo and Serengeti safaris and vehicle hire.

Masumin Tours & Safaris (☎ 250 0192, 250 3295; www.masumintours.com; Kenyatta Rd) Rubondo and Serengeti safaris.

Serengeti Services & Tours (☎ 250 0061, 250 0754; serengeti@mwanza-online.com; Post St) Rubondo and Serengeti safaris, vehicle hire and general travel assistance.

Sights & Activities

Central Mwanza has a vaguely oriental feel due to its many **mosques** and **Hindu temples**, and is worth a stroll, particularly the area around Temple St. Nearby is the bustling and chaotic **market**, where you can find almost anything you could want.

Also impressive are some of the surrounding **hills** and **boulders**, which offer stunning views over the town and lake. One to try is the large rock just west of Kenyatta Rd near New Mwanza Hotel. The large pile of boulders balancing precariously just offshore from Rock Beach Garden Hotel is **Bismarck Rock**, Mwanza's main landmark.

SAA NANE GAME RESERVE

This little **reserve** (admission Tsh800) is on a tiny island just off Capri Point. It's a peaceful getaway from the dust of town and ideal for bird-watching, marred only by its dejected-looking collection of caged animals. A boat departs several times daily from next to Hotel Tilapia (Tsh1000, 15 minutes). There's no food or lodging on the island. The reserve's office is on Capri Point Rd, about 200m north of Hotel Tilapia.

Sleeping

For information on accommodation northeast of Mwanza near Serengeti National Park's Ndabaka Gate, see under Serengeti National Park (p204).

BUDGET

Camping is possible at **Maganga Beach** (camping per person Tsh2000), on a pretty stretch of lake shore in Nyagezi, about 8km from town. There are no facilities, nor are food and drink available, and you'll need a vehicle to get there. Otherwise, the closest places for camping are Bujora Cultural Centre (p220), or near the Serengeti's Ndabaka Gate (p203).

There are many inexpensive guesthouses in the busy central area of town. All offer serviceable singles/doubles, most with mosquito nets and some with fan, for about Tsh2500/3500 with shared facilities, though most make their living from business by the hour. One of the (marginally) better ones: **Kishamapanda Guest House** (☎ 42523; cnr Uhuru & Kishamapanda Sts).

Much nicer are some of the hotels and hostels.

Christmas Tree Hotel (☎ 250 2001; off Karuta St; r Tsh12,000) This appealingly named establishment is good value. The spiffy rooms have a small double bed, hot water and TV. Some have nets, and there's a restaurant. The hotel is tucked away in the town centre just off busy Karuta St, from where it is signposted.

Hotel La-Kairo (☎ 250 0343/5; s/d Tsh20,000/24,000) Friendly and family-run, this is another good bet, though closer to mid-range than budget. Rooms are spotless, with fan, and the restaurant dishes up good local meals. It's in a small, leafy neighbourhood street about 4km out of town, just off the airport road and signposted.

St Dominic's (Makongoro) Hostel (☎ 250 0830; off Balewa Rd; s/d Tsh12,000/15,000, without bathroom Tsh4000/6000; breakfast Tsh1000) Staid and spartan, this church-run hostel has rooms with shared bathroom (no hot water), plus newer en suite ones (with hot water). It's about five minutes' walk north of the clock tower roundabout.

Lake Hotel (☎ 250 0658; Station Rd; ground fl s/d Tsh7200/8400, upstairs d Tsh15,000) This hotel is ageing and tatty, but its shortcomings are easy to overlook if you've just disembarked from a 40-hour haul on the Central Line train. Upstairs rooms – complete with trickling hot-water shower, fan and net – are best, and management let three people sleep in a double for no additional charge.

MID-RANGE & TOP END

Hotel Tilapia (☎ 250 0517, 250 0617; www.hoteltilapia .com; Capri Point; d/ste from US$80/100; ✍ ▯ ✍) The Tilapia is central Mwanza's best hotel, in a prime and breezy setting overlooking the water on the eastern side of Capri Point – especially beautiful when the morning or evening sun illuminates the surrounding rocks and hills. There's a raised lakeside deck, a business centre, several restaurants and your choice of rooms or bungalow-style suites. A good buffet breakfast is included in the price, and credit cards are accepted (5% surcharge).

Tunza Lodge (☎ 256 2215; enquiries@renair.com; s/tw/d US$45/55/60) An amenable anglers' lodge, with cosy cottages scattered over an expansive lawn sloping down to the lake, and a large restaurant (opposite). In addition to fishing, it arranges volleyball, waterskiing and other water sports. It's about 8km from town and 2km from the airport: from town, follow the airport road to the Ilemela *dalla-dalla* (minibus) station; turn left (no sign-

post), and continue down a dirt road about 2.5km to the lake, staying left at the forks. Public transport goes as far as Ilemela, from where it's a 20-minute walk, or you can arrange transfers with the lodge.

New Mwanza Hotel (☎ 250 1070/1; www.new mwanzahotel.com; cnr Post St & Kenyatta Rd; s/d Tsh50,000/60,000; ✍) This three-star place with five-star aspirations is the only 'proper' hotel in the town centre. The bland rooms have TV, and there's a terrace-level restaurant.

Wag Hill Lodge (☎ 0744-777086, 917974; www .waghill.com; per person full board & transfers to/from Mwanza US$250; ✍) For a delightful getaway, try the intimate and beautiful Wag Hill, which is worth the splurge, especially if you're interested in getting to know Lake Victoria's ecosystems, or in angling. It has just three small bungalows nestled into a forested hillside surrounded by the lake, and is completely tranquil, with only birds, monkeys and other local wildlife to keep you company. It's on a small peninsula outside of Mwanza, and they'll come and collect you from the Mwanza Yacht Club by boat. Fully equipped fishing is included in the price.

Eating & Drinking

For street food, try the stalls opposite the post office, the area along the train tracks, near the ferry terminals and the women near the train station who sell whole fried fish for under Tsh1000.

Kuleana Pizzeria (☎ 256 0566; Post St; meals Tsh2000; ✍ 9am-9pm) Good food – pizzas, sandwiches, yogurt, desserts, fresh-squeezed juices and more – and good vibes are the features here. The pizzeria serves as a vocational training centre run by the nearby Kuleana Centre for Children's Rights, and profits go to the centre.

Szechuan Mahal (☎ 40339; Kenyatta Rd; meals from Tsh6000; ✍ dinner) If the drab exterior doesn't put you off, the delicately seasoned Chinese food here is some of Mwanza's best cuisine.

Hotel Tilapia (☎ 250 0517, 250 0617; Capri Point; buffet Tsh4000, meals from Tsh4000; ✍ lunch & dinner) The Tilapia's popular weekend lunchtime barbecue – on a breezy terrace overlooking the lake – is an ideal excuse to while away an afternoon sipping a cold drink while gazing over the water. Downstairs are several other restaurants with lakeside seating and pricier à la carte dining.

Rock Beach Garden Hotel (meals from Tsh3500; ☺ lunch & dinner) You can usually rustle up a meal, but the main attraction is sipping sundowners on the lakeside terrace overlooking Bismarck Rock. Turn left one block west of the post office and continue along the dirt road running parallel to the water for about 500m, crossing the railroad tracks.

Tunza Lodge (☎ 256 2215; meals from Tsh4000, buffet Tsh8500; ☺ lunch & dinner) Tunza Lodge has a large restaurant with beef, fish, pasta and Indian dishes, and an outdoor Sunday afternoon barbecue buffet.

Sizzler (Kenyatta Rd; meals Tsh3000-5000; ☺ lunch & dinner) Sizzler's complete lack of atmosphere is compensated for by large portions and reasonably prompt service. The menu features homogenised Chinese, Indian and Western dishes.

Just Rumours (Post St) Mwanza's main bar and weekend discotheque, opposite Kuleana Pizzeria.

On hot days, locals head for **Salma Cone** (Bantu St; ☺ until 10pm), with soft-serve ice cream and fast food. Opposite is the **Food Square** (Bantu St; ☺ breakfast, lunch & dinner), with cheap meals.

SELF-CATERING
Imalaseko (Makongoro Rd) Near the clock tower; Mwanza's main supermarket.
Sabrina's (Nkrumah St) Off Uhuru St.

Shopping
Duka la Sanaa Handicraft Shop (Sheik Amin Rd) This small shop on the western edge of the market is run by a local women's cooperative. It has a small selection of leather goods and wood carvings, and is worth a quick stop.

Getting There & Away
AIR
There are daily flights to/from Dar es Salaam (US$125) and to/from Bukoba (US$70) on **Air Tanzania** (☎ 250 0046; Kenyatta Rd) and **Precision Air** (☎ 250 0819; pwmwz@africaonline.co.tz; Kenyatta Rd), with some of the Precision Air flights between Dar es Salaam and Mwanza going via Shinyanga. Precision also flies several times weekly between Kilimanjaro International Airport and Mwanza (US$145).

Coastal Aviation (☎ 256 0443, 256 0441; coastal mwanza@coastal.cc; at the airport) flies twice weekly between Mwanza and Rubondo (US$70), and is planning to start flights between Arusha and Mwanza via Seronera. **Auric Air Charters** (☎ 250 0096, 250 0128; www.auric air.com; cnr Post St & Kenyatta Rd), at the Dolphin Tours & Safaris office, has a scheduled flight three times weekly between Mwanza and Entebbe (US$150 one way). Once Mwanza's proposed new international airport comes into being, expect increased regional flights.

For air charters to Rubondo Island or elsewhere, contact Auric Air Charters, **RenAir** (☎ 256 2069, 256 2215; www.renair.com) at the airport, or Coastal Aviation.

BOAT
Passenger ferries connect Mwanza with Bukoba and with several islands in Lake Victoria, including Ukerewe and Maisome (for Rubondo island). For schedule and fare information see p327. A speedboat service between Mwanza and Bukoba is scheduled to start imminently, cutting the current sailing time by more than half; ask at North Port for an update.

Ferries to Bukoba use Mwanza's North Port, near the clock tower. For Ukerewe, most departures are from North Port, with sporadic smaller boats leaving from Mwaloni, about 2.5km north of the town centre off the airport road. Cargo boats to Port Bell (Uganda) and Kenya depart from Mwanza South Port, about 1.5km southeast of the centre; see p327.

To go by road from Mwanza anywhere west or southwest you'll need to cross the Mwanza Gulf between Mwanza and Sengerema. There are two ferries. The northernmost (Kamanga) ferry docks just south of the passenger ferry terminal at Mwanza North Port, and is the more reliable of the two, departing Mwanza at 8.30am, 10.30am, 12.30am, 2.30pm (except Sunday), 4.30pm and 6.30pm (per person/vehicle Tsh300/3600, 20 minutes). Departures from Kamanga are every two hours from 8am until 6pm, except there's no 2pm ferry on Sunday. If you are continuing from Kamanga to Sengerema or Geita, see if the Geita bus is in the vehicle queue lined up to board the ferry. If it is, it's worth buying your bus ticket before crossing to avoid the rush on the other side. If there's no bus, the only option is the *dalla-dallas*, which wait on the other side.

The more southerly Busisi ferry operates in theory until 10pm but shouldn't be counted on. Its eastern terminus is at Kikongo, about 30km south of Mwanza.

BUS

All departures are from the main bus stand near the market, except for Scandinavian Express buses, which depart from the **Scandinavian office** (☎ 250 3315; Rwagasore St) just south of the market; and Akamba buses, which depart from the **Akamba office** (☎ 250 0272), off Mtakuja St, and just north of the small footbridge near Majukano Hotel.

To Musoma, buses go throughout the day from 6am until about 2pm (Tsh3500, four hours); some continue to the Kenyan border.

To Geita, there's a daily bus, usually continuing to Biharamulo (Tsh6000), from where there are connections to Bukoba, Lusahunga and on to Benako and Ngara for the Rwanda and Burundi borders. To Benako and Ngara it's just as fast to go via Shinyanga and Kahama (Tsh6000, eight hours between Kahama and Benako). There are also weekly buses direct from Mwanza to Ngara (Tsh9500). To Muganza (for Rubondo island), there are several direct buses weekly (Tsh6000, eight hours).

To Bukoba, it's best to do the trip in stages via Biharamulo. The road journey is long and rough (until you get to Biharamulo, where it gets smoother), and almost everyone takes the ferry or flies.

To Tabora, the best bet is Mohammed Trans, which goes daily via Shinyanga (Tsh7500, seven hours), departing in each direction at 6.30am.

To Arusha/Moshi and Dar es Salaam, the best route is via Nairobi (Tsh38,000 plus US$20 for a Kenyan transit visa, about 30 hours to Dar es Salaam), and the best line is Scandinavian. Akamba also does the route. Alternatively, you can try the long and gruelling loop via Singida (Tsh28,500, two days), traversed by Tawfiq, or – for a fleeting safari – go on one of the several weekly buses that travel through the Serengeti (Tsh26,000, plus entry fees for Serengeti park and for Ngorongoro Conservation Area).

To Kigoma, there are three buses weekly, mostly via Biharamulo, with at least one weekly via Kahama and Shinyanga. Departures are about 5am and arriving the next day if you're lucky.

See p321 for details of buses to Kenya and Uganda.

TRAIN

Mwanza is the terminus of a branch of the Central Line from Dar es Salaam. See p332 for schedules and fares.

Getting Around
TO/FROM THE AIRPORT

Mwanza's airport is 10km north of town (Tsh5000 in a taxi). *Dalla-dallas* (Tsh150) leave from near the clock tower.

BUS & TAXI

Dalla-dallas for destinations along the Musoma road, including Kisesa and Igoma (for Bujora) depart from the Bugando Hill stand, southeast of the market, while those running along the airport road depart from near the clock tower. *Dalla-dallas* to Nyegezi depart from Nyerere Rd.

There are taxi stands near the market, at the intersection of Station and Kenyatta Rds in front of Fourways Travel, and in front of Szechuan Mahal restaurant.

CAR & MOTORCYCLE

All the companies listed under Travel Agencies arrange car rental (p217).

AROUND MWANZA
Sukuma Museum & Bujora Cultural Centre

If you're interested in learning about Sukuma culture, the **Sukuma Museum & Bujora Cultural Centre** (http://photo.net/sukuma; admission Tsh3000; ☯ 8am-6pm Mon-Sat, 1-6pm Sun) makes a worthwhile day trip from Mwanza. The centrepiece is an open-air museum where, among other things, you'll see traditional Sukuma dwellings, the house of a traditional healer, a wooden trough used for rainmaking potions and a blacksmith's house and tools. There is also a large map showing the old Sukuma kingdoms, and nearby a rotating cylinder illustrating different Sukuma systems for counting from one to 10. Traditionally, these systems were used by various Sukuma age-based groups as a sort of secret language or symbol of initiation. Each group – girls, boys, women, men – had its own counting system, which would be used within the

---

THE SUKUMA

The Sukuma – Tanzania's largest tribal group, with about 15% of the country's population – are renowned throughout the region for their pulsating dancing. Dancers are divided into two competing dance societies, the Bagika and the Bagulu, that travel throughout Sukumaland (the Sukuma heartland around Mwanza and southern Lake Victoria), competing. The culmination is at the annual Bulabo dance festival in Bujora, which begins each year on the religious feast of Corpus Christi (about 60 days after Easter) and lasts for about two weeks. The most famous dances are those using animals, including the Bagulu *banungule* (hyena dance) and the Bagika *bazwilili bayeye* (snake and porcupine dance). Before beginning, the dancers are treated with traditional medicaments to protect themselves from injury. (And it's not unheard of for the animals, too, to be given a spot of something to calm their tempers.)

---

group, but which would not be understood by members of any other group.

Also on the grounds is the **royal drum pavilion**, built in the shape of the stool used by Sukuma kings. On the pavilion's upper level is a collection of royal drums that are still played on church feast days, official government visits and at other special events. Traditionally, each Sukuma kingdom had a special place such as this one – though not on the same scale – for preserving its royal drums.

The round **church** in the centre of the museum was built in 1969 by David Fumbuka Clement, the Québecois missionary priest who founded the museum. Inside are some traditionally styled altar pieces. Although services (10am Sunday) are in Swahili, much of the singing is in Sukuma.

On request, the museum can organise performances of traditional drumming and dancing for a flat fee of Tsh40,000 per performance, regardless of group size. It's best to arrange this in advance, although sometimes you can organise things on the spot. It's also possible to arrange Sukuma drumming lessons. There are no set fees; you'll need to negotiate with the instructors, but don't expect it to be cheap. An English-speaking guide is available at the museum.

SLEEPING & EATING

There's **camping** (per person Tsh2000) on the grounds of the centre, and no-frills **rooms** (s/d without bathroom Tsh3000/6000) with mosquito nets and tiny windows. Bucket showers can be arranged, as can meals, with advance notice (Tsh1000 for breakfast, and Tsh3500 for lunch or dinner). Otherwise, you can bring your own food and cook it yourself, or make arrangements for staff to cook it. The closest market is in Kisesa, about 3km away.

GETTING THERE & AWAY

Bujora is about 20km east of Mwanza off the Musoma road. Take a *dalla-dalla* to Igoma, from where you can get a 4WD or pick-up on to Kisesa. Once in Kisesa, walk a short way along the main road until you see the sign for Bujora Primary School (Shule ya Msingi Bujora). Turn left at the sign and follow the small dirt road for about 2km to 3km to the cultural centre. There is no public transport along this road.

En route from Mwanza, around 2km past Igoma on the western side of the main road, is a graveyard for victims of the 1996 sinking of the Lake Victoria ferry MV *Bukoba*.

Ukerewe

The large and densely populated Ukerewe island is in the middle of Lake Victoria north of Mwanza. It is well off the beaten track, with no paved roads and – outside Nansio, the major town – no electricity. While there isn't much to 'do' here, the island makes an intriguing, offbeat diversion and, with its friendly people and rocky terrain broken by lake vistas and tiny patches of forest, it's an ideal place for simply wandering around and watching local life.

SLEEPING & EATING

Gallu Beach Hotel (☎ 028-251 5094; www.gallu.net; camping per person Tsh1500, d Tsh7000) This pleasant and unassuming guesthouse is the best accommodation on the island. There's also a camping area, and meals by arrangement. It's on the waterfront in Nansio, and just a short walk from the ferry terminal. Staff can help you organise excursions.

There are also several cheaper guesthouses in Nansio, with rooms from about Tsh3000.

LAKE VICTORIA

CHILDREN OF THE RAIN-MAKER

One of Ukerewe's most famous sons is Aniceti Kitereza (1896–1981), actually born near Mwanza on the mainland, but grandson of a Ukerewe chief. After a career spent as a translator (he read or spoke eight languages, including Greek and Latin), Kitereza set out to write the biography of his grandfather, King Machunda. The two-volume work – currently available only in German as *Die Kinder der Regenmacher* (Children of the Rain-maker) and *Die Schlangentöter* (The Snake-killer) – weaves priceless strands of local mythology, folk tales and traditional customs into the main family chronicle. Kitereza wrote originally in Kikewere, and later translated his work by hand into Swahili, though he did not live to see the book published.

GETTING THERE & AWAY

The MV *Nansio* sails daily except Sunday between Nansio and Mwanza's North Port, departing Nansio at 8.30am, and Mwanza at 2.30pm (Tsh3500/2000 for 2nd/3rd class, three hours). There are also usually some smaller boats from Mwaloni Port for about the same price.

It's also possible to reach Nansio from Bunda, about 30km north of the Serengeti's Ndabaka Gate on the Mwanza–Musoma road, which means that you can go from Mwanza to Ukerewe and then on towards Musoma or the Serengeti, or vice-versa, without backtracking. Via public transport, take any vehicle between Mwanza and Musoma and disembark at Bunda. From Bunda, you can get transport to Kibara-Kisorya, from where it's a short boat ride to Ukerewe. Both the Mwanza–Nansio and Bunda–Nansio ferries take vehicles; the Bunda–Nansio ferry runs every two to three hours, with the first departure from the mainland usually at 7am, and the last at 5.30pm.

There is little public transport on Ukerewe. A few vehicles meet boat arrivals; if you miss these, the only option is walking or bargaining for a lift on a bicycle.

RUBONDO ISLAND NATIONAL PARK

If you relish tranquil surroundings away from the crowds, Rubondo Island National Park, in the southwestern corner of Lake Victoria, is one of Tanzania's best kept secrets. In addition to its excellent birding, it offers fishing, quiet beaches and low-key but rewarding wildlife-watching. Almost 400 bird species have been identified here, including stately fish eagles, herons, storks, ibis, kingfishers and cormorants. Keeping them company is a wealth of butterflies, and populations of chimpanzees, hippos, crocodiles, giraffes and even elephants (the latter were introduced several decades ago). The island is also one of the few places in East Africa where you can observe the sitatunga, an amphibious antelope that likes to hide among the marshes and reeds along the shoreline. If you find yourself in the region, Rubondo is a complete change of pace from Tanzania's other parks, and well worth a detour.

In addition to Rubondo island, the park encompasses several smaller nearby islands. It was gazetted in 1977 with a total area of 460 sq km, around 240 sq km of which is land.

Information

Park entry fees are US$15/5 per adult/child aged five to 15 years. For camping fees, see p35. There is also a US$50 per week sport-fishing fee. The park is open year-round, but the best time to visit is from June to early November, before the rains set in.

For camp site bookings and information contact the senior park warden (PO Box 111, Geita). From Mwanza, this is best done via radio, arranged through any of the travel agencies listed in that section (p217). Park headquarters are at Kageye on the island's eastern side.

Both the park and Rubondo Island Camp (opposite) organise chimpanzee tracking. However, if your primary interest is chimps, your chances of sightings and close-up observation are much better in Gombe Stream or Mahale Mountains National Parks (see the Western Tanzania chapter, p230).

Sleeping

The park has an ordinary camp site and some nice double *bandas* (thatched-roof huts) on the lake shore just south of park headquarters; both should be booked in advance through the park warden. There's a tiny shop selling a few basics, but it's better to bring all essentials with you.

Rubondo Island Camp (☎ 027-254 4109; www .flycat.com; s/d full board, excursions extra US$180/280, s/d all-inclusive except fishing US$300/520; ☒) This intimate luxury camp has a wonderful lakeside setting, cosy en suite tents, tasty cuisine and a highly relaxing ambience. Excursions include guided walks, boat trips, and fishing. Ask about low season discounts.

Getting There & Away
AIR
Most guests staying at Rubondo Island Camp arrive via a chartered flight arranged through the camp. It costs about US$300/450 one way from Mwanza for a three-/five-seater plane. For charter companies, see p219.

BOAT
The cheapest, most adventurous and most time consuming way to reach the park is to travel by ferry or bus to one of the villages on the lake shore opposite Rubondo island, from where you can arrange a boat pick-up with park headquarters. The main villages for doing this are Muganza (on the mainland southwest of Rubondo), Nkome (southeast of Rubondo), and Maisome (on Maisome island, just east of Rubondo). For Muganza, there are several direct buses weekly from Mwanza along a rough but reasonable road. If you get stuck there for the night, there are a few basic guesthouses with rooms for about Tsh2000. For both Nkome and Maisome, there are occasional ferry connections; see p327. Nkome can also be reached by bus via a rough road (allow a full day from Mwanza); if you're driving you can leave your vehicle at the ranger post there, which is also where you can sleep until the boat comes to collect you.

You'll need to radio park headquarters in advance to let them know you'll be arriving this way; in Mwanza, travel agencies or the Saa Nane Game Reserve office can help you call, and there's also a radio at the police station in Muganza. Plan on paying about Tsh40,000 per boat from Muganza, and up to double this from Nkome or Maisome, although with some negotiating you may be able to get it for less. Local fishing boats don't generally enter Rubondo, though if you sort out the permissions in advance with park headquarters, the captains will give you a much better price deal (eg about Tsh10,000 from Maisome to Rubondo).

BUKOBA
☎ 028
Bukoba is a bustling town with an attractive waterside setting and amenable small-town feel, and makes a convenient stop if you're travelling between Tanzania and Uganda or Rwanda.

The surrounding Kagera region is home of the Haya people, known for their powerful kingdoms (see the boxed text, p225). Prior to the rise of the Haya kingdoms, Kagera was at the heart of a highly advanced early society known for its techniques of steel production. Various artefacts, including remnants of kilns estimated to be close to 2000 years old, indicate that steel production was well developed here long before equivalent techniques were known in Europe. Although there are no traces of this now in Bukoba, there is a small display on Iron Age findings from the region at the National Museum in Dar es Salaam.

The modern-day town of Bukoba traces its roots to 1890, when Emin Pasha (Eduard Schnitzer) – a German doctor and inveterate wanderer – arrived on the western shores of Lake Victoria as part of efforts to establish a German foothold in the region. Since then, the town has kept itself alive through a flourishing local coffee industry and a busy regional port (the second largest on the Tanzanian lake shore).

Information
INTERNET ACCESS
Bukoba Cybercafé (cnr Jamhuri & Kashozi Rds; per hr Tsh2000; ⊙ 8.30am-10pm)

MONEY
NBC (Jamhuri Rd) Changes cash and travellers cheques.

TELEPHONE
TTCL (⊙ 7.30am-9pm Mon-Fri, 8am-5pm Sat) For operator-assisted calls.

TRAVEL AGENCIES
Kiroyera Tours (☎ 222 0203; www.kiroyeratours.com; Sokoine St) An excellent, very clued-up agency opposite the market, giving new life to tourism in Bukoba and the surrounding Kagera region, and an essential stop if you're in Bukoba. It has a number of informative leaflets about the attractions in the surrounding area, and can organise cultural and historical outings in and around town.

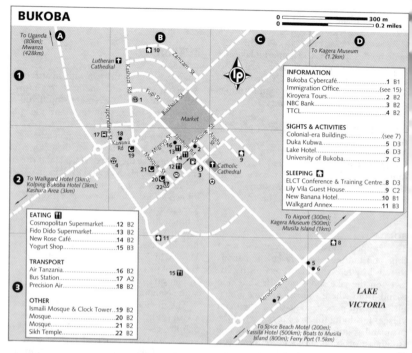

BUKOBA

0		300 m	
0		0.2 miles	

INFORMATION
Bukoba Cybercafé.................................**1** B1
Immigration Office.......................(see 15)
Kiroyera Tours.....................................**2** B2
NBC Bank..**3** B2
TTCL...**4** B2

SIGHTS & ACTIVITIES
Colonial-era Buildings.....................(see 7)
Duka Kubwa..**5** D3
Lake Hotel...**6** D3
University of Bukoba.........................**7** C3

SLEEPING
ELCT Conference & Training Centre.**8** D3
Lily Vila Guest House.........................**9** C2
New Banana Hotel............................**10** B1
Walkgard Annex................................**11** B3

EATING
Cosmopolitan Supermarket............**12** B2
Fido Dido Supermarket....................**13** B2
New Rose Café..................................**14** B2
Yogurt Shop.....................................**15** B3

TRANSPORT
Air Tanzania.....................................**16** B2
Bus Station.......................................**17** A2
Precision Air.....................................**18** B2

OTHER
Ismaili Mosque & Clock Tower.........**19** B2
Mosque..**20** B2
Mosque..**21** B2
Sikh Temple......................................**22** B2

Sights & Activities

Along the lake are some **colonial-era buildings**, now housing the university and some government offices. More intriguing are the scattered traces of the network of powerful Haya kingdoms that once held sway in this area (see the boxed text, opposite). Although the legacy of the kingdoms is preserved today primarily in oral tradition, there are still a few remnants of **royal dwellings** and other spots of interest that can be visited within a half-day's trip from town. Kiroyera Tours (p223) has information leaflets on the various options and can help you organise tours.

At the eastern edge of town near the lake is the old **Lake Hotel** – functioning now in name only – where Ava Gardner and Frank Sinatra reportedly enjoyed a drink or two when filming *Mogambo* in the area northwest of the Kagera River near the Uganda border. Just up the road towards town is the crumbling **Duka Kubwa** ('Big Shop'), which served as the local general store during the German colonial era, and is said to be Bukoba's oldest building.

KAGERA MUSEUM

This **museum** (☎ 222 0203; kmuseum@kiroyeratours.com; Nyamukazi area; admission US$2, guided tour Tsh2500 per group; ☒ 9.30am-6pm) houses a collection of top-notch wildlife photographs from the Kagera region by Danish wildlife photographer Dick Persson, as well as an intriguing collection of local tribal items. For a preview, look for the exhibition of wildlife photography by the same photographer in the National Museum in Dar es Salaam. The museum is on the far side of Bukoba's airstrip. The easiest way to get here is by following the lake shore past the airstrip. However, as you're officially not permitted to walk across the airfield, it's better to take the long way around, heading northeast along Sokoine St past the market, winding your way to the edge of town, and turning right at the signpost. Kiroyera Tours can sort you out with directions and a guide.

Sleeping

BUDGET

ELCT Conference & Training Centre (☎ 222 3121; elct-hotel@bukobaonline.com; Aerodrome Rd; s/d

US$20/30, d/tr without bathroom US$12/18) A good, long-standing place with clean, comfortable rooms and pleasant grounds along the airport road near the lake. Breakfast costs extra.

Spice Beach Motel (☎ 2220142; s/d Tsh8000/12,000) This small guesthouse is at the southeastern edge of town directly on the water, and not far from the port. There's one single with shared facilities and several small en suite doubles – ask for one facing the lake – and a restaurant.

New Banana Hotel (☎ 222 0861; Zamzam St; s/tw/d Tsh7500/8000/10,000) Rooms here are straightforward and clean, and the doubles have TV. Downstairs is a restaurant. The hotel is about 500m northeast of the bus stand.

Lily Vila Guest House (☎ 222 0402; d Tsh5500, s/d without bathroom Tsh2500/3500) A simple family-style guesthouse, with most rooms sharing a bathroom in common, and food available by prior arrangement. It's on a small, dirt lane behind the Catholic cathedral.

MID-RANGE

Yassila Hotel (☎ 222 1251; s/d Tsh20,000/30,000) A popular hotel near the port – if you're departing Bukoba via the MV *Victoria* and are up for a sprint, you can relax at Yassila's lakeside restaurant until the first whistle blows, and still make it on board before the boat pulls away from the dock. Rooms have TV, mini-fridge and air-con, and the restaurant serves up good tilapia grills and other dishes.

Walkgard Hotel (☎ 222 0935; www.walkgard .com; s/d/ste US$30/40/60; ❄ ☐ ☎) This imposing three-star place is Bukoba's top of the line, targeted primarily at local business clientele and conferences. Staff can help you organise car rental. It's worth checking out a few rooms, as size varies; all come with full breakfast, TV and telephone. The hotel is on a hill about 3km from the town centre in the Kashura area (Tsh2500 in a taxi). The same management runs **Walkgard Annex** (☎ 222 0935; s/d Tsh20,000/25,000) in the town centre, with quite acceptable rooms – all with fan, net and TV, and the best ones upstairs – and a restaurant. It's about 300m southeast of the telecom building on the western side of town.

Kolping Bukoba Hotel (☎ 222 0199; s/d/ste Tsh20,000/30,000/40,000) Just next to Walkgard Hotel, and giving it stiff competition. Rooms here are pleasant and just as good if not better value than at the Walkgard, and meals can be arranged.

THE HAYA

Bukoba is the heartland of the Haya people, and if you spend much time here, you'll undoubtedly make their acquaintance. The Haya, which today is one of Tanzania's largest tribes, also played a prominent role throughout the country's history. It had one of the most highly developed early societies on the continent, and by the 18th or 19th century was organised into eight different states or kingdoms. Each of these was headed by a powerful and often despotic *mukama* who ruled in part by divine right. It was the *mukama* who controlled all trade and who, at least nominally, owned all property, while land usage was shared among small, patrilineal communes. Order was maintained through a system of appointed chiefs and officials, assisted by an age group–based army. With the arrival of the colonial authorities, this political organisation began to erode. The various Haya groups splintered and many chiefs were replaced by persons considered more malleable and sympathetic to colonial interests.

In the 1920s, in the wake of growing resentment toward these propped-up leaders and to the colonial government, the Haya began to regroup and in 1924 founded the Bukoba Bahaya Union. This association was initially directed towards local political reform but soon developed into the more influential and broad-based African Association. Together with similar groups established elsewhere in the country – notably in the Kilimanjaro region and in Dar es Salaam – it constituted one of Tanzania's earliest political movements and was an important force in the drive towards independence.

Now, the Haya receive as much attention for their dancing – characterised by complicated foot rhythms, and traditionally performed by dancers wearing grass skirts and ankle rattles – and for their singing as for their history. Saida Karoli and Maua – popular female singers in the East African music scene – both come from the area around Bukoba.

Eating

The unassuming **New Rose Café** (Jamhuri Rd) is a local institution, with inexpensive meals and snacks. There's fresh yogurt at the small shop next to the Immigration building at the southern end of the road with the telecom building.

The restaurant at Yassila Hotel (see p225) is the main gathering spot, with lake views and tasty pepper steak, grilled tilapia and other dishes. Spice Beach Hotel is also good, with an equally nice setting and slow service. In town, try the restaurant at **Walkgard Annex** (meals from Tsh3500). Menus throughout feature grilled fish and local dishes, including the Haya staple *matoke* (cooked plantains).

For self-catering you can try **Fido Dido** (Jamhuri Rd) or **Cosmopolitan** (Jamhuri Rd).

Getting There & Away

AIR

There are daily flights to/from Mwanza (US$70) on **Precision Air** (☎ 222 0861; Bukoba Machinery Bldg; Kawawa Rd) and **Air Tanzania** (☎ 0748-737259; Global Travel, Jamhuri Rd), with connections to Dar es Salaam.

BOAT

There is passenger-ferry service between Bukoba and Mwanza on the MV *Victoria,* and soon, on a smaller, faster speedboat. For schedules and fares, see p327.

Fishing boats depart for tiny Musila Island, offshore from the airport, from just southwest of Spice Beach Motel.

BUS

Bukoba's roads are getting a facelift, and you can now go on good tarmac all the way to Kampala (Uganda). Heading south, the road is tarmac as far as Biharamulo. All the bus companies and their ticket offices are based at or near the bus stand at the western end of town.

Buses go daily to Biharamulo (Tsh6500), from where you can catch onward transport to Lusahunga, and from there on to Ngara or Benako and the Burundi and Rwanda borders.

To Kigoma, there's a weekly direct bus via Biharamulo and Kasulo, departing Fridays at 6am (Tsh12,000, at least 12 hours), but it's faster to go to Biharamulo and catch onward transport from there. Depending on the security situation, you may or may not be accompanied by an armed convoy between Lusahunga and Kigoma.

To Mwanza, you can try making your way in stages via Biharamulo, but it's better to take the ferry or fly.

To Uganda and Kenya, several buses (currently Tawfiq and Jaguar) go daily from Bukoba to Kampala. See p324 for details.

BUNDA
☎ 028

Bunda is a minor transport hub and you'll probably pass through here if you're heading to/from Kenya or Ukerewe island, or coming from the western Serengeti. The bus stand is along the main Mwanza–Musoma highway; nearby are a few basic and unappealing guesthouses with rooms for about Tsh2500. Better is **CN Motel** (☎ 262 1064; small/large s Tsh6000/9000), with clean singles; the extra Tsh3000 gets you a larger bed and a sit-down loo (versus the squat model in the smaller rooms). It's at the northern edge of town along the road to Musoma; meals can be arranged with advance notice.

MUSOMA
☎ 028

Musoma – attractive and usually overlooked – sits serenely on the eastern shore of Lake Victoria, firmly relegated to playing third-fiddle (behind Mwanza and Bukoba) among the Tanzanian lake shore settlements. Yet, if you happen to venture this way, the town – capital of the Mara region – makes an agreeable stop, with a bustling market, colourful fishing port and agreeable waterside setting. The surrounding countryside, marked by low hills dotted with large boulders, is a melting pot of cultures, with the Kuria, Jita, Luo, Taturu and many more all rubbing shoulders.

About 45km south of Musoma is Butiama, Julius Nyerere's home town. Nyerere attended primary school in the Mwisenge section of Musoma, about 1.5km west of town along the Makoko road. About 2km further along this road is the Makoko Language School (p308).

Information

The local NBC branch, four blocks south of the main street, changes cash and travellers cheques, and has an ATM. For Internet, try **Musoma Communications Centre** (☿ daily), just up from CRDB Bank, one block north of the main street.

There is a large army base in Musoma, and in many areas – particularly around Makoko and along the lake shore west of town – photography is prohibited.

Sights & Activities
MWALIMU JULIUS K NYERERE MUSEUM
The **Nyerere museum** (adult/child/student US$3/1/2; ☿ 9.30am-6pm), about 45km southeast of Musoma in Butiama, is highly recommended for anyone interested in the statesman's life and Tanzanian history. It contains memorabilia from the years leading up to Tanzanian independence and from the country's early post-independence days, as well as a large collection of photographs. Boxes of Nyerere's personal effects, including his diaries, a hand-written Swahili translation of part of Plato's *Republic,* and collections of his poetry are also there. Although these are not on display, you may be able to arrange with the curator to view them. A few hundred metres away from the museum is the Nyerere family home, and the graves of Nyerere and his parents.

To get to the museum by public transport, take a minibus to Nyasho (Tsh1000), from where you can get transport to Butiama (Tsh1000). Hiring a taxi will cost about Tsh15,000 return, including waiting time. If you are driving, there are two routes: follow the Mwanza road for approximately 35km to the signposted turn-off, from where it is 11km further down a dirt road; or follow the Mwanza road to Nyakanga, where you bear southeast along a shorter but rougher road to Butiama.

OTHER SIGHTS & ACTIVITIES
Not to be missed are the stunning **views** over Mara Bay at sunrise and sunset. One of the best spots for observing both is the narrow, breezy peninsula near Tembo Beach Hotel. The lively **fishing port** on the eastern edge of town is at its best in the early morning.

Although local boys plunge daily into the lake – especially from the small beach in Makoko – the waters are infested with bilharzia (*kichocho* in Swahili). To stay on the safe side, try the 25m **swimming pool** (day admission Tsh1500) at Peninsula Hotel.

A better way to explore the lake is to splash out on a night or two on **Lukuba island** (below). Lukuba island, also called Rukuba island, is northwest of Musoma and actually consists of a few islands (one with the lodge and the other, larger, one with a village) plus numerous tiny islets. It's possible to visit the larger of the islands via public boat as a day trip; see p228.

Sleeping
Tembo Beach Hotel (☎ 262 2887; d without/with bathroom Tsh11,000/16,500) Rooms here are reasonably clean, there's a small strip of sand out front, and the setting is ideal, with views of sunrise and sunset. It's also the main stop in town for overland trucks. The hotel is set on a narrow peninsula about 1.5km north of town; follow the road from the CRDB bank north along the edge of the lake.

Hotel Orange Tree (☎ 262 2651; Kawawa St; s/d Tsh6500/8500) A modest establishment on the eastern edge of town with basic but clean rooms and a good restaurant.

Afrilux Hotel (☎ 262 0031; s/d Tsh15,000/20,000; ⊠) This slightly garish, modern hotel is in a multistorey building about halfway between the lake and the bus stand in the town centre. Rooms are good value, and the restaurant has a large selection of local dishes and tasty curries.

Peninsula Hotel (☎ 264 0119, 264 2526; Makoko Rd; s/d/ste Tsh25,000/31,500/60,000; ⊠ ☏) The Peninsula, which hovers between two and three stars, is the main upmarket option in the town centre. Rooms are faded but plush in a 1970s sort of way, and there is hot water, air-con and attentive staff. Downstairs is a restaurant and across the street is a pool. The hotel is about 1km from the town centre on the Makoko road.

Lukuba Island Lodge (☎ 0744-090100, 027-254 8840; www.lukubaisland.com; per person full board plus transfers to/from Musoma US$230) If Robinson Crusoe were a moneyed angler, this relaxing and exclusive luxury retreat in the middle of Lake Victoria is undoubtedly where he would choose to spend his days. It makes an excellent getaway, with wonderfully rustic bungalows, and the chance for hiking, birding (over 70 bird species are at home here), boating and fully equipped fishing. Advance bookings are required; walks and local boat trips around the islands are included in the price.

Eating

Hotel Orange Tree (☎ 262 2651; Kawawa St; meals from Tsh2000; ☽ lunch & dinner) serves up good plates of grilled fish and rice. The more top-end **Peninsula Hotel** (☎ 264 0119, 264 2526; Makoko Rd; meals about Tsh4000; ☽ lunch & dinner) has more of the same, plus soups, spaghetti and other standards. **Mara Dishes Frys** (meals from Tsh1000), a local favourite around the corner from NBC bank, is good for plantains or chicken and chips. Further down the same street is a little no-name place selling Musoma's best *nyama choma* (seasoned roasted meat).

For self-caterers, the best-stocked shop is Kotra in the town centre. For yogurt, try the small *maziwa* (dairy) shop just off the main street near the market; ask for *maziwa mgando*.

Getting There & Away

AIR

The airfield is about 1km west of the market; there are currently no scheduled flights.

BOAT

Local boats, including those to villages along the lake shore, depart from the Mwigobero section of town near Afrilux Hotel. For Lukuba island, there's a public boat, departing from Musoma at 11am, noon and 3pm, and from Lukuba at 7.30am and 2pm (Tsh700, one to 1½ hours).

BUS

Frequent buses and minibuses connect Musoma and Mwanza, departing between about 6am and 2pm (Tsh3500, four hours). There are minibuses throughout the day to Sirari on the Kenyan border, where you can change to Kenyan transport. **Scandinavian Express** (☎ 262 0006), with its office near the bus stand, stops at Musoma on its Mwanza–Nairobi–Dar es Salaam route (Tsh36,000 between Musoma and Dar es Salaam).

Dalla-dallas run throughout the day between the town centre and the Makoko section of Musoma. The *dalla-dalla* stand is along the road between town and the airfield.

SHINYANGA

☎ 028

Shinyanga would probably be relegated to complete anonymity were it not the site of one of the world's largest diamond pipes

(about 45km northeast of town near Mwadui, and now operating at only a fraction of its former capacity). Apart from this, the town – with dusty streets and a scrappy atmosphere – has little to offer, other than as a possible overnight stop if you're travelling in the region. There's an NBC bank, and an Internet café, both on the main road.

Sleeping & Eating

The best places to stay are **Mwoleka Hotel** (☎ 276 2249, 276 3004; s/d from Tsh10,000/15,000) near the bus stand, and the similar but slightly less pretentious **Shinyanga Motel** (☎ 276 2458; r with fan Tsh15,000, with air-con & TV from Tsh20,000) near the train station. For something less expensive try **Maleko's Annex** (r without bathroom Tsh3500-5000) near the bus stand, or the better **Shellatone Hotel** (d Tsh7000) nearby.

For food, **Shita's** (meals from Tsh2000) has inexpensive, piping hot plates of rice and sauce and other local fare. Mwoleka Hotel also has a decent **restaurant** (meals from Tsh3000).

Getting There & Away

The best bus company is Mohammed Trans, which goes daily to Tabora (Tsh5500, six hours, departing by 7am, book in advance) and to Mwanza (Tsh3000, three hours, several departures between 6am and 8.30am).

SINGIDA

☎ 026

Pretty Singida is well away from Lake Victoria, but you'll probably pass through if you're travelling between Mwanza and Arusha via the rugged southwestern loop. It's also a possible detour from Babati and Mt Hanang (p190) for the adventurous.

The surrounding area is dotted with huge granite boulders and two lakes – Lake Singidani (just north of town), and the smaller Lake Kindai (to the south) – both of which attract flamingos, pelicans and many other water birds.

Thanks to all the through traffic, and to Singida's status as regional capital, the town has reasonably good infrastructure, including an **Internet café** (per hr Tsh2000) just north of the market, and an NBC bank, near the post office, on the northern side of town.

Sleeping & Eating

Stanley Hotel (☎ 250 2351; d Tsh12,000, s/d without bathroom Tsh6000/8000) This reliable, reasonable-value place near the bus stand has no-frills rooms and a popular restaurant serving up large portions of chicken and chips and other standard dishes.

Legho Singida Motel (☎ 250 2526; r Tsh11,500) Quieter than the Stanley, and one of the better places to stay. It's on the northern edge of town, with decent rooms, a nice garden and a restaurant.

Social Training Centre (☎ 250 3464; s without/with bathroom Tsh3500/10,000) A clean, simple, good-value place run by the Catholic Diocese of Singida. It's behind the TTCL building, and near the NSSF compound; meals can be arranged.

Shana Resort, just west of the market, has good juices and local dishes, while Florida has the usual assortment of snacks, chicken and fries.

Getting There & Away

There are at least two daily buses along the mostly unsealed route between Singida and Arusha (eight to 10 hours), but it's better to break the trip at Babati or Katesh (for Mt Hanang). The road on to Nzega and Shinyanga is rough and the journey to Mwanza can take several days. Daily buses also run between Singida and Dodoma (eight to 12 hours), but it's better to take the train (p332). There's also a daily direct bus between Singida and Dar es Salaam via Dodoma, departing in both directions at about 6am (14 to 20 hours).

Western Tanzania

HIGHLIGHTS

- Experiencing the primeval rhythms of nature in **Katavi** (p243), one of Africa's wildest and most remote parks

- Visiting wonderful **Mahale Mountains National Park** (p237) – the ultimate 'get-away-from-it-all' destination

- Mingling with the chimps at **Gombe Stream National Park** (p236)

- Kicking back on the shores of **Lake Tanganyika** (p239), or sailing towards Zambia on the *Liemba* ferry

- Following the old caravan routes to **Tabora** (p240) or tiny **Ujiji** (p236), or enjoying the modest creature-comforts and urban outpost ambience of **Kigoma** (p231)

The west is Tanzania's rough, remote frontier land, with few tourists, minimal infrastructure, vast trackless expanses crossed only by the ageing Central Line train and little to draw you here – unless you're interested in chimpanzees. For this, and for watching wildlife in one of Tanzania's most pristine settings, it's among the best spots on the continent.

At Gombe Stream National Park – Jane Goodall's world-renowned chimpanzee research station – and at the isolated and sublimely beautiful Mahale Mountains National Park, you can take advantage of the best opportunities anywhere to get close to our fascinating primate cousins. At wild Katavi National Park, you'll be just a speck in the surrounding universe of vast floodplains trammelled by thousands of buffaloes, as well as zebras, lions and more. Still looking for more? Those who are truly adventurous and have a healthy imagination can visit tiny Ujiji. Now it's a nondescript fishing village, but in its heyday, it was the terminus of one of East Africa's most important caravan routes linking Lake Tanganyika with Bagamoyo and the sea, an important dhow-building centre, and a way station for several European exploratory expeditions. Lake Tanganyika itself – the world's longest and second-deepest freshwater lake – is a scenic and useful transport route if you are heading to or from northern Zambia, and makes a welcome respite from dusty, bumpy roads, with some unforgettable sunset views.

Wherever you go, travel in western Tanzania is rugged, and you will need plenty of time. There are few roads (none of them good), and often the only transport choices are boat, train or truck. Outside of Kigoma and the national parks, the region is seldom visited, and has almost no tourist facilities.

National Parks & Reserves

Parks are western Tanzania's main attractions. Gombe Stream (p236) and Mahale Mountains (p237) parks are renowned as being among the best spots anywhere in Africa to observe chimpanzees at close range, while Katavi (p243) is one of the continent's last great frontier destinations, with pristine wilderness and abundant wildlife.

There are also several game reserves including Moyowosi, Kigosi, Ugalla River and Rukwa, although none are developed for tourism.

Dangers & Annoyances

The security situation at western Tanzania's border areas with Burundi and Rwanda ebbs and flows, due to the ongoing refugee crisis in western Tanzania. Get an update from your embassy before travelling here. Due to spates of banditry, some roads – eg Kasulu to Lusahunga – may require an armed escort if you'll be driving.

Getting There & Around

There are airports at Kigoma and Tabora, and airstrips in Katavi and Mahale Mountains parks.

Tanzania's far west has the worst roads of anywhere in the country. Even during the dry season, you'll need a 4WD, and good supplies of time, spares and mechanical knowledge to get around. While buses run along major routes, they're notoriously prone to breakdowns and journeys are long and rough. Apart from flying, train is the best way to travel although, here too, expect long delays and deviations from the published schedules. Along Lake Tanganyika, the *Liemba* ferry makes a good travel alternative.

KIGOMA
☎ 028

Sprawled along the lake shore about as far away from Dar es Salaam as you can get is Kigoma, a scrappy but agreeable town in a

WESTERN TANZANIA

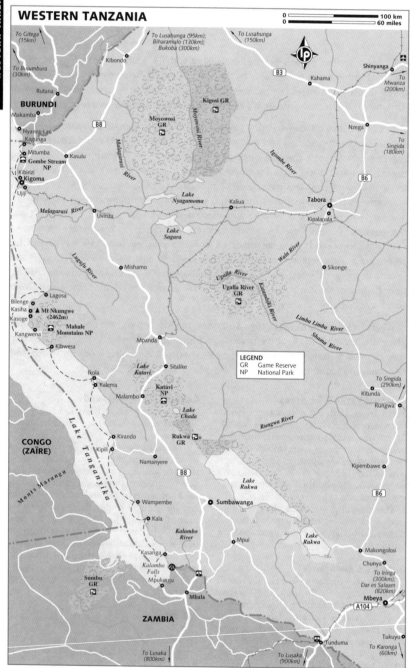

0 ———————— 100 km
0 ———————— 60 miles

To Gitega
(15km)

To Bujumbura
(30km)

Kibondo

To Lusahunga (95km);
Biharamulo (130km);
Bukoba (300km)

To Lusahunga
(150km)

B3

Kahama

Shinyanga

To
Mwanza
(200km)

BURUNDI

Rutana

Makamba

Nyanza-Lac
Kagunga

Mitumba
Gombe Stream
NP

Kibirizi
Kigoma

Ujiji

B8

Kasulu

Malagarasi River

Kigosi GR

Moyowosi
GR

Moyowosi River

Nzega

Igombe River

To
Singida
(180km)

B6

Malagarasi River

Uvinza

Lake
Nyagamoma

Kaliua

Tabora

Kipalapala

Lake
Sagara

Lagosa
River

Mishamo

Ugalla River

Ugalla River
GR

Wala River

Sikonge

Kalambuli River

Bilenge
Kasiha
Kasoge

Kangwena

Mt Nkungwe
(2462m)

Mahale
Mountains NP

Kibwesa

Mpanda

Limba Limba River

Shama River

To Singida
(290km)

Ikola

Kalema

Malambo

Lake
Katavi

Sitalike

Katavi
NP

Lake
Chada

LEGEND
GR   Game Reserve
NP   National Park

Kitunda

Rungwa

Kirando

Kipili

Namanyere

Rukwa
GR

Rungwa River

CONGO
(ZAÏRE)

Monts Marungu

Lake Tanganyika

B8

Wampembe

Kala

Lake
Rukwa

Sumbawanga

Kipembawe

B6

Kalambo
River

Mpui

Lake
Rukwa

Makongolosi

Chunya

To Iringa
(300km);
Dar es Salaam
(820km)

Kasanga

Kalambo
Falls

Mpulungu

Mbala

Sumbu
GR

Mbeya

A104

Tukuyu

ZAMBIA

To Lusaka
(800km)

To Lusaka
(900km)

Tunduma

To Karonga
(60km)

green and tropical waterside setting. In addition to being the regional capital, Kigoma is the most important Tanzanian port on Lake Tanganyika, the end of the line if you've slogged across the country on the Central Line train, and the best starting point for visits to Gombe Stream and Mahale Mountains parks. For much of Kigoma's history it was overshadowed by Ujiji to the south, only coming into its own with the building of the Central Line railway terminus. In recent years, with the upheavals in nearby Congo (Zaïre), Rwanda and Burundi, the surrounding area has become a major refugee centre and base for the attendant clutch of international aid organisations that are working in the region.

Information

CONSULATES
There are consulates for **Burundi** (Kakolwa St; 8.30am-4pm Mon-Fri) and **Congo (Zaïre)** (Kaya Rd; 8.30am-4pm Mon-Fri) – both southwest of the roundabout near the train station. See p317 for visa details.

IMMIGRATION OFFICE
An immigration officer is posted at the port on Wednesday to take care of immigration formalities for travellers departing for Zambia on the MV *Liemba*. Otherwise the immigration office is on the main road towards Ujiji, near the hospital.

INTERNET ACCESS
Baby Come 'n' Call (Lumumba St; per hr Tsh3000; 8am-8pm Mon-Sat) Just up from the train station.
Kigoma Hilltop Hotel (Lumumba St; per hr Tsh5000; 24hr) Expensive, but sometimes the only connection that works.

MEDICAL SERVICES
Baptist Mission Hospital (280 2241) Near the airport.

MONEY
NBC (Lumumba St) Changes cash and travellers cheques, and has an ATM.

POST & TELEPHONE
TTCL (Kiezya Rd) Operator assisted calls and postal services.

TRAVEL AGENCIES
To arrange boat rental, or visits to Gombe Stream and Mahale Mountains parks, contact the following:

Chimpanzee Safaris (280 4435/7; www.chimpan zeesafaris.com) Western Tanzania's main tour operator, run by Kigoma Hilltop Hotel.
Sunset Tours (280 2408; aqua@cats-net.com) A low-key group at Aqua Lodge.

Sights & Activities
Kigoma's lively **market** abounds with produce and is worth a stroll, as is the colourful fishing village of **Kibirizi**, which is 2km north of town and best visited in the early morning when the fishing boats pull in. In town, watch for the stately German-built **train station** at the base of Lumumba St.

The best place for relaxing is **Jakobsen's beach** (admission Tsh3000), which is actually two small, pretty coves reached via steps down a vegetated section of hillside about 5km southwest of town. There are a few *bandas* (thatched-roof hut with wooden or earthen walls for shade), and the water is bilharzia-free (see p338). West of Jakobsen's beach and about the same distance from town is **Zungu beach** (admission Tsh500), which is also nice, though 'beach' is a stretch, as there are only loose stones to sit on. Neither place has food or drink. Both are reached by heading west from town along the road past Kigoma Hilltop Hotel, keeping right at the small fork, until the sign for Zungu beach. Go right here and continue uphill for about 2.5km to a small fork. Jakobsen's is about 1.5km further, signposted to the right; Zungu beach is about 1km downhill to the left. Via public transport, catch a Katonga *dalla-dalla* (minibus) at the roundabout near the train station and ask the driver to drop you at the turn-off for Zungu beach, from where it's 30 to 40 minutes further on foot to either beach.

Sleeping
BUDGET
Lake Tanganyika Beach Hotel (280 2694; s/d Tsh8000/12,000) This hotel's setting is ideal – overlooking a long lawn sloping down to the lake – but the rooms have become quite run down. There's a reasonable restaurant, and a loud disco on Saturday nights. It's about 1km west of town, off Kakolwa Ave and past the port. The hotel is slated for renovations, so prices may rise along with standards.
Zanzibar Lodge (280 3306; r Tsh3500-9000) Cleaner and better value than Lake Tanganyika, as long as you don't mind being a bit

KIGOMA

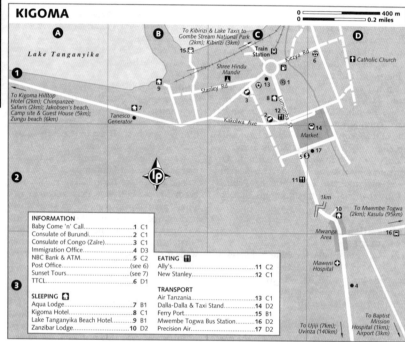

INFORMATION
Baby Come 'n' Call...........................1 C1
Consulate of Burundi........................2 C1
Consulate of Congo (Zaïre)..............3 C1
Immigration Office...........................4 D3
NBC Bank & ATM............................5 C2
Post Office.................................(see 6)
Sunset Tours...............................(see 7)
TTCL..6 D1

SLEEPING
Aqua Lodge....................................7 B1
Kigoma Hotel.................................8 C1
Lake Tanganyika Beach Hotel..........9 B1
Zanzibar Lodge.............................10 D2

EATING
Ally's..11 C2
New Stanley.................................12 C1

TRANSPORT
Air Tanzania................................13 C1
Dalla-Dalla & Taxi Stand.................14 D2
Ferry Port....................................15 B1
Mwembe Togwa Bus Station..........16 D2
Precision Air.................................17 D2

out of town. There are a variety of rooms, many with bathrooms, so it's worth checking out a few. For a quieter room, ask for one facing away from the road. It's about 2km from central Kigoma in the Mwanga area. Food is available, and *dalla-dallas* ply regularly to/from the centre.

Kigoma Hotel (Lumumba St; r with/without bathroom Tsh5000/3500) One of the cheapest places in the town centre, with a convenient location, grubby, noisy rooms, bucket baths and a sleazy bar.

There is very good camping at Jakobsen's beach (see right).

MID-RANGE & TOP END

Kigoma Hilltop Hotel (☎ 280 4435/6/7; www.kigoma .com; s/d full-board & airport pick-up US$90/140; ❄ 🖥 ⛵) Kigoma's best hotel by far, with a prime setting on an escarpment overlooking the lake, comfortable, good-value cottages complete with mini-fridge, TV and air-con, a pool (Tsh2000 for nonresidents) and its own private beach. There's also a good restaurant with Indian and Western dishes starting at Tsh4000, and the chance to do

water-skiing or parasailing. The lodge runs luxury tented camps in Mahale Mountains, Gombe Stream and (soon) Katavi parks, and can organise private safaris to all of these places.

Aqua Lodge (☎ 280 2408; aqua@cats-net.com; s/d Tsh15,000/18,000) A small, long-standing place with pleasant, good-value rooms, a restaurant with breakfast for Tsh2000 and meals around Tsh5000, and a low-key tour company that can arrange safaris to Gombe Stream and Mahale Mountains parks. It's at the western edge of town, opposite the Tanesco generator.

Jakobsen's Guest House (☎ 0741-534141; ferie land@hotmail.com; accommodation per family for 1st/ succeeding nights Tsh45,000/30,000, per additional adult Tsh10,000, electricity per hr Tsh2500) This comfortable private guesthouse is located well out of town near Jakobsen's beach (p233) and well away from everything else, and is generally rented out in its entirety rather than by room, though it may offer rooms on a space-available basis. It has three double and seven single beds divided among several rooms, a kitchen and two bathrooms and a quiet, cliff-top perch. The guesthouse is within a few minutes' walk of Jakobsen's Beach, where the same owners run a small and very nice **camp site** (camping per family for 1st/succeeding nights Tsh20,000/10,000) with ablutions, a grill, lanterns and water supply. For both camping and the guesthouse, bring all your own food from town.

Eating & Drinking

Ally's (Lumumba St; meals Tsh1000) is a local favourite, with piping hot *wali maharagwe* (rice and beans), or *ugali* (a staple made from maize or cassava flour, or both) and sauce. **New Stanley** (Kakolwa Ave; meals Tsh2500; ⓨ lunch & dinner) is several steps up in price and ambience, with reasonable grilled chicken/fish and other staples, plus a popular disco for post-meal entertainment.

If these don't suit, head to the restaurant at **Lake Tanganyika Beach Hotel** (see p233; meals Tsh3000; ⓨ lunch & dinner) – or better, skip the mediocre food and instead sit on the lawn and enjoy a drink at sundown. Alternatively, make your way up to **Kigoma Hilltop Hotel** (opposite; meals from Tsh6000; ⓨ lunch & dinner) for Kigoma's finest dining.

Getting There & Away

AIR
There are five flights weekly between Dar es Salaam and Kigoma, usually via Tabora, on **Precision Air** (☎ 280 4720, 280 3166). The office is just off the main road near NBC bank. **Air Tanzania** (☎ 280 2508) is at the roundabout near the train station, although it currently has no flights to Kigoma.

There are frequent charter flights between Kigoma, Mwanza and Arusha. Kigoma Hilltop Hotel is the best contact for booking, and for finding out about the availability of extra seats.

The airport is about 5km southeast of the town centre.

BOAT
Lake Ferries
The venerable MV *Liemba* plies between Kigoma and Mpulungu (Zambia), and the MV *Mwongozo* sails between Kigoma and Bujumbura (Burundi). For information and schedules see p325.

Lake Taxis
Lake taxis are small, wooden motorised boats, piled high with people and produce,

that connect villages along the lake shore as far north as the Burundi border, including a stop at Gombe Stream National Park. They are inexpensive, but offer no shade or other creature comforts. The lake taxis don't stop at Kigoma itself, but at Kibirizi village, about 2km north of Kigoma. The easiest way to get there is to follow the railway tracks north. Alternatively, follow the road uphill past the post office, turn left at the top and continue straight for about 2km (Tsh1500 in a taxi).

BUS
Roads from Kigoma in all directions are rough, and the security situation ebbs and flows, so think twice before travelling here by bus. For all long-distance lines, including buses to Biharamulo, Bukoba, Mwanza and other destinations near Lake Victoria, departures are from Mwembe Togwa, about 4km southeast of the town centre; follow the Ujiji road to the airport turnoff, from where it's about 700m down to the left.

To Mwanza, there are three buses weekly (Tuesday, Friday and Sunday), departing Kigoma about 5.30am (Tsh15,000, at least 20 hours). Most go via Lusahunga and Biharamulo, though there's usually one weekly taking the route via Kahama and Shinyanga. Service is frequently interrupted, especially during the rains, and prone to frequent breakdowns.

To Bukoba, there are several buses weekly, departing at 5.30am (Tsh12,000, 10 hours).

The road to Mpanda is quite feasible during the dry season (and sometimes during the rains as well), though there's no direct public transport apart from the occasional lorry.

TRAIN
The classic way to reach Kigoma (apart from sailing in on the MV *Liemba*) is with the ageing Central Line train from Dar es Salaam, Mwanza or Tabora. See p332 for schedules and fares.

Getting Around
Taxis between the town centre and Mwembe Togwa charge about Tsh2000. *Dalla-dallas* to Mwanga, Mwandigo (for Mwembe Togwa) and Ujiji run throughout the day, departing from the *dalla-dalla* stand in the town centre.

UJIJI

Tiny Ujiji, one of Africa's oldest market villages, earned its place in travel lore as the spot where explorer-journalist Henry Morton Stanley uttered his famously casual 'Dr Livingstone, I presume?'. The site where Stanley's encounter with Livingstone allegedly occurred is commemorated by a plaque set in a walled compound near a small garden. Nearby are two mango trees, which are said to have been grafted from the original tree that shaded the two men during their encounter. There's also a tiny and rather bleak **museum** (admission free, donation appreciated) housing a few pictures by local artists of Livingstone scenes. The site is signposted to the right of the main road coming from Kigoma – just ask for Livingstone and the *dalla-dalla* driver will make sure you get off at the right place.

Prior to Livingstone, Ujiji enjoyed prominence as the main settlement in the region (a status it lost only after the railway terminus was built at Kigoma), and as a major dhow-building centre. Burton and Speke also stopped here in 1858 before setting out to explore Lake Tanganyika. Thanks to its position as a terminus of the old caravan route to the coast, Ujiji still sports various Swahili traits, primarily in local building style.

Despite its glorious past, little remains today of Ujiji's former significance, and many people find the village decidedly underwhelming. But it's easy enough to reach from Kigoma and worth a stop if you're in the area. From the Livingstone compound, you can continue about 500m further along the same street to Ujiji's beach and small dhow port. No power tools are used in building the boats and construction methods are the same as they were generations ago.

Sleeping & Eating

There are a couple of very basic guesthouses along the main road, where you can enjoy bare-bones rooms and bucket bath for about Tsh1500. For food, there are some undistinguished local eateries along the main street.

Getting There & Away

Ujiji is about 8km south of the centre of Kigoma; *dalla-dallas* run between the two towns throughout the day (Tsh100).

GOMBE STREAM NATIONAL PARK

With an area of only 52 sq km, Gombe Stream is Tanzania's smallest national park. It is also the site of the longest-running study of any wild animal population in the world and, for those interested in primates, it's a fascinating place.

The Gombe Stream area was gazetted as a game reserve in 1943. In 1960 British researcher Jane Goodall arrived to begin a study of wild chimpanzees, and in 1968 Gombe was designated as a national park. Goodall's study is now in its fifth decade.

Gombe Stream's approximately 150 chimps are well habituated, and you can sometimes get to within 5m of them. In addition to observing the chimps, it's possible to swim in the lake or hike in Gombe's forest. Other animals you may see in the park include colobus and vervet monkeys, bushbucks, baboons, bushpigs and a variety of birdlife. If you're really interested in the chimpanzees, allow at least two days at Gombe.

Information

Entry fees are US$100/20 per 24 hours per adult/child aged seven to 15 years. Guides cost US$20 per group per day. Children aged under seven are not permitted in the park.

Gombe Stream can be visited year-round, although the chimps are often easier to find during the rainy season (between about February and June, and again in November and early December). Bookings for the hostel and resthouse can be made through Kigoma travel agencies, or directly through the **senior park warden** (☎ 028-280 2586). Park headquarters are on the beach at Mitumba Valley at the northern end of the park. All tourism activities are south of here at Kasekela, on the beach near the centre of the park, and this is where you'll need to disembark when you visit.

A visitors centre for Gombe Stream is set to open in Kigoma about 2km south of the NBC bank on the Mwanga road, up the hill to the left, behind the multistorey buildings, but it's still far from completion.

For photos, bring high-speed film for use in the forest; flashes aren't permitted.

Sleeping & Eating

There is a rather run-down **hostel** (per person US$10) with basic rooms and no nets, and a small, no-frills but somewhat nicer

resthouse (per person US$20), which has nets. Both are at Kasekela, on the beach near the centre of the park. An additional hostel is being planned. You can also **camp** (per person US$20) on the beach, although park staff don't recommend it because of the danger from baboons, and it doesn't save you any money anyway. If you do camp, don't underestimate the baboons, and bring a metal container for storing food. There's a small shop at park headquarters selling drinks and a few basics, and it's sometimes possible to arrange inexpensive grilled fish or other local meals with staff. Otherwise, bring whatever provisions you will need from Kigoma.

Gombe Luxury Tented Camp (☎ 280 4435/6/7; www.chimpanzeesafaris.com; per person all-inclusive US$400) This relaxing luxury camp is on the beach at Mitumba in the northern part of the park, and makes a good splurge if you want some comforts at the end of a hard, sweaty day tracking the chimps. It has comfortable en suite tents, good meals and a shady, waterside location that's much better than that of the park hostel and resthouse. It's run by Kigoma Hilltop Hotel in Kigoma, and they have transport-accommodation deals.

Getting There & Away

Gombe Stream is located on the shore of Lake Tanganyika, about 20km north of Kigoma. The only way to reach the park is by boat – either charter or lake taxi. Lake taxis to the park depart from Kibirizi (p235) between about noon and 3pm Monday to Saturday (Tsh1000, three to four hours). They return to Kibirizi in the morning (which means you'll need to spend two nights at the park if travelling by public transport), passing Gombe by around 8am. Park staff can help you wave down a boat.

Alternatively, you can arrange with local fishermen to charter a boat – and you'll be besieged with offers to do so – although this will be expensive. For a return trip, you may have to pay an advance for petrol (which should not be more than one-third of the total price), but don't pay the full amount until you have arrived back in Kigoma. It's common practice for local boat owners to try to convince you that there are no lake taxis, in an effort to get business.

Faster boats can be organised through Sunset Tours (p233; US$165 return per boat for up to 15 passengers, plus a US$80 per night stopover fee) and Kigoma Hilltop Hotel (p234; US$300 return per boat for up to 20 passengers, plus a US$50 per night stopover fee).

MAHALE MOUNTAINS NATIONAL PARK

It's difficult to imagine a more idyllic combination: clear, blue waters, white sand beaches backed by lushly forested mountains, some of the most challenging and intriguing wildlife-watching on the continent and a setting of such unrivalled remoteness that you're likely to have it all almost to

---

CHIMPANZEES

The natural habitat of Tanzania's chimpanzees (Pan troglodytes schweinfurthii) once extended along much of the western border of the country, throughout the Kigoma and Rukwa regions and into Burundi, Rwanda, Uganda and Congo (Zaïre). Deforestation and human population pressures have greatly reduced these areas, and today the chimps are found mainly in Gombe Stream National Park, and in and around Mahale Mountains National Park.

In addition to deforestation, the main threat to Tanzania's remaining chimp populations is illegal trafficking. Chimpanzees, which are coveted as pets, sought for medical research, and wanted for commercial zoos, command high prices on the black market. Yet, to capture a baby chimpanzee, all nearby adults must be killed. The result is many dead chimps, and many orphans. For young chimps that are recaptured from illegal traffickers, there is also the problem of reinte-gration. With few exceptions, chimps cannot be reintroduced to the wild in an area where there are other chimps living. While there are numerous groups working hard to halt illegal trafficking, the networks are entrenched, and it's an uphill battle that requires constant vigilance.

If you're considering visiting either Gombe Stream or Mahale Mountains parks, also remember that chimpanzees are susceptible to human diseases, so don't visit if you're ill. (And, if park officials get wind of a sniffle or the flu, you won't be allowed to enter.)

yourself. Mahale – Tanzania's most isolated park – stretches along the Lake Tanganyika shoreline about 130km south of Kigoma, with the misty and rugged Mahale range running down its centre. Like Gombe Stream to the north, Mahale is primarily a chimpanzee sanctuary, home to about 700 of our primate relatives, with roan antelopes, buffaloes, zebras and even some lions keeping them company (although the lions are seldom seen).

Mahale national park has been the site of an ongoing Japanese-sponsored primate research project since 1965, when the Kyoto University Africa Primatological Expedition initiated research here, and the chimpanzee communities that have been focal points of study are well habituated. While Mahale's size and terrain mean that it can take time (and some strenuous, steep and sweaty walking) to find them, almost everyone who spends at least a few days here comes away well rewarded.

Mahale Mountains was gazetted as a national park in 1980 with an area of around 1600 sq km. The park's highest peak is Mt Nkungwe (2462m), first climbed in 1939.

Information

Entry fees are US$50/20 per adult/child aged five to 15 years. For camping fees see p35. Children under seven aren't permitted in Mahale. Camping and park *bandas* can be booked through the **senior park warden** (PO Box 1374, Kigoma), or more easily through Kigoma Hilltop Hotel in Kigoma (p234), which can also help you contact park headquarters if you'll be arriving independently. Guide fees are US$20 per group (maximum six people).

Park headquarters, where fees are paid, are at Bilenge in the park's northwestern corner. About 10km south of here are Kasiha (site of the park camp site and *bandas*) and Kangwena beach (with two top-end camps). The park's eastern section is currently closed to tourists, although trail development is planned.

The park is open year-round, although during the rains it gets too muddy to do much walking, and the private camps close. There are no roads in Mahale; walking (and boating, along the shoreline) are the only ways to get around. Bring high-speed film for use in the forest; flashes aren't permitted.

Sleeping

There is a park **camp site** (per person US$20) and a cluster of quite nice double **bandas** (per person US$20) at Kasiha. For both, bring whatever you will need from Kigoma, as there's nothing available in the park.

Mahale Camp (www.nomad-tanzania.com; s/d all-inclusive US$610/970; ◯ mid-May–mid-March) This exclusive camp, in a superb setting on Kangwena beach, offers what is probably the ultimate getaway, if for no other reason than that it's so remote. Accommodation is in six rustic thatched tented *bandas* without electricity or running water, although solar power and bush showers mean you still have all the comforts. Children under 12 years are not permitted on chimpanzee-tracking walks. The camp can only be booked through upmarket travel agencies or safari operators, including some of those listed on p326 and p59.

Nkungwe Luxury Tented Camp (☎ 280 4435/6/7; www.chimpanzeesafaris.com; per person all-inclusive US$350) Nkungwe camp, run by Kigoma Hilltop Hotel in Kigoma, is on the beach north of Kangwena and about 1km north of Mahale Camp. It has six comfortable double tents, and makes a good-value alternative to Mahale Camp for those on more moderate budgets.

Getting There & Away

Getting to Mahale is half the fun, with the only ways in via charter aircraft or boat.

AIR

Flying in to Mahale treats you to some impressive aerial views of the Lake Tanganyika shoreline. The airstrip is just north of the park boundary at Sitolo. Charter flights from Kigoma and Arusha can be arranged through Kigoma Hilltop Hotel, Nomad Safaris, or any of the charter companies listed on p185. It's also worth checking with the camps themselves to see if there are any charters arriving with spare seats.

BOAT

Despite the lake's temperamental choppiness and the length of the journey, it's hard to beat the satisfyingly adventurous edge – and the impressive lake shore scenery – of journeying to Mahale via lake steamer. The MV *Liemba* stops at Lagosa (also called Mugambo), to the north of the park (US$25/20/15 in 1st/

LAKE TANGANYIKA

Stretching like a giant blue ribbon along Tanzania's western edge is Lake Tanganyika, the world's longest (670km) and second-deepest (over 1400m) lake. At somewhere between nine and 12 million years old, it is also one of the oldest lakes on the planet and, thanks to its age and ecological isolation, is home to an exceptional variety of fish. Most notable are its colourful cichlids, many of which are found nowhere else, and which make for some wonderful snorkelling in the lake's clear waters.

Lake Tanganyika is also fascinating from a human perspective. Several dozen tribal groups – spread throughout four countries – make their home along its shores, rubbing elbows with about 1000 (on the Tanzanian side) chimpanzees. During the late 18th and early 19th centuries, the lake was a major conduit for slaves and trade along the old caravan routes, while today its shores bustle with cross-border traders and refugees. The best way to get a feel for local life – centred around the countless fishing villages strung out along the shoreline – is to set off on the MV *Liemba*, which calls in at a string of small ports as it makes its way down the shoreline. There are very few docking jetties, so at each place where the *Liemba* pulls in, it's met by dozens of small boats which race their way out to the ferry, with boat owners and food vendors all jostling for custom from the passengers. At night, the whole scene is lit up by the glow of dozens of tiny kerosene lamps, waving precariously in the wind and waves.

Besides Kigoma (the largest town on the Tanzanian lake shore), Ujiji (one of the oldest lake shore settlements) and Lagosa (for Mahale Mountains National Park), ports of note include the old mission station of Kalema (Karema) and the pleasant village of Ikola, about 15km further north. At Kalema, the main point of interest is the old Catholic mission station, parts of which were originally a Belgian fort, before being handed over to the White Fathers in 1889. In Ikola – the only village in these parts with anything remotely tourist-oriented – there is the simple and helpful **Zanzibar Guest House** (r Tsh1500) with buckets of hot water on request and filling, inexpensive meals. The owners can help you organise a local boat to explore the surrounding lake shore and nearby rivers. From both Kalema and (better) Ikola, you can get transport to Mpanda.

2nd/3rd class, about 10 hours from Kigoma). From Lagosa, it's possible to continue with small local boats to park headquarters, about two hours further south, but not the best idea as the *Liemba* reaches Lagosa about 2am or 3am. (If you do decide to try this, there's a basic guesthouse in Lagosa where you can wait until dawn.) It's better to radio park headquarters in advance from Kigoma and arrange a pick-up. Kigoma Hilltop Hotel and the *Liemba* office in Kigoma can help with the radio call. The park boat costs US$50 per boat (for up to about 15 people, one way), although if the park is sending a boat up anyway, you may be able to negotiate something better. Coming from Mpulungu (Zambia) the *Liemba* passes Lagosa sometime between late Saturday night and early Sunday morning around 3am or 4am.

The other option is to charter a boat through either Kigoma Hilltop Hotel (US$1500 return per boat for up to 20 persons, plus US$50 per night stopover charge; about 10 hours) or Sunset Tours (US$960 per boat for up to eight people, including

two to three days waiting at Mahale). Kigoma Hilltop Hotel also has a faster, pricier speedboat, which cuts travel time by more than half.

UVINZA

Salt production has kept Uvinza on the map for at least several centuries, and the town is still one of Tanzania's major salt-producing areas. If you find yourself here, a highlight is visiting the local salt factory, which has been running since the 1920s. As so few travellers pass this way, staff will be happy to see you; permits can be arranged at the entry gate. For lodging, there are several no-frills guesthouses, including **Sibuondo Guest House** (r without bathroom Tsh5000) in the town centre.

Uvinza is about two hours southeast of Kigoma via the Central Line train. There's no regular public transport to/from the town, but the road towards Kigoma has been improved and is regularly traversed by lorries. Expect to pay about Tsh2500 for a lift from Uvinza to Kasulu, from where there are daily minibuses to Kigoma (Tsh2000). Trucks also run reasonably frequently between Uvinza and Mpanda, especially during the dry season (about Tsh5000, one day). There is little traffic on this road, and few supplies available en route, so stock up before setting off. If you're driving, check locally for an update on road conditions, but currently the best route to Kigoma is along the track heading west shortly after the salt factory, which joins with the Kigoma–Kasulu road before Kigoma. There's also a longer route heading northwest from Uvinza, then branching west towards Kigoma about 10km before Kasulu.

TABORA

☎ 026

Tabora – a sleepy town basking in the shade of numerous mango and flame trees – was once a major trading centre along the old caravan route connecting Lake Tanganyika with Bagamoyo and the sea. Known in early days as Kazeh, it was the domain of famed Nyamwezi king Mirambo, as well as headquarters of infamous slave trader Tippu

Tib (p241). A string of European explorers passed through its portals, most notably Stanley and Livingstone, and Burton and Speke. Stanley, waxing lyrical over the town, noted that it contained 'over a thousand huts and tembes, and one may safely estimate the population…at five thousand people.' After the Central Line railway was constructed, Tabora became the largest town in German East Africa.

By the turn of the 19th century, Tabora had also become an important mission station. It soon also gained prominence as a regional educational centre – a reputation that it has somewhat managed to retain even today – and Julius Nyerere attended school here.

Although it's hard to shake the initial impression of the town as a dusty backwater, Tabora is still an important transport junction where the Central Line branches for Mwanza and Kigoma. It's also the traditional heartland of the Nyamwezi (People of the Moon), one of Tanzania's largest tribal groups. If you're travelling by train you'll probably need to spend at least a day here.

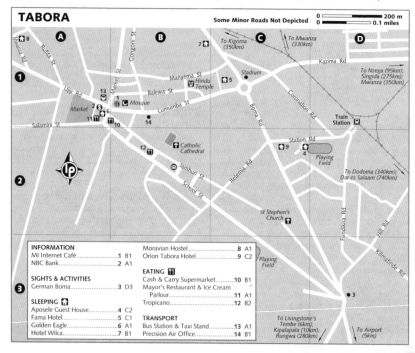

TABORA

Some Minor Roads Not Depicted

INFORMATION		
MI Internet Café	1	B1
NBC Bank	2	A1

SIGHTS & ACTIVITIES		
German Boma	3	D3

SLEEPING ☐		
Aposele Guest House	4	C2
Fama Hotel	5	C1
Golden Eagle	6	A1
Hotel Wilca	7	B1

Moravian Hostel	8	A1
Orion Tabora Hotel	9	C2

EATING ☐		
Cash & Carry Supermarket	10	B1
Mayor's Restaurant & Ice Cream		
Parlour	11	A1
Tropicano	12	B2

TRANSPORT		
Bus Station & Taxi Stand	13	A1
Precision Air Office	14	B1

TIPPU TIB

Tippu Tib (also Tippu Tip), whose real name was Hamed bin Mohamed el Murjebi, was one of East Africa's most infamous slave traders, notorious for his ruthless cruelty. He was born around 1830 in Zanzibar as the son of a wealthy plantation owner from Tabora. While still young, Tippu Tib began to assist his father with trade and soon came to dominate an extensive area around Lake Tanganyika that stretched well into present-day Congo (Zaïre). At the height of his power in the late 19th century, he had trading stations strung out across eastern Congo and Tanzania. Tippu Tib knew some of the European explorers and assisted Livingstone and Stanley with their expeditions. In 1887 Stanley persuaded him to become governor of the eastern region of the Congo although the undertaking was short-lived. In 1890 Tippu Tib left his base in the Congo for Zanzibar, where he died in 1905. His house still stands in Zanzibar Town near Africa House Hotel, although it is not open to visitors. Tippu Tib wrote an autobiography which has been published in Swahili, English and German.

Information

MI Internet Café (Lumumba St) Just east of the bus stand.
NBC Bank (Market St) Changes cash and travellers cheques; an ATM is planned.

Sights & Activities

There are a few buildings dating back to the German era, including the **train station** and the old **boma**, at the end of Boma Rd. The main attraction, however, is **Livingstone's tembe** (flat-roofed Arabic-style house; admission Tsh1500), about 6km southwest of town in Kwihara, off the Kipalapala road. It was here that Livingstone stayed in 1872 after being found by Stanley in Ujiji, and the house – now a small museum – is full of his memorabilia, including some letters, a diary and other items. To get here, take any *dalla-dalla* heading to Kipalapala and have them drop you at the turnoff (to the right, when coming from Tabora), from where it's about 2km further on foot. Taxis from town charge about Tsh7000 return. Once at the tembe, you'll need to find the caretaker to let you in – he lives about 500m before; ask anyone in the village for 'Livingstone' and they'll point you in the right direction.

Sleeping

Orion Tabora Hotel (☎ 260 4369; oriontbrhotel@spider sat.net; cnr Boma & Station Rds; s/d Tsh24,000/30,000) The old railway hotel, which was very nicely restored and is now the best place in town by far. All rooms have TV and nets, there's a good restaurant, a well-stocked bar and a veranda from where you can watch the passing scene. The hotel was originally built by a German baron as a hunting lodge, before its later reincarnation as the Railway

Hotel, and still has lots of atmosphere. Staff are very accommodating if you're travelling by train and there is usually someone around to let you in for pre-dawn train arrivals.

Hotel Wilca (☎ 5397; Boma Rd; s/d Tsh7200/8500) After Orion Tabora Hotel, this small place is Tabora's nicest establishment. Rooms are clean and quiet (all with nets), and there's a good restaurant and a small garden. It's at the northeastern edge of town along Boma Rd.

Moravian Hostel (☎ 260 4710; Mwanza Rd; s/tw Tsh5000/6000, tw without bathroom Tsh3000) The best shoestring deal, with spartan rooms, all twin-bedded with nets. Breakfast costs Tsh1000, and other meals can be arranged with advance notice. It's northwest of the centre and about 2.5km from the train station. Head to Lumumba St and turn right just behind the market. The hostel is about 300m down on the right, next to the church.

Golden Eagle (☎ 260 4623; Jamhuri St; s without bathroom Tsh5500, tw Tsh9000, with TV from Tsh15,000) Rather run-down but reasonable rooms with fan, food and a convenient location near the bus stand.

Other recommendations:

Aposele Guest House (☎ 260 4510; s/d Tsh3500/5000, d without bathroom Tsh3000) The best of the cheap guesthouses, with large, no-frills rooms on a small side street off Station Rd, and just a few minutes' walk from the train station. Food is available.

Fama Hotel (☎ 260 4657; s/d Tsh6000/8000, d with TV Tsh10,000) Clean, quiet rooms, a good restaurant and a convenient central location just off Lumumba Rd.

Eating

Of the hotel restaurants, the best is at **Orion Tabora Hotel** (see left; meals from Tsh3500; ✏ breakfast, lunch & dinner) followed by the restaurants at **Fama Hotel** (meals Tsh2500) and **Hotel Wilca** (meals from Tsh3500).

Mayor's Restaurant & Ice Cream Parlour (cnr Market & School Sts; snacks from Tsh500, meals Tsh1000; ☺ breakfast, lunch & dinner) This is a great stop for snacks, including fresh pineapple juice and soft-serve ice cream, plus samosas and light meals. **Tropicano** (School St; snacks from Tsh500; ☺ until 7pm) lack's Mayor's ambience, but has a similar menu.

For self-catering try **Cash & Carry Supermarket** (☎ 260 4327; Jamhuri St).

Getting There & Away

AIR

Precision Air (☎ 260 4818; Lumumba St) stops at Tabora five times weekly on its flight between Dar es Salaam and Kigoma. The airline's office is near the market. The airport is about 5km south of town.

BUS

Mohammed Trans runs between Tabora and Mwanza, departing daily in each direction at 6.30am (Tsh7500, 7½ hours). If you're heading east, you can disembark at Nzega (which is also serviced daily by 4WDs), and then catch a bus on to Singida, though this means an overnight in Nzega. It's possible to drive between Tabora and Mbeya (4WD only), but it's a long slog, and the route is serviced by three to four buses weekly during the dry season. To Kigoma, there's no public transport except the train.

TRAIN

Tabora is the main Central Line junction for trains north to Mwanza, west to Kigoma and south to Mpanda. For schedule and fare information see p332. Trains from Mpanda reach Tabora about 3am, trains from Kigoma and Mwanza arrive by about 5am, and trains from Dar es Salaam reach Tabora by about 9pm. Travelling between Kigoma and Mwanza, you will need to spend the day in Tabora, and to reconfirm your onward reservation.

Getting Around

The main taxi stand is at the edge of the bus station, at the corner of Market St and Ujiji Rd. Taxis meet all train arrivals, and charge Tsh1000 from the station to the town centre. If you arrive in the middle of the night,

ask the driver to wait until you're sure that there's someone around at your hotel to let you in.

MPANDA
☎ 025
This small and somewhat scruffy town is of interest mainly as a starting point for visits to Katavi National Park. It's also the terminus of a branch of the Central Line railway, and a useful junction town if you're heading inland from Lake Tanganyika.

Sleeping & Eating

Super City Hotel (☎ 282 0459; s/d from Tsh2500/3000) The main place to stay, with clean rooms, all with nets, and a decent but slow restaurant. It's along the Sumbawanga road at the southern edge of town. To get here from the train station, follow the tracks to the end, then take the first left and look for the multistorey building.

Slightly cheaper, but less conveniently located, is **Moravian Hostel** (☎ 282 0187; s/d without bathroom Tsh2000/2500), just northeast of the centre, with no-frills rooms, meals, and a bucket of hot water for bathing.

Getting There & Away

BUS

4WDs to Katavi National Park and Sumbawanga depart in the mornings from in front of Super City Hotel. Sumry bus line departs Mpanda for Sumbawanga (Tsh7500, seven hours) by around midday on Tuesday, Thursday and Saturday, after waiting for the train.

Trucks ply the route towards Uvinza and Kigoma fairly regularly, especially during the dry season; allow at least 12 hours. The train is the best option to Kigoma.

From Mpanda southwest to Kalema and Ikola (the main Lake Tanganyika ports in this area), there are occasional lorries which are usually timed to coincide with arrivals of the *Liemba* ferry.

TRAIN

There is a branch of the Central Line that connects Mpanda with Tabora via Kaliua. For schedule and fare information see p332. If you're heading to Kigoma or Mwanza from Mpanda, you will need to spend at least a day in Tabora or Kaliua. You can wait for the connection at Kaliua, but as there are few guesthouses and little to do, most travellers continue on to Tabora and wait there.

KATAVI NATIONAL PARK

Katavi, about 35km southwest of Mpanda, is Tanzania's third-largest park and one of its most unspoiled wilderness areas. For travellers seeking an alternative to more popular destinations elsewhere in the country, it is the ultimate – and most rugged – safari experience. Katavi's predominant feature is its enormous flood plain, whose vast, grassy expanses cover much of the northern section of the park. The plains are broken by the Katuma river and several seasonal lakes, which support huge populations of hippos, plus crocodiles and a wealth of birds (over 400 bird species have been identified in Katavi thus far). In the west and centre of the park, the floodplains yield to vast tracts of brush and woodland, which are the best areas for sighting roan and sable antelopes; together with Ruaha National Park, Katavi is one of the few places where you have a decent chance of spotting both.

The park comes to life in the dry season, when the river and lakes dry up and huge herds of buffalo, elephants, lions, zebras, giraffes and many more make their way to the remaining pools and streams. At these times, it's hard not to feel that you've reached the heart of Africa, vast, uncontainable and pulsing to the primeval rhythms of the wild.

Katavi was originally gazetted in 1974 with an area of 2253 sq km. In 1997 it was extended to about 4500 sq km and, together with the contiguous Rukwa Game Reserve, encompasses a conservation area covering 12,500 sq km. Because of its remote location and completely under-publicised attractions, the park receives very few visitors. You'll probably have the place to yourself, and are almost guaranteed to see animals.

Information

Entry fees are US$15/5 per adult/child aged five to 15 years. For information on camping fees see p35.

Katavi is open year-round, but should only be visited during the dry season, between June and November/December, with the peak months for wildlife watching from late July to October. **Park headquarters**

(ktnp@afsat.com), for hut bookings, entry fee payments and other information, is just off the main road, about 1.5km south of Sitalike, on the park's northern edge.

Wildlife viewing is permitted in open vehicles, and park vehicles can be hired, if they aren't being used by staff. Rates are US$1 per kilometre with a minimum charge of US$100, plus guide fees. It's also possible to drive in the park with your own vehicle. While it's not required to bring a guide along in the original (western) section of the park, it's highly recommended. In the newer (eastern) section there are only rough bush tracks and you'll need an armed ranger.

Walking safaris are permitted with an armed ranger. For any safaris in Katavi, bring along thick, long-sleeved shirts and trousers, preferably in khaki or other drab shades (avoid anything bright, very contrasting or very dark), as protection against tsetse fly bites.

Sleeping

There are several ordinary camp sites in the park, including the well-situated Chada Campsite near Lake Chada; Ikuu Campsite at Ikuu ranger post northwest of Lake Chada; and Lake Katavi Campsite near Lake Katavi, just west of the Sumbawanga–Mpanda road. For those without a tent, there is the small (six-bed) Chief Nsalamba Resthouse, about 2km from park headquarters, where a camp site and double-bedded tourist *bandas* are also being constructed. For the camp sites, you will have to bring everything you'll need with you, including sleeping bag, food and drinking water (or purifying tablets). The resthouse near park headquarters has blankets. In Sitalike village just outside the park gate, the only option is the new **Katavi Hippo Garden Hotel** (r per person US$30).

Chada Katavi Camp (www.nomad-tanzania.com; s/d all-inclusive US$590/930; Jun-Oct & mid-Dec–mid-Mar) This tented camp is one of the most exclusive in Katavi in terms of setting and atmosphere. Its feel is rustic and unbeatable – mixing a classic safari ambience with the bare minimum of amenities – and the location overlooking the Chada floodplains is superb. It's an absolute must for the well-heeled, ruggedly inclined safari connoisseur. The camp has just seven double tents, each with bush shower and solar-powered lighting and can only be booked through top-end travel agencies.

Katavi Wildlife Camp (☎ 0748-237422, 0744-237 422; www.tanzaniasafaris.info; s/d all-inclusive US$410/700) This is a comfortable, rustic camp in a prime setting near Ikuu ranger post, with spacious en suite tents overlooking the floodplains, top-notch guides and very good cuisine. It's owned by Foxes African Safaris (p63), which also runs camps in Ruaha and Mikumi, and they offer some excellent combination itineraries.

Katavi Tented Camp (☎ 280 4435/6/7; www .chimpanzeesafaris.com; per person all-inclusive US$350; ✉ mid-May–mid-Feb) A new camp, under the same ownership as Kigoma Hilltop Hotel (p234), and scheduled to open soon.

Flycatcher Safaris (www.flycat.com) This long-established Swiss-run outfit offers Katavi itineraries based out of their own temporary camp, and can arrange combination itineraries taking in Katavi, Mahale Mountains and Rubondo Island National Parks, as well as other destinations in Tanzania. Prices are mid-range to top end.

Getting There & Away
AIR
There are airstrips for charter flights in Mpanda, Sitalike and at Ikuu ranger post near Lake Chada.

BUS
Any bus running between Mpanda and Sumbawanga will drop you at the gate, where you can arrange vehicle rental. Alternatively, it's sometimes possible to find a lift with one of the park vehicles that come frequently to Mpanda for supplies. If you are driving, the closest petrol stations are in Mpanda and Sumbawanga.

SUMBAWANGA
☎ 025
The peppy and surprisingly pleasant capital of the Rukwa region is set on the fertile Ufipa plateau at about 1800m altitude in the far southwestern corner of the country. While there's little reason to make the town a destination in itself, Sumbawanga is a useful stopping point if you're travelling between Zambia or Mbeya and Katavi National Park. The market is a good place for stocking up (there's nothing to rival it

until you get to Mpanda or Mbeya), and the climate can be refreshingly cool, especially in the evenings. The surrounding Ufipa plateau, which lies at around 2000m, cradled between the eastern and western branches of the Great Rift Valley, is home to an ecologically important mixture of forests and montane grasslands.

East of Sumbawanga, below the escarpment, is the vast, shallow Lake Rukwa (p270).

Sleeping & Eating
Moravian Conference Centre (☎ 280 2853/4; conf cen@atma.co.tz; Nyerere Rd; standard s/d Tsh5000/10,000, executive s/d Tsh10,000/20,000) Sumbawanga's best value, with clean rooms and inexpensive meals. Breakfast is not included in the price of standard rooms. It's about 1km from the town centre along the road to the Regional Block area.

Upendo View Hotel (☎ 280 2242; Kiwelu Rd; d Tsh6500) Rooms are clean and fairly spacious, and the central location just southeast of the bus stand is convenient; the main disadvantage (if you want to sleep) is that it doubles as Sumbawanga's main nightspot, with a loud and popular disco on Friday and Saturday night. Meals are available from about Tsh1500.

Zanzibar Guest House (☎ 280 0010; d Tsh5000, s/d without bathroom Tsh2500/3500) Cheap and quieter than Upendo View; the en suite rooms are worth the splurge. It's just a few minute's walk from the bus stand, off Kiwelu Rd and south of Upendo View Hotel.

Forestway Country Club (☎ 280 2800; Nyerere Rd; r Tsh20,000) Sumbawanga's only proper hotel, with clean rooms and a good restaurant. It's about 2km from town along Nyerere Rd in the Regional Block area, past the Moravian Conference Centre (Tsh1500 in a taxi from the bus stand).

Sim's Restaurant (Kiwelu Rd; meals Tsh1000) A perennially popular place just opposite Upendo View Hotel, with a good, cheap menu featuring all the standards.

Getting There & Away
Sumry line buses run daily between Mbeya and Sumbawanga via Tunduma (for Zambia), departing in each direction between 6am and 7am (Tsh7500, six hours, book in advance). To Mpanda, Sumry has buses departing Sumbawanga at 1pm on Mon-

day, Wednesday and Friday (Tsh7500, seven hours). There are also daily 4WDs departing from the petrol station on the main road starting about 7am (Tsh8000). The road passes through Katavi National Park, though it's not necessary to pay park fees if you are just in transit.

KASANGA & KALAMBO FALLS

Plunging in a long, regal chute about 212m down the Rift Valley escarpment into Zambia are the Kalambo Falls. In addition to being Africa's second highest single-drop waterfall, the area is also important archaeologically, as the site of some major Stone Age finds.

The main access route to the falls is from Zambia, via Mbala. It's also possible to reach the falls from Kasanga, which is about 120km southwest of Sumbawanga on Lake Tanganyika and the last (or first) stop in Tanzania on the MV *Liemba* (see p326). From Kasanga, you'll need to get a lift towards the falls, and then walk for about four hours in each direction.

There is a very basic **guesthouse** (r without bathroom Tsh1500) in the Muzei section of Kasanga.

Trucks go sporadically between Sumbawanga and Kasanga, and a bus meets the *Liemba* arrivals (Tsh3500, up to nine hours). These arrivals can be anywhere between midnight and 6am, although the boat often remains at the dock until dawn. You're allowed to stay on board during this time, but the boat pulls out without much warning, so ask staff to wake you in time to disembark.

Southern Highlands

HIGHLIGHTS

- Sitting at dawn by the river in **Ruaha National Park** (p262), taking in the magnificence of the wild

- Watching lions in **Mikumi National Park** (p255)

- Cooling off under the spray of Sanje Falls in **Udzungwa Mountains National Park** (p257)

- Exploring off the beaten track in **Iringa** (p259), **Songea** (p274) or around **Mbeya** (p268)

- Getting away from it all on the shores of **Lake Nyasa** (p271)

Green, mist-shrouded hills rolling into the horizon, lively markets overflowing with produce, striking baobab-studded landscapes, jacaranda-lined streets and wildlife galore are among the attractions that await you in Tanzania's scenic and often overlooked Southern Highlands.

Officially, the Highlands begin at the Makambako Gap, about halfway between Iringa and Mbeya, and extend southwards into Malawi. Here, the term is used to designate the entire region along the mountainous chain running between Morogoro in the east and Lake Nyasa and the Zambian border in the west. In addition to being beautiful, the Highlands are also one of Tanzania's most important agricultural areas, producing a large proportion of the country's maize, as well as coffee, tea and other crops.

Perched off the northern edge of the highlands on the central Tanzanian plateau is dusty, arid Dodoma, Tanzania's official capital. To the east, near Morogoro, the lush Uluguru Mountains are home to the matrilineal Luguru people, plus many unique plant and bird species. Just southwest of here is the easily accessed Mikumi National Park, as well as Udzungwa Mountains National Park, an offbeat destination for hikers. Further west, past Iringa, is sublime and unspoiled Ruaha National Park, with stunning riverine scenery and one of Africa's largest elephant populations. The heart of the Southern Highlands is in the country's southwestern corner, which is filled with secluded valleys, rolling hills and verdant mountains that cascade down to the tranquil and seldom-trodden shores of Lake Nyasa.

While many travellers pass through the Southern Highlands en route to or from Malawi or Zambia, few stop along the way, even though there is much of interest. Facilities in most places are more than adequate and main roads are in generally good condition.

National Parks & Reserves

The Southern Highland's impressive array of parks includes Mikumi (p255) and Ruaha (p262) for wildlife watching, and Udzungwa Mountains (p257) for hiking. Mikumi is part of the Selous ecosystem; Ruaha is also part of a much larger ecosystem, which encompasses the adjoining Rungwa and Kisigo Game Reserves. For a profusion of spring wildflowers, head to the soon-to-be-declared Kitulo National Park (p271).

THE SOUTHERN HIGHLANDS

For more about the Southern Highlands region, see www.southernhighlandstz.org, or get a copy of Liz de Leyser's excellent *A Guide to the Southern Highlands of Tanzania*, available at many bookstores and hotels for Tsh5000.

Getting There & Around

There are airstrips in many towns, though no scheduled flights to anywhere except Ruaha National Park.

Getting around by road is quite straightforward, thanks to the good tarmac highway from Dar es Salaam southwest into Zambia, with tarmac branch routes leading to Songea and to Kyela, and between Morogoro and Dodoma. Apart from these, everything is unsealed.

Several ferries run on Lake Nyasa, with sporadic connections between towns on the Tanzanian side, and between Tanzania and Malawi; see p325.

DODOMA

☎ 026 / pop 150,000

Arid Dodoma sits in not-so-splendid isolation in the geographic centre of the country, at a height of about 1100m. Although

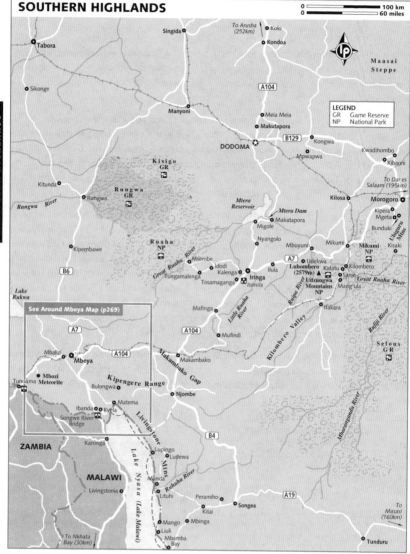

SOUTHERN HIGHLANDS

LEGEND
GR — Game Reserve
NP — National Park

the town was located along the old caravan route that connected Lake Tanganyika and Central Africa with the sea, it remained little more than a large village until the construction of the Central Line railway just after the turn of the 20th century.

Since 1973 Dodoma has been Tanzania's official capital and headquarters of the rul-

ing CCM party. According to the original plan, the entire government was to move to Dodoma by the mid-1980s, and the town was to be expanded to ultimately encompass more than 300,000 residents, all living in smaller independent communities set up along the lines of the *ujamaa* (familyhood) village. The plans proved unrealistic for a

ARIADNE VAN ZANDBERGEN

Elephants under an acacia bush, Tarangire National Park (p199)

ARIADNE VAN ZANDBERGEN

Lone giraffe in front of Mt Meru (p194)

Hippos swimming in Lake Magadi in the Ngorongoro Crater (p208), Ngorongoro Conservation Area

DAVID WALL

ARIADNE VAN ZANDBERGEN

Giraffes in the Katavi National Park (p243)

JASON EDWARDS

Waves lapping the shore of Lake Tanganyika (p239) on Tanzania's western border

JASON EDWARDS

Olive baboon and young, Gombe Stream National Park (p236)

Watching for the local chimp population of Mahale Mountains National Park (p237)

ARIADNE VAN ZAND

variety of reasons, including a lack of any sort of viable economic base and an insufficient water supply, and have therefore been abandoned. Today, although the legislature meets in Dodoma – hence the periodic profusion of 4WDs along its dusty streets – Dar es Salaam remains the unrivalled economic and political centre of the country.

There's little reason to come to Dodoma. However, if you find yourself here, it's not a bad place to spend a day or two. With its grandiose street layout and the imposing architecture of many church and government buildings – all sharply contrasting with the slow-paced reality of daily life – it's easy to get the feeling that the town is dressed in clothes that are several sizes too big.

Orientation

From the bus stand, the main (Dar es Salaam) road heads west into the centre of town where it meets Kuu St at a large roundabout. Just south of here are the railway tracks, after which everything turns to small dusty lanes. To the north, a warren of small avenues run off Kuu St into the busiest part of town, with the market and lots of shops. Further north is the airfield, and to the north and east are several large and rather bare residential areas and a few hotels.

Information

EMERGENCY & MEDICAL SERVICES

Aga Khan Hospital (☎ 232 1789; Sixth St; ✆ 8am-8pm Mon-Sat, 9am-noon Sun) On a small side street just northeast of Food Junction.

Mission Aviation Fellowship (☎ 235 2810/6; Dodoma Airfield) Evacuation assistance in medical emergencies.

Twins Chemist (☎ 232 1511; cnr Kuu St & Mpwapwa Rd; ✆ 8am-9pm Mon-Sat, 10am-9pm Sun)

INTERNET ACCESS

Aladdin's Cave (per hr Tsh1000; ✆ 9.30am-1pm & 3.30-8.30pm Tue-Sun, 9.30am-1pm Mon)

RAL Internet Café (Kuu St; per 80min Tsh1000; ✆ 8am-9pm Mon-Sat, 2-9pm Sun) Just north of the main roundabout.

MONEY

NBC (Kuu St) Changes cash and travellers cheques, and has an ATM.

POST

Main post office (Railway St) Just west of the train station.

Dangers & Annoyances

Because Dodoma has so many government buildings, photography is prohibited in most areas of town.

Sights & Activities

MUSEUM OF GEOSCIENCES

This rather forlorn **museum** (Nyumba ya Mayonyesho ya Madini; adult/child Tsh500/100; ✆ 8am-3.30pm Mon-Fri) contains rock samples and geological information on the entire country, and is worth a stop if you are geologically inclined. It's inside the compound of the Ministry of Energy and Minerals, behind New Dodoma Hotel.

OTHER ATTRACTIONS

There's a small swimming pool and a squash court at **Climax Swimming Club** (admission Tsh1500; ✆ noon-7pm Tue-Thu, noon-9pm Fri, 10am-9pm Sat, noon-8pm Sun), situated about 2.5km west of the city centre.

Lion Rock, which overlooks Dodoma from the northeast, makes a decent hike (about 45 minutes to the top). There have been some muggings here, so don't bring any valuables and go in a group. To get to the base, ask any *dalla-dalla* (minibus) driver heading out on the Arusha road to drop you nearby, or take a taxi. If driving, hire a guard to watch your vehicle. The enticing-looking hill to the southwest of town near the swimming pool is off limits because of the nearby prison.

If you're intrigued by religious architecture, Dodoma has several places of interest, including the **Anglican church** in the town centre, the large **Lutheran cathedral** opposite, the **Ismaili mosque** nearby and the enormous **Catholic cathedral** just west along the railroad tracks.

The **parliament** *(Bunge)* is housed in a modern complex on the eastern edge of town just off the Dar es Salaam road. It's possible to observe when it's in session; bring your passport along.

Dodoma is the centre of Tanzania's tiny wine industry, and there are vineyards throughout the surrounding area, originally started by Italian missionaries in the early 20th century. Most of what is produced is for church use, and the commercially available vintage won't win awards any time soon. However, it's possible to visit some of the wineries to see the production process.

SOUTHERN HIGHLANDS

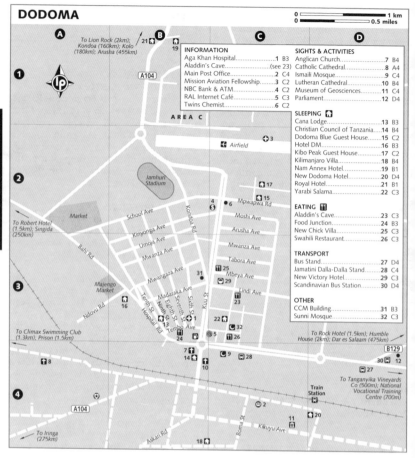

DODOMA

INFORMATION
Aga Khan Hospital.....................1 B3
Aladdin's Cave.....................(see 23)
Main Post Office.....................2 C4
Mission Aviation Fellowship.....3 C2
NBC Bank & ATM.....................4 C2
RAL Internet Café.....................5 C3
Twins Chemist.....................6 C2

SIGHTS & ACTIVITIES
Anglican Church.....................7 B4
Catholic Cathedral.....................8 A4
Ismaili Mosque.....................9 C4
Lutheran Cathedral.....................10 B4
Museum of Geosciences.....11 C4
Parliament.....................12 D4

SLEEPING
Cana Lodge.....................13 B3
Christian Council of Tanzania.....14 B4
Dodoma Blue Guest House.....15 C2
Hotel DM.....................16 B3
Kibo Peak Guest House.....17 C2
Kilimanjaro Villa.....................18 B4
Nam Annex Hotel.....................19 B1
New Dodoma Hotel.....................20 D4
Royal Hotel.....................21 B1
Yarabi Salama.....................22 C3

EATING
Aladdin's Cave.....................23 C3
Food Junction.....................24 B3
New Chick Villa.....................25 C3
Swahili Restaurant.....................26 C3

TRANSPORT
Bus Stand.....................27 D4
Jamatini Dalla-Dalla Stand.....28 C4
New Victory Hotel.....................29 C3
Scandinavian Bus Station.....30 D4

OTHER
CCM Building.....................31 B3
Sunni Mosque.....................32 C3

The closest one to Dodoma is **Tanganyika Vineyards Company**, about 2km southeast of town, off the Dar es Salaam road.

Dodoma is also a good springboard to Kolo (180km north) and its centuries-old **rock paintings** (p190).

Sleeping

Water supplies are erratic, so expect bucket baths at the cheaper hotels. Also, hotels fill up whenever parliament is in session, so don't be surprised if you need to try several before finding a room.

BUDGET

Christian Council of Tanzania (CCT; ☎ 232 1682; s/d Tsh4500/9000, r without bathroom Tsh4500) This is the most convenient budget lodging in town, with a central location (at the main roundabout, next to the Anglican church), tatty but tolerable rooms with mosquito nets, and buckets of hot water for bathing on request. Breakfast costs extra; other meals can be arranged with advance notice.

Kibo Peak Guest House (☎ 232 2902; s Tsh7000, s with TV Tsh10,000) Clean, reasonable-value rooms with fan and net, and an almost exclusively male clientele. It's about 1km north of the main roundabout off Mpwapwa Rd (reached via Kuu St).

Dodoma Blue Guest House (☎ 234 2085; Mpwapwa Rd; r Tsh10,000) Just around the corner from Kibo Peak, and of similar standard. Rooms have nets and small double beds.

Other recommendations:

Yarabi Salama (r without bathroom Tsh2500) The cheapest recommendable option near the bus station, with very basic rooms and a friendly proprietor. It's about a 10-minute walk west of the bus stand, and two blocks east of Kuu St.

Kilimanjaro Villa (☎ 235 2258; s/d without bathroom Tsh4000/5000) Has friendly staff, basic, stuffy rooms and a small bar. It's on a quiet side street behind the High Court.

MID-RANGE & TOP END

New Dodoma Hotel (Dodoma Rock Hotel; ☎ 232 1641; dodomahotel@kicheko.com; Railway St; s/d with fan Tsh35,000/50,000, s/d with air-con Tsh50,000/75,000; meals Tsh4000-6000; ✖ ☐ ☎) The former Railway Hotel has been renovated and is now Dodoma's most upmarket option, with attentive staff, a large inner courtyard, pleasant rooms and a restaurant with a good-value, if uninspired, dinner buffet.

Humble House (☎ 235 2261; hhousetz@yahoo.com; Area E; s/d Tsh10,000/12,000; meals Tsh3000; ☐) This B&B-style place run by the Anglican church is a welcome change from Dodoma's profusion of homogenised mid-range hotels. Rooms (some with Western-style sit-down toilets, others with the squat version, and two sharing bathroom) are good value. There's also a small garden for relaxing lunch/dinner on request and – soon – an Internet connection. It's mainly an option if you have your own transport, as it's buried away in a maze of dirt lanes in Area E (also known as Ipagala), and signposted from the Dar es Salaam road about 2.5km east of town.

National Vocational Training Centre (NVTC, VETA; ☎ 232 2181; s/d Tsh13,000/17,000, s without bathroom Tsh8500; meals from Tsh3500) Another good alternative to the standard hotel scene, with simple, clean rooms, professional staff and a restaurant. It's set in pleasant grounds about 2km east of the centre off the Dar es Salaam road.

Cana Lodge (☎ 232 1199; costerki@yahoo.com; Ninth St; s/ste Tsh10,000/40,000, d Tsh13,000-18,000) A new and spotless place with small, sterile rooms and a restaurant.

There are a plethora of other mid-range hotels, all with clean, bland rooms with mosquito net, TV and bathroom, and all remarkably similar in price and standards. They include the following:

Nam Annex Hotel (☎ 232 2255; Area C; s/d Tsh15,000/20,000) Decent rooms in new and old wings, a restaurant and an unreliable water supply. It's just north of the airfield, and 30 minutes on foot from the centre of town.

Royal Hotel (☎ 230 0343; s/d Tsh12,000/15,000, without bathroom Tsh10,000/12,000) Just across the main road from Nam Annex Hotel and similar, but newer.

Robert Hotel (☎ 230 0306, 230 2252; s Tsh7000-18,000) In the Kizota area, about 3km west of town on the Singida road. There's a large poster of Switzerland dominating the reception, to remind you of where you aren't.

Hotel DM (☎ 232 1001; s/d Tsh12,000/17,000, without bathroom Tsh8000/10,000) At the base of Mwangaza Ave, near Majengo market.

Rock Hotel (☎ 232 0027; rockyhotel2003@yahoo.com; s/d Tsh15,000/18,000) About 2km east of town on the Dar es Salaam road.

Eating

Aladdin's Cave (snacks Tsh500-1500; ✆ 9.30am-1pm Mon, 9.30am-1pm & 3.30-8.30pm Tue-Sun) Great milkshakes, soft-serve ice cream and other snacks. It's one block east of Kuu St, north of the Ismaili mosque.

Swahili Restaurant (meals from Tsh1500; ✆ lunch & dinner) This is a good place to mix with locals, and it has a wide selection of inexpensive Indian snacks and standard fare, including yogurt and a few vegetarian dishes. It's near the roundabout and one block north of the Dar es Salaam road.

Food Junction (Tembo Ave; meals from Tsh1000; ✆ 8.30am-3.30pm & 6.45-10pm Mon-Sat) This popular spot for budget meals serves chicken and rice, and various Indian snacks. It's near the main roundabout, two blocks west of Kuu St.

New Chick Villa (Kuu St; ✆ until 6.30pm) Another local favourite, with the usual assortment of snacks, chicken and chips.

Shopping

Dodoma is noted for its crafts, including *marimbas* (musical instruments played with the thumb), *vibuyu* (carved gourds), wooden stools and other items made by the local Gogo people. Sisal crafts are available from the prison to the west of town with an advance order.

Getting There & Away
AIR

There are currently no commercial flights to Dodoma. If you arrive on a charter, the airfield is about 2km north of the main roundabout (Tsh1500 in a taxi).

BUS

The best connection to/from Dar es Salaam is with Scandinavian Express, with daily departures in each direction at 9.15am (luxury Tsh9000) and 11am (ordinary Tsh6500), both taking six hours. Scandinavian buses depart from their terminal about 1km east of town along the Dar es Salaam road. There are several other daily buses to Dar es Salaam that depart from the main bus station, with the last departure at about 11am.

To Iringa, there's a daily bus via Makatapora; for details see p261.

To Kondoa, Satellite Coach has daily buses departing from the main bus stand in Dodoma about noon daily (Tsh4000, four to five hours). From Kondoa, it's easy to get onward transport to Kolo. Alternatively, there's a bus departing from New Victory Hotel off Kuu St, diagonally opposite the CCM building, at 6am Monday, Wednesday and Saturday to Kondoa, and then continuing on to Kolo (Tsh5000). Going in the other direction, there is a direct bus from Kolo to Dodoma on Sunday, Tuesday and Thursday, departing Kolo about 3.30am, reaching Kondoa by 5am, and then continuing to Dodoma.

To Singida, it's best to take the train (p332). Otherwise, there are direct buses (Tsh5000, at least eight hours) coming from Dar es Salaam that pass Dodoma's main bus station about noon, although they are often full.

The *dalla-dalla* stand, known as Jamatini, is on the Dar es Salaam road just east of the Ismaili mosque.

TRAIN

Dodoma lies on the Central Line connecting Dar es Salaam with Kigoma and Mwanza. Departures from Dodoma westwards are about 8am, and about 6pm eastwards. There's also a spur line between Dodoma and Singida; see p332 for more.

MOROGORO
☎ 023

Bustling, sprawling Morogoro would be a fairly scruffy town were it not for its verdant setting at the foot of the Uluguru Mountains, which brood over the landscape from the southeast. The surrounding area is one of the country's breadbaskets, home to the prestigious Sokoine University (Tanzania's

national agricultural institute) and a major educational and mission station. While there's a dearth of tourist attractions in Morogoro itself, it's an unpretentious place and a good introduction to Tanzanian life outside Dar es Salaam. Just outside town is some easily arranged hiking.

Information
IMMIGRATION OFFICE
The immigration office is signposted about 200m south of the main road, though officials usually ask you to go to Dar es Salaam to handle visa extensions.

INTERNET ACCESS
Morogoro Internet Café (Mahenge St; per hr Tsh1000; ⏰ 9am-7pm) Next to Princess Lodge.
Wats Internet Café (Mahenge St; per hr Tsh1000; ⏰ 8.30am-9pm) Diagonally opposite Princess Lodge.

MEDICAL SERVICES
Bede Pharmacy (☎ 260 0333; Mahenge St)
Morogoro Medical Stores Pharmacy (☎ 4251; Old Dar es Salaam Rd) Also open Sunday mornings.

MONEY
NBC (Old Dar es Salaam Rd) Changes cash and travellers cheques, and has an ATM.

POST & TELEPHONE
You'll still find a few old four-digit telephone numbers in Morogoro. If they don't work, try adding 260 at the beginning.
Main post office (Old Dar es Salaam Rd) With cardphones nearby.

Sights & Activities
The best thing to do is head into the hills outside town for hiking. With your own clubs, you could try the **golf course** opposite Morogoro Hotel. The **market** sometimes has good deals on textiles.

Morogoro is also a logical base for excursions to Mikumi National Park (p255), although you'll need to have your own vehicle or rent one in Dar es Salaam, as they're difficult to find in Morogoro.

Sleeping
BUDGET
Princess Lodge (☎ 4122, 0744-319159; Mahenge St; r without bathroom Tsh7000) This is the best shoestring option, with clean, small rooms, all with double bed, fan and net, plus helpful

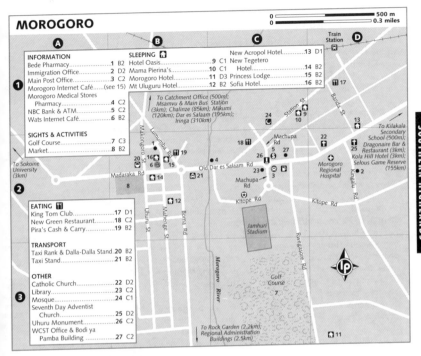

MOROGORO

INFORMATION
Bede Pharmacy	1	B2
Immigration Office	2	D2
Main Post Office	3	C2
Morogoro Internet Café	(see 15)	
Morogoro Medical Stores Pharmacy	4	C2
NBC Bank & ATM	5	C2
Wats Internet Café	6	B2

SIGHTS & ACTIVITIES
Golf Course	7	C3
Market	8	B2

SLEEPING
Hotel Oasis	9	C1
Mama Pierina's	10	C1
Morogoro Hotel	11	D3
Mt Uluguru Hotel	12	B2
New Acropol Hotel	13	D1
New Tegetero Hotel	14	B2
Princess Lodge	15	B2
Sofia Hotel	16	B2

EATING
King Tom Club	17	D1
New Green Restaurant	18	C2
Pira's Cash & Carry	19	B2

TRANSPORT
Taxi Rank & Dalla-Dalla Stand	20	B2
Taxi Stand	21	B2

OTHER
Catholic Church	22	D2
Library	23	C2
Mosque	24	C1
Seventh Day Adventist Church	25	D2
Uhuru Monument	26	C2
WCST Office & Bodi ya Pamba Building	27	C2

management and a good restaurant downstairs. It's one block in from the main road in the town centre.

Sofia Hotel (☎ 260 4848; Mahenge St; s/d Tsh12,000/15,000, without bathroom Tsh6000/7000) A long-standing place with small, clean rooms and a restaurant. It's diagonally opposite Princess Lodge.

Mt Uluguru Hotel (☎ 260 4153, 260 3489; d Tsh15,000) This nondescript multistorey hotel is worth a look for its convenient location. Rooms are reasonable (ask for one with a view) and there's an inexpensive restaurant and a large outdoor bar. It's south of the main road, just off Mahenge St.

New Tegetero Hotel (☎ 3398; Madaraka Rd; r Tsh5800) The New Tegetero, in a drab highrise building on the busy main street, looks like a bit of a dump, but the price is right and there's cheap food downstairs. Breakfast costs extra.

Mama Pierina's (Station St; d Tsh9000) The location is quieter and nicer than that of New Tegetero, but rooms – all with nets and fan, and set around a tiny garden – are well past their prime and have paper-thin walls. At-

tached is a restaurant serving large portions of unexciting food.

MID-RANGE & TOP END

Hotel Oasis (☎ 4178, 3010; hoteloasistz@morogoro .net; Station St; s/d/tr US$35/40/50;) The Oasis is the best bet in the town centre, with pleasant, good-value rooms – all with fan, air-con, TV and small fridge – plus grassy grounds, efficient staff and a busy restaurant. The room price includes a good breakfast buffet.

New Acropol Hotel (☎ 3403, 0744-309410; new acropolhotel@morogoro.net; s/d from US$42/48;) This slick, upmarket, B&B-style hotel is popular with expats. It has a handful of spacious rooms (all with TV and large double bed) and a classy restaurant (p255). It's about 300m east of the centre on Old Dar es Salaam Rd.

Kola Hill Hotel (☎ 260 4394, 260 3707; r with fan/ air-con US$35/45;) The uninspired rooms at this hotel – all are doubles or twins, and some have TV – are redeemed by the setting in a green and quiet semirural area about 3km east of the centre, and the hotel

HIKING IN THE ULUGURU MOUNTAINS

Rising up from the plains just southeast of Morogoro are the Uluguru Mountains, which belong to the Eastern Arc chain and contain some of Africa's oldest original forest; certain areas are estimated to be about 25 million years old. The mountains are also notable for hosting an impressive variety of birds, plants and insects, including many unique species such as the Uluguru bush shrike. The only comparable mountain-forest area in East Africa, as far as age and endemism are concerned, is the Usambaras (p152).

The main tribal group in the mountains are the matrilineal Luguru, who earn their living primarily through subsistence agriculture, and who have managed to maintain much of their rich traditional culture intact. Due to the high population density in the Ulugurus, most of the original forest cover has been depleted – you'll see this immediately on the hillsides – with only a few small protected patches remaining on the upper slopes. Accompanying the deforestation has been severe erosion. Despite this, the mountains offer rewarding hiking, and are well worth exploration if you're in the area. Come prepared with a jacket, as it can rain at any time of year.

From Morogoro, the most popular route is to **Morningside**, an old German mountain hut to the south of town at about 1000m. The path, which can easily be done in half a day return, starts at the regional administration buildings about 3km south of Morogoro at the end of Boma Rd. From here, a track leads uphill and then curves to the right through small farm plots and degraded forest before reaching the Morningside hut. It's possible to camp at Morningside with your own tent and supplies; there's a small waterfall nearby. Once at Morningside, it takes another 40 minutes or so to reach the border of the Uluguru North Forest Reserve. It's generally not permitted to continue beyond here, because of sensitivities about the Bondwe Peak communications tower higher up the slopes.

Another possibility from town is the hike to **Lupanga Peak** (2147m), the highest point in the immediate vicinity, although views from the top are obscured by the forest. The starting point is at Kilakala Secondary School, 1km east of town off Old Dar es Salaam Rd. The trek is detailed in the Uluguru tourist-information booklet mentioned following; allow about five hours return. Since part of the hike is in the forest reserve, you'll need to first get a permit (Tsh4000) from the Catchment Office in Morogoro. It's 1.5km north of the town centre on the road to Msamvu junction, in an unmarked building on the left just after crossing the second set of railway tracks. If you have access to a 4WD, there are several good walks from Bunduki, about 2½ to three hours drive south of Morogoro.

The Wildlife Conservation Society of Tanzania (WCST), in collaboration with the Uluguru Mountains Biodiversity Conservation Project, has published the very helpful *Tourist Information for the Uluguru Mountains*, with detailed route descriptions and information on places to stay. It's for sale at the **WCST office** (☎ 023-3122; uluguru@morogoro.net; 1st fl, Bodi ya Pamba Bldg, Old Dar es Salaam Rd) in the centre of Morogoro, or can be downloaded for free (www.africanconservation.com/uluguru; click on Contents, then on Section 4). The WCST office is also the best place to arrange a guide.

is a reasonable choice if you have your own transport. Meals are available. It's about 300m off Old Dar es Salaam Rd along the Bigwa *dalla-dalla* route, with the turn-off signposted opposite the Teachers' College Morogoro.

Morogoro Hotel (☎ 3270/1/2; Rwegasore Rd; s/d from US$20/25) Once a Morogoro institution, this place is now well past its prime. Accommodation is in bungalows that have seen better days, although the location – in appealing green grounds about 1.5km off the main road, opposite the golf course – goes some way to compensate. It's popular for weddings and other functions on weekends, which can mean loud music until late.

Eating & Drinking

Princess Lodge (☎ 4122, 0744-319159; Mahenge St; meals Tsh2000; ◷ breakfast, lunch & dinner) Bright and friendly, this place is the best bet for local dishes, with efficient service and meals promised in '30 minutes or less'.

New Green Restaurant (☎ 4021; Station St; meals from Tsh3000; ◷ lunch & dinner, closed dinner Sun) A long-standing establishment with Indian dishes, grilled chicken and a few vegetarian choices.

Dragonaire Bar & Restaurant (☎ 0748-470713; ☺ lunch & dinner daily, breakfast Sat & Sun) Nice, green grounds, a good mix of locals and expats, and delicious pizzas on weekends. Accommodation is planned. It's signposted about 2.5km east of town, and about 700m off the Old Dar es Salaam Rd.

New Acropol Hotel (☎ 3403, 0744-309410; newacro polhotel@morogoro.net; ☺ closed Mon) Morogoro's classiest restaurant, the New Acropol has *nouvelle cuisine*–style meals, a well-stocked bar and excellent local coffee (you can also buy some to bring home).

King Tom Club (Station St; meals Tsh1000; ☺ 7am-11pm) Grilled pork, *ugali* and beer are the features – actually the only offerings – at this colourful local hang-out. It's near the train station, with seating under *bandas* (thatched-roof hut) in an outdoor garden.

For self-catering, try **Pira's Cash & Carry** (Lumumba Rd), just north of the main road.

Getting There & Away
BUS
The main bus station is about 3km north of town on the main Dar es Salaam road in Msamvu, about 300m east of the roundabout (Tsh1500 in a taxi and Tsh150 in a *dalla-dalla*).

Scandinavian Express buses go daily to Dodoma, Mikumi, Iringa, Mbeya and Dar es Salaam, but as none originate in Morogoro it's best to book in advance. The Scandinavian office is at the bus station. To Dar es Salaam, there are also many local buses, from 5.45am until about 4pm (Tsh2000, 3½ hours).

There are several buses, including Hood, that do the route to Arusha daily (Tsh7500, nine hours), but none are recommended.

To Tanga, there is a direct bus daily (Tsh4000, five hours), departing by 8am.

The main *dalla-dalla* stand is in front of the market, where there is also a taxi rank.

TRAIN
Morogoro is on the Central Line (p332), but to Dar es Salaam it's several hours faster to travel by bus.

MIKUMI NATIONAL PARK
Mikumi, part of the vast Selous ecosystem, is Tanzania's fourth-largest national park. It's also the most accessible from Dar es Salaam, and – with almost guaranteed sightings of wildlife – makes an ideal destination for a budget safari, or for those who don't have much time. Within its 3230 sq km, set between the Uluguru Mountains to the north and the Lumango Mountains to the southeast, Mikumi hosts buffaloes, giraffes, elephants, lions, zebras, leopards, crocodiles and more, and chances are high that you'll see a good sampling of these within a short time of entering the park.

The best and most reliable viewing is around the Mkata floodplains, to the northwest of the main road. Among other attractions here are the Hippo Pools, where you can watch these lumbering behemoths at close range, plus do some fine birding.

To the south, Mikumi is contiguous with Selous Game Reserve, although there's currently no official road linking the two and only minimal road development for driving around. More feasible is a combination of Mikumi with Udzungwa National Park, which is about a two-hour drive south.

Mikumi is an important educational and research centre. Among the various projects being carried out is an ongoing field study of yellow baboons, which is one of just a handful of such long-term primate studies on the continent.

Information
Entry fees are US$15/5 per adult/child aged five to 15 years. For camping fees see p35. Mikumi can be visited year-round, though it's best in the dry season – during the rainy season (from about December to April) some areas become inaccessible. For information and camp-site bookings, contact the **senior park warden** (☎ 023-262 0498). Foxes African Safaris, which runs two lodges in the park, has safari vehicles for its guests. Otherwise, you'll need to either have your own vehicle to visit the park, or arrange an organised tour. Guided walking safaris can be arranged at the park entrance.

Sleeping
The park has four ordinary camp sites, for which you'll need to be self-sufficient. The two closest to the park headquarters have toilet facilities, and one has a shower. There is a special camp site near Choga Wale in the north of the park; permission to camp elsewhere can be requested from park headquarters, and is charged at special camp-site

rates. There is also a hostel for students, which must be reserved in advance through park headquarters; bring your own food and other supplies.

Foxes Safari Camp (☎ 0748-237422, 0744-237422; www.tanzaniasafaris.info; s/d all-inclusive US$280/470; ☕) This camp, operated by the same family that operates Ruaha River Lodge (in Ruaha National Park), is attractively set on a rocky outcrop in a good wildlife-viewing area in Mikumi's far north. It's the most intimate camp in the park, with just eight en suite tents and wide views over the surrounding Mkata plains. It's also the one with the most authentic wilderness feel – set 13km inside the park's northeastern boundary, and accessed via a signposted turn-off about 25km northeast of the main park gate. Walks and fly camping can be arranged.

Kikoboga (☎ 022-2600352/4; obhotel@acexnet.com; s/d full board US$120/200; ☕) Kikoboga, about 500m northeast of the park gate, has nice stone cottages spread out on a grassy field frequented by grazing zebras and gazelles. Given its proximity to the highway, it's not a wilderness experience, but the animals don't seem to mind, and you'll probably see plenty from your front porch.

Vuma Tented Camp (☎ 0748-237422, 0744-237422; www.tanzaniasafaris.info; s/d all-inclusive US$280/470; ☕) An attractive, easily accessed and popular camp set on a rise about 7km south of the main road, and under the same management as Foxes Safari Camp. The 16 tented en suite cottages each have a double and a single bed, the mood is relaxed and the cuisine is good. The turn-off is diagonally opposite the park entry gate.

Also see Sleeping options in Mikumi town (right), 23km west.

Getting There & Around
BUS
Although getting to the gate of Mikumi is easy via public transport (take any of the buses running along the Morogoro–Iringa highway and ask the driver to drop you), there is no vehicle rental at the park, so you'll need your own car unless you've arranged otherwise with one of the lodges. It's often possible to see animals along the road side if you're passing through on a bus, especially if you travel in the early morning or evening, but the buses move too fast for decent viewing. The best budget way to visit

the park is on one of the frequent special deals offered by Coastal Travels and other Dar es Salaam–based tour operators, or to take the bus to Mikumi town and organise transport to the park through Genesis Motel (see below).

CAR
The park gate is about a four-hour drive from Dar es Salaam; speed limits on the section of main highway inside the park are controlled (70km/h during the day and 50km/h at night). Some roads in Mikumi's northern section are accessible with a 2WD during the dry season, but in general 4WD is best.

TRAIN
For a good splurge, take the private luxury train run by Foxes African Safaris between Dar es Salaam and Kidatu (about 40km south of Mikumi town); see p302.

MIKUMI
☎ 023
Mikumi is the last of the lowland towns along the Dar es Salaam–Mbeya highway before it starts its climb up into the hills and mountains of the Southern Highlands. The town itself is stretched out along a few kilometres of highway, and has an unmistakable truck-stop feel. It's of interest almost exclusively as a transit point for visits to the Mikumi or Udzungwa Mountains National Parks, though it's quite possible to visit both without overnighting here.

Sleeping & Eating
Genesis Motel (☎ 262 0461; camping with shower Tsh3000, r per person Tsh15,000) This small hotel is located on the edge of Mikumi town, directly on the main highway and about 2.5km east of the Ifakara junction. The setting is noisy and a bit too close to the truck stops to be enjoyable, but rooms are fine for the price, staff are helpful and there's a decent restaurant (Mikumi's best). It's also a good place to organise budget safaris to Mikumi park (from US$30 to US$50 per person, transport only) and transport to Udzungwa Mountains park.

Kilimanjaro Village Inn (☎ 262 0429; d from Tsh8500, s/d without bathroom Tsh3500/6000) A reliable budget place with an assortment of reasonable, no-frills rooms and a restaurant.

It's about 1km east of the Ifakara junction, and just west of the railway tracks.

Getting There & Away

Minibuses heading towards Udzungwa Mountains National Park (Tsh2000, two hours) leave throughout the day from the Ifakara junction just south of the highway. Direct buses on the Dar es Salaam–Mbeya route stop along the main highway just east of the Ifakara junction. Few buses originate in Mikumi, so you'll need to stand on the road side and wait until one comes by with space.

Going west, the best bet is Scandinavian Express from Dar es Salaam, which passes Mikumi daily on its routes to Iringa, Mbeya and Songea, beginning about 9.30am. There is also a direct bus from Kilombero to Iringa, passing Mikumi about 5.30am. Going east, buses to Dar es Salaam start to pass Mikumi from 8.30am.

UDZUNGWA MOUNTAINS NATIONAL PARK

Towering steeply over the Kilombero Plains about 350km southwest of Dar es Salaam are the wild, lushly forested slopes of the Udzungwa Mountains, portions of which are protected as part of Udzungwa Mountains National Park. In addition to an abundance of unique plants, the park is home to a healthy population of primates (10 species – more than in any of Tanzania's other parks) and makes an intriguing offbeat destination for anyone botanically inclined or interested in hiking well away from the crowds.

The going can be tough in parts: the trail network is limited, and those trails that do exist are often muddy, steep, humid and densely overgrown. Infrastructure is rudimentary and you'll need to have your own tent and do your hiking accompanied by a guide. But the night-time symphony of forest insects, the rushing of countless streams and waterfalls and the views down over the plains compensate. Plus, because the Udzungwas aren't on the way to anywhere, relatively few travellers pass this way and you'll probably have most trails to yourself.

The park was gazetted in 1992 with an area of 1900 sq km. Among its residents are the rare Iringa red colobus, the Sanje

> **DID YOU KNOW?**
>
> The Udzungwas' high degree of endemism and biodiversity is due, in large part, to the area's constant climate over millions of years, which has given species a chance to evolve. Another factor is the Udzungwas' altitudinal range. From the low-lying Kilombero Valley south of the park (at approximately 200m) to Luhombero Peak (the park's highest point at 2579m), there is continuous forest, making this one of the few places in Africa with continuous rainforest over such a great span.

crested mangabey and the Udzungwa forest partridge, which has been sighted near the park's boundaries. While there are also elephants, buffaloes, leopards, hippos and crocodiles, these – particularly hippos and crocodiles – are primarily in the park's southwest and are seldom seen along the main hiking routes.

There are no roads in Udzungwa; instead, there are about five major, and several lesser, hiking trails winding through various sections of the park. Most trails are on the eastern side of the park, although development is starting in the west. The most popular route is a short (three to five hours) but steep circuit from Sanje village through the forest to **Sanje Falls**, where swimming and camping are possible. More satisfying is the two-night, three-day (or two long days, if you're fit) hike up to **Mwanihana Peak** (2080m), the park's second-highest point. The challenging four- to five-day trail from Mang'ula to **Luhombero Peak** is currently not cleared, although it's worth checking with park headquarters for an update on this, as well as about the six-day **Lumemo Trail**, and shorter day trails planned for the baobab-studded northwestern corner of the park around Mbatwa Ranger Post.

Information

Entry fees are US$15/5 per adult/child aged five to 15 years. For camping fees, see p35. Porter fees range between Tsh3000 and Tsh6000 per day, depending on the trail.

The park is best visited between June and October. For all hikes, you'll need to be accompanied by a guide (US$15 per day, or US$25 for an armed ranger guide necessary for longer hikes). For birding, bring your own field guide along, as none are available at the park. For overnight hikes, allow an extra day at Mang'ula to organise things, and time to get from park headquarters to the trailheads.

The entrance gate, **park headquarters** (☎ 023-262 0224; www.udzungwa.org) and the senior park warden's office are located in Mang'ula, 60km south of Mikumi town along the Ifakara road. There are plans to open an entry post at Udekwa village, on the western side of the park, which would be useful if you are coming from Iringa or want to climb Luhombero Peak from the west, though for now, all visitors must pass by Mang'ula.

There's a tiny market in Mang'ula near the train station, and another small one in town to the north of the station, both with only limited selections. It's a good idea to stock up on major items in Dar es Salaam or Morogoro and – if you'll be staying in the park for a while – to bring a supply of dried fruit and nuts to supplement the bland locally available offerings. You can usually find bottled water near the markets.

Sleeping

There are three rudimentary camp sites near park headquarters, one with a shower and the others near a stream, though visitors rarely stay at them as they cost US$20 per person for the most basic facilities, versus Tsh2000 for the nearby Udzungwa Mountain View Hotel. You'll need a tent and all your own supplies. The main site is signposted about 100m south of the park gate. There are also several camp sites along the longer trails.

Udzungwa Mountain View Hotel (☎ 023-262 0260; camping Tsh2000, r per person Tsh15,000; meals about Tsh4500) This hotel, under the same management as Genesis Motel in Mikumi, is the best choice. Rooms are basic but clean, the forested setting is pleasant and the restaurant is surprisingly good. It's about 500m south of the park entrance, along the road.

Twiga Hotel (☎ 023-262 0239; r with/without bathroom Tsh5000/4000) Twiga has scruffy, no-frills rooms that are several notches down from those at Udzungwa Mountain View, though they are arguably better shoestring value. Meals can be arranged. It's just outside the park gate, about 200m off the road and signposted.

Getting There & Away
BUS

Minibuses and pick-ups run several times daily between Mikumi town (from the *dalla-dalla* stand on the Ifakara road just south of the main highway) and Kilombero, where you'll need to wait for onward transport towards Mang'ula. However, it's faster to wait for one of the larger direct buses coming from either Dar es Salaam or Morogoro to Ifakara, which pass Mikumi any time from about 8.30am to about 2pm. Going in the other direction, there are several departures each morning from Ifakara, passing Mang'ula any time from about 8am to noon; park staff can help you with the connection. The fare between Mang'ula and Mikumi is Tsh2500.

From both Dar es Salaam and Morogoro there are several buses daily to Ifakara and Mahenge via Mang'ula, departing between 6.30am and 10am (Tsh5500, seven to eight hours from Dar to Mang'ula).

From Iringa to Kilombero, there is one bus daily in each direction, departing around midday from Iringa and by 5am from Kilombero.

Allow plenty of time to get from the park gate (where you pay your entry fee) to Sanje village, 10km to the north, which is the trailhead for a few of the hikes. There are sporadic minibuses between Mang'ula and Sanje (Tsh500) and the occasional lorry. With luck, you may be able to arrange a lift on a park vehicle (Tsh10,000 one way). If you decide to walk, the only route is along the main road. Allow a day to get from Mang'ula to the western side of the park by road; you'll need your own transport or else take your chances on being able to arrange something with park staff.

TRAIN

Tazara ordinary trains stop at Mang'ula. The station is about a 30-minute walk from park headquarters; if you make advance arrangements, staff from the hotels will meet you. Express trains stop only at Ifakara, about 50km further south, and two hours by bus to Mang'ula. Much better is to take the private luxury train operated by Foxes African Safaris, which follows the Tazara line along the northern border of the Selous to Kidatu, about 25km north of the park gate; see p302.

IRINGA

☎ 026

With its bluff-top setting, jacaranda-lined streets and highland feel, Iringa is instantly likeable, and one of the most agreeable stops along the Dar es Salaam–Mbeya highway. The town, which is perched at a cool 1600m on a cliff overlooking the valley of the Little Ruaha River, was initially built up by the Germans at the turn of the century as a bastion against the local Hehe people. Now Iringa is a district capital, an agricultural centre and the gateway to Ruaha National Park.

Information

INTERNET ACCESS

JM Business Consulting (Uhuru Ave; per hr Tsh500; ☽ 8am-9.30pm Mon-Sat, 10am-9.30pm Sun)
MR Hotel (☎ 270 2006, 270 2779; www.mrhotel.co.tz; Mkwawa Rd; per hr Tsh1000; ☽ 7.30am-9.30pm)
Top Internet Café (Uhuru Ave; per 70 min Tsh1000; ☽ 8am-9pm) Near Hasty Tasty Too.

MEDICAL SERVICES

Aga Khan Health Centre (Jamat St; ☽ 8am-6pm Mon-Fri, 8am-2pm Sat & Sun) Next to the Lutheran cathedral.

MONEY

NBC (Uhuru Ave) Opposite the Catholic cathedral. Changes cash and travellers cheques and has an ATM.

TELEPHONE

JM Business Consulting (Uhuru Ave) Offers cheap Internet dialling and lets you receive calls without charge.
TTCL Next to the post office, just off Uhuru Ave.

TOURIST INFORMATION

Hasty Tasty Too (☎ 270 2061; shaffinhaji@hotmail .com; Uhuru Ave) The best place to organise budget vehicle safaris to Ruaha.

Sights & Activities

Iringa's colourful **market** is piled high with fruits and vegetables, plus countless other wares, including large, locally made Iringa baskets, and is well worth a stroll. Nearby, in front of the police station, is a **monument** to the Africans who fell during the Maji Maji uprising between 1905 and 1907. West along this same street is Iringa's main trading area, dominated by the impressive German-built **Ismaili Mosque** with its distinctive clock tower.

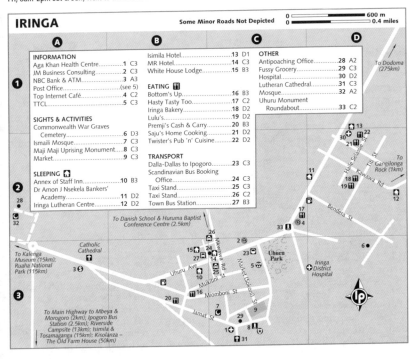

IRINGA

Some Minor Roads Not Depicted

0 ___ 600 m
0 ___ 0.4 miles

INFORMATION		
Aga Khan Health Centre...............1	C3	
JM Business Consulting................2	C3	
NBC Bank & ATM............................3	A3	
Post Office......................................(see 5)		
Top Internet Café...........................4	C2	
TTCL..5	C3	

SIGHTS & ACTIVITIES		
Commonwealth War Graves		
Cemetery..................................6	D3	
Ismaili Mosque................................7	C3	
Maji Maji Uprising Monument....8	C3	
Market...9	C3	

SLEEPING		
Annex of Staff Inn.......................10	B3	
Dr Amon J Nsekela Bankers'		
Academy..................................11	D2	
Iringa Lutheran Centre...............12	D2	

Isimila Hotel................................13	D1	
MR Hotel.....................................14	C3	
White House Lodge.....................15	B3	

EATING		
Bottom's Up................................16	B3	
Hasty Tasty Too..........................17	C2	
Iringa Bakery..............................18	D2	
Lulu's..19	D2	
Premji's Cash & Carry.................20	B3	
Saju's Home Cooking..................21	D2	
Twister's Pub 'n' Cuisine............22	D2	

TRANSPORT		
Dalla-Dallas to Ipogoro............23	C3	
Scandinavian Bus Booking		
Office......................................24	C3	
Taxi Stand...................................25	C3	
Taxi Stand...................................26	C2	
Town Bus Station........................27	B3	

OTHER		
Antipoaching Office....................28	A2	
Fussy Grocery..............................29	C3	
Hospital......................................30	D2	
Lutheran Cathedral.....................31	C3	
Mosque.......................................32	A2	
Uhuru Monument		
Roundabout.............................33	C2	

CHIEF MKWAWA

Mkwawa, chief of the Hehe and one of German colonialism's most vociferous resisters, is a legendary figure in Tanzanian history. He is particularly revered in Iringa, near which he had his headquarters. Under Mkwawa's leadership during the second half of the 19th century, the Hehe became one of the most powerful tribes in central Tanzania. They overpowered one group after another until, by the late 1880s, they were threatening trade traffic along the caravan route from western Tanzania to Bagamoyo. In 1891, after several attempts by Mkwawa to negotiate with the Germans were rejected, his men trounced the colonial troops in the infamous battle of Lugalo, just outside Iringa on the Mikumi road. The next year, Mkwawa's troops launched a damaging attack on a German fort at Kilosa, further to the east.

The Germans placed a bounty on Mkwawa's head and, once they had regrouped, initiated a counterattack in which Mkwawa's headquarters at Kalenga were taken. Mkwawa escaped, but later, in 1898, committed suicide rather than surrender to a contingent that had been sent after him. His head was cut off and the skull sent to Germany, where it sat almost forgotten (though not by the Hehe) until it was returned to Kalenga in 1954. The return of Mkwawa's remains was due, in large part, to the efforts of Sir Edward Twining, then the British governor of Tanganyika. Today, the skull of Mkwawa and some old weapons are on display at the Kalenga museum.

The grave of Chief Mkwawa is about 40km outside Iringa and signposted about 11km off the main road to Ruaha National Park.

Keeping watch over town from the northeast is **Gangilonga Rock** (gangilonga means 'talking stone' in Hehe), which is where Chief Mkwawa often meditated and where he learned that the Germans were after him. It's an easy climb to the top, rewarded by wide views over town.

Southeast of town is a **Commonwealth War Graves Cemetery** with graves of the deceased from both world wars.

Sleeping
BUDGET
Riverside Campsite (☎ 272 5280/2; phillips@africaonline.co.tz; camping per person Tsh2500, tent rental Tsh2000) Riverside Campsite, 13km northeast of Iringa on the main road, has a lovely setting on the banks of the Little Ruaha River and all the basics for camping, including hot showers and cold drinks. To get here, take a *dalla-dalla* heading towards Ilula and ask the driver to drop you off (Tsh400). It's signposted and about 1.5km off the main road. Meals are available also (Tsh1500 for breakfast and Tsh2500 for lunch or dinner). Tents are sometimes available to rent and overland groups are welcome. Bring your own food supplies.

Iringa Lutheran Centre (☎ 270 2489; Kawawa Rd; d Tsh5000, s/d without bathroom Tsh2500/3500) This is a good shoestring option with relatively clean rooms, and food available on request. Breakfast costs Tsh500. It's on the north-

eastern edge of town, about 700m from the main road.

The **Annex of Staff Inn** (☎ 270 0165; Uhuru Ave; r Tsh7500-15,000) is a local favourite, along the main road near the bus station, with no-frills, somewhat-overpriced rooms and meals. For something cheaper, the same management also runs the less-appealing **White House Lodge** (☎ 270 0165; s/d without bathroom Tsh4000/6000) at the northern edge of the bus stand.

MID-RANGE & TOP END
Huruma Baptist Conference Centre (☎ 270 1532, 270 0184/2; camping per person with shower Tsh2500, s/d Tsh10,000/20,000) This place is set on large grounds about 3km from the town centre down Mkwawa Rd, near the Danish School. Rooms, while past their prime, are spacious, a few have mosquito nets, and filling, inexpensive meals are available. It's about a 25-minute walk from the town centre; *dalla-dallas* run every hour or so from the bus station, beginning about 7am, and will drop you at the junction 200m away from the conference centre.

MR Hotel (☎ 270 2006, 270 2779; www.mrhotel.co.tz; Mkwawa Rd; s/d/ste US$25/32/37; meals Tsh4000; 🔀 🖳) This good multistorey hotel next to the bus station has the corner on the business travellers' market, with efficient staff, modern rooms and a restaurant. It also organises car rental, Ruaha safaris and other excursions, including to Mtera Dam.

Isimila Hotel (☎ 270 1194; Uhuru Ave; s/d/ste Tsh9000/ 11,500/18,000) Some things never change and this hotel is one of them, looking almost exactly the same as it did almost a decade ago. Rooms are OK and reasonable value, plus there's an acceptable restaurant. It's past the Bankers' Academy at the northern end of town.

Dr Amon J Nsekela Bankers' Academy (☎ 270 2431; Uhuru Ave; s/ste Tsh8000/12,000) A former school that is as staid as its name would suggest, with clean but soulless rooms and an institutional ambience. The singles have one small bed and the suites have a double bed. It's on the main road at the northern end of town. There's no food.

Eating

Hasty Tasty Too (☎ 270 2061; shaffinhaji@hotmail .com; Uhuru Ave; snacks & meals from Tsh500; ◷ 7.30am-8pm) One of Iringa's highlights, Hasty Tasty Too has good breakfasts, yogurt, shakes and reasonably priced main dishes, plus an amenable mix of local and expat clientele. The owner is a wealth of information on the area and very helpful with arranging budget safaris to Ruaha. It also packs great toasted sandwiches to go and can arrange food if you're planning to camp in the park.

Saju's Home Cooking (Haile Selassie St; snacks & meals from Tsh500; ◷ 7am-11pm) This homy, family-run eatery makes a good stop for cheap local food. It's at the northern end of town, on a small lane running parallel to the main road.

Lulu's (☎ 270 2122; snacks & meals from Tsh500; ◷ 8.30am-3pm & 6.30-9pm Mon-Sat) The Greek-owned Lulu's is a quiet and friendly place with a varied menu selection, including soft-serve ice cream, and a nice umbrella-shaded outdoor seating area. It's one block southeast of the main road, just off Kawawa Rd. Next to Lulu's is Iringa Bakery, with fresh rolls and bread.

Twister's Pub 'n' Cuisine (Haile Selassie St; meals from Tsh2500; ◷ 11am-11pm Tue-Sun) Next to Saju's Home Cooking, Twister's has Indian, Western and a few Chinese dishes.

Bottom's Up (cnr Miskitini & Miomboni Sts; meals Tsh4000; ◷ lunch Tue-Sun, dinner daily) Atmosphere here is minimal and the place could use a good airing, but the food (a mix of Chinese and Indian dishes) is quite OK. It's on the 2nd floor of a large two-storey building just south of the main road.

For self-catering head to **Premji's Cash & Carry** (☎ 270 2296; Jamat St).

Getting There & Away

To catch any bus not originating in Iringa, you'll need to go to the main bus station at Ipogoro, about 3km southeast of town below the escarpment (Tsh1000 in a taxi from town), where the Morogoro–Mbeya highway bypasses Iringa. This is also where you'll get dropped off if you're arriving on a bus continuing towards Morogoro or Mbeya. *Dalla-dallas* to Ipogoro leave from the edge of Uhuru Park in town. All buses originating in Iringa start at the bus station in town, and stop also at Ipogoro to pick up additional passengers.

Scandinavian Express has three daily buses to Dar es Salaam, leaving at 6.30am, 9am and 10.30am (Tsh7500, 7½ hours); book in advance at the Scandinavian booking office, opposite the bus station in town.

To Mbeya, there's a bus departing daily at about 6am (Tsh6000, four to five hours). Otherwise, you can book a seat on the Scandinavian bus from Dar es Salaam that passes Iringa (Ipogoro) about 1pm, or just show up at the station and take your chance that there will be space.

To Njombe, there's one bus daily, departing in the morning from the town bus station. There are no direct buses to Songea from Iringa so you'll need to change in Njombe. For both Njombe and Songea, it's faster to wait for the Scandinavian bus from Dar es Salaam.

To Dodoma, there's a daily bus departing about 8am in each direction (Tsh6000, 10 to 12 hours), going via Nyangolo and Makatapora. Otherwise, all transport is via Morogoro. Driving to Dodoma via Makatapora in a private car, allow five to six hours.

Getting Around

Dalla-dalla stands are opposite the bus station and along the edge of Uhuru Park. Taxi ranks are along the small road between the bus station and the market, in front of MR Hotel, and at the Ipogoro bus station.

AROUND IRINGA
Isimila Stone-Age Site

About 15km outside of Iringa, off the Mbeya road, is **Isimila** (admission Tsh1000), where in the late 1950s archaeologists unearthed one of the most significant Stone Age finds ever identified. The tools found at the site are estimated to be between 60,000 and 100,000 years old. Although the display itself is not particularly exciting, the surrounding area is worth the journey, with bizarrely eroded sandstone pillars, and it's a popular weekend picnic spot.

Isimila is signposted off the main road to the left, and is an easy bicycle ride from Iringa. Otherwise, take a *dalla-dalla* heading towards Tosamaganga and ask to be dropped off at the Isimila turn-off, from where it's a 20-minute walk to the site. Taxis charge about Tsh5000 for the return trip.

A good detour on bicycle is to nearby **Tosamaganga**, a pretty hill-top town with a hospital and a mission station.

Kalenga

About 15km from Iringa on the road to Ruaha National Park is the famed former Hehe capital of Kalenga. It was here that Chief Mkwawa (see the boxed text, p260) had his headquarters until Kalenga fell to the Germans in the 1890s, and it was here that he committed suicide rather than succumb to the German forces. The small **Kalenga Historical Museum** (admission Tsh1500) contains Mkwawa's skull and a few other relics from the era. It's just off the park road and signposted.

Mtera Dam

This dam, about 120km north of Iringa off the Dodoma road, forms a huge reservoir for the waters of the Great Ruaha River as it flows out of the Southern Highlands and through Ruaha National Park on its way to join the Rufiji in Selous Game Reserve. Nearby is one of Tanzania's major hydroelectric power stations. With help from the Danish aid agency Danida, the small village of Migole, on the southeastern edge of the reservoir, has begun a cultural tourism programme that's easy to do as a day or overnight excursion from Iringa. Activities centre around the rustic **Chapuya Camp** (s/d with breakfast US$25/30, full board US$40/60, day visit full board per person US$15, village development fee per group per visit US$15), where you can go out in local boats (US$25 per half-day), take guided walks, and see various activities, such as basket weaving. Book through MR Hotel in

Iringa. There's also excellent angling at the dam, notably for tiger fish, though you'll need your own gear. The brush and reed landscapes along the shoreline also attract many water birds. Drinking water is available, but otherwise you should come with your own drinks.

RUAHA NATIONAL PARK

Ruaha National Park, together with neighbouring Rungwa and Kisigo Game Reserves and several smaller conservation areas, forms the core of a wild and extended ecosystem covering about 40,000 sq km and providing home to one of Tanzania's largest elephant populations. In addition to the elephants, which are estimated to number about 12,000, the park (Tanzania's second-largest) hosts large herds of buffaloes, as well as greater and lesser kudus, Grant's gazelles, wild dogs, ostriches, cheetahs, roan and sable antelopes, and more than 400 different types of birds. Bird life is especially prolific along the Great Ruaha River, which winds through the eastern side of the park, as are hippos and crocodiles.

Ruaha is notable for its wild and – around the Great Ruaha River – striking topography. Much of it is undulating plateau averaging about 900m in height with occasional rocky outcrops, and mountains in the south and west reaching to about 1600m and 1900m, respectively. Running through the park are several 'sand' rivers, most of which dry up completely during the dry season, when they are used by wildlife as corridors to reach areas where water remains.

Although the area around the camps on the eastern side of the park gets full during the high season, Ruaha receives relatively few visitors by comparison with the northern parks. Large sections are unexplored, and during much of the year you will have the place to yourself. Set aside as much time as you can spare to visit; it's not a place to be discovered on a quick in-and-out trip.

Information

Entry fees are US$15/5 per adult/child aged five to 15 per 24-hour period; multiple entries permitted. For accommodation fees, see p35.

There are two official entry points to the park, one at the main gate about 8km inside the park boundary on its eastern side, and the other at Msembe airstrip, about 6km northeast of the main gate, where visitors arriving by plane can pay their entry fees. **Park headquarters** (kudu@bushlink.co.tz; PO Box 369, Iringa) are at Msembe.

The road network in Ruaha is good, and the park can be visited at any time of year. The driest time is between June and November, and this is when it's easiest to spot wildlife along the river beds. Lodges are often booked to capacity during July and August. During the rainy season, some areas become impassable and there are fewer animals along the river, although enough roads remain open to make a visit worthwhile, and birding is especially good.

Except for the period from February to May, all the lodges organise walks (most between two and six hours), as does the park for those staying in the camp sites or *bandas*. Park rates for walks are US$25 per group (up to six people, and likely to be increased) for up to six hours; book in advance.

Sleeping

Ruaha River Lodge (☎ 0748-237422, 0744-237422; www.tanzaniasafaris.info; s/d all-inclusive US$280/470) This classy but unpretentious lodge is directly on the river, about 15km inside the park gate, and is run by the Fox family, who have several decades of experience in Ruaha. The cosy and inviting stone *bandas* are built on and around a kopje, with wonderful views over the water, where more often than not you'll gaze out over hippos and other animals. There's an elevated central dining area with equally good panoramas, and the overall ambience is attentive and low-key. Excursions include vehicle safaris and guided walks; fly camping can be arranged, and there are very reasonable drive-in rates available.

Mwagusi Safari Camp (☎ UK 44-20-8846 9363; tropicafrica.uk@virgin.net; s/d all-inclusive US$380/620; ✹ Jun-Mar) Mwagusi is an exclusive and highly regarded luxury tented camp in a top-notch wildlife-viewing location – favoured by elephants, among other visitors – on the Mwagusi Sand River about 20km inside the park gate. The atmosphere is intimate, with just 16 beds, there are superb views from the tents, and the quality of guiding is some of the best you'll find anywhere. Walks and other excursions can be arranged.

Mdonya Old River Camp (☎ 022-211 7959/60; safari@coastal.cc; s/d all inclusive US$290/480) The relaxed, rustic and comfortable Mdonya Old River Camp is in the western part of the park, about 1½ hours drive from Msembe – far enough away that you're likely to have wildlife watching to yourself even during high season. There are just eight tents, set in the shade on the bank of the Mdonya Sand River, and guided walks are possible. It's run by Coastal Travels in Dar es Salaam (p62). While not as luxurious as some of the other camps, if you take advantage of Coastal's specials – including a 'last minute' deal that offers a 50% discount on combined accommodation-flight packages for bookings less than 72 hours before departure – Mdonya Old River offers quite good value for a Ruaha safari. The camp is closed from one week after Easter through to June.

Jongomeru Camp (www.ccafrica.com; per person all-inclusive US$370) This exclusive camp, under the Conservation Corporation Africa umbrella, is set off on its own in the remote southwestern part of the park, about 60km from Msembe on the banks of the Jongomeru Sand River. The eight spacious en suite tents are among the most upmarket that you'll find in this part of Tanzania, and boast verandas and furnishings made from recycled wood. Apart from luxuriating in your surroundings, one of the nicest aspects of this camp is that you're unlikely to see any other visitors, no matter what time of year you go there. The camp is closed during April and May.

With your own transport, it's also possible to stay outside the park boundaries. The **Tandala Tented Camp** (☎ 026-270 3425, 023-260 1569; tandala@iwayafrica.com; per person full board US$65) is a pleasant new camp just outside the park boundary along the Tungamalenga road shortly before it joins the park access road, and about 12km from the park gate. Accommodation is in raised tents, and the camp can help you arrange vehicle rental to Ruaha, as well as guided walks in the area bordering the park. Park fees are only payable on the days you actually enter Ruaha.

In Tungamalenga village, about 35km from the park gate, is the friendly **Tungamalenga Camp** (☎ 026-278 2198/6; tungcamp@yahoo .com; camping US$5, r per person with breakfast/full board US$15/30; meals Tsh5000). There are simple en suite *bandas* set around a tiny garden (where you can pitch your tent), running water, kitchen facilities and a restaurant serving local dishes. If you arrive in Tungamalenga by bus, the camp has a vehicle that you can rent (about US$100 per day to the main gate area).

Ruaha has good facilities for do-it-yourself safaris. There are two ordinary camp sites, both about 9km northwest of park headquarters, and about 1.5km apart. Neither camp site has water; the only facilities are pit toilets, so you will need to be self-sufficient. There are about five special camp sites, all located well away from the Msembe area. The park also maintains several *bandas* near the river and about 2km from headquarters – there are several doubles and two larger family *bandas* accommodating four to five people each. Water is available for showers and the park sells soft drinks and a few basics, but otherwise you will need your own supplies. There is also a hostel for students and a resthouse, which is usually reserved for staff but is open to the public, space permitting. For all park accommodation, including ordinary camp sites, it's best to book in advance (through the senior park warden at park headquarters), especially during the high season.

If you are already in Iringa and want to book a camp site or *banda*, the antipoaching office on the edge of town can help you with its radio. To get here, head west out of town on the road to Ruaha. Take the first right after the roundabout at the edge of town, and then the first left. About 200m down on the left is a white mosque. Opposite, in an unsigned building, is the antipoaching office.

Getting There & Away
AIR
There are airstrips at both Msembe and Jongomeru.

Coastal Aviation flies from both Dar es Salaam and Zanzibar to Ruaha via Selous Game Reserve (US$300 one way from Dar es Salaam or Zanzibar, US$270 from Selous Game Reserve), and with sufficient demand, has flights between Ruaha and Arusha (US$300) and Ruaha and Kilwa (US$360). Foxes African Safaris (p63) has a plane based in Ruaha for flights to Katavi (US$400), Dar es Salaam (US$300), Arusha

(US$300), Selous (US$270), Mikumi and other destinations on request.

BUS
There's no public transport to Ruaha. A bus goes daily between Iringa and Tungamalenga, departing Iringa at 1pm and Tungamalenga at 3am (Tsh2500, 3½ to five hours). From Tungamalenga, there is nothing other than the occasional park vehicle, or the option of renting a vehicle from Tungamalenga Camp. Another option is to get a lift with one of the supply trucks that go several times weekly from Iringa to park headquarters. Ask around at the market for the schedule of the vehicles, or at Fussy Grocery near the market opposite the Lutheran cathedral. However, unless you are staying at one of the lodges this leaves you with the problem of getting around once at Ruaha, as the park doesn't rent out vehicles.

The best contact for arranging budget safaris is Hasty Tasty Too (p259). The owner can organise transport (from a very reasonable US$130 per vehicle per day, five persons maximum, for two days and one night) and, if you're travelling alone or in a small group, can sometimes put you in touch with other travellers who are interested in visiting the park.

CAR & MOTORCYCLE
Ruaha is about 115km from Iringa. The road is unsealed, but in decent condition. About 58km before reaching the park, the road forks; both sides go to Ruaha, and the distance is about the same each way. If you want to pass through Tungamalenga, take the left fork. The right fork is maintained by the park and is in marginally better condition.

Roads in Ruaha are in good condition, which makes it one of the better parks to visit during the rainy season. The closest petrol station is at Iringa.

IRINGA TO MAKAMBAKO
From Iringa, the Tanzam highway continues southwest, winding its way gradually up, past dense stands of pine, before reaching the junction town of Makambako. About 85km out of Iringa is **Mafinga**, the turn-off point to reach the forested highlands around **Mufindi**, which are laced with small streams and known for their tea estates and trout fishing.

Kisolanza – The Old Farm House (www.kisolanza .com; camping per person with hot showers US$3, self-catering chalets US$15-25, cottages per adult/child half board US$50/12) is a gracious farm homestead about 40km southwest of Iringa and about 1km off the main road to Mbeya. It comes highly recommended, both for its accommodation and for its cuisine. There are two camping grounds, one for overlanders and one for private vehicles; two-person chalets with linen and kitchens; and pleasant cottages (two doubles and one quintuple). There is also a shop selling home-grown vegetables and fruit, meat, fish, eggs and bread. On the opposite side of the road, near the river, is Kisolanza's **picnic site** (adult/ child Tsh500/250), which has shade, tables, grill and toilet. Scandinavian Express and other buses will drop you at the turn-off.

The genteel **Foxes Southern Highlands Lodge** (☎ 0748-237422, 0744-237422; www.tanzaniasafaris .info; s/d full board plus activities US$120/160), vaguely reminiscent of a transplanted Scottish country estate, is set amid the hills and tea plantations around Mufindi. It's a worthwhile detour if your idea of relaxation is spending the evening in front of a crackling fire, falling asleep at night in a cosy cabin, fishing for rainbow trout or walking. From Mafinga, it's 45km further south; pick-ups can be arranged.

Mafinga itself has a collection of unmemorable guesthouses, one of the better of which is the **White House Executive Lodge** (d Tsh9000).

MAKAMBAKO

Makambako is a bleak and windy junction town where the road from Songea meets the Dar es Salaam–Mbeya highway. It's also a stop on the Tazara railway line. Geographically, the area marks the end of the Eastern Arc mountain range and the start of the Southern Highlands. If you get stuck overnight here, your only choices are **Lutheran Centre Hotel & Guest House** (☎ 273 0047; s/d without bathroom Tsh2000/3000), on the main road opposite the train station, or the more expensive **Uplands Hotel** (☎ 273 0201; r Tsh10,000), also on the main road, about 500m west of the junction.

The bus fare between Makambako and Mbeya is Tsh2500, although drivers often ask for twice this. Large buses from Dar es Salaam begin to pass Makambako from about 2.30pm; otherwise, you'll need to take 30-seaters or minibuses.

MBEYA

☎ 025

The thriving town of Mbeya sprawls at about 1700m in the shadow of Loleza Peak, in a gap between the verdant Mbeya mountain range to the north and the Poroto mountains to the southeast. It was founded in 1927 as a supply centre for the gold rush at Lupa, to the north, but today owes its existence to its position on the Tazara railway line and the Tanzam highway, and its status as a major trade and transit junction between Tanzania, Zambia and Malawi. The surrounding area, in addition to being highly scenic, is also a major farming region, with coffee, tea, bananas and cocoa all grown here. While the town centre is on the scruffy side (especially around the bus station), the cool climate, jacarandas and views of the hills compensate, and there are dozens of good excursions nearby.

Information
INTERNET ACCESS
Nane Information Centre (per hr Tsh500; ✆ 8am-10pm) On the western side of the market square.

MEDICAL SERVICES
Aga Khan Medical Centre (☎ 250 2043; ✆ 8am-8pm Mon-Sat, 8am-1pm Sun) Just north of the market.

MONEY
NBC (cnr Karume & Kaunda Aves) Changes travellers cheques with purchase receipts; an ATM is planned.

TOURIST INFORMATION
Sisi Kwa Sisi Grass Roots Information Centre & Tour Guides (☎ 0744-463471, 0744-087689; sisikwasisitours@hotmail.com; ✆ 9am-1pm & 2-4pm Mon-Fri) Near the rhino statue between the market and the bus station. This is a clued-up local group that provides information and guides for various attractions in the Mbeya area, and is the best contact for arranging excursions and car hire. Rates average Tsh15,000 per person per day.

Dangers & Annoyances
As a major transport junction, Mbeya attracts many transients, particularly in the area around the bus station. Watch your luggage here and avoid walking alone through the small valley behind the station. Also around the bus station, and in the area near

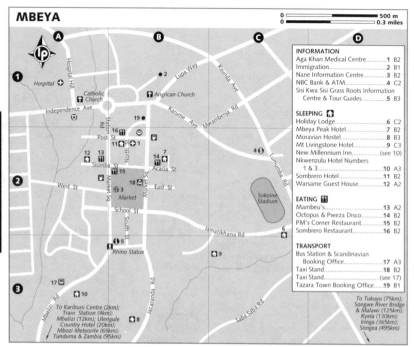

MBEYA

| | | | 0 | 500 m |
| | | | 0 | 0.3 miles |

INFORMATION
Aga Khan Medical Centre..........1 B2
Immigration................................2 B1
Nane Information Centre..........3 B2
NBC Bank & ATM......................4 C2
Sisi Kwa Sisi Grass Roots Information
   Centre & Tour Guides..........5 B3

SLEEPING
Holiday Lodge.............................6 C2
Mbeya Peak Hotel.....................7 B2
Moravian Hostel.........................8 B3
Mt Livingstone Hotel.................9 C3
New Millennium Inn............(see 10)
Nkwenzulu Hotel Numbers
   1 & 3..................................10 A3
Sombrero Hotel.........................11 B2
Warsame Guest House.............12 A2

EATING
Mambeu's...................................13 A2
Octopus & Pweza Disco...........14 B2
PM's Corner Restaurant...........15 B2
Sombrero Restaurant................16 B2

TRANSPORT
Bus Station & Scandinavian
   Booking Office....................17 A3
Taxi Stand..................................18 B2
Taxi Stand..........................(see 17)
Tazara Town Booking Office.....19 B1

To Tukuyu (75km);
Songwe River Bridge
& Malawi (125km);
Kyela (130km);
Iringa (365km);
Songea (495km)

---

the information office, it's common to be approached by impostor guides saying they work for Sisi Kwa Sisi. Although some may be legitimate, don't make any arrangements with anyone until actually going into the office. If the office is closed, you can recognise official guides by their Sisi Kwa Sisi T-shirts.

Sleeping
BUDGET
Karibuni Centre (☎ 250 3035; mec@atma.co.tz; camping per double tent Tsh2000 plus per person Tsh1000; d/tr/q Tsh10,000/12,000/14,000; meals about Tsh3000; ☯ restaurant 7am-9pm Mon-Fri, lunch Sat) This clean, quiet and popular mission-run place is in an enclosed compound where you can also pitch a tent. Rooms, most of which are en suite, are good value, and there's a pleasant restaurant. It's 3km southwest of the town centre, and about 10 minutes on foot from the *dalladalla* stop for transport into town. Watch for the signpost along the north side of the main highway and about 500m west of the first junction coming from Dar es Salaam. From the turn-off, head through what looks like an empty lot for about 300m to the gate.

Holiday Lodge (☎ 250 2821; Jamatikhana Rd; s/d Tsh6000/7500) A cheery, whitewashed local guesthouse with clean rooms – some with bathroom – and a restaurant. It's just off the main road behind the large Rift Valley Hotel, about 10 minutes' walk from the market area, and about 15 minutes on foot from the bus stand.

Moravian Hostel (☎ 250 2643, 250 3626; Jacaranda Rd; s Tsh6000, d without bathroom Tsh3600) This long-standing budget place is slowly sliding past its prime, with no-frills rooms (breakfast costs extra), and meals sometimes available on order. It's about 800m south of the market, and not safe to walk to, especially at night (Tsh1000 in a taxi from town).

Other recommendations:
Warsame Guest House (☎ 0744-311086; Sisimba St; s/d without bathroom Tsh2000/3000) This is one of Mbeya's cheapest options, with surprisingly decent rooms (no nets), grubby shared facilities and a central location just northwest of the market.

New Millennium Inn (☎ 250 0599; Mbalizi Rd; s without/with bathroom Tsh5000/6500) Located directly opposite the bus station, convenient if you have an early bus. Rooms are small, noisy and reasonably clean; there's no food.

Nkwenzulu Hotel Number 1 (☎ 250 2225; Mbalizi Rd; s/d Tsh6500/7500, without bathroom Tsh5500/6500) Next to New Millennium Inn and of similar standard, this hotel is not to be confused with the grubbier Nkwenzulu Hotel Number 3, which is at the base of the small hill and is the closest place to get a meal.

MID-RANGE & TOP END

Mbeya Peak Hotel (☎ 250 3473; Acacia St; s/d/ste Tsh12,000/15,000/30,000; meals Tsh3500) With a central, sunny setting and decent rooms, some with views over the hills, this is one of the better-value choices. It's on a small side street about 300m east of the market. There's also a restaurant with garden seating.

Sombrero Hotel (☎ 250 3636, 0744-087 800; Post St; r US$25) The Sombrero, about to open when we passed through, is Mbeya's newest hotel, with spotless rooms in a high-rise. All have TV, and an Internet connection is planned. The owner also runs a tour company, and can assist with car rental and organising excursions. It's in the town centre opposite Sombrero Restaurant.

Mt Livingstone Hotel (☎ 0741-350484; Jamatikhana Rd; s/d/ste Tsh20,000/30,000/45,000) Once the *grande dame* of Mbeya's hotels, but today very faded. Rooms, most done up in various brown tones, are comfortable enough, and there's an uninspired restaurant. It's about 200m off Jamatikhana Rd.

Utengule Country Hotel (☎ 256 0100; s/tw/ste US$45/80/120; ⚑) This attractive lodge is set on a coffee plantation in the hills about 20km west of Mbeya. Rooms – lined up along a grassy lawn with sunset views – are spacious and comfortable, and there's a fireplace in the common area – wonderful on chilly nights. If you have your own transport, Utengule makes a cosy base for exploring the surrounding region. Take the Tunduma road west from Mbeya for about 12km to Mbalizi, where there's a signposted turn-off to the right. Follow this road for 8.5km, keeping left at the first fork. The lodge is signposted to the right. Via public transport, take any Tunduma-bound *dalla-dalla* to Mbalizi, from where sporadic pick-ups will take you within about 2km of the lodge. Credit cards are accepted.

Eating & Drinking

Sombrero Restaurant (☎ 250 3636; Post St; mains Tsh2500-3500; ⚐ breakfast, lunch & dinner) A lively place, serving up large portions of vegetarian curry, spaghetti bolognaise and other dishes for very reasonable prices.

Utengule Country Hotel (☎ 256 0100; meals Tsh8500; ⚐ lunch & dinner) The place to go for fine dining, with a delicious daily set menu or á la carte, and a convivial bar.

Octopus (Acacia St; meals Tsh5000) Offers a good selection of grills, and Pweza disco is next door.

PM's Corner Restaurant (cnr Sisimba St & Market Sq; meals Tsh1000) and Mambeu's, just opposite, are local staples, with inexpensive *ugali*, chips, chicken and the like.

For self-catering, try the small shops around the market area, most of which have reasonable selections of boxed juices, tinned cheese and the like.

Getting There & Away

BUS

Scandinavian Express has two buses daily to Dar es Salaam at 6.30am (Tsh13,500, 12 hours) and 7am (Tsh15,500), going via Iringa and Morogoro, which should be booked in advance at their office at the bus station. Sumry line is the next best bet, with a daily departure at 6.30am (Tsh13,500).

Not recommended, the Hood line departs direct to Arusha at 5am (Tsh25,000, 16 hours).

There are a few small buses to Njombe each morning (Tsh4500, four hours). Better is Super Feo, which departs daily at 5.30am to Njombe (Tsh5500, four hours) and Songea (Tsh10,000, eight hours).

Dalla-dallas go several times daily from Mbeya to Tukuyu (Tsh700), Kyela (Tsh1500) and Malawi. For Itungi, you'll need to change vehicles in Kyela. There is also daily transport between Mbeya and the Malawi border, where you can pick up Malawian transport heading to Karonga and beyond. To Lilongwe, there's a bus several times weekly (currently Monday, Wednesday and Friday), departing Dar es Salaam at 5am, reaching Mbeya between 3pm and 4pm, and then continuing to Lilongwe. For more on connections between Mbeya and Malawi, see p321.

Minibuses go daily to Tunduma, on the Zambian border (Tsh2500, two hours), where you can change to Zambian transport; the Scandinavian bus between Dar es Salaam and Tunduma passes Mbeya in the late afternoon. To Lusaka, the best connections

THE MBOZI METEORITE

The Mbozi meteorite (also known as Mbosi) is one of Tanzania's more arcane attractions, and is seldom visited by travellers. Yet the site is scientifically significant and makes an interesting stop if you are geologically inclined. The meteorite, with an estimated weight of about 25 metric tons, a length of about 3m, and a height of about 1m, is the fourth largest in the world. Scientists are unsure of when it hit the earth, but it is assumed to have been many thousands of years ago, since there are no traces of the crater that it must have made when it fell, nor any local legends regarding its origins. Although the site was only discovered by outsiders in 1930, it had been known to locals for centuries but not reported because of various associated taboos.

Like most meteorites, the one at Mbozi is composed primarily of iron (90%), with about 8% nickel and traces of phosphorous and other elements. It was declared a protected monument by the Tanzanian government in 1967. It is now mounted on a small pedestal and is under the jurisdiction of the Department of Antiquities. The meteorite's dark colour is due to its high iron content, while its burnished look comes from the melting and other heating that occurred as the meteorite hurtled through the atmosphere towards Earth.

Mbozi is about 65km southwest of Mbeya. To reach the site you will need your own vehicle. From Mbeya, follow the main road towards Tunduma. About 50km from Mbeya there is a sign-posted turn-off to the left. From here, it's 13km further down a dirt road (no public transport). During the wet season, you'll need a 4WD. Otherwise, a 2WD can get through without difficulty, except perhaps for a tiny stream about 2km before the meteorite. There is a caretaker and an informative leaflet for sale with details on the meteorite. There is no charge for visiting.

are on Scandinavian, which runs four times weekly between Dar es Salaam and Lusaka via Mbeya (Tsh35,000 between Mbeya and Lusaka); see p321.

To Sumbawanga, Sumry goes daily at 5.30am and 7am (Tsh7500, six hours). For Mpanda, you'll need to change vehicles in Sumbawanga; plan on spending the night there, since most vehicles to Mpanda depart Sumbawanga in the morning.

To Tabora, there are three to four buses weekly during the dry season, going via Chunya and Rungwa.

TRAIN

Tickets for all classes can be booked at the Tazara town booking office near the post office, which is open (in theory) from 7.30am to 3pm Monday to Friday. Otherwise, book at the **station** (7.30am-12.30pm & 2-5pm Mon-Fri, 10.40am-12.40pm & 2-4pm Sat).

See p332 for schedules and fares between Mbeya and Dar es Salaam, and p332 for information about connections with Zambia.

Getting Around

Taxis park at the bus station and near the market. The Tazara station is 4km out of town on the Tanzania–Zambia highway (Tsh2000 in a taxi). *Dalla-dallas* from the

road in front of Nkwenzulu Hotel Number 1 run to the station and to Mbalizi, but the ones to the station are often too full if you have luggage.

AROUND MBEYA
Loleza & Mbeya Peaks

Watching over Mbeya from the north is **Loleza Peak** (2656m, and also known as Mt Kaluwe), which can be climbed as an easy half-day hike. There's an antenna at the top, so you can't go to the summit, but the views are still good. The walk begins on the road running north from town past the hospital, and should be done in the company of a Sisi Kwa Sisi guide.

Just west of Loleza is **Mbeya Peak** (2820m), the highest peak in the Mbeya range and a good day hike. There are several routes you can take. One goes from Mbalizi junction, about 12km west of town on the Tunduma road. Take a *dalla-dalla* to Mbalizi, get out at the sign for Utengule Country Hotel, head right, and follow the dirt road for about 1km to a sign for St Mary's Seminary. Turn right here and follow the road up past the seminary to Lunji Farm, and then up to the peak. With a vehicle, you can park at Lunji Farm and go the remaining way on foot. For an alternative route, proceed as above, but ignore the turn-off to the semi-

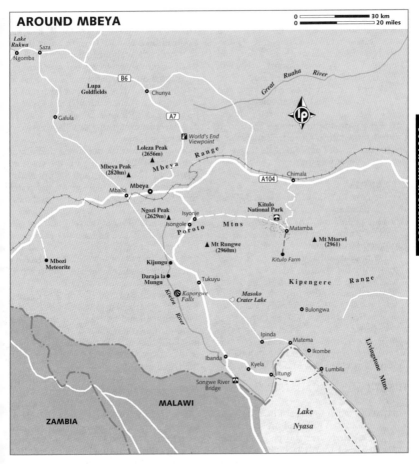

AROUND MBEYA

nary and keep walking along the road from Mbalizi towards Utengule Country Hotel. Just after the seminary turn-off you'll see a tiny bridge. Continue past two more small bridges to an unmarked dirt path heading off to the right, 2.7km from Mbalizi junction. This path winds its way towards the peak, though you'll probably need to ask locals to point out the way as it forks several times. Allow five to six hours for the return trip, a bit less for the slightly shorter Lunji Farm route. There's also another, longer route from Mbeya, beginning near Lolozi Secondary School to the west of town. For all routes, bring along a guide from Sisi Kwa Sisi or Utengule Country Hotel.

Chunya

This old gold-mining town came to life during the height of the 1920s gold rush, after which it declined to its present status as something of a ghost town. Although Chunya itself has little of inherent interest, it makes part of an interesting and adventurous loop to Lake Rukwa if you have your own transport and extra time on your hands. From Mbeya, head northeast along the edge of the Mbeya escarpment, passing the impressive **World's End Viewpoint**, with views over the Usangu catchment area (source of the Great Ruaha River) and some beautiful views out over the escarpment en route. Once in Chunya, where there is a basic guesthouse, it's possible to continue via Saza and Ngomba to the shores of Lake Rukwa, although there are no facilities en route. You can return the same way, or alternatively, at Saza, head south via Galula and Utengule Country Hotel towards Mbeya on a slightly shorter but rougher road.

Pick-ups go daily between Mbeya and Chunya (three hours), but it's likely you'll need to overnight in Chunya as return transport departs in the mornings. The rough routes from Chunya north to Rungwa and on to either Tabora or Singida are traversed by several buses weekly.

Lake Rukwa

Remote Lake Rukwa is a large salt lake notable for its many water birds and its large crocodile population. The northern section is part of Rukwa Game Reserve, which is contiguous with Katavi National Park. As the lake has no outlet, its water level varies significantly between the wet and dry seasons. It rarely exceeds about 3m in depth, and sometimes splits into two separate lakes separated by swamplands. Visits are only practical with a 4WD, and even then access to the shore is difficult. The main approaches are from Sumbawanga, or from Mbeya via Chunya and Saza to Ngomba, on the lake shore. There are no facilities.

TUKUYU
☎ 025

Tukuyu is a small town set in the heart of a beautiful area of hills and orchards near Lake Nyasa. There are many potential hikes in the area, but tourist facilities are minimal, so for anything you undertake, you'll be on your own.

NBC in the centre of town changes cash and travellers cheques, and you can get online at **Siaki Internet Café** (per hr Tsh1000), diagonally opposite the bank.

Hiking

The best way to arrange hikes is through the Sisi Kwa Sisi tourist office in Mbeya. The most amenable months for hiking are from July to October; during the wet season paths get very muddy. Following are brief outlines of a few routes. Topographical maps of the area are available from the Surveys & Mapping Division in Dar es Salaam, and the booklet *A Guide to the Southern Highlands of Tanzania* has detailed descriptions.

To the east of the main road between Tukuyu and Mbeya is 2960m **Mt Rungwe**. You can hike up and down in a day if you start early; allow about 10 hours. The climb starts from Rungwe Secondary School, signposted off the Mbeya road about 15km north of Tukuyu. A guide can be arranged at Rungwe, or better, through Sisi Kwa Sisi in Mbeya. Mt Rungwe can also be reached as a day hike from Isongole village between Tukuyu and Mbeya.

Somewhat further northwest and about 7km west of the main road is the volcanic **Ngozi Peak** (2620m) with it's impressive, deep-blue lake lying 200m below the crater rim. The lake is the subject of several local legends. To get here via public transport, take any *dalla-dalla* travelling between Mbeya and Tukuyu and ask to be dropped off; there's a small sign for Ngozi at the turn-off. Once at the turn-off, if you haven't come with a guide, you'll be approached by locals offering their services; the going rate is about Tsh1000. From Mbeya, Sisi Kwa Sisi charge Tsh15,000 for the whole excursion, including transport, guide fees and lunch. If you're short on time, you can go about half the distance from the main road to Ngozi by vehicle, and then walk the remainder.

South of Ngozi, and also west of the main road, is **Kijungu** (Cooking Pot), where the Kiriwa River tumbles through a rocky gorge. Nearby is **Daraja la Mungu** (Bridge of God), a natural bridge estimated to have been formed around 1800 million years ago by water flowing through cooling lava that spewed out from the nearby Rungwe volcano. The bridge spans a small waterfall. Further south along the river are the pretty **Kaporogwe Falls**.

Sleeping & Eating

Landmark Hotel (☎ 255 2400; s/d/tw Tsh20,000/ 25,000/30,000) This new and nice hotel has modern rooms, all with TV and hot water, and there's a good restaurant. It's the unmissable two-storey building at the main junction.

Langboss Lodge (☎ 255 2080; d Tsh4000, s/d without bathroom Tsh2000/3000) The Langboss was long Tukuyu's only accommodation, and is still the main shoestring option. It's about 1km east of the town centre; from the small roundabout at the top of town, head straight and then right. Rooms are basic, with no hot water, and meals can be arranged with lots of advance notice.

Lutengano Moravian Centre (camping Tsh2000 plus per small/large car per night Tsh1000/2500, s without bathroom Tsh2500, tr Tsh3500) This no-frills place off the main road north of Tukuyu has a handful of simple rooms with nets, plus large grounds where you can pitch a tent, and is sometimes used by overland trucks. Meals can be arranged (Tsh1000 for breakfast and Tsh1500 for lunch/dinner), or you can use the kitchen; advance bookings are recommended. Head north from Tukuyu for about 3km to the signposted turn-off on the western side of the road, from where it's 7km down a dirt road. There's a pick-up from Tukuyu (Tsh500) daily except Sunday, departing from the minibus station near the market about 2pm, and returning the next morning.

Getting There & Away

Minibuses run several times daily between Tukuyu and both Mbeya (Tsh1000, one to 1½ hours along a scenic, tarmac road) and Kyela (Tsh1000, one hour).

Two roads connect Tukuyu with the northern end of Lake Nyasa. The main tarmac road heads southwest and splits at Ipanda, with the western fork going to Songwe River Bridge and into Malawi, and the eastern fork to Kyela and Itungi port. A secondary dirt road that was being rehabilitated as we passed through heads southeast from Tukuyu to Ipinda and then east towards Matema.

KITULO PLATEAU

Nestled at about 2600m in the highlands northeast of Tukuyu is this flower-clad plateau, part of which is protected as the soon-to-be-formalised **Kitulo National Park**. During the rainy season from about November until April, it explodes in a profusion of colour, with orchids (over 40 species have been identified thus far), irises, aloes, geraniums and many more flowers carpeting its grassy expanses. Rising up from the plateau, in addition to the flowers, is Mt Mtorwi (2961m), one metre higher than Mt Rungwe, and southern Tanzania's highest peak. While Kitulo lacks the raw drama of the Serengeti plains and is unlikely to ever be a fixture on tourist itineraries, it's

well worth a visit if you are in the area and enjoy walking or things botanical. The best months for seeing the orchids – the plateau's most renowned residents – are December to March, which is also when hiking is at its muddiest.

There's currently only the most rudimentary infrastructure, and park fees (to be set at US$15 per person) are not yet being collected. For any hiking, you'll need to be self-sufficient with food and water, and carry a GPS. Camping is possible at Kitulo Farm, and once the park gets going, there will be several other sites.

The best access is via Chimala, about 80km east of Mbeya along the main highway. From here, turn south at the park signpost on the western edge of town and continue another 42km on a rough road that climbs over a seemingly endless series of hairpin turns to the sizable settlement of Matamba (where park staff are temporarily based), the park's **Mwakipembo Gate** and **Kitulo Farm**, which is the planned site for park headquarters. Pick-ups go as far as Matamba, where there are a couple of basic guesthouses. From here, you'll need to walk or have your own transport; allow about six to seven hours on foot between Matamba and Kitulo Farm. It's also possible to reach the plateau from a signposted turn-off near Isyonje, along the Tukuyu road, heading east and southeast from there along a rough track to Kitulo Farm.

Sisi Kwa Sisi in Mbeya is the best contact for organising visits.

LAKE NYASA

Lake Nyasa (also known as Lake Malawi) is Africa's third-largest lake after Lake Victoria and Lake Tanganyika. It's more than 550km long, up to 75km wide and as deep as 700m in parts. It also has a high level of biodiversity, containing close to one third of the world's known cichlid species. The lake is bordered by Tanzania, Malawi and Mozambique. The Tanzanian side is rimmed to the east by the Livingstone Mountains, whose green, misty slopes form a stunning backdrop. Few roads reach the towns strung out between the mountains and the shore along the lake's eastern side. While the mountains are incredibly beckoning to hikers, you'll need to be completely self-sufficient (including tent and water filter) and carry a GPS. Sisi Kwa Sisi in Mbeya organises a one- or two-day hike from the mission station of Bulongwa (reached via *dalla-dalla* from Njombe) to Matema, which offers some superb views as you make your way down to the lake shore. A longer version of this hike is also possible, starting near the Kitulo park gate. Another possibility is taking a *dalla-dalla* from Njombe to Ludewa, from where you could make your way down to Lupingu and wait for the MV *Iringa*. Once at the shoreline, note that both hungry, cerebral malaria–carrying *falciparum* mosquitoes and hungry crocodiles are real hazards, so take the appropriate precautions.

Other places of interest around the Tanzanian side of the lake include the following (from north to south).

Kyela
☎ 025

There's no reason to linger in this scruffy, nondescript transit town unless your boat arrives late at Itungi and you need somewhere to spend the night. Photography is prohibited in most areas of town.

SLEEPING & EATING
Makete Half London Guest House (☎ 254 0459; s Tsh4500) Rooms here are basic but clean, with mosquito nets, one medium-sized bed and bathrooms. There are no doubles. It's in the centre of town, opposite the Scandinavian Express bus office.

Rooms at the **Pattaya Hotel** (☎ 254 0015; s/d Tsh5500/6000) have either one or two large beds, but otherwise are similar to those at the Makete. It's on the same road as the Makete and the Scandinavian bus office, and about 300m in from the corner (heading northwest). One block north you'll find the **Steak Inn Restaurant** (meals from Tsh500).

GETTING THERE & AWAY
Scandinavian Express departs daily at 6am to Dar es Salaam (Tsh17,000) from its office, opposite Makete Half London Guest House. If you're heading to Tukuyu and Mbeya (Tsh1500), you can take the Scandinavian bus; otherwise there are several minibuses departing daily from the minibus stand about two blocks north of Pattaya Hotel. Pick-ups run daily between Kyela and Itungi, in rough coordination with boat arrivals and departures.

Itungi
Itungi, about 11km southeast of Kyela, is the main port for the Tanzanian Lake Nyasa ferry service. There is no accommodation, and photography is forbidden. Pick-ups run sporadically to and from Kyela (Tsh200). For ferry schedules and fares, see p325.

Matema
☎ 025

This quiet lake-side settlement is the only spot on northern Lake Nyasa that has any sort of tourist infrastructure, and it makes an ideal spot to relax for a few days. You can arrange rides in local canoes, hike to some small waterfalls and caves nearby or lounge on the beach. On Saturdays, there's a lively **pottery market** at Lyulilo village, about 1.5km east of the Lutheran Guest House along the lake shore, where Kisi pots from Ikombe are sold. There's nowhere in Matema to change money, so bring enough shillings with you.

SLEEPING & EATING
Matema Lake Shore Resort (☎ 250 4178; mec@atma .co.tz; camping per person with shower Tsh3000, 3-, 4- & 5-bed r US$15-30, d without/with bathroom US$8/25) This good place, on the beach about 300m past the Lutheran Guest House, has two en suite chalets, each of which can accommodate up to five people, and two smaller en suite cottages, with some triples and a quad. There's no restaurant, but it's easy and cheap to arrange grilled fish and other meals with staff; there's also a grill, with a nominal charge for charcoal use. You can also arrange bookings through the Karibuni Centre in Mbeya.

Lutheran Guest House (d Tsh8400, tr/q without bathroom Tsh6200/13,200) Rooms at this charmingly dilapidated beach-side place are simple, but clean and adequate, and food can be arranged with advance notice. Before heading down, check with the **Lutheran mission** (☎ 255 2597/8) in Tukuyu, just downhill from the NBC bank, to be sure space is available.

GETTING THERE & AWAY
Boat
The MV *Iringa* (p327) stops at Matema on its way from Itungi port down the eastern lake shore, reaching Matema in mid-afternoon. Note that the MV *Songea* (p325) doesn't stop here, which means you'll need to head back to Itungi port if you're going to Malawi.

Bus

To get to Matema from Tukuyu, take a pick-up from the roundabout by the NBC bank to Ipinda (Tsh1700, two hours); departures are in the morning, usually around 8am. Although drivers sometimes say they are going all the way to Matema, generally they go only as far as Ipinda. About 20km out of Tukuyu en route to Ipinda is the scenic Masoko Crater Lake, into which fleeing Germans allegedly dumped a small fortune of gold pieces and coins during WWI. From Ipinda, pick-ups run sporadically to Matema (Tsh1500, 35km), departing around 2pm, which means you'll need to wait around Ipinda for a while. Departures from Matema back to Ipinda are in the morning. Chances are better on weekends for finding a lift between Matema and Ipinda with a private vehicle. If you get stuck in Ipinda, there are several basic guesthouses.

There are also sporadic pick-ups from Kyela to Ipinda (Tsh1500), a few of which then continue on to Matema. From Kyela, it's also fairly easy to hire a vehicle to drop you off.

Car & Motorcycle

If you are heading to Matema in your own vehicle, the usual route from Tukuyu is via Ipinda (not via Kyela). During the dry season, and with a 4WD, it's also possible to take the main road from Tukuyu to Kyela, and then head east along a signposted, bad road to Ipinda and on to Matema. The Lutheran Mission in Tukuyu can arrange transport between Tukuyu and Matema for about US$65 per vehicle one way (about US$100 return, including waiting time).

Ikombe

The tiny village of Ikombe is notable for its clay pots, which are made by the local Kisi women and sold at markets in Mbeya and elsewhere in the region. It's reached via dugout canoe from Matema. There are no tourist facilities.

Liuli

Liuli is the site of an old and still active Anglican mission and the small St Anne's mission hospital, the major health faci'ity on the eastern lake shore. It's also notable for a (with some imagination) sphinx-like rock lying just offshore, which earned the settlement the name of Sphinxhafen during the German era. There's no accommodation, other than what you can arrange with villagers.

Mbamba Bay

The relaxing outpost of Mbamba Bay is the southernmost Tanzanian port on Lake Nyasa. With its low-key ambience and attractive beach fringed by palm, banana and mango trees, it makes a good spot to spend a few days waiting for the ferry, or as a change of pace if you have been travelling inland around Songea or Tunduma.

SLEEPING & EATING

Neema Lodge (Mama Simba's; Mbamba Bay 3; r without bathroom Tsh5000) The best value-for-money option in town, Neema Lodge has basic but adequate rooms, a friendly proprietor, a nice water-side setting and meals. To get here, turn left just before the bridge as you enter town.

Nyasa View (d without bathroom Tsh6000) Also not bad, though the rooms here aren't really worth the price difference compared with those at the Neema. Meals can be arranged. To get here, continue straight through town after the bridge, towards the beach.

Both places can help organise boat hire for exploring the nearby shoreline.

GETTING THERE & AWAY

There are occasional direct vehicles from Songea, usually coordinated with ferry arrivals, but generally you will need to change vehicles at Mbinga. It's Tsh2500 for each of the two legs of the trip, sometimes more during the wet season when the Mbamba Bay–Mbinga section is only traversed by 4WDs. With luck, the journey takes five to six hours, longer during the rains.

For details of ferry services between Mbamba Bay and Itungi port see p325. For ferry connections with Nkhata Bay, see p327.

From Mbamba Bay northbound, there are occasional 4WDs to Liuli mission station. Between Liuli and Lituhi there is no public transport and little traffic, and from Lituhi northwards, there is no road along the lake, only a footpath. There's also a rough track leading from Lituhi southeast towards Kitai and Songea, which opens the possibility for an interesting loop.

Entering or leaving Tanzania via Mbamba Bay, you will need to stop at the immigration post/police station near the boat landing to take care of passport formalities; it's possible to buy Tanzanian visas here.

MBINGA
☎ 026

This peppy, self-assured town lies en route between Songea and Mbamba Bay in the heart of one of Tanzania's major coffee-producing areas. If travelling via public transport, it's likely you'll need to change vehicles here. The main points of interest are the large, new Catholic cathedral and the panoramic road leading down to Mbamba Bay and Lake Nyasa.

For accommodation and dining, try **Mbicu Hotel** (☎ 264 0168; r Tsh7500), with spiffy rooms and a restaurant. It's on the edge of town along the Songea road.

NJOMBE
☎ 026

The workaday town of Njombe, about 240km north of Songea, is a district capital and regional agricultural centre. It would be completely unmemorable but for its highly scenic setting on the eastern edge of the Kipengere mountain range at almost 2000m. In addition to giving it the reputation of being Tanzania's coldest town, this perch provides wide vistas over hills that seem to roll into the horizon. While it's all quite inviting for walking, there's no tourist infrastructure at all, so anything you undertake will need to be completely on your own steam and with a GPS. For a few suggestions for walks see p271 or the *A Guide to the Southern Highlands of Tanzania* (see the boxed text, p247).

Sleeping

Chani Motel (☎ 278 2357; s/d Tsh8500/10,500) Njombe's best, with running water (usually hot) and meals. It's about 2km north of town and about 500m off the main road, signposted to the west.

For budget lodging, try **Lutheran Centre Guest House** (☎ 278 2403; s/d without bathroom Tsh2000/3500), about 700m south of the bus stand along the main road in the Lutheran church compound, or **Mbalache Guest House** (☎ 278 2164; r without bathroom Tsh2500), on the main road near the bus stand.

The only choice in between is the faded **Milimani Motel** (☎ 278 2408; r Tsh5500), about 1km south of the bus stand along the main road.

Getting There & Away

There are small 30-seater buses and minibuses that go daily between Njombe and Songea (Tsh4500, three to four hours) and to Makambako, where you can get transport to Mbeya. There's also at least one direct 30-seater bus to Mbeya (about Tsh3500). Between Njombe and Songea, it's sometimes possible to get a seat on Scandinavian Express (Tsh4500), although the buses usually run full.

Pick-ups go daily to both Bulongwa (departing Njombe about 10am) and Ludewa (departing by 8am).

SONGEA
☎ 025

Songea, just over 1000m in altitude, is capital of the surrounding Ruvuma region. Although not big, it's a bustling, pleasant place, and if you've just come from Tunduru or Mbamba Bay, it will seem like a major metropolis. The main ethnic group here is the Ngoni, who migrated into the area from South Africa during the 19th century, subduing many smaller tribes along the way. Songea takes its name from one of their greatest chiefs, who was killed following the Maji Maji rebellion (see the boxed text, opposite), and is buried about 1km from town near the Maji Maji museum.

NBC, on the street behind the market, changes cash and travellers cheques, and has an ATM. There's an Internet connection at **Valongo Internet Café** (per hr Tsh2000; ☒ 9am-6pm), just down from NBC, near the market and towards the main road.

Sights & Activities

Songea's colourful **market** along the main road is worth a visit. The impressive **carved wooden doors** on the cathedral diagonally opposite the bus stand are also worth a look, as are the **wall paintings** inside.

About 1km from the centre of town, off the Njombe road, is the small **Maji Maji museum** (admission free but donation appreciated; ☒ daily), which is quite run down but still interesting. Behind the museum is the tomb of Chief Songea. The museum is kept locked; ask for the caretaker,

THE MAJI MAJI REBELLION

The Maji Maji rebellion, which was the strongest local revolt against the colonial government in German East Africa, is considered to contain some of the earliest seeds of Tanzanian nationalism. It began about the turn of the 20th century when colonial administrators set about establishing enormous cotton plantations in the southeast and along the railway line running from Dar es Salaam towards Morogoro. These plantations required large numbers of workers, most of whom were recruited as forced labour and required to work under miserable salary and living conditions. Anger at this harsh treatment and long-simmering resentment of the colonial government combined to ignite a powerful rebellion. The first outbreak was in 1905 in the area around Kilwa, on the coast. Soon all of southern Tanzania was involved, from Kilwa and Lindi in the southeast to Songea in the southwest. In addition to deaths on the battlefield, thousands died of hunger brought about by the Germans' scorched earth policy, in which fields and grain silos in many villages were set on fire. Fatalities were undoubtedly exacerbated by a widespread belief among the Africans that enemy bullets would turn to water before reaching them, and so their warriors would not be harmed – hence the name Maji Maji (*maji* means 'water' in Swahili).

By 1907, when the rebellion was finally suppressed, close to 100,000 people had lost their lives. In addition, large areas of the south were left devastated and barren, and malnutrition was widespread. The Ngoni, a tribe of warriors much feared by their neighbours, put up the strongest resistance to the Germans. Following the end of the rebellion, they continued to wage guerrilla-style war until 1908, when the last shreds of their military-based society were destroyed. In order to quell Ngoni resistance once and for all, German troops hung about 100 of their leaders and beheaded their most famous chief, Songea.

Among the effects of the Maji Maji uprising were a temporary liberalisation of colonial rule and replacement of the military administration with a civilian government. More significantly, the uprising promoted development of a national identity among many ethnic groups and intensified anticolonial sentiment, kindling the movement towards independence.

who lives nearby. To get to the museum from town, take the first tarmac road to the right after passing the CRDB bank, and continue about 200m. The museum entrance is on the left; look for the large archway.

About 30km west of town, in Peramiho, is a large Benedictine **monastery**, where you can buy home-made cheese, sausage and sometimes ice cream. There are some pleasant walks in the surrounding area.

Sleeping & Eating

Songea has numerous budget hotels, but very little by way of mid-range quality.

Don Bosco Hostel (d without bathroom Tsh4000) Spartan rooms and a central location are the attractions at this hostel. It's just off the main road, behind the Catholic church and near the bus stand.

Annex of Yapender Hotel (☎ 260 2855; s/d Tsh7000/8500) The slickest budget option in the town centre, though it's still quite basic. Rooms are clean and with en suite, and there's a restaurant. From the bus stand, head uphill 400m past the market, take the first right (watch for the sign for the Lu-

theran church) and continue about 300m to the end of the dirt lane.

White House Holiday Inn (☎ 260 0892; s/d Tsh7500/9000, s without bathroom Tsh5000; meals Tsh2500) If you have your own transport, this isn't a bad choice. Rooms are small but clean and reasonably pleasant, and there's a decent restaurant serving lunch and dinner. It's about 2.5km north of the centre of town, along the Njombe road, in the Bomba Mbili section of town, and is signposted.

Angoni Arms Hotel (☎ 260 2219, 0745-512373; r Tsh15,000) The only choice approaching mid-range is the Angoni Arms Hotel, with clean en suite rooms with hot water, and a restaurant. It's about 1km from the market, along the Tunduru road.

The **Anglican Church Hostel** (☎ 260 0693; s/d Tsh3000/3500, without bathroom Tsh2000/2500) has clean rooms with mosquito nets, set in a relatively quiet area northwest of the main road. Next door is a small **restaurant** (meals Tsh500-2000; ☑ 6am-8pm). Nearby, on the road leading into the hostel grounds, are ovens where you can buy fresh bread in the afternoons. To get to the hostel, head uphill from the bus stand, past the market to the Tanesco building. Go left and wind your way back about 400m to the Anglican church compound.

Villamoss Bakery, along the road leading down to Annex of Yapender Hotel, sells good rolls, pastries and home-made yogurt.

Thanks to the German missionary influence, you can buy sausage in Songea; look for the small 'wurst' sign on the main road about 300m west of the bus stand.

Getting There & Away

Scandinavian Express departs daily at 6am (ordinary) and 6.15am (luxury) for Dar es Salaam (Tsh15,000/17,000 ordinary/luxury, 12 to 13 hours); your best bet is to book in advance.

Super Feo travels to and from Mbeya, departing at 6am daily in each direction (Tsh10,000, eight hours).

To Njombe, there are several minibuses and pick-ups daily, with most departures in the morning; better is to take Scandinavian or Super Feo and have them drop you there.

For Mbamba Bay, transport goes daily to Mbinga (Tsh3500, four hours), departing at 8am and again at 10am. From Mbinga, you can get onward transport to Mbamba Bay (Tsh3000). Although some drivers in Songea will say they are going all the way to Mbamba Bay, few do, so plan on changing in Mbinga. During the wet season, when the trip often needs to be done with 4WDs, prices rise to Tsh8000 for the journey.

TUNDURU

Dusty, remote Tunduru, halfway between Songea and Masasi, is in the centre of an important gemstone-mining region, with a bit of a Wild West feel. The town is also a truck and transit stop, and you'll need to spend at least one night here if travelling between Songea and Masasi. The better guesthouses are at the western end of town. There are plenty to choose from; all are around the same standard.

Four-wheel drives to Songea also congregate at the western end of town. Reserve a seat for onward travel when you arrive in Tunduru, as the vehicles fill up quickly.

Getting There & Away

The road from Tunduru in either direction is in poor condition, particularly between Tunduru and Songea, and it's sometimes impassable during the wet season, although thanks to recent rehabilitation work it's better than it was. There's at least one bus (and sometimes also a 4WD) daily between Tunduru and Masasi, departing about 5am (seven to 10 hours). Between Tunduru and Songea, the main options are 4WDs, which go daily (Tsh15,000, eight to 11 hours, departing Tunduru between 3am and 7am), as well as usually one bus (Tsh9000, departing at 6am). If you are staying at a guesthouse near the 4WD 'station' you can arrange for the driver to come and wake you before departure. There is little en route, so bring food and water with you.

Southeastern Tanzania

SOUTHEASTERN TANZANIA

HIGHLIGHTS

- Drifting off to sleep to the sound of hippos grunting in the **Rufiji River** (p298)

- Diving amidst corals and colourful fish in the waters around **Mafia** (p294), or gazing at the stars from your own private tree house on nearby **Chole** (p297)

- Exploring traces of bygone days at the old Swahili trading towns of **Mikindani** (p283), **Kilwa Kivinje** (p293) and **Lindi** (p287)

- Visiting the ruins of the famed medieval city-state of **Kilwa Kisiwani** (p291)

- Setting off via public transport down the coast for the ultimate backpacker's **adventure journey** (p278)

Time seems to have stood still in Tanzania's remote southeast. It lacks the development and bustle of points further north, tourists are an almost nonexistent species, and Arusha's crush of 4WDs and safari companies is so far removed that it might as well be in another country. Yet it's here, in this often forgotten corner, where you can get into the beat of the bush with nothing in-between, step back into a fascinating time-warp of centuries of Swahili history and experience adventure at every turn. Vast, seemingly uninhabited savanna landscapes stretch into the horizon, white sand beaches shimmer under an unrelenting sun, shoals of colourful fish flit past amazing coral formations in Tanzania's two marine parks at Mafia and Mnazi Bay, and immense herds of wildlife roam the untrammelled expanses of Selous Game Reserve. On the isolated Makonde plateau, carvers skilfully shape wood into distinctive styles that have become famous throughout the region, while the ruins on Kilwa Kisiwani offshore and a collection of old Swahili coastal towns testify to days when this part of the continent was the centre of trading networks stretching to the Far East.

Despite its attractions, it's likely you'll have much of the southeast to yourself. Away from Mafia island and the Selous, where a full range of amenities is available, travel is rough and rugged. And, while there are good air connections to major destinations, infrastructure otherwise is undeveloped and road journeys can be long and hard. During the Mozambican war the southeast was considered to be a sensitive border zone and many areas were off limits to tourists. As a result – although travel restrictions have long since been lifted – the region remains in many ways traditional and reserved.

National Parks & Reserves

Selous Game Reserve (p298) sprawls over much of southeastern Tanzania, although only the northern sector is open for tourism. In the far south along the Ruvuma River are tiny Lukwika-Lumesule and Msangesi Game Reserves (p285) – offbeat destinations for intrepid travellers with lots of time – while along the coast are Mafia island (p296) and Mnazi Bay (p284) Marine Parks.

Getting There & Around

Mtwara, Mafia, Selous Game Reserve and Kilwa Masoko are easily reached by scheduled flights.

The road from Dar es Salaam south is tarmac to the Rufiji River, where there's now a bridge, unsealed and rough, but being rehabilitated, to Lindi and then tarmac to Mtwara. Buses ply the route year-round, except in the heaviest rains, and there's also a ship between Dar es Salaam and Mtwara. Dhows are an option for the adventurous between other coastal towns. Inland, apart from a stretch of tarmac between Mtwara and Masasi, everything is dirt, and minibuses or old 4WDs are the only public transport.

MTWARA

☎ 023

Sprawling Mtwara is southeastern Tanzania's major town. It was first developed after WWII by the British as part of the failed East African Groundnut Scheme to alleviate a post-war shortage of plant oils. Grand plans were made to expand Mtwara, then an obscure fishing village, into an urban centre of about 200,000 inhabitants. An international airport and Tanzania's first deep-water harbour were built, and the regional colonial administration was relocated here from nearby Lindi. Yet, no sooner had this been done than the groundnut scheme – plagued by conceptional difficulties and an uncooperative local climate – collapsed and everything came to an abrupt halt. While Mtwara's port continued to play a significant role in the region over the next decades as an export channel for cashews, sisal and other products, development of the town came to a standstill.

In recent years Mtwara has had something of a second wind, with a revival of interest in the tourism potential of the southeast. While lacking the historical appeal of nearby Mikindani and other places along the coast, it has decent infrastructure, easy access and

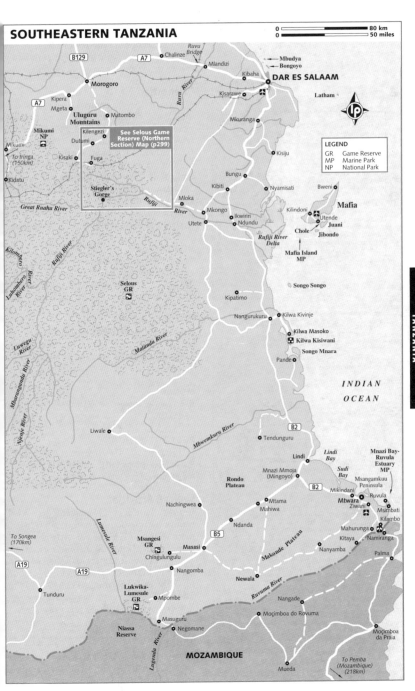

SOUTHEASTERN TANZANIA

0 — 80 km
0 — 50 miles

B129
A7
Chalinze
Ruvu Bridge
Mlandizi
Kibaha
→ Mbudya
→ Bongoyo
DAR ES SALAAM
Morogoro
Kisarawe
Kipera
Mgeta
A7
Uluguru Momtains
Matombo
Latham
LP
Mikumi NP
Kilengezi
Mkuranga
Mikumi
Dutumi
To Iringa (150km)
Kisaki
Fuga
Kisiju
Kidatu

LEGEND
GR — Game Reserve
MP — Marine Park
NP — National Park

Bungu
Great Ruaha River
Stiegler's Gorge
Rufiji
Kibiti
Nyamisati
Bweni
Mafia
Mloka
Mkongo
Kilindoni
Utende
Juani
River
Ikwiriri
Ndundu
Chole
Jibondo
See Selous Game Reserve (Northern Section) Map (p299)
Utete
Rufiji River Delta
Rufiji River
Mafia Island MP

Kilombero River
Lahombero River
Selous GR
Songo Songo
Kipatimo
Nangurukuru
Kilwa Kivinje
Kilwa Masoko
Kilwa Kisiwani
Songo Mnara
Luwegu River
Matandu River
Pande

Mbarangandu River
Njenje River
INDIAN OCEAN

Liwale
Mbwemkuru River
B2
Tendunguru
Lindi
Lindi Bay
Mnazi Bay-Ruvula Estuary MP
Mnazi Mmoja (Mingoyo)
Sudi Bay
Msangamkuu Peninsula
Rondo Plateau
Mikindani
Ruvula
Nachingwea
Mtama
Mahiwa
B2
Mtwara
Ziwani
Msimbati
Lumesule River
Ndanda
Kilambo
To Songea (170km)
B5
Mahurunga
Kitaya
Namiranga
Msangesi GR
Masasi
Makonde Plateau
Nanyamba
A19
Chingulungulu
Nangomba
Newala
Palma
A19
Ruvuma River
Tunduru
Lukwika-Lumesule GR
Mpombe
Nangade
Lugenda River
Masuguru
Moçimboa do Rovuma
Niassa Reserve
Negomane
Moçimboa da Praia
MOZAMBIQUE
Mueda
To Pemba (Mozambique) (218km)

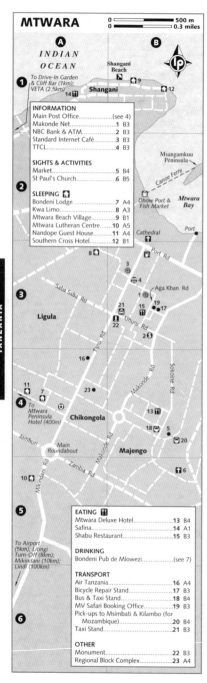

MTWARA

INDIAN
OCEAN

INFORMATION
Main Post Office....................(see 4)
Makonde Net.............................1 B3
NBC Bank & ATM.....................2 B3
Standard Internet Café.............3 B3
TTCL...4 B3

SIGHTS & ACTIVITIES
Market......................................5 B4
St Paul's Church.......................6 B5

SLEEPING
Bondeni Lodge.........................7 A4
Kwa Limo.................................8 A3
Mtwara Beach Village...............9 B1
Mtwara Lutheran Centre.........10 A5
Nandope Guest House.............11 A4
Southern Cross Hotel..............12 B1

EATING
Mtwara Deluxe Hotel..............13 B4
Safina.....................................14 A1
Shabu Restaurant....................15 B3

DRINKING
Bondeni Pub de Mlowezi.......(see 7)

TRANSPORT
Air Tanzania...........................16 A4
Bicycle Repair Stand...............17 B3
Bus & Taxi Stand....................18 B4
MV Safari Booking Office........19 B3
Pick-ups to Msimbati & Kilambo (for
    Mozambique).....................20 B4
Taxi Stand..............................21 B3

OTHER
Monument..............................22 B3
Regional Block Complex..........23 A4

a relaxed pace, and makes a good starting point for exploring the region. It's also the main entry/exit point if you're combining travels in Tanzania and Mozambique.

Orientation
Mtwara is loosely centred around a business and banking area to the northwest, near Uhuru and Aga Khan Rds, and the market and bus stand about 1.5km away to the southeast. The main north–south street is Tanu Rd. In the far northwest on the sea, and about 3.5km from the bus stand, is the Shangani quarter, with a small beach and several guesthouses. In Mtwara's far southeastern corner, just past the market, are the lively areas of Majengo and Chikongola.

Information
Tide tables are available at the port: after entering the port area, but before reaching the gate, turn right and go behind the buildings to the harbour master's office.

INTERNET ACCESS
Makonde Net (per hr Tsh1000; 8.30am-6pm Mon-Sat, 9am-2pm Sun) Just off Aga Khan Rd in the town centre.
Standard Internet Café (Tanu Rd; per hr Tsh500; 8am-9pm)

MONEY
NBC (Uhuru Rd) Changes cash and travellers cheques, and has an ATM.

POST & TELEPHONE
TTCL (Tanu Rd; 7.45am-12.45pm & 1.30-4.30pm Mon-Fri, 9am-12.30pm Sat) Operator-assisted domestic and international calls, and a card phone.

Sights & Activities
In town there's a lively **market** with a small traditional-medicine section next to the main building. Much of Mtwara's fish comes from Msangamkuu on the other side of Mtwara Bay, and the small **dhow port** and adjoining **fish market** are particularly colourful in the early morning and late afternoon. The **beach** in Shangani is popular for swimming on weekends (high tide only).

Sleeping
BUDGET
Drive-In Garden & Cliff Bar (camping per person Tsh2000) A shady, secure spot for camping, with friendly, helpful management, and an

ARIADNE VAN ZANDBERGEN

Small forest-fringed waterfall, Udzungwa Mountains National Park (p257)

Burchell's zebra in Ruaha National Park
(p262)

ARIADNE VAN ZANDBERGEN

Sandstone pillars at Isimila Stone-Age
site (p261), Iringa

ARIADNE VAN ZANDBERGEN

Breakfast stop on rocks at Stiegler's Gorge (p298) on the Rufiji River, Selous Game Reserve

A young boy from Kilwa
Kivinje prepares small fish for
smoking, Lindi (p287)

Arabic fort (p292), Kilwa Ruins, Kilwa Kisiwani

Reputedly the home of Dr David Livingstone who
spent time in Mikindani (p283) in 1866

inexpensive restaurant and small bar in the same grounds. It's in Shangani: go left at the main junction and follow the road paralleling the beach for about 1.5km to the small signpost on your left. The same owners are planning to open a budget guesthouse, so check with them for an update.

Mtwara Lutheran Centre (☎ 233 3294; Mikindani Rd; dm Tsh2500, s Tsh10,000, d without bathroom Tsh5000) A good budget choice, with decent rooms (most with nets), and fairly reliable water and electricity supplies. The rooms vary, so it's worth checking a few. Meals (Tsh4500) can be arranged with advance notice.

Nandope Guest House (☎ 233 4060; r without bathroom Tsh3000) One of the cheapest options, with no-frills rooms, some with mosquito nets. It's about 400m west of Tanu Rd, down the unsealed road near the police station.

Bondeni Lodge (☎ 233 3669; s/d Tsh8000/10,000) No-frills block-style rooms, all with fan and net, lined up next to a tiny courtyard. Next door is a popular outdoor pub. It's just up from Nandope Guest House.

Kwa Limo (☎ 233 3570; s Tsh7000) Kwa Limo is mainly a restaurant-bar, with a row of no-frills cement block rooms opposite the eating area. It's about 250m west of Tanu Rd down the dirt path opposite the post office.

Mtwara Beach Village (☎ 233 3670; d Tsh12,000) Another restaurant/bar, with a couple of tatty rooms in the back corner of the property. It's on the beach in Shangani (go right at the main junction for about 500m).

MID-RANGE

VETA (☎ 233 4094; s/ste Tsh15,000/35,000; 🏊) Good-value rooms, all with a large bed, TV and

views over the water, plus a popular restaurant, with mains from Tsh2500, open for lunch and dinner. It's in Shangani, about 200m back from the water (though there's no swimming beach here). From the T-junction in Shangani, go left and continue for about 3km. There's no public transport; taxis charge Tsh3000 from town.

Mtwara Peninsula Hotel (☎ 0741-502431; s with fan Tsh15,000, tw/d with air-con Tsh25,000; 🍴) This hotel, which caters to a local business clientele, is the only option approaching mid-range in the town centre. Rooms are reasonable, and there's a restaurant serving up rice and fish, and sometimes a few other dishes, under a large *banda* (thatched-roof hut). It's on a dusty backstreet 1km west of Tanu Rd past Nandope Guest House.

Southern Cross Hotel (☎ 233 3206, 0741-506047; www.msemo.com; s/d US$30/50; meals Tsh4000) This place, scheduled to open soon, promises to be Mtwara's best option. It's directly overlooking the sea at the eastern end of Shangani beach, with a relaxing seaside terrace restaurant and (soon) a handful of good-value rooms. Diving and bicycle rental are planned, and profits from the hotel are to be channelled into primary healthcare services in the Mtwara region.

Eating

The fish market at the Msangamkuu boat dock is good for street food, selling grilled *pweza* (octopus), *vitambua* (rice cakes) and other delicacies.

Of the hotel restaurants mentioned under Sleeping, the one at VETA is the best. **Kwa Limo** (☎ 233 3570; nyama choma Tsh1000; 🍴 lunch &

ST PAUL'S CHURCH

If you happen to be in the lively Majengo area of Mtwara, it's worth stopping in at St Paul's church to view its remarkable artwork. The entire front and side walls are covered with richly coloured biblical scenes painted by a German Benedictine priest, Polycarp Uehlein. These paintings, which took about two years to complete, are part of a series by the same artist decorating churches throughout southern Tanzania and in a few other areas of the country, including churches in Nyangao, Lindi, Malolo, Ngapa and Dar es Salaam. In addition to their style and distinctive use of colour, the paintings are notable for their universalised portrayal of common biblical themes. The themes were chosen to assist churchgoers to understand the sermons and to relate the biblical lessons to their everyday lives.

During the years he has worked in Tanzania, Father Polycarp has taught several African students. The best known of these is Henry Likonde from Mtwara, who has taken biblical scenes and 'Africanised' them. You can see examples of Likonde's work in the small church at the top of the hill in Mahurunga, south of Mtwara near the Mozambican border, and in the cathedral in Songea.

dinner) has reasonable *nyama choma* (seasoned roasted meat), and at **Mtwara Beach Village** (☎ 233 3670; meals Tsh2500) you can arrange grilled fish and other meals with lots of time (allow up to two hours).

Better are **Shabu Restaurant** (Aga Khan Rd; meals Tsh1000; ☺ 8am-10pm Mon-Sat, Sun 8am-1pm) in the town centre, serving local dishes, snacks and delicious fresh yogurt, and **Mtwara Deluxe Hotel** (meals Tsh2000; ☺ lunch & dinner) near the bus stand, with good Indian and other dishes.

Litingi (☎ 233 3635; off Mikindani road; meals from Tsh3000; ☺ dinner) is a bit out of town, but worth the drive for some good Indian food. To get here, follow the Mikindani road for 9km to the signposted turn-off, from where it's 2km further to Litingi. Taxis from Mtwara cost Tsh4000. Mikindani *dalla-dallas* (minibuses) can drop you by the turn-off, but you'll need to find a lift back as *dalla-dallas* don't run late at night.

For self-caterers: there are several reasonably useful shops along Uhuru Rd. Better is **Safina** (Container Shop; ☺ 8am-9pm), at the main junction in Shangani, with a good selection of basics, plus cold drinks.

Drinking & Entertainment

Popular places for a drink include Bondeni Pub de Mlowezi next to Bondeni Lodge (p281), Safina (see above) and the pleasant Drive-In Garden & Cliff Bar (p280). For dancing, there's a disco at **Litingi** (above; admission Tsh500) on Friday and Saturday evenings.

Shopping

Mtwara and outlying villages are good places for buying Makonde carvings, although many carvers only work on commission. A good place to start is the family of carvers on the Mikindani road under the second tree after the airport turn-off.

Getting There & Away

AIR

There are flights each day between Mtwara and Dar es Salaam (US$89) on **Air Tanzania** (☎ 233 3147; Tanu Rd; ☺ closed during flight arrivals & departures).

BOAT

The MV *Safari* sails roughly weekly between Dar es Salaam and Mtwara; see p85. The **booking office** (☎ 233 3591, 233 3550; Aga Khan St) is just up from Shabu's restaurant.

BUS

All long-distance buses depart from the main bus stand just off Sokoine Rd near the market; most departures are in the morning.

To Masasi, buses depart approximately hourly between 6am and 2pm (Tsh3000, five to six hours); once in Masasi you'll need to change vehicles for Tunduru and Songea.

To Lindi (Tsh2000, three hours), there are two buses daily, departing Mtwara between 9am and 11am. There is also a post bus, departing Mtwara at around noon daily except Tuesday. Departures in the other direction are in the mornings, so it doesn't work to visit Lindi as a day trip on public transport.

Direct buses to Newala (Tsh4500, six to eight hours) use the southern route via Nanyamba. Departures from Mtwara are between 6am and 8am daily, except during the wet season when services are more sporadic. It's also possible to reach Newala via Masasi, although this often entails an overnight stay in Masasi.

To Dar es Salaam, there are buses four times weekly (Tsh15,000, about 20 hours, sometimes longer), departing Mtwara any time between morning and early afternoon, and from Dar es Salaam by 8am. Book in advance as these buses fill up quickly.

To Mozambique, there are several pick-ups daily to Mahurunga and the Tanzanian immigration post at Kilambo (Tsh2500), departing Mtwara between 8am and 11am. Departures are from the eastern side of the market in front of the yellow Aaliyah Trading Company building. For information on crossing the Ruvuma River, see p323. The best places for updated information on the ferry are the Old Boma and Ten Degrees South, both in Mikindani (opposite).

CAR & MOTORCYCLE

If you're driving to/from Dar es Salaam, there are petrol stations in Kibiti, Ikwiriri, Nangurukuru, Kilwa Masoko, Lindi and Mtwara.

Getting Around

Taxis to or from the airport (6km southeast of the main roundabout) cost Tsh5000. There are taxi ranks at the bus stand, and near the CCM building at the corner of

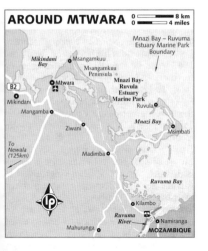

AROUND MTWARA

Mnazi Bay – Ruvuma
Estuary Marine Park
Boundary

Mikindani
Bay
Msangamkuu
Msangamkuu
Peninsula
B2
Mtwara
Mnazi Bay-
Ruvula
Estuary
Marine Park
Mikindani
Ruvula
Mangamba
Mnazi Bay
Ziwani
Msimbati
To
Newala
(125km)
Madimba
Ruvuma Bay
Kilambo
Ruvuma
River
Namiranga
Mahurunga
MOZAMBIQUE

Uhuru and Tanu Rds; the cost for a town trip is Tsh1000 (Tsh2000 from the centre to Shangani).

There are a few *dalla-dallas* running along Tanu Rd to and from the bus stand.

Bicycle is the best way to get around town. To arrange a rental, ask at the market or at one of the nearby bicycle shops, or at the small bicycle-repair stand off Aga Khan Rd.

MIKINDANI
☎ 023

Mikindani is a quiet, charming Swahili town with a long history, lots of coconut groves and a picturesque bay. Although easily visited from Mtwara, it makes an ideal base for exploring the surrounding area.

Mikindani gained prominence early on as a major dhow port and terminus for trade caravans from Lake Nyasa. By the late 15th century, these networks extended across southern Tanzania as far as Zambia and present-day Congo (Zaïre). Following a brief downturn in fortunes, trade – primarily in slaves, ivory and copper – again increased in the mid-16th century as Mikindani came under the domain of the Sultan of Zanzibar. In the 19th century, following the ban on the slave trade, Mikindani fell into decline until the late 1880s when the German colonial government made the town its regional headquarters and began large-scale sisal, coconut, rubber and oilseed production in the area. However, the boom was not to last.

With the arrival of the British and the advent of larger ocean-going vessels, Mikindani was abandoned in favour of Mtwara's superior harbour, and now – almost a century later – seems not to have advanced much beyond this era. Much of the town has been designated as a conservation zone, and life today centres around the small dhow port, which is still a hub for local coastal traffic.

For David Livingstone fans, the famous explorer spent a few weeks in the area in 1866 before setting out on his last journey.

Information
The closest banking facilities are in Mtwara.

The Old Boma has a helpful tourist information office, and is the best place for organising walking tours of town, and excursions in the area.

Sights & Activities
The imposing German **boma**, built in 1895 as a fort and administrative centre, has been beautifully renovated as a hotel (see below). Even if you're not staying here, it's worth taking a look, and climbing the tower for superb **views** over the town.

Down the hill from the boma is the old **slave market**, which now houses several craft shops. Unfortunately, it was less accurately restored than the boma, and lost much of its architectural interest when its open arches were filled in. The original design is now preserved only on one of Tanzania's postage stamps.

The **prison ruins** are opposite the jetty, and nearby is a large, hollow baobab tree that was once used to keep unruly prisoners in solitary confinement.

Apart from the various historical buildings, it's well worth just strolling through town to soak up the atmosphere and see the numerous carved Zanzibar-style doors. With more time, you can make your way up Bismarck Hill, rising up behind the Old Boma, for some good views.

Sleeping & Eating
Old Boma at Mikindani (☎ 233 3875, 0742-767642; www.mikindani.com; r with half board without/with balcony US$89/109, tr ste US$179; 🌊) This beautifully restored building is on a hill overlooking town and Mikindani Bay. It offers spacious, high-ceilinged doubles and top-end standards, and is well worth a splurge. In fact,

it's so nice that it might be worth coming to Mikindani just to stay here for a night or two. For those on a mid-range or top-end budget, the hotel makes an excellent base for exploring the surrounding area, and can organise excursions. There is also a swimming pool and a 'sunset terrace' overlooking the bay. Travellers cheques and credit cards (with 24-hours notice) are accepted.

Ten Degrees South Lodge (☎ 0748-855833; www .eco2.com; r without bathroom US$15-25; meals Tsh4000; ◷ restaurant lunch & dinner) A great budget travellers' base, with completely refurbished rooms – all with large beds and nets – and a very good restaurant-bar under a shady thatched *banda* with a popular Saturday evening barbecue. Diving can be arranged through **ECO2** (www.eco2.com), which is based at the hotel, and staff can help with excursions in the area.

Mikindani Yacht Club (contact through ECO2; admission Tsh2500, snacks from Tsh1500) Snacks and light meals, and a good place to hire a boat for the day.

Getting There & Away

Mikindani is 10km from Mtwara along a sealed road, and an easy bike ride. Minibuses (Tsh200) run between the two towns throughout the day.

MNAZI BAY–RUVUMA ESTUARY MARINE PARK

Tanzania's newest marine park encompasses a narrow sliver of coastline extending from Msangamkuu peninsula (just north and east of Mtwara) in the north to the Mozambique border in the south. In addition to about 5000 people, it provides home to over 400 marine species and an impressive array of delicate coastal ecosystems. Although still very much in its initial stages, it's ultimately hoped that the park will be the core of a conservation area extending as far south as Pemba in Mozambique.

The heart of the new conservation area is **Msimbati Peninsula**, together with the bordering Mnazi Bay. Among its attractions: an excellent beach that ranks as one of the best in the country, a string of (mostly unexplored) offshore reefs, and a complete lack of crowds. Most visitors head straight to the tiny village of **Ruvula**, which is about 7km beyond Msimbati village along a sandy track (or along the beach at low tide), where you'll find the finest stretch of sand in the area. In addition to its beach, Ruvula is notable as the spot where British eccentric Latham Leslie-Moore built his house and lived until 1967 when he was deported after agitating for independence for the Msimbati Peninsula. (To Leslie-Moore, deportation seemed a better solution than being subjected to the government of the newly independent Tanzania.) His story is chronicled in John Heminway's *No Man's Land*, and in *Africa Passion*, a documentary film. Today, Leslie-Moore's house stands in ruins; the property is privately owned. Offshore, northwest of Ruvula, are several small islands inhabited by fishing communities.

Msangamkuu Peninsula, at the northern edge of the marine park and best reached from Mtwara, boasts a fishing village, an attractive beach and snorkelling (bring your own equipment).

Marine park entry fees are US$10 per day (US$5/free for children from five to 16 years/ under five), and are collected at the marine park gate at the entrance to Msimbati village. To arrange diving, contact **ECO2** (www .eco2.com), based at Ten Degrees South Lodge in Mikindani, which is also the best source of updated information on the park.

Ruvula Sea Safari (camping per person Tsh5000, bandas per person full board Tsh30,000) The only place to stay, with rustic *bandas*, and the beach at your doorstep. A few basic supplies are available in Msimbati village, but if you're camping, stock up in Mtwara, and bring a torch.

Getting There & Away

There is at least one pick-up daily in each direction between Mtwara and Msimbati (Tsh1500, one hour), departing Mtwara by or before 11am from the eastern side of the market. Departures from Msimbati are around 6am. On weekends, many of Mtwara's foreign residents head towards Msimbati, and it's usually quite easy to find a lift.

Driving from Mtwara, take the main road from the roundabout south for 4km to the village of Mangamba, branch left at the signpost onto the Mahurunga road and then continue about 18km to Madimba. At Madimba, turn left again and continue for 20km to Msimbati; the road is unsealed, but in good condition. If you are cycling, the major village en route is Ziwani, which has a decent market.

There isn't any public transport between Msimbati and Ruvula. On weekends, it is sometimes possible to hitch a lift. Otherwise, arrange a lift on a bicycle with one of the locals, or walk along the beach at low tide.

Dhows and canoes make the trip between the Shangani dhow port dock in Mtwara and Msangamkuu peninsula throughout the day (Tsh100, about 15 minutes with favourable winds).

LUKWIKA-LUMESULE & MSANGESI GAME RESERVES

These tiny game reserves are hidden away in the remote hinterlands southwest and west of Masasi. They're officially off-limits during the July to December hunting season (thanks to local hunting concessions), and unofficially off-limits during much of the rest of the year due to the rains. If you're keen on heading down this way, late June is the best time to come.

Lukwika-Lumesule is the more interesting of the two. It's separated from Mozambique's wild Niassa Reserve by the Ruvuma River, and animals frequently wade across the border. With luck you may see elephants, sable antelopes, elands, greater kudus, crocodiles and hippos. The main challenge, apart from getting around the reserve, is figuring out a way to spot the animals through the often very dense vegetation.

Because Msangesi reserve has no permanent water source, its wildlife concentrations are often low. It's rumoured to have buffaloes, elands, zebras, sable antelopes and duikers, though it's unlikely you'll spot many of these.

Reserve officials are eager to have visitors – so much so that admission to both reserves is free at the time of writing. However, before arriving, you'll need to get a letter of permission from the **reserve warden** (☎ 023-251 0364; PO Box 42, Masasi). In Mtwara you can get information on the reserve from the Office of Natural Resources in the Regional Block complex (go to the small white building at the back).

Sleeping & Eating

There are a few simple *bandas* at each reserve, which need to be booked in advance with the reserve warden in Masasi. You'll need to bring everything with you, including food and drinking water. Water for bathing is normally available at Lukwika-Lumesule, but not at Msangesi. Camping is permitted with your own tent. There is currently no charge for either the *bandas* or for camping.

Getting There & Away

The entry point into Lukwika-Lumesule is about 2.5km southwest of Mpombe village on the northeastern edge of the reserve, and reached via Nangomba village, 40km west of Masasi.

To reach Msangesi from Masasi, follow the Tunduru road west to the Masasi airfield. Turn right, and continue to Chingulungulu, the last village before the reserve.

There is no regular public transport to either reserve, although you may sometimes be able to get a lift with a vehicle from the reserve warden's office in Masasi. Otherwise, you'll need your own 4WD transport. During the dry season, it's possible to drive around Lukwika-Lumesule, following a road running along its periphery. Getting around in Msangesi is more difficult. The road is not maintained and is sometimes impassable. The Old Boma at Mikindani (p283) organises three-day/two-night trips to Lukwika-Lumesule for US$500 per person for two people.

MAKONDE PLATEAU & AROUND

This seldom-visited plateau, much of which lies between 700m and 900m above sea level, is home to the Makonde people, famed throughout East Africa for their exotic wood carvings (see the boxed text, p286). With its comparative isolation, scattered settlements and seeming oblivion to developments elsewhere in the country, it in many ways epitomises southeastern Tanzania, and offers rewarding exploration.

Newala
☎ 023

Dusty, bustling Newala is the major settlement on the plateau. Thanks to its perch at 780m altitude, it offers a pleasantly brisk climate, and wonderful views over the Ruvuma River valley and into Mozambique. At the edge of the escarpment on the southwestern side of town is the old German boma (now the police station) and nearby, the impressive Shimo la Mungu (Hole of God) viewpoint. There are also numerous

SOUTHEASTERN TANZANIA

THE MAKONDE

The Makonde people, known throughout East Africa for their woodcarvings, are one of Tanzania's largest ethnic groups. They originated in northern Mozambique, where many still live, and began to make their way northwards during the 18th and 19th centuries. The Mozambican war sparked another large influx, with up to 15,000 Makonde crossing the border during the 1970s and 1980s in search of a safe haven and employment. Today, although the Makonde on both sides of the Ruvuma River are considered to be a single ethnic entity, there are numerous cultural and linguistic differences between the two groups.

Like many tribes in this part of the region, the Makonde are matrilineal. Children and inheritances normally belong to the woman, and it's common for husbands to move to the village of their wives after marriage. Settlements are widely scattered – possibly a remnant of the days when the Makonde sought to evade slave raids – and there is no tradition of a unified political system. Each village is governed by a hereditary chief and a council of elders.

Due to their isolated location, the Makonde have remained largely insulated from colonial and post-colonial influences, and are considered to be one of Tanzania's most traditional groups. Even today most Makonde still adhere to traditional religions, with the complex spirit world given its fullest expression in their carvings.

Traditionally, the Makonde practised body scarring and while it's seldom done today, you may see older people with markings on their face and bodies. It's also fairly common to see elderly Makonde women wearing a wooden plug in their upper lip, or to see this depicted in Makonde artwork.

Most Makonde are subsistence farmers, and there is speculation as to why they chose to establish themselves on a waterless plateau. Possible factors include the relative safety that the area offered from outside intervention (especially during slave trading days), and the absence of the tsetse fly.

---

paths along which you can make your way down to the river. If you plan to do this it's not a bad idea to carry your passport (which you'll need to carry around anyway in Newala, given its proximity to the border), and arrange a local guide. Bicycles can be rented near the market.

SLEEPING & EATING

Country Lodge Bed & Breakfast (☎ 241 0355; Masasi road; s/d Tsh7000/10,000, s without bathroom Tsh5000; meals Tsh3000) The best choice in town. Rooms have nets, most have a bathroom, and the doubles have two large beds. There's also a decent restaurant, with the usual array of standard dishes plus better fare with an advance order. It's about 600m from the bus stand, on the road to Masasi.

For something cheaper, there are several less-expensive guesthouses in the market–bus stand area, with no-frills rooms with shared bathroom for about Tsh2500, and cheap eateries nearby.

New Acapulco (meals Tsh1000) Opposite the Chamber of Commerce, and good for inexpensive local food during the day. The normal menu is chicken and *ugali*, but other dishes can be arranged in advance.

GETTING THERE & AWAY

Daily buses run from Newala to Mtwara and to Masasi (Tsh2500, three hours). There is also usually at least one vehicle daily between Newala and Mtama, on the Masasi–Mtwara road. All roads from Newala are unsealed. The journeys to Masasi and Mtama offer beautiful views as you wind down the side of the plateau.

Masasi
☎ 023

Masasi, a bustling district centre and birthplace of Tanzanian President Benjamin Mkapa, stretches out along the main road off the edge of the Makonde plateau against a backdrop of impressive granite hills. It's notable primarily as a transport hub for onward travel along the wild road west towards Tunduru, or north to Nachingwea and Liwale. The history of the modern settlement dates to the late 19th century, when the Anglican Universities' Mission to Central Africa (UMCA) came from Zanzibar to establish a settlement of former slaves here.

About 70km east of Masasi on the road to Mtwara is **Mahiwa**, the site of one of WWI's bloodiest battles in Africa, in which more than 2000 lost their lives.

Masasi is also the gateway for visiting Lukwika-Lumesule and Msangesi reserves (see p285). The **reserve warden's office** (☎ 251 0364; PO Box 42, Masasi) is located on the Newala road, a few hundred metres southeast of the Mtwara road, near the immigration office. Ask for *Mali Asili* (Natural Resources).

SLEEPING & EATING

Two of the better guesthouses are **Holiday Guest House** (d Tsh5500) at the western end of town near the petrol station, and **Sayari Hotel** (☎ 251 0095; r Tsh8700), at the eastern end of town near the post office.

For something cheaper, try Top Ten Guest House, about 1km east of the bus stand on the main road, or Masasi Hotel, opposite the petrol station, both with doubles sharing facilities for about Tsh3000.

Both the Masasi and Sayari Hotels have restaurants. Otherwise, there's street food available near the market.

GETTING THERE & AWAY

The bus stand is at the far western end of Masasi on the Tunduru road. If you're arriving from Mtwara, ask the driver to drop you off at your hotel or at the petrol station to avoid having to walk back into town.

The road between Masasi and Mtwara is mostly paved and, generally, is in good condition. Buses travel between the two towns approximately hourly between 6am and 2pm most days.

To Tunduru, the road is in bad condition and it can take up to 12 hours to cover the 200km stretch. 4WDs and the occasional bus travel this stretch most days during the dry season. During the wet season, departures are more sporadic and prices are higher.

Nachingwea

Nachingwea is a small, nondescript town about 50km north of Masasi. Should you find yourself here en route to or from Masasi, **New Paris** (r without bathroom Tsh2500), behind the bus station, has rooms and meals. There is at least one bus daily to and from Masasi.

Ndanda

Ndanda is a small town about 40km northeast of Masasi off the edge of the Makonde plateau. It's dominated by a large Benedic-tine monastery, founded by German missionaries in the late 19th century. Adjoining the monastery is a hospital, which serves as the major health clinic for the entire surrounding region. About a 45-minute walk south (uphill) from the monastery is a small dam with clean water for swimming.

Nuru Ndanda Hotel (s/d without bathroom Tsh2500/3000) is diagonally opposite the hospital at the bus stand, and has basic rooms and a tiny restaurant.

There are buses daily between Masasi and Ndanda, or any vehicle along the main road will drop you.

LINDI
☎ 023

In its early days, Lindi was part of the Sultan of Zanzibar's domain, a terminus of the slave caravan route from Lake Nyasa, regional colonial capital, and the main town in southeastern Tanzania. The abolishment of the slave trade and the rise of Mtwara as a local hub sent Lindi into a slow decline, from which it has yet to recover, although it again moved briefly into the limelight in the early 20th century when dinosaur bones were discovered nearby (see the boxed text, p289).

Today, Lindi is a lively, pleasant place, and worth wandering around for a day or so to get into life on the coast. Although it's not nearly as atmospheric as Kilwa Kivinje further north, its small dhow port still bustles with local coastal traffic, a smattering of carved doorways and crumbling ruins line the dusty streets, and a Hindu temple and Indian merchants serve as a reminder of once-prosperous trade routes to the east.

Salt production is the main local industry, announced by the salt flats lining the road into town. There's also a sisal plantation in Kikwetu, near the airfield. The coral reef running from south of Lindi to Sudi Bay hosts abundant marine life, and has been proposed as a possible protected marine area.

Information

INTERNET ACCESS

Internet Café (Amani St; per hr Tsh2000; ⏰ 9am-7pm) Near Muna's restaurant, a few blocks up from the harbour.

MEDICAL SERVICES

Brigita Dispensary (☎ 220 2679; Makonde St) An efficient, Western-run clinic, and the best place for medical emergencies.

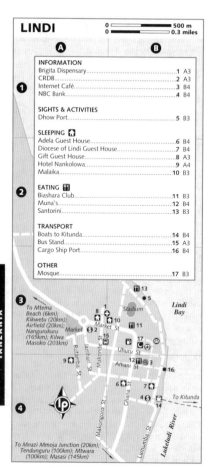

LINDI

0   500 m
0   0.3 miles

INFORMATION
Brigita Dispensary...1 A3
CRDB..2 A3
Internet Café..3 B4
NBC Bank..4 B4

SIGHTS & ACTIVITIES
Dhow Port..5 B3

SLEEPING
Adela Guest House...6 B4
Diocese of Lindi Guest House..........................7 B4
Gift Guest House...8 A3
Hotel Nankolowa..9 A4
Malaika...10 B3

EATING
Biashara Club..11 B3
Muna's...12 B4
Santorini...13 B3

TRANSPORT
Boats to Kitunda...14 B4
Bus Stand..15 A3
Cargo Ship Port..16 B4

OTHER
Mosque...17 B3

---

ruins of an Arab tower and the occasional carved doorway. Much livelier is the small **dhow port** on palm-fringed Lindi Bay. From the hills in town there are good views over large stands of palm trees and Lindi Bay, and across the Lukeludi River to **Kitunda peninsula** – ask locals to point you in the direction of Mtanda, Wailes or Mtuleni neighbourhoods. On Kitunda itself, which was formerly a sisal estate, there's nothing much now other than a sleepy village, but it's a pleasant enough spot for wandering around.

About 6km north of town off the airfield road is **Mtema beach**, which is usually empty except for weekends and public holidays. Take care with your valuables.

Sleeping

Malaika (☎ 220 2880; Market St; s/d Tsh7500/9000) Malaika, one block east of the market, is the best bet in town. Rooms are clean, no-frills and fine, with net and fan, and there's a decent restaurant.

Gift Guest House (☎ 220 2462; cnr Market & Makonde Sts; r without bathroom Tsh5000) Just down Market St from Malaika, and a decent, more basic, alternative if Malaika is full.

Adela Guest House (Ghana St; r without bathroom Tsh4000) Another budget standby, with basic rooms with net and fan. It's just off the main road that goes towards Mtwara, near the Msinjaili primary school.

Hotel Nankolowa (☎ 220 2727; Rutamba St; s Tsh7000, s/d without bathroom Tsh5000/5500) Small, basic and clean rooms. Breakfast is served in a cheery dining room, and other meals can be arranged with advance notice.

Diocese of Lindi Guest House (☎ 220 2288; r Tsh12,000) This place has spacious, breezy rooms near the waterfront, but is generally open only to church or aid workers. Advance bookings are required.

Eating & Drinking

While Lindi isn't distinguished for its dining options, you can get some delicious grilled fish. Otherwise, the menu is usually chicken with rice or *ugali*. Places to try include the good **Muna's** (Amani St; meals Tsh2000), just up from the harbour; **Biashara Club** (Market St; meals Tsh1500), a small place near the stadium with outdoor tables; and **Santorini** (meals from Tsh1500), which is behind the stadium in the Mikumbi area, and a good place for a drink or an evening meal. The

MONEY
CRDB (Market St) By the main roundabout near the market; changes cash, and travellers cheques at a high commission.
NBC (Lumumba St) On the waterfront; changes cash and travellers cheques.

TELEPHONE
There are card phones at Hotel Nankolowa and at the post office.

Sights & Activities

The most interesting part of town is the historical section along the waterfront, though there's little here to remind you of the town's more glorious past, and it can't compare with Kilwa Kivinje for time-warp ambience. Watch for the remains of the old German boma,

cheapest food is at the bus stand, where there's a row of stalls dishing up grilled chicken and chips, plus a few stools to sit and watch the passing scene.

Getting There & Away
AIR
There are currently no flights to Lindi, but some should start soon. For an update, check with Precision Air (p327), which was doing the route before. The airfield is about 20km north of town.

BOAT
Cargo boats along the coast, including to Dar es Salaam, call at the port near NBC bank, although they generally don't take passengers. The dhow port is about 800m further up the coast.

Boats across the Lukeludi River to Kitunda sail throughout the day from in front of NBC.

BUS
Buses to Mtwara depart daily from the **bus station** (cnr Makonde & Uhuru Sts) at 5am, 8am (post bus) and sometimes again at around 11am.

To Masasi (Tsh3000), buses depart at around 5am, 11am and 1pm daily. Otherwise, minibuses go throughout the day to Mnazi Mmoja (Mingoyo, Tsh1000), where you can get onward transport to Masasi until

---

BRACHIOSAURUS BRANCAI

Tendunguru, about 100km northwest of Lindi, is the site of one of the most significant palaeontological finds in history. From 1909 to 1912, a team of German palaeontologists unearthed the remains of more than a dozen different dinosaur species, including the skeleton of *Brachiosaurus brancai*, the largest known dinosaur in the world. The Brachiosaurus skeleton is now on display at the Museum of Natural History in Berlin. Scientists are not sure why so many dinosaur fossils were discovered in the region, although it is thought that flooding or some other natural catastrophe was the cause of their death.

Today, Tendunguru is of interest mainly to hardcore palaeontologists. For visitors, there is little to see and access to the site is difficult, even with your own vehicle.

---

about 2pm. Mnazi Mmoja has only the grubbiest of guesthouses, so plan your travels to avoid staying there overnight.

For Dar es Salaam, there are direct buses daily, departing Lindi by 8am and reaching Dar es Salaam the next day (usually stopping overnight at the Rufiji River). There are no direct buses from Lindi to Kilwa Masoko or Kilwa Kivinje. To get to either of these places you'll need to catch the Dar es Salaam bus and get out at Nangurukuru (Tsh5500, six to seven hours), from where you can get onward transport. Once the tarmac road is completed between Lindi and Dar es Salaam, expect all this information to change.

The main taxi rank is at the bus stand.

KILWA MASOKO
☎ 023

Kilwa Masoko (Kilwa of the Market) is a small coastal market centre about halfway between Dar es Salaam and Mtwara. More significantly, it's the springboard for visiting the impressive ruins of the 15th-century Arab settlements at Kilwa Kisiwani and Songo Mnara, and as such, the gateway into one of the most significant eras of East African coastal history.

Thanks to a major archaeological/tourism initiative by the French and Japanese governments, Kilwa is finally starting to come into its own after decades spent languishing in oblivion. While the town still isn't much, it will undoubtedly become an increasingly popular destination as tourism along the coast picks up.

The National Microfinance Bank, on the main road, changes cash but not travellers cheques; there's no Internet connection.

Sights & Activities
On the eastern edge of town is **Jimbizi Beach**, a good stretch of sand dotted with the occasional baobab tree; it's reached via a path that heads downhill by the Masoko Urban Health Centre. Better is the long, beautiful palm-fringed beach at **Masoko Pwani**, about 4km northeast of town, and best reached by bicycle. This is also where Kilwa Masoko gets its fish, and the colourful harbour area is worth a look, especially in the early morning and late afternoon. About 85km northwest of Kilwa at Kipatimo are some extensive limestone **caves**.

KILWA MASOKO

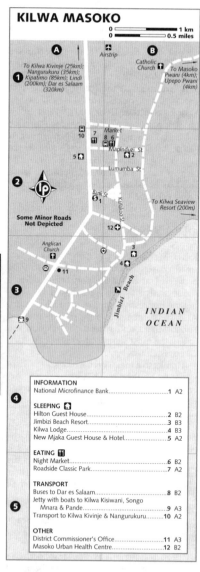

Sleeping

BUDGET

New Mjaka Guest House & Hotel (☎ Kilwa 89; Main Rd; s without bathroom Tsh3000, s/d banda Tsh5000/10,000) No-frills rooms, with a reliable water supply and Western-style toilets. Next door are nicer *bandas*, some with two rooms sharing a common area and others standard doubles.

Hilton Guest House (Mapinduzi St; r without/with bathroom Tsh2500/3500) Strictly shoestring, with basic rooms, fans, nets and squat toilets. It's 300m east of the main road, near the market.

MID-RANGE

Kilwa Seaview Resort (☎ Kilwa 144, 022-265 0250; www.kilwa.net; s/d/tr US$50/60/65) A recommended place, with spacious, breezy A-frame cottages perched along a small escarpment at the eastern end of Jimbizi beach. All six cottages overlook the water, just a few minutes' walk from the beach, and there's a restaurant that's built around a huge baobab tree and serves up tasty soups, grilled fish and other meals. Driving, the access turnoff is signposted from the main road. By foot, the quickest way to get here is to make your way past the police barracks and health clinic to Jimbizi Beach, at the end of which is a small path leading up to the cottages.

Kilwa Lodge (☎ 240 2397, 0748-205586; kilwa lodge@iwayafrica.com; Jimbizi beach; per person full board US$65; 🛏 🏊) An angling camp in the centre of Jimbizi beach with rustic en suite cabins set back from the water and a few beachside chalets, plus a popular beachside bar. The camp has its own plane for charters (US$90 one way Dar es Salaam–Kilwa), a vehicle for hire, sea kayaks, diving (US$40 per dive) and fully-equipped big game fishing (from US$350 to US$800 per boat per day, depending on boat and location). They can also organise overnight 'island cruises' including diving and fishing for US$1600 per boat (four-person) per day, all-inclusive. The big game fishing season runs from late July to early April.

Upepo Pwani (www.upepo-pwani.com; camping/ bandas per person without bathroom US$3/20) A camping and overlanders place on a wonderful stretch of beach at Masoko Pwani, about 4km north of Kilwa Masoko. It was under construction when we passed through, but a restaurant and simple beachside *bandas* are planned, in addition to camping. It's run by **Kilwa Safari** (☎ UK 0870-442 2571; www.kilwa-safari .com), which runs overland trips in southern Tanzania and northern Mozambique, and which channels some of its profits into the local community.

Jimbizi Beach Resort is a new upmarket place under construction on Jimbizi Beach, next door to Kilwa Ruins.

Eating & Drinking

Both New Mjaka and Hilton have restaurants, which do fish, chicken or meat with rice from Tsh1500, although it is a rare day when you will have a choice of all three. Better is **Roadside Classic Park** (Main Rd; meals from Tsh1000) diagonally opposite New Mjaka, with tasty local food, outdoor seating and a popular bar. Kilwa's lively and atmospheric night market, between the main street and the market, sells inexpensive fish and other snacks from dusk onwards.

For something more upmarket, both Kilwa Seaview Resort and Kilwa Ruins have good, reasonably priced restaurants (meals about Tsh4000), and Kilwa Ruins' bar is the main spot for meeting other travellers.

Getting There & Away

AIR

Coastal Aviation has three flights weekly from Dar es Salaam to Kilwa via Mafia, with a minimum of two passengers (US$110 one way Dar es Salaam to Kilwa, US$70 one way Mafia to Kilwa). The airstrip is about 2km north of town along the main road.

BOAT

There are no scheduled passenger-boat services to and from Kilwa Masoko. Dhows are best arranged in Kilwa Kivinje (see p293). Boats to Kilwa Kisiwani, Songo Mnara and Pande leave from the jetty at the southern end of town.

BUS

Rehabilitation work is under way on the road from the Rufiji River south to Kilwa Masoko, and it should be easily passable year-round.

To Nangurukuru (Tsh1500, one hour) and Kilwa Kivinje (Tsh1000, 45 minutes), pick-ups depart several times daily from the main road just up from the market.

To Dar es Salaam, there is a daily bus (that stops also at Kilwa Kivinje), departing in each direction at about 5am (Tsh6000, nine to 10 hours). Buses from Kilwa depart from the market, and should be booked in advance. Departures in Dar es Salaam are from the Temeke bus stand, with smaller buses also departing from Mbagala (take a *dalla-dalla* to 'Mbagala Mwisho'), along the Kilwa road.

Coming from Dar es Salaam it's also possible to get a bus heading to Lindi or Mtwara and get out at Nangurukuru junction, from where you can get local transport to Kilwa Kivinje (Tsh500, 11km) or Kilwa Masoko (35km), although this will be more expensive since buses from Dar es Salaam generally charge the full Lindi or Mtwara fare. This doesn't work as well heading north, as buses from Mtwara are often full when they pass Nangurukuru.

To go south from Kilwa, you'll have to go first to Nangurukuru, from where there is a vehicle most mornings to Lindi. From Lindi, it's easy to find onward transport towards Mtwara, although as most vehicles leave in the morning, you may need to spend a night there.

KILWA KISIWANI

Basking in the sun just offshore from Kilwa Masoko is Kilwa Kisiwani (Kilwa on the Island) – today a quiet fishing village, but in its heyday the seat of sultans, and centre of a vast trading network linking the old Shona kingdoms and the gold fields of Zimbabwe with Persia, India and China. Ibn Battuta, the famed traveller and chronicler of the medieval world, visited Kilwa in the early 14th century and described the town as being exceptionally beautiful and well constructed. At its height, Kilwa's influence extended north past the Zanzibar Archipelago, and south as far as Sofala on the central Mozambican coast.

Kilwa's glory days are well in the past, but the ruins of the settlement – together with the ruins on nearby Songo Mnara – are among the most significant groups of Swahili buildings on the East African coast and a Unesco World Heritage site. Thanks to funding from the French and Japanese governments, major rehabilitation work is under way, and the most significant sections of the ruins are in an impressive state of repair, and more accessible than they have been in decades.

History

The coast near Kilwa Kisiwani has been inhabited for several thousand years, and artefacts from the Late and Middle Stone Age have been found on the island. Although the first settlements in the area date to around AD 800, Kilwa remained a relatively undistinguished place until the early 13th century. At this time, trade links developed with Sofala, 1500km to the south in present-day Mozambique. Kilwa came to control Sofala and to dominate its lucrative gold trade, and before long it had become the most powerful trade centre along the Swahili coast.

In the late 15th century, Kilwa's fortunes began to turn. Sofala freed itself from the island's dominance, and in the early 16th century Kilwa came under the control of the Portuguese. It wasn't until more than 200 years later that Kilwa regained its independence and became a significant trading centre again, this time as an entrepôt for slaves being shipped from the mainland to the islands of Mauritius, Réunion and Comoros. In the 1780s, Kilwa came under the control of the Sultan of Oman. By the mid-19th century, the local ruler had succumbed to the sultan of Zanzibar, the focus of regional trade shifted to Kilwa Kivinje on the mainland, and the island town entered a decline from which it never recovered.

Information

To visit the ruins, you will need to get a permit (Tsh1500 per person) from the **District Commissioner's office** (Halmashauri ya Wilaya ya Kilwa; ☽ 7.30am-3.30pm Mon-Fri) in Kilwa Masoko, diagonally opposite the post office. Go to Room 13, or ask for Ofisi ya Utamaduni (Antiquities Office); the permit is issued while you wait. To maximise your chances of finding the right person, it's best to go in the morning. On weekends, the hotels can help you track down the permit officer, who is usually quite gracious about issuing permits outside of working hours. You'll also need to be accompanied by a guide to visit the island; these can be arranged through the Antiquities Office, or through your hotel.

For detailed information about the ruins in English, ask at the District Commissioner's office to see a copy of HN Chittick's informative manuscript. The National Museum in Dar es Salaam has a small but worthwhile display on the ruins at Kilwa Kisiwani.

There's no accommodation on the island.

The Ruins

The ruins at Kilwa Kisiwani are in two groups. When approaching Kilwa Kisiwani, the first building you'll find is the **Arabic fort**. It was built in the early 19th century by the Omani Arabs, on the site of a Portuguese fort dating from the early 16th century. To the southwest of the fort are the ruins of the **Great Mosque**, which has now been completely restored. Some sections of the mosque date to the late 13th century, although most are from additions made to the building in the 15th century. In its day, this was the largest mosque on the East African coast. Further southwest and behind the Great Mosque is a smaller **mosque** dating from the early 15th century. This is considered to be the best preserved of the buildings at Kilwa, and has been made even more impressive by the restoration work. To the west of the small mosque are the crumbling remains of the **Makutani**, a large, walled enclosure in the centre of which lived some of the sultans of Kilwa. It is estimated to date from the mid-18th century.

Almost 1.5km from the fort along the coast is **Husuni Kubwa**, once a massive complex of buildings covering almost a hectare and, together with nearby **Husuni Ndogo**, the oldest of Kilwa's ruins. The complex, which is estimated to date from the 12th century or earlier, is set on a hill and must have once commanded great views over the bay. Now much of the original layout has been cleaned up and brought back to life, including an octagonal bathing pool. Husuni Ndogo is smaller than Husuni Kubwa and is thought to date from about the same time, although archaeologists are not yet sure of its original function. To reach these ruins, you can walk along the beach at low tide, or follow the slightly longer inland route.

Getting There & Away

Local boats go from the port at Kilwa Masoko to Kilwa Kisiwani (Tsh200) whenever there are passengers – usually only in the early morning, about 7am, which means you'll need to arrange your permit the day before. To charter your own boat costs Tsh1000 one way (Tsh10,000 return for a boat with a motor). There is a Tsh300 port fee for tourists. With a good wind, the trip takes about 20 minutes.

SONGO MNARA

Tiny Songo Mnara, about 8km south of Kilwa Kisiwani, contains ruins at its northern end – including of a palace, several mosques and numerous houses – that are believed to date from the 14th and 15th centuries. They are considered in some respects to be more significant architecturally than those at Kilwa Kisiwani – with one of the most complete town layouts along the coast, although they're much less visually impressive. Just off the island's western side, at **Sanje Majoma**, are additional ruins dating from the same period. The small island of **Sanje ya Kati**, between Songo Mnara and Kilwa Masoko, has some lesser ruins of a third settlement in the area, also believed to date from the same era. The ruins at Songo Mnara are included in the ongoing rehabilitation project, with clearing scheduled to start soon.

There's nowhere to sleep on Songo Mnara. The Kilwa Kisiwani permit includes Songo Mnara.

The best way to get to Songo Mnara is via motorboat from Kilwa Masoko, arranged through the District Commissioner's office. A round-trip excursion costs Tsh30,000, including fuel. Alternatively, there's a much cheaper motorised local dhow that departs by 6am most mornings from Kilwa Masoko to Pande, and will stop on request at Songo Mnara. The boat returns to Kilwa Masoko the same day, departing Pande about 1pm. Dhows between Kilwa Masoko and Songo Mnara take about two hours with a decent wind.

After landing at Songo Mnara, you'll need to wade through mangrove swamps before reaching the island proper.

KILWA KIVINJE

Kilwa Kivinje (Kilwa of the Casuarina Trees) owes its existence to Omani Arabs from Kilwa Kisiwani who set up a base here in the early 19th century following the fall of the Kilwa sultanate. By the mid-19th century the settlement had become the hub of the regional slave trading network, and by the late 19th century, a German administrative centre. With the abolishment of the slave trade, and German wartime defeats, Kilwa Kivinje's brief period in the spotlight came to an end. Today it's a crumbling, moss-covered and highly atmospheric relic of the past with a Swahili small-town feel and an intriguing mixture of German colonial and Omani Arab architecture.

The most interesting section of town is around the old **German boma**. The boma itself is completely dilapidated, but it's worth picking your way through the rubble and climbing the stairs to the first floor for the view towards the water. The street behind the boma is lined with small houses, many with carved Zanzibar-style doorways. Nearby is a **mosque**, which locals claim has been in continuous use since the 14th century, and a warren of back streets where you can get an excellent slice of coastal life, with children playing on the streets, and women sorting huge trays of dagga for drying in the sun. Just in from here on the water is the bustling **dhow port**, where brightly painted vessels set off for Songo Songo, Mafia and other coastal ports of call.

The best way to visit Kilwa Kivinje is as an easy day trip from Kilwa Masoko. Overnight options are limited to a clutch of non-descript guesthouses near the market, all with rooms for about Tsh2000, and all rivalling each other in grubbiness. Among the better ones: King Wardo and Mziwanda near the market and New Sudi Guest House on the main road.

Getting There & Away

Kilwa Kivinje is reached by heading about 25km north of Kilwa Masoko along a sealed road, and then turning in at Nangurukuru for about 5km further. Pick-ups travel several times daily to/from Kilwa Masoko, and the bus between Dar es Salaam and Kilwa Masoko also stops at Kilwa Kivinje.

Dhows sail regularly from Kilwa Kivinje to both Dar es Salaam and Mtwara, although the journey to both destinations is long and not recommended; every year several boats capsize. Expect to pay about Tsh5000 for trips in either direction. There are also dhows to Mafia (about Tsh5000), although for this, it's much better to take a bus up the coast towards Dar es Salaam and get a boat at Kisiju. See p298 for more details.

The road between Nangurukuru and Kilwa Masoko is mostly good tarmac.

SONGO SONGO

Coconut palms, low shrub vegetation, about 3500 locals, lots of birds, a good beach and a natural-gas field are the main attractions on this four sq km island. Together with several surrounding islets, Songo Songo is an ecologically important area for nesting sea turtles and marine birds and, in the event that you find yourself here, it offers some rewarding birding.

There's nowhere to stay, other than what can be arranged through friendly locals, but before planning this, ask around to see if visitors are still welcome on the island now that the gas project is getting under way. The best beach is in Songo Songo's southeastern corner, reached through a coconut plantation.

Songo Songo lies 25km northeast of Kilwa Kivinje, from where it can be reached by dhow. Songo Songo's natural gas field has been targeted for exploitation as part of the Songo Songo Gas to Electricity Project, and there are frequent charter flights; check with Dar es Salaam-based air charter operators, or Coastal Aviation (p327), which stops here frequently on its Kilwa–Mafia run.

MAFIA

Mafia island – a green wedge of land surrounded by turquoise waters, small islets and glinting white sandbanks – has remained well off the beaten track for years, undiscovered by all except deep-sea fishing aficionados,

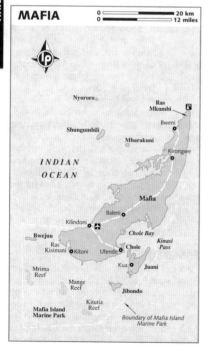

and a trickle of visitors seeking out its relaxing pace. While it's unlikely to ever draw the crowds that Zanzibar does, it has a relaxing tropical ambience unique among Tanzania's other coastal destinations, and is becoming an increasingly popular destination. Among the island's attractions: a complete lack of hustle and bustle, impressive coral formations and shoals of brightly coloured fish, several excellent hotels, an intriguing traditional culture and enough ruins to keep you busy exploring for an afternoon. Green and hawksbill turtles also find Mafia enticing, and have breeding sites along the island's eastern shores, as well as on the nearby islands of Juani and Jibondo. To protect these and other local ecosystems, the entire southeastern part of the island, together with offshore islets and waters, has been gazetted as a national marine park.

History

Mafia island is part of the Mafia Archipelago, which also includes Juani island to the southeast, Chole (between Mafia and Juani, and measuring just 1km in length), Jibondo, south of Juani, and at least a dozen other islets and sandbars. The archipelago first rose to prominence between the 11th and 13th centuries in the days when the Shirazis controlled much of the East African shoreline. Thanks to its central buffer position between the Rufiji River delta and the high seas of the Indian Ocean, it made an ideal trading base, and the local economy soon began to thrive. One of the first settlements was built during this era at Ras Kisimani, on Mafia's southwestern corner, followed by another at Kua on Juani.

By the time the Portuguese arrived in the early 16th century, Mafia had lost much of its significance and had come under the sway of the Sultan of Kilwa. In the early 18th century, the island's fortunes revived, and by the mid-19th century it had come within the domain of the powerful Omani sultanate, under which it flourished as a trade centre linking Kilwa to the south and Zanzibar to the north. It was during this era that the coconut palm and cashew plantations that now cover much of the island were established.

Following an attack by the Sakalava people from Madagascar, Mafia's capital was moved from Kua to tiny Chole island, nearby. Chole's importance rapidly grew, and it soon became known as Chole Mjini (Chole City), while the main island of Mafia was referred to as Chole Shamba (roughly, the Chole hinterlands). Mafia's administrative seat continued on Chole throughout the German colonial era. It was later moved to Kilindoni on the main island by the British, who used Mafia as a naval and air base.

Today farming and fishing are the main sources of livelihood for Mafia's approximately 45,000 residents (most of whom live on the main island), and you'll find cassavas, cashews and coconuts in abundance.

Orientation

Kilindoni – where all boats and planes arrive – is Mafia's hub, with the bank, port, market, small shops and a few budget guesthouses. The only other settlement of any size is Utende, about 15km southeast of Kilindoni on Chole Bay, where Mafia's top-end hotels are located. The Utende–Chole Bay area is also the base for the Mafia Island Marine Park and for diving. The rest of the island is dotted with scattered villages and lots of coconut trees.

Information

INTERNET ACCESS
Internet Café (per hr Tsh1500; ☼ 9am-9pm) On Utende road, in the town centre.

MEDICAL SERVICES & EMERGENCIES
For malaria tests, there's a village clinic on Chole island. For treatment or for other serious ailments, you'll need to go to Dar es Salaam.

MONEY
National Microfinance Bank (Airport road) Near the main junction; changes cash only (US dollars, euros and pounds).

TELEPHONE
Telephone calls can be made at New Lizu Hotel in Kilindoni. For mobiles, Vodacom now covers Mafia.

TOURIST INFORMATION
Pole Pole Resort's airport office doubles as a tourist information office.

Sights & Activities
It doesn't take too much imagination to step through Mafia's coconut plantations back

into centuries past, with **village life** here going on much as it did during the island's Shirazi-era heyday. Chole island is a good place to start exploring, especially around its crumbling but picturesque **ruins**, which date from the 19th century. Also on Chole, thanks to the efforts of a local women's group who bought the area where an important nesting tree is located, is now what is probably East Africa's only **fruit bat sanctuary** (Comoros lesser fruit bat). Juani island, just southeast of Chole also has ruins, primarily of five mosques dating from a Shirazi settlement during the 18th and 19th centuries, although they are largely covered and overgrown.

Much of Mafia is surrounded by mangroves, and the island is not known for its beaches. But, if you want some sand and swimming, the Chole Bay hotels can arrange excursions to a pristine and idyllic **sandbank** nearby. With more time, you can make your way through the coconut groves to the beach at Ras Kisimani. You can also arrange excursions – either with the Chole Bay hotels, or with Sunset Resort Camp (p296) – to the islets and sandbanks surrounding Mafia to the south and west.

At **Ras Mkumbi**, Mafia's wild and windswept northernmost point, there's a **lighthouse** dating to 1892, as well as the nice **Kanga beach** and a forest that's home to monkeys, blue duikers and lots of birds, among others.

DIVING & SNORKELLING
The main reasons to come to Mafia for diving are the excellent corals, the impressive variety of fish, including numerous pelagics, and the relaxing dive ambience; diving is usually done from motorised dhows, and since there are no crowds, there's no pressure to rush back for other waiting divers. There are several sites in Chole Bay, which is diveable year-round, plus seasonal diving outside the bay. In addition to Chole Bay, the main areas are Kinasi Pass and along the eastern fringing reefs. Most of the Chole Bay hotels (p297) organise diving and snorkelling, including certification courses, at prices similar to those in the Zanzibar Archipelago (see the boxed text, p94).

FISHING
Mafia has long been popular for deep-sea fishing, and is known especially for its tuna,

MAFIA ISLAND MARINE PARK

Mafia Island Marine Park – the largest marine protected area in the Indian Ocean (around 822 sq km) – shelters a unique complex of estuarine, mangrove, coral reef and marine channel ecosystems. These include the only natural forest on the island and close to 400 fish species. There are also about 10 villages within the park's boundaries with an estimated 15,000 to 17,000 inhabitants – all of whom depend on its natural resources for their livelihoods. As a result, the park has been classified as a multi-use area, with the aim of assisting local communities to develop sustainable practices that will allow conservation and resource use to coexist.

The park isn't set up for tourism, especially at the budget level. The main way to explore it is to organise a diving excursion with one of the hotels at Chole Bay. If you have your own gear, the park office may be able to help you out with snorkelling or set you up with a local fisherman to take you out.

Entry into the marine park area (payable by everyone, whether you dive or not) costs US$10 per day, or US$5 for children from five to 16 years. The fees are collected at a barrier gate across the main road about 1km before Utende, and can be paid in any major currency, cash or travellers cheques. Save your receipt, as it will be checked again when you leave. The **park office** (☎ 023-240 2690; wwfmafia@bushlink.co.tz) is in Utende, just north of Pole Pole Resort.

marlin, sailfish and other big-game fish. Conditions are most favourable between September and March, with June and July the least-appealing months due to strong winds. The best contact is Kinasi Lodge (opposite), which offers light sport fishing, and big game fishing from the island's northern tip.

Within the marine park, fishing is prohibited in much of Chole Bay, in Kinasi Pass, along the eastern edge of the island to the north of Chole Bay, along the eastern and southern edges of Juani, along the eastern edge of Jibondo, and around the Mange and Kitutia reefs. Sport fishing is permitted elsewhere within the marine park, although there's a maximum weight limit for most species. Spear-gun and harpoon fishing are prohibited. Licences are organised by the hotels for those booking through them. Otherwise, they can be arranged through park headquarters.

Sleeping & Eating

BUDGET

All of Mafia's budget accommodation is in Kilindoni.

Harbour View Resort (☎ Mafia 92; s without bathroom & with fan Tsh7500; d with/without bathroom Tsh15,000/12,000; ✂) Clean, good-value rooms in a smart house overlooking the harbour; food can be arranged. Head down the hill in Kilindoni and go into the port area; turn left, and follow the waterside road for about 500m to Harbour View.

Sunset Resort Camp (☎ 240 2522, ext 45; carpho 2003@yahoo.co.uk; camping per person US$7, bandas per person without bathroom US$10) This good place has nice camping on a lawn set on a cliff above the water, and clean bucket showers. There's also a small gazebo for watching the sunset, a few simple twin-bedded *bandas* and meals (Tsh3500 to Tsh5000) on order. About a 10-minute walk down the cliff side is a small beach, and the owner is helpful with arranging excursions to outlying islands and elsewhere. It's about 2km from the town centre, behind the hospital (Tsh1500 in a taxi).

New Lizu Hotel (☎ 240 2683; s/d without bathroom Tsh5000/10,000) Reasonable rooms (no frills, no nets), bucket baths, good cheap food and a convenient location at the main junction in Kilindoni, about a five-minute walk from the airfield.

MID-RANGE & TOP END

All the Chole Bay hotels offer discounts during the low season and for children, and all except Mafia Island Lodge are closed in April and May. All are also within the marine park area, which means – whether you intend to go diving or not – you will need to pay the US$10 per person per entry day fee.

Mafia Island Lodge (☎ 022-211 7959/60; info@ mafialodge.com; Utende; s/d US$39/60, full board US$65/100, renovated d US$80; airport transfers per person one way US$10; ✂ 💻) The former government hotel, this lodge is set on a long lawn sloping down to a nice, palm-studded beach, and is a recommended choice if your budget or tastes don't stretch to a stay at one of its more upmarket neighbours. There's a mix of renovated rooms (scheduled to open soon) and standard rooms, all lined up at the top of the lawn about 300m in from the water, and all good value and relaxing despite the backdrop of 1970s architecture. The main restaurant overlooks Chole Bay and serves up tasty meals featuring seafood and Italian cuisine. A beachside bar and restaurant are planned. Staff can help you arrange excursions, and there's a resident PADI/NAUI dive instructor.

Pole Pole Resort (☎ 022-260 1530; www.polepole .com; s/d full board & airport transfers US$228/350) This beautiful place is set amidst the palm trees and tropical vegetation on a long hillside overlooking Chole Bay. One of the best things about it is the bungalows – spacious, breezy, constructed completely of natural materials, and all with large private verandas ideal for curling up with a good book or listening to the wind rustling the palms. There's also an open-sided *duara* (gazebo) where you can while away the afternoons sipping a drink and gazing out over the water, and the overall ambience is a good balance between luxury and lack of pretension. Meals are made primarily with organic ingredients and are delicious. Excursions (all upmarket) include camping trips to Bwejuu, day and overnight trips to Mafia's far north (where you may even be able to arrange to sleep at the lighthouse), and adventure outings to the Rufiji River Delta. For relaxation afterwards, Pole Pole has a resident masseuse. The lodge manages several community development projects in nearby villages aimed at supporting local schools and protecting the environment.

Kinasi Lodge (☎ 022-284 2525, 0741-242977; www.mafiaisland.com; s/d full board & airport transfers US$165/280; 🏊) This is another top-notch choice, with 12 stone and thatch cottages set around a long, manicured hillside sloping down to Chole Bay, and a genteel, subdued ambience. There's an intimate open lounge area with satellite TV, a small beach and windsurfing rentals, plus a fully equipped dive centre, with the pool for instruction. Kinasi offers a number of intriguing excursions, including an upmarket camping trip to Mafia's northern tip (where the lodge

is building a luxury bush camp), as well as packages combining visits to Mafia with Zanzibar, the Selous, and boating along the Rufiji River.

Chole Mjini (info@cholemjini.com; s/d full board US$150/300, village fee per person per day US$10) If your idea of the ultimate getaway is sleeping in the treetops in a rustic but comfortable ambience, Chole Mjini, on tiny Chole island, is the place to stay. Accommodation is in six imaginatively designed tree houses (a couple of which are actually lower stilt houses), each set on its own with views over the bay, the mangroves, or the Chole ruins, and each accommodating up to three people. Although the tree houses have a range of amenities, there's no electricity, and there's no bathroom up above – you'll need to come down to ground level, where each tree house has its own outdoor shower garden and rustic, but hygienic, toilet facilities. Dining focuses around simple, tasty seafood-based meals, and diving can be arranged. Children under two cannot be accommodated. Transfers to the airport cost Tsh20,000 per vehicle. The management is very involved in the local community, with a portion of earnings channelled back into health and education projects.

N'gombeni Coconut Estate Guest Cottage (☎ 0745-670900; coconut@iwayafrica.com; per house per night US$100) This spacious six-person self-catering house is set in tranquil grounds in the middle of a working coconut plantation, with simple, spotless rooms, a kitchen and a veranda. It's ideal for longer-term stays, holing up to work on that novel you've always dreamed of writing, or simply for something a bit out of the ordinary for families or small groups. The cottage is in the N'gombeni area, about 3km south of Kilindoni (which is the closest place for food and supplies), and about a 40-minute walk from the closest beach. There's no public transport, so to get to/from town, you'll need to make arrangements for pickups with a taxi driver. Discounted long-term rates are available, and there's room for a few extra beds.

Getting There & Away
AIR
Coastal Aviation flies daily between Dar es Salaam and Mafia (US$70), and (with a minimum of two passengers) between

Mafia and Kilwa Masoko (US$70), both with connections on to Zanzibar, Selous Game Reserve and Arusha. The other option is Kinasi Lodge, which has its own aircraft for guests, with seats open on a space-available basis to non-guests.

All the Chole Bay hotels arrange airfield transfers for their guests (included in the room price, except as noted).

BOAT

There are no regular scheduled boats to/ from Mafia. Dhows go to the island from several points along the coast. The best connections are from Kisiju, 45km southeast of Mkuranga on the Dar es Salaam–Mtwara road. If you want to do this, take a *dalla-dalla* from Dar es Salaam to Mtoni-Mtongani, which is about 8km south of the city along the Kilwa road, from where several pick-ups daily go to Kisiju (Tsh2000, two hours). Alternatively, take any bus on the Dar es Salaam–Mtwara route and get off at Mkuranga, from where you can get a pick-up to Kisiju.

From Kisiju, boats – usually sailing boats, sometimes grimier motorboats – leave every day or two except Sunday for Mafia, and charge about Tsh4000. Departures depend on the tides and are generally before dawn. The usual procedure is to arrive in Kisiju in the late afternoon, board the boat at about 9pm and sleep on it until departure. With good winds, you should arrive in Mafia by late afternoon, although the trip can take much longer. If the winds turn, the captain may stop for a night at Koma island (no facilities), about one-third of the way between Kisiju and Mafia. Going in the other direction, boats leave from the port at Kilindoni. The boarding procedure and departure times are the same as at Kisiju.

Getting Around

Dalla-dallas connect Kilindoni with Utende and Bweni, usually with one vehicle daily in each direction. On the Kilindoni–Utende route (Tsh1000), vehicles depart Kilindoni at about 1pm and Utende at about 7am. Departures from Kilindoni to Bweni are usually at about 1pm, and from Bweni at about 7am. In Kilindoni the *dalla-dalla* stop is on the road that goes down to the port.

In Kilindoni it's also possible to hire pick-ups to take you around the island, but you'll need to bargain hard. Expect to pay about Tsh15,000 return between Kilindoni and Utende.

The other option is bicycle. If you bring your own, bring a mountain bike, as none of Mafia's roads are tarmac. To rent a local bicycle, ask around at the market in Kilindoni. The going rate is about Tsh500 per hour for a heavy single-speed.

Between Utende and Chole, most of the Chole Bay hotels provide boat transport for their guests. Local boats charge Tsh100 one way. From Chole, it's possible to walk to Juani at low tide. Local boats can be chartered to Jibondo and the other islands, and there is also a sporadic local service. Expect to pay from Tsh3000, depending on the destination.

SELOUS GAME RESERVE

At the heart of Tanzania's forgotten south is the Selous – a vast 48,000 sq km wilderness area stretching over more than 5% of the mainland. It is Africa's largest wildlife reserve, and Tanzania's most extensive protected area, although the extended ecosystems of Ruaha National Park and the Serengeti come close. It's also home to large herds of elephants, plus buffaloes, crocodiles, hippos, wild dogs, an amazing diversity of birds and some of Tanzania's last remaining black rhinos. Bisecting it is the **Rufiji River**, king of Tanzania's rivers, which winds its way more than 250km from its source in the highlands through the Selous to the sea, and boasts one of the largest water-catchment areas in East Africa. En route, it cuts a path past woodlands and grasslands and stands of borassus palm, and provides the chance for some unparalleled water-based wildlife watching. In the river's delta area, which lies outside the reserve opposite Mafia island, the reddish-brown freshwater of the river mixes with the blue salt water of the sea, forming striking patterns, and providing habitats for many dozens of bird species, passing dolphins and more.

In the northwestern part of the reserve is the impressive **Stiegler's Gorge**, which averages 100m in depth, and is named after a Swiss explorer who was killed here by an elephant in 1907.

Although the number of tourists visiting Selous is gradually increasing, it remains low in comparison with Tanzania's northern

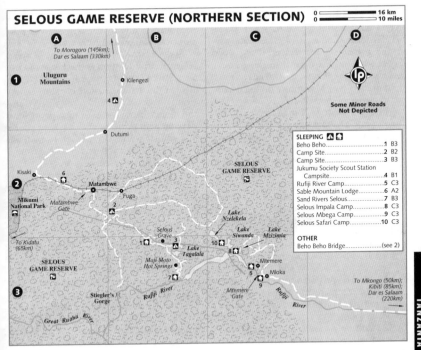

SELOUS GAME RESERVE (NORTHERN SECTION)

0 — 16 km
0 — 10 miles

To Morogoro (145km);
Dar es Salaam (330km)

Uluguru
Mountains

Kilengezi

Some Minor Roads
Not Depicted

Dutumi

Kisaki

Matambwe

Mikumi
National Park

Matambwe
Gate

Fuga

SELOUS
GAME RESERVE

Lake
Nzelekela

To Kidatu
(65km)

Selous
Grave

Lake
Tagalala

Lake
Siwanda

Lake
Mzizimia

SELOUS
GAME RESERVE

Maji Moto
Hot Springs

Mtemere

Mloka

Stiegler's
Gorge

Rufiji River

Mtemere
Gate

Rufiji
River

To Mkongo (50km);
Kibiti (85km);
Dar es Salaam
(220km)

Great Ruaha River

SLEEPING

Beho Beho	.....1 B3
Camp Site	.....2 B2
Camp Site	.....3 B3
Jukumu Society Scout Station	
Campsite	.....4 B1
Rufiji River Camp	.....5 C3
Sable Mountain Lodge	.....6 A2
Sand Rivers Selous	.....7 B3
Selous Impala Camp	.....8 C3
Selous Mbega Camp	.....9 C3
Selous Safari Camp	.....10 C3

OTHER

Beho Beho Bridge	.....(see 2)

parks, and the congestion of the north is refreshingly absent. The Selous' wildlife concentration and diversity are also generally considered to be lower than in some of the northern parks, although it's hard to remember this when you're sitting in a boat in the middle of the Rufiji River, watching elephants playing in the water just a few hundred metres in front of you, or counting several dozen hippos along the river banks from the doorway of your safari tent.

Another major advantage of the Selous is that you can explore it by boat or on foot – a welcome change of pace if you've been cooped up in 4WD vehicles on dusty roads during other parts of your travels. Boat safaris down the Rufiji or on the reserve's lakes are offered by most of the camps and lodges. Most also organise walking safaris, usually three-hour hikes near the camps, or further afield, with the night spent at a fly camp.

Only the section of the reserve north from the Rufiji River is open for tourism; large areas of the south have been zoned as hunting concessions.

History

Parts of the reserve were set aside as early as 1896, although it was not until 1922 that it was expanded and given its present name (after Frederick Courteney Selous, the British explorer who was killed in the reserve during WWI). The area continued to be extended over the next several decades until 1975 when it assumed its current boundaries. In more recent years there has been ongoing discussion of plans to link Selous Game Reserve with the Niassa Reserve in Mozambique, with the first stages of the project – including establishment of a wildlife corridor – set to start in the near future.

Information

Admission to the game reserve costs US$30 (US$5/free for children aged between six and 15/five and under), plus a vehicle fee of US$30 per day. Camping fees at established (ordinary) camp sites are US$20 per person (US$5/free for children between five and 15/under five). Camping at special camp sites costs US$40 for adults (US$10/free for children aged between five and 15/under five). There is also an additional fee of US$20 per day for a wildlife guard – mandatory in camping areas. Guide fees are US$10 per day (US$15 outside normal working hours and US$20 on walking safaris). The reserve's headquarters is at Matambwe on the north-western edge of the Selous.

The best time to visit the reserve is from June to late October, during the cool, dry season, and in January and February when the rains break and the landscape is green and in flower. Much of the reserve is inaccessible between March and May as a result of the heavy rains, and many of the tourist camps close for at least part of this time, usually during April and May. If you do visit in the wet season, the main challenge will be getting yourself to the reserve, as roads are sometimes impassable and airstrips too soft for landing. You'll also need to keep your itinerary and expectations flexible, and be prepared for a bit of mud.

Both the Mtemere and Matambwe Gates are open from 6am to 6pm daily. The booklet *Selous Game Reserve: The Travel Guide* by Drs Rolf Baldus and Ludwig Siege is an excellent source of background information on the region. It also has descriptions of safari routes in the reserve, and information and tips on wildlife viewing. It's available at bookshops, and at camps in the Selous for about Tsh12,000. An earlier edition, *Selous: Africa's Largest & Wildest Game Reserve,* is equally good, in case you find any copies sitting around.

Sleeping

All of the Selous lodges and upmarket camps offer boat safaris (some on the Rufiji River, others on Lake Tagalala), wildlife drives and guided walks.

BUDGET

There are two ordinary camp sites, one at Beho Beho bridge about 12km southeast of Matambwe, and one at Lake Tagalala, roughly midway between Mtemere and Matambwe. Each has a pit toilet, but otherwise there are no facilities. For both, you will need to be self-sufficient, including having drinking water. Special camp sites can be arranged in the area between Mtemere Gate and Lake Manze (northeast of Lake Tagalala). Contact the Wildlife Division in

advance for bookings and information on permitted locations. You'll need to be self-sufficient at these camps as well.

About 60km north of Matambwe between Kilengezi and Dutumi is the **Jukumu Society Scout Station Campsite** (camping per person Tsh5000). It's run by an association of game scouts from villages surrounding the reserve and the money earned is used to support local development projects, antipoaching efforts and similar work. There is a pit toilet and bathing area, and water is available from a small nearby waterfall.

It's also possible to pitch your tent just east of Mtemere Gate at Selous Mbega Camp, which also has some good backpacker deals; see left and below.

MID-RANGE

Selous Mbega Camp (☎ 022-265 0250; www.selous -mbega-camp.com; camping per person US$10, s/d full board US$135/190, s/d 'backpackers' special for those arriving by public bus at Mloka US$70/100, excursions extra) This laid-back camp is conveniently located about 500m outside the eastern boundary of the Selous near Mtemere Gate and about 3km from Mloka village. It's an excellent budget choice, with eight pleasant tents set in the foliage a bit back from the riverbank. Each has three beds, a bathroom and veranda. There's also a tree house overlooking a water hole, and a small camping ground (for which you'll need to be self-sufficient with food). Excursions – including boat safaris, wildlife drives and walks – cost US$30 per person, plus reserve fees where applicable. The camp is open year-round. Pick-ups and drop-offs to and from Mloka are free.

Sable Mountain Lodge (☎ 022-211 0507; www .saadani.com; s/d full board US$170/250, all-inclusive US$260/430; 🏊) The friendly and relaxed Sable Mountain Lodge is about halfway between Matambwe Gate and Kisaki village on the northwestern boundary of the reserve, in an area known for its elephants. The cosy and comfortable en suite stone cottages all have views. There are also two more luxurious honeymoon cottages, a tree house overlooking a water hole, a spring-water swimming pool and a snug for stargazing – the ultimate in relaxation. In addition to walking safaris and wildlife drives, the lodge offers a good combined wildlife drive and boat safari on Lake Tagalala, and night drives outside the reserve. Free pick-ups and drop-offs are provided to the Kisaki train station and staff are very helpful if you're travelling independently. Open year-round.

Rufiji River Camp (☎ 022-212 8662/3; www.hippo tours.com; s/d all-inclusive US$295/470; ☒) This long-standing and unpretentious camp has a fine location on a wide bend in the Rufiji River about 1km inside Mtemere Gate. The 20 en suite tents all have river views, there's a sunset terrace and a small library. Activities include boat safaris, and half-day walking safaris with the possibility of staying overnight at a fly camp; prices include park fees. It's one of the few places that is willing to accommodate visitors year-round (with advance notice during the rainy season).

Selous Impala Camp (☎ 022-211 7959/60; www .coastal.cc; s/d all-inclusive US$430/700) The attractive Selous Impala Camp is beautifully set on the river bank near Lake Mzizimia amidst borassus palms and other vegetation. With just six tents, it's one of the smallest of the Selous camps, and quite good value if you take advantage of some of Coastal Travels' (p62) favourably priced flight and accommodation deals.

TOP END

Sand Rivers Selous (www.nomad-tanzania.com; s/d all-inclusive US$590/930) Beautiful Sand Rivers Selous, set splendidly on its own on the Rufiji River south of Lake Tagalala, is the Selous' most exclusive option, with some of Tanzania's most renowned wildlife guides. Its eight luxurious stone cottages are all completely open in front with full river views. Bookings can only be made through upmarket travel agents. Nomad, who run the camp, also offer superlative walking safaris of up to six days based out of mobile fly camps.

Selous Safari Camp (www.ccafrica.com; per person all-inclusive US$400; ☒) A luxurious camp set on a side arm of the Rufiji overlooking Lake Nzelekela, with 12 spacious, widely spaced tents, a lofty, raised dining and lounge area and impeccable service.

Beho Beho (☎ 022-260 0352; www.behobeho.com; d all-inclusive US$800; ☒) Beho Beho, set on a rise northwest of Lake Tagalala and away from the river, has spacious stone and thatch *bandas* with large verandas overlooking the plains. Boat safaris are done on Lake Tagalala, which is an excellent birding

location, as well as being notable for its resident populations of hippos and crocodiles.

Getting There & Away

AIR

Coastal Aviation and ZanAir have daily flights linking Selous Game Reserve with Dar es Salaam (US$120 one way), Zanzibar (US$130) and (via Dar es Salaam) Arusha, with connections to other northern circuit airstrips. Coastal also has flights between the Selous and Mafia (US$120), plus three flights weekly between Selous and Ruaha National Park (US$270). Flights into the Selous are generally suspended during the March to May wet season. All lodges provide airfield transfers.

BUS

Akida and Mwera bus lines have buses daily between Dar es Salaam's Temeke bus stand (departing from the Sudan Market area) and Mloka village, about 10km east of Mtemere Gate (Tsh4000, seven to nine hours). Departures in both directions are at 5am. From Mloka, you can usually find a ride with a vehicle from the reserve for the remainder of the trip or, better, arrange a pick-up with one of the camps in advance. There's no accommodation in Mloka, and hitching within the Selous isn't permitted, so you'll need to have a lodge booking.

CAR & MOTORCYCLE

You'll need a 4WD in the Selous. There's no vehicle rental at the reserve and motorcycles aren't permitted.

To get here via road, there are two options. The first is to take the Dar es Salaam to Mkongo road, via Kibiti, and then on to Mtemere (250km). The road is mostly tarmac as far as Kibiti and unsealed but in good condition to Mkongo. The stretch from Mkongo to Mtemere (75km) is sometimes impassable during heavy rains. Allow about eight hours from Dar es Salaam.

Alternatively, you can go from Dar es Salaam to Kisaki via Morogoro and then onto Matambwe via a scenic, but longer, 350km route through the Uluguru Mountains. Allow at least nine hours for the journey, sometimes more. This route is sometimes impassable during heavy rains and a 4WD is required at any time of the year. From Dar es Salaam, the road is good tarmac as far as Morogoro. Once in Morogoro, take the Old Dar es Salaam road east towards Bigwa. About 3km or 4km from the centre of town, past the Teachers' College Morogoro and before reaching Bigwa, you will come to a fork in the road, where you bear right. From here, the road becomes steep and rough as it winds its way through the Uluguru Mountains onto a flat plain, which is usually the most difficult section to pass during the rains due to poor drainage. Shortly before Kisaki there is often – except for at the height of the dry season – a small river to cross, which isn't usually too much of a problem, apart from the steep bank on the far side. Allow five to eight hours for the stretch from Morogoro to Matambwe, depending on the season. If you are coming from Dar es Salaam and want to bypass Morogoro, there is an unsignposted left-hand turn-off via Mikese, about 25km east of town on the main Dar es Salaam road that meets up with the Kisaki road at Msumbisi.

Coming from Dar es Salaam, the last petrol station is at Kibiti (about 100km northeast of Mtemere Gate), although supplies aren't reliable; coming from the other direction, at Morogoro (about 160km from the Matambwe ranger post). Occasionally you may find diesel sold on the road side at Matombo, 50km south of Morogoro, although supplies aren't reliable. If you plan to drive around the Selous you will need to bring sufficient petrol supplies with you as there is none available at any of the lodges.

TRAIN

Train is a good option, especially if you're staying on the western side of the reserve or if you can splurge on the private train (see later in this section). All Tazara trains stop at Kisaki, which is about five to six hours from Dar es Salaam, and the first stop for the express train, and ordinary trains stop at Kinyanguru and Fuga stations (both of which are closer to the central camps) and at Matambwe (near Matambwe Gate). All the lodges will do pick-ups. For schedules, see p332.

It works best to take the train from Dar es Salaam to Selous Game Reserve. If you decide to do it the other way around, be prepared for delays of up to 20 hours going back to Dar es Salaam. The lodges can help you monitor the train's progress with their radios.

For a treat, **Foxes African Safaris** (☎ 0748-237422, 0744-237422; www.safariexpress.info) operate a private luxury train from Dar es Salaam, following the Tazara line along the northern border of the Selous (where it's quite likely you'll see animals) to Kidatu, 25km north of the entry gate for Udzungwa Mountains National Park, and stopping at Kinyanguru, Fuga, Matambwe and Kisaki stations en route. Departures in both directions are in the morning on Sunday, Tuesday and Friday (four to five hours to Fuga station, about seven hours to Kidatu; US$120/180 one way/return between Dar es Salaam and stations in the Selous).

Directory

CONTENTS

ACCOMMODATION

Tanzania boasts a wide range of accommodation options, ranging from humble cinderblock rooms with communal bucket bath to some of Africa's most luxurious safari lodges. Most mid-range and top-end hotels consider July, August and the Christmas/New Year holidays to be high season, and sometimes levy a 'peak-season' charge on top of regular high-season rates. During the March to early June low season, it's often possible to negotiate significant discounts – sometimes up to 50% – on room prices. A residents' permit also entitles you to discounts at some hotels.

PRACTICALITIES

- Tanzania uses the metric system for weights and measures.

- You can access electricity (220-250V AC, 50Hz) with British-style three-square-pin or two-round-pin plug adaptors.

- English-language newspapers available include the dailies *Guardian* and *Daily News* and the weeklies *Business Times, Financial Times* and the *East African*. The international newspaper the *International Herald Tribune* is also available.

- Radio Tanzania is the government-aligned national station, broadcasting in English and Swahili. BBC's World Service and Deutsche Welle transmit in English and Swahili.

Most sleeping listings in this book are divided into budget, mid-range and top-end categories. Budget rooms cost less than Tsh15,000, mid-range range from Tsh20,000 to Tsh100,000 and top-end rooms are more than Tsh100,000.

Camping

It's a good idea to carry a tent if you're planning to travel off the beaten track, and it can save you some money in and around the northern parks (though camping in the parks costs at least $20 per person per night).

NATIONAL PARKS

All the national parks have camp sites, designated as either 'ordinary' or 'special'. Ordinary camp sites have toilets (usually pit latrines), and sometimes a water source. Most ordinary camp sites are in reasonable condition, and some are very pleasant. Special camp sites are smaller, and more remote and rugged than ordinary sites, with no facilities at all. The idea is that the area remains as close to pristine as possible. Unlike ordinary camp sites, which don't require bookings, they must be booked in advance. They are also twice as expensive as ordinary camp sites. In most cases, once you make a booking, the special camp site is reserved exclusively for your group. For either type of camp site, plan on being completely self-sufficient, including taking your own drinking water.

Most parks also have simple huts or *bandas*, several have basic resthouses, and many northern circuit parks have hostels. For camping prices, see p35.

ELSEWHERE

There are camp sites in or near most major towns, near many of the national parks, and in some scenic locations along a few of the main highways (ie Dar es Salaam–Mbeya, and Tanga–Moshi); prices average US$3 to US$5 per person per night (or up to US$8 for those near national parks). Camping away from established sites is generally not advisable. If you are in a rural area and want to pitch your tent, seek permission first from the village head or elders. Camping is not permitted on Zanzibar. Camping prices quoted in this book are per person per night except as noted. For more on fly camps and permanent and luxury tented camps see right.

Guesthouses

Almost every Tanzanian town has at least one basic guesthouse. At the bottom end of the spectrum, expect a cement-block room – often small and poorly ventilated, and not always very clean – with a foam mattress, shared bathroom facilities (often long-drop toilets and bucket showers), and sometimes a fan and/or mosquito net. Rates for this type of place average Tsh2000 to Tsh4000 per room per night. The next level up gets you a cleaner, decent room, often with a bathroom (although not always with running or hot water). Prices for a single/double room with bathroom average about Tsh6000/8000.

For peace and quiet, guesthouses without bars are the best choice. In many towns, water is a problem during the dry season, so don't be surprised if your only choice at budget places is a bucket bath. Also, many of the cheaper places don't have hot water. This is a consideration in cooler areas, especially during winter, although most places will arrange a hot bucket if you ask. In Swahili, the word *hotel* or *hoteli* does not mean accommodation, instead it means food and drink. The more common term used for accommodation is *guesti*, or guesthouse, or more formally, *nyumba ya kulala wageni*.

There are numerous mission hostels and guesthouses, primarily for missionaries and aid-organisation staff, though a few are willing to accommodate travellers if space is available.

In coastal areas, you'll find *bandas*, or bungalows – small thatched-roof structures with wooden or earthern walls – ranging from simple huts to luxurious en suite affairs, and often built directly on the sand with the sea at your doorstep.

Hotels & Lodges

All larger towns have one or several mid-range hotels with en suite (widely referred to in Tanzania as 'self-contained') rooms, hot water, and a fan or an air conditioner. Facilities range from not so great to quite good value, and prices range from US$20 to US$80 per person.

Tanzania also has an impressive array of top-end hotels and lodges with all the amenities you would expect for the price you pay – from US$80 to US$200 or more per person per night. On the safari circuits there are some wonderful and very luxurious lodges costing from US$100 to US$500 per person per night, although at the top end of this spectrum prices are usually all-inclusive (which generally means accommodation, full board and activities).

At many of the parks, you'll come across 'permanent tented camps' or 'luxury tented camps'. These offer comfortable beds in (often spacious) canvas tents, with screened windows and most of the comforts that you would get in a hotel room, but with more of a wilderness feel. Most tents also have private bathrooms with running water, as well as generator-provided electricity for at least part of the evening. In contrast to permanent tented camps, which are designed to stay in the same place from season to season, 'mobile' or 'fly' camps are temporary camps set up for one or several nights, or perhaps just for one season. In the Tanzanian context, fly camps are often used for longer walking safaris away from the main tented camp or lodge, or to give you the chance for an even closer, more intimate bush experience. Although fly camps are a bit more rugged than permanent luxury tented camps (ie they may not have running water or similar features), they are invariably quite comfortable and fully cater to

---

ACCOMMODATION PRICES

Except as noted, accommodation prices in this book include bathroom and continental breakfast (coffee/tea, bread, jam and sometimes an egg). Many lodges and luxury camps in or near national parks quote all-inclusive prices, which means accommodation and full board plus excursions such as wildlife drives, short guided walks or boat safaris. Park entry fees and airport transfers can also be included, though you should clarify as details can vary significantly. When excursions are included, the standard is for two per day – one in the morning and one in the afternoon – with additional excursions incurring an extra charge. If you're not interested in organised excursions, ask for accommodation-only prices.

---

their guests with bush-style showers (where an elevated bag or drum is filled with solar-heated water) and other amenities. They are also often more expensive than regular tented camps or lodges, since provisions must be carried to the site.

ACTIVITIES
Bird-Watching
The Tanzanian air is filled with the chirping and twittering of more than a thousand bird species, and it's an excellent destination for ornithologists. In addition to the national parks, top birding spots include the eastern Usambara Mountains (p152), Lake Victoria (p213) and Lake Eyasi (p211). Useful websites include the **Tanzania Bird Atlas** (http://tanzaniabirdatlas.com/), the **Tanzania Bird Checklist** (www.tanzaniabirding.com/bird_checklists.htm), and the **Tanzania Hotspots** page on (www.camacdonald.com/birding/africatanzania.htm).

Boating, Sailing & Kayaking
Local dhow trips can be arranged from various places along the coast; for more on the realities of dhow travel, see the boxed text, p328. Better is to contact one of the coastal or island hotels, many of which have nice dhows that can be chartered for cruises. Catamarans and sailboats can be chartered on Zanzibar and Pemba, and Dar es Salaam, Tanga and Mikindani have yacht clubs.

Selous Game Reserve (p298) is the best place for boat safaris; there are also possibilities at Saadani Game Reserve (p143), and Arusha National Park (p191) has canoe safaris.

For upmarket trips down the Rufiji River and across the channel to Mafia island, contact Pole Pole Resort or Kinasi Lodge (p297).

Chimpanzee Tracking
Tanzania is the best destination in Africa for observing chimpanzees. Gombe Stream National Park (p236) and Mahale Mountains National Park (p237) have both hosted international research teams for decades, and are the places to go if you're interested in observing our primate cousins at close range. It's also possible to see chimpanzees at Rubondo Island National Park (p222).

Cycling
In rural areas, cycling is an agreeable way to get to know the country. For more information, see p327.

Diving
Slide beneath the surface of Tanzania's turquoise seas, and a whole new world opens up as shadowy manta rays float by in the depths, barracuda swim slowly past brightly coloured coral and dolphins cavort in the swells.

If you've ever thought about learning to dive, or want to brush up on your skills, Tanzania is a good place to do it, with the best diving around Zanzibar, Pemba and Mafia islands, where you'll also find an array of diving operators. There's also diving along the coast north of Dar es Salaam (p88), and in the southeast around Msimbati and Mtwara in the largely unexplored waters of the Mnazi Bay–Ruvuma Estuary Marine Park (p284).

Attractions throughout include extensive coral reefs, rich marine life, interesting wrecks in sheltered waters and a good mix of conditions. Also see the boxed text, p94.

Fishing
Mafia, the Pemba channel and the waters around Zanzibar have long been insider tips in deep sea fishing circles, and upmarket hotels in these areas are the best places to arrange charters. Other contacts include Ras Kutani (p90), which organises fishing excursions in the waters north of Mafia, and

Kilwa Lodge (p290), in Kilwa Masoko, are two other angler-friendly establishments.

Lake Victoria is renowned for its fishing, particularly for Nile perch. The best contacts here are Lukuba Island Lodge (p227), Rubondo Island Camp (p223) and Wag Hill Lodge (p218). In Dar es Salaam, anglers can inquire at Msasani Slipway (p83), at the Dar es Salaam Yacht Club, or at White Sands Hotel (p89).

Hiking & Trekking

The Usambara Mountains around Lushoto (p154) offer logistically easy and highly enjoyable walking. Other good hiking areas include the lush Udzungwa Mountains (p157), the Crater Highlands (p206), where you can hike through Maasai lands, surrounded by rugged Rift Valley vistas, and the much tamer eastern Usambara Mountains around Amani Nature Reserve (p152), where there's a network of trails. Mt Hanang (p190), southwest of Arusha, has a straightforward, satisfying climb to the top, while the Pare (p158) and Uluguru Mountains (see the boxed text, p254) both offer rewarding hiking and good introductions to local cultures for anyone who doesn't mind being self-sufficient and roughing things a little. For something more challenging, few excursions can rival the trek to the top of Mt Kilimanjaro (p172). The climb up Mt Meru (p194) is also challenging, and notable for its exceptional beauty.

If you plan to hike while in Tanzania, it's worth investing in a copy of Lonely Planet's *Trekking in East Africa*, which covers the possibilities in more detail.

Wildlife Watching

Tanzania is one of Africa's premier wildlife watching destinations, and a safari here is likely to be one of the highlights of your travels. Among the main draws: unparalleled scenery, a superlative wilderness ambience (especially in the southern parks) and sense of space, and an exceptional array and concentration of wildlife. For more, see the Safaris chapter (p37), and the wildlife special section.

BUSINESS HOURS

Business hours are listed inside the front cover, with exceptions noted in the individual listings. In addition to regular bank-ing hours, most forex bureaus remain open until 5pm Monday to Friday, and until noon on Saturday. Many shops and offices close for one to two hours between noon and 2pm, and – especially in coastal areas – on Friday afternoons for mosque services.

CHILDREN

Tanzanians tend to be very friendly and helpful towards children, and travelling here with young ones is unlikely to present any major problems. The main concerns are likely be the presence of malaria, the scarcity of decent medical facilities outside major towns, the length and safety risks involved in many road journeys, and the difficulty of finding clean, decent bathrooms outside mid-range and top-end hotels.

It's a good idea to travel with a blanket to spread out and use as a make-shift nappy changing area. Processed baby foods, powdered infant milk, disposable nappies and similar items are available in major towns, but otherwise carry your own wipes, as well as food (avoid feeding your children street food). Informal childcare is easy to arrange, the best bet is to ask at your hotel. Child seats for hire cars and safari vehicles are generally not available unless arranged in advance.

Some wildlife lodges have restrictions on accommodating children under 12; otherwise, most hotels are family friendly. Many places – including all national parks – offer significant discounts for children on entry fees and accommodation or camping rates although you'll need to specifically ask about these, especially if you're booking through a tour operator. Children under two or three years of age often stay free, and for those up to 12 years old sharing their parents' room you'll pay about 50% of the adult rate. Even in hotels without special rates, triple rooms are commonly available for not too much more than a double room. Mid-range and top-end places often have pools, or grassy areas where children can play.

In beach areas, keep in mind the risks of hookworm infestation in populated areas, and bilharzia infection in lakes. Other things to watch out for are sea urchins at the beach, and thorns and the like in the brush.

For protection against malaria, bring along mosquito nets for your children and ensure that they sleep under them, and check with your doctor regarding the use of malarial prophylactics. Bring long-sleeved shirts and trousers for dawn and dusk.

Wildlife watching is suitable for older children who have the patience to sit for long periods in a car, but less suitable for younger ones. For children who enjoy walking, one of the best destinations is the area around Lushoto (p157), where the relaxed pace and lack of traffic combine for a family-friendly ambience. Coastal destinations are another good bet, because of the beaches, and there are several water amusement parks near Dar es Salaam (p89).

Lonely Planet's *Travel with Children* by Cathy Lanigan is full of tips for keeping children and parents happy while on the road.

CLIMATE CHARTS

Tanzania's climate is determined in large part by the monsoon winds, which bring rains in two major periods. During the *masika* (long rains), from mid-March to May, it rains heavily almost every day, although seldom for the whole day. The lighter *mvuli* (short rains), fall during November, December and sometimes into January. Otherwise, altitude is the main factor to take into account. The climate along the coast is tropical, with relatively high humidity, while the central plateau tends to be somewhat cooler and arid. In the lush mountainous areas of the northeast and southwest, temperatures occasionally drop below 15°C at night during

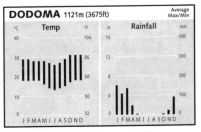

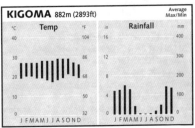

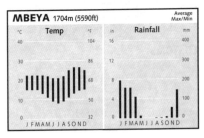

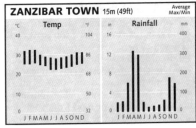

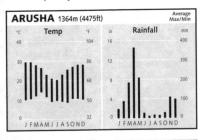

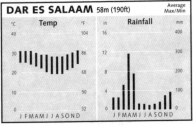

June and July, and you should be prepared for rain at any time of year. The coolest months throughout the country are from June to October, and the warmest from December to March.

COURSES
Language

Tanzania is the best place in East Africa to learn Swahili. Schools (many of which can arrange home stays) include:

DIRECTORY

Baptist Academy Swahili Language School
(☎ 026-270 0184/2986; hbcc@maf.or.tz) At Huruma
Baptist Conference Centre (p260).
ELCT Language & Orientation School (elct_language
_school@yahoo.com; PO Box 740, Morogoro, c/o Lutheran
Junior Seminary)
Institute of Swahili & Foreign Languages (Map
p98-9; ☎ 024-223 0724, 223 3337; takiluki@zanlink
.com; PO Box 882, Zanzibar, attn: Department of Swahili
for Foreigners; Vuga Rd, Zanzibar Town) Also see www
.glcom.com/hassan/takiluki.html.
Julius Nyerere Cultural Centre (Nyumba ya Sanaa;
☎ 022-213 3960; Ohio St, Dar es Salaam) Next to Royal
Palm Hotel; courses offered in conjunction with KIU, above.
KIU Ltd (☎ 022-285 1509; www.swahilicourses.com) At
various locations in Dar es Salaam.
Makoko Language School (☎ 028-264 2518;
swahilimusoma@juasun.net) In Makoko neighbourhood,
on the outskirts of Musoma.
MS Training Centre for Development Cooperation
(☎ 027-255 3837/8; www.mstcdc.or.tz) About 15km
outside Arusha, near Usa River.
University of Dar es Salaam (☎ 022-241 0757;
www.udsm.ac.tz/kiswahilicourses.html) In Dar es Salaam.

CUSTOMS

Exporting seashells, coral, ivory and turtle
shells is illegal. You can export a maximum
of Tsh2000 without declaration. There's no
limit on the importation of foreign currency; amounts over US$10,000 must be
declared.

DANGERS & ANNOYANCES

Tanzania is in general a safe, hassle-free
country, and can be a relief if you've recently
been somewhere like Nairobi. That said,
you do need to take the usual precautions.
Avoid isolated areas, especially stretches of
beach, and in cities and tourist areas take a
taxi at night. When using public transport,
don't accept drinks or food from someone
you don't know, and be sceptical of anyone
who comes up to you on the street asking
you whether you remember them from the
airport, your hotel or wherever.

In tourist areas – especially Arusha,
Moshi and Zanzibar – touts and flycatchers can be extremely aggressive, especially
around bus stations and budget tourist hotels. Do everything you can to minimise
the impression that you're a newly arrived
tourist. Duck into a shop if you need to get
your bearings or look at a map, and don't
walk around any more than necessary with

TRAVEL ADVISORIES

Government travel advisories are a good
source of updated security information,
and should be looked at before travel to
Tanzania:

- Australia – www.dfat.gov.au/zw-cgi
  /view/Advice/Tanzania

- Canada – www.voyage.gc.ca/dest/ctry
  /reportpage-en.asp

- UK – www.fco.gov.uk

- US – www.travel.state.gov/travel/index

---

your luggage. While looking for a room,
leave your bag with a friend or reliable hotel
rather than walking around town with it.
Buy your bus tickets a day in advance (without your luggage) and, when arriving in a
new city, take a taxi from the bus station
to your hotel. Be very wary of anyone who
approaches you on the street, at the bus
station or in your hotel offering safari deals,
and never pay any money for a safari or trek
in advance until you've thoroughly checked
out the company.

In western Tanzania along the Burundi
border, there are sporadic outbursts of banditry and political unrest. Get an update
from your embassy before travelling there.

A few more tips:

- Avoid external money pouches, dangling
  backpacks and camera bags, and leave
  jewellery, fancy watches, personal stereos
  and the like at home. Carry your passport, money and other documents in a
  pouch against your skin, hidden under
  loose-fitting clothing. Or, better, store
  valuables in a hotel safe, if there's a reliable one, ideally inside a pouch with a
  lockable zip to prevent tampering.

- Arriving for the first time at major bus stations, especially in Arusha, can be a fairly
  traumatic experience, as you'll probably
  be besieged by touts as you get off the bus,
  all reaching to help you with your pack
  and trying to sell you a safari. Have your
  luggage as consolidated as possible, with
  your valuables well hidden under your
  clothes. Try to spot the taxi area before
  disembarking, and make a beeline for it.
  It's well worth a few extra dollars for the
  fare, rather than attempting to walk to
  your hotel with your luggage.

Take requests for donations from 'refugees', 'students' or others with a grain of salt. Contributions to humanitarian causes are best done through an established agency or project.

Keep the side windows up in vehicles when stopped in traffic, and keep your bags out of sight, eg, on the floor behind your legs.

When bargaining or discussing prices, don't do so with your money or wallet in your hand.

DISABLED TRAVELLERS

While there are few facilities for the disabled, Tanzanians are generally quite accommodating, and willing to offer whatever assistance they can as long as they understand what you need. Disabled travel is becoming increasingly common on the northern safari circuit, and Abercrombie & Kent and several other tour operators listed on p326 cater to disabled travellers. Some considerations:

While newer lodges often have wheelchair accessible rooms (noted in individual listings), few hotels have lifts (elevators), and many have narrow stairwells. This is particularly true of Stone Town on Zanzibar, where stairwells can be steep and narrow. Grips or railings in the bathrooms are extremely rare.

Many park lodges and camps are built on ground level. However access paths – in an attempt to maintain a natural environment – are sometimes rough or rocky, and rooms or tents raised, so it's best to inquire about access before booking.

As far as we know, there are no Braille signboards at any parks or museums, nor any facilities for deaf travellers.

Minibuses are widely available both on Zanzibar and on the mainland, and can be chartered for transport and customised safaris. Large or wide-door vehicles can also be arranged through car-rental agencies in Dar es Salaam, and with Arusha-based tour operators. Throughout the country, taxis are usually small sedans, and buses are not wheelchair equipped.

One of the most helpful starting points is **Accessible Journeys** (www.disabilitytravel.com), with northern circuit safari itineraries for disa-

bled travellers. Other entities to check with – all of which disseminate travel information for the mobility impaired – include **Access-Able Travel Source** (www.access-able.com); **Mobility International** (www.miusa.org); **National Information Communication Awareness Network** (www.nican.com.au); and **Holiday Care** (www.holidaycare.org.uk). In Tanzania, the main organisations are the **Tanzania Association for the Disabled** (Chawata; ☎ 0744-587376; chawatahq@hotmail.com) in Dar es Salaam, with branches elsewhere in the country; and the **Zanzibar Association of the Disabled** (☎ 024-223 3719; uwz@zanzinet.com) in Zanzibar Town.

DISCOUNT CARDS

A student ID will get you a 50% discount on train fares.

EMBASSIES & CONSULATES
Tanzanian Embassies & Consulates

Tanzanian representation in the region and around the world includes the following:
Australia Sydney (☎ 02-9261 0911; www.tanzaniaconsul.com; Level 3, 185 Liverpool St, Sydney, NSW 2000); Perth (☎ 08-9322 6222; legal@murcia.com.au; Level 25, QV1 Building, 250 St George's Terrace, Perth WA 6000). The Sydney embassy covers NSW, VIC, ACT and Tasmania, the Perth embassy SA, NT and QLD.
Canada (☎ 0613-232 1500; tzottawa@synapse.net; 50 Range Rd, Ottawa, Ontario KIN 8J4)
France (☎ 01-5370 6370, 4755 0546; tanzanie@infonie.fr; 13 Ave Raymond Poincare, 75116 Paris)
Germany (☎ 030-303 0800; www.tanzania-gov.de; Eschenallee 11, 14050 Berlin-Charlottenburg)
Italy (☎ 06-334 85801; www.tanzania-gov.it; Viale Cortina d'Ampezzo 185, Rome)
Japan (☎ 03-425 4531; tzrepjp@japan.co.jp; 21-9, Kamiyoga 4, Chome Setagaya-Ku, Tokyo 158)
Kenya Nairobi (☎ 02-331056, 331104; tanzania@users.africaonline.co.ke; Reinsurance Plaza, 9th fl, between Tarifa Rd & Aga Khan Walk, Nairobi); Mombasa Consulate (tancon@users.africonline.co.ke; Palli House, Nyerere Ave)
Mozambique (☎ 01-490110; Ujamaa House, 852 Ave Mártires de Machava, Maputo)
The Netherlands (☎ 0180-320 939; Parallelweg Zuid 215, 2914 LE Nieuwerkerk aan den Ijssel)
Rwanda (tanzarep@rwandatell.rwandal.com; 15 Avenue Paul VI, Kigali)
South Africa (☎ 012-342 4393; tanzania@cis.co.za; PO Box 56572, Arcadia 0007, Pretoria)
Uganda (☎ 256-41-256292, 256272; tzrepkla@imul.com; 6 Kagera Rd, Kampala)
United Kingdom (☎ 020-7499 8951; www.tanzania-online.gov.uk; 43 Hertford St, London W1Y 8DB)

USA Washington (☎ 1-202-939 6125; www.tanzania embassy-us.org; 2139 R St, NW, Washington DC); New York Consulate (☎ 1-212-972 9160; 205 East 42nd St, New York, NY)
Zambia (☎ 01-253320, 227698; tzreplsk@zamnet.zm; Ujamaa House, 5200 United Nations Ave, Lusaka)

Tanzania also has diplomatic representation in Belgium (Brussels), China (Beijing), Congo (Zaïre) (Kinshasa), Egypt (Cairo), Ethiopia (Addis Ababa), India (New Delhi), Nigeria (Lagos), Sweden (Stockholm), Switzerland (Geneva) and Zimbabwe (Harare). There's no Tanzanian high commission in Malawi.

Embassies & Consulates in Tanzania
Australians can contact the Canadian embassy (www.embassy.gov.au/). Except as noted, most are open from about 8am to at least 3pm, often with a midday break. Visa information is given for Tanzania's neighbours; applications for all should be made in the morning. Embassies and consulates in Dar es Salaam include the following:
Belgium (Map p73; ☎ 211 4025, 211 2503; daressalaam@diplobel.org; 5 Ocean Rd, Upanga)
Burundi (Map p73; Lugalo St, Upanga; ☺ 8am-5pm Mon-Fri) One-month single-entry visas cost US$45 plus two photos and are issued within 24 hours. Burundi also has a consulate in Kigoma (p233).
Canada (Map p74; ☎ 211 2831; www.dfait-maeci .gc.ca/tanzania; 38 Mirambo St)
Congo (Zaïre) (Map p73; Maliki Rd, Upanga; ☺ 8.30am-3pm Mon-Fri) One-month single-entry visas cost US$50, require two photos, and are available within three days. You'll need a letter from an employer, tour operator or embassy explaining your purpose. The consulate in Kigoma (p233) issues visas within 24 hours, and without a letter, but with lots of questions.
France (Map p73; ☎ 266 6021; www.ambafrance -tz.org; Ali Hassan Mwinyi Rd)
Germany (Map p74; ☎ 211 7409 to 7415; www.dares salam.diplo.de/en/Startseite.html; cnr Mirambo & Garden Sts)
India (Map p73; ☎ 260 0714; www.hcindiatz.org; 1349 Haile Selassie Rd, Masaki)
Ireland (Map p73; ☎ 260 2355/6, 266 6211; iremb@raha.com; 1131 Msasani Rd) Just off Haile Selassie Rd, near the International School.
Italy (Map p73; ☎ 211 5935; www.italdipldar.org in Italian; 316 Lugalo St, Upanga)
Kenya (Map p73; ☎ 270 1747; 14 Ursino, cnr Kawawa & Old Bagamoyo Rds; ☺ 8am-2.30pm Mon-Fri) One-month single-entry visas cost Tsh50,000 (no photos required), and are issued within 24 hours.

Malawi (Map p74; ☎ 0748-481740; 1st fl, Zambia House, cnr Ohio St & Sokoine Dr; ☺ 8am-3pm Mon-Fri) Many nationalities, including USA and UK, don't require visas. For those that do, one-month single-entry visas cost US$70 plus two photos and are issued within 24 hours.
Mozambique (Map p74; ☎ 211 6502; 25 Garden Ave; ☺ 8am-3pm Mon-Fri) One-month single-entry visas cost US$40/35 for same-day/two-day service, plus two photos. Visas are also issued at the Mozambique consulate in Zanzibar Town (p97).
Netherlands (Map p74; ☎ 211 000; www.netherlands -embassy.go.tz; cnr Mirambo St & Garden Ave)
Oman (Map p98-9; ☎ 223 0066; Vuga Rd, Zanzibar Town)
Rwanda (Map p73; ☎ 211 5889; 32 Ali Hassan Mwinyi Rd, Upanga; ☺ 8am -3.30pm Mon-Fri) One-month single-entry visas cost US$45 plus two photos, and are ready within three days.
Uganda (Map p73; ☎ 266 7009; 25 Msasani Rd, near Oyster Bay Primary School; ☺ 8.30am-4.30pm Mon-Fri) Three-month single-entry visas cost US$30 plus two photos and are issued the same day.
UK (Map p74; ☎ 211 0101; bch.dar@fco.gov.uk; cnr Mirambo & Garden Sts)
USA (Map p73; ☎ 266 8001; http://usembassy.state .gov/tanzania; Old Bagamoyo & Kawawa Rds)
Zambia (Map p74; ☎ 212 5529; Zambia House, cnr Ohio St & Sokoine Dr; ☺ visa applications 9am-11am, visa pick-ups 2pm-3pm, Mon-Fri) Three-month single-entry visas cost Tsh25,000-43,000 depending on nationality, and require two photos. They're processed the same day.

FESTIVALS & EVENTS
The best festivals and celebrations in Tanzania are the small-scale ones that aren't announced anywhere, such as being invited to a wedding in a small town, or to a rite of passage celebration. Getting away from the tourist haunts and into the villages, and mingling with Tanzanians is the best way to find out about these. Events that draw more attention include the following:

JANUARY
Music Crossroads Southern Africa (www.jmi.net /activities/crossroads/) A showcase for young musical talent from throughout southern and East Africa; times and locations vary, but the most recent festivals have been held in Dar es Salaam.

FEBRUARY
Sauti za Busara (☎ 024-223 2423; busara@zanlink .com) A three-day music and dance festival centred around all things Swahili, traditional and modern; dates and location vary.

MARCH

Kilimanjaro Marathon (www.kilimanjaromarathon
.com) Something to do around the foothills, just in case
climbing to the top of the mountain isn't enough; it's held
in February or March, and the start and finish points are
in Moshi.

JULY

Festival of the Dhow Countries (www.ziff.or.tz)
A two-week extravaganza of dance, music, film and
literature from Tanzania and other Indian Ocean countries,
with the **Zanzibar International Film Festival** as its
centrepiece; held in early July.

Mwaka Kogwa A four-day festival held in late July to
mark Nairuzim (the Shirazi New Year); festivities are best in
Makunduchi (p123) on Zanzibar.

SEPTEMBER

Bagamoyo Arts Festival (www.sanaabagamoyo
.com) This fun festival involves a week of traditional
music, dance, acrobatics, poetry reading and more,
featuring local and regional ensembles. It is held in late
September.

FOOD

For more on the fine art of dining well in
Tanzania, see the Food & Drink chapter
(p65).

Eating listings in this book are ordered
by price as follows: budget (under Tsh5000),
mid-range (Tsh5000 to Tsh10,000) and top
end (over Tsh10,000). Supplementing what
you'll find in restaurants is an abundance of
fresh tropical fruits and a reasonably good
selection of vegetables, both available at
markets throughout the country.

GAY & LESBIAN TRAVELLERS

From an official point of view, homosexual-
ity is illegal in Tanzania, incurring penalties
of up to 14 years imprisonment. While pros-
ecutions rarely occur, discretion is advised as
gay sexual relationships are culturally taboo,
and public displays of affection, whether between people of the same or opposite sex, are
frowned upon. Traditionally, gay travellers
have experienced few particular difficulties.
However, in early 2003, a demonstration was
staged in Dar es Salaam by an influential
Muslim organisation protesting the anticipated arrival of a large group of gay tourists
from the USA. The tour group's visit was
ultimately postponed due to other factors,
and there have been no further incidents, so
hopefully this was only an isolated incident.

In general, Zanzibar, followed by Arusha,
tend to be more tolerant of gay relationships,
at least privately, than areas that see fewer
visitors.

The website www.purpleroofs.com/africa
/tanzaniata.html lists a number of gay or
gay-friendly tour companies in the region
which may be able to help you plan your
trip. For all-inclusive packages, try **Atlan-
tis Events** (www.atlantisevents.com) or **David Tours**
(www.davidtours.com).

HOLIDAYS

Government holidays tend to be quiet affairs, with all businesses closed, but if you're
in the right place at the right time, you may
catch parades and other events. Christian religious feasts invariably centre around beautiful church services and singing. Eid al-Fitr
and the other Muslim holidays are colourful anywhere, but particularly on Zanzibar,
where you'll be treated to the sight of entire
families dressed up and celebrating, processions in the streets and other festivities.

New Year's Day 1 January
Zanzibar Revolution Day 12 January
Easter March/April – Good Friday, Holy Saturday and
Easter Monday
Union Day 26 April
Labour Day 1 May
Saba Saba (Peasants' Day) 7 July
Nane Nane (Farmers' Day) 8 August
Independence Day 9 December
Christmas 25 December
Boxing Day 26 December

The dates of Islamic holidays depend on the
moon, and are known for certain only a few
days in advance. They fall about 11 days earlier each year, and include the following:

Eid al-Kebir (Eid al-Haji) Commemorates the moment
when Abraham was about to sacrifice his son in obedience
to God's command, only to have God intercede at the last
moment and substitute a ram instead. It coincides with the
end of the pilgrimage (*hajj*) to Mecca.

Eid al-Fitr The end of Ramadan, and East Africa's most
important Islamic celebration; celebrated as a two-day
holiday in many areas.

Eid al-Moulid (Maulidi) The birthday of the Prophet
Mohammed.

Ramadan The annual 30-day fast when adherents do not
eat or drink from sunrise to sunset.

Approximate dates for these events are
shown following. Although Ramadan is not

a public holiday, restaurants are often closed during this time on Zanzibar and in other coastal areas.

Event	2005	2006	2007
Ramadan begins	5 Oct	24 Sep	13 Sep
Eid al-Fitr (end of Ramadan, two day holiday)	3 Nov	24 Oct	13 Oct
Eid al-Kebir (Eid al-Haji)	21 Jan	10 Jan	31 Dec (2006)
Eid al-Moulid	21 Apr	11 Apr	31 Mar

INSURANCE

Travel insurance covering theft, loss and medical problems is highly recommended. Before choosing a policy, spend time shopping around, as those designed for short package tours in Europe may not be suitable for the wilds of Tanzania. Also be sure to read the fine print, as some policies specifically exclude 'dangerous activities', which can mean scuba diving, motorcycling and even trekking. A locally acquired motorcycle licence isn't valid under some policies. Some policies pay doctors or hospitals directly, while others require you to pay on the spot and claim later. If you have to claim later, keep all documentation. Most importantly, check that the policy covers an emergency flight home.

Before heading to Tanzania, it's well worth taking out a membership with the **African Medical & Research Foundation** (Amref; www.amref.org; Nairobi emergency lines ☎ 254-2-501280, 602492, satellite fax 000873 761 298080; Nairobi head office ☎ 254-2-501301; Dar es Salaam branch office ☎ 022-211 6610, 212 7187, 211 5832; Ali Hassan Mwinyi Rd just north of Bibi Titi Mohammed Rd; Canada national office ☎ 416-961 6981; amref@web.apc.org). This entitles you to emergency regional evacuation by the Flying Doctors' Society of Africa, which operates 24-hour air ambulance service based out of Wilson airport in Nairobi. A two month membership costs US$25/50 for evacuations within a 500km/1000km radius of Nairobi. The 1000km membership encompasses the entire East African region, except for southernmost Tanzania around Songea, Tunduru and Mtwara.

INTERNET ACCESS

Most travellers make constant use of Internet cafés and free Web-based email such as Yahoo (www.yahoo.com) or Hotmail (www.hotmail.com).

If you're travelling with a notebook or hand-held computer, be aware that your modem may not work once you leave your home country. The safest option is to buy a reputable 'global' modem before you leave home, or buy a local PC-card modem if you're spending an extended time in any one country. For more information on travelling with a portable computer, see www.teleadapt.com.

Tanzania is online, with numerous Internet cafés in Dar es Salaam and Zanzibar and at least one or two in major towns. The exception to this is parts of southern and western Tanzania, where connections are few and far between. Prices range from less than Tsh500 per hour in Dar es Salaam to about Tsh2000 per hour in outlying areas. Top-end hotels also have Internet access, though don't expect to be able to connect while on safari.

If you're travelling with a laptop, you'll be able to hook up at top-end hotels and the occasional mid-range hotel (take a universal adaptor for the modem).

See p11 for helpful websites for planning your Tanzanian travels.

LEGAL MATTERS

Apart from traffic offences such as speeding and driving without a seatbelt (mandatory for driver and front seat passengers), the main area to watch out for is drug use and possession. Marijuana (*bangi* or *ganja*) is widely available in some areas, and is frequently offered to tourists on the street in places like Zanzibar and Dar es Salaam – almost always as part of a setup involving the police or fake police. If you're caught, expect to pay a large bribe to avoid arrest or imprisonment. In Dar es Salaam, the typical scheme is that you'll be approached by a couple of men who walk along with you, strike up a conversation and try to sell you drugs. Before you've had a chance to shake them loose, policemen (sometimes legitimate, and sometimes not) suddenly appear and insist that you pay a huge fine for being involved in the purchase of illegal drugs. Protestations to the contrary are generally in vain, and there's often little you can do other than instantly hightailing it in the opposite direction if you smell this scam coming. If you are caught, insist on going to the nearest police station before paying anything, and whittle the bribe down as low as you can. Initial demands can be as high as US$300, but if you're savvy, you should be able to get away with under US$50.

MAPS

Good country maps include those published by Nelles (1:1,500,000) and Harms-ic, both available in Tanzania and elsewhere. Harms-ic also publishes maps for Lake Manyara National Park and the Ngorongoro Conservation Area.

The **Surveys and Mapping Division's Map Sales Office** (cnr Kivukoni Front & Luthuli St, Dar es Salaam; ◷ 8am-2pm Mon-Fri), sells dated topographical maps (1:50,000) for mainland Tanzania, although individual sheets covering popular areas are often out of stock. Topographical maps for Zanzibar and Pemba are available in Stone Town (p97).

An excellent series of attractive, colourful maps, hand-drawn by a man named Giovanni Tombazzi and marketed under the name MaCo, cover Zanzibar, Arusha and many northern Tanzania parks. They're available for about US$5 in bookshops in Dar es Salaam, Arusha and Zanzibar Town.

MONEY

Tanzania's currency is the Tanzanian shilling (Tsh). There are bills of Tsh10,000, 5000, 1000, 500 and 200, and coins of Tsh200, 100, 50, 20, 10, five and one shilling(s). For exchange rates, see the table inside the front cover. For information on costs, see p9.

The best currency to bring is US dollars in a mixture of cash and travellers cheques, large and small denominations, plus a Visa card for withdrawing money from ATMs.

ATMs

Standard Chartered (with branches in Dar es Salaam, Arusha, Moshi and Mwanza) and Barclays (Dar es Salaam and Arusha) have ATMs that allow you to withdraw shillings with a Visa card to a maximum of Tsh400,000 per day. Some ATMs also accept MasterCard. All are open 24 hours in theory, though in practice they're frequently out of service. The machines also have a tendency to keep your card if you delay in entering the password or enter it incorrectly. If this happens, all have emergency numbers that you can call, to retrieve the card the next business day.

Black Market

There's essentially no black market for foreign currency. You can assume that the frequent offers you'll receive on the street to change at high rates of exchange are a set-up.

WAYS TO SAVE

Whatever your budget, some tips if you're trying to save money:

▪ Travel in the low season, and always ask about children's discounts.

▪ Travel in a group (four is ideal) for organised treks and safaris.

▪ Keep your schedule flexible to take advantage of last minute deals.

▪ Stay outside park boundaries to save the daily entry fee, especially at those parks and reserves where you can do wildlife excursions outside the boundaries, or where the entry fee is valid for multiple admissions within a 24-hour period.

▪ Enter parks in the middle of the day: as fees are calculated on a 24-hour basis, you'll be able to enjoy prime evening and morning wildlife viewing hours for just one day's payment.

▪ Camp whenever possible.

▪ Focus on easily accessed parks and reserves to minimise transportation costs.

▪ Use public transport.

▪ Do Cultural Tourism Programs rather than wildlife safaris.

▪ Eat local food.

▪ Stock up on food and drink in major towns to avoid expensive hotel fare and pricey shops in tourist areas.

▪ Offer to pay in cash – sometimes this may result in a discount.

Cash

US dollars are the most convenient foreign currency and get the best rates, although euros, British pounds and other major currencies are readily accepted in Dar es Salaam, Arusha and Zanzibar. With dollars, you'll get higher rates for US$100 and US$50 bills than for smaller denominations.

Credit Cards

Some top-end hotels, tour operators, and a few mid-range establishments accept credit cards – most with a 5% to 10% commission – though their use isn't common.

You can get cash advances at poor rates against Visa or MasterCard in Dar es Salaam, Arusha and Zanzibar Town.

Exchanging Money

You can change cash and travellers cheques with a minimum of hassle at banks or foreign exchange (forex) bureaus in all major towns and cities; rates and commissions vary, so it pays to shop around. Forex bureaus are usually quicker, less bureaucratic and offer higher rates for cash, although many smaller towns don't have them. The most useful bank for changing money is National Bank of Commerce (NBC), with branches throughout the country, many with ATMs. Banks in small towns usually change cash only, and all charge commissions for travellers cheques (NBC's are by far the lowest, at about 0.5% of the transaction amount; others go as high as US$40 per transaction, minimum.) Throughout the country, banks and forex bureaus are closed from noon Saturday until Monday morning.

In order to reconvert Tanzanian shillings to hard currency at the end of your trip, it's a good idea to save at least some of your exchange receipts, though they are seldom checked. The easiest places to reconvert currency are at the airports in Dar es Salaam and Kilimanjaro. Otherwise you can convert at forex shops or banks in major towns.

In theory, it's required for foreigners to pay for accommodation, park fees, organised tours, upmarket hotels and the Zanzibar ferries in dollars. If you have an excess of shillings, it's usually possible to pay in shillings at roughly the going rate. You'll need shillings for food, taxis, souvenirs and for some budget guesthouses.

Taxes

Tanzania has a 20% value-added tax (VAT) that's usually included in quoted prices.

Tipping

Tipping is generally not practised in small, local establishments, especially in rural areas. However, in major towns and in establishments frequented by tourists, tips are expected. Some top-end places include a service charge in the bill. Otherwise, depending on the situation, either rounding out the bill, or about 10% is standard, assuming the service warrants it. On treks and safaris, it's common practice to tip drivers, guides, porters and other staff. For guidelines on amounts see p38 for safaris and p173 and p194 for treks.

Travellers Cheques

Travellers cheques can be easily cashed in major towns, less easily elsewhere. Exchange rates are slightly lower than for cash, and most hotels don't take them as direct payment. Most banks and forex bureaus require you to show the original purchase receipt before exchanging the cheques.

PHOTOGRAPHY & VIDEO
Film & Equipment

Print film, including Kodak and Fuji, is sold in major towns and tourist areas (about Tsh3500 for a roll of 100ASA/36 exposures). Slide film (Kodak and Fuji, 100ASA) is available in Dar es Salaam (about Tsh9000 for 36 exposures), on Zanzibar, in Arusha and other tourist areas. Faster speeds are difficult to find.

For developing print film, most local pros either use Burhani in Dar es Salaam or send their film to Nairobi or elsewhere. Dar es Salaam is the only place to process slide film, although here, too, most professionals send their film to Nairobi, or develop it elsewhere.

Serious wildlife photography requires an SLR (single lens reflex) camera, which can take long focal-length lenses. Zoom lenses are good as you can frame your shot easily to get the best composition; a 200mm lens is the minimum you will need for good close-up shots. Telephoto (fixed focal-length) lenses give better results than zoom lenses, although you'll be limited by having to carry a separate lens for various focal lengths. For both zoom and telephoto lenses you'll need 200ASA or 400ASA film. Whatever equipment you take, be sure that it's in a bag protecting it from dust and knocks. Also make sure your travel insurance policy covers your camera in case it is stolen.

Lonely Planet's *Travel Photography: A Guide to Taking Better Pictures* by Richard I'Anson is full of helpful tips for taking photographs while on the road.

Tips & Restrictions

Always ask permission first before photographing people and always respect their wishes. In many places, locals will ask for a fee before allowing you to photograph them, which is fair enough, although rates are high these days – from Tsh1000 in tourist areas.

Don't take photos of anything connected with the government and the military, including army barracks, land and people anywhere close to army barracks. Government offices, post offices, banks, ports, train stations and airports are also off limits.

POST

Postage via airmail to the USA/Australia/ Europe costs from Tsh600/800/500 and is reasonably reliable, but don't send any valuables.

There's poste restante service in all major towns, with a charge of Tsh200 per received letter. Mail is held for at least one month.

SHOPPING

Tanzania has an enticing selection of crafts, ranging from basketry and woodcarvings to textiles and paintings. Craft centres and artist cooperatives in major towns have a wide variety and prices are very reasonable. Things to look for include Makonde carvings (best purchased in Dar es Salaam or Mtwara); Tingatinga paintings (the best buys are in Dar es Salaam); Singida baskets (the best are in the villages around Singida, but these villages are difficult to reach, so try craft shops in Dar es Salaam and Arusha); and *vibuyu* (carved gourds) and Gogo woodcarvings (both sold in Dodoma). There are also some wonderful textiles, primarily the *kanga* – the traditional cloth garment worn by many Tanzanian women, with Swahili sayings printed along the edge – and the heavier *kitenge* (Zanzibar Town has some great buys). Dar es Salaam is a good place to shop for textiles, especially batiks. For more unusual choices, look for some of the crafts made by children from recycled wires, soft-drink cans and the like.

When buying woodcarvings, remember most of the pieces marketed as ebony are really *mpinga* (African blackwood), while others are simply lighter wood that has been blackened with dye or shoe polish. Rubbing the piece with a wet finger, or smelling it, should tip you off. When assessing quality, look at the attention that has been given to detail and the craftsmanship. With textiles, spread them out to check for flaws or uneven cuts.

Bargaining

Bargaining is expected by vendors in tourist areas, particularly souvenir vendors, except in a limited number of fixed-price shops. However, at markets and other venues away from tourist areas, and for non-tourist items, the price quoted to you will often be the 'real' price – so in these situations don't immediately assume that the quote you've been given is too high.

There are no set rules for bargaining, other than that it should always be conducted in a friendly and spirited manner. Before starting, it's worth shopping around for a while to get a feel for the 'value' of the item you want. Asking others what they have paid can also be helpful. Once you start negotiating, if things become exasperating, or seem like a waste of time, politely take your leave. Sometimes sellers will call you back if they think their stubbornness has been counterproductive. Very few will pass up the chance of making a sale, however thin the profit. If the vendor won't come down to a price you feel is fair, it means that they aren't making a profit, or that too many high-rolling foreigners have passed through already.

SOLO TRAVELLERS

While you may be a minor curiosity in rural areas, especially solo women travellers, there are no particular problems with travelling solo in Tanzania, whether you're male or female. Times when it is advantageous to join a group are for safaris and treks – when going in a group can be a significant cost-saver – and when going out at night. If you go out alone at night, take taxis and use extra caution, especially in urban and tourist areas. Whatever the time of day, avoid isolating situations, including lonely stretches of beach. Also see Women Travellers, opposite.

TELEPHONE

You can make domestic and international calls from Tanzania Telecom offices in all major towns (usually located near the post office), or from private communications shops. Local calls are cheap – about Tsh100 per minute. Costs for domestic long-distance calls vary depending on distance, but average about Tsh1000 for the first three minutes plus Tsh500 per minute thereafter. Calls to mobile phones cost Tsh500 per minute. International calls start about US$2 per minute (less evenings and weekends), though in a few places, there's much cheaper Internet dialling for about half this price. There are card phones in major towns (buy cards during business hours at TTCL or at shops near the phones) but for international calls, even with the most expensive card (Tsh7500, 150 units), you'll only get a few minutes to talk.

Mobile Phones

Mobile (cell) phones are very common. The rapidly expanding network covers major towns throughout the country, plus a wide arc encompassing most of the north and northeast. In the south, west and centre, you often won't get a signal once you're away from the larger towns. Mobile phone numbers are six digits, preceded by (0)741 (Mobitel), (0)744 and (0)745 (Vodacom), (0)748 (Celtel) or (on Zanzibar) (0)747. To reach a mobile telephone number from outside Tanzania, dial the country code, then the mobile phone code without the initial 0, and then the six-digit number. From within Tanzania, keep the initial 0 and don't use any other area code.

All the companies sell pre-paid starter packages, and top-up cards are on sale at shops throughout the country. Vodacom has the widest call range. If you're bringing your own phone, check with your home company about using it in Tanzania.

Phone Codes

Tanzania's country code is ☎ 255. To make an international call, dial ☎ 000, followed by the country code, local area code (without the initial '0') and telephone number.

Most telephone numbers are seven digits, although there are still a few five-digit numbers around. Area codes must be used whenever you dial long-distance. They are given in the regional chapters.

TIME

Time in Tanzania is GMT/UTC plus three hours. There is no daylight saving. See the World Time Zones map, p343.

Tanzanians use the Swahili system of telling time, in which the first hour is *saa moja (asubuhi)*, corresponding with 7am. Counting begins again with *saa moja (jioni)* (the first hour, evening, corresponding with 7pm). Although most will switch to the international clock when speaking English with foreigners, confusion sometimes occurs, so ask people to confirm whether they are using *saa za kizungu* (international time) or *saa za kiswahili* (Swahili time). Signboards with opening hours are often posted in Swahili time.

TOILETS

Toilets vary from standard long-drops to full-flush luxury conveniences that spring up in the most unlikely places. Almost all mid-range and top-end hotels sport flushable sit-down types, although at the lower end of the price range, toilet seats are a rare commodity. Budget guesthouses often have squat-style toilets – sometimes equipped with a flush mechanism, otherwise with a bucket and scoop.

Cleanliness levels vary; if you go in expecting the worst, you'll often be surprised that they're not all that bad. Toilets with running water are a rarity outside major hotels. If you see a bucket with water nearby, use it for flushing. Paper (you'll invariably need to supply your own) should be deposited in the can that's usually in the corner.

Many upmarket bush camps have 'dry' toilets – just a fancy version of the long drop with a Western-style seat perched on top – though it's all generally quite hygienic. When trekking it's a good practice to burn your toilet paper before burying it.

TOURIST INFORMATION

The **Tanzania Tourist Board** (TTB; www.tanzania -web.com) has offices in Dar es Salaam (p76) and Arusha (p179). In the UK, the Tanzania Tourist Board is represented by the **Tanzania Trade Centre** (☎ 0207-407 0566; director@tanzatrade .co.uk; 80 Borough High St, London, SE1 1LL). In the USA, the TTB representative is **The Bradford Group** (☎ 212-447 0027; tanzania@bradfordmarketing .org; 347 Fifth Ave, Suite 610, New York, NY 10016).

VISAS

Almost everyone needs a visa, which currently cost between US$20 and US$50, depending on nationality, for a single-entry visa valid for up to three months. It's best to get the visa in advance (and necessary if you want multiple entry), though they're currently issued at Dar es Salaam and Kilimanjaro airports, and at most border crossings (US dollars cash only, single-entry only). Some embassies require you to show proof of an onward ticket before they'll issue a visa, though a flight itinerary will usually suffice.

Visa Extensions

One month is the normal visa validity, and three months the maximum. For extensions within the three-month limit, there are immigration offices in all major towns; the process is free and straightforward. Extensions after three months are difficult – you'll usually need to leave the country and apply for a new visa.

WOMEN TRAVELLERS

Tanzania is a relatively easy place to travel, either solo or with other women, especially when compared with parts of North Africa, South America and certain Western countries. You're not likely to encounter any more specifically gender-related problems than you would anywhere else in the world, and more often than not, you'll meet only warmth, hospitality and sisterly regard, and find that you receive special treatment that you probably wouldn't be shown if you were a male traveller. That said, you'll inevitably attract some attention, especially if you're travelling alone, and there are some areas where caution is essential. Following are a few tips:

- Dress modestly: trousers or a long skirt, and a conservative top with a sleeve. Tucking your hair under a cap or scarf, or tying it back, also helps.
- Use common sense, trust your instincts and take the usual precautions when out and about. Try to avoid walking alone at night. Avoid isolated areas during both daytime and evening hours, and be particularly cautious on beaches, many of which can become quickly deserted.
- If you find yourself with an unwanted suitor, creative approaches are usually effective. For example, explain that your husband (real or fictitious) or a large group of friends will be arriving imminently at that very place. Similar tactics are also usually effective in dealing with the inevitable curiosity that you'll meet as to why you might not have children and a husband, or if you do have them, why they are not with you. The easiest response to the question of why you aren't married is to explain that you are still young (*bado kijana*), which whether you are or not will at least have some humour value. Just saying *bado* ('not yet') to questions about marriage or children should also do the trick. As for why your family isn't with you, you can always explain that you will be meeting them later.
- Seek out local women, as this can enrich your trip tremendously. Good places to try include tourist offices, government departments or even your hotel, where at least some of the staff are likely to be formally educated young to middle-aged women. In rural areas, starting points include women teachers at a local school, or staff at a health centre.

WORK

The most likely areas for employment are the safari industry, tourism, dive masters and teaching. For safari, diving and tourism-related positions, competition is stiff and the best way to land something is to get to know someone already working in the business.

Work and residency permits should be arranged through the potential employer or sponsoring organisation, and residency permits normally need to be applied for from outside Tanzania. Be prepared for lots of bureaucracy. Most teaching positions are voluntary, and best arranged through voluntary agencies or mission organisations at home.

Some places to start your search: **Voluntary Service Overseas** (VSO; www.vso.org.uk), which can provide placements for young professionals, and **Volunteer Abroad** (www.volunteer abroad.com), with numerous volunteer listings for Tanzania.

Transport

GETTING THERE & AWAY

ENTERING THE COUNTRY

As long as you have a visa (p317), Tanzania is straightforward to enter. There are no vaccination requirements, including yellow fever, although there are several you should consider (p334).

Passport

Other than needing a visa (p317), there are no entry restrictions for any nationalities.

AIR
Airports & Airlines

Tanzania's major air hub is **Dar es Salaam International Airport** (code DAR; ☎ 022-284 2461, 022-284 4371, ext 2001), with a modest array of services including an Internet connection, souvenir shops (the best are in the international departures lounge) and several forex bureaus. **Kilimanjaro International Airport** (code JRO; ☎ 027-255 4252, 027-255 4707; www .kilimanjaroairport.co.tz), midway between Arusha and Moshi, handles an increasing number of international flights and is the best option if you'll be concentrating on Arusha

---

THINGS CHANGE

The information in this chapter is particularly vulnerable to change. Check directly with the airline or a travel agent to make sure you understand how a fare (and ticket you may buy) works, and be aware of the security requirements for international travel. Shop carefully. The details given in this chapter should be regarded as pointers and are not a substitute for your own careful, up-to-date research.

---

and the northern safari circuit. It has forex and an Internet connection, and shouldn't be confused with the smaller **Arusha Airport** (code ARK), about 8km west of Arusha, which handles some domestic flights. There are also international flights to/from **Zanzibar International Airport** (code ZNZ). **Mwanza Airport** (code MWZ) and **Mtwara Airport** (code MYW) handle some regional flights.

Air Tanzania (airline code TC; in Arusha ☎ 027-250 3201/3, in Dar es Salaam 022-211 8411, 284 4239, in Zanzibar 0747-412 139; www.airtanzania.com; hub Dar es Salaam International Airport) is the national airline. It has been partially acquired by South African Airways and services are generally efficient and reliable. Current regional and international destinations include Nairobi, Moroni (Comores), Entebbe and Johannesburg, plus numerous other connections from Johannesburg, including Cape Town, Durban and Harare. Credit cards are accepted at the Dar es Salaam office only.

Regional and international carriers flying to/from Tanzania include the following (all with offices in and servicing Dar es Salaam, except as noted):

Air India (airline code AI; ☎ 022-215 2642; www.air india.com; hub Mumbai)

Airkenya (airline code REG; ☎ 027-250 2541, in Nairobi 601727; www.airkenya.com; hub Nairobi)

British Airways (airline code BA; ☎ 022-211 3820, 022-284 4082; www.britishairways.com; hub Heathrow Airport, London)

EgyptAir (airline code MS; ☎ 022-211 0333; www.egypt air.com.eg; hub Cairo International Airport)

Emirates Airlines (airline code EK; ☎ 022-211 6100; www.emirates.com; hub Dubai International Airport)

Ethiopian Airlines (airline code ET; ☎ 022-211 7063, in Arusha 027-250 6167, 027-250 7512; www.flyethiopian .com; hub Addis Ababa). Also serves Kilimanjaro International Airport (KIA).

Kenya Airways (airline code KQ; ☎ 022-211 9376/7, in Zanzibar 024-223 8355; www.kenya-airways.com; hub Jomo Kenyatta International Airport, Nairobi)

KLM (airline code KL; ☎ 022-213 9790/1, in Arusha 027-250 8062/3; www.klm.com; hub Schiphol Airport, Amsterdam) Also serves KIA.

Linhas Aéreas de Moçambique (airline code TM; ☎ 022-213 4600; www.lam.co.mz; hub Mavalane International Airport, Maputo)

Oman Air (airline code OMA; in Zanzibar ☎ 024-223 8308; www.oman-air.com; hub Seeb International Airport, Muscat) Also serves Zanzibar International Airport.

Precision Air (airline code PW; ☎ 022-212 1718, 022-284 3547, in Arusha 027-250 2818, 027-250 6903, in Zanzibar 024-223 4520; www.precisionairtz.com; hub Dar es Salaam) In partnership with Kenya Airways; flights from Nairobi to Dar es Salaam, Kilimanjaro and Zanzibar, with connections elsewhere in Tanzania. Credit cards accepted at the Arusha office.

South African Airways (airline code SA; ☎ 022-211 7044; www.flysaa.com; hub Johannesburg International Airport)

Swiss International Airlines (airline code LX; ☎ 022-211 8870; www.swiss.com; hub Kloten Airport, Zurich)

Yemenia Yemen Airways (airline code IY; ☎ 022-212 6036; www.yemenairways.net; hub Sana'a International Airport)

Tickets

Fares from Europe and North America are highest in December and January, and again between mid-June and late August. They're lowest from March to May, except around the Easter holidays. London is the main discount airfare hub. It's often easier to find discounted fares into Nairobi, where you can then make your way overland into Tanzania. Online ticket sellers include the following:

Cheapflights (www.cheap-flights.co.uk) With links to UK-based online travel agents.

Flight Centre (www.flightcentre.com)

Flights.com (www.eltexpress.com)

Microsoft Expedia (www.expedia.co.uk, www.expedia.ca)

OneTravel.com (www.onetravel.com)

STA Travel (www.statravel.com)

Travel.com.au (www.travel.com.au) For travel from Australia.

Travelocity (www.travelocity.com, www.travelocity.ca)

COURIER FLIGHTS

Courier fares can be a bargain, although you may be allowed carry-on luggage only

and have limited flexibility with flight dates and times. The **International Association of Air Travel Couriers** (www.aircourier.co.uk) and the **Air Courier Association** (www.aircourier.org) are good places to start looking; for both you'll need to pay a modest membership fee to access their fares. Note that many advertised courier fares are one way only.

INTERCONTINENTAL (RTW) TICKETS

Intercontinental (round-the-world) tickets give you a limited period (usually a year) to circumnavigate the globe. You can go anywhere that the carrying airline and its partners go, as long as you stay within the set mileage or number of stops, and don't backtrack. However, as Tanzania and other East African destinations generally aren't part of standard RTW packages, you'll probably need to pay extra to include them. Plan on from about UK£1200 from the UK and from about A$2600 from Australia.

Travel agents can put together 'alternative' RTW tickets, which are more expensive, but more flexible, than standard RTW itineraries. For a multiple-stop itinerary without the cost of a RTW ticket, consider combining tickets from two low-cost airlines.

Online RTW ticket sellers include the following:

Airbrokers (www.airbrokers.com) For travel originating in North America.

Airtreks (www.airtreks.com) For travel originating in North America.

Oneworld (www.oneworld.com) An airline alliance offering RTW packages.

Roundtheworldflights.com (www.roundtheworld flights.com) For travel originating in the UK.

Star Alliance (www.staralliance.com) An airline alliance offering RTW packages.

Africa

Useful airlines and connections include the following:

Air Madagascar (www.airmadagascar.mg) Antananarivo (Madagascar) to Nairobi, from where you can connect to Tanzania.

Air Tanzania (www.airtanzania.com) Connections between Moroni (Comoros), Johannesburg, Nairobi, Harare, Entebbe, Lusaka and Dar es Salaam or Zanzibar.

Auric Air (www.auricair.com) Entebbe to Mwanza.

Cameroon Airlines (www.cameroon-airlines.com) Douala to Addis Ababa, from where you can connect on Kenya Airways or Ethiopian Airlines to Dar es Salaam.

TRANSPORT

EgyptAir (www.egyptair.com.eg) Cairo to Dar es Salaam via Entebbe.

Emirates (www.emirates.com) Cairo to Dar es Salaam via Dubai.

Ethiopian Airlines (www.flyethiopian.com) Abidjan, Lagos, Cairo, Entebbe and Kigali to Addis Ababa, and then on to Dar es Salaam or Kilimanjaro.

Kenya Airways (www.kenya-airways.com) Abidjan, Cairo, Douala, Harare, Johannesburg, Khartoum, Lilongwe and other cities to Nairobi, with connections to Dar es Salaam and Zanzibar.

Linhas Aéreas de Moçambique (www.lam.co.mz) Maputo to Dar es Salaam via Pemba (Mozambique)

Precision Air (www.precisionairtz.com) Mombasa and Nairobi to Zanzibar, Dar es Salaam, Kilimanjaro and Arusha.

Rwandair Express (www.rwandair.com) Kigali to Kilimanjaro.

SAA (www.flysaa.com) Johannesburg to Dar es Salaam.

Sample one-way fares/durations to Dar es Salaam include Cairo (US$470, six hours), Maputo (US$325, five hours) and Johannesburg (US$480, four hours). Always ask about return excursion fares for intra-African flights, as they are frequently significantly cheaper than standard return fares.

Ticket discounters:

Flight Centres (☎ 02-210024; fcswwat@arcc.or.ke) In Kenya.

Flight Centre (☎ 011-327 5355, 021-939 4280, 0860-400 727; www.flightcentre.co.za) In South Africa.

Let's Go Travel (☎ 02-340331; www.lets-go-travel.net) In Kenya.

STA Travel (☎ 011-447 5414, 021-418 6570; www.statravel.co.za) In South Africa.

Asia

Popular connections from Asia are via Singapore and the United Arab Emirates, or via Mumbai, from where there are connections to Dar es Salaam on Kenya Airways and Air India (about US$550 one way). Ethiopian Airlines (via Addis Ababa) also flies this route. Oman Air is worth checking for flights from Zanzibar to Bombay or Madras via Muscat. Ticket discounters:

Phoenix Services Hong Kong (☎ 2722 7378)

Shoestring Travel Hong Kong (☎ 2723 2306)

STA Travel Bangkok (☎ 02-236 0262, ext 211-214; www.statravel.co.th); Singapore (☎ 6737 7188; www.statravel.com.sg)

STIC Travels New Delhi (☎ 011-2335 7468; www.stictravel.com)

Traveller Services Hong Kong (☎ 2375 2222; www.taketraveller.com)

Australia & New Zealand

There are no direct flights from Australia or New Zealand to anywhere in East Africa. However, from Australia, Qantas (from Sydney and Perth) and South African Airways (from Perth) have several flights weekly to Johannesburg, from where you can connect to Dar es Salaam (from about A$3000). Other options include: Emirates via Dubai to Dar es Salaam (around A$2260); Qantas or Air India via Mumbai (Bombay); and Air Mauritius via Mauritius and Nairobi. A RTW ticket is another possibility (see p319). Ticket discounters include **Flight Centre** (☎ 131 600; www.flightcentre.com.au) and **STA Travel** (☎ 1300 733 035; www.statravel.com.au), both with branches around the country.

From New Zealand, try Emirates via Dubai (around NZ$2740) or Qantas and South African Airways via Sydney and Johannesburg (about NZ$2900). RTW tickets from New Zealand start at about NZ$3000. **Flight Centre** (☎ 09-309 6171; www.flightcentre.com) and **STA Travel** (☎ 0508-782872; www.statravel.co.nz) both have branches throughout the country.

The USA & Canada

Most flights from North America are via Europe; there are few bargain deals. Expect to pay from US$1300 (for tickets through consolidators or discount agencies) to well over US$3000 return, depending on the season and your starting point. Fares offered by Canadian discounters tend to be around 10% more expensive than those sold in the USA.

The cheapest routing is generally to London on a discounted transatlantic ticket, where you can then purchase a separate ticket on to Tanzania. Most of the airlines mentioned under The UK & Continental Europe, following, also offer direct fares from North America.

A roundabout but occasionally cheaper alternative is South African Airways from New York or Atlanta to Johannesburg, from where you can connect to Dar es Salaam (from about US$1200 return for the transcontinental portion of the trip). Other options include EgyptAir between New York and Dar es Salaam via Cairo, Ethiopian Airways between New York and Dar es Salaam via Rome and Addis Ababa, and Kenya Airways together with **Virgin Atlantic** (www.virgin-atlantic.com) from New York to Dar es Salaam via London and Nairobi.

Discount ticket sellers:

Flight Centre (☎ 888-967 5355; www.flightcentre.ca) In Canada.

STA Travel (☎ 800-781 4040; www.statravel.com) In the USA.

Travel CUTS (☎ 800-667 2887; www.travelcuts.com) In Canada.

The UK & Continental Europe

Return tickets between London and Dar es Salaam cost from about UK£400 return. From Continental Europe, low-season return fares start about €700. There are more frequent flights and sometimes better deals available to Nairobi, so check these out as well. Charter flights, especially from London, are also worth investigating. Flights from Europe are heavily booked between late June and late August, so reserve well in advance. The lowest fares are usually for travel between January and May.

The main European airlines to check out are Swiss, KLM and British Airways. Non-European carriers include Kenya Airways (via Nairobi), Egypt Air (via Cairo), Ethiopian Airlines (via Addis Ababa), Emirates (via Dubai) and Yemen Airways (via Sana'a). Oman Air flies between London and Zanzibar via Muscat.

In the UK, most travel agents are registered with the **Association of British Travel Agents** (ABTA; www.abta.com). Tickets from unregistered bucket shops are riskier but sometimes cheaper. London is the best place to buy a ticket, but specialist agencies elsewhere in the UK can provide comparable value. Discount ticket agencies in the UK:

Africa Travel Centre (☎ 020-7387 1211; www.africatravel.co.uk)

Bridge the World (☎ 0870 444 7474; www.b-t-w.co.uk)

North-South Travel (☎ 01245-608291; www.northsouthtravel.co.uk)

STA Travel (☎ 0870-1600 599; www.statravel.co.uk)

Trailfinders (☎ 020-7938 3939; www.trailfinders.com)

Travel Bag (☎ 0870 890 1456; www.travelbag.co.uk)

Agencies to try for discounted fares from Continental Europe:

Kilroy Travels (www.kilroytravels.com) Germany (☎ 030-310 0040); Netherlands (☎ 020-524 5100)

Nouvelles Frontières (nationwide ☎ 08 25 00 08 25, in Paris ☎ 01 45 68 70 00; www.nouvelles-frontieres.fr) In France.

OTU Voyages (☎ 01 40 29 12 12; www.otu.fr) In France.

SSR (☎ 01-261 2954; www.ssr.ch) In Switzerland.

STA Travel (☎ 01805-456 422, 030-20 16 50 63; www.statravel.de) In Germany.

LAND
Bus

Buses cross the borders between Tanzania and Kenya, Malawi, Uganda and Zambia. Apart from sometimes lengthy waits at the border for passport checks, there are usually no hassles. At the border, you'll need to disembark on each side to take care of visa formalities, then reboard your bus and continue on. Visa fees are not included in bus ticket prices for trans-border routes. It's also possible to travel to/from all of Tanzania's neighbours by minibus or (for Kenya) shared taxis. Most main routes go direct, but sometimes you'll need to walk across the border and change vehicles on the other side.

Car & Motorcycle

If you're arriving via car or motorcycle, you'll need the vehicle's registration papers and your licence (p330), plus pay for a temporary import permit at the border (Tsh20,000 for one month) and a one-time fuel levy (Tsh5000). You'll also need a *carnet de passage en douane*, which acts as a temporary waiver of import duty. The carnet – arranged through your local automobile association – should also specify any expensive spare parts that you'll be carrying.

Most rental companies don't permit their vehicles to cross international borders; should you find one that does, arrange the necessary paperwork with it in advance.

For road rules, see p331.

Most border posts don't have petrol stations or repair shops; head to the nearest large town.

Burundi

The main crossing is at Kobero Bridge between Ngara and Muyinga (Burundi). Although the border is officially open, the security situation ebbs and flows, so get an update from your embassy first. The road between Kigoma and Lusahunga in particular is subject to occasional banditry, and it's sometimes necessary to travel in a convoy.

The trip is done in stages via Lusahunga, from where there are vehicles north towards Biharamulo and Lake Victoria and southeast via Kahama towards Nzega or Shinyanga. The road from Nzega to the Burundi border via Ngara is in fairly good condition. Time your travels so that if you need to overnight in Tanzania, it will be in either Biharamulo or Kahama, rather than in Lusahunga or other less-safe points near the border.

Kenya

With the exception of the Serengeti–Masai Mara crossing, there is public transport across all Tanzania–Kenya border posts.

BORDER CROSSINGS

The main route to/from Kenya is the sealed road connecting Arusha and Nairobi via the heavily travelled Namanga border post (open 24 hours). There are also border crossings at Horohoro, north of Tanga; at Taveta, east of Moshi; at Illassit, northeast of Moshi; at Bologonya in the northern Serengeti; and at Isebania, northeast of Musoma.

TO/FROM MOMBASA
Bus

Scandinavian Express goes daily between Dar es Salaam and Mombasa, departing Dar es Salaam at 7.30am and Mombasa at 8.30am (Tsh17,000, 10 hours). Buses between Tanga and Mombasa depart each morning (Tsh5000, four to five hours).

Car

The road is well sealed between Dar es Salaam and Tanga, potholed between Tanga

---

BORDER HASSLES

At the Namanga border post watch out for touts – often claiming they work for the bus company – who tell you that it's necessary to change money, to pay a fee or to come over to 'another building' to arrange the necessary payments to enter Tanzania/Kenya. Apart from your visa, there are no border fees, payments or exchange requirements for crossing, and the rates being offered for money exchange are well below the norm.

---

and the border at Horohoro, and in good condition from the border to Mombasa.

TO/FROM NAIROBI
Bus

Scandinavian Express goes daily between Dar es Salaam and Nairobi via Arusha, departing in each direction at 6.45am (Tsh35,000, 13 hours). Both Scandinavian Express and Akamba also have daily buses between Mwanza and Nairobi (Tsh15,000 to Tsh19,000, 12 to 14 hours).

Between Arusha or Moshi and Nairobi, the most popular option is one of the daily shuttle buses, which depart daily at 8am and 2pm in each direction (five hours). Main companies include the following:

Davanu Arusha (☎ 027-250 1242, 027-250 3761; davanutz@habari.co.tz; Goliondoi Rd, Arusha, with a branch at Mt Meru Hotel); Nairobi (☎ 254-2-222 002, 217 178; davanu@nbnet.co.ke; 4th fl, Windsor House, University Way, with a desk at the New Stanley Hotel)

Impala Arusha (☎ 027-250 7197; impala@cybernet .co.tz; Impala Hotel, cnr Moshi & Old Moshi Rds, Arusha); Nairobi (☎ 254-2-271 7373; Silver Springs Hotel)

Riverside Arusha (☎ 027-250 2639, 027-250 3916; riverside_shuttle@hotmail.com; Sokoine Rd, Arusha, with a branch at Mt Meru Hotel); Nairobi (☎ 254-2-229 618, 241 032; Pan African Insurance House, 3rd fl, Room 1, Kenyatta Ave)

All charge about US$25 one way, and with a little prodding, it's easy enough to get the residents' price (US$10). In Arusha, all companies drop you at Mt Meru Hotel, as well as at their offices. In Nairobi, drop offs are at centrally located hotels and at Jomo Kenyatta International Airport. For pick ups in Nairobi, if you book in advance, they'll meet your flight. Otherwise you can contact the shuttles through the tourist information desk in the international arrivals area. Confirm the drop-off point when booking, and insist on being dropped off as agreed. Also watch out for touts who may board the bus at the New Stanley Hotel (Nairobi) and insist that it's the end of the line to drum up business for waiting taxis.

Regular buses link Arusha and Nairobi daily (Tsh9000, six to seven hours), departing between 6.30am and 8am, and sometimes also in the afternoon about 2pm. Departures in Arusha are from the bus station; in Nairobi most are from Accra Rd.

Taxi

Shared taxis go between the Arusha bus station and the Namanga border (Tsh2500) throughout the day, starting at 6am. Most are nine-seater sedans that do the journey at hair-raising speeds. At Namanga, you'll have to walk a few hundred metres across the border, and then catch one of the frequent *matatus* (Kenyan minivans) or share taxis to Nairobi (about US$5). From Nairobi, the *matatu* and share-taxi depots are on Ronald Ngala St, near the River Rd junction.

TO/FROM VOI

Minibuses go daily between Moshi and Voi, or you can do the trip in stages via Taveta on the border. There are also occasional direct buses between Moshi and Mombasa via Voi, although most reach Mombasa in the middle of the night.

TO/FROM MASAI MARA

There's no public transport between the northern Serengeti and Kenya's Masai Mara Game Reserve, and only East African residents and citizens can cross here. If you're a resident and are exiting Tanzania here, you're supposed to take care of immigration formalities in Seronera, to the south. Entering Tanzania from Masai Mara, park fees are payable at the Lobo ranger post, about halfway between the border and Seronera.

TO/FROM KISII
Bus

Minibuses go daily between Musoma and the Sirari/Isebania border post, where you can change to Kenyan transport for Kisii, and then on to Kisumu or Nairobi. Scandinavian Express and Akamba also pass Kisii on their daily runs between Mwanza and Nairobi (Tsh15,000 to Tsh19,000, 12 to 14 hours between Mwanza and Nairobi), with some buses continuing on to Arusha and Dar es Salaam.

Car

The road is good tarmac from Mwanza to the border, and on into Kenya.

Malawi
BORDER CROSSINGS

The only crossing is at **Songwe River bridge** (🕒 7.30am-6pm Tanzanian time, 6.30am-5pm Malawi time), southeast of Mbeya.

BUS

Buses go three times weekly (currently Monday, Wednesday and Friday) between Dar es Salaam and Lilongwe, departing Dar es Salaam about 5am (Tsh40,000, 27 hours). A better choice is to take Scandinavian from Dar es Salaam to Mbeya, and get onward transport there. From Mbeya, buses depart several times a week in the afternoon, arriving in Lilongwe the next day (Tsh26,000). There are also daily minibuses connecting both Mbeya and Kyela with the border, although verify that your vehicle is really going all the way to the border, as some stop at Ibanda, 7km before. Once at the border, there's about a 300m walk to the Malawian side, from where there are minibuses to Karonga. There's also one bus daily between the border and Mzuzu, departing the border by mid-afternoon and arriving by evening. Many vehicles and trucks ply between Mbeya and Karonga, so it's easy to find a lift.

Coming from Malawi, the best option is to take a minibus from the border to Mbeya, and then get an express bus onwards from there towards Dar es Salaam. This means overnighting in Mbeya, as buses to Dar es Salaam depart Mbeya between 6am and 7am.

CAR

The road from Mbeya to Karonga is good tarmac, and rough from Karonga south towards Chiweta.

Mozambique
BORDER CROSSINGS

There are no bridges over the Ruvuma River (the border). The main crossing is at Kilambo (south of Mtwara), where there is a sometimes-operational ferry. It's also possible to get your passport stamped on the crossing between Newala and Moçimboa do Rovuma (Mozambique). If you travel by boat, there are border officials at Msimbati (Tanzania) and at Palma and Moçimboa da Praia (Mozambique). It's also reportedly possible to get stamped in at the crossing between Songea and Nova Madeira (Mozambique); otherwise, there's an immigration office in Songea.

BUS

Pick-ups depart Mtwara daily between 7am and 9am to the Kilambo border post

(Tsh2000, one hour) and on to the Ruvuma, which is crossed via dugout canoe (Tsh2000, 10 minutes to over an hour, depending on water levels, and dangerous during heavy rains). On the Mozambique side, there are usually two pick-ups daily to the Mozambique border post (about 4km further) and on to Moçimboa da Praia (US$7, four hours), with the last one departing by about noon. If you get stuck at the Ruvuma, there's a bedbug-ridden guesthouse on a sandbank in the middle of the river; camping on the Mozambique side is a better option.

The Ruvuma crossing is notorious for pickpockets. Keep an eye on your belongings, especially when getting into and out of the boats, and keep up with the crowd when walking to/from the river bank.

The border crossing south of Newala is rarely used and entails long walks on both sides (up to 25km in Tanzania, and at least 10km in Mozambique). The main Mozambique town is Moçimboa do Rovuma, from where there's a daily vehicle to Mueda.

Further west, you can make your way from Songea to the Ruvuma via sporadic public transport and on foot. Once in Mozambique, there's a truck every other day from the Ruvuma to Lichinga via Nova Madeira and Macaloge.

CAR

The road from Mtwara to the border is in reasonably good condition. There's a vehicle ferry at Kilambo, which operates at high tide (Tsh500/20,000 per person/large vehicle), though the captain has been known to skip off and leave vehicles waiting for several days. Get an update first at the Old Boma or Ten Degrees South Lodge (both in Mikindani, p283), or **Russell's Place** (Cashew Camp; ☎ in Mozambique 082-686273; russellbott@yahoo .com) in Pemba (Mozambique).

In Mozambique, the road is unsealed, but in reasonable condition during the dry season, from the border to Palma, a mix of tarmac and good graded dirt from Palma to Moçimboa da Praia, and tarmac from there to Pemba.

Rwanda
BORDER CROSSINGS

The main crossing is at Rusumu Falls, southwest of Bukoba. Although there have been no problems recently, due to a long history of instability in this region it's worth getting an update before setting off.

BUS

Daily pick-ups go between Benako (30km southwest of the border) and Rusumu Falls border post; see p220 for connections to Benako. At the border, walk across the bridge to the Rwandan border post, where minibuses go to Kibungo and on to Kigali (US$5, three hours). There are also occasional direct buses between Mwanza and Kigali.

CAR

A 4WD with high clearance is essential on the Tanzanian side.

Uganda
BORDER CROSSINGS

The main post is at Mutukula, northwest of Bukoba. There's another crossing further west at Nkurungu, but the road is bad and sparsely travelled.

BUS

Scandinavian goes daily between Dar es Salaam and Kampala via Nairobi (Tsh40,000, 25 hours). Jaguar and Tawfiq go daily between Bukoba and Kampala, departing Bukoba about 7am (Tsh9500, five to six hours). Departures from Kampala are at 7am and usually again at about 1.30pm. From Kampala, Tawfiq continues on to Nairobi and Dar es Salaam (Tsh36,000 plus transit visas for Uganda (US$15) and Kenya (US$20), 36 hours), though if you're headed to Nairobi it's better to sleep in Kampala and get another bus the next day as the Tawfiq bus arrives late at night.

From Mwanza, the best connections are on Akamba, which goes three times weekly to/from Kampala (Tsh18,000, 19 hours). It's also possible to do the trip in stages, via Kisii, in Kenya (where you'll probably need to overnight), and Kisumu.

The road on both sides of the Mutukulu border post is good tarmac.

Zambia
BORDER CROSSINGS

The main **crossing** (☺ 7.30am-6pm Tanzania time, 6.30am-5pm Zambia time) is at Tunduma, southwest of Mbeya. There's also a crossing at Kasesha, between Sumbawanga and Mbala (Zambia).

BUS
Scandinavian goes on Tuesday, Thursday, Saturday and Sunday between Dar es Salaam and Lusaka via Mbeya, departing at 5.15am (Tsh48,000, 24 hours). Departures from Lusaka are at 5pm on Monday, Wednesday, Friday and Saturday. Otherwise, minibuses go frequently between Mbeya and Tunduma (Tsh2500, two hours), where you walk across the border for Zambian transport to Lusaka (US$20, 18 hours). The road from Dar es Salaam into Zambia is good tarmac.

TRAIN
The Tanzania–Zambia (Tazara) line links Dar es Salaam with Kapiri Mposhi in Zambia (Tsh55,000/39,100/31,500 1st/2nd/economy class, about 40 hours) twice weekly via Mbeya and Tunduma. Departures from Dar es Salaam are at 4pm Tuesday and Friday, and from Kapiri Mposhi at 3pm on the same days. Students with ID get a 50% discount. From Kapiri Mposhi to Lusaka, you'll need to continue by bus.

Tazara also has slower ordinary trains between Dar es Salaam and Mbeya (p332) and between Kapiri Mposhi and Nakonde (on the Zambian side of the Zambia–Tanzania border), departing Kapiri Mposhi at 4.30pm Monday and Nakonde at 4.15pm on Tuesday (about 20 hours).

SEA & LAKE
There's a US$5 port tax for travel on all boats and ferries from Tanzanian ports.

Burundi
FERRY
MV *Mwongozo* sails weekly at night between Kigoma and Bujumbura (US$30/25/20 for 1st/2nd/3rd class, payment in US dollars cash only, 11 hours).

LAKE TAXI
Security situation permitting, you can take a lake taxi from Kibirizi (just north of Kigoma) to the Burundi border (p235). Once there, walk a few kilometres to the border, from where there are minibuses to Nyanza-Lac and Bujumbura.

Congo (Zaïre)
There's currently no passenger service to/from Congo (Zaïre).

Kenya
DHOW
Dhows sail sporadically between Pemba, Tanga and Mombasa; the journey can be long and rough. Ask at the ports in Tanga, or in Mkoani or Wete on Pemba for information on sailings. In Kenya, ask at the port in Mombasa, or at Shimoni.

FERRY
There's no passenger ferry service on Lake Victoria between Tanzania and Kenya. Occasional cargo boats depart Mwanza for Kenya that are sometimes willing to take passengers. Inquire at the Mwanza South port about sailings.

Malawi
The MV *Songea* sails between Mbamba Bay and Nkhata Bay (Malawi), departing Mbamba Bay on Friday, and Nkhata Bay on Saturday (US$10/4 1st/economy class, four to five hours). The schedule is highly variable and sometimes cancelled completely.

Mozambique
DHOW
Dhows between Mozambique and Tanzania (12 to 30 or more hours) are best arranged at Msimbati or Moçimboa da Praia (Mozambique).

FERRY
The official route between southwestern Tanzania and Mozambique is via Malawi on the *Songea* ferry between Mbamba Bay and Nkhata Bay (above), and then from Nkhata Bay on to Likoma island (Malawi), Cóbuè and Metangula (both in Mozambique) on the ferry **Ilala** (in Malawi ☎ 01-587311; ilala@malawi .net). Unofficially, there are small boats that sail along the eastern shore of Lake Nyasa between Tanzania and Mozambique. However, Lake Nyasa is notorious for its severe and sudden squalls, and going this way is risky.

Uganda
There's no passenger-ferry service, but it's relatively easy to arrange passage between Mwanza and Kampala's Port Bell on cargo ships (about 16 hours). On the Ugandan side, you'll need a letter of permission from the railway station director (free). Ask for the managing director's office, on the 2nd floor of the building next to Kampala's

railway station. In Mwanza, a letter isn't required, but you'll need to check in with the immigration officer at the South Port. Expect to pay about US$20, including port fees. Crew are often willing to rent out their cabins for a negotiable extra fee.

Zambia

The venerable MV *Liemba*, which has been plying the waters of Lake Tanganyika for the better part of a century, connects Kigoma with Mpulungu in Zambia weekly (US$55/45/40 for 1st/2nd/economy class US dollars cash only, at least 40 hours). Stops include Lagosa (for Mahale Mountains National Park), Karema (southwest of Mpanda) and Kasanga (southwest of Sumbawanga). Departures from Kigoma are on Wednesday afternoon, reaching Mpulungu Friday morning. Departures from Mpulungu are Friday afternoon. Food is available, but it's best to bring some supplements and drinking water. First class is quite comfortable, with two reasonably clean bunks and a window. Second-class cabins (four bunks) and economy-class seating are poorly ventilated and uncomfortable – better to find deck space than economy-class seating. Keep watch over your luggage, and book early if you want a cabin – Monday morning is your best bet.

There are docks at Kigoma and Kasanga, but at many smaller stops you'll need to disembark in the middle of the lake into small boats that take you to shore – a bit of an adventure (or nerve-wracking, depending on your perspective) at night, if the lake is rough or if you have a heavy pack.

Elsewhere in the World
FREIGHTERS

Several cargo shipping companies sailing between Europe and East Africa have passenger cabins. Expect to pay from about UK£1350 one way for a 23-day journey from Felixstowe (UK) to Dar es Salaam via the Suez Canal. Useful contacts:

Freighter World Cruises Inc (☎ 800-531 7774, 626-449 3106; www.freighterworld.com) Based in the USA.
Strand Voyages (☎ 020-7836 6363; www.strandtravel.co.uk) In the UK.

For route and shipping-line information, check the quarterly **Reed Travel Group** (in the UK ☎ 01582-600111) *OAG Cruise & Ferry Guide*. Durban is a good place to look for a lift on private yachts sailing up the East African coast, including to Tanzanian ports.

TOURS

Dozens of tour and safari companies organise package tours to Tanzania. While it's generally cheaper to organise your tour with a Tanzania-based company, this may be outweighed by the convenience of organising things in advance with a company in your home country. For safari and trekking operators, see p59.

Australia & New Zealand
Africa Travel Centre Australia (☎ 02-9267 3048; level 11, 456 Kent St, Sydney, NSW 2000); New Zealand (☎ 09-520 2000; 21 Remuera Rd, Newmarket, Auckland)
African Wildlife Safaris (☎ 03-9696 2899, 1300-363302; www.africanwildlifesafaris.com.au) Discount air tickets and safaris.
Peregrine Travel (☎ 03-9663 8611; www.peregrine.net.au) Everything from overland truck tours to top-end wildlife safaris.

The UK
Abercrombie & Kent (☎ 0845-070 0610; www.abercrombiekent.co.uk) Top-end tours and safaris.
Dragoman (☎ 0870-499 4475; www.dragoman.co.uk) Overland tours.
Explore Worldwide (☎ 01252-760000; www.exploreworldwide.com) Small group tours, treks and safaris.
Footprint Adventures (☎ 01522-804929; www.footprint-adventures.co.uk) Treks and safaris.
Gane & Marshall (☎ 020-8441 9592; www.ganeandmarshall.co.uk) Top-end tours and safaris.
Guerba (☎ 01373-826611; www.guerba.com) Overland tours.
Safari Drive (☎ 01488-71140; www.safaridrive.com) Self-drive safaris in Serengeti National Park and Ngorongoro Conservation Area.

The USA & Canada
African Adventures (☎ 678-478 3812; www.africanadventures.com) Northern circuit treks and safaris.
Born Free Safaris (☎ 800-372 3274, 818-981 7185; www.bornfreesafaris.com) Safaris and tours.
Explorateur Voyages (☎ 514-847 1177; www.explorateur.qc.ca in French) Northern circuit treks and safaris.
Fresh Tracks (☎ 800-267 3347, 416-922 7584; www.freshtracks.com) Northern circuit safaris.
International Expeditions (☎ 800-633 4734, 205-428 1700; www.ietravel.com) Top-end safaris.
Thomson Family Adventures (☎ 800-262 6255, 617-923 2004; www.familyadventures.com) Family-friendly safaris and tours.

GETTING AROUND

AIR
Airlines in Tanzania

The national airline, **Air Tanzania** (www.airtanzania.com; Arusha ☎ 027-250 3201/3; Dar es Salaam Map p74; ☎ 022-211 8411, 022-284 4293; Zanzibar ☎ 024-223 0213) has reliable flights connecting Dar es Salaam with Mwanza, Bukoba, Zanzibar and Kilimanjaro, and probably several more destinations soon. Other airlines flying domestically, all with solid reputations, their connections are listed following. All also do charters.

Air Excel (☎ 027-254 8429, 027-250 1597; reservation@airexcelonline.com) Arusha, Serengeti, Lake Manyara, Dar es Salaam, Zanzibar.

Coastal Aviation (☎ 022-284 3293, 022-284 2877, 022-211 7959, 0744-325673; www.coastal.cc) Arusha, Dar es Salaam, Kilwa Masoko, Lake Manyara NP, Mafia, Mwanza, Pemba, Ruaha NP, Rubondo Island NP, Saadani GR, Selous GR, Serengeti NP, Tanga, Tarangire NP, Zanzibar.

Precision Air (☎ 022-212 1718, 022-213 0800, in Arusha 027-250 2818, 027-250 6903, in Zanzibar 024-223 4520/1, in Mwanza 028-250 0819; www.precisionairtz .com) Arusha, Bukoba, Dar es Salaam, Kigoma, Mwanza, Shinyanga, Tabora, Zanzibar.

Regional Air Services (☎ 027-250 4477, 207-250 2541; www.airkenya.com/docs/regair3.htm) Arusha, Kilimanjaro, Lake Manyara NP, Serengeti NP (Seronera, Grumeti & Klein's Camp).

ZanAir (☎ 024-223 3670/8; www.zanair.com) Arusha, Dar es Salaam, Lake Manyara NP, Mafia, Pemba, Selous GR, Serengeti NP, Tarangire NP, Zanzibar.

BICYCLE

Main sealed roads aren't good for cycling, as there's often no shoulder and traffic moves dangerously fast. However, many of Tanzania's secondary roads are ideal, although distances are long, and the most satisfactory cycling is often from a fixed base (eg the western Usambaras around Lushoto, or anywhere on Pemba). For point-to-point journeys, you'll need to plan well and carry basic supplies, including water (at least 4L), food, a water filter, at least four spare inner tubes, a spare tyre and plenty of tube patches.

Throughout the country, cycling is best well away from urban areas, in the early morning and late afternoon, and in the drier winter season (from June to August/September). When calculating daily dis-

tances, plan on taking a break from the midday heat, and don't count on covering as much territory as you might in a northern European climate.

Mountain bikes are best for flexibility and local terrain, and should be brought from home. Bikes available for rental (about Tsh400 per hour, check at hotels and markets) are usually heavy single speeds or beat-up mountain bikes.

Other planning considerations include rampaging motorists (a small rear-view mirror is worthwhile), sleeping (bring a tent) and punctures (thorn trees are a problem in some areas). Cycling isn't permitted in national parks or wildlife reserves.

In theory, bicycles can be transported on minibuses and buses, though many drivers are unwilling. For express buses, you'll need to make advance arrangements to stow your bike in the hold. Bicycles can be transported on the Zanzibar ferries and any of the lake ferries for no additional cost. The highly recommended **International Bicycle Fund** (www .ibike.org/bikeafrica) organises cycling tours in Tanzania and provides information. Green Footprint Adventures (p60) organises rides around Lake Manyara National Park, and also rents mountain bikes and equipment.

BOAT
Dhow

Main routes include those connecting Zanzibar and Pemba with Dar es Salaam, Tanga, Bagamoyo and Mombasa; those connecting Kilwa Kivinje, Lindi, Mikindani and Mtwara with other coastal towns; and between Mafia and the mainland. Officially, foreigners are prohibited on non-motorised dhows, and on any dhows between Zanzibar and Dar es Salaam; captains are subject to heavy fines if they're caught, and may be unwilling to take you.

Ferry

Ferries operate on Lake Victoria, Lake Tanganyika and Lake Nyasa, and between Dar es Salaam, Zanzibar and Pemba. There's a US$5 port tax per trip on most routes. For

TRANSPORT

DHOW TRAVEL

With their billowing sails, graceful forms and long histories, these ancient sailing vessels have become a symbol of East Africa for adventurous travellers. Even the name has a certain allure, evoking images of nights spent under the stars sailing through distant archipelagos. Yet, despite their romantic reputation, the realities of dhow travel can be quite different.

If the wind is with you and the water calm, a dhow trip can be enjoyable, and will give you a better sense of the centuries of trade that shaped East Africa's coastal communities during the days when dhows reigned supreme. However, if you're becalmed miles from your destination, if seas turn rough, if the boat is leaking or overloaded, if it's raining, or if the sun is very strong, the experience will be much less pleasant.

Places to arrange dhow trips include Msimbati (p284), Mikindani (p283), Kilwa Kivinje (p293) and Bagamoyo (p138). To experience dhow travel with a bit more comfort (and fewer risks), many coastal hotels have their own boats or can help you arrange a boat locally for a short sail.

Some things to keep in mind if you decide to give a local dhow a try:

- Be prepared for rough conditions. There are no facilities on board, except possibly a toilet hanging off the stern. As sailings are wind and tide dependent, departures are often during the predawn hours.

- Journeys often take much longer than anticipated; bring plenty of extra water and sufficient food.

- Sun block, a hat and a covering are essential, as is waterproofing for your luggage and a rain jacket.

- Boats capsize and people are killed each year. Avoid overloaded boats and don't set sail in bad weather.

- Travel with the winds, which blow from south to north from approximately July to September and north to south from approximately November to late February.

Note that what Westerners refer to as dhows are called either *jahazi* or *mashua* by Tanzanians. *Jahazi* are large, lateen-sailed boats. *Mashua* are similar in design, although smaller, and often with proportionately wider hulls and a motor. The *dau* has a sloped stem and stern. On lakes and inland waterways, the *mtumbwi* (dugout canoe) is in common use. Coastal areas, especially Zanzibar's east-coast beaches, are good places to see the *ngalawa* (outrigger canoe).

details of ferries between Dar es Salaam and Zanzibar, see p84.

LAKE VICTORIA

The MV *Victoria* departs Mwanza at 10pm on Tuesday, Thursday and Sunday (Tsh16,500/14,500/11,300/10,600 for 1st class/2nd-class sleeping/2nd-class sitting/3rd class plus port tax, nine hours). Departures from Bukoba are at 9.30pm Monday, Wednesday and Friday. First class has two-bed cabins, and 2nd-class sleeping has six-bed cabins. Second-class sitting isn't very comfortable, so if you can't get a spot in 1st class or 2nd-class sleeping, the best bet is to buy a 3rd-class ticket. With luck, you may then be able to find a comfortable spot in the 1st-class lounge. First- and 2nd-class cabins fill up quickly in both directions, so book as

soon as you know your plans. Food is available on board. A smaller, faster speedboat is expected to begin service imminently, which will at least halve the transit time.

The MV *Butiama* sails between Mwanza and Nkome, to the northwest of Geita (Tsh6100/4300 for 2nd/3rd class), with numerous stops en route, including at Maisome island. Departures from Mwanza are at 8.30am Saturday, arriving at Nkome about 6pm. Departures from Nkome are at 8am Sunday. At 8.30am Wednesday the *Butiama* departs Mwanza for Nyamirembe (northeast of Biharamulo) with a stop en route at Maisome island (14 hours). Departures from Nyamirembe are at noon on Thursday.

For information on the MV *Nansio* between Mwanza and Ukerewe island, see p222.

LAKE TANGANYIKA

For the MV *Liemba* schedule between Kigoma and Mpulungu (Zambia), see p326. See p325 for ferry schedules between Kigoma and Bujumbura (Burundi).

LAKE NYASA

In theory, the MV *Songea* departs Itungi port about 1pm on Thursday and makes its way down the coast via Lupingu, Manda, Lundu, Mango and Liuli (but not via Matema) to Mbamba Bay (Tsh14,000/8000 for 1st/economy class, 18 to 24 hours). It then continues across to Nkhata Bay in Malawi, before turning around and doing the return trip. This schedule is highly unreliable and frequently interrupted.

The smaller MV *Iringa* services lake-side villages between Itungi and Manda (about halfway down the Tanzanian lake shore), departing Itungi about noon on Tuesday and stopping at Matema, Lupingu and several other ports en route, before turning back again on Wednesday for the return trip. Schedules are very fluid and change often; the best places to get an update for both the *Iringa* and the *Songea* are with Sisi Kwa Sisi in Mbeya (p265), or at one of the hotels in Matema (p272).

BUS

Major long-distance routes have a choice of express and ordinary buses. Express buses make fewer stops, are less crowded than ordinary buses and depart on schedule. Some have air-con and toilets, and the nicest ones are called 'luxury' buses. On secondary routes, the only option is ordinary buses, which are often packed to overflowing, make many stops and run to a less rigorous schedule.

For popular routes, book your seat in advance, although you can sometimes get a place by arriving at the bus station an hour prior to departure. Scandinavian and Royal Coach fill up quickly on all routes, and should be booked at least one day in advance. Each bus line has its own booking office, usually at or near the bus station.

Most express buses have a compartment below for luggage. Otherwise, stow your pack under your seat or at the front of the bus, where there's usually space near the driver.

Prices are basically fixed, although overcharging isn't unheard of. Most bus stations are chaotic, and at the ones in Arusha and other tourist areas you'll be incessantly hounded by touts. Buy your tickets at the office, and not from the touts, and don't believe anyone who tries to tell you there's a luggage fee.

For short stretches along main routes, express buses will drop you, though you'll often be required to pay the full fare to the next major destination.

Major bus companies and a sampling of their destinations:

Dar Express (Map p74) Arusha, Dar es Salaam.
Royal Coach (Map p74) Arusha, Dar es Salaam.
Scandinavian Express (Map p73; www.scandinaviagroup.com) Arusha, Dar es Salaam, Dodoma, Iringa, Kampala (Uganda), Kyela, Mbeya, Mombasa (Kenya), Morogoro, Nairobi (Kenya), Njombe, Songea.

Other lines, none distinguished, include Takrim/Tawfiq (Arusha, Bukoba, Kampala, Mwanza, Nairobi, Singida), Jaguar (Bukoba, Kampala) and Sumry (Mbeya, Sumbawanga). You can book tickets online for Scandinavian Express routes, but need to collect (and pay for) your ticket at least three days prior to the journey date.

Minibus & Shared Taxi

For taking shorter trips away from the main routes, the choice is often between 30-seater buses ('Coasters' or *thelathini*) and *dalla-dallas* (minibuses). Both options come complete with chickens on the roof, bags of produce wedged under the seats and no leg room. Shared taxis are relatively rare, except in northern Tanzania near Arusha. Like ordinary buses, minibuses and shared taxis leave when they're full; they're probably the least safe of the various transport options.

CAR & MOTORCYCLE

Unless you have your own vehicle and are familiar with driving in East Africa, it's relatively unusual for travellers to tour mainland Tanzania by car. More common is to focus on a region, and then arrange local transport through a tour or safari operator. On Zanzibar it's easy and fairly economical to hire a car or motorcycle for touring.

Bringing Your Own Vehicle

For requirements on bringing your own vehicle, see p321.

TRANSPORT

Driving Licence
On the mainland you'll need your home driving licence or (preferable) an international driving licence. On Zanzibar you'll need an international driving licence, or a permit from Zanzibar (p112), Kenya, Uganda or South Africa.

Fuel & Spare Parts
Petrol costs about Tsh950 per litre in Dar es Salaam (Tsh750 for diesel), more inland. Filling and repair stations are readily available in major towns, but scarce elsewhere, so tank up whenever you get the opportunity and carry basic spares. For travel in remote areas and in national parks, carry jerry cans with extra fuel.

Hire
DAR ES SALAAM
Dar es Salaam has a modest array of car-rental agencies, none outstanding. Daily rates for 2WD start about US$40, excluding fuel, plus US$20 to US$30 for insurance and tax. Prices for 4WD range from US$70 to US$150 per day plus insurance (US$30 to US$40 per day), fuel and driver (US$15 to US$35 per day). There's also a 20% value added tax.

For anything outside the city, most companies require 4WD. Also, most don't permit self-drive outside of Dar es Salaam, and none presently offer unlimited kilometres. Per-kilometre charges average US$0.50 to

US$1. Clarify what the company's policy is in the event of a breakdown.

Avis (Map p74; ☎ 022-211 5381; avis@skylinktanzania .com; Skylink Travel & Tours, Ohio St) Opposite Royal Palm Hotel, with a branch in Arusha.

Business Rent-a-Car (Map p74; ☎ 022-212 2852; www.businessrent-a-car.com; Kisutu St)

Evergreen Car Rentals (Map p73; ☎ 022-218 2107, 022-218 5419; evergreen@raha.com; cnr Nkrumah St & Nyerere Rd)

Hertz (Map p74; ☎ 022-212 2130, 022-212 2363; hertz@cats-net.com; Royal Palm Hotel, Ohio St)

ELSEWHERE IN TANZANIA
You can rent 4WD vehicles in Arusha, Mwanza, Zanzibar Town and other centres through travel agencies, tour operators and hotels. Except on Zanzibar, most come with driver. Rates average US$70 to US$120 per day plus fuel, less on Zanzibar (where it's also easy to rent motorcycles and minibikes, and arrange car rental privately). Clarify before setting out who bears responsibility for repairs.

Insurance
Unless you're covered from other sources such as your credit card, it's worth taking the full coverage offered by rental companies.

Road Conditions & Hazards
Around 20% of Tanzania's road network is sealed, including the roads from Dar es

---

PERILS OF THE ROAD

Road accidents are probably your biggest safety risk while travelling in Tanzania, with speeding buses being among the worst offenders. Road conditions are poor and driving standards leave a lot to be desired. Overtaking blind is a big problem, as are high speeds. Your bus driver may in fact be at the wheel of an ageing, rickety vehicle with a cracked windshield and marginal brakes on a winding, potholed road. However, he'll invariably be driving as if he were piloting a sleek racing machine coming down the straight – nerve-wracking to say the least. Impassioned pleas from passengers to slow down usually have little effect, and pretending you're sick often is counterproductive. Many vehicles have painted slogans such as *Mungu Atubariki* (God Bless Us) or 'In God we Trust' – probably in the hope that a bit of extra help from above will see the vehicle safely through the day's runs.

To maximise your chances of happy and uneventful travels, try to stick with more reputable bus companies such as Scandinavian Express and Royal Coach. Also, if you have a choice, it's usually better to go with a full-sized bus than a minibus or 30-seater bus.

Buses aren't permitted to drive at night in Tanzania, which is just as well, though at least in the dark you can't see the road swerving before you. On most routes, the last departure is generally timed so that the bus should reach its destination by evening (assuming that all goes well). For cross-border routes, departures are usually timed so that night driving will be done once outside Tanzania.

CULTURAL TOURISM PROGRAM

To see local life away from the organised safari scene, it's well worth trying a Cultural Tourism Program (CTP) tour. These are 'community-owned' ventures spread in various places around the country, including Ng'iresi, Ilkidin'ga, Mulala, Monduli Juu, Mkuru and Longido (all accessed from Arusha), Machame (Moshi), Marangu, Engaruka, Mto Wa Mbu and Gezaulole (near Dar es Salaam), the Usambara Mountains (near Lushoto), and the northern and southern Pare Mountains, Pangani and Kisangara (near Mwanga in northeastern Tanzania). They range in length from a few hours to a few days, and usually centre around light hikes or other activities, with the focus on experiencing local cultures.

Some of the tours are a bit rough around the edges, but others are well organised, and they're great for getting to know Tanzania at the local level. Most have various 'modules' available, from half a day to several nights. Fees (listed in the regional chapters) are reasonable and a portion of the income supports community projects such as school or well construction. Per-person costs decrease with increasing group size. Payments should be made on site; always ask for a receipt.

Tours should be arranged directly with the local coordinator, although there's a CTP representative at the tourist information office in Arusha (p179) who can help with those in the Arusha area and with general information.

Salaam to Arusha via Chalinze, and from Dar es Salaam to Mbeya via Morogoro and Iringa. The road from Dar es Salaam south to Mtwara is in the process of being sealed. Secondary roads range from good to nearly impassable, depending on the season and when they were last maintained. For the majority of trips outside major towns you will need 4WD.

Hazards include vehicles overtaking blind on curves, pedestrians and animals on the road, and children running onto the road.

Road Rules
In theory, driving is on the left, and traffic already in roundabouts has the right of way. Unless otherwise posted, the speed limit is 80km/h; on some routes, including Dar es Salaam to Arusha, police have radar. Tanzania has a seat-belt law for drivers and front-seat passengers. The official traffic-fine penalty is Tsh20,000.

Motorcycles aren't permitted in national parks, except for the section of the Dar es Salaam–Mbeya highway passing through Mikumi park and on the road between Sumbawanga and Mpanda via Katavi National Park.

HITCHING
Hitching in Tanzania is generally slow going. It's prohibited inside national parks, and is usually fruitless around them. That said, in remote areas, hitching a lift with truck drivers may be your only transport option. Expect to pay about the same or a bit less than the bus fare for the same route, with a place in the cab costing about twice that for a place on top of the load. To flag down a vehicle, hold out your hand at about waist level, palm to the ground, and wave it up and down.

Expat workers or well-off locals may also offer you a ride. Payment is usually not expected, but you should still offer some token of thanks, such as making a contribution for petrol on longer journeys.

As in other parts of the world, hitching is never entirely safe, and we don't recommend it. Travellers who hitch should understand that they are taking a potentially serious risk. If you do hitch, you'll be safer doing so in pairs and letting someone know of your plans.

LOCAL TRANSPORT
Dalla-Dalla
Local routes are serviced by *dalla-dallas* (minibuses) and, in rural areas, pick-up trucks or old 4WDs. Prices are fixed and inexpensive – from Tsh100 for local town runs. The vehicles make many stops and are invariably extremely crowded. Accidents are frequent, particularly in minibuses. Many are caused when the drivers race each other to an upcoming station in order to collect new passengers. Destinations are either posted in the front window, or called out by the driver's assistant, who also col-

TRANSPORT

lects fares. If you have a large backpack, think twice about getting on a *dalla-dalla*, especially at rush hour, when it will make the already crowded conditions even more uncomfortable for the other passengers.

Taxi

Taxis, which have white plates on the mainland and a *'gari la abiria'* (passenger vehicle) sign on Zanzibar, can be hired in all major towns. None have meters, so agree on the fare with the driver before getting in. The standard rate for short town trips is Tsh1000. In Dar es Salaam and major towns, many drivers have an official price list, although rates shown on it are significantly higher than what is normally paid. If you're unsure of the price, ask locals what it should be and then use this as a base for negotiations. For half-day hire around major cities, expect to pay from around Tsh15,000. For longer trips away from town, negotiate the fare based on distance, petrol costs and road conditions, plus a fair profit for the driver.

TOURS

For safari and trekking operators, see p59. For local tour operators, see listings in the regional chapters.

TRAIN

Tanzania has two rail lines: **Tazara** (☎ 022-286 0340/4, 022-286 5339; www.tazara.co.tz; cnr Nyerere & Nelson Mandela Rds, Dar es Salaam) links Dar es Salaam with Kapiri Mposhi in Zambia via Mbeya and Tunduma; and the Tanzanian Railway Corporation's **Central Line** (Map p73; ☎ 022-211 7833; www.trctz.com; cnr Railway St & Sokoine Dr, Dar es Salaam) links Dar es Salaam with Kigoma and Mwanza via Morogoro, Dodoma and Tabora. There is a branch of the Central Line that links Tabora with

Mpanda; there's also passenger service on the Dodoma–Singida spur.

Tazara is more comfortable and efficient, but on both lines, breakdowns and long delays – up to 12 hours or more – are common. That said, both lines see a small but steady stream of travellers, many of whom thoroughly enjoy the trips.

Classes

There are three classes: 1st class (two- or four-bed compartments); 2nd-class sleeping (six-bed compartments); and economy class (benches, usually very crowded). Some trains also have a '2nd-class sitting section', with one seat per person. Men and women can only travel together in the sleeping sections by booking the entire compartment.

Reservations

Tickets for 1st and 2nd class should be reserved at least several days in advance, although occasionally you'll be able to get a seat on the day of travel. Economy-class tickets can be bought on the spot.

Schedules & Costs

Both lines are undergoing renovations and management changes, so expect schedule and price changes.

TAZARA

Tazara runs three trains weekly: two 'express' trains between Dar es Salaam and Kapiri Mposhi in Zambia via Mbeya; and an 'ordinary' train between Dar es Salaam and Mbeya.

For more on the express trains see p325. Ordinary trains depart Dar es Salaam at 10am Monday, reaching Mbeya the next day (Tsh24,500/18,400/12,200 for 1st/2nd/economy class, 24 hours); departures from Mbeya are at 12.20pm Monday.

Destination	1st class	2nd-sleeping class	2nd-sitting class	Economy class
Dar es Salaam to Kigoma	Tsh45,200	Tsh33,100	–	Tsh15,000
Dar es Salaam to Mwanza	Tsh44,600	Tsh32,600	Tsh17,700	Tsh18,800
Dar es Salaam to Tabora	Tsh32,700	Tsh24,200	Tsh13,000	Tsh11,000
Mwanza to Tabora	Tsh17,600	Tsh13,600	Tsh7200	Tsh6400
Tabora to Mpanda	Tsh16,300	Tsh12,600	–	Tsh6000
Dodoma to Singida	Tsh10,400	Tsh6900	–	–

CENTRAL LINE

Central Line trains depart Dar es Salaam at 5pm Tuesday, Friday and Sunday for both Kigoma and Mwanza (splitting at Tabora). In theory, both journeys take about 40 hours, though it's often much longer. Trains from both Mwanza and Kigoma to Dar es Salaam depart at 6pm Tuesday, Thursday and Sunday.

Trains between Tabora and Mpanda (about 14 hours) depart Tabora at 9pm Monday, Wednesday and Friday, and depart Mpanda at 1pm Tuesday, Thursday and Saturday.

Trains depart Dodoma for Singida (about 11 hours) at 10am Wednesday, Friday and Sunday. Departures from Singida are at 8am Monday, Thursday and Saturday.

TRANSPORT

Health Dr Caroline Evans

CONTENTS

As long as you stay up to date with your vaccinations and take basic preventive measures, you're unlikely to succumb to most of the health hazards covered in this chapter. While Tanzania has an impressive selection of tropical diseases on offer, it's more likely you'll get a bout of diarrhoea or a cold than a more exotic malady. The main exception to this is malaria, which is a real risk throughout the country.

BEFORE YOU GO

A little predeparture planning will save you trouble later. Get a check-up from your dentist and your doctor if you have any regular medication or chronic illness, eg high blood pressure and asthma. You should also organise spare contact lenses and glasses (and take your optical prescription with you); get a first-aid and medical kit together; and arrange necessary vaccinations.

Travellers can register with the **International Association for Medical Advice to Travellers** (IAMAT; www.iamat.org), which provides directories of certified doctors. If you'll be spending much time in remote areas (ie anywhere away from Dar es Salaam, Arusha and Zanzibar), you should consider doing a first-aid course (contact the Red Cross or St John Ambulance) or attending a remote medicine first-aid course, such as that offered by the **Royal Geographical Society** (www.wilderness medicaltraining.co.uk).

If you bring medications with you, carry them in their original (labelled) containers. A signed and dated letter from your physician describing all medical conditions and medications, including generic names, is also a good idea. If carrying syringes or needles, be sure to have a physician's letter documenting their medical necessity.

INSURANCE

Find out in advance if your insurance plan will make payments directly to providers or reimburse you later for overseas health expenditures. Most doctors in Tanzania expect payment in cash. It's vital to ensure that your travel insurance will cover any emergency transport required to get you at least as far as Nairobi (Kenya), or – preferably – all the way home, by air and with a medical attendant if necessary. It's worth taking out a temporary membership with the African Medical & Research Foundation (Amref; p312).

RECOMMENDED VACCINATIONS

The **World Health Organization** (www.who.int/en/) recommends that all travellers be covered for diphtheria, tetanus, measles, mumps, rubella, polio and hepatitis B, regardless of their destination. The consequences of these diseases can be severe and outbreaks do occur.

According to the **Centers for Disease Control and Prevention** (www.cdc.gov), the following vaccinations are recommended for Tanzania: hepatitis A, hepatitis B, rabies and typhoid, and boosters for tetanus, diphtheria and measles. While a yellow-fever vaccination certificate is not officially required to enter the country unless you're coming from an infected area, carrying one is also advised; check with your doctor before travelling, and also see p339.

MEDICAL CHECKLIST

It's a very good idea to carry a medical and first-aid kit with you, to help yourself in the case of minor illness or injury. Following is a list of items to consider packing:

- antibiotics eg ciprofloxacin (Ciproxin) or norfloxacin (Utinor)

- antidiarrhoeal drugs (eg loperamide)
- acetaminophen (paracetamol) or aspirin
- anti-inflammatory drugs (eg ibuprofen)
- antihistamines (for hay fever and allergic reactions)
- antibacterial ointment (eg Bactroban) for cuts and abrasions (prescription only)
- antimalaria pills
- bandages, gauze, gauze rolls and tape
- scissors, safety pins, tweezers
- pocket knife
- DEET-containing insect repellent for the skin
- permethrin-containing insect spray for clothing, tents, and bed nets
- sun block
- oral rehydration salts
- iodine tablets (for water purification)
- sterile needles, syringes and fluids if travelling to remote areas
- acetazolamide (Diamox) for altitude sickness (prescription only)
- self-diagnostic kit that can identify if malaria is in the blood from a finger prick

INTERNET RESOURCES

A good place to start is the **Lonely Planet website** (www.lonelyplanet.com). The World Health Organization publishes the helpful *International Travel and Health,* available free at www.who.int/ith. Other useful websites include **MD Travel Health** (www.mdtravelhealth.com) and **Fit for Travel** (www.fitfortravel.scot.nhs.uk).

Government travel-health websites:
- Australia: www.dfat.gov.au/travel
- Canada: www.hc-sc.gc.ca/pphb-dgspsp/tmp-pmv/pub_e.html
- UK: www.doh.gov.uk/traveladvice/index.htm
- USA: www.cdc.gov/travel

FURTHER READING

- *A Comprehensive Guide to Wilderness and Travel Medicine* by Eric A Weiss (1998)
- *Healthy Travel* by Jane Wilson-Howarth (1999)
- *Healthy Travel Africa* by Isabelle Young (2000)
- *How to Stay Healthy Abroad* by Richard Dawood (2002)
- *Travel in Health* by Graham Fry (1994)
- *Travel with Children* by Cathy Lanigan (2004)

IN TANZANIA

AVAILABILITY & COST OF HEALTH CARE

Good, Western-style medical care is available in Dar es Salaam. However, for serious matters, you'll need to go to Nairobi (Kenya), which is the main destination for medical evacuations from Tanzania, or return home. Elsewhere, reasonable-to-good care is available in Arusha, Moshi, Zanzibar and in some mission stations, including Kigoma and Songea. If you have a choice, try to find a private or mission-run clinic, as these are generally better equipped than government ones. If you fall ill in an unfamiliar area, ask staff at a top-end hotel or resident expatriates where the best nearby medical facilities are, and in an emergency contact your embassy. All towns have at least one clinic where you can get an inexpensive malaria test and, if necessary, treatment.

Pharmacies in Dar es Salaam and major towns are generally well stocked for commonly used items, and usually don't require prescriptions; always check expiry dates. In villages, selection is limited, although you can get chloroquine (for malaria) and paracetamol almost everywhere. Fansidar (an antimalarial medication) is also relatively easy to obtain, although antimalarials in general, as well as drugs for chronic diseases, should be brought from home. Some drugs for sale in Tanzania might be ineffective: they might be counterfeit or might not have been stored under the right conditions. The most common examples of counterfeit drugs are antimalaria tablets and expensive antibiotics, such as ciprofloxacin. Also, the availability and efficacy of condoms cannot be relied upon; they might not be of the same quality as in Europe or Australia and might have been incorrectly stored.

There is a high risk of contracting HIV from infected blood transfusions. The **Blood-Care Foundation** (www.bloodcare.org.uk) is a good source of safe blood, which can be transported to any part of the world within 24 hours.

INFECTIOUS DISEASES

Following are some of the diseases that are found in Tanzania, though with a few basic preventive measures, it's unlikely that you'll succumb to any of these.

Cholera

Cholera is usually only a problem during natural or artificial disasters, eg war, floods or earthquakes, although small outbreaks can also occur at other times. Travellers are rarely affected. It is caused by a bacteria and spread via contaminated drinking water. The main symptom is profuse watery diarrhoea, which causes debilitation if fluids are not replaced quickly. An oral cholera vaccine is available in the USA, but it is not particularly effective. Most cases of cholera could be avoided by close attention to good drinking water and by avoiding potentially contaminated food. Treatment is by fluid replacement (orally or via a drip), but sometimes antibiotics are needed. Self-treatment is not advised.

Diphtheria

Diphtheria is spread through close respiratory contact. It usually causes a temperature and a severe sore throat. Sometimes a membrane forms across the throat and a tracheotomy is needed to prevent suffocation. Vaccination is recommended for those likely to be in close contact with the local population in infected areas but is more important for long stays than for short-term trips. The vaccine is given as an injection alone or with tetanus, and lasts 10 years. Self-treatment: none.

Filariasis

Filariasis is caused by tiny worms migrating in the lymphatic system, and is spread by a bite from an infected mosquito. Symptoms include localised itching and swelling of the legs and/or genitalia. Treatment is available. Self-treatment: none.

Hepatitis A

Hepatitis A is spread through contaminated food (particularly shellfish) and water. It causes jaundice and, although it is rarely fatal, it can cause prolonged lethargy and delayed recovery. If you've had hepatitis A, you shouldn't drink alcohol for up to six months afterwards, but once you've recovered, there won't be any long-term problems. The first symptoms include dark urine and a yellow colour to the whites of the eyes. Sometimes a fever and abdominal pain might be present. Hepatitis A vaccine (Avaxim, VAQTA, Havrix) is given as an injection: a single dose will give protection for up to a year, and a booster after a year gives 10-year protection. Hepatitis A and typhoid vaccines can also be given as a single-dose vaccine, hepatyrix or viatim. Self-treatment: none.

Hepatitis B

Hepatitis B is spread through sexual intercourse, infected blood and contaminated needles. It can also be spread from an infected mother to her baby during childbirth. It affects the liver, causing jaundice and sometimes liver failure. Most people recover completely, but some people might be chronic carriers of the virus, which could lead eventually to cirrhosis or liver cancer. Those visiting high-risk areas for long periods, or those with increased social or occupational risk, should be immunised. Many countries now routinely give hepatitis B as part of childhood vaccination. It is given singly or can be given at the same time as hepatitis A.

A course will give protection for at least five years. It can be given over four weeks or six months. Self-treatment: none.

HIV

Human immunodeficiency virus (HIV), the virus that causes acquired immune deficiency syndrome (AIDS), is a major problem in Tanzania, with infection rates averaging about 8%, and much higher in some areas. The virus is spread through infected blood and blood products, by sexual intercourse with an infected partner and from an infected mother to her baby during childbirth and breastfeeding. It can be spread through 'blood to blood' contact, such as with contaminated instruments during medical, dental, acupuncture and other body-piercing procedures, and through sharing used intravenous needles. At present there is no cure; medication that might keep the disease under control is available, but these drugs are too expensive, or unavailable, for the overwhelming majority of Tanzanians. If you think you might have been infected with HIV, a blood test is necessary; a three-month gap after exposure and before testing is required to allow antibodies to appear in the blood. Self-treatment: none.

Malaria

Malaria is endemic throughout most of Tanzania (except at altitudes higher than

2000m, where the risk of transmission is low), and a major health scourge. Infection rates are higher during the rainy season, but the risk exists year-round, and it is extremely important to take preventive measures, even if you will just be in the country for a short time.

Malaria is caused by a parasite in the bloodstream spread via the bite of the female anopheles mosquito. There are several types, falciparum malaria being the most dangerous and the predominant form in Tanzania. Unlike most other diseases regularly encountered by travellers, there is no vaccination against malaria (yet). However, several different drugs are used to prevent malaria, and new ones are in the pipeline. Up-to-date advice from a travel-health clinic is essential, as some medication is more suitable for some travellers than others (see right). The pattern of drug-resistant malaria is changing rapidly, so what was advised several years ago might no longer be the case.

SYMPTOMS

The early stages of malaria include headaches, fevers, generalised aches and pains, and malaise, which could be mistaken for flu. Other symptoms can include abdominal pain, diarrhoea and a cough. Anyone who develops a fever in Tanzania or within two weeks after departure should assume malarial infection until a blood test proves negative, even if you have been taking antimalarial medication. If not treated, the next stage could develop within 24 hours, particularly if falciparum malaria is the para-

site: jaundice, then reduced consciousness and coma (also known as cerebral malaria) followed by death. Treatment in hospital is essential, and the death rate might still be as high as 10% even in the best intensive-care facilities.

SIDE EFFECTS & RISKS

Many travellers are under the impression that malaria is a mild illness, that treatment is always easy and successful, and that taking antimalarial drugs causes more illness through side effects than actually getting malaria. Unfortunately, this is not true. Side effects of the medication depend on the drug being taken. Doxycycline can cause heartburn and indigestion; mefloquine (Larium) can cause anxiety attacks, insomnia and nightmares, and (rarely) severe psychiatric disorders; chloroquine can cause nausea and hair loss; and proguanil can cause mouth ulcers. These side effects are not universal and can be minimised by taking medication correctly, eg with food. Also, some people should not take a particular antimalarial drug, eg people with epilepsy should avoid mefloquine, and doxycycline should not be taken by pregnant women or children younger than 12.

If you decide that you really don't want to take antimalarial drugs, you must understand the risks and be obsessive about avoiding mosquito bites. Use nets and insect repellent, and report any fever or flu-like symptoms to a doctor as soon as possible. Some people advocate homeopathic preparations against malaria, such as Demal200, but as yet there is no conclusive evidence

---

ANTIMALARIAL A TO D

- **A** – Awareness of the risk. No medication is totally effective, but protection of up to 95% is achievable with most drugs, as long as other measures have been taken.

- **B** – Bites: avoid at all costs. Sleep in a screened room, use a mosquito spray or coils and sleep under a permethrin-impregnated net at night. Cover up at night with long trousers and long sleeves, preferably with permethrin-treated clothing. Apply appropriate repellent to all areas of exposed skin in the evenings.

- **C** – Chemical prevention (ie antimalarial drugs) is usually needed in malarial areas. Expert advice is needed as resistance patterns can change, and new drugs are in development. Not all antimalarial drugs are suitable for everyone. Most antimalarial drugs need to be started at least a week in advance and continued for four weeks after the last possible exposure to malaria.

- **D** – Diagnosis. If you have a fever or flu-like illness within a year of travel to a malarial area, malaria is a possibility, and immediate medical attention is necessary.

that this is effective, and many homeopaths do not recommend their use. Malaria in pregnancy frequently results in miscarriage or premature labour, and the risks to both mother and foetus during pregnancy are considerable. Travel in Tanzania when pregnant should be carefully considered.

STAND-BY TREATMENT

If you will be away from major towns, it's worth carrying emergency stand-by treatment. However, this should be viewed as emergency treatment only and not as routine self-medication, and should only be used if you will be far from medical facilities and have been advised about the symptoms of malaria and how to use the medication. If you do resort to emergency self-treatment, seek medical advice as soon as possible to confirm whether the treatment has been successful. In particular, you want to avoid contracting cerebral malaria, which can be fatal within 24 hours. As mentioned on p335, self-diagnostic kits, which can identify malaria in the blood from a finger prick, are available in the West, and worth investing in.

Meningococcal Meningitis

Meningococcal infection is spread through close respiratory contact and is more likely in crowded places, such as dormitories, buses and clubs. While the disease is present in Tanzania, infection is uncommon in travellers. Vaccination is recommended for long stays and is especially important towards the end of the dry season (see p307). Symptoms include a fever, severe headache, neck stiffness and a red rash. Immediate medical treatment is necessary.

The ACWY vaccine is recommended for all travellers in sub-Saharan Africa. This vaccine is different from the meningococcal meningitis C vaccine given to children and adolescents in some countries; it is safe to be given both types of vaccine. Self-treatment: none.

Onchocerciasis (River Blindness)

This disease is caused by the larvae of a tiny worm, which is spread by the bite of a small fly. The earliest sign of infection is intensely itchy, red, sore eyes. It's rare for travellers to be severely affected. Treatment undertaken in a specialised clinic is curative. Self-treatment: none.

Poliomyelitis

This disease is generally spread through contaminated food and water. It is one of the vaccines given in childhood and should be boosted every 10 years, either orally (a drop on the tongue) or else as an injection. Polio can be carried asymptomatically (ie showing no symptoms) and could cause a transient fever. In rare cases it causes weakness or paralysis of one or more muscles, which might be permanent. Self-treatment: none.

Rabies

Rabies is spread via the bite or lick of an infected animal on broken skin. It is always fatal once the clinical symptoms start (which might be up to several months after an infected bite), so post-bite vaccination should be given as soon as possible. Post-bite vaccination (whether or not you've been vaccinated before the bite) prevents the virus from spreading to the central nervous system. Consider vaccination if you'll be travelling away from major centres (ie anywhere where a reliable source of post-bite vaccine is not available within 24 hours). Three preventive injections are needed over a month. If you have not been vaccinated you'll need a course of five injections starting 24 hours, or as soon as possible, after the injury. If you have been vaccinated, you'll need fewer post-bite injections, and have more time to seek medical help. Self-treatment: none.

Schistosomiasis (Bilharzia)

This disease is a risk throughout Tanzania. It's spread by flukes (parasitic flatworm) that are carried by a species of freshwater snail, which then sheds them into slow-moving or still water. The parasites penetrate human skin during swimming and then migrate to the bladder or bowel. They are excreted via stool or urine and could contaminate fresh water, where the cycle starts again. Swimming in suspect freshwater lakes (including Lake Victoria) or slow-running rivers should be avoided. Symptoms range from none to transient fever and rash, and advanced cases might have blood in the stool or in the urine. A blood test can detect antibodies if you might have been exposed, and treatment is readily available. If not treated, the infection can cause kidney failure or permanent bowel damage. It's not possible for you to infect others. Self-treatment: none.

Tuberculosis (TB)

TB is spread through close respiratory contact and occasionally through infected milk or milk products. BCG vaccination is recommended if you'll be mixing closely with the local population, especially on long-term stays, although it gives only moderate protection against TB. TB can be asymptomatic, only being picked up on a routine chest X-ray. Alternatively, it can cause a cough, weight loss or fever, sometimes months or even years after exposure. Self-treatment: none.

Trypanosomiasis (Sleeping Sickness)

This disease is spread via the bite of the tsetse fly. It causes headache, fever and eventually coma. There is an effective treatment. Self-treatment: none.

Typhoid

This is spread through food or water contaminated by infected human faeces. The first symptom is usually a fever or a pink rash on the abdomen. Septicaemia (blood poisoning) can sometimes occur. A typhoid vaccine (typhim Vi, typherix) will give protection for three years. In some countries, the oral vaccine Vivotif is also available. Antibiotics are usually given as treatment, and death is rare unless septicaemia occurs. Self-treatment: none.

Yellow Fever

Although Tanzania (including Zanzibar) no longer officially requires you to carry a certificate of yellow-fever vaccination unless you're arriving from an infected area (which includes Kenya), it's still sometimes asked for at some borders, and is a requirement in some neighbouring countries. When trying to decide whether to get jabbed or not, remember that yellow fever exists in Tanzania, and the vaccine is recommended for almost all visitors by the **Centers for Disease Control and Prevention** (www.cdc.gov/travel/yb/countries/Tanzania.htm).

Yellow fever is spread by infected mosquitoes. Symptoms range from a flu-like illness to severe hepatitis (liver inflammation), jaundice and death. The yellow-fever vaccination must be given at a designated clinic and is valid for 10 years. It is a live vaccine and must not be given to immunocompromised or pregnant travellers. Self-treatment: none.

TRAVELLERS' DIARRHOEA

It's not inevitable that you'll get diarrhoea while travelling in Tanzania, but it's certainly likely. Diarrhoea is the most common travel-related illness, and sometimes can be triggered simply by dietary changes. To help prevent diarrhoea, avoid tap water, only eat fresh fruits or vegetables if cooked or peeled, and be wary of dairy products that might contain unpasteurised milk. Although freshly cooked food can often be a safe option, plates or serving utensils might be dirty, so be selective when eating food from street vendors (make sure that cooked food is piping hot all the way through). If you develop diarrhoea, be sure to drink plenty of fluids, preferably an oral rehydration solution. A few loose stools don't require treatment but if you start having more than four or five stools a day you should start taking an antibiotic (usually a quinoline drug, such as ciprofloxacin or norfloxacin) and an antidiarrhoeal agent (such as loperamide) if you are not within easy reach of a toilet. If diarrhoea is bloody, persists for more than 72 hours or is accompanied by fever, shaking chills or severe abdominal pain, seek medical attention.

Amoebic Dysentery

Contracted by eating contaminated food and water, amoebic dysentery causes blood and mucus in the faeces. It can be relatively mild and tends to come on gradually, but seek medical advice if you think you have the illness as it won't clear up without treatment (which is with specific antibiotics).

Giardiasis

This, like amoebic dysentery, is caused by ingesting contaminated food or water. The illness usually appears a week or more after you have been exposed to the offending parasite. Giardiasis might cause only a short-lived bout of typical travellers' diarrhoea, but it can also cause persistent diarrhoea. Ideally, seek medical advice if you suspect you have giardiasis, but if you are in a remote area you could start a course of antibiotics.

ENVIRONMENTAL HAZARDS
Altitude Sickness

Lack of oxygen at altitudes above 2500m affects most people. The effect may be mild or severe and occurs because less oxygen reaches the muscles and the brain at high altitudes, requiring the heart and lungs to compensate by working harder. Symptoms of Acute Mountain Sickness (AMS) usually develop during the first 24 hours at altitude but may be delayed for up to three weeks. Mild symptoms include headache, lethargy, dizziness, sleeping difficulties and loss of appetite. AMS may become more severe without warning and can be fatal. It is a significant risk for anyone – no matter what their fitness level – who tries to ascend Mt Kilimanjaro or Mt Meru too rapidly. Severe symptoms include breathlessness; a dry, irritative cough (which may progress to the production of pink, frothy sputum); severe headache; lack of coordination and balance; confusion; irrational behaviour; vomiting; drowsiness; and unconsciousness. There is no hard-and-fast rule as to what is too high: AMS has been fatal at 3000m, although 3500m to 4500m is the usual range.

Treat mild symptoms of AMS by resting at the same altitude until recovery, which usually takes a day or two. Paracetamol or aspirin can be taken for headaches. If symptoms persist or become worse, however, immediate descent is necessary; even descending just 500m can help. Drug treatments should never be used to avoid descent or to enable further ascent.

The drugs acetazolamide and dexamethasone are recommended by some doctors for the prevention of AMS; however, their use is controversial. They can reduce the symptoms, but they may also mask warning signs and cause severe dehydration; severe and fatal AMS has occurred in people taking these drugs. In general we do not recommend them for travellers.

To prevent AMS, try the following:

- Ascend slowly – have frequent rest days, spending two to three nights at each rise of 1000m. If you reach a high altitude by trekking, acclimatisation takes place gradually and you are less likely to be affected than if you fly or drive directly to an area of high altitude.
- It is always wise to sleep at a lower altitude than the greatest height reached during the day if possible ('climb high, sleep low'). Also, once above 3000m, care should be taken not to increase the sleeping altitude by more than 300m per day.
- Drink lots of fluids. Mountain air is dry and cold and moisture is lost as you breathe. Evaporation of sweat may occur unnoticed and result in dehydration.
- Eat light, high-carbohydrate meals for more energy.
- Avoid alcohol as it increases the risk of dehydration.
- Avoid sedatives.

Heat Exhaustion

This condition occurs after heavy sweating and excessive fluid loss with inadequate replacement of fluids and salt, and is primarily a risk in hot climates when taking unaccustomed exercise before full acclimatisation. Symptoms include headache, dizziness and tiredness. Dehydration is already happening by the time you feel thirsty – aim to drink sufficient water to produce pale, diluted urine. Self-treatment: fluid replacement with water and/or fruit juice, and cooling the body with cold water and fans. The treatment of the salt-loss component consists of consuming salty fluids (as in soup) and adding a little more table salt to foods than usual.

Heatstroke

Heat exhaustion is a precursor to the much more serious condition of heatstroke. In this case there is damage to the sweating mechanism, with an excessive rise in body temperature; irrational and hyperactive behaviour; and, eventually, loss of consciousness and death. Rapid cooling by spraying the body with water and fanning is ideal. Emergency fluid and electrolyte replacement is usually also required by intravenous drip.

Hypothermia

Too much cold can be just as dangerous as too much heat. If you are trekking at high altitudes, such as on Mt Kilimanjaro or Mt Meru, you'll need to have appropriate

TRADITIONAL MEDICINE *Mary Fitzpatrick*

According to some estimates, at least 80% of Tanzanians rely in part or in whole on traditional medicine, and close to two thirds of the population have traditional healers as their first point of contact in the case of illness. The *mganga* (traditional healer) holds a revered position in many communities, and traditional medicinal products are widely available in local markets. In part, the heavy reliance on traditional medicine is because of the comparatively high costs of conventional Western-style medicine, and because of prevailing cultural attitudes and beliefs, but also because it sometimes works. Often, though, it's because there is no other choice. In northeastern Tanzania, for example, it is estimated that while there is only one medical doctor to 33,000 people, there is a traditional healer for approximately every 150 people. While the ratio is somewhat better countrywide (one medical doctor to about 20,000 people), hospitals and health clinics are concentrated in urban areas, and most are limited in their effectiveness because of insufficient resources and chronic shortages of equipment and medicines.

While some traditional remedies seem to work on malaria, sickle cell anaemia, high blood pressure and some AIDS symptoms, most traditional healers learn their art by apprenticeship, so education (and consequently application of knowledge) is often inconsistent and unregulated. At the centre of efforts to address problems arising from this is the **Institute of Traditional Medicine** (www.muchs.ac.tz; Muhimbili Medical Centre, Dar es Salaam). Among other things, the institute is studying the efficacy of various traditional cures, and promoting those that are found to be successful. There are also local efforts to create healers' associations, and to train traditional practitioners in sanitation and various other topics. On a broader scale, the Organisation of African Unity has declared 2001 to 2010 the Decade of Traditional Medicine in Tanzania and across the continent.

HEALTH

clothing and be prepared for cold, wet conditions. Even in lower areas, such as the Usambara Mountains, the rim of Ngorongoro Crater or the Ulugurus, conditions can be wet and quite chilly.

Hypothermia occurs when the body loses heat faster than it can produce it and the core temperature of the body falls. It is surprisingly easy to progress from being very cold to being dangerously cold due to a combination of wind, wet clothing, fatigue and hunger, even if the air temperature is above freezing. It is best to dress in layers; silk, wool and some of the new artificial fibres are all good insulating materials. A hat is important, as a lot of heat is lost through the head. A strong, waterproof outer layer (and a 'space' blanket for emergencies) is essential. Carry basic supplies, including food that contains simple sugars to generate heat quickly and fluid to drink.

Symptoms of hypothermia are exhaustion, numb skin (particularly of the toes and fingers), shivering, slurred speech, irrational or violent behaviour, lethargy, stumbling, dizzy spells, muscle cramps and violent bursts of energy. Irrationality may take the form of sufferers claiming they are warm and trying to take off their clothes.

To treat mild hypothermia, first get the person out of the wind and/or rain, remove their clothing if it's wet and replace it with dry, warm clothing. Give them hot liquids – not alcohol – and high-kilojoule, easily digestible food. Do not rub victims: allow them to slowly warm themselves instead. This should be enough to treat the early stages of hypothermia. The early recognition and treatment of mild hypothermia is the only way to prevent severe hypothermia, which is a critical condition.

Insect Bites & Stings

Mosquitoes might not always carry malaria or dengue fever, but they (and other insects) can cause irritation and infected bites. To avoid these, take the same precautions as you would for avoiding malaria (see p337). Bee and wasp stings cause real problems only to those who have a severe allergy to the stings (anaphylaxis), in which case, carry an adrenaline (epinephrine) injection.

Scorpions are found in arid areas. They can cause a painful bite that is sometimes life-threatening. If bitten by a scorpion, take a painkiller. Medical treatment should be sought if the victim collapses.

Bed bugs are often found in hostels and cheap hotels. They lead to very itchy, lumpy bites. Spraying the mattress with crawling insect killer after changing the bedding will get rid of them.

Scabies is also frequently found in cheap accommodation. These tiny mites live in the skin, particularly between the fingers. They cause an intensely itchy rash. The itch is easily treated with Malathion and permethrin lotion from a pharmacy; other members of the household also need to be treated to avoid spreading scabies, even if they do not show any symptoms.

Snake Bites
Basically, avoid getting bitten! Don't walk barefoot or stick your hand into holes or cracks. However, 50% of those bitten by venomous snakes are not actually injected with poison (envenomed). If bitten by a snake, do not panic. Immobilise the bitten limb with a splint (such as a stick) and apply a bandage over the site, with firm pressure – similar to bandaging a sprain. Do not apply a tourniquet, or cut or suck the bite. Get medical help as soon as possible so an anti-venin can be given if needed.

Water
Unless your intestines are well accustomed to Tanzania, don't drink tap water that hasn't been boiled, filtered or chemically disinfected (such as with iodine tablets). Also avoid drinking from streams, rivers and lakes unless you've purified the water first. The same goes for drinking from pumps and wells – some do bring pure water to the surface, but the presence of animals can still contaminate supplies.

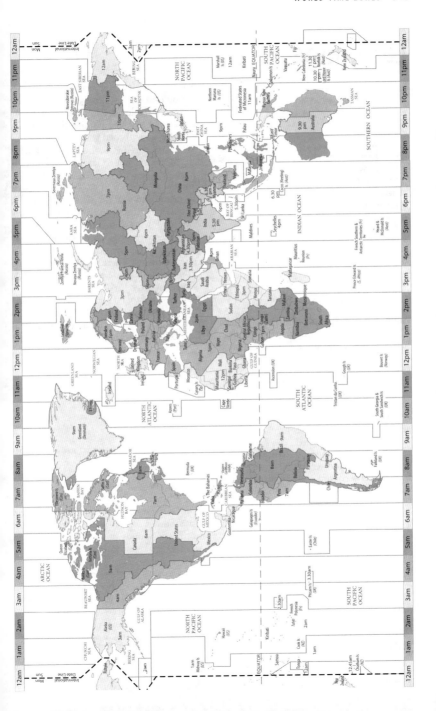

Language

CONTENTS

Along with English, Swahili is the official language of Tanzania. Standard Swahili is based on the variety of the language spoken in Zanzibar Town, although there are several other dialects. Written Swahili – the language of newspapers, textbooks and literature – usually conforms to that spoken on the East African coast.

Although Swahili may seem a bit daunting at first, its structure is fairly regular and pronunciation uncomplicated. You'll soon discover that just a handful of basic words will go a long way, and will rapidly break down barriers between you and the many people you meet on your travels in Tanzania.

If your time is limited, concentrate first on the greetings (of critical importance in Tanzanian society), and then on numbers (very useful when negotiating with market vendors, taxi drivers etc). The words and phrases included in this chapter will help you get started. For a more comprehensive guide to the language, get hold of Lonely Planet's Swahili Phrasebook. Good luck and Safari njema! (happy travels).

PRONUNCIATION

Perhaps the easiest part of learning Swahili is the pronunciation. Every letter is pronounced, unless it's part of the consonant combinations discussed in the 'Consonants' section below. If a letter is written twice, it is pronounced twice – mzee (respected elder) has three syllables: m-ZE-e. Note that the 'm' is a separate syllable, and that the double 'e' indicates a lengthened vowel sound.

Word stress in Swahili almost always falls on the second-to-last syllable.

Vowels

Correct pronunciation of vowels is the key to making yourself understood in Swahili. If the following guidelines don't work for you, listen closely to how Swahili speakers pronounce their words and spend some time practising. There's also a useful audio pronunciation guide available on the Yale website: www.yale.edu/swahili/.

Remember that if two vowels appear next to each other, each must be pronounced in turn. For example, kawaida (usual) is pronounced ka-wa-EE-da.

a as in 'calm'
e as the 'ey' in 'they'
i as the 'ee' in 'keep'
o as in 'go'
u as the 'oo' in 'moon'

Consonants

Most consonants in Swahili have equivalents in English. The only one that might be a bit unusual for an English speaker is the sound ng. It can be a bit tricky at first, but with a little practice it should come easily – say 'sing along' a few times and then drop the 'si', and that's how it sounds at the beginning of a word. The sounds th and dh occur only in words borrowed from Arabic.

r Swahili speakers make only a slight distinction between r and l; use a light 'd' for 'r' and you'll be pretty close.
dh as 'th' in 'this'
th as 'th' in 'thing'
ny as the 'ni' in 'onion'
ng as in 'singer'
gh like the 'ch' in Scottish loch
g as in 'get'
ch as in 'church'

ACCOMMODATION

Where's a ...?	... iko wapi?
camping ground	uwanja wa kambi
guesthouse	gesti
hotel	hoteli
youth hostel	hosteli ya vijana

Can you recommend cheap lodging?
Unaweza kunipendekezea malazi rahisi?

What's the address?
Anwani ni nini?

Do you have a ... room?	Kuna chumba kwa ...?
single	mtu mmoja
double	watu wawili, kitanda kimoja
twin	watu wawili, vitanda viwili
triple	watu watatu

How much is it per day/person?
Ni bei gani kwa siku/mtu?

Can I see the room?
Naomba nione chumba?

Where's the bathroom?
Choo iko wapi?

Where are the toilets?
Vyoo viko wapi?

I'll take it.
Nataka.

I'm leaving now.
Naondoka sasa.

CONVERSATION & ESSENTIALS

Greetings are probably the most important vocabulary for a traveller to Tanzania. It's worth taking the time to familiarise yourself with the few we include here.

Jambo is a pidgin Swahili word, used to greet tourists who are presumed not to understand the language. There are two possible responses: *Jambo* (meaning 'Hello, now please speak to me in English'), and *Sijambo* (or 'Things aren't bad with me, and I'm willing to try a little Swahili').

If people assume you can speak a little Swahili, greetings may involve one or a number of the following exchanges:

How are you?	Hujambo?
(to one person)	
I'm fine.	Sijambo.
How are you all?	Hamjambo?
We're fine.	Hatujambo.

The word *habari* (meaning 'news') can also be used for general greetings. You may hear the word *salama* substituted for *habari*, or the *habari* may be dropped altogether.

How are you?	Habari?
How are you all?	Habari zenu?
What's the news?	Habari gani?
Good morning.	Habari za asubuhi?
Good day.	Habari za leo?
Good afternoon.	Habari za mchana?
Good evening/night.	Habari za jioni?
What's happening with you?	Habari yako?

By memorising these three simple words, you can reply to almost anything:

Good.	Nzuri.
Fine.	Salama.
Clean.	Safi.

There is also a respectful greeting for elders:

Greetings.	Shikamoo.
(response)	Marahaba.

Once you've dealt with all the appropriate greetings, you can move onto other topics:

What's your name?	Jina lako nani?
My name is ...	Jina langu ni ...
Where are you from?	Unatoka wapi?
I'm from ...	Natoka ...
I like ...	Ninapenda ...
I don't like ...	Sipendi ...

Farewells are generally short and sweet:

Goodbye.	Kwa heri.
Until tomorrow.	Kesho.
Later on.	Baadaye.
Good night.	Usiku mwema.

And a few basics never hurt ...

Yes.	Ndiyo.
No.	Hapana.
Please.	Tafadhali.
Thank you (very much).	Asante (sana).
You're welcome.	Karibu.
Excuse me.	Samahani.
Sorry.	Pole.
Just a minute.	Subiri kidogo.

SIGNS

Mahali Pa Kuingia	Entrance
Mahali Pa Kutoka	Exit
Maelezo	Information
Imefunguliwa	Open
Imefungwa	Closed
Ni Marufuku	Prohibited
Polisi	Police
Choo/Msalani	Toilets/WC
Wanaume	Men
Wanawake	Women

DIRECTIONS

Where's ...?	... iko wapi?
It's straight ahead.	Iko moja kwa moja.

Turn ...	Geuza ...
at the corner	kwenye kona
at the traffic lights	kwenye taa za barabarani
left	kushoto
right	kulia

behind	nyuma ya
in front of	mbele ya
near	karibu na
next to	jirani ya
opposite	ng'ambo ya

EMERGENCIES

Help!	Saidia!
There's been an accident!	Ajali imetokea!
Call the police!	Waite polisi!
Call a doctor!	Mwite daktari!
I'm lost.	Nimejipotea.
Leave me alone!	Niache!

HEALTH

I'm sick.	Mimi ni mgonjwa.
It hurts here.	Inauma hapa.

I'm allergic to ...	Nina mzio wa ...
antibiotics	viuavijasumu
aspirin	aspirini
bees	nyuki
nuts	kokwa
peanuts	karanga

antiseptic	dawa ya kusafisha jeraha
condoms	kondom
contraceptives	kingamimba

insect repellent	dawa la kufukuza wadudu
iodine	iodini
painkillers	viondoa maumivu
thermometer	pimajoto
water purification tablets	vidonge vya kusafisha maji

LANGUAGE DIFFICULTIES

Do you speak (English)?
Unasema (Kiingereza)?
Does anyone speak (English)?
Kuna mtu yeyote kusema (Kiingereza)?
What does (asante) mean?
Neno (asante) lina maana gani?
Yes, I understand.
Ndiyo, naelewa.
No, I don't understand.
Hapana, sielewi.
Could you please write ... down?
Tafadhali ... andika?
Can you show me (on the map)?
Unaweza kunionyesha (katika ramani)?

NUMBERS

0	sifuri
1	moja
2	mbili
3	tatu
4	nne
5	tano
6	sita
7	saba
8	nane
9	tisa
10	kumi
11	kumi na moja
12	kumi na mbili
13	kumi na tatu
14	kumi na nne
15	kumi na tano
16	kumi na sita
17	kumi na saba
18	kumi na nane
19	kumi na tisa
20	ishirini
21	ishirini na moja
22	ishirini na mbili
30	thelathini
40	arobaini
50	hamsini
60	sitini
70	sabini
80	themanini
90	tisini
100	mia moja
1000	elfu

PAPERWORK

name	*jina*
nationality	*raia*
date of birth	*tarehe ya kuzaliwa*
place of birth	*mahali pa kuzaliwa*
sex/gender	*jinsia*
passport	*pasipoti*
visa	*viza*

QUESTION WORDS

Who?	*Nani?*
What?	*Nini?*
When?	*Lini?*
Where?	*Wapi?*
Which?	*Gani?*
Why?	*Kwa nini?*
How?	*Namna?*

SHOPPING & SERVICES

department store	*duka lenye vitu vingi*
general store	*duka lenye vitu mbalimbali*
I'd like to buy ...	*Nataka kununua ...*
I'm just looking.	*Naangalia tu.*
How much is it?	*Ni bei gani?*
Can I look at it?	*Naomba nione.*
I don't like it.	*Sipendi.*
That's too expensive.	*Ni ghali mno.*
Please lower the price.	*Punguza bei, tafadhali.*
I'll take it.	*Nataka.*
Do you accept ...?	*Mnakubali ...?*
credit cards	*kadi ya benki*
travellers cheques	*hundi ya msafiri*
more	*zaidi*
less	*chache zaidi*
Where's (a/the) ...?	*... iko wapi?*
bank	*benki*
market	*soko*
tourist office	*maarifa kwa watalii*
... embassy	*ubalozi ...*
hospital	*hospitali*
post office	*posta*
public phone	*simu ya mtaani*
public toilet	*choo cha hadhara*
telecom centre	*telekom*

TIME & DATES

What time is it?	*Ni saa ngapi?*
It's (ten) o'clock.	*Ni saa (nne).*
morning	*asubuhi*
afternoon	*mchana*
evening	*jioni*
today	*leo*
tomorrow	*kesho*
yesterday	*jana*
Monday	*Jumatatu*
Tuesday	*Jumanne*
Wednesday	*Jumatano*
Thursday	*Alhamisi*
Friday	*Ijumaa*
Saturday	*Jumamosi*
Sunday	*Jumapili*
January	*mwezi wa kwanza*
February	*mwezi wa pili*
March	*mwezi wa tatu*
April	*mwezi wa nne*
May	*mwezi wa tano*
June	*mwezi wa sita*
July	*mwezi wa saba*
August	*mwezi wa nane*
September	*mwezi wa tisa*
October	*mwezi wa kumi*
November	*mwezi wa kumi na moja*
December	*mwezi wa kumi na mbili*

TRANSPORT
Public Transport

What time is the ... leaving?
... inaondoka saa ngapi?
Which ... goes to (Mbeya)?
... ipi huenda (Mbeya)?

bus	*basi*
minibus	*daladala*
plane	*ndege*
train	*treni*

When's the ... (bus)?
(Basi) ... itaondoka lini?

first	*ya kwanza*
last	*ya mwisho*
next	*ijayo*

A ... ticket to (Iringa).
Tiketi moja ya ... kwenda (Iringa).

1st-class	*daraja la kwanza*
2nd-class	*daraja la pili*
one-way	*kwenda tu*
return	*kwenda na kurudi*
cancelled	*imefutwa*
delayed	*imeche leweshwa*
platform	*stendi*
ticket window	*dirisha la tiketi*
timetable	*ratiba*

Private Transport

I'd like to hire a/an ...	*Nataka kukodi ...*
bicycle	*baisikeli*
car	*gari*
4WD	*forbaifor*
motorbike	*pikipiki*

Are you willing to hire out your car/motorbike?
Unaweza kunikodisha gari/pikipiki yako?
(How long) Can I park here?
Naweza kuegesha hapa (kwa muda gani)?
Is this the road to (Embu)?
Hii ni barabara kwenda (Embu)?
Where's a petrol station?
Kituo cha mafuta kiko wapi?
Please fill it up.
Jaza tangi/tanki.
I'd like ... litres.
Nataka lita ...

diesel	*dizeli*
leaded/unleaded	*risasi/isiyo na risasi*
I need a mechanic.	*Nahitaji fundi.*
I've had an accident.	*Nimepata ajali.*
I have a flat tyre.	*Nina pancha.*
I've run out of petrol.	*Mafuta yamekwisha.*

The car/motorbike has broken down (at Chalinze).
Gari/pikipiki ime haribika (Chalinze).
The car/motorbike won't start.
Gari/pikipiki haiwaki.
Could I pay for a ride in your truck?
Naweza kulipa kwa lifti katika lori lako?
Could I contribute to the petrol cost?
Naweza kuchangia sehemu ya bei ya mafuta?
Thanks for the ride.
Asante kwa lifti.

TRAVEL WITH CHILDREN

I need a/an ...	*Nahitaji ...*
Is there a/an ...?	*Kuna ...?*
baby change room	*chumba cha kuvalia mtoto*
baby seat	*kiti cha kitoto*
child-minding service	*anayeweza kumlea mtoto*
children's menu	*menyu kwa watoto*
disposable nappies/ diapers	*nepi*
(English-speaking) babysitter	*yaya (anayesema Kiingereza)*
highchair	*kiti juu cha mtoto*
potty	*choo cha mtoto*
stroller	*kigari cha mtoto*

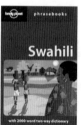

Also available from Lonely Planet:
Swahili Phrasebook

Glossary

ASP – Afro-Shirazi Party

banda – thatched-roof hut with wooden or earthen walls
bangi – marijuana
bao – a board game widely played in East Africa, especially on Zanzibar
baraza – the stone seats seen along the outside walls of houses in Zanzibar's Stone Town, used for chatting and relaxing
boma – a fortified living compound; in colonial times, an administrative office
bui-bui – black cover-all worn by some Islamic women outside the home

chai – tea
chakula – food
Chama Cha Mapinduzi (CCM) – Party of the Revolution (Tanzania's governing political party)
choo – toilet
Cites – UN Convention on International Trade in Endangered Species
Civic United Front (CUF) – Tanzania's main opposition party

dada – sister; often used as a form of address
dalla-dalla – minibus
Deutsch-Ostafrikanische Gesellschaft (DOAG) – German East Africa Company
dhow – ancient Arabic sailing vessel
duka – small shop or kiosk

fly camp – camp away from main tented camps or lodges, usually a bit more rugged than permanent luxury tented camps (ie may not have running water)
forex – foreign exchange (bureau)

ganja – see *bangi*
gongo – distilled cashew drink

hodi – called out prior to entering someone's house; roughly meaning 'may I enter?'
hotel/hoteli – basic local eatery

jamaa – clan, community

kahawa – coffee
kaka – brother; often used as a form of address, and to call the waiter in restaurants
kanga – printed cotton wrap-around worn by many Tanzanian women; Swahili proverbs are printed along the edge of the cloth

kanzu – white robe-like outer garment worn by men – often for prayer – on the Zanzibar Archipelago and in other Swahili areas
karanga – peanuts
karibu – welcome
kidumbak – an offshoot of *taarab* music, distinguished by its defined rhythms and drumming, and hard-hitting lyrics
kikoi – cotton linen wrap-around traditionally worn by men in coastal areas
kitenge – similar to a *kanga,* but usually a larger, heavier piece of cloth with no Swahili proverb
kofia – a cap, usually of embroidered white linen, worn by men on the Zanzibar Archipelago and in other Swahili areas
kwaya – church choir music

maandazi – doughnut
masika – long rains
matatu – Kenyan minivan
matoke – cooked plantains
mbege – banana beer, popular around Marangu
mgando – see *mtindi*
mihrab – the prayer niche in a mosque showing the direction to Mecca
mishikaki – meat kebabs
moran – Maasai warrior
mpingo – African blackwood
mtindi – cultured milk product similar to yogurt
mvuli – short rains
Mwalimu – teacher; used to refer to Julius Nyerere
mzungu – white person, foreigner (pl wazungu)

nazi – fermented coconut wine
NCA – Ngorongoro Conservation Area
NCAA – Ngorongoro Conservation Area Authority
ndugu – brother, comrade
ngoma – dance and drumming
northern circuit – the popular northern safari route, including Serengeti, Tarangire, Arusha and Lake Manyara National Parks and the Ngorongoro Conservation Area

ordinary camp site – type of national park camp site, with basic facilities, generally including latrines and a water source

papasi – literally 'a tick'; used on Zanzibar to refer to street touts
pweza – octopus, usually served grilled, at night markets and street stalls

shamba – farm plot
shehe – village chief

shetani – style of figurative art embodying images from the spirit world

shikamoo – Swahili greeting of respect, used for elders or anyone in a position of authority; the response is 'marahaba'

southern circuit – primarily Selous Game Reserve and Ruaha National Park, also Mikumi and Udzungwa Mountains National Parks

special camp site – type of national park camp site, more remote than *ordinary camp sites*, with no facilities at all

TAA – Tanganyika Africa Association, successor of the African Association and predecessor of *TANU*

taarab – Zanzibari music combining African, Arabic and Indian influences

Tamofa – Tanzania-Mozambique Friendship Association

Tanapa – Tanzania National Parks Authority

TANU – Tanganyika (later, Tanzania) African National Union

TATO – Tanzanian Association of Tour Operators

Tazara – Tanzania–Zambia Railway

tilapia – Nile perch

Tingatinga – Tanzania's best-known style of painting, developed in the 1960s by Edward Saidi Tingatinga; traditionally in a square format with colourful animal motifs against a monochrome background

TTB – Tanzania Tourist Board

ugali – maize and/or cassava meal pap

uhuru – freedom; also the name of Mt Kilimanjaro's highest peak

ujamaa – familyhood, togetherness

umoja – unity

Unguja – Swahili name for Zanzibar island

vibuyu – carved gourds

vitambua – rice cakes

wali – cooked rice

ZIFF – Zanzibar International Film Festival

ZNP – Zanzibar Nationalist Party

ZPPP – Zanzibar & Pemba People's Party

ZTC – Zanzibar Tourist Corporation

Behind the Scenes

THIS BOOK

This is the 3rd edition of Lonely Planet's *Tanzania*. The 1st edition of this book (entitled *Tanzania, Zanzibar & Pemba*) was researched and written by Mary Fitzpatrick, with contributing author David Else. Mary also updated the 2nd edition, with Sean Pywell updating the Wildlife Guide. For this edition Mary was again at the helm, fully researching and updating the text. Dr Caroline Evans wrote the Health chapter.

THANKS from the Author

Mary Fitzpatrick Thanks go first and foremost to Rick, for his enthusiasm, support and encouragement, and for the countless hours of assistance on the road and at home, and to Christopher, for his patience and wonderful sense of humour. Thank you also to those in Cairo whose daily thoughtfulness brightened many days during the writing of this book.

In Tanzania, I'm indebted to numerous people for their time, and assistance with information and logistics. In particular I'd like to express my appreciation to Nasr (Babu) Hamiduddin, Dr Rolf Baldus, Katavi Chief Park Warden Stephano Qolli, Dr Hubert Krischke, Susan and Sanjay Pandit, Dr Hildegard Vogt, Mathias J. Lema, Dick Persson, Steven Broadbent and Mike Beckner. Many thanks also to all those who wrote in with updates and information, especially Sue Jaggar and Kenny Blackmore.

There is a Swahili saying which, roughly translated, reads: 'If you are going to give someone a bowl of porridge, then give them a full bowl, not just half'. Time and again, Tanzanians I met while researching – and whose names I'll probably never know – put this adage into practice, going out of their way to help me when they did not have to, and when it may have inconvenienced them. For this, my sincere gratitude.

CREDITS

This book was commissioned by Hilary Rogers in Lonely Planet's Melbourne office. Joanne Newell wrote the brief and Will Gourlay assessed the manuscript. *Tanzania* 3 was coordinated by Katie Lynch (editorial) and Daniel Fennessy (cartography). Michael Ruff laid out the book and Laura Jane designed the colour pages and did the cover artwork. Gerilyn Attebery designed the cover. Overseeing production were Rachel Imeson (with assistance from Charles Rawlings-Way) as project manager, Melanie Dankel as managing editor and Shahara Ahmed as managing cartographer. Quentin Frayne coordinated the language content. A talented team of editors, proofers, cartographers and designers assisted on this project: Andrew Bain, Imogen Bannister, Sasha Baskett, Adrienne Costanzo, Hunor Csutoros, Brooke Lyons, Lucy Monie and Jacqui Saunders. Thanks also to Fiona Siseman.

THANKS from Lonely Planet

Many thanks to the hundreds of travellers who used the last edition and wrote to us with helpful hints, useful advice and interesting anecdotes:

A Betty Abang, Alan Adorni, Paul Aelen, Ameet Aggarwal, Monica Aggarwal, Daniel Albert, Enrico Alberti, Donald & Ileens Allen, Katie Amadon, Thorsten Amft, Christine Amon, Jayne Andrews, Linda Arthur, Malcolm Arthur, Nick & Sarah Atkinson, Robert Augustino,

---

THE LONELY PLANET STORY

The story begins with a classic travel adventure: Tony and Maureen Wheeler's 1972 journey across Europe and Asia to Australia. There was no useful information about the overland trail then, so Tony and Maureen published the first Lonely Planet guidebook to meet a growing need.

From a kitchen table, Lonely Planet has grown to become the largest independent travel publisher in the world, with offices in Melbourne (Australia), Oakland (USA) and London (UK). Today Lonely Planet guidebooks cover the globe. There is an ever-growing list of books and information in a variety of media. Some things haven't changed. The main aim is still to make it possible for adventurous travellers to get out there – to explore and better understand the world.

At Lonely Planet we believe travellers can make a positive contribution to the countries they visit – if they respect their host communities and spend their money wisely. Every year 5% of company profit is donated to charities around the world.

Vincent Aupers **B** Adam Bairu, Gayle Baker, Sandrine Bareigts, Juan Carlos Barrera, Tracy E Bartley, Andrea & Alessandra Barucchello, Rachel Bassignani, Susan & Ken Batten, Berry Beersen, Valena E Beety, Ozsel Beleli, Pamela Berghegen, Renee Bernard, Christine Berndt, Daniela Bertoglio, Fremon Best, Ruth Bevington, Amei Binns, Suzan Bloemscheer, Rik Blondeel, David Bolton, Allan & Beth Boorer, Magnus Bostrom, Ernst Brand, Marek Brejl, Luis Paulo Bresciani, Brandy Brewster, Anna Brown, Dianne Brown, Graham Brown, Douglas Buchalter, Tina Buckley, Frank Bult **C** Linda & Mark Campbell, Jo Campion, Inigo Campo, Mike Carlson, Brigitte Carron, Bruno Cassiers, W G Caudwell, Carolynn Chaput, Nikka Clinton, Lynne Cole, Cindy Collins, Liz Collins, Peter Collins, Deirdre Connolly, Hilary Connor, Carrie Cook, David Cooke, Monique Coolen, Andrea Cooper, Lucy Cooper, Kent Correll, Joanne Crawford, Ron Czajkowski **D** Alison Davis, Anke de Boer, Peter, Paul & Marijke de Heer, Roland De Jong, Silvia de Verga, Femke, Natascha & Sietze de Wijs, Jody Delichte, Martijn Derks, Mike Dewsbury, Kathleen Diina, Alexandra Dilsky, Brian Dixson, Marjan Dixson, Ryan Drake-Lee, Niels Drent, Kate Duffy **E** Adrian Easthope, Clare Edgington, Hugh Edwards, Robert Eppinga **F** Holger Fabig, Brian Fagan, Caryll Fagan, Helen M Farebrother, Suzie Fendick, Jana Fialova, Christoph Finck, Anne Fitzpatrick, James Forbes, Rosa Fouassier, Jamie Fox, J P Frejci, Laura Frew, Margit Friedrich, Christl Fuchslechner, Rüdiger Funk **G** Krystyna Gade, Francisco Garcia, Megan Gibbons, Anna Gigli, Andrew Gill, Christophe Gimmler, Bettina Gloggler, David Godfrey, Lionel Gonzalez, David Goodman, Erik Gorter, Yves Gounin, Calixte Govaarts, Emmanuelle Grand, Carles Gras, Nicolas Gravoin, Kenneth Gray, Anton Grenholm, Gwendoline Griffiths, Michael Grill, Gabriele & Kaspar Grossenbacher **H** Joya Halder, Tony Hales, Aengus Hallinan, Rupert Hallowes, Nicholas Hancock, Sam Hannah-Rankin, Lorraine Hanover, Christian Hansen, Helle Hansen, Josephine Harden, Chris Harker, Brigit Harte, Emma Hartwig, Jianhui He, Theresa Heasman, Colleen Heenan, Kirsten Hellevang, Akseli Hemminki, Consuela & Vincent Hendriks, Rachel Hill, Simon Hill, Claudia Hirtbach, Margaret Hoff, Parker Holden, Nicolas & Sarah Holl, Javier Huarte Osacar, Jonathan Hyatt **J** George Jackson, Latifa Jackson, Ginger Jackson-Gleich, Sue Jaggar, Ingela Jansson, Line Jeppesen, Thomas Johansen, Craig Johnson, Warren Johnson, Steve Jordan, Sine Wanda Jorgensen, Jasvinder Josen, Charles L Joyce, Stipo Jurcevic **K** Hanne Kaergaard, Liesbeth Kager, Bart Kakoschke, Christina Kalsto, Ray Kang, Veronika Karl, Russell Karlson, Berit Karlsson, Liselott Karlsson, Dennis Kavanagh, Pavla Kazbundova, Christina Keinhenis, Sharon Kellner, Megan Kennedy, Laura Kerr, Yongjin Kim, Mary Kipling, Lulu Kirschenmann, Susan Kirwan, Tore Kleist, Lara Knudsen, Johanna Kolehmainen, Rina Kor, Marian Korecek, Klaudia Kovacs, Didi Kriel, Roger & Cecilie Kristiansen, Sacha Krustulovic, Rastislav Kulich, Rosemarie Kullik, Laura Kyrke-Smith **L** Howard Lambert, Tony & Judy Lamborn, Christine Landolt, Regina Lang, Pierre Laoureux, Kirstie Le Bouedec, P Ledroit, Simon Lethem, Sasha Lezhnev, Michael Lieberherr, Yvette Lievens, Mike Linder, Benoit & Amelie Lomont, Michael Lousada, Chris Lovett, Jeremy Lown, Walt Lueder, Luc Lugghe, Diderik Lund, Lisbeth Lynggaard **M** Geralyn Macfadyen, Neil Mackenzie, Monica Mackey, Steve Mackey, Larry MacKillop, Tammy MacMillan, Dan Mallaber, Rajnil Mallik,

Jack Mann, Alex Manning, Sabine Mantsch, Dr Mario Mariani, Michal Markus, Peter Marnoch, Perry Martin, Javier Martinez-Pardo, Terumi Mascarenhas, Agusti Mascaro, Audrey Mason, Branka Matanovic, Margaret McGowan-Smyth, Noelle McGrady, Ross McKenzie, Judy McKinley, Janet McNicol, S McNutt, Andrea Meier, Brenda Meier, Matthias Meixner, Iciar Melia Fullana, C A Menken, Sonja Merljak, Mark Meulenbroeks, Lesley Meyer, Scotty Meyers, Roger Michel, Rachel Miller, Joel Mog, Toby Monk, Cara Moody, Leah Morgan, Wendy Morrison, Lisa & Ute Mueller, Stefan Mueller, Sytske Mulder, P Mulhern, Ana Murillo, Brendon Murray **N** Jeroen Nales, Britta Narum, David Nason, Seen Yee Neo, Eva Nerga, Britta Neumann, Rainer Neumann, John Nevison, Alex Nikolic, Camilla Nordstrom, Sarah Norton, Brian Novy **O** Flora O'Callaghan, Sheila O'Connor, Mark & Mae-Cy Ogden, Tim Ozinga **P** Anna Palbom, Jenny Paley, David & Libby Palmer, Colin Pearson, Maria Jose Permayner, Kaia Peterka, Elizabeth Pfifer, Sven Piertner, Maes Pieter, Chris Pilley, Dominique Pin, Robert Pinter, Gemma Pitcher, Jacco Pols, Sofie Ponsaerts, Nathan Popp, William Post, Denis Powell, Val Presten **Q** Mark Quandt, Simon Quinn **R** Michael Rankin, Benjamin Ray, Helen Reeves, Adir Regev, Richard Reinisch, James Reynolds, Saskia Rietdijk, Marieke Rijkers, Pamela Riley, Jeremie Robert, Lorna Robinson, Heiko Roemhild, Hilde Rosseland, Johanness Rwanzo **S** Evert Saladin, Anin Sam, Adam Sandell, Allan Sander, Marianne Saralegui, Amelia Savino, Lindsey Schatzberg, Polly Schmincke, Florence Schnydrig, Lotte Schreiber, Paul Schulte, John Schwarzkopf, Chris Scobie, John Sebastian, Beate Selbig, Diane Senior, Susan Sgarlat, D Sharman, Stephen Simblet, Barun Sinha, Malin Sjoblom, Martin Skjoldebrand, Sebastian

SEND US YOUR FEEDBACK

We love to hear from travellers – your comments keep us on our toes and help make our books better. Our well-travelled team reads every word on what you loved or loathed about this book. Although we cannot reply individually to postal submissions, we always guarantee that your feedback goes straight to the appropriate authors, in time for the next edition. Each person who sends us information is thanked in the next edition – and the most useful submissions are rewarded with a free book.

To send us your updates – and find out about Lonely Planet events, newsletters and travel news – visit our award-winning website: **www.lonelyplanet.com/feedback**

Note: We may edit, reproduce and incorporate your comments in Lonely Planet products such as guidebooks, websites and digital products, so let us know if you don't want your comments reproduced or your name acknowledged. For a copy of our privacy policy visit www.lonelyplanet.com/privacy

Slania, Jennifer Slater, Ella Sloman, Stephan Smout, Carolien Spaans, Marjan Spaans, Kim Staats, Henrik Stabell, Katie Stanley, Johannes Starostzik, Margrethe Stensland, Asheri Stephen, Bill & Ann Stoughton, Richard Strickland, John Strong, Lee Suter, Steph & Juan Svendsen, Oscar Svensson, Peter Swanson **T** Ramon Tak, Dawn Talbert, Martin Taylor, Mary Taylor, Claudia Thomas, Sandra Timmermans, Aiko Tomikawa, Helena Tong, Stephen Totterman, Barry Tremblay, Tabitha Tuckett, Abigail Turner, Michael Turner, Nicola Turner, Jenny Turunen **U** Shaun Unger **V** Dave Valliere, Nelleke van de Wiel, Bart van den Eijnden, Olaf van Ginneken, Rogier van Hulten, Heleen van Loenen, Simone van Slooten, Eline Verbruggen, Charolette Verheijdt, Rob Verschoor, Jan Verstricht, Christina von Borcke, Carna von Hove, Theo von Laufenberg, Ties Vrenssen **W** Craig Walker, Katie Walsh, Elke Walter, Wolf Walter, Andy Ward, Hannah Ward, Dorenda Warnaar, Craig Wealand, Leann Webb, Jens Weissenburger, Manuel Welsch, Guy Westoby, Savini Wijesingha, Kris Wilde, Merlin Williams, Lisa Womersley, Caroline Woollin, Chris Worrall, Birgitta & Jan Wreeby, Mike Wrigglesworth, Paul Wright, Susie Wright **Y** Pablo Yee **Z** Andreas Zahner, Ommi Zahran, Su Zhang, Jan A Zijlstra

ACKNOWLEDGEMENT

Index

000 Map pages
000 Location of colour photographs

368

MAP LEGEND

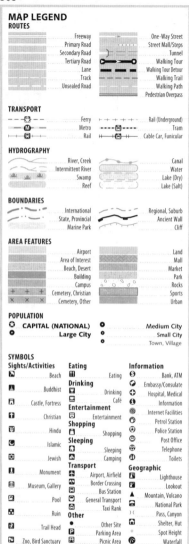

ROUTES

Freeway
Primary Road
Secondary Road
Tertiary Road
Lane
Track
Unsealed Road

One-Way Street
Street Mall/Steps
Tunnel
Walking Tour
Walking Tour Detour
Walking Trail
Walking Path
Pedestrian Overpass

TRANSPORT

Ferry
Metro
Rail

Rail (Underground)
Tram
Cable Car, Funicular

HYDROGRAPHY

River, Creek
Intermittent River
Swamp
Reef

Canal
Water
Lake (Dry)
Lake (Salt)

BOUNDARIES

International
State, Provincial
Marine Park

Regional, Suburb
Ancient Wall
Cliff

AREA FEATURES

Airport
Area of Interest
Beach, Desert
Building
Campus
Cemetery, Christian
Cemetery, Other

Land
Mall
Market
Park
Rocks
Sports
Urban

POPULATION

◎ CAPITAL (NATIONAL)
● Large City
● Medium City
● Small City
● Town, Village

SYMBOLS

Sights/Activities
Beach
Buddhist
Castle, Fortress
Christian
Hindu
Islamic
Jewish
Monument
Museum, Gallery
Pool
Ruin
Trail Head
Zoo, Bird Sanctuary

Eating
Eating

Drinking
Drinking
Café

Entertainment
Entertainment

Shopping
Shopping

Sleeping
Sleeping
Camping

Transport
Airport, Airfield
Border Crossing
Bus Station
General Transport
Taxi Rank

Other
Other Site
Parking Area
Picnic Area

Information
Bank, ATM
Embassy/Consulate
Hospital, Medical
Information
Internet Facilities
Petrol Station
Police Station
Post Office
Telephone
Toilets

Geographic
Lighthouse
Lookout
Mountain, Volcano
National Park
Pass, Canyon
Shelter, Hut
Spot Height
Waterfall

LONELY PLANET OFFICES

Australia
Head Office
Locked Bag 1, Footscray, Victoria 3011
☎ 03 8379 8000, fax 03 8379 8111
talk2us@lonelyplanet.com.au

USA
150 Linden St, Oakland, CA 94607
☎ 510 893 8555, toll free 800 275 8555
fax 510 893 8572, info@lonelyplanet.com

UK
72-82 Rosebery Ave,
Clerkenwell, London EC1R 4RW
☎ 020 7841 9000, fax 020 7841 9001
go@lonelyplanet.co.uk

Published by Lonely Planet Publications Pty Ltd
ABN 36 005 607 983

© Lonely Planet 2005

© photographers as indicated 2005

Cover photographs: Zebras, one 'talking' into the other's ear, Tanzania, Purdy Matt/Lamberti/Getty Images (front); Dhows moored in the Dhow Harbour, Zanzibar, Steve Davey/LPI (back). Many of the images in this guide are available for licensing from Lonely Planet Images: www.lonelyplanetimages.com

All rights reserved. No part of this publication may be copied, stored in a retrieval system, or transmitted in any form by any means, electronic, mechanical, recording or otherwise, except brief extracts for the purpose of review, and no part of this publication may be sold or hired, without the written permission of the publisher.

Printed through The Bookmaker International Ltd
Printed in China

Lonely Planet and the Lonely Planet logo are trademarks of Lonely Planet and are registered in the US Patent and Trademark Office and in other countries.

Lonely Planet does not allow its name or logo to be appropriated by commercial establishments, such as retailers, restaurants or hotels. Please let us know of any misuses: www.lonelyplanet.com/ip

Although the authors and Lonely Planet have taken all reasonable care in preparing this book, we make no warranty about the accuracy or completeness of its content and, to the maximum extent permitted, disclaim all liability arising from its use.